RECOVERING A COVENANTAL HERITAGE:

Essays in Baptist Covenant Theology

Edited by
Richard C. Barcellos, Ph.D.

RBAP
Palmdale, CA

Copyright © 2014 Richard C. Barcellos. All rights reserved.

Scripture quotations taken from the Holy Bible, English Standard Version® (ESV®), copyright © 2001 by Crossway Bibles, a publishing ministry of Good News Publications. Used by permission. All rights reserved.

Scripture taken from the NEW AMERICAN STANDARD BIBLE®, Copyright® 1960, 1962, 1963, 1968, 1971, 1972, 1973, 1975, 1977, 1995 by The Lockman Foundation. Used by permission.

THE HOLY BIBLE, NEW INTERNATIONAL VERSION®, NIV® Copyright © 1973, 1978, 1984, 2011 by Biblica, Inc.® Used by permission. All rights reserved worldwide.

Official copyright notice for the BibleWorks fonts:
BWHEBB, BWHEBL [Hebrew]; BWGRKL, BWGRKN, and BWGRKI [Greek] Postscript® Type 1 and TrueType™ fonts Copyright © 1994-2012 BibleWorks, LLC. All rights reserved. These biblical Greek and Hebrew fonts are used with permission and are from BibleWorks, software for biblical exegesis and research.

Requests for information should be sent to:

RBAP
349 Sunrise Terrace
Palmdale, CA 93551
rb@rbap.net
www.rbap.net

No part of this publication may be reproduced, stored in a retrieval system, or transmitted in any way by any means, electronic, mechanical, photocopy, recording, or otherwise, without the prior permission of RBAP except as provided by USA copyright law.

Printed in the United States of America.

Cover design and formatted for print by Cameron Porter.

ISBN-13: 978-1499714487
ISBN-10: 1499714483

Recovering a Covenantal Heritage is more than a book title; it is a welcomed clarion call for modern Reformed Baptists. I am grateful to God for our Presbyterian brethren and the sea of books, tracts, and treatises on Covenant Theology they have produced over the years. However, Baptists have a distinct covenantal heritage, and that heritage has been underrepresented in Reformed thinking and publication. This volume serves to clarify Baptist distinctives, outlines our place in Reformation history, identifies us as more than merely 'Deep Water' Presbyterians, distinguishes us from Dispensationalists, modern Calvinistic (non Reformed) Baptists and New Covenant Baptists, and, in the end exalts Christ as the redeemer of God's elect. May it receive a wide and thorough reading, and spark a renewal of distinct Reformed Baptist theology!

Voddie Baucham
Pastor of Preaching at Grace Family Baptist Church
Author of *Joseph and the Gospel of Many Colors*

For many people around the world, the Baptist heritage is associated with a voluntaristic faith whereby the individual believer chooses to believe, is baptized and works his way through his spiritual journey where his personal tastes lead him to go. This is indeed the way in which many Baptists are embodying what it means to be Baptist. However, this is a relatively new development in the history of Protestantism as well as being a flawed picture of the Evangelical faith. This marvelous collection of essays expounds a historically older and theologically better version of the Baptist heritage. By recovering a covenantal theology that is central to biblical revelation, this book helps to re-signify the Baptist identity by grounding it in the biblical-covenantal framework and by showing its organic relationship to the Reformed faith.

Leonardo De Chirico
Istituto di Formazione Evangelica e Documentazione
Padova, Italy

For over a century, Baptist pastors and scholars have tended to either downplay the biblical covenants or interpret them through the lens of Dispensationalism. The past generation has witnessed a fresh interest in covenantal thought in Baptist life, especially among Calvinistic Baptists, though as yet we have no consensus. One of the recent contributions to this discussion is the thesis that seventeenth-century Baptists advanced a version of federal theology that differed in important respects from their paedobaptist friends, but that also stands apart from more recent theological projects such as New Covenant Theology. *Recovering a Covenantal Heritage* is a thoughtful contribution to this discussion that deserves a close read by all Calvinistic Baptists who are interested in covenant thought. My prayer is that the Lord would use books like this to grant us greater consensus as we seek to rightly interpret the Word of God and shepherd healthy congregations that closely reflect the teachings of that Word.

Nathan A. Finn, Ph.D.
Associate Professor of Historical Theology and Baptist Studies
Southeastern Baptist Theological Seminary
Wake Forest, NC

Over the last few years, an increasing number of pastors and scholars who self-identify with the Particular Baptist movement in seventeenth-century England have begun to reconsider the structure of the salvation history as outlined by the biblical covenants. Dissatisfied with Dispensationalism, "new covenant" theology, and the assumptions of the Westminster Confession of Faith, they have turned to the second of the Particular Baptist confessions of faith (1677/1689) and to the theological writings of the community which produced it. As they have done so, these pastors and scholars have found themselves returning to important emphases in early Baptist writing. The chapters collected in this volume represent some of the most important first-fruits of this enquiry – based on an old, but startlingly new, call to consider the developing revelation of the covenant of grace.

Crawford Gribben
Professor of Early Modern British History
School of History and Anthropology
Queen's University
Belfast
Author of *The Irish Puritans: James Ussher and the Reformation of the Church* and *The Puritan Millennium: Literature and Theology, 1550-1682* (Revised Edition) (Studies in Christian History and Thought)

Here is a book worth digging your teeth into and it has come at the right time in the global growth of the Reformed Baptist movement. Covenant theology is to soteriology what a foundation is to any building. It anchors salvation deep into the immovable rock of eternity and gives it stability as it towers right across history. You go wrong here and the rest will go wrong. Conversely, a robust covenant theology ensures a robust understanding of our great salvation. Therefore, this scholarly work, written from a Reformed Baptist perspective, is worth all the effort you will put into reading it. Put your thinking cap on and go for it!

Conrad Mbewe
Pastor of Kabwata Baptist Church
Lusaka, Zambia
Editor of *Reformation Zambia*
Author of *Foundations for the Flock*
Chancellor of African Christian University

This is a thoroughly enjoyable book. The variety of authors provides much diversity in approach, content, and interest but not contradictory stances. Each chapter serves as a reaffirmation and complementary statement to the others. Study of people, study of ideas, study of confessions, exegetical and theological analyses, and careful interaction with other covenantal approaches provides a marvelous introductory education to this vital subject. This kind of work, provided by so many excellent researchers and writers, gives a coherent framework within which to comprehend the biblical doctrines of God's redemptive person and his redemptive work that we hold in such holy love. I wish I had had such a book when I began my theological journey. A sincere thank you to all the contributors.

Tom J. Nettles
Professor of Church History, retired
The Southern Baptist Theological Seminary

It is encouraging to discover that after many years of neglect Baptists are again giving serious attention to the doctrine of the covenant. We owe much to our North American brethren for the way in which this study has been developed, both exegetically and historically. As the title suggests, it is a recovery of lost ground. Significant leaders such as John Gill and Andrew Fuller in the eighteenth century and Charles Haddon Spurgeon in the nineteenth were covenant theologians. Recent study has brought to light important material from the seventeenth century, much of which has been unavailable, gathering dust in a few specialist libraries although the fruits of this early work were evident in both London Confessions of that century. A fascinating side-light has been the work of John Owen who although a paedobaptist was developing aspects of covenant theology close to that of the Particular Baptist pioneers. Recently Greg Nichols has made a major contribution to this subject with his work, *Covenant Theology*. In this volume, we have the work of twelve other contemporary scholars brought together. I warmly welcome this work for all who wish to understand classic Particular Baptist thinking on this important subject.

Robert W. Oliver
Visiting Professor of Church History,
Puritan Reformed Theological Seminary, Grand Rapids
Author of *History of the English Calvinistic Baptists 1771-1892*

Table of Contents

Preface 11
    Richard C. Barcellos, Ph.D.

Introduction 13
    James M. Renihan, Ph.D.

Historical

1. A Brief Overview of Seventeenth-Century Reformed
   Orthodox Federalism 19
       Richard C. Barcellos, Ph.D.

2. Covenant Theology in the First and Second London
   Confessions of Faith 45
       James M. Renihan, Ph.D.

3. By Farther Steps: A Seventeenth-Century Particular
   Baptist Covenant Theology 71
       Pascal Denault, Th.M.

4. The Puritan Argument for the Immersion of Believers:
   How Seventeenth-Century Baptists Utilized the
   Regulative Principle of Worship 109
       G. Stephen Weaver, Jr., Ph.D.

5. The Antipaedobaptism of John Tombes 127
       Michael T. Renihan, Ph.D.

6. The Abrahamic Covenant in the Thought of John Tombes ... 159
       Michael T. Renihan, Ph.D.

7. John Owen on the Mosaic Covenant 175
       Thomas E. Hicks, Jr., Ph.D.

8. A 'Novel' Approach to Credobaptist and Paedobaptist
   Polemics 193
       Jeffrey A. Massey

Biblical

9. The Fatal Flaw of Infant Baptism: The Dichotomous
   Nature of the Abrahamic Covenant. 223
      Jeffrey D. Johnson, D.Min.

10. The Difference Between the Old and New Covenants:
    John Owen on Hebrews 8:6. 257
       John Owen, D.D.

11. The Newness of the New Covenant (Part 1). 325
       James R. White, Th.D.

12. The Newness of the New Covenant (Part 2) 357
       James R. White, Th.D.

13. Acts 2:39 in its Context (Part 1): An Exegetical Summary. 383
    of Acts 2:39 and Paedobaptism
       Jamin Hübner, Th.D.

14. Acts 2:39 in its Context (Part 2): Case Studies in
    Paedobaptist Interpretations of Acts 2:39. 417
       Jamin Hübner, Th.D.

15. An Exegetical Appraisal of Colossians 2:11-12. 449
       Richard C. Barcellos, Ph.D.

Biblical-Theological

16. Reformed Baptist Covenant Theology and
    Biblical Theology 475
       Micah and Samuel Renihan

Scripture Index 507

Name and Subject Index 517

Preface

This book is offered with the intent to further the discussion on covenant theology among Baptists and paedobaptists. It in no way pretends to be a fully worked-out Baptist covenant theology. It contains essays by thirteen different authors who do not necessarily advocate the fine details of every contribution, something that is quite common with multiple-author works.

A few words about the book's structure may be helpful. After the Preface and Introduction, the first main section is historical. It seeks to set a historical-theological context for the reader. I have found it to be the case, quite often, that covenant theology is understood to be the sole property of paedobaptists. However, anyone familiar with the Particular Baptists of the seventeenth century, their writings, and the Second London Confession of Faith (1677/89), know otherwise.[1] The first section of this work seeks to show this and displays some continuity with the work of non-Baptists of that era.

The second section of this work discusses various biblical issues related to covenant theology, primarily from a Baptist perspective.[2] Issues covered from a distinctly Baptist perspective include: the Abrahamic Covenant, the newness of the New Covenant, and the expositions of Acts 2:38-39 and Colossians 2:11-12, two crucial texts in this discussion. We have solicited the help of John Owen on the differences between the Old and New Covenants. The reason for this is two-fold: first, it is clear from the primary, Particular Baptist sources of the seventeenth century that Owen's view was substantially that of most of the Baptists of that day; and second, Nehemiah Coxe, most likely the co-editor (and senior editor?) of the 2LCF and author of the major seventeenth-century Particular Baptist work on God's covenants, pointed his readers to Owen on

---

[1] The Second London Confession of Faith (1677/89) will be abbreviated 2LCF hereinafter.

[2] The one exception is John Owen, who was a paedobaptist.

this issue. This being the case, Owen's thesis reflects the view of the Baptist theologians behind the 2LCF.

The third section of the book, though the shortest, seeks to put things together, though certainly not in any comprehensive sense.

A word on the Introduction seems to be in order as well. Once the entire work was written, I asked Dr. James M. Renihan to write an Introduction that would help the reader understand the importance of this work in its historical and theological context.

On a personal note, as I have studied this subject over the years, I keep finding my thinking corrected many times by older writers – Baptists and paedobaptists. Several years ago, I came to the conclusion that I did not understand chapter 7, "Of God's Covenant," of the 2LCF properly. This may or may not be the case with the reader. Either way, let me encourage you, especially if you claim the 2LCF, to read and think carefully through the arguments of this book. I think they are crucial to understand and important to further the discussions that are presently taking place among Baptists and paedobaptists.

I want to thank Patrick McWilliams for helping with the editing of this book. His keen eye detected many necessary changes in the 11th hour.

Cameron Porter must be mentioned. He formatted the text for print and designed the cover in his "spare" time.

It is my hope that this work will both challenge and instruct Baptist readers and introduce paedobaptists into part of the thought-world of Baptist covenant theology.

The Editor
Richard C. Barcellos, Ph.D.
Grace Reformed Baptist Church
Palmdale, CA

Introduction

Twenty-first century Baptists in North America are the children of the twentieth century. While this might seem like a truism, it is nevertheless of great importance to understand Baptist self-identity. It would be a fascinating study to investigate all of the different ways that this notion works itself out. We must, however, limit ourselves to the task at hand. One might adapt the phrase and apply it specifically to this book by saying that twenty-first century Baptists in America are the children of the reductionist and non-covenantal theological trends among twentieth-century Baptists.

From their beginnings in the seventeenth century, Baptists on both sides of the Atlantic were thoroughly covenantal.[1] Formulating their doctrine in the familiar terms of Reformed orthodoxy, they built a theological system that was easily recognized by all of the strands of churches coming out of the Reformation. This commitment was expressed in their Confessions, their published books, and may be seen in surviving manuscript documents as well. While it would be an exaggeration to say that covenantalism was a 'central dogma' (a mistaken notion when applied to most theological systems), it is nonetheless clear that our fathers recognized the foundational nature of covenant theology and built their system on its basis. To use B. B. Warfield's term, it was the "architectonic principle"[2] of their confessional understanding. As late as 1881, William Cathcart, editor of the very

---

[1] While our interest and focus is on Particular Baptist history and theology, this statement may be made of General Baptists as well. The General Baptist *Orthodox Creed* of 1678 clearly articulates a covenantal doctrine in its Article XVI, which is very similar in content to both the 2LCF and Westminster Confession of Faith (WCF) 7. See William Lumpkin, *Baptist Confessions of Faith* (Valley Forge, PA: Judson Press, 1959), 307.

[2] B. B. Warfield, *The Westminster Assembly and its Work* (1931; reprint, Grand Rapids: Baker, 1981), 56. Warfield's comment applies directly to WCF, but since 2LCF and the Philadelphia Confession (along with its other American iterations – Charleston, etc.) are direct descendants, it appropriately applies to these as well.

important *Baptist Encyclopedia* could state, "In England and America, churches, individuals, and Associations, with clear minds, with hearts full of love for the truth . . . have held with veneration the Articles of 1689."[3] While this statement is (in my opinion) somewhat exaggerated in its breadth[4] and optimism, the very fact that it could be made in such an important work is telling. The basic covenantal structure of the 2LCF was still, at that late date, received widely by Baptists north and south of the Mason-Dixon Line.

By 1920, this statement could no longer be made. Very few, if any of the churches in the Northern and Southern Baptist Conventions, remained committed to the old confessional theology.[5] Baptists were swept away by powerful movements, each of which challenged and altered their theological commitments. We shall comment on four: Revivalism, Modernism, Fundamentalism, and Dispensationalism.

Revivalism has its roots in the Second Great Awakening, a cross-denominational movement flourishing in the early nineteenth century. In a review of Iain Murray's *Revival and Revivalism*, Bobby Jamieson identifies two major alterations in theological understanding related to the development of 'revivalism' – a new view of conversion and a shift in evangelistic practice.

> The result of these two shifts is that church leaders began to regard revival as something that could be infallibly secured through the use of proper means – "proper" being whatever would induce an immediate decision or external token of decision.[6]

---

[3] William Cathcart, *The Baptist Encyclopedia* (Philadelphia: Everts, 1881), 266.

[4] Cathcart could hardly bring himself to acknowledge the various strands of General or Freewill Baptists.

[5] It is true that some churches in the Primitive Baptist tradition maintained some appreciation for the older theology, but they tended to be insular and plagued by their own unique theological disputes and trajectories. The result was idiosyncratic doctrines and practices that did not in reality (despite their loud protestations otherwise) reflect the emphases of the Baptist fathers.

[6] Bobby Jamieson, *Book Review: Revival and Revivalism* in 9Marks Journal, March-April 2012, found at http://www.9marks.org/books/book-review-revival-and-revivalism, accessed 28 March, 2013.

Among other things, this change moved the focus of ministry away from theological and exegetical preaching to methods and schemes aimed at the production of numerical results. An attendant consequence was the diminishing importance of theology as it was replaced by external measurements. Ministerial effectiveness was calculated numerically. What does covenant theology matter if it doesn't directly contribute to the desired product?

Modernism is a term with many referents. For the sake of this essay, I employ it as a marker describing the slow movement from a high view of the authority of Scripture and commitment to the 'catholic' doctrines of Christianity, to various stages of doubt about these matters. Rooted in German liberalism, the proponents of this view, men such as William Newton Clarke and Walter Rauschenbusch, put forward a new form of Christianity, very much *unlike* the older orthodoxy. It undermined the testimony of Scripture and postulated a denuded form of Christian faith. In the south, the more conservative E. Y. Mullins proposed a stripped-down experience-oriented faith and paved the way for nearly a century of liberalism at the seminary he served as president, Southern Seminary in Louisville, KY. In each case, the details of covenant theology were irrelevant to the formulation of modern faith. Vast swaths of Baptists were lost to the well-established theological pattern.

The reaction to the surging wave of modernism was fundamentalism. Contrary to popular opinion, it was, in its origins, largely, a northern, urban, and intellectual phenomenon Many of its earliest leaders were ministers in downtown churches located in large northern cities – New York, Boston, Baltimore, Chicago and even Toronto. These men were members of the Northern Baptist Convention, concerned with the inroads of modernism in the denominational schools. As they fought battles to restore theological orthodoxy to the Convention, they found themselves marginalized and outmaneuvered by the (largely) liberal-dominated denominational staff. In 1922, W. B. Riley, pastor of the First Baptist Church of Minneapolis, proposed that the Northern Baptist Convention adopt the New Hampshire Confession as something of a minimal standard for faith. His proposal was rejected, and even this basic statement was lost to Baptist life. In response, Fundamentalists narrowed the field of battle to a few essential doctrines, and fought a losing battle, ultimately producing more separatist groupings such as the General Association of Regular Baptists (1932) and the Conservative Baptist Association (1947). Once again, covenant theology was neglected as doctrines considered more central – the virgin birth and bodily resurrection of Jesus Christ as examples – became the focal point of defense and (believing) Baptist identity. Robust confessionalism, which would have incorporated a well-developed covenant theology, was replaced by abbreviated doctrinal statements. The result was a profound weakening in Baptist theology.

But perhaps the most important factor in the demise of Baptist covenantalism is Dispensationalism. A modern system, developed first by John Nelson Darby in nineteenth-century Ireland and England, it quickly swept across the ocean and was adopted by evangelicals of many stripes.[7] Postulating a series of 'dispensations' in which God's method of self-revelation and his expectations for man differ, it divided the Bible into various epochs. Each of these periods incorporated divergent tasks for men. Here is the definition as given in the *New Scofield Reference Bible*:

> A dispensation is a period of time during which man is tested in respect to his obedience to some specific revelation of the will of God.
>
> Three important concepts are implied in this definition: (1) a *deposit* of divine revelation concerning God's will, embodying what God requires of man in his conduct; (2) man's *stewardship* of this divine revelation, in which he is responsible to obey it; and (3) a *time-period*, often called an

---

[7] Though many people equate Dispensationalism with Baptist theology, historically this is an exaggeration. Among the early leaders of the movement, C. I. Scofield was a Congregationalist and later joined the Southern Presbyterian denomination, Arno Gaebelein a Methodist, James Gray was a Reformed Episcopalian, and A. T. Pierson a Presbyterian.

"age," during which this divine revelation is dominant in the testing of man's obedience to God.[8]

Darby seems to have developed this system based upon his reading of 2 Timothy 2:15, which says "Study to shew thyself approved unto God, a workman that needeth not to be ashamed, rightly dividing the word of truth" (KJV). To him, the latter phrase of this text requires some form of division in Scripture. His solution was to postulate the dispensations, or ages of history, as periods which segmented the history recorded in the Bible. In itself, this view necessitates discrete epochs in redemptive history, units of time with different standards and requirements based on revelation. It is exactly the opposite of covenantalism which seeks to emphasize the unity of God's purpose in the history of salvation.

It is breathtaking to recognize how quickly Dispensationalism overwhelmed evangelical churches, especially among Baptists. In one sense it is not surprising, since the vacuum created by Fundamentalism was quickly filled by a new and seemingly vibrant system of interpretation. It was advocated by popular preachers and adopted by the disseminators of Christian literature.

Revivalism began the process of turning people from a thoughtful and theological faith to an experience-oriented belief. Modernism brought new ideas into the churches. Fundamentalism circled the wagons and reduced the faith to a few requisite doctrines. And Dispensationalism swept in to fill the void. In every case, covenantalism was shunted to the side, and Baptists lost their rightful heritage. A beautiful system of faith was exchanged for a novelty.

This book is one small attempt to correct this problem. It consists of three sections, historical, exegetical and theological. It is an attempt to demonstrate that this rich legacy must be recovered and reasserted. Not only were our fathers thoroughly covenantal, we must be too. History, theology, and exegesis are all on the side of covenantalism. For too long, Baptists have followed the false

---

[8] E. Schuyler English, ed., *The New Scofield Reference Bible* (New York: OUP, 1967), 3, footnote at Genesis 1:28 heading, emphasis in original.

roads of Revivalism, the diminished pathways of Fundamentalism, and the dead-end street of Dispensationalism. The time has come to restore exegetical and theological rigor and vigor to our churches and ministries.

Iain Murray has stated that part of the problem with the change in Baptist beliefs "has to be attributed to the shortage of published records."[9] Baptists were not aware of their history and surely this must include the writings of preceding generations. Sadly, this same observation continues to apply. Even today, while many paedobaptist writings from past generations have been reprinted and are available, this cannot be said of early Baptist writings. Some of the noteworthy printing houses have provided us with useful reprints, but these publishers have paedobaptist commitments and have largely neglected writings outside their own traditions. This is not to criticize, simply to identify causes. It does, however, point out a fault among Baptists. *We* have not given the time or effort to recovering our lost heritage. Some headway has been made,[10] but much more needs to be done. This lacuna has resulted in twenty-first century Baptist books with a theology (or often *without* any theology) that bears little or no resemblance to the vigorous confessional beliefs of the past. Some may laud this but we view it as a serious deficiency. This book is a small step towards recovering that lost heritage. May the Lord use it for his glory and the good of the churches.

James M. Renihan, Ph.D.
Institute of Reformed Baptist Studies
Westminster Seminary, CA

---

[9] Iain Murray, *Revival and Revivalism* (Edinburgh: Banner of Truth, 1994), 301.

[10] For example, several of Benjamin Keach's volumes are available from Kregel and Solid Ground Christian Books, and even more importantly Nehemiah Coxe's *Discourse of the Covenants* has been reprinted by RBAP, available at www.rbap.net.

CHAPTER 1
A Brief Overview of Seventeenth-Century Reformed Orthodox Federalism
Richard C. Barcellos, Ph.D.*

It is no secret that various seventeenth-century Reformed orthodox theologians articulated theology utilizing a federal or covenantal model. There are many sources (primary and secondary) available for the contemporary reader which amply display and discuss this model.[1] We will examine briefly a few of the more important

---

*Richard C. Barcellos, Ph.D., is pastor of Grace Reformed Baptist Church, Palmdale, CA (www.grbcav.org), and author of *The Family Tree of Reformed Biblical Theology: Geerhardus Vos and John Owen – Their Methods of and Contributions to the Articulation of Redemptive History*, *Better than the Beginning: Creation in Biblical Perspective*, and *The Lord's Supper as a Means of Grace: More than a Memory*. This chapter is a slightly revised section from the author's *The Family Tree of Reformed Biblical Theology* and is used with permission.

[1] For instance, for primary sources see Herman Witsius, *The Economy of the Covenants Between God and Man: Comprehending A Complete Body of Divinity, Two Volumes* (Escondido, CA: The den Dulk Christian Foundation, Reprinted 1990); Nehemiah Coxe and John Owen, *Covenant Theology From Adam to Christ* (Owensboro, KY: RBAP, 2005); Samuel Bolton, *The True Bounds of Christian Freedom* (Edinburgh: The Banner of Truth Trust, Reprint edition of 1978); Edward Fisher, *The Marrow of Modern Divinity: In Two Parts – Part I. the Covenant of Works and the Covenant of Grace; Part II. An Exposition of the Ten Commandments* (Edmonton, AB, Canada: Still Water Revival Books, Reprint edition of 1991); Francis Turretin, *Institutes of Elenctic Theology, Volume Two* (Phillipsburg, NJ: P&R Publishing, 1994); and for secondary works see A. T. B. McGowan, *The Federal Theology of Thomas Boston* (Edinburgh: Rutherford House, 1997); John Von Rohr, *The Covenant of Grace in Puritan Thought* (Atlanta: Scholars Press, 1986); John L. Girardeau, *The Federal Theology: Its Import and Its Regulative Influence* (Greenville, SC: Reformed Academic Press, 1994); Charles S. McCoy and J. Wayne Baker, *Fountainhead of Federalism: Heinrich Bullinger and the Covenantal Tradition* (Louisville: Westminster/John Know Press, 1991); Mark W. Karlberg, *Covenant Theology in Reformed Perspective: Collected Essays and Book Reviews in Historical, Biblical, and Systematic Theology* (Eugene, OR: Wipf and Stock Publishers, 2000); Lyle D. Bierma, *German Calvinism in the Confessional Age: The Covenant Theology of Caspar Olevianus* (Grand Rapids: Baker Book House, 1996); Rowland S. Ward, *God & Adam: Reformed Theology and The*

federal theologians of the seventeenth century to introduce readers to the world of seventeenth-century federal or covenant theology. This brief survey understands federal theology as a method and not as a distinct school.²

Federal or covenant theology did not begin in the seventeenth century. The seventeenth-century Reformed orthodox built upon the labors of their Reformed predecessors, who built upon the labors of others before them. Such theologians as Zwingli, Bullinger, Calvin, Ursinus, Olevianus, Rollock, Perkins, Ames, and Ball all played key roles in the early development of federal theology.³ We will look briefly at some of the key contributors to the development of federalism in the early and late seventeenth

---

Creation Covenant – An Introduction to the Biblical Covenants – A Close Examination of the Covenant of Works (Wantirna, Australia: New Melbourne Press, 2003); Peter Golding, *Covenant Theology: The Key of Theology in Reformed Thought and Tradition* (Ross-shire, Scotland: Christian Focus Publications, 2004); Peter Lillback, *The Binding of God: Calvin's Role in the Development of Covenant Theology* (Grand Rapids: Baker Academic, 2001); Willem J. van Asselt, *The Federal Theology of Johannes Cocceius (1603-1669)* (Leiden, Boston, Koln: Brill, 2001); John Murray, "Covenant Theology" in *Collected Writings, Volume Four* (Edinburgh: The Banner of Truth Trust, 1982), 216-40; Geerhardus Vos, "The Doctrine of the Covenant in Reformed Theology" in Richard B. Gaffin, Jr., editor, *Redemptive History and Biblical Interpretation* (Phillipsburg, NJ: P&R Publishing, 1980), 234-67.

² Cf. Willem J. van Asselt, "The Fundamental Meaning of Theology: Archetypal and Ectypal Theology in Seventeenth-Century Reformed Thought," *Westminster Theological Journal (WTJ)* 64 (2002): 323, where he notes, "This should warn us against any facile juxtaposition of federal-biblical theology with scholastic-dogmatic theology..." 'This' in context refers to the fact that many late sixteenth- and seventeenth-century Reformed theologians utilized Junius' classification of archetypal and ectypal knowledge. Van Asselt claims that this is true of continental Reformed theologians as well as some English Puritans. John Owen makes such distinctions in his *Biblical Theology* (Pittsburgh: Soli Deo Gloria, 1994). (Cf. Chapter 8 of my *The Family Tree of Reformed Biblical Theology*, Owen, *Biblical Theology*, Chapter 3 Book I, and Sebastian Rehnman, *Divine Discourse: The Theological Methodology of John Owen* (Grand Rapids: Baker Academic, 2002), 57-71 for an extended discussion as it relates to Owen.). Once again, this is further evidence that Reformed scholasticism was a complex method and not a static system of theology. Reformed orthodox theologians could be and were often both scholastic and federal.

³ For a well-referenced treatment of the history of federal theology in the post-Reformation era see Ward, *God & Adam*. Cf. also Golding, *Covenant Theology*, 13-66.

century, and even into the eighteenth century, to provide a wider context to introduce the reader to the thought-world of post-Reformation federalism. This should assist the reader as he continues through this volume. Knowing the historical-theological issues of the most productive era of the formulation of federal or covenant theology (among paedobaptists and Particular Baptists) will introduce readers to the ways and means utilized in such formulations and help understand some of the post-Reformation confessional statements and the biblical and theological issues at stake.

William Perkins

William Perkins, a late sixteenth-century English theologian, was a theology professor at Christ College, Cambridge.[4] He is known by some as the father or chief architect of English Puritanism. He had several works of note, especially his *The Art of Prophesying* and *A Golden Chaine*. *The Art of Prophesying* was a hermeneutical and homiletical handbook which influenced English and American Puritanism.[5] Those who influenced Perkins' theology most were men like John Calvin, Peter Martyr Vermigli, Theodore Beza, Jerome Zanchi, Casper Olevianus, and Franciscus Junius.[6] Perkins utilized Ramist logic while articulating his theology. Peter Ramus was a sixteenth-century French logician and philosopher who simplified Aristotelianism and developed a system of analysis that was utilized by the Cambridge Puritans and passed on to their heirs. Ramism analyzed discourse by defining and dividing. Axioms were divided into two parts or dichotomies. Divisions could be subdivided down to their smallest units. As an effect of humanism in Ramist logic, there was an emphasis on practicality.

---

[4] Donald K. McKim, "Perkins, William (1558-1602)" in Donald K. McKim, editor, *Encyclopedia of the Reformed Faith* (*ERF*) (Louisville and Edinburgh: Westminster/John Knox Press, 1992), 274-75.

[5] Donald K. McKim, "Perkins, Williams (1558-1602)" in Donald K. McKim, editor, *Dictionary of Major Biblical Interpreters* (*DMBI*) (Downers Grove, IL: InterVarsity Press, 2007), 815.

[6] McKim, "Perkins" in McKim, editor, *DMBI*, 815.

This contribution of Ramism in Puritanism created the tendency in Puritan exegesis of Scripture to create sermons under two main considerations – exposition/doctrine and use.[7]

William Ames

William Ames, a student of Perkins at Christ College, Cambridge, became professor of theology at the University of Franeker, the Netherlands in 1622. Ames' major work was his *The Marrow of Theology*.[8] This work was very influential among various groups of Protestants in the seventeenth century, including Baptists. It follows Perkins' utilization of Ramist logic in the articulation of theology. Ames has been called the "chief architect of the federal theology."[9]

Ames was Johannes Cocceius' (see below) theology professor and could have been the source behind two of his contributions to federalism – (1) a mediating position on the relation between the *ordo salutis* and the *historia salutis* and (2) the concept of a progressive abrogation of the covenant of works.[10] Commenting on Ames' teaching on the relation between the *ordo* and *historia salutis*, van Vliet says, "The horizontal movement and the vertical "strikes" are continually in a state of intersection; predestination and covenant meet in unity."[11] In his discussion on "The Administration of the Covenant of Grace before the Coming of Christ" Ames combines aspects of the *ordo salutis* with aspects of the *historia salutis*. He does this in the three major Old Testament redemptive-

---

[7] Cf. McKim, "Perkins" in *DMBI*, 816 and McKim, "Ramus, Peter (1515-1572)" in *ERF*, 314.

[8] William Ames, *The Marrow of Theology* (Durham, NC: The Labyrinth Press, 1983).

[9] Jan van Vliet, "Decretal Theology and the Development of Covenant Thought: An Assessment of Cornelis Graafland's Thesis with a Particular View to Federal Architects William Ames and Johannes Cocceius," *WTJ* 63 (2001): 405 and 414. Van Vliet is quoting Perry Miller.

[10] Cf. van Vliet, "Decretal Theology and the Development of Covenant Thought," 416 for a fascinating discussion suggesting this very thing.

[11] van Vliet, "Decretal Theology and the Development of Covenant Thought," 415.

historical epochs: from Adam to Abraham,[12] from Abraham to Moses,[13] and from Moses to Christ.[14] In each redemptive-historical epoch, Ames shows how the stages of the *ordo salutis* were exemplified or as Ames says, "adumbrated."[15]

Ames held to what van Vliet calls "a form of [the progressive] abrogation of the covenant of works."[16] Commenting on the New Covenant, Ames says:

> 4. The testament is new in relation to what existed from the time of Moses and in relation to the promise made to the fathers. But it is new not in essence but in form. In the former circumstances the form of administration gave *some evidence of the covenant of works*, from which this testament is essentially different.[17]

While discussing Christian freedom under the New Covenant, Ames continues, "9. Freedom comes, first, in doing away with government by law, or *the intermixture of the covenant of works*, which held the ancient people in a certain bondage."[18] Ames viewed the Old Covenant as containing elements of the covenant of works which are not included in the New Covenant. This could be where Cocceius first heard of the progressive abrogation of the covenant of works, though in seed form. Cocceius' theory of progressive abrogation will be discussed below.

Finally, Ames' method of articulating the covenant of grace was chronological or along redemptive-historical lines.[19] He also saw the promise of the redeemer in Genesis 3:15.[20]

---

[12] Ames, *The Marrow of Theology*, 203 (XXXVIII:14-19).
[13] Ames, *The Marrow of Theology*, 204 (XXXVIII:20-28).
[14] Ames, *The Marrow of Theology*, 204-5 (XXXVIII:30-5).
[15] Ames, *The Marrow of Theology*, 203 (XXXVIII:29).
[16] van Vliet, "Decretal Theology and the Development of Covenant Thought," 418.
[17] Ames, *The Marrow of Theology*, 206 (XXXVIII:4). Emphasis added.
[18] Ames, *The Marrow of Theology*, 206 (XXXVIII:9). Emphasis added.
[19] Cf. Ames, *The Marrow of Theology*, 202-10 (XXXVIII and XXXIX) and van Vliet, "Decretal Theology and the Development of Covenant Thought," 416.
[20] Ames, *The Marrow of Theology*, 203 (XXXVIII:14).

Johannes Cocceius

One of the most important and controversial Reformed orthodox federal theologians of the seventeenth century was Johannes Cocceius (1603-1669), a student of Ames.[21] Though German born, Cocceius lived most of his life in The Netherlands. He attended the University of Franeker from 1626-1629. He ended his teaching career as professor of theology at Leiden from 1650-1669. He wrote commentaries, works on philology, dogmatics, ethics, and his famous *Summa doctrinae de foedere et testament Dei* (*Doctrine of the Covenant and Testament of God*) in 1648.[22] This was the classic continental federal theology. "By means of the concept of *foedus* he sought to do justice, also in systematic theology, to the historical nature of the biblical narrative."[23] Some of his followers (i.e., Cocceians) sought to integrate elements of Cartesian philosophy into his federalism, "in spite of Cocceius's rejection of such a union."[24] Integrating covenant and kingdom he "developed a theology of history, or in his own words, "a prophetic theology.""[25] Cocceius held a controversial view of the Sabbath, which was

---

[21] Cf. William Klempa, "Cocceius, Johannes (1603-1669)" in Donald K. McKim, editor, *ERF*, 73-74; Willem J. van Asselt, "Cocceius, Johannes" in McKim, editor, *DMBI*, 315-20; Willem J. van Asselt, "Cocceius Anti-Scholasticus?" in Willem J. van Asselt and Eef Dekker, editors, *Reformation and Scholasticism: An Ecumenical Enterprise* (Grand Rapids: Baker Academic, 2001), 227-51; van Asselt, *The Federal Theology of Johannes Cocceius (1603-1669)*, 23-33; Willem J. van Asselt, "Structural Elements in the Eschatology of Johannes Cocceius," *Calvin Theological Journal* (*CTJ*) 35 (2000): 76-104; Willem J. van Asselt, "The Doctrine of the Abrogations in the Federal Theology of Johannes Cocceius (1603-1669)," *CTJ* 29 (1994): 101-16; McCoy and Baker, *Fountainhead of Federalism*, 63-79; Jan van Vliet, "Decretal Theology and the Development of Covenant Thought: An Assessment of Cornelis Graafland's Thesis with a Particular View to Federal Architects William Ames and Johannes Cocceius," *WTJ* 63 (2001): 393-420.

[22] It is of interest to note that the most famous "Biblical Theologian" of the seventeenth-century Reformed orthodox also wrote a work on Dogmatics.

[23] van Asselt, "Cocceius, Johannes" in McKim, editor, *DMBI*, 315.

[24] van Asselt, "Cocceius, Johannes" in McKim, editor, *DMBI*, 315.

[25] van Asselt, "Cocceius, Johannes" in McKim, editor, *DMBI*, 318; cf. van Asselt, "Structural Elements in the Eschatology of Johannes Cocceius," 85ff. for a discussion on Cocceuis' doctrine of the epochs of the church as he found them in the book of Revelation and his fascination with the number seven in Scripture.

confronted by Voetius and his followers, as well as issues of continuity and discontinuity between the Old and New Testaments.[26]

Cocceius' view of the covenant of works infused eschatology into his theology from the Garden of Eden.[27] "The covenant of works opened up the possibility of a history with an eschatological prospect."[28] Paradise "was a symbol and pledge of a 'better habitation.'"[29] He was not the only Reformed orthodox to argue in this manner. If fact, as we shall see, the intersection of protology and eschatology through the doctrine of the covenant of works was quite common. Cocceius viewed the covenant of works not as a contract, "but rather *amicitia*, friendship – a concept that has medieval roots and which extends back into classical antiquity."[30] He viewed God's covenant as "essentially monopleuric" (i.e., one-sided) and yet assuming a dipleuric (i.e., two-sided) character once man engaged himself and concurred with God's "covenantal initiative."[31]

He held a very unique view of progressive revelation in that he saw the covenant of works progressively abrogated as salvation history unfolded and advanced.[32] Van Asselt comments:

> One of the most peculiar constructions in the theological system of Johannes Cocceius certainly is the doctrine of the so-called abrogations. This doctrine, which is closely connected with the doctrine of the covenant of works and the covenant of grace, occurs in both systematic main works of Cocceius: *in the Summa Doctrinae de Foedere et Testamento Dei* of 1648 (§58) and in the *Summa Theologiae ex Scripturis*

---

[26] van Asselt, "Cocceius, Johannes" in McKim, editor, *DMBI*, 316-17.
[27] van Asselt, *The Federal Theology of Johannes Cocceius*, 264.
[28] van Asselt, "Structural Elements in the Eschatology of Johannes Cocceius," 82.
[29] van Asselt, *The Federal Theology of Johannes Cocceius*, 264.
[30] van Asselt, *The Federal Theology of Johannes Cocceius*, 24, n. 3.
[31] van Asselt, *The Federal Theology of Johannes Cocceius*, 39.
[32] Cf. van Asselt, *The Federal Theology of Johannes Cocceius*, 271-87 for an extensive discussion.

repetita of 1662 (cap. 31 §1). Briefly formulated, this doctrine describes some five degrees (*gradus*) by which God leads man into eternal life and by which the consequences of the violation of the covenant of works through the Fall are gradually abrogated.[33]

Cocceuis' five degrees of abrogation were: (1) by the fall, (2) by the covenant of grace revealed through the first promise of salvation (Genesis 3:15)[34] and its subsequent unfolding in both testaments, (3) by the incarnation, (4) by the intermediate state, and (5) by the eternal state.[35] These degrees or stages of abrogation combine the *historia salutis* with the *ordo salutis*. Indeed, van Asselt says, "…the historical and the existential moments are combined."[36] Each epoch of the *historia salutis* has a corresponding state of condition in the *ordo salutis*.[37] Cocceius saw movement and development along salvation-historical lines and sought to give expression to that via the slow but certain abrogation of the covenant of works and the slow but certain increasingly fulfilled covenant of grace. His views gave the appearance of driving a wedge between issues of forgiveness and justification in the Old and New Testaments and, thus, his theory was rejected firmly by Voetius and his followers. Van Asselt argues that the Cocceians themselves failed to develop their teaching in a manner that accurately reflected Cocceius' thought and, thus, "the doctrine of abrogations as a means of

---

[33] van Asselt, "The Doctrine of the Abrogations in the Federal Theology of Johannes Cocceius (1603-1669)," 101; cf. also van Asselt, "Structural Elements in the Eschatology of Johannes Cocceius," 83.

[34] van Asselt, *The Federal Theology of Johannes Cocceius*, 58.

[35] van Asselt, "The Doctrine of the Abrogations in the Federal Theology of Johannes Cocceius (1603-1669)," 107-08; van Asselt, "Structural Elements in the Eschatology of Johannes Cocceius," 83; van Asselt, *The Federal Theology of Johannes Cocceius*, 271-72.

[36] van Asselt, "The Doctrine of the Abrogations in the Federal Theology of Johannes Cocceius (1603-1669)," 110.

[37] van Asselt, "The Doctrine of the Abrogations in the Federal Theology of Johannes Cocceius (1603-1669)," 110 and van Asselt, *The Federal Theology of Johannes Cocceius*, 278-82. Cf. the discussion in van Vliet, "Decretal Theology and the Development of Covenant Thought," 412ff.

coordination of salvation history and *ordo salutis* broke down, it became obsolete and so disappeared in Coccieian theology."[38]

Despite his oddities, Cocceius' major contribution was the further development of the utilization of the concept of covenant throughout redemptive history (and even predating it via the *pactum salutis*) and articulating his theology in a more historical-linear fashion, though certainly not exclusively. He moved from the *pactum salutis* to the covenants of works and grace. "One of the most important features of Cocceius' theology is what we shall refer to as his *historical method*."[39] Cocceius viewed redemptive history as covenantal history and progressive. He utilized the *analogia Scripturae* and *analogia fidei*, as well as analogy, typology,[40] and "his so-called prophetic exegesis"[41] method of interpreting and applying prophecy. Through his view of the abrogations, "Cocceius brought about a powerful dynamism in his view of the covenant, which simultaneously lent it a strong eschatological orientation."[42] Cocceius saw revelation as redemptive, progressive, and eschatological from its inception.[43]

---

[38] van Asselt, "The Doctrine of the Abrogations in the Federal Theology of Johannes Cocceius (1603-1669)," 116.

[39] van Asselt, *The Federal Theology of Johannes Cocceius*, 291.

[40] van Asselt, *The Federal Theology of Johannes Cocceius*, 56.

[41] van Asselt, "Structural Elements in the Eschatology of Johannes Cocceius," 78.

[42] van Asselt, "Structural Elements in the Eschatology of Johannes Cocceius," 83, cf. *Ibid.*, 102, where van Asselt says of Cocceius, "…historical dynamics are of central importance to him."

[43] McCoy called Cocceius "the most eminent theologian of the federal school" (cf. McCoy, "Johannes Cocceius: Federal Theologian" in *Scottish Journal of Theology* 16 (1963): 352) and (we think wrongly) "*not* scholastic " (cf. McCoy, "Johannes Cocceius: Federal Theologian," 353). McCoy's analysis of Cocceius is fraught with Barthian presuppositions. For instance, he says, "God's Word, which is primarily Jesus Christ, is revealed through Scripture, not in the words alone, but from faith to faith under the illumination of the Holy Spirit." Cf. McCoy, "Johannes Cocceius: Federal Theologian," 355. "The language of Scripture places before us in its words only metonymy, metaphor and the like; God gives the message." Cf. McCoy, "Johannes Cocceius: Federal Theologian," 358. In the article just referenced, McCoy devotes a whole section to trying to prove that Cocceius was anti-scholastic. However, cf. van Asselt, "Cocceius Anti-Scholasticus?" in van Asselt and Eef

Nehemiah Coxe

Nehemiah Coxe was a Particular Baptist.[44] He is important in our brief survey for at least four reasons: (1) Coxe was the co-editor (and most likely the "senior" editor) of the Particular Baptist 2LCF;[45] (2) Coxe agreed with John Owen and other seventeenth-century Reformed orthodox theologians on the function of the covenant of works as it related to the Mosaic covenant in redemptive history;[46] (3) Coxe authored *A Discourse of the Covenants that God made with men before the Law*, which is structured after the federal model, utilizes Reformed orthodox theological nomenclature, concepts, and sources, and is semantically Reformed orthodox, except portions of his exposition of the Abrahamic covenant(s);[47] and (4) Coxe introduces us to the seventeenth-century Particular Baptist formulation of covenant theology.

Coxe's treatise discusses God's covenant with Adam, God's covenant with Noah, and God's covenant(s) with Abraham.[48] It is constructed in a linear-historical trajectory from creation, to fall, to redemption in typical federal fashion.

Dekker, editors, *Reformation and Scholasticism*, 231-51 where he challenges and puts to rest McCoy's anti-scholastic interpretation of Cocceius.

[44] For a brief biography cf. James M. Renihan, "An Excellent and Judicious Divine: Nehemiah Coxe" in Nehemiah Coxe and John Owen, edited by Ronald D. Miller, James M. Renihan, and Francisco Orozco, *Covenant Theology From Adam to Christ* (Palmdale, CA: Reformed Baptist Academic Press, 2005), 7-24; James M. Renihan, "Confessing the Faith in 1644 and 1689" in *Reformed Baptist Theological Review* (*RBTR*) III:1 (July 2006): 33ff.; and Michael A. G. Haykin, *Kiffin, Knollys and Keach* (Leeds, England: Reformation Today Trust, 1996) for an introduction to three key Particular Baptists of the seventeenth century.

[45] Cf. Renihan, "An Excellent and Judicious Divine: Nehemiah Coxe," 19-21 and Renihan, "Confessing the Faith in 1644 and 1689," 33ff.

[46] Cf. Richard C. Barcellos, "John Owen and New Covenant Theology" in Coxe and Owen, *Covenant Theology*, 353-54. Coxe himself defers to Owen in Coxe and Owen, *Covenant Theology*, 30.

[47] Cf. Coxe and Owen, *Covenant Theology*, 71-140.

[48] For an outline of Coxe's treatise where this can be observed easily see Richard C. Barcellos, "Appendix One: Outline of Coxe" in Coxe and Owen, *Covenant Theology*, 313-15.

Coxe held a robust federal view of the covenant of works. He called it the covenant of creation,[49] covenant of works,[50] covenant of friendship,[51] and a covenant of rich bounty and goodness.[52] He held that God created Adam in his image with the law written in his heart. It was the sum of this law that was promulgated on Mount Sinai and delivered more briefly by our Lord "who reduced it to two great commandments respecting our duty both to God and our neighbor…"[53] Added to this moral law was "a positive precept in which he charged man not to eat of the fruit of one tree in the midst of the garden of Eden."[54] The covenant of works or creation was not co-extensive with creation but an addition to it. Coxe says:

> In this lies the mystery of the first transaction of God with man and of his relationship to God founded on it. This did not result immediately from the law of his creation but from the disposition of a covenant according to the free, sovereign, and wise counsel of God's will. Therefore, although the law of creation is easily understood by men (and there is little controversy about it among those that are not degenerate from all principles of reason and humanity), yet the covenant of creation, the interest of Adam's posterity with him in it, and the guilt of original sin returning on them by it, are not owned by the majority of mankind. Nor can they be understood except by the light of divine revelation.[55]

It is not from any necessity of nature that God enters into covenant with men but of his own good pleasure. Such a privilege and nearness to God as is included in covenant

---

[49] Coxe and Owen, *Covenant Theology*, 39, 46, 49, 53, 58.
[50] Coxe and Owen, *Covenant Theology*, 45, 49, 53.
[51] Coxe and Owen, *Covenant Theology*, 49, 51. This seems to be dependent upon Cocceius.
[52] Coxe and Owen, *Covenant Theology*, 49.
[53] Coxe and Owen, *Covenant Theology*, 43. For a brief survey of the highly nuanced view of the functions of the Decalogue in redemptive history in Reformed orthodoxy see Appendix Two of my *The Family Tree of Reformed Biblical Theology*.
[54] Coxe and Owen, *Covenant Theology*, 43.
[55] Coxe and Owen, *Covenant Theology*, 49.

interest cannot immediately result from the relationship which they have to God as reasonable creatures, though upright and in a perfect state.[56]

Adam had "the promise of an eternal reward on condition of his perfect obedience to these laws."[57] The tree of life functioned sacramentally, as "a sign and pledge of that eternal life which Adam would have obtained by his own personal and perfect obedience to the law of God if he had continued in it."[58] Adam's violation of the positive precept of Genesis 2:17 was also a violation of "that eternal law that is written in his heart."[59]

Coxe sees the covenant of grace introduced via the promise of the gospel first revealed in Genesis 3:15. The 2LCF, 7.3 says, "This Covenant [the covenant of grace in context; cf. 7.2] is revealed in the Gospel; first of all to Adam in the promise of Salvation by the seed of the woman…"[60] In his *Discourse of the Covenants*, he says:

> 11. It was from this design of love and mercy that when the Lord God came to fallen man in the garden in the cool of the

---

[56] Coxe and Owen, *Covenant Theology*, 36.

[57] Coxe and Owen, *Covenant Theology*, 44, 51. Coxe gives three proofs with discussion for the promise of an eternal reward on pages 45-46.

[58] Coxe and Owen, *Covenant Theology*, 45. Coxe justifies this function of the tree of life as follows: "The allusion that Christ makes to it in the New Testament (Revelation 2:7). …The method of God's dealing with Adam in reference to this tree after he had sinned against him and the reason assigned for it by God himself [i.e., Genesis 3:22ff.]. …This also must not be forgotten: that as Moses' law in some way included the covenant of creation and served for a memorial of it (on which account all mankind was involved in its curse), it had not only the sanction of a curse awfully denounced against the disobedient, but also a promise of the reward of life to the obedient. Now as the law of Moses was the same in moral precept with the law of creation, so the reward in this respect was not a new reward, but the same that by compact had been due to Adam, in the case of his perfect obedience." Here Coxe is articulating Owen's (and others') view of the function of the covenant of works under the Mosaic covenant.

[59] Coxe and Owen, *Covenant Theology*, 43, 51.

[60] Cf. *A Confession of Faith Put Forth by the Elders and Brethren of many Congregations of Christians (baptized upon Profession of their Faith) in London and the Country, Printed in the Year, 1677* (Auburn, MA: B&R Press, Facsimile edition, 2000), 27.

day, and found him filled with horror and shame in the consciousness of his own guilt, he did not execute the rigor of the law on him. Instead he held a treaty with him which issued in a discovery of grace. By this a door of hope was opened to him in the laying of a new foundation for his acceptance with God and walking well pleasing before him.

1. For in the sentence passed on the serpent (which principally involved the Devil whose instrument he had been in tempting man, and who probably was made to abide in his possession of the serpent until he had received this doom, Genesis 3:15) there was couched a blessed promise of redemption and salvation to man. This was to be worked out by the Son of God made of a woman, and so her seed, and man was to receive the promised salvation by faith and to hope in it. In this implied promise was laid the first foundation of the church after the fall of man which was to be raised up out of the ruins of the Devil's kingdom by the destruction of his work by Jesus Christ (1 John 3:8).[61]

Coxe adds later:

> From the first dawning of the blessed light of God's grace to poor sinners faintly displayed in the promise intimated in Genesis 3:15, the redeemed of the Lord were brought into a new relation to God, in and by Christ the promised seed, through faith in him as revealed in that promise.[62]

This understanding of Genesis 3:15 gives Coxe's work a Christocentric flavor from the beginning. In the first paragraph, he says:

> The great interest of man's present peace and eternal happiness is most closely concerned in religion. And all true religion since the fall of man must be taught by divine

---

[61] Coxe and Owen, *Covenant Theology*, 55.
[62] Coxe and Owen, *Covenant Theology*, 59.

revelation which God by diverse parts and after a diverse manner[63] has given out to his church. He caused this light gradually to increase until the whole mystery of his grace was perfectly revealed in and by Jesus Christ in whom are hid all the treasures of wisdom and knowledge. God, whose works were all known by him from the beginning, has in all ages disposed and ordered the revelation of his will to men, his transactions with them, and all the works of his holy providence toward them, with reference to the fullness of time and the gathering of all things to a head in Christ Jesus. So in all our search after the mind of God in the Holy Scriptures we are to manage out inquiries with reference to Christ. Therefore the best interpreter of the Old Testament is the Holy Spirit speaking to us in the new. There we have the clearest light of the knowledge of the glory of God shining on us in the face of Jesus Christ, by unveiling those counsels of love and grace that were hidden from former ages and generations.[64]

Not only is this statement programmatic for a Christocentric understanding of Scripture, it also reflects the fact that Coxe viewed special revelation as progressive. The 2LCF, 7.2 says, "This covenant is revealed in the Gospel; first of all to Adam in the promise of Salvation by the seed of the woman, and afterwards by farther steps, until the full discovery thereof was completed in the new Testament." Coxe saw Christ as the hermeneutical center and focal-point of the whole Bible (i.e, *scopus Scripturae* [the scope of the Scriptures]).

Coxe utilized Reformed orthodox theological nomenclature and concepts. For instance, in the preface of his work, Coxe says:

> The usefulness of all divine truth revealed in the Holy Scriptures and the great importance of what particularly

---

[63] Here he is dependent upon Beza. Cf. Coxe and Owen, *Covenant Theology*, 33, n. 1.

[64] Coxe and Owen, *Covenant Theology*, 33.

concerns those *federal* transactions which are the subject of the following treatise are my defense for an essay to discover the mind of God in them.[65]

He held clearly to a covenant of redemption between the persons of the Trinity before the world began.[66] In the first chapter of his work, he briefly discusses the monopleuric (i.e., God's sovereign initiation or proposal[67]) and dipleuric (i.e., man's restipulation[68]) nature of covenantal engagements between God and men. Coxe defines the "general notion of any covenant of God with men" as follows: "A declaration of his sovereign pleasure concerning the benefits he will bestow on them, the communion they will have with him, and the way and means by which this will be enjoyed by them."[69] Covenantal engagements spring from God's "condescending love and goodness."[70] Covenant is not co-extensive with creation.[71] God sovereignly proposes covenants with men in order to bring them to an advanced or better state than they are currently in and ultimately "to bring them into a blessed state in the eternal enjoyment of himself."[72] Adam "was capable of and made for a greater degree of happiness than he immediately enjoyed

---

[65] Coxe and Owen, *Covenant Theology*, 29. Emphasis added.

[66] Cf. Coxe and Owen, *Covenant Theology*, 54 and 2LCF 7.3 and 8.1.

[67] Cf. Coxe and Owen, *Covenant Theology*, 35 and Richard A. Muller, *Dictionary of Latin and Greek Theological Terms* (Grand Rapids: Baker Book House, Second Printing, September 1986, 1985), 122, where he says, "**foedus monopleuron…**: *one-sided or one-way covenant*; the covenant as bestowed by God and exhibiting his will toward man."

[68] Cf. Coxe and Owen, *Covenant Theology*, 35 and Muller, *Dictionary*, 120, where he says, "**foedus dipleuron…**: *two-sided or two-way covenant*; *Foedus dipleuron*, therefore, indicates, not the covenant in itself or in its underlying requirements, but rather the further relationship of God and man together in covenant, and particularly the free acceptance on the part of man of the promise of God and of the obedience required by the covenant."

[69] Coxe and Owen, *Covenant Theology*, 36. Coxe is quoting or paraphrasing Cocceuis' *Doctrine of the Covenant and Testament of God* (cf. Coxe and Owen, *Covenant Theology*, 36, n. 7).

[70] Coxe and Owen, *Covenant Theology*, 36.

[71] Cf. Coxe and Owen, *Covenant Theology*, 36, and 49 both quoted above.

[72] Coxe and Owen, *Covenant Theology*, 36.

[which] was set before him as the reward of his obedience by that covenant in which he was to walk with God."[73] Coxe even held the view that "Moses' law in some way included the covenant of creation and served for a memorial of it..."[74] This was the view of both Ames and Cocceius above, as well as John Owen.[75] Finally, Coxe utilized typology in a manner similar to others in his day.[76]

Coxe utilized Reformed orthodox sources. In his "Preface to the Reader" he acknowledges John Owen's commentary on Hebrews 8. Coxe had thought about continuing his treatment of God's federal transactions with man by dealing with the Mosaic covenant, however, Owen's treatment of these issues satisfied him.[77] Coxe quotes or references many Reformed orthodox theologians throughout his work: for instance, Beza,[78] Cocceius,[79] Rivet,[80] Ainsworth,[81] Strong,[82] Pareus,[83] Owen,[84] Whiston,[85] and Junius.[86]

---

[73] Coxe and Owen, *Covenant Theology*, 47.
[74] Coxe and Owen, *Covenant Theology*, 46.
[75] Cf. Owen, *Works*, XXII: 78, 80, 81, 142 and Richard C. Barcellos, "John Owen and New Covenant Theology: Owen on the Old and New Covenants and the Functions of the Decalogue in Redemptive History in Historical and Contemporary Perspective" in *RBTR* I:2 (July 2004): 12-46, which includes discussion and proof of Owen's view.
[76] Cf. Coxe and Owen, *Covenant Theology*, 45 (the tree of life as a type of the eschatological state), 47-48 (Adam as a type of Christ), 57 (the garments or coats of skin as a type of imputed righteousness), and 62-64 (the Ark as a type of Christ or the church).
[77] Coxe and Owen, *Covenant Theology*, 30. Coxe said, "That notion (which is often supposed in this discourse) that the old covenant and the new differ in substance and not only in the manner of their administration, certainly requires a larger and more particular handling to free it from those prejudices and difficulties that have been cast on it by many worthy persons who are otherwise minded. Accordingly, I designed to give a further account of it in a discourse of the covenant made with Israel in the wilderness and the state of the church under the law. But when I had finished this and provided some materials also for what was to follow, I found my labor for the clearing and asserting of that point happily prevented by the coming out of Dr. Owen's third volume on Hebrews. There it is discussed at length and the objections that seem to lie against it are fully answered, especially in the exposition of the eighth chapter. I now refer my reader there for satisfaction about it which he will find commensurate to what might be expected from so great and learned a person."
[78] Coxe and Owen, *Covenant Theology*, 33.
[79] Coxe and Owen, *Covenant Theology*, 34, 36.

Coxe articulated a Reformed orthodox view of the covenant of works, along with his Particular Baptist view of the covenant of grace[87] and the function of the covenant of circumcision made with Abraham. He understood revelation to be progressive and Christo-climactic. Christ, for Coxe, was the *scopus* of Scripture. Coxe also articulated a view of the Garden of Eden that we have seen before: God offered an eternal reward of unbroken communion and future blessedness with him to Adam. In other words, Adam had an eschatology; protology is eschatological in Coxe's federal scheme.

Herman Witsius

The Dutch theologian Herman Witsius (1636-1708) served several congregations as pastor then became professor of theology, serving "at Franeker (1675-1680), then at Utrecht (1680-1698), and finally at Leiden (1698-1707)."[88] He published his famous *The Economy of the Covenants Between God and Man Comprehending A Complete Body of Divinity*[89] in 1677. It was offered as somewhat of a peace effort between the Voetians and Cocceians.[90] According to Ramsey and

---

[80] Coxe and Owen, *Covenant Theology*, 33, 84, 86.
[81] Coxe and Owen, *Covenant Theology*, 61, 86.
[82] Coxe and Owen, *Covenant Theology*, 77.
[83] Coxe and Owen, *Covenant Theology*, 77.
[84] Coxe and Owen, *Covenant Theology*, 108.
[85] Coxe and Owen, *Covenant Theology*, 111.
[86] Coxe and Owen, *Covenant Theology*, 126.
[87] Coxe's view of the covenant of grace had distinct Particular Baptist nuances to it. Cf. Chapters 2, 3, and 16 below.
[88] Herman Witsius, *The Economy of the Covenants Between God and Man Comprehending A Complete Body of Divinity*, Two Volumes (Escondido, CA: The den Dulk Christian Foundation, Reprinted 1990). For a brief biographical sketch see D. Patrick Ramsey and Joel R. Beeke "Introduction: The Life and Theology of Herman Witsius (1636-1706)" in *An Analysis of Herman Witsius's The Economy of the Covenants* (Grand Rapids: Reformation Heritage Books and Fearn, Ross-shire, Scotland: Christian Focus Publications, 2002), vi.
[89] Ramsey and Beeke "Introduction: The Life and Theology of Herman Witsius (1636-1706)" in *An Analysis of Herman Witsius's The Economy of the Covenants*, iii-xxiv.
[90] See the discussion above for the issues at stake and Ramsey and Beeke "Introduction: The Life and Theology of Herman Witsius (1636-1706)," vi.

Beeke, "In governing his systematic theology by the concept of covenant, Witsius uses Cocceian methods while maintaining essentially Voetian theology."[91] "Witsius wrote his *magnum opus* on the covenants to promote peace among Dutch theologians who were divided on covenant theology."[92] His *Economy of the Covenants* contains four books: Book I – The Covenant of Works; Book II – The Covenant of Redemption; Book III – The Covenant of Grace (*ordo salutis*); and Book IV – The Covenant of Grace (*historia salutis*).[93]

Witsius starts his *magnum opus* by discussing divine covenants in general.[94] He offers a brief study of the etymology of the Hebrew and Greek words for covenant.[95] He then states "the nature of the covenant of God with man" in these words:

> A covenant of God with man, is an agreement between God and man, about the way of obtaining consummate happiness; including a combination of eternal destruction,

---

[91] Ramsey and Beeke "Introduction: The Life and Theology of Herman Witsius (1636-1706)," vii.

[92] Ramsey and Beeke "Introduction: The Life and Theology of Herman Witsius (1636-1706)," x.

[93] Cf. Ramsey and Beeke "Introduction: The Life and Theology of Herman Witsius (1636-1706)," xi for a slightly different, though essentially the same breakdown.

[94] Cf. Richard A. Muller, "The Covenant of Works and the Stability of Divine Law in Seventeenth-Century Reformed Theology: A Study in the Theology of Herman Witsius and Wilhelmus A` Brakel," in *CTJ* 29 (1994): 80, where he says, "The Reformed orthodox understanding of covenant rested on a complex of exegetical, etymological, theological, and legal considerations that evidence concern for the text of scripture, the culture of the Jews and other ancient Near Eastern peoples, the linguistic and cultural transition from Hebrew into Greek and Latin, the Christian exegetical tradition, and the doctrinal appropriation of ancient covenant language in the light of other fundamental theological questions – notably the relationship of Adam and Christ, the *imago Dei*, the problem of original righteousness and original sin, the history of salvation recorded in Scripture, and the distinction of law and gospel."

[95] Witsius, *Economy of the Covenants*, 1:42-44. Cf. Muller, "The Covenant of Works and the Stability of Divine Law in Seventeenth-Century Reformed Theology," in *CTJ* 29 (1994): 81.

with which the contemner of the happiness, offered in that way, is to be punished.[96]

He argues that covenants are comprised of a promise, a condition, and a sanction.[97] The covenant of works, or nature, or of the law[98] is "an agreement between God and Adam…by which God promised eternal life and happiness…, if he [i.e., Adam] yielded obedience…; threatening him with death if he failed but in the least point: and Adam accepted this condition."[99] Here we see Witsius utilizing the concepts of monopleurism[100] and dipleurism as did Coxe. Muller comments:

> In their understanding of both covenants, moreover, both Witsius and a` Brakel bear witness to a resolution of the seeming problem of monopleuric and dipleuric definitions of covenant — and, in so doing, evidence yet another aspect of continuity with the intentions of the Reformers. Over against the view which has tended to set monopleuric against dipleuric definitions, as if the former indicated a reliance on the doctrine of election and the latter an almost synergistic emphasis on human responsibility, the lengthy etymological and exegetical discussion offered by Witsius indicates that all covenants between God and human beings are founded on divine initiative and are, in that sense, monopleuric. At the same time, these covenants, once made, bespeak a mutuality: The human partner must in some way

---

[96] Witsius, *Economy of the Covenants*, 1:45.

[97] Witsius, *Economy of the Covenants*, 1:46. Cf. Muller, "The Covenant of Works and the Stability of Divine Law in Seventeenth-Century Reformed Theology," in *CTJ* 29 (1994): 84.

[98] Witsius, *Economy of the Covenants*, 1:50.

[99] Witsius, *Economy of the Covenants*, 1:50. Cf. Muller, "The Covenant of Works and the Stability of Divine Law in Seventeenth-Century Reformed Theology," in *CTJ* 29 (1994): 75-101.

[100] Cf. Muller, "The Covenant of Works and the Stability of Divine Law in Seventeenth-Century Reformed Theology," in *CTJ* 29 (1994): 85.

consent to the covenant and exercise responsibility within it.[101]

A hint of Edenic eschatology can be seen here as well. Adam was to keep the law of nature, which is comprised of the Decalogue in substance[102] and was "implanted …at his creation,"[103] as well as keep the positive precept forbidding him from eating of the tree of the knowledge of good and evil (Genesis 2:16-17).[104] Witsius sees Adam in a probationary state and capable of arriving at a higher, more blessed state of existence. He says:

> That man was not yet arrived at the utmost pitch of happiness, but [was] to expect a still greater good, after his course of obedience was over. This was hinted by the prohibition of the most delightful tree, whose fruit was, of any other, greatly to be desired; and this argued some degree of imperfection in that state, in which man was forbid the enjoyment of some good.[105]

The more blessed state of existence was "eternal life, that is the most perfect fruition of himself [i.e., God], and that forever, after finishing his course of obedience…"[106] This promise of life flowed out of God's goodness and bounty and not out of any strict necessity.[107] The Garden of Eden, according to Witsius, was a pledge, a type, a symbol, both temporary and anticipatory of a better state yet to be enjoyed.[108] In other words, protology is, as we have seen in other Reformed orthodox theologians, eschatological.

---

[101] Muller, "The Covenant of Works and the Stability of Divine Law in Seventeenth-Century Reformed Theology," in *CTJ* 29 (1994): 86.
[102] Witsius, *Economy of the Covenants*, 1:62.
[103] Witsius, *Economy of the Covenants*, 1:60.
[104] Witsius, *Economy of the Covenants*, 1:60, I:68ff.
[105] Witsius, *Economy of the Covenants*, 1:69; cf. also 1:123-24.
[106] Witsius, *Economy of the Covenants*, 1:73.
[107] Witsius, *Economy of the Covenants*, 1:76ff.
[108] Witsius, *Economy of the Covenants*, 1:106ff., esp. 1:109.

Witsius cites Hosea 6:7 as proof that Adam broke covenant with God in the Garden when he sinned.[109] Adam's sin brought him and the entire human race to spiritual ruin.[110]

The covenant of redemption is the pre-temporal foundation for the temporal covenant of grace.[111] The covenant of grace is made between God and the elect.[112] It is first revealed in Genesis 3:15[113] and then progressively unfolded in five redemptive-historical epochs: Adam to Noah; Noah to Abraham; Abraham to Moses; Moses to Christ; and the New Testament.[114]

Book IV is where Witsius follows a more *historia salutis* model. Genesis 3:15 is the first promise of the gospel and the first revelation of the covenant of grace. This crucial text is programmatic for Witsius. His exposition of Genesis 3:15 covers twenty pages.[115] He then traces the covenant of grace through Noah, Abraham, Moses, and the prophets. Witsius holds that the Mosaic covenant cannot be viewed simply as a covenant of grace or works. It is a national covenant, subservient to both the covenants of works and grace. Witsius says, "It was a *national covenant* between God and Israel...[It] supposed a covenant of grace...and the doctrine of the covenant of works..."[116]

Witsius, as others we have surveyed, is somewhat typical in his articulation of federalism. He starts with the covenant of works. Adam sins and brings ruin upon himself and the entire human race. Because of God's pre-temporal purpose to save the elect through a Mediator, he reveals his purposes of grace through the first gospel promise in Genesis 3:15. This gospel promise is progressively expanded through various historical types[117] and through explicit

---

[109] Witsius, *Economy of the Covenants*, 1:135.
[110] Witsius, *Economy of the Covenants*, 1:146ff.
[111] Witsius, *Economy of the Covenants*, 1:165.
[112] Witsius, *Economy of the Covenants*, 1:281ff.
[113] Witsius, *Economy of the Covenants*, 2:108ff.
[114] Witsius, *Economy of the Covenants*, I:313-16.
[115] Witsius, *Economy of the Covenants*, 2:108-28.
[116] Witsius, *Economy of the Covenants*, 2:186.
[117] Witsius, *Economy of the Covenants*, 2:188-231.

Old Testament prophecies and culminates in our Lord Jesus Christ, the *scopus* of Scripture.

Jonathan Edwards

Though Edwards was neither European nor seventeenth-century Reformed orthodox, he wrote within that theological tradition and was very aware of the intellectual currents of his day.[118] Probably America's greatest theologian to date, Edwards was a prolific student and writer. He was somewhat unique in that he utilized a pre-critical hermeneutic, though living during the early days of the emerging critical era.[119]

In 1739 Edwards preached a series of sermons that ended up being slightly revised and published in 1774 as *A History of the Work of Redemption, containing the outlines of a Body of Divinity, including a view of Church History, in a method entirely new*.[120] In this work, Edwards sought, first, to discuss the redemptive story-line of the Bible in its scriptural order and then to give a history of the church as the implications of redemption accomplished applied throughout history. In his Preface, he says this body of divinity is unique in that it is written in the form of a history in order to show the most remarkable events "from the fall to the present time" and even to the end of the world which are "adapted to promote the work of redemption…"[121]

Edwards' *History of Redemption* is divided into three periods: I. From the Fall to the Incarnation; II. From Christ's Incarnation to His Resurrection; and III. From Christ's Resurrection to the End of the World. Each period is further subdivided. The first period contains these subheadings: from the fall to the flood, from the flood to Abraham, from Abraham to Moses, from Moses to David, from

---

[118] D. A. Sweeney, "Edwards, Jonathan *(1703-1758)*" in McKim, editor, *DMBI*, 397.

[119] Sweeney, "Edwards, Jonathan *(1703-1758)*" in McKim, editor, *DMBI*, 399.

[120] Cf. Jonathan Edwards, *The Works of Jonathan Edwards*, Volume One (Edinburgh: The Banner of Truth Trust, reprinted 1990), 532-619.

[121] Edwards, *Works*, 1:532. We will focus on the sections dealing with biblical history alone.

David to the Babylonian Captivity, and from the Babylonian Captivity to the incarnation of Christ. The biblical section is approached in a linear fashion, tracing the biblical history of redemption chronologically.

From the outset of the first period in Edwards' scheme, his Christocentricity is clear and ample. He says, "As soon as man fell, Christ entered on his mediatorial work."[122] Christ's mediatorial work is founded in the covenant of redemption where "He stood engaged with the Father to appear as man's mediator, and to take on that office when there should be occasion, from all eternity."[123]

His Christocentricity is further displayed, when he says that "the gospel was first revealed on earth, in these words, Gen. iii. 15."[124] "This was the first revelation of the covenant of grace; the first drawing of the light of the gospel on earth."[125] Edwards viewed redemptive history as Christocentric and progressive. "Thus you see how that gospel-light which dawned immediately after the fall of man, gradually increases."[126] He utilized typology to see Christ progressively revealed in the Old Testament until the fullness of time had come.

The incarnation and subsequent life, death, and resurrection of Christ were climactic events in Edwards' thought. The second period, from the incarnation to the resurrection, is

> the most remarkable article of time that ever was or ever will be. Though it was but between thirty and forty years, yet more was done in it than had been done from the beginning of the world to that time.[127]

Edwards even has traces of doctrinal formulations seen as far back as Ames. He intersects *historia salutis* with *ordo salutis*, though

---

[122] Edwards, *Works*, 1:536.
[123] Edwards, *Works*, 1:536.
[124] Edwards, *Works*, 1:537.
[125] Edwards, *Works*, 1:537.
[126] Edwards, *Works*, 1:546.
[127] Edwards, *Works*, 1:572.

he extends what he calls "the work of redemption" to the end of the world. He says:

> And here, by the way, I would observe, that the increase of gospel-light, and the progress of the work of redemption, as it respects the church in general, from its erection to the end of the world, is very similar to the progress of the same world and the same light, in a particular soul, from the time of its conversion, till it is perfected and crowned in glory. Sometimes the light shines brighter, and at other times more obscurely; sometimes grace prevails, at other times it seems to languish for a great while together; now corruption prevails, and then grace revives again. But in general grace is growing: from its first infusion, till it is perfected in glory, the kingdom of Christ is building up in the soul. So it is with respect to the great affair in general, as it relates to the universal subject of it, and as it is carried on from its first beginning, till it is perfected at the end of the world.[128]

Edwards also sees a two-fold utility of the Decalogue as given by God to Moses: (1) as "a new exhibition of the covenant of works"[129] and (2) as a rule of life.[130] Commenting on "God's giving the moral law in so awful a manner at mount Sinai,"[131] he says:

> And it was a great thing, whether we consider it as a new exhibition of the covenant of works, or given as a rule of life.
> The covenant of works was here exhibited as a schoolmaster to lead to Christ, not only for the use of that nation, under the Old Testament, but for the use of God's church throughout all ages of the world...
> If we regard the law given at mount Sinai – not as a covenant of works, but – as a rule of life, it is employed by

---

[128] Edwards, *Works*, 1:539-40.
[129] Edwards, *Works*, 1:547.
[130] Edwards, *Works*, 1:548.
[131] Edwards, *Works*, 1:547.

the Redeemer, from that time to the end of the world, as a directory to his people, to show them the way in which they must walk, as they would go to heaven: for a way of sincere and universal obedience to this law is the narrow way that leads to life.[132]

Though Edwards' title includes the words "in a method entirely new," some elements contained in this work have precedent in seventeenth-century Reformed orthodoxy. Edwards articulated redemptive history in a federal model. He held to the covenants of redemption, works, and grace. He saw the gospel first revealed in Genesis 3:15 and then progressively amplified in the Old Testament until the climactic event of the incarnation occurred along with its necessary redemptive accompaniments.

Conclusion

The intent of this brief survey is to introduce readers to the thought-world of the most productive era in the history of the church for the formulation of federal or covenant theology. Among the theologians surveyed above, there is both continuity and discontinuity of thought. The lone Particular Baptist, Nehemiah Coxe, clearly utilized the formulations of others in his day, yet departing at crucial points. The various Particular Baptist departures will become more evident in the chapters immediately following (2-9, but especially 2-3). However, the chapters dealing with biblical and biblical-theological issues (9-16) will pick up on some of the same issues brought up in this chapter and, especially, in the chapters that immediately follow.

---

[132] Edwards, *Works*, I:547-48. Edwards presents a two-fold utility of the moral law given at Sinai. The way in which he presents the material may lead some to think he is presenting two mutually exclusive positions; either "a new exhibition of the covenant of works" or "a rule of life." I think it better to take it as both/and. For a discussion on the highly nuanced views of the Reformed orthodox on the functions of the Decalogue in redemptive history see Richard C. Barcellos, "John Owen and New Covenant Theology," 12-46.

A Brief Overview of Seventeenth-Century Reformed Orthodox Federalism

As will become evident, the seventeenth-century Particular Baptists were not merely immersing Presbyterians, as a friend of mine once said. Neither did they formulate their version of federal theology in order to avert the hand of persecution. Their formulation was based on biblical exegesis and the redemptive-historical theological synthesis of those exegetical labors. Their views had much in common with paedobaptist federalism, though their formulation departed at crucial points and did so with clearly stated reasons. The chapters that follow attempt to identify and discuss some of those reasons.

A Brief Overview of Seventeenth-Century Reformed Orthodox Federalism

Chapter 2
Covenant Theology in the First and Second London Baptist Confessions
James M. Renihan, Ph.D.*

In the introduction to his monograph on seventeenth-century Antinomianism, *Blown by the Spirit*, David Como says that "antinomianism cannot be understood apart from the puritan community as a whole." Arguing that Antinomianism developed in contradistinction to mainstream Puritanism, he seeks to demonstrate that the movement was "a rejection of many of the most hallowed priorities of puritan religiosity."[1] Como's methodology is sound, recognizing that context explains much, even, or perhaps especially, when differences arise.

A study of covenant theology in the two Particular Baptist London Confessions must follow the same approach. The theological views expressed in those Confessions did not arise immediately, without reference to the religious climate of that period, but flowed out of a larger doctrinal milieu, a setting ignored at great peril. This may be confirmed in multiple ways. For example, both Confessions were penned by men steeped in the theological discourse of the day. Their religious faith was nurtured in the world of English Puritanism. We know that they sat under the preaching of well-known ministers, maintained friendly relations with some of the most famous theologians of their day, and some were trained at the Universities where theology faculties

---

* James M. Renihan, Ph.D., Trinity Evangelical Divinity School, is Dean and Professor of Historical Theology at the Institute of Reformed Baptist Studies, Westminster Seminary, CA.

[1] David Como, *Blown by the Spirit: Puritanism and the Emergence of an Antinomian Underground in Pre-Civil-War England* (Stanford: Stanford University Press, 2004), 29.

were dominated by Puritans.[2] Similarly, when these early Baptists wished to declare their *common agreement* with the Puritans around them, rather than creating new doctrinal standards, they employed and edited well-known paedobaptist Confessions in order to highlight the many doctrines held in common with the broader Puritan movement.[3]

The *First London Confession* (1LCF) is a seminal statement of Particular Baptist faith and practice.[4] A product of the political and religious upheavals of early 1640s London, it was an attempt by seven small and relatively new churches to mitigate growing concerns about their doctrines and intentions in the metropolis. Religious toleration was virtually unknown, and rumors abounded that this burgeoning group of illegal congregations held nefarious views similar to the execrated Anabaptists of Münster in northern Germany. Cries for the civil magistrate to take action were sounding forth. The situation was certainly volatile, and the representatives of the churches determined that the best course of action would be an honest declaration of their faith, hoping that this act would convince their concerned opponents of their peaceful orthodoxy. The 1644 edition of the Confession was their first attempt. It was criticized by some leading opponents resulting in a revised edition published in 1646.

---

[2] See for example, William Orme, ed., *Remarkable Passages in the Life of William Kiffin* (London: Burton and Smith, 1823), 3-5, where Kiffin attributes his conversion to hearing John Davenport and John Norton (among others); Hanserd Knollys (and William Kiffin), *The Life and Death of that Old Disciple of Jesus Christ, and Eminent Minister of the Gospel, Mr. Hanserd Knollys* (London: 1692), 3. Knollys matriculated at Katherine Hall, Cambridge, while Richard Sibbes was Master and Thomas Goodwin a Fellow. For an account of the friendships maintained during the 1640s, see Murray Tolmie, *The Triumph of the Saints: The Separate Churches of London 1616-1649* (Cambridge: CUP, 1977), 56. I have provided pointers to biographical material for the Baptists cited in this chapter.

[3] See James M. Renihan, "Confessing the Faith in 1644 and 1649" in *RBTR* III:1 (January 2006), 27-47.

[4] The material in this and the next paragraph is taken from James M. Renihan, *True Confessions: Baptist Documents in the Reformed Family* (Owensboro, KY: RBAP, 2004), 3-4.

The method used in writing this Confession (and its successor) is important to notice. The document(s) are not *de novo*[5] productions, but rather adaptations of important theological works already extant. The broad framework for the 1LCF is drawn from the *1596 True Confession* of an English Separatist church which was gathered in exile in The Netherlands, and probably composed by Henry Ainsworth. This was supplemented by many excerpts from *The Marrow of Divinity*, an important theological work penned by the leading theologian of the exiles and separatists (and well-respected by non-separating Puritans as well), William Ames, and significant quotations from the 1603 document *The Points of Difference* probably co-authored by Ainsworth, and some other sources.[6] The influence of the 1596 Separatist Confession is pervasive in the 1644 London Confession. A comparison of the first eleven articles of each Confession demonstrates that the Baptists relied upon the order and substance of the earlier Separatist document. From article twelve to article twenty of the 1LCF, the Baptists have continued to follow the order of the *True Confession* through its article sixteen, but added four articles to further explicate the Mediatorship of Christ in his offices of prophet, priest, and king. Articles twenty-one through thirty-two in the Baptist Confession are then added, delineating many issues pertinent to soteriology. Articles thirty-three through thirty-five mirror articles seventeen through nineteen of the *True Confession*, while articles thirty-six through fifty-two only occasionally echo its statements, since they deal more fully with the distinctive aspects of early Baptist ecclesiology and church polity. It is clear that these Baptists were satisfied that much of the theology of this older Confession reflected their own beliefs.

---

[5] Latin for new or from the beginning.

[6] On the sources of the 1LCF see *True Confessions* as well as Jay Travis Collier, "The Sources Behind the First London Confession" in *American Baptist Quarterly* XXI:2 (June 2002), 197-214; Stanley A. Nelson, "Reflecting on Baptist Origins: The London Confession of Faith of 1644" in *Baptist History and Heritage* XXIX:2 (April 1994), 33-46; and James M. Renihan, "An Examination of the Possible Influence of Menno Simons' *Foundation Book* upon the Particular Baptist Confession of 1644" in *American Baptist Quarterly* XV:3 (September 1996), 191-210.

The Confession was quickly scrutinized by important religious authorities of London who examined it to determine its orthodoxy. These men were motivated to find every possible deviation from the standard maintained by Parliament in the Church of England.[7] It is fascinating to notice their strictures. Largely, they are of minor and expected points of disagreement – baptism, the ministry, and the relation of church and state. One of these critics, Daniel Featley, a member of the Westminster Assembly and self-appointed heresy-hunter, said this of the 1644 Confession:

> if we give credit to this Confession and the Preface thereof, those who among us are branded with that title [i.e., Anabaptist], are neither Heretics, nor Schismatics, but tender hearted Christians: upon whom, through false suggestions, the hand of authority fell heavy, whilst the Hierarchy stood: for, they neither teach free-will; nor falling away from grace with the *Arminians*, nor deny original sin with the *Pelagians*, nor disclaim Magistracy with the *Jesuites*, nor maintain plurality of Wives with the *Polygamists*, nor community of goods with the *Apostolici*, nor going naked with the *Adamites*, much less aver the mortality of the soul with the *Epicures* and *Psychophannichists*: and to this purpose they have published this confession of Faith, subscribed by sixteen persons, in the name of seven Churches in *London*.[8]

A paragraph later he makes this amazing comment:

---

[7] Thomas Edwards, *The First and Second Part of Gangraena* (London: Ralph Smith, 1646) 108-09; Daniel Featley, *The Dipper's Dip't*, Robert Baillie, *Anabaptisme, the True Fountaine of Independency, Antinomy, Brownisme, Familisme* . . . (London: Samuel Gellibrand, 1647); Ephraim Pagitt, *Heresiography* (London: William Lee, 1648) 38-39. Featley's criticisms may be summarized in this way: 1. That the Baptists in article 31 seem to imply that the right to earthly possessions is founded in grace, not nature; 2. That article 38 speaks against the support of ministers by the state; objections 3., 4., and 5. all deal with believer's baptism; 6. That the Baptists allowed non-ordained men to preach. Pagitt's strictures are the same as Featley's.

[8] Daniel Featley, *The Dippers Dip't* (London: Richard Royston, 1660, seventh edition) 177-78.

> We read in *Diodorus Sculus,* of certain creatures about the shores of *Nilus* not fully formed; and in a Stone-cutters shop we see here the head of a man, there all the upper parts carved, and in a third place a perfect statue; so it seems to me, that these Anabaptists are but *in fieri,* (as the Schools speak) not *in facto esse*: like the fish and Serpents in the middle of *Nilus,* not fully shaped, like a Statue in a Stone-cutters shop, not finished: they are Anabaptists but in part, not in whole. Be it so, for I desire to make them better then worse, then they are . . . .[9]

Apart from six specific minor criticisms, he finds no fault in the statements of doctrine expressed in the 1LCF. This is of great importance, for it aids us in understanding the theological context of the Confession. Featley was motivated to find error; instead he finds vast agreement and minor differences, and he hopes that in pointing out the dissimilarities, he might make the "Anabaptists" better, that is, even more orthodox than they already state.

This orthodoxy may be attributed (beyond the obvious fact that these men truly believed these things) to the documents upon which the 1LCF is based. They too carry the stamp of mainstream Reformed thought. Henry Ainsworth, in the preface to the *1596 True Confession* (the most important source for the 1LCF) wrote:

> We testify by these presents unto all men, and before them to take knowledge hereof, that we have not forsaken any one point of the true Ancient Catholic and Apostolic faith professed in our land: but hold forth the same grounds of Christian religion with them still, agreeing likewise herein, with the Dutch, Scottish, German, French, Helvetian, and all other Christian reformed Churches round about us, whose Confessions published, we call to witness our agreement

---

[9] Featley, *The Dippers Dip't*, 178-79. *In fieri* carries the sense "in process or becoming"; *in facto esse,* "in acquisition."

with them, in matters of greatest moment, being conferred with these Articles of our faith following.[10]

This was an important claim. In the face of persecution (Ainsworth's congregation had been forced to flee to The Netherlands), the shared orthodoxy of this pilgrim church was vital. By this statement, Ainsworth and his people were seeking to position themselves within the established Reformed tradition, making it evident that the persecution directed towards them was not in any way based upon heterodoxy in catholic doctrines, but rather in matters of worship and church order mandated by the Bishops of the Church of England. It was to these they objected. In some sense – in terms of the common doctrines expressed in both documents – this claim could be made by the authors of the 1LCF as well. In this sense, it is an orthodox Reformed Confession. John Spilsbury, whose name is affixed to both the 1644 and 1646 editions of the 1LCF, on the first page of his *A Treatise Concerning the Subject of Baptisme*, mentions matters of agreement with his paedobaptist brothers:

> And for some things in the beginning, I shall pass over briefly, they not much concerning the point in hand. As the Scriptures being a perfect rule of all things, both for faith and order; this I confess a truth. And for the just and true consequence of Scripture, I do not deny; and the covenant of life lying between God and Christ for all his elect, I do not oppose ...."[11]

---

[10] [Henry Ainsworth], *An Apologie or Defence of Such True Christians as are commonly (but unjustly) Called Brownists* (1604), 7.

[11] J[ohn] S[pilsbury], *A Treatise Concerning the Lawfull Subject of Baptisme* (London: 1643), 1. This material is the same in the enlarged version of this *Treatise* published in 1652. See James Renihan, "John Spilsbury, (1593-c. 1662/1668" in Michael A. G. Haykin, ed., *The British Particular Baptists 1638-1910* (Springfield, MO: Particular Baptist Press, 1998), 21-37. He should not be confused with two paedobaptists, father and son, of the same name. John Spilsbury Sr. was a fellow of Magdalen College, Oxford, and was for many years minister in Bromsgrove, Worcestershire. His son was a dissenting minister in Kidderminster. Cf. Walter Wilson, *The History and Antiquities of Dissenting Churches and Meeting Houses in*

All of this is to say that there is a theological provenance to both Baptist Confessions.[12] They cannot and must not be read apart from this context. Both largely reflect the setting from which they emerge. To treat them in any other fashion is to commit the anachronistic fallacy.

Covenant Theology in the 1LCF

The First London Confession may be outlined like this:

Introduction: Paragraph 1
Unit 1: God, Paragraphs 2-6
    Trinity 2
    Decrees 3
    Creation & Fall 4
    Redemption & Judgment 5&6
Unit 2: Scripture, 7&8
    Canon 7
    Christ is the theme 8
Unit 3: Christ, 9-20
    His Person 9
    Mediator 10-13
    3-fold office 14
    Prophet 15-16
    Priest 17-18
    King 19-20
Unit 4: The Blessings of Salvation, 21-32
    Rooted in Christ's Death 21
    Faith 22
    Preservation 23
    Effectual calling 24
    Against preparationism 25

London, Westminster and Southwark, (London: For the Author, 1808), 2:55-56. The son apparently married the daughter of John Eckels, the Particular Baptist pastor in Bromsgrove. See R. L. Greaves and Robert Zaller, *Biographical Dictionary of British Radicals* (Brighton: Harvester, 1984), 3:194.

[12] The provenance of the 2LCF will be investigated below.

  Christian life dependence on the power of God 26
  Union with God and adoption 27
  Justification 28
  Sanctification 29
  Peace with God/reconciliation 30
  The tension between this world and the world to come 31
  The saints' dependence on Christ throughout this life 32
Unit 5: The Church 33-47
  Universal/Visible 33
  Promises made to the church 34
  Necessity of the church 35
  Independency 36
  Duties of Ministers 37
  Ministerial Support 38
  Baptism: General statement 39
  Immersion and its signification 40
  Administration of baptism 41
  Church Discipline 42
  Every member is subject to discipline 43
  Ministers and members: all have a part 44
  Gifted Brothers 45
  Members should maintain membership through difficulties 46
  Associations 47
Unit 6: The Civil Magistrate 48-53
  God ordained 48
  King and Parliament 49
  Toleration and their demeanor under it 50
  Demeanor under opposition/persecution 51
  Maintaining the distinctions of society 52
  God and Caesar 53

We are mostly interested in the first four units. Our method will be to seek to explain the language of the 1LCF through the writings of contemporary, seventeenth-century Baptist authors.

  Though the word "covenant" is not used extensively in the document, the concept is at the very root of the theology described.

Covenant Theology in the First and Second London Baptist Confessions

After an introductory paragraph and several important statements about God, his purposes in the world, and the centrality of Scripture, paragraph x explicitly introduces the language of "covenant." We are told that Jesus Christ (who is the theme of Scripture, paragraphs viii and ix) is the "mediator of the new Covenant, even the everlasting covenant of grace."[13] This phrase alerts the reader to the fact that covenant theology must be viewed through the lens of Jesus Christ. He is the one who accomplishes the purposes of God. A careful reading of paragraph xi set in its theological context demonstrates that the Baptists adhered to the current scheme of Reformed covenant theology. The earlier part speaks of the eternal trinitarian covenant or plan of God for the salvation of men (often called the *pactum salutis*) and the latter part addresses the historical accomplishment of this plan (often called the *historia salutis*). Father, Son, and Spirit are each included in this work. The "appointment" of Christ is "from everlasting" (i.e., covenantal).

Paragraph xii moves the thought further, explaining the earlier part of the previous statement. Jesus Christ was called by God to serve in this role as mediator according to a "special covenant" (1644) or "special promise" (1646 revision). This change deserves mention. In the literature of the day, the term covenant was employed with two nuanced senses: contract or compact and promise. When it is changed from "covenant" to "promise" in the revised edition of the 1LCF xii, it is to emphasize the promissory nature of this covenant. What is described here is not a mutual intratrinitarian *contract*, but rather a gracious trinitarian *promise* of salvation in Christ. Robert Purnell wrote:

> if we would . . . know when this covenant was made with Christ for us, let us weigh that text, Ephesians 1:4, *We are chosen in him, before the foundation of the world*. Now if election be before the foundation of the world (sure it is) then also by the same ground the covenant or promise was made before the foundation of the world, for the word doth prove the one

---

[13] 1LCF/1646 abbreviates this language but states the same doctrine.

as well as the other; these promises were made first to Christ on our behalf, before they are made to us, because the whole work of our redemption and salvation, was transacted between the Father and the Son, before the foundation of the world, and is afterwards revealed to us in due time, as is evident, Titus 1:2, 2 Timothy 1:9.[14]

Later in the same work, he said, "The covenant and promise of grace, are built upon the unchangeable purpose of God . . . ."[15] Purnell's statements shed light on the entire structure of the 1LCF up to this point. The forward movement from the doctrine of God must be followed by statements about the accomplishment of redemption, all of which is done according to an eternal covenant. In no way does this change introduce doctrinal novelty; it is a refinement. Especially important to note is that paragraph xii (as well as much of the following material) is not present in the *1596 True Confession*, but actually is drawn directly from William Ames' *The Marrow of Sacred Divinity*.[16] The Baptists were not afraid to adopt the covenant theology of the most mainstream of Puritan theologians in their common Confession.

Writing in 1649, another signatory of the 1LCF, Samuel Richardson, explained:

> the word *Covenant*, imports a mutual agreement of two parties to perform each of them the things agreed upon; for it cannot be a Covenant, unless there be something to be done on both parties; and therefore a promise differs from a Covenant, in that a promise may tie one party only, as all

---

[14] Robert Purnell, *A Little Cabinet Richly Stored* (London: Thomas Brewster, 1657), 29, 83. Purnell was an elder in the Broadmead, Bristol Church until his death in 1666. See Roger Hayden, ed., *The Records of a Church of Christ in Bristol, 1640-1687* (Bristol: Bristol Record Society, 1974), 19-27.

[15] Purnell, *A Little Cabinet Richly Stored*, 19-27.

[16] William Ames, *The Marrow of Sacred Divinity* (London: Henry Overton, 1642), 82-87. Paragraphs xiii, xv, xvi and xvii do have parallels in the *True Confession*. Interestingly, at one point in xiv, Ames seems to follow the wording of the *True Confession*! This material is set out in parallel columns in Renihan, *True Confessions*, 15-24.

free and absolute promises doe; but a conditional promise differs nothing from the nature of a Covenant.[17]

Richardson's point is that the covenant of grace is, on the one hand, a promise to the elect, but on the other, a covenant between God and Christ. Believers are not a part of those who keep the conditions on either side. In this way, the same arrangement may be called by either term, depending on the context. When viewed from the divine perspective, describing the eternal acts of God, it is properly a covenant. When viewed, however, from the prospect of the salvation of sinners, it is more properly called a promise. It is an important but helpful distinction, and explains the use of the language in the 1LCF.

Christopher Blackwood, prominent in the 1640s, wrote at length about the nature of the covenants. He argues that apart from the Noahic, Davidic and Levitical covenants "there are two other Covenants most considerable." These are "a carnal typical covenant, called old" and what Scripture calls "the second covenant . . . or the new covenant . . . or the better covenant of which Christ was the surety." In response to the query "What is this new Covenant?" Blackwood replies:

> It is God's free promise, whereby he promiseth not only pardon of sins and eternal life to them that are elect . . . but also doth promise to take away the stony heart and to give them a new heart and new spirit and to put his laws in their minds and write them in their hearts.[18]

Paragraphs xiii through xxxii flesh out many important aspects of this doctrine. Only Christ may fill the threefold office of mediator, defined as prophet, priest, and king. Each role is for the benefit of the elect and the accomplishment of this eternal

---

[17] Samuel Richardson, *Divine Consolations; or The Teachings of God in Three Parts* (London: M. Simmons, 1649), 221-22. For Richardson, see Greaves and Zaller, *BDBR*, 3:93-95.

[18] Christopher Blackwood, *A Soul-Searching Catechism* (London: Giles Calvert, 1653), 37-38. See Greaves and Zaller, *BDBR*, 1:69-70.

covenant/promise of God. In their ignorance, believers need a teacher who is fully divine and entirely human; in their alienation from God, they need a priest, not after the Aaronic order, but according to Melchizedek, to make sacrifice and intercede for the people; and because of their inabilities, they need a king to govern and guard and protect and strengthen them. All of this is done so that God's purpose is accomplished. The entire section is intricately woven and must be read forward and backward, recognizing the theological interdependence of concepts.

The objects of these gracious covenantal acts planned in eternity and accomplished in history are believers. Paragraphs xxix and xxx return to the term "covenant" in order to emphasize the sovereign nature of all the privileges they enjoy. This too fits the doctrinal writings of the day. In 1652, Henry Lawrence stated:

> The great benefit of this New Covenant in opposition to the Old, lies in this, that in the New Covenant God doth not only propound the terms, but engages himself to perform the condition, whereas the Old Covenant set before you life and death, good and evil, but engaged you to the performance of good without assistance (for the Law was without you) or to the suffering of evil. But in the New Covenant, the Law is within, written on your hearts, by which you are made holy and disposed for all good.[19]

Salvation is, from first to last, an act of a gracious God who acts for his own glory and for the good of his people. He plans their salvation, accomplishes it in Christ, and grants them a gracious disposition to serve him in thankfulness. One thinks of the famous structure of the Heidelberg Catechism.

The doctrine of the covenant, however, is not yet exhausted. Believers are not saved in isolation. Another blessing of the

---

[19] Henry Lawrence, *A Plea for the use of Gospel Ordinances* (London: Livewell Chapman, 1652), 22. The word "without" simply means "outside." Lawrence wrote in defense of believer's baptism in the mid 1640s. See Greaves and Zaller, *BDBR*, 2:175-76.

covenant is the church, the place of God's covenantal presence, xxxiv. It is there that he acts to save and keep the elect. The church is the recipient of promises, signs (baptism and the Lord's Supper), love, blessings, and protection. All types of men (xxxv) are called there so that they might enjoy the privileges meted out through this body. These blessings are not found in the world (which is a different kingdom, xlviii etc.), but only within the covenantal community.

When viewed holistically and against the backdrop of the theological horizon of the day, it becomes obvious that an orthodox, covenantal divinity is central to the doctrinal progress of the 1LCF. It is no wonder that Thomas Edwards and Daniel Featley, along with others, could recognize and (in a sense) approve the broad theological structure of this Confession. It was (and is) a member of the classic Reformed family of covenant theology. Throughout, the 1LCF employs the current terminology as one might find it in, for example, William Ames. While its covenant theology is dispersed and not neatly summarized as in the 2LCF, it nevertheless reflects contemporary beliefs among the Puritan/Separatist and Reformed scholastic thinkers of the day.[20]

Covenant Theology in the 2LCF[21]

The *Second London Baptist Confession of Faith* of 1677/89 along with its predecessor of 1644/46, are perhaps the two most influential Baptist Confessions in existence.[22] In many ways, the more recent Confession eclipses the earlier in importance, for by 1689 the 1LCF had become scarce, so much so that one of the key subscribers to the 2LCF stated that he had not previously seen the earlier document. It was the latter text which quickly became the standard

---

[20] See also Michael James Novak, *Thy Will Be Done: The Theology of the English Particular Baptists, 1638-1660*. Unpublished Thesis (Ph.D.), Harvard University, 1979.

[21] Much of the following material is taken from or based upon my yet unnamed, forthcoming exposition of the 2LCF.

[22] Taken from Renihan, *Confessing the Faith*, 33-34.

of Calvinistic Baptist orthodoxy in England, North America, and today, in many parts of the world.

This Confession, influential as it is, may perhaps best be understood against its historical and theological backgrounds. It did not appear *de novo*, the product of a sudden burst of theological insight on the part of an author or authors, but in the tradition of good Confession making, it is largely dependent on the statements of earlier Reformed Confessions. A quick glance will demonstrate that it is based, to a large degree, on that most Puritan of documents, the *Westminster Confession of Faith* of 1647 (WCF). A closer inspection will reveal that it is even more intimately related to the revision of the WCF made by John Owen and others in 1658, popularly known as the *Savoy Declaration and Platform of Polity*. In almost every case the editors of the Baptist Confession follow the revisions of the Savoy editors when they differ from the Westminster document. In addition, the Baptists make occasional use of phraseology from the 1LCF. When all of this material is accounted for, there is very little left that is new and original to the 2LCF.

This heavy dependence on previous sources was very much part of the purpose of the composition of the Confession. In the epistle "To the Judicious and Impartial Reader" attached to the first edition of the Confession, the editors state:

> And forasmuch as our method, and manner of expressing our sentiments, in this, doth vary from the former [i.e. the First London Confession] (although the substance of the matter is the same) we shall freely impart to you the reason and occasion thereof. One thing that greatly prevailed with us to undertake this work, was (not only to give a full account of ourselves, to those Christians that differ from us about the subject of Baptism, but also) the profit that might from thence arise, unto those that have any account of our labors, in their instruction, and establishment in the great truths of the Gospel; in the clear understanding, and steady belief of which, our comfortable walking with God, and fruitfulness before him, in all our ways, is most neerly

concerned; and therefore we did conclude it necessary to express our selves the more fully, and distinctly; and also to fix on such a method as might be most comprehensive of those things which we designed to explain our sense, and belief of; and finding no defect, in this regard, in that fixed on by the assembly [i.e., the Westminster Assembly], and after them by those of the Congregational way [i.e., the Savoy Synod], we did readily conclude it best to retain the same *order* in our present confession: and also, when we observed that those last mentioned, did in their confession (for reasons which seemed of weight both to themselves and others) choose not only to express their mind in words concurrent with the former in sense, concerning all those articles wherein they were agreed, but also for the most part without any variation of the terms we did in like manner conclude it best to follow their example in making use of the very same words with them both, in these articles (which are very many) wherein our faith and doctrine is the same with theirs, and this we did, the more abundantly, to manifest our consent with both, in all fundamental articles of the Christian Religion, as also with many others, whose orthodox confessions have been published to the world; on the behalf of the Protestants in divers Nations and Cities: and also to convince all, that we have no itch to clogge Religion with new words, but do readily acquiesce in that form of sound words, which hath been, in consent with the holy Scriptures, used by others before us, hereby declaring before God, Angels, & Men, our hearty agreement with them, in that wholesome Protestant Doctrine, which with so clear evidence of Scriptures they have asserted: some things indeed, are in some places added, some terms omitted, and some few changed, but these alterations are of that nature, as that we need not doubt, any charge or suspition of unsoundness in the faith, from any of our brethren upon account of them.[23]

---

[23] *A Confession of Faith,* unnumbered pages 2-5 of "To the Judicious and

The Baptists were concerned to demonstrate to all that their doctrinal convictions had been, from the very start, orthodox and in most ways identical with those of the Puritans around them. In both of their Confessions, the Baptists purposely used existing documents in order to evidence their concurrence with much of current theological thinking. In the quote above, they argue that the doctrines expressed in both Baptist Confessions are the same,[24] but they have chosen to base the newer Confession upon the more recent and widely available documents of Westminster and Savoy. In doing this, they were declaring with some vigor their own desire to be placed in the broad stream of English Reformed confessional Christianity.

This methodology provides us with some insight into understanding the Confession and its teaching. When it concurs with these other documents, it may be read as an endorsement of the views espoused by those Presbyterians and Independents who subscribed those documents, and of the theological works they published in defense of the confessional statements. Thus, if one wonders how the Baptists understood the doctrine of the decree of God, or justification, or the application of the law to people's consciences, or how they worked out the implications of the teaching on the perseverance of the saints, one may consult the writings of paedobaptist Puritans with much profit. Of course, not every word of every author is necessarily a fair representation of their views, but in general, their method implies substantial theological agreement with the writings of their orthodox contemporaries.

It is helpful to analyze the structure or framework of the Confession itself. I have constructed the outline to reflect the central nature of the *covenant* and *Christian Liberty* in the Confession's theology. As I have reflected on the contents of the Confession, it

---

Impartial Reader."

[24] See Renihan, "Confessing the Faith," 39-43; James M. Renihan, "Bound to Keep the First Day of the Week: Covenant Theology, the Moral Law, and the Sabbath among the first English Particular Baptists" *Reformed Baptist Theological Review* III:2 (July, 2006), 51-76. It is essential that the reader understand the fact that there are no significant doctrinal differences between these two Confessions.

seems to me that the notion of the covenant is central to the structure and contents of the document.

Outline of the 2LCF

I. First Principles (Chapters 1-6)
   A. The Scriptures (Chapter 1)
   B. The Doctrine of God (Chapters 2-3)
      1. God's Nature
      2. God's Decree
   C. Creation (Chapters 4-6)
      1. Creation
      2. Providence
      3. Sin
II. The Covenant (Chapters 7-20)
   A. The Covenant Defined (Chapter 7)
   B. The Covenant Servant: Christ the Mediator (Chapter 8)
   C. The Covenantal Setting: Free Will (Man's will as created; fallen — in need of covenantal grace; renewed — exercising covenantal grace; and perfected) (Chapter 9)
   D. The Covenant Blessings (God's Acts) (Chapters 10-13)
      1. Effectual Calling
      2. Justification
      3. Adoption
      4. Sanctification
   E. The Covenant Graces (Man's Acts) (Chapters 14-18)
      1. Faith (14:2 — Covenant of Grace)
      2. Repentance (15:2 & 5 — Covenant of Grace)
      3. Good Works
      4. Perseverance (17:2 — Covenant of Grace)
      5. Assurance
   F. The Means of Receiving the Covenant (Chapters 19-20)
      1. God's Law (19:6, 2x — not under a Covenant of Works)
      2. God's Gospel (20:1 — Covenant of Works broken)
III. God-centered Living: Freedom and Boundaries (Chapters 21-30)
   A. The Basis: Liberty of Conscience (Chapter 21)
   B. Principles

Covenant Theology in the First and Second London Baptist Confessions

1. The Worship of God (Chapters 22-23)
      a. The Practice of Worship
      b. The Day of Worship
      c. Vows
   2. Civil Government (Chapter 24)
   3. Marriage (Chapter 25)
   4. The Church (Chapters 26-30)
      a. Universal
      b. Local
      c. Fellowship
      d. Sacraments
IV. The World to Come (Chapters 31-32)
   A. The Intermediate and Resurrection States
   B. The Last Judgment

The doctrine of the covenant of grace is profoundly integrated into the theological statements, and even the structure, of the 2LCF. B. B. Warfield recognized this fact long ago:

> The architectonic principle of the Westminster Confession is supplied by the schematization of Federal theology, which had obtained by this time in Britain, as on the continent, a dominant position as the most commodious mode of presenting the corpus of Reformed doctrine.[25]

What was true of the WCF is also true of the 2LCF. This outline of the 2LCF demonstrates that the technical covenantal terminology is centered on three sections of the Confession, leading to the main points of Roman numeral II in the outline.

Observe, for example, the earliest occurrences. In chapter 7, the 2LCF adopts the substance of the WCF/Savoy language in their parallel chapters, while renaming the chapter "Of God's Covenant." In Chapter 8, the 2LCF follows the Savoy introduction of the idea of a covenant of redemption into the first sentence of the chapter, thus placing the work of Christ the mediator in a covenantal context. No

---

[25] Warfield, *The Westminster Assembly and its Work*, 56.

direct use is made of the term covenant until chapters 14, 15 and 17, all of which describe blessings granted to men in salvation. Chapters 19 and 20 return to the language of the covenant of works, chapter 19 asserting twice that believers are not under the law as a covenant of works, and chapter 20 incorporating the new material introduced by Savoy on the Gospel.

Chapter 9 presents what may at first appear to be an interesting problem. Does its presence disturb the flow of thought necessary to maintain this argument? In a word, no. If one looks closely, one will notice that it deals with a fundamentally important issue: man's relation to covenantal grace at the various stages (or states) of his existence. Chapter 9:2 speaks to fallen man's need for covenantal grace, and 9:3 speaks to renewed man's exercise of covenantal grace. This is essentially the structure of the following chapters.[26]

Chapters 10-18 all deal with facets of covenantal relations, not unlike the general description given in 7.2 as follows:

> Moreover Man having brought himself under the curse of the Law by his fall, it pleased the Lord to make a Covenant of Grace wherein he freely offereth unto Sinners, Life and Salvation by Jesus Christ, requiring of them Faith in him, that they may be saved; and promising to give unto all those that are ordained unto eternal Life, his holy Spirit, to make them willing, and able to believe.

Chapters 10-13 view the covenant relationship from God's point of view – the things that he does – and chapters 14-18 detail the

---

[26] Cf. Nehemiah Coxe, *A Discourse of the Covenants* (London: Nathaniel Ponder, 1681), 10-11, "That as all the Worship and Obedience that God hath required of, and accepted from the Children of Men, hath been upon *Covenant-Terms*; so their Ability, or moral capacity, of walking in well-pleasing before him, hath been also given to them, or wrought in them, pursuant to the ends of their Covenant-Relation; and therefore must be the inseperable Adjunct (not of the *bare proposal* of a Covenant to them, but) of that Covenant-Interest in which they have been stated . . . ." A slightly modernized version may be found in Nehemiah Coxe and John Owen, *Covenant Theology: From Adam to Christ* (Palmdale, CA: RBAP, 2005), 38-39. For biographical information on Coxe see Coxe and Owen, *Covenant Theology*, 7-24.

covenant relationship from man's perspective – that which man does in response to God's gracious acts.

Nehemiah Coxe describes the basis of this structure:

> 2. The notion of a covenant adds assurance to that of a promise, since it implies a special bond of favor and friendship which belongs to federal-interest and relation. For a covenant is the foundation of a special relationship between the parties involved in it. The kind and benefit of this relationship is determined by the covenant itself and its nature, promises, and end.

> 6. Yet this restipulation (and consequently, the way and manner of obtaining covenant blessings, as well as the right by which we claim them) necessarily varies according to the different nature and terms of those covenants that God at any time makes with men. If the covenant be of works, the restipulation must be by doing the things required in it, even by fulfilling its condition in a perfect obedience to its law. Suitably, the reward is of debt according the terms of such a covenant. (Do not understand it of debt absolutely but of debt by compact.) But if it be a covenant of free and sovereign grace, the restipulation required is a humble receiving or hearty believing of those gratuitous promises on which the covenant is established. Accordingly, the reward or covenant blessing is immediately and eminently of grace.[27]

Defining a covenant was not an issue for the Baptists. When Nehemiah Coxe sought to provide definitions, he sent his readers off to the Reformed scholars Johannes Cocceius and Andrew

---

[27] Coxe and Owen, *Covenant Theology*, 36-38.

Rivet.[28] The fundamental issues of covenant theology were held in common across the baptismal divide.

Although the doctrine permeates the theology of the Confession, the basic doctrine of covenant theology is found in chapter 7. Space will not permit a thorough exposition of the entire text of the 2LCF; a summary of the key elements must suffice.

In chapter 7, the first paragraph describes the necessity of covenant. As noted above, Coxe recognized that covenant was the divinely chosen vehicle through which contact and communication would be made with humanity. This was true with Adam[29] and is likewise true of all his posterity. The necessity of covenant is rooted in the Creator/creature distinction, but not in man's finitude. Rather, God's incomprehensibility is the basis. The profound doctrine of God expressed in chapter 2 must come to mind. God is a unique category of Being, and must stoop to reach his creatures. In creating man, God's intention was that Adam might be the king of the new world, purposing to bless the man and his descendants with the reward of life. As a result, God condescends to man by way of covenant.

The second paragraph teaches that this distance between Creator and creature is complicated by Adam's fall into sin. Since man brought curse and damnation upon himself by his disobedience, it was necessary for God to enter again into covenant with man on a very different basis than before the fall – now he acts in grace. The nature of this covenant is entirely different from the pre-lapsarian circumstance, for the Lord sovereignly makes a

---

[28] Coxe and Owen, *Covenant Theology*, 34. See Johanne Coccejo, *Summa Doctrinae de Foedere et Testamento del Explicata* (1654), 1-13; Andreae Rivet, *Theologicae & Scholasticae Exercitationes CXC in Genesin* (1633), 271.

[29] While the 2LCF omits the phrase "Covenant of Works" in Chapters 6 and 7, it clearly endorses this notion in 20:1. There are several interesting reasons for this early omission which will be explored in detail in my forthcoming book. In short, I will say that the Particular Baptists in no way rejected the concept. The omission in chapter 7 is basically (though not exclusively) rooted in the fact that the focus of the chapter and the following chapters is on the accomplishment of salvation via covenant. They are *forward looking* and positive in their development of the heads of covenantal soteriology.

Covenant Theology in the First and Second London Baptist Confessions

covenant, acting for the salvation of humans. Nehemiah Coxe explains the idea:

> The tenders of life in the gospel are full of grace, the command to believe, equal and rational; and the promise of life to the believer sure and steadfast: Election is a secret and hidden thing, as to the concernment of particular persons in it, which belongeth unto God; and as none can know their election of God before faith, so it is no way necessary that they should do so in order to believing: for revealed things belong unto us and our children, and we are bound to attend them in that same order in which God hath revealed them: Now in the gospel is the salvation of God revealed to lost sinners, and they, simply considered as such, commanded to accept of it upon the terms proposed to them; none are called to believe under the formal consideration of elect persons; but as *weary* and *heavy laden sinners; undone thirsty sinners*; in which terms every one sensible of his condition by nature, finds himself presently, and equally with others concerned.[30]

By the covenant, God calls sinners to believe, promising to give them eternal life.

The third paragraph describes how this covenant of grace is revealed. It is important to note that the 2LCF does not follow Savoy here but rather significantly alters both the WCF and Savoy. The covenant theology of the 2LCF is not simply a rehash of WCF and/or Savoy. In fact, it differs significantly. The 2LCF statement is briefer but, at the same time, is far more comprehensive than either of the paedobaptist statements. Its paragraph 3 is a wonderful redemptive-historical overview of the covenantal purpose of God in the gospel. One might expect that Baptists would be more historically sensitive in their formulation, and that is exactly the case. Their emphasis on the forward movement of redemptive history, especially in their sensitivity to the distinct subjects of

---

[30] Nehemiah Coxe, *Vindiciae Veritatis* (London: Nathaniel Ponder, 1677), 34.

Covenant Theology in the First and Second London Baptist Confessions

circumcision and baptism and their role as positive laws within specific historical covenants, brought an awareness of the progress from one covenant to another. While the paedobaptists, in the WCF and Savoy 7.5, begin their formulations at Sinai,[31] the Baptists begin in Genesis 3:15 and see covenantal development from that starting point. In this sense, the 2LCF restores the inceptive redemptive-historical focus we have noted in the 1LCF. It is important to remember that the 2LCF incorporated a great deal of material from 1LCF. Both Confessions articulate a forward-moving purpose of God, revealed in Scripture, fulfilled in Christ, applied to the believer. The use of the earlier material demonstrates both that the later Baptists understood the continuity of the documents and their theology.

The Baptist doctrine of the covenant is somewhat simpler than is that of the Presbyterians and/or Independents. The necessity of a covenant is rooted in man's creaturehood, not his fall (this is confessed in all three – WCF and Savoy as well as the 2LCF). Even Adam, as a creature, could not attain a "reward of life" apart from divine condescension (cf. 7.1). Thus, God's relationship with Adam was covenantal (i.e., federal). In 7.2, there is an assertion that man brought himself under "the curse of the law." But what law? It could not be the law of Moses. Rather, it was the law of nature given to Adam, the federal head of the race. In this way, men are addressed as law-breakers (or even covenant-breakers) in Adam, and the promise of the gospel – the covenant of grace – is addressed to all men. It was progressively revealed in history (7.3), and based

---

[31] WCF 7.5, "This covenant was differently administered in the time of the law, and in the time of the gospel: under the law, it was administered by promises, prophecies, sacrifices, circumcision, the paschal lamb, and other types and ordinances delivered to the people of the Jews, all foresignifying Christ to come; which were, for that time, sufficient and efficacious, through the operation of the Spirit, to instruct and build up the elect in faith in the promised Messiah, by whom they had full remission of sins, and eternal salvation; and is called the Old Testament." Savoy 7.5, "Although this covenant hath been differently and variously administered in respect of ordinances and institutions in the time of the law, and since the coming of Christ in the flesh; yet for the substance and efficacy of it, to all its spiritual and saving ends, it is one and the same; upon the account of which various dispensations, it is called the Old and New Testament."

upon the determination of God to save men in a new covenant, with another covenant head – Christ. No one can stand before God in innocence as did Adam – they all need Christ. The Baptists eliminated and avoided any language that suggests that men are guilty of violating the law of Moses. They need to be saved because they violate the law of nature.

As a result, men are covenant breakers in Adam. This is very similar to the New Testament methodology of preaching the gospel. How did the apostles address the lost? They tailored their message to their audiences. When they were among the Jews, they showed how the Law and the prophets pointed to Christ. But when they were with Gentiles, they went all the way back to creation (cf. Acts 14:15-18; 17:22ff.). This is the same with Paul's method in Romans. When he describes the Gentile world and its sins, he does not do so in terms of the Jewish law, but rather in terms of the violation of the knowledge of God.

When viewed against the context of the WCF/Savoy material, one is able to see that the Baptists wanted to retain the notion of covenant theology while at the same time framing it in a more historical cast. No one should say that the Baptist doctrine is identical to the Presbyterian, because it is not. But neither is the Independent doctrine the same as the Presbyterian. In fact, the Baptist doctrine is a major advance on the Presbyterian doctrine. It is not simply an alteration and/or modification of the earlier doctrine. The Particular Baptists understood that theology is integrative, and that the formulation and/or expression of one *locus* of theology can have profound impact on other *loci*. This is the genius of the Baptists' Confession (even if one thinks that they are wrong) – they saw the implications that one doctrine can have on another, and sought to express their theology in consistent formulations.

The covenant theology of the rest of the Confession may be summarized. In fulfillment of the eternal purposes of God, Christ is appointed mediator (8.1), another doctrine previously expressed in the 1LCF. Christ redeems elect individuals, and in time brings them to salvation. In chapters 10-13, this is accomplished by the divine acts of calling, justification, adoption, and sanctification. These are followed (in the confessional order) by the acts of faith, repentance, good works, perseverance, and assurance. Even these must be understood in the light of the previous sovereign covenantalism. No one is able to believe, repent, do good works, persevere or enjoy assurance apart from the priority of the divine acts. In this way, all of the blessings of salvation fit within a covenantal framework.

Conclusion

When viewed within their theological contexts, it is evident that the Particular Baptist version of covenant theology articulated in the two London Confessions shared a great deal with the formulations of the Reformed and Puritan divines around them. But at the same time, it took on a decidedly redemptive-historical character, recognizing the forward movement of the purposes of God in the outworking of his decrees. In both documents, covenant theology is cast in a forward looking frame. It is about the planning and accomplishment of salvation, according to the sovereign purpose of God, carried out in the person and work of Christ and applied to the elect by the work of the Holy Spirit. From first to last, salvation is covenantal, graciously given by the Lord to his people.

Although their theology was steeped in the familiar categories of their day, there can be no doubt that the Baptists framed their covenant theology to fit their ecclesiological purposes. It was here that the differences are evident, as they would only offer the sign of baptism to professing believers, just as admission to church membership was limited to these same people. This is most clearly demonstrated in the third paragraph of the 2LCF chapter 7, which explicitly depicts an advancing redemptive-historical perspective. While their Confessions do not directly address questions of the relationship between the Old and New Covenants, they consistently recognized that the Old Covenant was in some sense a republication of the covenant of works, not, according to Benjamin Keach "to justify them, or to give them eternal life . . ." but rather to "reveal the wisdom of God" and to show the nature of the righteousness once possessed by humanity and now required by

God for justification."[32] In this way, men may know that only Christ brings salvation.

In Particular Baptist theology, the doctrine of the divine covenants was a source of great joy and comfort. Two quotations, one from a subscriber to the 1LCF and the second from a signatory to the 2LCF, make the point:

> ... to make a new covenant with the soul is to write the Law of God in a mans heart, and in his mind, and to infuse saving knowledge and faith, by which God unites the soul to himself, and so pardons all his sins, and without any condition considered in the creature, binds over himself to be their God freely in Christ, and binds over himself to own them to be his people. And only thus, and no otherwise, is God said to make his new covenant, with a poor soul.[33]

Many years later, in the introduction to a funeral sermon preached upon the death of Henry Forty (a signatory of the 1646 edition of the 1LCF), Benjamin Keach said these words, a fitting conclusion to our study.

> The subject treated on ... is of the highest concernment .... This covenant being ... support, salvation, and consolation ... both in ... life and in death.... This covenant is the only city of refuge, for a distressed soul, to fly to for sanctuary, when all the billows and waves of temptations run over him, or Satan doth furiously assault him: If we fly to this armory, we can never want weapons to resist the Devil, nor doubt of success against him.[34]

---

[32] Benjamin Keach, *The Everlasting Covenant, a Sweet Cordial for a Drooping Soul* (London: H. Barnard, 1699), 7-8. For Keach see Austin Walker, *The Excellent Benjamin Keach* (Dundas: Joshua Press, 2004) and D. B. Riker, *A Catholic Reformed Theologian: Federalism and Baptism in the Thought of Benjamin Keach, 1640-1704*, Portland, Wipf and Stock, 2010).

[33] Thomas Patient, *The Doctrine of Baptism and the Distinction of the Covenants* (London: Henry Hills, 1654), 80. For Patient see Greaves and Zaller, *BDBR* 3:12-13.

[34] Keach, *Everlasting Covenant*, unnumbered verso of title page.

CHAPTER 3
By Farther Steps:
A Seventeenth-Century Particular Baptist Covenant Theology
Pascal Denault, Th.M.*

Covenant theology is at the core of Reformed thought. In the seventeenth century, Particular Baptists developed their own understanding of covenant theology. Their view was at the same time similar and distinct from their fellow paedobaptist contemporaries. In this chapter, we will present seventeenth-century Particular Baptist federalism.[1] We will use the following headings: 1) The Particular Baptist understanding of the Covenant of Works; 2) The Particular Baptist understanding of the Covenant of Grace; 3) The Particular Baptist understanding of the Abrahamic Covenant; 4) The Particular Baptist understanding of the Mosaic Covenant; and 5) The Particular Baptist understanding of the New Covenant. A brief conclusion will close our study.

The Particular Baptist understanding of the Covenant of Works

The seventeenth-century Particular Baptists endorsed the broadly accepted view among Reformed theologians concerning the covenant of works. This particular view considered that a covenant was made with Adam, representing his posterity, in the beginning identified as the covenant of works. It consisted of two elements: if Adam obeyed, he and his posterity after him would have attained

---

* Pascal Denault, Th.M., is pastor of the Evangelical Reformed Baptist Church, St. Jerome, Quebec, Canada.

[1] This chapter is an abbreviated version of the author's published work *The Distinctiveness of Baptist Covenant Theology: A Comparison Between Seventeenth-Century Particular Baptist and Paedobaptist Federalism* (Vestavia Hills, AL: Solid Ground Christian Books, 2013).

eternal life and would have been sealed in justice; on the other side, his disobedience would be the entrance of death and place Adam and all of his posterity under condemnation. The covenant of works provided no way to expiate the offense. In Reformed theology, the covenant of works is seen as the foundation for the "retributive" justice of God, whereby obedience begets blessing and disobedience brings malediction. It is the covenant of works that founded the principle "do this and you shall live" (Lev. 18:5; Gal 3:12) as well as the principle "the wages of sin is death" (Rom. 6:23). Under the covenant of works, eternal life cannot be given freely, it must be earned. But now, because of sin, the covenant of works is ineffective in giving life; it can only bring death (Gal. 3:21; Rom. 8:3).

Before the fall, man benefited from a relationship with his Creator wherein, by virtue of the covenant of works, God was his God. While remaining under the obligation of obeying God because of this covenant, fallen man lost his covenantal privileges which ensured him of God's favour and found himself, from then on, under God's wrath. While God remained God for all men even after the fall, sin made it so that he was no longer their God in a favorable covenantal connection. John Owen summarizes the Puritan conception of the covenant of works after the fall as follows: "And man continued under an obligation to dependence on God and subjection to his will in all things. ...But that especial relation of mutual interest by virtue of the first covenant ceased between them."[2]

The abundant references to the covenant of works in the Baptists' writings leave no doubt concerning their shared conception of it with other Reformed theologians. It is, however, remarkable to note that the 2LCF removed much of the explicit mention of the covenant of works that was to be found in the Westminster and Savoy Confessions.[3] The only place where it is

---

[2] John Owen, "An Exposition of Hebrews 8:6-13: Wherein, the nature and differences between the Old and New Covenants is discovered" in Coxe and Owen, *Covenant Theology*, 281.

[3] Here are the paragraphs of the 2LCF where the references to the covenant of works were removed. 6.1; 7.2; 19.1; those that make reference to the covenant of

directly referenced in the Particular Baptists' Confession is in chapter 20, paragraph 1.[4] This ought not to be interpreted as an indication that they rejected the doctrine of the covenant of works; they did not. Also, certain formulations that can be found in these sister Confessions were rejected in the 2LCF to avoid ambiguous wording.[5] Thus, we should not conclude that the Particular Baptists rejected the doctrine of the covenant of works in their Confession.

The Baptists' view of the origin, nature, and function of the covenant of works was the same as the rest of the Puritans. However, they had a divergent opinion regarding the relationship between the covenant of works and the Old Covenant. Most of the paedobaptist theologians of the seventeenth century understood that "not under law but under grace" (Rom. 6:14) simply meant not to be under the covenant of works, but under the covenant of grace. For example, Herman Witsius explains that to be "under the curse of the law" (Gal. 3.10) does not mean to be under the Old Covenant, but under the covenant of works: "But many things prove that nothing is meant by the curse, but the curse of the Covenant of Works."[6]

The Westminster and Savoy Confessions call the covenant of works "the first covenant" and the covenant of grace "the second covenant."[7] This terminology is ambiguous because the New Testament makes a comparison between a first and second covenant, not to designate the covenant of works and the covenant

---

works without naming it: 4.3; 7.2; 19.1, 2; and those where the expression "covenant of works" can be found: 19.6 (2x); 20.1.

[4] "Covenant of works" is used twice in 19:6; however, it does not refer to the covenant of works made with Adam, but rather to the concept of such a covenant.

[5] For a more complete discussion of this topic and the ambiguities in question cf. Samuel Waldron, *A Modern Exposition of the 1689 Baptist Confession of Faith* (Darlington, UK and Webster, NY: Evangelical Press, 1989), 94-96. In his course, *Baptist Symbolics*, Dr. James Renihan explains that the focal point of chapter 7 of the 2LCF is not exactly covenant theology, broadly speaking, but rather the salvation of the elect. This chapter was edited so that all of the emphasis was put on the plan of salvation.

[6] Herman Witsius, *The Economy of the Covenants Between God and Man* (Kingsburg CA: The den Dulk Christian Foundation, Reprinted 1990), 1:359.

[7] Cf. Chapter 7, paragraphs 2 and 4 of these confessions.

By Farther Steps: A 17th Century Particular Baptist Covenant Theology

of grace, but in comparing the Old and New Covenants (cf. Heb. 8-9). This understanding of the paedobaptists did not consider the Old and New Covenants as being antithetical. John Ball, for example, writes, "Some make the Old and New Testament, as the Covenant of works and grace, opposite in substance and kind, and not in degree alone: and that to introduce an unfound distinction."[8]

The Baptists accepted, with no problem, that the word law, used as an antithesis to the word grace, would refer to the covenant of works. Paragraph 2 of Chapter 7 of the 2LCF reads, "Moreover, man having brought himself under the curse of the law by his fall…" The Baptists, however, refused to deny the continuity between the covenant of works and the Old Covenant. For them, the law/grace antithesis reflected the Old/New Covenant antithesis. This understanding is obvious in this quote from Benjamin Keach:

> Though evident it is that God afterwards more clearly and formally repeated this Law of Works to the People of Israel […] though not given in that Ministration of it for Life, as before it was to Adam; yet as so given, it is by St. Paul frequently called the Old Covenant, and the Covenant of Works, which required perfect Obedience of all that were under it.[9]

Keach and the other Baptists believed that the covenant of works was reaffirmed in the Old Covenant, but for different reasons than when it was initially given to Adam. Contrary to most of the paedobaptists, the Particular Baptists understood the New Testament law/grace contrast as a contrast between the Old and New Covenants. For these paedobaptists, the expression "the curse of the law" referred directly to the covenant of works, while for the Baptists, it referred to the covenant of works, but as being

---

[8] John Ball, *A Treatise of the Covenant of Grace* (Dingwall, UK: Peter and Rachel Reynolds, Reprinted 2006 [1645]), 93.

[9] Benjamin Keach, *The Display of Glorious Grace: Or, The Covenant of Peace Opened. In Fourteen Sermons* (London: Printed by S. Bridge, 1698), 15.

reaffirmed or republished in the Old Covenant. Therefore, in order to maintain unity and continuity between the Old and New Covenants, these paedobaptists had to reject the unity and continuity between the covenant of works and the Old Covenant. The distinctiveness of the Particular Baptists' view regarding the covenant of works resided in the relationship between this covenant and the Old Covenant as being similar rather than distinct. We will develop this point further when we address the nature of the Old Covenant.

The Particular Baptist understanding of the Covenant of Grace

The paedobaptist model: "one covenant under two administrations"

To fully grasp the Baptist understanding of the covenant of grace, it is important to compare it with the seventeenth-century majority position held by paedobaptists. The common view of the covenant of grace among Reformed theologians since the beginning of the Reformation up to the end of the seventeenth century was the notion that it was administered respectively by the Old and New Covenants. This paradigm, one covenant under two administrations, made the Old and New Covenants to be seen only as two different administrations of the same covenant, rather than two different covenants in themselves. This notion was definitively rooted in the broader Reformed theology. The Westminster terminology is a witness of that fact, when it says, "This covenant [i.e., the covenant of grace] was differently administered in the time of the law and in the time of the gospel…"[10]

In order to explain the difference between the Old and New Covenants, Reformed paedobaptists used a fundamental distinction between the substance and the administration in each of these covenants. This distinction allowed them to acknowledge that the Old and New Covenants were different in form but not different in substance. For example, Herman Witsius wrote in 1677:

---

[10] WCF, 7.5.

> It is a matter of the greatest moment, that we learn distinctly to consider the Covenant of Grace, either as it is in its *substance* or essence, as they call it, or as it is in divers ways proposed by God, with respect to *circumstantials*, under different economies. If we view *the substance* of the covenant, it is but only one, nor is it possible it should be otherwise. ...But if we attend to the circumstances of the covenant, it was dispensed *at sundry times and in divers manners*, under various economies, for the manifestation of the manifold wisdom of God.[11]

Not only did the distinction between the substance and circumstance allow the paedobaptists to affirm the unity of the covenant of grace without denying the existence of divergences between the Testaments, it also allowed them to justify the mixed nature of the people of God (made up of both the regenerate and the non-regenerate) within the covenant of grace. This is fundamental to paedobaptism. By distinguishing the substance from the administration, the paedobaptists had a category for the non-elect within the covenant of grace and thereby made a place for the natural posterity of believers. The external administration of the covenant of grace would, therefore, contain the regenerate and the non-regenerate, while its internal substance would only contain the regenerate or the soteriologically elect.

In the very formulation "one covenant under two administrations," we find the *substance/circumstance* distinction. First, there is *one covenant* (invisible substance) *under two administrations* (visible circumstance). This distinction is implicit in all of paedobaptist federalism and it is fundamental to it. For example, William Ames, discussing the differences between the Old and New Covenants, uses this distinction. He says, "The [new] testament is new in relation to what existed from the time of Moses

---

[11] Herman Witsius, *The Economy of the Covenants*, 1:291.

and in relation to the promise made to the fathers. But it is new not in essence but in form."[12]

In distinguishing between the essence and the form (substance/administration), Ames confines the newness of the New Covenant to its external form, its substance being the same as the Mosaic Covenant. Consequently, for Ames and his paedobaptist contemporaries, there is identity of substance between the Old and New Covenants.[13] On the basis of this continuity, the paedobaptists established their principle of posterity by which the natural descendents of believers are integrated into the covenant of grace.

The identity of substance between the Old and New Covenants constituted the theological foundation of paedobaptism. Under the Old Covenant, natural descendents were included in the covenant based on Genesis 17:7. If the New Covenant is substantially identical to the Old, this principle of posterity must continue. For example, Francis Turretin, in defending the identity of substance between the Old and New Covenants on the basis of the unity of the covenant of grace, affirmed the perennial nature of the principle "I will be your God and the God of your posterity after you":

> Second, in particular, from all the parts of the Covenant of Grace which were the same in both cases. Such is the clause of the covenant that God will be our God and the God of our seed; for as it had already been proposed to Abraham (Gen. 17.7) and renewed to Moses in a vision (Ex. 3.15) and

---

[12] William Ames, *The Marrow of Theology* (Grand Rapids: Baker, 1997 [1629]), 206.

[13] Paedobaptist federalism was characterized by the identity between the Old and New Covenants. Jeffrey D. Johnson, in *The Fatal Flaw of the Theology Behind Infant Baptism* (Conway, AR: Free Grace Press, 2010), in chapter 3, demonstrates that the notion of continuity of essence between the Old and New Covenants was taught by the main paedobaptist theologians from the Reformation until the present day: Uldrich Zwingli, Henry Bullinger, John Calvin, Caspar Olevianus, Zacharia Ursinus, Thomas Cartwright, John Preston, Thomas Blake, John Ball, William Ames, Johannes Cocceius, Johannes Wollebius, Herman Witsius, Charles Hodge, James Buchanan, Robert Dabney, John Murray, Edward Young, James Bannerman, O. Palmer Robertson, Robert Reymond. This list is not exhaustive, but it is certainly representative.

frequently in legislation, confirmed in the captivity and after it (Ezk. 36.28), so no other was proposed in the Covenant of Grace as the foundation of all blessings, spiritual as well as celestial (Mt. 22.32; 2 Cor 6.16; Rev 21.3).[14]

The Baptists did not deny the principle of natural posterity under the Old Covenant. However, they considered the importation of this principle under the New Covenant to be a fallacy dependent upon an artificial and arbitrary construction of the covenant of grace.[15] They had to prove that the paedobaptists were wrong to establish a unity of substance between the Old and New Covenants. This was a great challenge, because the unity of the substance of the covenant of grace was seen as self-evident (something the Baptists also believed) and sufficient to justify the importation of the Old Covenant principle of natural posterity under the New Covenant (which was rejected by the Baptists).

The Baptist model: a covenant revealed progressively and formally concluded

In rejecting the paedobaptist model of the covenant of grace, the Baptists did not want to do as the Socinians, who had rejected the

---

[14] Francis Turretin, *Institutes of Elenctic Theology* (Phillipsburg, NJ: P&R Publishing, 1992), 2:195. Cf. also Thomas Goodwin, "A Discourse on Election" *The Works of Thomas Goodwin*, Volume 9 (Grand Rapids: Reformation Heritage Books, 2006 [1682]), 428ff. Goodwin attempts to explain that the "covenantal" privilege "I will be your God and the God of your posterity after you" was reserved for Abraham as "the father of all believers," but that it is also the privilege of all children of Abraham to also have their own posterity counted in the covenant of grace.

[15] They also believed the paedobaptists did not apply this principle in a manner which was coherent with the way in which it was applied under the Abrahamic covenant. Nehemiah Coxe explains: "They [the paedobaptists] generally narrow the terms of covenant interest…by limiting it to the immediate offspring. Yet in this covenant [the Abrahamic covenant] it was not restrained like this but came just as fully on remote generations. They also exclude the servants and slaves of Christians, with the children born of them, from that privilege which they suppose they enjoyed under the Old Testament in being sealed with the sign or token of the covenant of grace." Cf. Coxe and Owen, *Covenant Theology*, 106.

covenant of grace itself and Reformed theology as a whole. They wanted to distance themselves from the latter and identify with Reformed orthodoxy. The Baptists maintained unity with the paedobaptists by affirming the unity of the covenant of grace. Particular Baptist theology subscribed fully to the notion of their being only one covenant of grace in the Bible, which brings together all who are saved as one people. The 2LCF clearly teaches this doctrine.

First, in the 2LCF 7.2, "Of God's Covenant," we read:

> Moreover, man having brought himself under the curse of the law by his fall, it pleased the Lord to make a covenant of grace, wherein He freely offers unto sinners life and salvation by Jesus Christ.

The Baptists considered that the covenant of grace started immediately after the fall and that the substance of this covenant, even under the Old Testament, was salvation through faith in Jesus Christ. Paragraph 3 leaves no doubt that they believed the gospel started with Adam.

> This covenant is revealed in the gospel; first of all to Adam in the promise of salvation by the seed of the woman, and afterwards by farther steps, until the full discovery thereof was completed in the New Testament.

In Chapter 11, paragraph 6, regarding justification, the Baptists explicitly refute Socinian theology, saying, "The justification of believers under the Old Testament was, in all these respects, one and the same with the justification of believers under the New Testament." Then, in Chapter 21, paragraph 1a, "Of Christian Liberty and Liberty of Conscience," the Baptists maintained that the substance of salvation was the same under both covenants:

> The liberty which Christ hath purchased for believers under the gospel, consists in their freedom from the guilt of sin, the condemning wrath of God, the rigour and curse of the law,

and in their being delivered from this present evil world, bondage to Satan, and dominion of sin, from the evil of afflictions, the fear and sting of death, the victory of the grave, and everlasting damnation: as also in their free access to God, and their yielding obedience unto Him, not out of slavish fear, but a child-like love and willing mind.

All which were common also to believers under the law for the substance of them…

Thirty years before the publication of the 2LCF, Henry Lawrence, in his treatise on baptism, affirmed the unity of the covenant of grace under the two testaments:

> I confess there are some things of common equity, the rule of life was the same then that now, and the same Christ that now is, was the salvation of the elect, such things therefore as are of such common nature, may be illustrated and inferred from one Testament to another.[16]

Edward Hutchinson, quoting John Owen, affirmed the unity and continuity of the covenant of grace by affirming the unity and continuity of the Church of the Old and New Testaments:

> Hence it was, that at the coming of the Messiah there was not one Church taken away and another set up in the room thereof, but the Church continued the same in those that were the children of Abraham according to the faith. The Christian Church is not another Church, but the very same that was before the coming of Christ, having the same faith with it, and interested in the same Covenant.[17]

---

[16] Henry Lawrence, *Of Baptism* (London: Printed by F. Macock, 1659 [1646]), 83.

[17] Quoted by Edward Hutchinson, *A Treatise Concerning the Covenant and Baptism* (London, Printed for Francis Smith, 1676), 33.

By using Owen's words, Hutchinson demonstrated that the credobaptists shared the same conviction as the paedobaptists regarding the unity of the covenant of grace. The Baptists had this conviction from the beginning. John Spilsbury, who was the pastor of the first Calvinist Baptist Church and who published the oldest treatise of Baptist covenant theology affirmed:

> The Church of God under the old testament and that now under the new, for nature are one, in reference to the Elect of God, called to the faith, and by the Spirit of grace united to Christ, as the branches to their vine.[18]

Although the Baptists believed in the unity of the covenant of grace, like their interlocutors, and though they wanted to maintain unity with them, they rejected the *one covenant under two administrations* model.

The Baptists saw a unity of substance in the covenant of grace from Genesis to Revelation, but they didn't see this same unity between the Old and the New Covenants. They therefore did not accept the idea that those two covenants were two administrations of the same covenant. Nehemiah Coxe expresses this fundamental Baptist conviction well: "…the Old Covenant and the new differ in substance and not only in the manner of their administration."[19] Consequently, the vast majority of them rejected the theology of one covenant of grace under two administrations.[20]

---

[18] John Spilsbury, *A Treatise Concerning the Lawfull Subject of Baptisme* (London: By me J.S., 1643), 20.

[19] Coxe and Owen, *Covenant Theology*, 30.

[20] It is interesting to note that John Smyth supported the doctrine of one covenant of grace under two administrations. This indicates that the General Baptists and the majority of the Particular Baptists did not arrive at credobaptism through the same reasoning nor based on the same theological foundation. Smyth writes, "Remember that there be alwaies a difference put betwixt the covenant of grace; and the manner of dispensing it, which is twofold: the form of administring the covenant before the death of Christ, which is called the old testament; and the forme of administring the covenant since the death of Christ which is called the new Testament of the kingdome of heaven." From *Principles and Inferences concerning the Visible Church*, 1607; quoted in: Paul S. Fiddes, *Tracks and Traces,*

The rejection or acceptance of this model had important repercussions on the formulation of covenant theology. John Owen writes:

> Here then arises a difference of no small importance, namely, whether these [the Old and New Covenants] are indeed two distinct covenants, as to the essence and substance of them, or only different ways of the dispensation and administration of the same covenant.[21]

The understanding of the nature and function of the Old and New Covenants depended on this question.

In comparing the Confessions of Faith, it becomes evident that the Particular Baptists rejected the paedobaptist model of the covenant of grace:

1689 (7:3)	Savoy (7:5)	Westminster (7:5-6)
This Covenant is revealed in the Gospel; first of all to Adam in the promise of Salvation by the seed of the woman, and afterwards by farther steps, until the full	Although this covenant hath been differently and variously administered in respect of ordinances and institutions in the time of the law, and since the coming of Christ in the flesh; yet for the substance and	This covenant was differently administered in the time of the law, and in the time of the gospel: under the law, it was administered by promises, prophecies, sacrifices, circumcision, the paschal

Baptist Identity in Church and Theology (Eugene, OR: Wipf & Stock, 2003), 26. We must, however, admit that certain Calvinist Baptist authors sometimes spoke of "the administrations of the covenant of grace," but what they meant by this terminology was different from paedobaptist theology.

[21] Coxe and Owen, *Covenant Theology*, 179.

discovery thereof was completed in the New Testament; and it is founded in that Eternal Covenant transaction, that was between the Father and the Son, about the Redemption of the Elect; and it is alone by the Grace of this Covenant, that all of the posterity of fallen Adam, that ever were saved, did obtain life and a blessed immortality; Man being now utterly incapable of acceptance with God upon those terms, on which Adam	efficacy of it, to all its spiritual and saving ends, it is one and the same; upon the account of which various dispensations, it is called the Old and New Testament.	lamb, and other types and ordinances delivered to the people of the Jews, all foresignifying Christ to come; which were, for that time, sufficient and efficacious, through the operation of the Spirit, to instruct and build up the elect in faith in the promised Messiah by whom they had full remission of sins, and eternal salvation; and is called the Old Testament. Under the gospel, when Christ, the substance, was exhibited, …and is called the New Testament. There are not therefore two covenants of

stood in his state of innocency.		grace, differing in substance, but one and the same, under various dispensations.

This is the most discordant passage of these Confessions. Knowing that the Baptists made every effort to follow the Westminster standards as much as possible when they wrote their Confession, the originality of their formulation of the covenant of grace is highly significant. It is obvious that the authors of the 2LCF completely avoided any formulation reminiscent of the *one covenant under two administrations* model that we find in the other two Confessions. This absence must be interpreted as a rejection of the theology behind this formulation and not as an omission or an attempt at originality. The Baptists' opinion regarding the paedobaptist model of the covenant of grace concords exactly with that of John Owen who states it thus:

> ...we may consider that Scripture does plainly and expressly make mention of two testaments, or covenants, and distinguish between them in such a way, that what is spoken can hardly be accommodated to a twofold administration of the same covenant.[22]

We have just seen what seventeenth-century Particular Baptist federalism was not. Let us now examine what it was. By rejecting the notion of a covenant of grace under two administrations, the Baptists were in fact rejecting only half of this concept: they accepted, as we have previously seen, the notion of one single covenant of grace in both testaments, but they refused the idea of the two administrations. For a large majority of the Baptists, there was only one covenant of grace, which was revealed from the Fall in a progressive way until its full revelation and conclusion in the

---

[22] Coxe and Owen, *Covenant Theology*, 186.

New Covenant. This model is clearly expressed in the 2LCF 7.3, which reads:

> This covenant is revealed in the gospel; first of all to Adam in the promise of salvation by the seed of the woman, and afterwards by farther steps, until the full discovery thereof was completed in the New Testament.

Upon first impression, this formulation does not seem to be radically different from that of the paedobaptists, since they also recognized the progressive revelation of the covenant of grace. However, in studying Particular Baptist theology in its historical context, it becomes evident that this formulation of the covenant of grace had a meaning that was very specific and fundamentally different from the paedobaptist understanding.

The first particularity is found in the difference between the notion of administration and that of revelation. The Baptists believed that before the arrival of the New Covenant, the covenant of grace was not formally given, but only announced and promised (revealed). This distinction is fundamental to the federalism of the 2LCF. Nehemiah Coxe explains:

> It must also be noted that although the Covenant of Grace was revealed this far to Adam, yet we see in all this there was no formal and express covenant transaction with him. Even less was the Covenant of Grace established with him as a public person or representative of any kind. But as he obtained interest for himself alone by his own faith in the grace of God revealed in this way, so must those of his posterity that are saved.[23]

This specification is highly significant and plays a determining role in Particular Baptist federalism. For Coxe, the covenant of grace was not concluded when God revealed it to Adam. John Owen explains why the covenant of grace could not be considered a

---

[23] Coxe and Owen, *Covenant Theology*, 57.

formal covenant before the establishment of the New Covenant, but was confined to the stage of a promise:

> It lacked its solemn confirmation and establishment, by the blood of the only sacrifice which belonged to it. Before this was done in the death of Christ, it had not the formal nature of a covenant or a testament, as our apostle proves, Heb. 9:15-23. For neither, as he shows in that place, would the law given at Sinai have been a covenant, had it not been confirmed with the blood of sacrifices. To that end the promise was not before a formal and solemn covenant.[24]

The distinction between the revelation and the administration of the covenant of grace finds its whole meaning when the second element of Particular Baptist federalism is added to it, that is to say, the full revelation of the covenant of grace in the New Covenant. If the Westminster federalism can be summarized in *one covenant under two administrations*, that of the 2LCF would be *one covenant revealed progressively and concluded formally under the New Covenant*.

The Baptists believed that no covenant preceding the New Covenant was the covenant of grace. Before the arrival of the New Covenant, the covenant of grace was at the stage of promise. According to Benjamin Keach, the expression "the covenants of the promise" that can be found in Ephesians 2:12 refers back to the covenant of grace.[25] The promise in question was the covenant of grace. If we are talking about a promise, this implies that it was not yet accomplished and was not yet in the form of a testament or a covenant. The Baptists believed that the New Covenant was the accomplishment of the promise or, in other words, the accomplishment of the covenant of grace. This doctrine is expressed in the following way in the 2LCF, "This covenant is revealed in the gospel; first of all to Adam…and afterwards by farther steps, until the full discovery thereof was completed in the New Testament." The New Testament brings the full revelation of the covenant of

---

[24] Coxe and Owen, *Covenant Theology*, 185.
[25] Keach, *The Display of Glorious Grace*, 182.

grace since the New Covenant is its accomplishment. The Baptists considered that the New Covenant, and it alone, was the covenant of grace.[26]

John Spilsbury affirmed this notion, saying, "Again, it's called the promise, and not the Covenant; and we know that every promise is not a covenant: there being a large difference between a promise and a covenant."[27] Spilsbury speaks of the covenant of grace that God revealed to Abraham and he declares that at this stage, it was not yet a formal covenant, but a promise.

This distinction (revealed/concluded) summarized the difference between the covenant of grace in the Old Testament and the covenant of grace in the New Testament. In the Old, it was revealed, in the New, it was concluded (fully revealed according to the expression of the 2LCF). In doing the exegesis of Hebrews 8:6, John Owen concentrates on the verb νομοθετέω ("established") to explain the difference between the covenant of grace before and after Jesus Christ. He arrives at the same theological conclusions of the Particular Baptists:

> This is the meaning of the word νενομοθέτηται, ..."reduced into a fixed state of a law or ordinance." All the obedience required in it, all the worship appointed by it, all the privileges exhibited in it, and the grace administered with them, are all given for a statute, law, and ordinance to the church. That which before lay hid in promises, in many things obscure, ...was now brought to light; and that covenant which had invisibly, in the way of promise, put forth its efficacy under types and shadows, was now solemnly sealed, ratified, and confirmed, in the death and

---

[26] In seventeenth-century Particular Baptist theology, we find an equivalency between the covenant of grace and the New Covenant, and this, from the 1LCF, in paragraph 10, where we read, "Jesus Christ is made the mediator of the new and everlasting covenant of grace." The expression "the new and everlasting covenant of grace" includes both the covenant of grace and the New Covenant. Thus, there is a distinction, without separation between the covenant of grace and the New Covenant.

[27] Spilsbury, *A Treatise Concerning the Lawfull Subject of Baptisme*, 26.

resurrection of Christ. *It had before the confirmation of promise, which is an oath; it had now the confirmation of a covenant, which is blood.* That which before had no visible, outward worship, proper and peculiar to it, is now made the only rule and instrument of worship to the whole church, nothing being to be admitted in that respect but what belongs to it, and is appointed by it. The apostle intends this by νενομοθέτηται, the "legal establishment" of the New Covenant, with all the ordinances of its worship. On this the other covenant was disannulled and removed; and not only the covenant itself, but all that system of sacred worship in accordance with which it was administered. ...When the New Covenant was given out only in the way of a promise, it was consistent with a form of worship, rites and ceremonies, and those composed into a yoke of bondage which belonged not to it. And as these, they were inconsistent with it when it was completed as a covenant; for then all the worship of the church was to proceed from it, and to be conformed to it.[28]

Before the establishment (νενομοθέτηται) of the New Covenant, the covenant of grace did not have a concrete manifestation, any cultus or ceremony; it was not a covenant, but a promise revealed in an obscure manner under temporary types and shadows. Before Christ, the covenant of grace was announced; after Christ, it was decreed (νενομοθέτηται).

The covenant of grace, in this specific sense, was not given to Adam or to Abraham. Owen writes, "...this covenant, as here considered, is not understood the promise of grace given to Adam absolutely; nor that to Abraham, which contained the substance and matter of it, the grace exhibited in it, but not the complete form of it as a covenant."[29] God did not conclude the covenant of grace with Adam any more than he did with Abraham; he revealed the substance of the covenant to them, but it was only concluded

---

[28] Coxe and Owen, *Covenant Theology*, 173-74. Italics added.
[29] Coxe and Owen, *Covenant Theology*, 239.

through Jesus Christ, in his sacrifice. Nehemiah Coxe affirms the same thing:

> ...in the wise counsel of God things were so ordered that the full revelation of the Covenant of Grace, the actual accomplishment of its great promises, and its being filled up with ordinances proper to it, should succeed the covenant made with Israel after the flesh.[30]

This understanding was radically different from that of the majority of paedobaptists in the seventeenth century.

Benjamin Keach ratifies this view of the covenant of grace when he describes its four sequences: 1) It was first decreed in past eternity, 2) It was secondly revealed to man after the Fall of Adam and Eve, 3) It was executed and confirmed by Christ in his death and resurrection, and 4) It becomes effective for its members when they are joined to Christ through faith.[31] The particularity of this *historia salutis* is the distinction between the revelation and the execution of the covenant of grace. Those who were saved before Christ were saved because of an oath; those who were saved after him were saved because of a covenant. The Epistle to the Hebrews makes this distinction when it bases the faith of believers in the Old Covenant on the oath that God made to Abraham (Heb. 5:17-18). However, the assurance of the believers of the New Covenant rests on a testament that is the achieved work of Christ (Heb. 7-9).

In order to clarify our comparison of paedobaptist and Particular Baptist federalism, here are two charts of their respective understandings.

---

[30] Coxe and Owen, *Covenant Theology*, 91.
[31] Benjamin Keach, *The Everlasting Covenant* (London: Printed for H. Barnard, 1693), 17.

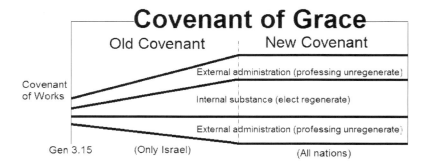

Paedobaptist chart

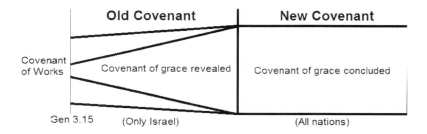

Baptist chart

So far we have seen two different understandings of the covenant of grace and of its relationship to the Old and New Covenants. The paedobaptist model perceived it as being under two successive administrations called the Old and New Covenants. By distinguishing between the covenant (substance) and its administrations (circumstance), paedobaptists established a foundation which was essential to them: they could maintain natural heirs and spiritual heirs within the same covenant, the first having part in the administration only and the second having part in both the administration and the substance of the covenant of grace. Paedobaptist federalism and ecclesiology were based on this distinction.

By Farther Steps: A 17th Century Particular Baptist Covenant Theology

The Particular Baptist understanding rested on another fundamental distinction: one between the phase where the covenant of grace was revealed and the phase where it was concluded. The revealed phase corresponded to the period preceding the death of Christ and the concluded phase corresponded to the time that followed. Therefore, Particular Baptists considered that no other covenant, besides the New Covenant, was the covenant of grace. They still recognized that it had been revealed under all the covenants since the fall, but distinguished between the actual substance of these covenants and the covenant of grace itself.

These two formulations of federalism were at the root of all the divergences between the paedobaptists and the Particular Baptists of the seventeenth century. Their understandings of the covenant of grace led them toward different hermeneutics and theological formulations. We will now concentrate on the Particular Baptist understanding of the covenant of grace and see how through it they perceive the function of the Abrahamic and Mosaic Covenants.

The Particular Baptist understanding of the Abrahamic Covenant

> What I mean is this: The law, introduced 430 years later, does not set aside the covenant previously established by God and thus do away with the promise. For if the inheritance depends on the law, then it no longer depends on the promise; but God in his grace gave it to Abraham through a promise. (Gal. 3:17-18)[32]

To this important passage of biblical covenant theology, the Particular Baptists applied their own paradigm of the covenant of grace (revealed/concluded). The covenant of grace was revealed to Abraham, but the formal covenant that God concluded with him at this point was not the covenant of grace, but the covenant of circumcision that the Baptists considered to be in essence a further

---

[32] Scripture citations are from the NIV.

development of the Old Covenant.[33] In harmony with the Baptist paradigm of the covenant of grace, Galatians 3:17-18 does not affirm that God gave his grace to Abraham through the covenant, but through the promise. In other words, the Abrahamic Covenant contained a promise; this promise was the revelation of the covenant of grace.

In order to properly define the Abrahamic Covenant, the Baptists insisted on the dualistic nature of this covenant: Abraham possessed a physical posterity as well as a spiritual posterity (Rom. 9:6-8; Gal. 4:22-31); there was an external circumcision of the flesh and an internal circumcision of the heart (Rom. 2:28-29); there was a promised land here on earth and a heavenly kingdom (Heb. 11:8-10). The Baptist pastor Hercules Collins taught this doctrine in his catechism. "We must know the Covenant made with Abraham had two parts: first, a spiritual, which consisted in God's promising to be a God to Abraham, and all his Spiritual-Seed in a peculiar manner…"[34]

The paedobaptists and the Baptists mutually recognized this dualism, but in a completely different way. The paedobaptists considered this dualism within one covenant. According to them, this covenant included a physical reality, external and earthly, combined with a spiritual reality, internal and celestial, exactly as in their understanding of the covenant of grace wherein there was an internal substance and an external administration. Although they recognized that the posterity of Abraham was both physical and spiritual at the same time, the paedobaptists refused to see two posterities, because, according to them, Abraham had only one posterity made up of the mixed people of the covenant of grace. This point was crucial, because if Abraham had two distinct posterities, the Baptists were right not to mix the natural (unregenerate) posterity and the spiritual (regenerate) posterity of Abraham. Inversely, if Abraham had only one mixed posterity, the

---

[33] See below under the heading "The Particular Baptist understanding of the Mosaic Covenant" for an explanation.

[34] Collins presents the physical and natural aspect of the Abrahamic Covenant. Cf. "An Orthodox Catechism: Being the Sum of Christian Religion, Contained in the Law and Gospel" in Renihan, *True Confessions*, 257.

paedobaptists were right to include those who were saved and those who were not saved in the covenant of grace. Samuel Petto, a paedobaptist, had understood this critical concern:

> Hence see the true meaning of Gal. 3.16. *To Abraham and his seed were the Promises made: he saith not unto seeds, as of many, but as of one, and to thy seed, which is Christ*: i.e. Always *Abraham* had but one seed, Christ, and those that are Christ's, and are of the Faith as to Justification, he never had two seeds for that end; in the times of the Old Testament there was but one seed, not two seeds, one by the Law, and another by Promise, but only one in Christ by Promise…
>
> And so it is not in the least mentioned to exclude Infants, as a fleshly seed, from an ecclesiastical seed, nor to repeal any priviledge or limit to cut them off from what they had before the coming of Christ…[35]

The paedobaptists refused to separate the dualities of the Abrahamic Covenant in order to preserve their model of the covenant of grace which integrated them. The covenant of grace, to include children, had to include both earthly and heavenly realities at the same time. Baptist theologians understood that if they kept these dualities united in the same covenant, they no longer had any reason to reject the paedobaptist model of the covenant of grace. In fact, if the covenant of grace revealed to Abraham included both his physical and spiritual posterity at once, why would it have been otherwise under the New Covenant? Therefore, not only did Particular Baptist theology make the distinction between the physical and spiritual posterities of Abraham, but it also strictly separated them into two separate categories. The Baptists saw two posterities in Abraham, two inheritances and consequently two covenants.

---

[35] Samuel Petto, *Infant Baptism of Christ's Appointment* (London: Printed for Edward Giles, 1687), 37-38.

Galatians 4:22-31 constitutes a key passage of Particular Baptist federalism. In it we read:

> [22] For it is written that Abraham had two sons, one by the slave woman and the other by the free woman. [23] His son by the slave woman was born according to the flesh, but his son by the free woman was born as the result of a divine promise. [24] These things are being taken figuratively: The women represent two covenants. One covenant is from Mount Sinai and bears children who are to be slaves: This is Hagar. [25] Now Hagar stands for Mount Sinai in Arabia and corresponds to the present city of Jerusalem, because she is in slavery with her children. [26] But the Jerusalem that is above is free, and she is our mother. [27] For it is written: "Be glad, barren woman, you who never bore a child; shout for joy and cry aloud, you who were never in labor; because more are the children of the desolate woman than of her who has a husband." [28] Now you, brothers and sisters, like Isaac, are children of promise. [29] At that time the son born according to the flesh persecuted the son born by the power of the Spirit. It is the same now. [30] But what does Scripture say? "Get rid of the slave woman and her son, for the slave woman's son will never share in the inheritance with the free woman's son." [31] Therefore, brothers and sisters, we are not children of the slave woman, but of the free woman.

From this passage, Nehemiah Coxe understood, not that the posterity of Abraham was of a mixed nature, but that Abraham had two distinct posterities and that it was necessary to determine the inheritance of each of these posterities on the basis of their respective promises. He writes:

> Abraham is to be considered in a double capacity: he is the father of all true believers and the father and root of the Israelite nation. God entered into covenant with him for both of these seeds and since they are formally distinguished from one another, their covenant interest must necessarily be

different and fall under a distinct consideration. The blessings appropriate to either must be conveyed in a way agreeable to their peculiar and respective covenant interest. And these things may not be confounded without a manifest hazard to the most important articles in the Christian religion.[36]

This understanding was vigorously affirmed amongst all Particular Baptist theologians and characterized their federalism from its origin. Spilsbury writes, "There was in *Abraham* at that time a spirituall seed and a fleshly seed. Between which seeds God ever distinguished through all their Generations."[37] On the allegory in Galatians 4, Henry Lawrence comments:

> Here you have a distinction as it were of two *Abrahams*, a begetting *Abraham*, and a believing *Abraham*, and also of two seeds, the children of the flesh, that is by carnal generation onely, and the children of the promise… Now, saith he, those only, which according to that of which Isaac was a type, are born by promise, those & those only are counted for the seed, Rom. 9:8.[38]

If Abraham had two distinct posterities, and they were non-mixed, and if they were in a relationship with God by way of covenant, these two posterities had to find themselves in two distinct covenants. Consequently, several Particular Baptists considered that God had concluded two covenants in Abraham: the covenant of grace in Genesis 12 with Abraham and his spiritual posterity (the believers) and the covenant of circumcision in Genesis 17 with Abraham and his natural posterity (the circumcised, which included believers). This does not mean that the Baptists saw two formal Abrahamic Covenants. The Baptists, as we have seen, considered that the covenant of grace did not manifest

---

[36] Coxe and Owen, *Covenant Theology*, 72-73.
[37] Spilsbury, *A Treatise Concerning the Lawfull Subject of Baptisme*, 6.
[38] Lawrence, *Of Baptism*, 90, 91.

itself as a formal covenant before the establishing of the New Covenant. They did not consider that the covenant of grace was formally established with Abraham in Genesis 12, 15, or 17, but that it was only revealed and promised to him. They saw only one formal Abrahamic Covenant: the covenant of circumcision established in Genesis 17, all the while clearly differentiating this covenant from the promise (i.e., the covenant of grace) that God had previously made. This distinction between the promise revealed to Abraham and the covenant concluded with Abraham is unequivocal for John Spilsbury:

> Again, its called the promise, and not the Covenant; and we know that every promise is not a covenant: there being a large difference between a promise and a covenant. And now let it be well considered what is here meant by the promise, and that is Gods sending of the Messias, or the seed in whom the Nations should be blessed; and so the sending of a Saviour or Redeemer unto Israel.[39]

It is in this way that the Particular Baptists understood that there were two covenants with Abraham, not two formal covenants, but a promise that revealed the covenant of grace followed by the covenant of circumcision. In light of Galatians 4:22-31, the theologians of the 2LCF considered that the two covenants that came from Abraham (Hagar and Sara) were the Old and New Covenants. The covenant of circumcision, Hagar, corresponded to the Old Covenant; a covenant of works established with the physical posterity of Abraham. The covenant of the promise, Sara, corresponded to the New Covenant; the covenant of grace revealed to Abraham and concluded with Christ and the spiritual posterity of Abraham (Gal. 3:29).

The fundamental divergence between the paedobaptists and the Particular Baptists regarding the Abrahamic Covenant was found here. The first did not view Ishmael and Isaac, Hagar and Sara, the promise and circumcision, the Old and the New Covenant

---

[39] Spilsbury, *A Treatise Concerning the Lawfull Subject of Baptisme*, 26.

separately. They united these dualities within the same covenant of grace that possessed at the same time a physical and spiritual reality, an internal substance and an external administration. This system was self sufficient, but it could not harmonize itself naturally with the biblical data, in particular, to the fact that there was not one, but two covenants in Abraham (Gal. 4:24).

The second, basing themselves on the exegesis of Galatians 4:22-31, separated the dualities contained in Abraham in such a way as to recognize that two covenants came from the patriarch.

It is also important to explain how the intertwinement of Abraham's seeds worked in the Baptist understanding of the Abrahamic Covenant. Nehemiah Coxe explains how certain promises made to the spiritual posterity of Abraham were sometimes presented in terms which led to the expectation of an immediate blessing for his natural posterity:

> It will readily be granted that some of those promises that ultimately respect the spiritual seed and spiritual blessings are sometimes given to Abraham under the cover of those terms that have an immediate respect to his natural seed and temporal blessings as types of the other. ...But only this much will fairly follow from it: that the apostle argues from the carnal seed as typical to the spiritual seed as typified by it.[40]

The posterities of Abraham were, therefore, often intertwined in their manifestation, but they were always ontologically distinct. Another reason for this intertwining comes from the fact that the posterities of Abraham were not necessarily distinct when it came to their subjects. One and the same person could be both a physical and spiritual heir of Abraham. This explains that two categories of promises could be made to the same people without these promises being the essence of the same covenant of grace.

That the physical and spiritual descendents of Abraham had received common promises did not mean that these promises had

---

[40] Coxe and Owen, *Covenant Theology*, 76.

the same value for each of these posterities. For example, the promise of being their God had a different meaning for each posterity, as Edward Hutchinson writes, "Now to both seeds, doth God promise to be a God, but in a different manner and respect."[41]

Another important reason, we believe, that the covenant of grace was intertwined with the covenant of circumcision comes from God's placing his promise under the custody of the Old Covenant in order to preserve it (Gal. 3:23). From this moment, the promise (i.e., the covenant of grace) could no longer be separated from the covenant of circumcision (i.e., the Old Covenant). We will develop this point further as we examine the Mosaic Covenant.

The Particular Baptist understanding of the Mosaic Covenant

The Particular Baptists saw the Mosaic Covenant to be the elaborate form of the Old Covenant already in existence since Abraham and even before. Thomas Patient writes representatively, "But it is clear to me that in substance, the same covenant of ceremonial obedience which was given to Moses when the people came out of Egypt, the same was given to Adam's generation."[42]

> [19]Why, then, was the law given at all? It was added because of transgressions until the Seed to whom the promise referred had come. The law was given through angels and entrusted to a mediator. [20]A mediator, however, implies more than one party; but God is one. [21]Is the law, therefore, opposed to the promises of God? Absolutely not! For if a law had been given that could impart life, then righteousness would certainly have come by the law. [22]But Scripture has locked up everything under the control of sin, so that what was promised, being given through faith in Jesus Christ, might be given to those who believe. [23]Before the coming of this faith, we were held in custody under the law, locked up

---

[41] Hutchinson, *A Treatise Concerning the Covenant and Baptism*, 26.

[42] Thomas Patient, *The Doctrine of Baptism, And the Distinction of the Covenants* (London: Printed by Henry Hills, 1654), beginning of Chapter 10.

until the faith that was to come would be revealed. 24So the law was our guardian until Christ came that we might be justified by faith. (Gal. 3:19-24)

According to the Apostle, the goal of the covenant made with the physical posterity of Abraham (i.e. the Old Covenant or the law) was to lead to Christ. This end was accomplished in at least three ways, according to the seventeenth-century Particular Baptists: 1) by preserving both the messianic lineage and the covenant of grace; 2) by pointing typologically towards Christ; and 3) by imprisoning everything under sin in order that the only means to obtain the promised inheritance was through faith in Christ.

This third way of leading to Christ corresponded to the understanding the Baptists had of the nature of the Old Covenant. They saw it not as a covenant of grace, but as a covenant of works, that is, a covenant whose blessings or curses were determined by the obedience or the disobedience of its members.

Many paedobaptists viewed the Mosaic Covenant as being unconditional. However, certain paedobaptists, as well as most Particular Baptists, did not share this point of view since they saw the Old Covenant as a covenant of works (i.e., a conditional covenant). Let us examine the relationship between the Old Covenant and the covenant of works given to Adam.

The covenant of works concluded at creation required man's perfect obedience. The blessing of this covenant depended entirely on the works or obedience of Adam. It provided no mercy or expiation in case of disobedience, but only death. This was not the case with the Old Covenant. The Scriptures present this covenant as being a covenant of redemption; the Old Covenant was based on a priesthood (Heb. 7:11). In a certain way, it was planned that the people would sin and that it would subsist nonetheless, thanks to the Levitical system of sacrifices. John Ball even relies on the fact that the Old Covenant planned for the forgiveness of sins, something the covenant of works could never have done, to prove that it was not a covenant of works, but of grace.[43]

---

[43] Ball, *A Treatise of the Covenant of Grace*, 108.

Samuel Petto, who did consider the Mosaic Covenant as being conditional, recognized that it could not be strictly the same covenant of works established at creation:

> [T]he covenant of works with the first Adam being violated, it was at an end as to the promising part; it promised nothing; after once it was broken, it remained in force only as to its threatening part, it menaced death to all the sinful seed of Adam, but admitted no other into it who were without sin, either to perform the righteousness of it, or to answer the penalty; it had nothing to do with an innocent person, after broken, for it was never renewed with man again, as before.[44]

Nothing, under the covenant of works, provided for the reparation of sin through the substitution of a righteous person. In this way, the Old Covenant was very different from the covenant of works. Nevertheless, under the Old Covenant, there was a principle belonging to the covenant made with Adam: "Keep my decrees and laws, for the person who obeys them will live by them" (Lev. 18:5).

How did the Particular Baptists, and certain paedobaptists along with them, conceive the nature of the Old Covenant if it was not *the* covenant of works, while being *a* covenant of works? What was the relationship between the covenant of works given to Adam and the Old Covenant made with Israel? Benjamin Keach affirms that there was, between the two of them, continuity but not uniformity:

> True, there was another Edition or Administration of it [i.e., the covenant of works] given to *Israel*. which tho' it was a covenant of works, *i.e. Do this and live*, yet it was not given by the Lord to the same End and Design, as the Covenant

---

[44] Samuel Petto, *The Great Mystery of the Covenant of Grace* (1820; reprint, Stoke-on-Trent, UK: Tentmaker Publications, 2007), 131-32.

was given to our first parents, viz. It was not given to justifie them, or to give them eternal Life.⁴⁵

A few years later, Keach published a collection of sermons on the covenant of grace in which he reiterated that the covenant of works was reaffirmed by the Old Covenant, but to a different end than at the time of its initial proclamation:

> Though evident it is that God afterwards more clearly and formally repeated this Law of Works to the People of Israel …though not given in that Ministration of it for Life, as before it was to Adam; yet as so given, it is by St. Paul frequently called the Old Covenant, and the Covenant of Works, which required perfect Obedience of all that were under it.⁴⁶

This specification constituted an essential characteristic of Particular Baptist federalism, specifically that the covenant of works, after the fall, was never again used for the descendents of Adam as "a law …that could impart life" (Gal. 3:21). This does not mean that the covenant of works had no further use, nor that it was absent from the covenants that God established with his people. On the contrary, it was reaffirmed, but in a new way; it was placed at the core of a covenant of redemption and was employed to different ends. According to this conception then, the Old Covenant was not exactly the equivalent of the covenant of works although it reaffirmed it. In agreement with the covenant of works, the Old Covenant demanded a perfect obedience to the law of God,⁴⁷ but

---

⁴⁵ Keach, *The Everlasting Covenant*, 7.
⁴⁶ Keach, *The Display of Glorious Grace*, 15.
⁴⁷ The slightest disobedience to the law constituted a sin punishable by death (Rom. 6:23), but not necessarily a transgression of the Old Covenant. It is necessary to make the distinction between the requirements of the law of works affirmed under the Old Covenant and the requirements of the Old Covenant itself towards Israel. The maintaining of the Old Covenant depended on the Levitical priesthood (Heb. 7:11) and not on absolute obedience. God planned for his commandments to be transgressed while maintaining his covenant. The Old Covenant was, therefore, not given to Israel as a covenant of life (Gal 3:21). However, it held this function for

contrary to the covenant of works, the Old Covenant was based on a sacrificial system for the redemption of sinners.[48] The covenant of works reaffirmed in the Old Covenant made this sacrificial system absolutely necessary since all sinners transgressed the law. However, the sacrifices of the Old Covenant could not accomplish the righteousness of the law effectively; that is why they only had a typological and temporary value. As long as they were offered, these sacrifices recalled that the requirements of the law were not satisfied, since sin still subsisted, and that this law weighed on the members of the Old Covenant like a curse (cf. Heb. 10:1-14). It is under this law that Christ was born (Gal. 4:4) and it is this same law (i.e. the covenant of works reaffirmed in the Old Covenant) that Christ fulfilled by his obedience (Rom. 5:19-20) and it is the curse of this law which he endured by his death (Gal. 3:13). Christ, therefore, accomplished the Old Covenant perfectly.

Therefore, the Old Covenant was, for the people of Israel, a typological covenant, earthly and conditional, designed to lead them to Christ and not to the covenant of works as such. The Old Covenant, while being different from the covenant of works, reaffirmed it, not so that Israel would look for life by this means,

---

Christ. This is why Samuel Petto considered that the Old Covenant did not have the same function for Israel as for Christ. For Israel it was a national covenant by whose conditions she received blessings and curses in its land (Deut. 28). For Christ, it was a covenant of works for which he had to accomplish righteousness actively and passively (Rom. 5:18-20; 8:3-4; Gal. 3:13; 4:4-5). Petto writes, "The Sinai law was not given as a covenant of works to Israel. It was designed to be a covenant of works as to be accomplished by Jesus Christ, as will appear afterwards; but the end of the Lord was not that it should be so to Israel." Cf. Petto, *The Great Mystery of the Covenant of Grace*, 113. This point is crucial in understanding the nature of the Old Covenant, its relationship to the covenant of works, its requirements for Israel as the covenant people and its accomplishment in Jesus Christ as the last Adam.

[48]After the fall, the covenant of works is no longer found as a law of life, because it would have been impossible for sinners to subsist within it and obtain life through it because of sin (cf. Rom. 8:3; Gal. 3:21). The covenant of works was maintained after the fall, thanks to the Old Covenant where it functioned on a new basis – a sacrificial system. This sacrificial system did not start with Aaron, but immediately after the fall and was in effect at the time of the Patriarchs (Gen. 3:21; 4:4; 8:20; 22:13; 46:1), until it was fully developed in the law of Moses.

but so that Christ would accomplish it. The Old Covenant was, therefore, not only necessary to lead to Christ but it was necessary so that he could accomplish salvation for God's Israel. Samuel Petto explains this important point:

> Indeed, I think, one great end of God in bringing Israel under this Sinai covenant, was to make way for Christ, his being born or made under the law, in order to the fulfilling of it for us. I do not see how (by any visible dispensation) Jesus Christ could have been born actually under the law, if this Sinai covenant had not been made; for the covenant of works with the first Adam being violated, it was at an end as to the promising part; it promised nothing; after once it was broken, it remained in force only as to its threatening part, it menaced death to all the sinful seed of Adam, but admitted no other into it who were without sin, either to perform the righteousness of it, or to answer the penalty; it had nothing to do with an innocent person, after broken, for it was never renewed with man again, as before: therefore, an admitting an innocent person (as Jesus Christ was) into it, must be by some kind of repetition or renewing of it, though with other intendments than at first, viz. that the guilty persons should not fulfil it for themselves, but that another, a surety, should fulfil it for them.[49]

This explanation from Petto demonstrates how he himself, and most of the Particular Baptists, considered that the covenant of works was reaffirmed with a different goal than at its first promulgation. The covenant of works did not provide a substitution to satisfy its righteousness; no one could obey in Adam's place nor suffer his punishment. God, therefore, reaffirmed the covenant of works in another covenant that allowed for a righteous person to substitute himself for sinners. Not only was the Old Covenant not *against* the promises of God (Gal. 3:21), but it was given specifically *for* the accomplishment of these promises (Gal.

---

[49] Petto, *The Great Mystery of the Covenant of Grace*, 131-32.

3:22-24). Without being itself a covenant of grace, the Old Covenant was given because of the covenant of grace and with a view to its accomplishment. Is this what the apostle John wanted to underline by declaring: "Out of his fullness we have all received grace in place of grace already given. For the law was given through Moses; grace and truth came through Jesus Christ" (John 1:16-17)? The law given by Moses was *a* grace to lead to *the* grace accomplished by Jesus Christ.

The Particular Baptist understanding of the New Covenant

In the Particular Baptist perspective, the identity of the New Covenant could not be separated from the covenant of grace. That is why much of what has been said already in this chapter defines the Baptist view of the New Covenant. We will only further develop what could be seen as a distinct aspect of the Baptist perspective – the newness of the New Covenant.

The newness of the New Covenant, according to the paedobaptist approach, was confined to the external aspects of the covenant and did not touch on its internal substance. This is exactly what the great Reformed theologian Francis Turretin said. "It is called "new" not as to the substance of the covenant (which is the same in both) but: (1) as to the circumstances and mode."[50]

John Owen, in agreement with Particular Baptist theology, explains that the unconditional nature constituted the newness of the New Covenant:

> A covenant properly is a compact or agreement on certain terms mutually stipulated by two or more parties. As promises are the foundation and rise of it, as it is between God and man, so it comprises also precepts, or laws of obedience, which are prescribed to man on his part to be observed. *But in the description of the covenant here annexed* [i.e., the New Covenant], *there is no mention of any condition on the part of man, of any terms of obedience prescribed to him, but*

---

[50] Turretin, *Institutes of Elenctic Theology*, 2:232.

> *the whole consists in free, gratuitous promises, as we will see in the explication of it.*[51]

The unconditional nature constitutes the radically new and unique element of the New Covenant. For the credobaptists, the New Covenant was radically new since no other formal covenant before it was unconditional.

The promises of the Old Covenant were preceded by an "if" that made them conditioned on man's obedience, while the promises of the New Covenant were marked by a divine monergism:

> [33]"This is the covenant I will make with the people of Israel after that time," declares the Lord. "I will put my law in their minds and write it on their hearts. I will be their God, and they will be my people. [34] No longer will they teach their neighbour, or say to one another, 'Know the Lord,' because they will all know me, from the least of them to the greatest," declares the Lord. "For I will forgive their wickedness and will remember their sins no more." (Jer. 31:33-34)

The three elements that make up the substance of the New Covenant are works supremely operated by God and are presented in the indicative mood, not the conditional. None of these promises depends on a condition that had first to be met by man. The unconditional nature of this covenant made it a radically new covenant. Thomas Patient explains that what made the New Covenant "intransgressable," contrary to the Old Covenant which could be transgressed (Gen. 17:14), was this unconditional character:

> For, as I have shown before, it is impossible that the New *Covenant can be broken because it is an absolute covenant made on no condition to be fulfilled by the creature. But the Lord works*

---

[51] Coxe and Owen, *Covenant Theology*, 259. Italics added.

"both to will and to do of His good pleasure" in this covenant. Therefore, *"it is not in him that willeth, nor in him that runneth, but in God Who shows mercy."*[52]

However, the Baptists did not conceive of the unconditional nature of the New Covenant as coming from the abolition of the covenant of works. On the contrary, the New Covenant was unconditional, according to them, since the covenant of works was accomplished. Thus, the New Covenant was unconditional for all its members, but it was not for its mediator – Christ. Benjamin Keach expresses this understanding:

> 1. As it refers to Christ, or to his part, and Work therein; and as thus it was a Conditional Covenant, Christ receives all for us, wholly upon the account of his own Desert, or Merits.
>
> 2. But whatsoever we receive by virtue of this Covenant, it is wholly in a way of Free Grace and Favor, through his Merits, or through that Redemption we have by his Blood: But take it either ways, 'tis of Grace.[53]

Not only did the newness of the New Covenant consist in its unconditional nature, but also in that all its members would participate in the substance of the covenant of grace. "No longer will they teach their neighbour, or say to one another, 'Know the Lord,' because they will all know me, from the least of them to the greatest," declares the Lord" (Jer. 31:34). In this regard, John Owen

---

[52] Patient, *The Doctrine of Baptism, And the Distinction of the Covenants*, chapter 9, argument 6. The italics are from the author.

[53] Keach, *The Display of Glorious Grace*, 173. Similarly, John Bunyan, in a section entitled "The conditions of the New Covenant" presents the conditional aspect of this covenant; in another section entitled "Christ completely fulfilled the conditions of the New Covenant," he demonstrates that it is not the believer, but only Christ who guarantees the success of this covenant and ensures its blessings to its members. Cf. John Bunyan, "The Doctrine of the Law and Grace Unfolded" in *The Works of John Bunyan* (Edinburgh/Carlisle, PA: Banner of Truth Trust, 1991), 1:524, 534.

writes, "Where there is not some degree of saving knowledge, there no interest in the New Covenant can be pretended."[54]

The Scriptures declare that the substance of the New Covenant can be summarized in three blessings: the law written on the heart, the personal and saving knowledge of God, and the forgiveness of sins which constitute the basis of the other two blessings and of the whole New Covenant. God takes great care in saying that this substance would not be the inheritance of only some amongst his people, but of all his people inclusively: "'because they will all know me, from the least of them to the greatest,' declares the Lord."

Conclusion

In this chapter, we have tried to put forth the majority Particular Baptist understanding of federal theology. In order to present this view of federalism, we have compared it to seventeenth-century paedobaptist federal theology. The latter conceived the covenant of grace upon a substance/administration hermeneutic, which leads to the "one covenant under two administrations" (OT/NT) structure. The Particular Baptist construction of the covenant of grace was rather established by a "revealed/concluded" (promise/fulfillment) structure, progressively revealed in the Old Testament by "the covenants of the promise" and concluded in the New Testament by the institution of the New Covenant as the promised covenant of grace fulfilled. These two different understandings of the covenant of grace determined the rest of the differences between the seventeenth-century Particular Baptist and paedobaptist theologies.

---

[54] Coxe and Owen, *Covenant Theology*, 299.

Chapter 4
The Puritan Argument for the Immersion of Believers: How Seventeenth-Century Baptists Utilized the Regulative Principle of Worship
G. Stephen Weaver, Jr., Ph.D.*

In 1544, in a treatise presented to the Imperial Diet at Speyer, the Genevan Reformer John Calvin articulated what has come to be known as the regulative principle of worship.[1] In his tract on *The Necessity of Reforming the Church*, Calvin wrote that "God disapproves of all modes of worship not expressly sanctioned by His Word."[2] Later in the same essay, Calvin drew the appropriate conclusion that "it ought to be sufficient for the rejection of any mode of worship, that it is not sanctioned by the command of God."[3] By this standard, Calvin and the other Reformers rejected much of the accretions in the worship and practice of the Roman Catholic Church from the medieval period. But whatever forms of "fictitious worship" Calvin had in mind when he penned those

---

* G. Stephen Weaver, Jr. is pastor of Farmdale Baptist Church, Frankfort, KY, and Ph.D., The Southern Baptist Theological Seminary. His dissertation is entitled, "Hercules Collins: Orthodox, Puritan, Baptist," and he's the co-editor of *Devoted to the Service of the Temple: Piety, Persecution, and Ministry in the Writings of Hercules Collins* published by Reformation Heritage Books and *An Orthodox Catechism* published by RBAP.

[1] For the historical context of Calvin's writing of the tract, see Bruce Gordon, *Calvin* (New Haven, CT: Yale University Press, 2009), 163-64. While Calvin's tract remains a classic treatment of the regulative principle, the Swiss Reformer Huldrych Zwingli is often credited with being the first to apply the principle to the worship of the church in Zurich.

[2] John Calvin, "The Necessity of Reforming the Church," in *Tracts Related to the Reformation*, Vol. 1. Translated by Henry Beveridge. (Edinburgh: The Calvin Translation Society, 1844), 128.

[3] Calvin, "The Necessity of Reforming the Church," 133.

words, it apparently did not include infant baptism which was retained in the Reformed church of Geneva. Likewise in 1648, when the Puritan Jeremiah Burroughs (1599-1646) offered the definitive treatment of the regulative principle in his volume titled *Gospel Worship*,[4] the practice of believer's baptism by immersion seems to have been the farthest thing from his mind. The English Baptist historian Thomas Crosby, however, used this paedobaptist's own words to argue for just that (i.e., believer's baptism) in his preface to the first volume of his *The History of the English Baptists*.[5] In so doing, Crosby, who was himself the son-in-law of the prominent seventeenth-century Particular Baptist pastor Benjamin Keach, was merely following the pattern of seventeenth-century Baptists in arguing for believer's baptism by immersion.

The Puritans were known for their strict adherence to and application of the Reformation's regulative principle of worship. In their recent book *A Puritan Theology*, Joel Beeke and Mark Jones defined this principle as stating "that nothing that is not explicitly commanded or sanctioned by example in the New Testament should be allowed in Christian worship."[6] They went on to say that in either Puritan times or today "those who adhere to the regulative principle believe that God is offended by unauthorized, man-made additions to His worship. ...The Puritans believed that these additions are sinful and irreverent, suggesting that Scripture is not sufficient."[7] In the mid- to late-seventeenth century a group of dissenters arose who viewed themselves as heirs to the Puritan tradition and who utilized this exact same argument to argue for believer's baptism by immersion. This chapter will demonstrate how the writings of the seventeenth-century Baptists utilized the

---

[4] One example of Burroughs' statement of the regulative principle: "I say that all things in God's worship must have a warrant out of God's Word. It must be commanded; it's not enough that it is not forbidden." Jeremiah Burroughs, *Gospel Worship* (Morgan, PA: Soli Deo Gloria Publications, 1990), 11.

[5] Thomas Crosby, *The History of the English Baptists*, Volume I (London, 1738), xi-xiii.

[6] Joel R. Beeke and Mark Jones, *A Puritan Theology: Doctrine for Life* (Grand Rapids, MI: Reformation Heritage Books, 2012), 851.

[7] Beeke and Jones, *A Puritan Theology*, 851.

same type of arguments used by the Reformers and the Puritans to argue against their paedobaptist position.

These early Baptists believed that although baptism may have been largely lost for centuries, it had now been recovered as a direct result of the renewed emphasis on the authority and sufficiency of the Word of God in the Protestant Reformation. Their Puritan-like zeal for worship regulated by God's Word drove them to reject what they perceived as the human innovation of infant baptism. In so doing, they were never more true to the spirit of Puritanism.

Defining Puritanism

I have been intentionally provocative by titling this chapter "The Puritan Argument for Immersion of Believers." Admittedly, the terms "Puritan" and "Puritanism" have been notoriously difficult to define.[8] As John Coffey has admitted, "Historians have agonized over its definition."[9] Disagreements exist among scholars over almost every conceivable question related to the definition of Puritanism. For the purposes of this essay, I am using an admittedly rather general definition of Puritanism. I am using the term to refer to that basic Puritan characteristic or instinct to draw all their faith and practice from the Scriptures. In his definition of Puritanism in *The Worship of the English Puritans*, Horton Davies defined a Puritan as one "who longed for further reformation in England according to the Word of God."[10] Similarly, John Brown referred to "the fundamental idea of puritanism in all its manifestations" as being "the supreme authority of Scripture

---

[8] For example, see Brian H. Cosby, "Toward a Definition of 'Puritan' and 'Puritanism': A Study in Puritan Historiography," *Churchman* 122:4 (2008), 297-314; and Ian Hugh Clary, "Hot Protestants: A Taxonomy of English Puritanism," *Puritan Reformed Journal* 2:1 (2010), 41-66.

[9] John Coffey, "Puritanism, evangelicalism and the evangelical protestant tradition," in Michael A. G. Haykin and Kenneth J. Stewart, eds., *The Advent of Evangelicalism: Exploring Historical Continuities* (Nashville: B&H Academic, 2008), 255.

[10] Horton Davies, *The Worship of the English Puritans* (Morgan, PA: Soli Deo Gloria Publications, 1997), 11.

brought to bear upon the conscience."[11] It is to this "fundamental idea of puritanism" which sought to bring the authority of Scripture to bear upon every aspect of life that the Particular Baptists of the seventeenth century were firmly committed. They, therefore, saw themselves as Puritans in their application of the regulative principle to the issue of baptism.

The English historian Christopher Hill called the seventeenth century "the century of revolution." Perhaps most subversive of all in this age of revolution, according to Hill, were the Baptists whose "theological starting point...meant that each individual...decided for himself what Church he would belong to."[12] The concept of a church composed solely of baptized believers was championed by John Smyth and Thomas Helwys as early as 1609. The mode of immersion, however, was probably not practiced until shortly before 1641[13] when it was argued for in print for the first time by the General Baptist Edward Barber.[14] Throughout the rest of the seventeenth century a number of books and tracts were published on this subject.[15] It is beyond the scope of this article to examine all of the defenses of baptism by seventeenth-century Baptists, instead it is hoped that by examining three works written over a forty-five

---

[11] John Brown, *The English Puritans: The Rise and Fall of the Puritan Movement* (Ross-shire, Scotland: Christian Focus Publications, 1998), 17.

[12] Christopher Hill, *The Century of Revolution* (London: Routledge Classics, 2006), 166.

[13] The date of the introduction of baptism by immersion is a disputed matter. For the most recent scholarship on this discussion, see Stephen Wright, *The Early English Baptists, 1603-1649* (Woodbridge, UK: The Boydell Press, 2006), 75-110; and Wm. Lloyd Allen, "Baptist Baptism and the Turn toward Believer's Baptism by Immersion: 1642" in *Turning Points in Baptist History: A Festschrift in Honor of Harry Leon McBeth*, ed. Michael E. Williams, Sr. and Walter B. Shurden (Macon, GA: Mercer University Press, 2008), 34-48.

[14] Edward Barber, *A Small Treatise of Baptisme, or, Dipping. Wherein Is Cleerely Shewed that the Lord Christ Ordained Dipping for those only that professe Repentance and Faith* (1641).

[15] For a helpful listing of some of these works written by Particular Baptists, see "Appendix 5: Some Other Seventeenth-Century Particular Baptist Works on Believer's Baptism" in Austin Walker, *The Excellent Benjamin Keach* (Dundas, Onatrio: Joshua Press, 2004), 383-85.

The Puritan Argument for the Immersion of Believers

year period by the first three successive pastors of London's oldest Baptist church, we can perhaps gain an understanding of the kinds of arguments which these early Baptists marshaled in favor of their positions.

Three Particular Baptist Pastors Considered

The three pastors whose works are under consideration in this essay are John Spilsbury, John Norcott, and Hercules Collins. Spilsbury[16] (1593-c. 1662/1668) was the first pastor of London's oldest Baptist church.[17] According to B. R. White, Spilsbury was the first of the Particular Baptists to "preach and practice believer's baptism" and his *A Treatise Concerning the Lawfull Subject of Baptisme* (1643) was "the first known publication on the subject by a Calvinist."[18] Spilsbury was one of the original signers, and perhaps the author,[19] of the *First London Confession of Faith* (1644).[20] Spilsbury's work was largely apologetic, the majority of it being a response to objections made by paedobaptists who saw believer's baptism as a novel practice. He published a second edition of his treatise on baptism in 1652 which was "corrected and enlarged by the Author."[21] This edition will be the one examined for the purpose of this study.

---

[16] Spilsbury is sometimes spelled Spilsbery.

[17] For a biographical and theological sketch of Spilsbury, see James M. Renihan, "John Spilsbury (1593-c.1662/1668)" in Michael A. G. Haykin, ed., *The British Particular Baptists: 1638-1910* (Springfield, MO: Particular Baptist Press, 1998), 1:21-37.

[18] B. R. White, *The English Baptists of the Seventeenth Century* (London: The Baptist Historical Society, 1996), 72.

[19] James Renihan states that "several authors hypothesize" that Spilsbury was either the author or co-author of the *First London Confession*. He cites A. C. Underwood, R. L. Greaves, and W. L. Lumpkin as supporting this view. "John Spilsbury (1593-c. 1662/1668)," 24.

[20] Available in William L. Lumpkin, *Baptist Confessions of Faith* (Valley Forge, PA: Judson Press, 1969), 153-71.

[21] John Spilsbery, *A Treatise Concerning the Lawfull Subject of Baptism* (London: Henry Hills, 1652), title page.

John Norcott (1621-1676) was the second pastor of the Wapping congregation, having followed Spilsbury upon his death in either 1662 or 1668. Norcott contributed to the seventeenth-century literature on baptism with his *Baptism Discovered Plainly and Faithfully, According to the Word of God* (1672). This was the only work which he ever published, but it had a long life, being reprinted ten times.[22] The last edition was published over two hundred years after the first printing and was "Corrected and Somewhat Altered" by Charles Haddon Spurgeon.[23] Whereas Spilsbury's work was largely a response to paedobaptist critiques, Norcott's work was a much more positive biblical treatment of the subject of baptism. For the purpose of this study, the second edition of *Baptism Discovered Plainly and Faithfully* (1675) which was published in Norcott's lifetime will be the edition used.

Hercules Collins (1647-1702) served as the third pastor of London's oldest Baptist church.[24] Collins' principal work on baptism was titled *Believers-Baptism from Heaven, and of Divine Institution* and at 139 pages it is the largest of the three works examined in this chapter, more than double the size of either Spilsbury or Norcott's works.[25]

The early English Baptists argued for believer's baptism by immersion based upon what Spilsbury would call "the plain testimony of Scripture."[26] Spilsbury would therefore reject infant baptism, since "there is neither command, or Example in all the

---

[22] 1675, 1694, 1700, 1709, 1721, 1722, 1723, 1740, 1801, and 1878.

[23] John Norcott, *Baptism Discovered Plainly and Faithfully, According to the Word of God* (London: Passmore & Alabaster, 1878), title page.

[24] For details on the life of Hercules Collins see Michael A. G. Haykin "The Piety of Hercules Collins (1646/7-1702)" in *Devoted to the Service of the Temple: Piety, Persecution, and Ministry in the Writings of Hercules Collins*, ed. Michael A. G. Haykin and Steve Weaver (Grand Rapids: Reformation Heritage Books, 2007), 1-30.

[25] Hercules Collins, *Believers-Baptism from Heaven, and of Divine Institution. Infants-Baptism from Earth, and Human Invention* (London, 1691).

[26] Spilsbery, *A Treatise Concerning the Lawfull Subject of Baptism*, unnumbered page 3 of "The Epistle to the Reader."

New Testament for such practise."[27] Similarly, Collins rejected infant baptism because, as he said, "We have neither precept nor example for that practice in all the Book of God."[28] Likewise John Norcott would argue that sprinkling could not serve as a substitute for dipping, because…

> God is a jealous God, and stands upon small things in matters of Worship; 'tis likely Nadab and Abihu thought, if they put fire in the Censer, it might serve, though it were not fire from the Altar; but God calls it strange fire, and therefore he burns them with strange fire, Leviticus 10:2-3.[29]

These Baptist pastors sought to apply the regulative principle more thoroughly than had Calvin or Burroughs and the Reformed/Puritan tradition which they represented. In general, they argued in three different ways for believer's baptism by immersion based upon what John Spilsbury would call "the plain testimony of Scripture."[30]

Arguments for Believer's Baptism by Immersion

English Baptists in the seventeenth century used three main types of arguments from Scripture. First, they argued from the meaning of the Greek word *baptizo*. Second, they argued from Great Commission texts. Third, they argued from New Testament example texts.

---

[27] Spilsbery, *A Treatise Concerning the Lawfull Subject of Baptism*, unnumbered page 3 of "The Epistle to the Reader."
[28] Hercules Collins, *An Orthodox Catechism* (London: 1680), 26-27.
[29] John Norcott, *Baptism Discovered Plainly & Faithfully, According to the Word of God* (1672), 19.
[30] Spilsbery, *A Treatise Concerning the Lawfull Subject of Baptism*, unnumbered page 3 of "The Epistle to the Reader."

The Puritan Argument for the Immersion of Believers

Definition of baptizo

In the *First London Confession* of 1644, in the formation of which Spilsbury played a large role, "the way and manner" of baptism is said to be "dipping or plunging the whole body under water."[31] This is said to be the case because the "signe, must answer the thing signified."[32] The thing signified was threefold, namely, the "washing of the whole soule in the bloud of Christ"; "the death, buriall, and resurrection" of Christ; and the future physical resurrection of believers.[33] In his "Epistle to the Reader" in his treatise on baptism, Spilsbury notes that the word *baptizo*, translated "baptism," means "to dipp, wash, or to plunge one into the water."[34] This, he says, "is the judgement of the most and best learned in the land," as well as seen "in all the Common Dictionaries."[35] This was clearly foundational for Spilsbury. For him, the word *baptizo* simply meant immersion. Thus, any attempt to deny this doctrine was a rejection of "the plain testimony of Scripture."[36] Similarly, in the General Baptist Edward Barber's *A Small Treatise of Baptisme, or, Dipping*, one is hard-pressed to even find the word "baptism" after the title page. In the subsequent pages, Barber virtually always substitutes the word "dipping," or a variant, for "baptism."[37] For these first two Baptist defenders of immersion, the meaning of the word *baptizo* was an important part of their argument for baptism by immersion.

---

[31] Lumpkin, *Baptist Confessions of Faith*, 167.
[32] Lumpkin, *Baptist Confessions*, 167.
[33] Lumpkin, *Baptist Confessions*, 167.
[34] Spilsbery, *A Treatise Concerning the Lawfull Subject of Baptism*, unnumbered page 3 of "The Epistle to the Reader."
[35] Spilsbery, *A Treatise Concerning the Lawfull Subject of Baptism*, unnumbered page 3 of "The Epistle to the Reader."
[36] Spilsbery, *A Treatise Concerning the Lawfull Subject of Baptism*, unnumbered page 3 of "The Epistle to the Reader."
[37] For example, Matthew 28:19 is rendered, "Goe and make Disciples, all Nations, dipping them in the Name of the Father, and of the Sonne, and of the Holy Spirit." Barber, *A Small Treatise of Baptisme*, 1.

Both Norcott and Collins devoted entire chapters to their belief "that baptism is dipping."[38] Norcott plainly asserts, "The Greek Βαπτιζω" [*baptizo*] means "to plunge, to overwhelm."[39] "Thus," he says, "Christ was plunged in water."[40] Further, they "did baptize in Rivers."[41] Therefore, he asked, "what need it be in a River, and where there was much water, would not a little in a Bason serve to sprinkle the face?"[42] Norcott goes on to show that the truths which baptism signifies only make sense if baptism is a complete plunging underneath the water. "Baptism signifies the Burial of Christ." Norcott therefore concludes, "Now we do not reckon a man buried, when a little earth is sprinkled on his face: but he is buried when covered, thus you are buried in Baptism."[43] Likewise, "Christ's sufferings are called a Baptism" and "when Christ suffered he was plunged into pains; ...from head to foot in pain."[44] Norcott summarizes his findings:

> Thus you see the place where they were Baptized, was a River, their Action, they went down into the Water; then being in the Water, they were Baptized; this was where was much Water. The end was to shew forth Christs Burial. Now if there be not a Burial under water to shew Christs Burial, the great end of the Ordinance is lost, but we are Buried by Baptism.[45]

As with Spilsbury, so too for Norcott, the word baptism means dipping or immersion.

---

[38] Chapter IV of Norcott, *Baptism Discovered Plainly and Faithfully*, 16-21 and chapter III of Collins, *Believers-Baptism from Heaven*, 11-20.
[39] Norcott, *Baptism Discovered Plainly and Faithfully*, 16.
[40] Norcott, *Baptism Discovered Plainly and Faithfully*, 16.
[41] Norcott, *Baptism Discovered Plainly and Faithfully*, 17.
[42] Norcott, *Baptism Discovered Plainly and Faithfully*, 17.
[43] Norcott, *Baptism Discovered Plainly and Faithfully*, 17.
[44] Norcott, *Baptism Discovered Plainly and Faithfully*, 17.
[45] Norcott, *Baptism Discovered Plainly and Faithfully*, 19.

Hercules Collins begins his chapter on "What Baptism is"[46] by first stating what baptism is not. Collins bluntly declares that baptism is "not sprinkling, dropping, or pouring of Water."[47] Instead, "Baptism is an external washing, plunging or dipping a profest Believer, in the Name of the Father, Son, and Holy Ghost."[48] The *Second London Confession of Faith* of 1689, of which Collins was a principal signer, states equally as bluntly that "Immersion, or dipping of the person in water, is necessary to the due administration of this ordinance."[49]

After stating his conviction that baptism is immersion, Collins proceeds to set out the evidence for his belief. The first evidence that baptism means immersion is taken from the fact that "the word Baptize in the New Testament is taken from the word Dip in the Old."[50] In other words, the Hebrew equivalent (*tabal*) of the word translated "baptize" (*baptizo*) in the New Testament is always translated "dip" in the Old Testament. This Hebrew word is translated as *baptizo* in the Septuagint. A second evidence is that the "end of the Ordinance sheweth Baptism to be dipping,"[51] namely, the death, burial, and resurrection of Christ. There is, Collins says, "no manner of similitude and likeness between Christ's Death and Burial, with sprinkling a little Water on the Face." However, "burying in the Water is as lively a Similitude and Likeness of Jesus Christ's Death, as the breaking Bread, and pouring out the Wine is at the Lord's Table."[52] Collins further argues that baptism is immersion by a series of examples and metaphors in a similar manner as Norcott had done previously.[53] Collins, therefore, concludes very similarly:

---

[46] Chapter III, also labeled "That Baptism is dipping" in the "The Contents."
[47] Collins, *Believers-Baptism from Heaven*, 11.
[48] Collins, *Believers-Baptism from Heaven*, 11.
[49] Lumpkins, *Baptist Confessions*, 291.
[50] Collins, *Believers-Baptism from Heaven*, 12.
[51] Collins, *Believers-Baptism from Heaven*, 15.
[52] Collins, *Believers-Baptism from Heaven*, 15.
[53] Although Collins rearranges and expands upon Norcott's work on baptism, the dependence is obvious in certain places, such as here.

Thus you see the Places where the Apostles Baptized, were in Rivers, and where was much Water: You see their Act and Posture, they went down into the Water; you see their End was, to exhibit and shew forth Christ's Death, Burial, and Resurrection.[54]

In answer to the possible question "Why Sprinkling will not do as well as Dipping?," Collins answers with five reasons:

> 1. Because that is another thing than Christ hath commanded; and 'tis high presumption to change God's Ordinances. ...
> 2. In so doing, we lose the End of the Ordinance, which as aforesaid, is to shew forth the Death and Resurrection of Christ.
> 3. We must keep the Ordinances as they were delivered unto us; as Moses was to make all things according to the Pattern shewed him in the Mount.
> 4. God is a Jealous God and stands upon small things in Matters of Worship: Had Moses and Aaron but lifted up a Tool upon the Altar of ruff Stone to beautify it, they would have polluted it, because contrary to the Command.
> 5. This hath no likeness to the holy Examples of Christ and his Apostles.[55]

Beside the above text Collins adds a marginal note more directly referencing the regulative principle:

> Tis a known Maxim, to practice anything in the Worship of God, as an Ordinance of his, without an Institution, ought to be esteemed Will-worship & Idolatry. And that there is a necessity for Scripture-Authority to warrant every Ordinance and Practice in Divine Worship, is owned by

---

[54] Collins, *Believers-Baptism from Heaven*, 19.
[55] Collins, *Believers-Baptism from Heaven*, 19-20.

Luther, Austin, Calvin, Basil, Theoph. Tertul, Mr. Ball; and in the 6th Article of the Church of England; also Bellarmine.[56]

For Collins then, it was the regulative principle of worship which required the rejection of infant baptism.

For Spilsbury, Norcott, and Collins, indeed, it was enough that the word *baptizo* meant to dip, plunge, or immerse. Any other mode was a "human invention" and therefore was rebellion against Christ, the Lord of the church. Collins speaks for all the early Baptists when he gives the reason for writing his book on baptism. His purpose was:

> to display this Sacrament in its apostolic primitive purity, free from the adulterations of men, a sin which God charged upon the learned Jews, that they made void the commands of God by their traditions. O that none of the learned among the Gentiles, especially those of the Reformed churches, may be charged with setting up men's inventions in the room of Christ's institutions.[57]

Great Commission texts

The main way in which the early Baptists argued from Great Commission texts was in regard to the proper order of faith and baptism. Just as preaching the gospel precedes baptism in the Great Commission texts, so too belief in the gospel on the part of the individual should precede their own baptism. Since infants are incapable of understanding and responding to the gospel message in faith, they are not fit, or "lawfull" subjects for baptism. John Spilsbury argues that if Matthew 28:19 were "well considered, and rightly understood" it "would stop mens mouthes for ever having a word to say for the baptizing of infants."[58] This is because "here teaching goes before baptizing, and presupposeth understanding

---

[56] Collins, *Believers-Baptism from Heaven*, 20.
[57] Collins, *Believers-Baptism from Heaven*, 7.
[58] Spilsbery, *A Treatise Concerning The Lawfull Subject of Baptism*, 46.

and faith in that which is taught."[59] Spilsbury then cites Mark 16:15-16 and declares that these verses "clearly manifest that infants are not the subjects of baptism appointed by Christ; for all the external benefits and privileges of the gospel are given onely to external and visible faith."[60] Elsewhere, Spilsbury even more forcefully says:

> God hath ordained in the Gospel preaching and believing to go before baptizing, as Matt. 28:18, with Mark 16:15-16. And that way or order which hath not God of its Author, and found in the records of Christ, with his image and superscription upon it, let us say as sometime he did, "Give to Caesar that which is Caesars, and to God that which is Gods;" so say I, give to Antichrist his baptizing of infants, and to Christ his baptizing of believers.[61]

In this way, Spilsbury used the Great Commission texts to show that faith in the message of the gospel must precede baptism, which makes infant baptism impossible since infants are incapable of faith.

Both John Norcott and Hercules Collins contain expositions of a Great Commission text as the starting point for their works on baptism. Norcott lays a foundation for his rejection of infant baptism by an exposition of Matthew 28:18-20 in which he breaks down the text into eight sections. In this chapter, Norcott makes repeated references to the order of teaching and then baptizing without making the application to infant baptism. He simply states, "when you have taught them, then baptize them."[62] In his concluding considerations, Norcott urges his readers to "[c]onsider, whether it be safe to admit of Consequences against an express Rule, Matt. 28:19, 'Teach and baptize'."[63] Clearly, Norcott sees this divine order as forming "an express Rule" that forbids the practice of infant baptism.

---

[59] Spilsbery, *A Treatise Concerning The Lawfull Subject of Baptism*, 46.
[60] Spilsbery, *A Treatise Concerning The Lawfull Subject of Baptism*, 46.
[61] Spilsbery, *A Treatise Concerning The Lawfull Subject of Baptism*, 46.
[62] Norcott, *Baptism Discovered Plainly and Faithfully*, 10.
[63] Norcott, *Baptism Discovered Plainly and Faithfully*, 58.

Whereas Norcott appeals to the Great Commission as recorded in Matthew 28:19-20, Collins begins his discourse on water baptism with the parallel text of Mark 16:16. The text simply states, "He that believeth, and is baptized, shall be saved." Collins very specifically spells out the significance of this text. "Here is first Faith," he writes, "then Baptism."[64] Collins then explains the implication of this order:

> Therefore to baptize before there be any appearance of Faith, is directly contrary unto this unerring standing Rule, and doth reflect upon our Lord and Lawgiver, as if he spoke rashly and inconsiderately, putting that first which should be last, and that last which should be first.[65]

Collins then proceeds to give two doctrines from the Great Commission. Doctrine 1: "It's the unalterable Will of Jesus Christ, who is King and Law-giver to his Gospel-Church, that all Persons believe before they are baptized."[66] Doctrine 2: "It's the indispensable Duty of all true Believers to be Baptized."[67] Collins calls baptism an indispensable duty for believers, he says, "because I know of no Place where our Lord hath left this to the Liberty of Believers to do it, or leave it undone, as best pleaseth them."[68] For early Baptists such as Collins, this was a serious issue. They were not Baptist by default, but by clear conviction. Only one of such deep conviction on this matter could appeal so fervently as Collins did:

> Therefore if this be your Lord and Savior's Will, Believers, pray obey him. In your Prayers you desire you may be enabled to do his Will on Earth as it is in Heaven: This is one part of his Divine Will; Your Redeemer was willing to be

---

[64] Collins, *Believers-Baptism from Heaven*, 8.
[65] Collins, *Believers-Baptism from Heaven*, 8.
[66] Collins, *Believers-Baptism from Heaven*, 9.
[67] Collins, *Believers-Baptism from Heaven*, 9.
[68] Collins, *Believers-Baptism from Heaven*, 9.

baptized in Blood for your Salvation, and will not you be baptized in Water, in obedience to his Commission?[69]

For these men baptism was not optional for the believer. They argued just as strongly for the necessity of believers being baptized as they did against the baptism of infants. Their hermeneutic required them to do so.

New Testament example texts

Another type of biblical text used by the early Baptists in their defense of believer's baptism was the examples of baptisms performed in the New Testament. These examples include both the baptism of Jesus by John the Baptist, but also the numerous examples of baptisms in the book of Acts. Most of the arguments based on these examples are short and to the point, but they are sprinkled throughout these texts and deserve some treatment here.

John Norcott begins his treatise on baptism in the very first chapter with an account of the baptism of Christ in the river of Jordan. Norcott uses the baptism of Jesus to demonstrate that baptism is dipping. The fact that Matthew 3:4 says that Jesus came "up out of the water" proves that Jesus was immersed beneath the water. Else, "had he not been down, 'twould not have bin said he went up."[70] "We never say," Norcott continued, "one goes out of the house when he never was in. So Christ could not be said to come out of the water, had he not been in."[71]

Likewise, Hercules Collins cites John 3:23, which states, "John the Baptist baptized in Enon, because there was much water there." To which Collins responds, "if Sprinkling would have done, there had been no need of much Water nor Rivers."[72] Collins elsewhere argues along with Norcott that if Jesus went up out of the water, "common sense signifies" that "He first went down...into the

---

[69] Collins, *Believers-Baptism from Heaven*, 9.
[70] Norcott, *Baptism Discovered Plainly and Faithfully*, 5.
[71] Norcott, *Baptism Discovered Plainly and Faithfully*, 5.
[72] Collins, *Believers-Baptism from Heaven*, 16.

water."[73] This is further seen in the examples from the times of the apostles. "Thus you see the Places where the Apostles Baptized, were in Rivers, and where was much Water: You see their Act and Posture, they went down into the Water."[74] In addition to these references, both Norcott and Collins devote an entire chapter to a listing of Scriptures without commentary that mentions baptism.[75] Many of these are further examples of individuals baptized as believers.

Early Baptists often appealed to the examples of the baptism administered by John, the baptism of Jesus, and the numerous examples of baptism in the book of Acts. Often these texts were merely listed, the argument seemingly being that the overwhelming number of such texts should convince their paedobaptist adversaries. These texts were used both to demonstrate the proper mode of baptism, immersion, and the proper order of baptism, faith preceding water baptism.

Conclusion

In his *An Orthodox Catechism* published in 1680, Hercules Collins' response to the question, "Doth the Scripture any where expressly forbid the baptizing of infants?" reveals the commitment which he would later argue for in his book on baptism. Collins replied:

> It is sufficient that the Divine Oracle commands the baptizing of believers, unless we will make ourselves wiser than what is written. Nadab and Abihu were not forbidden to offer strange fire, yet for so doing they incurred God's wrath, because they were commanded to take fire from the altar.[76]

---

[73] Collins, *Believers-Baptism from Heaven*, 18.
[74] Collins, *Believers-Baptism from Heaven*, 19.
[75] Norcott, *Baptist Discovered Plainly and Faithfully*, 48-51 and Collins, *Believers-Baptism from Heaven*, 72-76.
[76] Hercules Collins, *An Orthodox Catechism: Being the Sum of Christian Religion, Contained in the Law and Gospel* (London, 1680), 27.

This logic by Collins mirrors that of Calvin, who said, "It ought to be sufficient for the rejection of any mode of worship, that it is not sanctioned by the command of God."[77] This same commitment was shared by all the early Baptists. The earliest Particular Baptists writing on the subject shared Collins' commitment to worship ordered by Scripture. Of infant baptism, John Spilsbury would write:

> For sure I am, there is neither command, or Example in all the New Testament for such practise, as I know, and whatsoever is done in the worship of God, in obedience to Christ, without his command, or apparent example approved of by Christ, is of man, as a voluntary will-worship, after the commandments and doctrines of man; the which Christ testifies as against a vain thing.[78]

Likewise, John Norcott would argue that sprinkling could not serve as a substitute for dipping because "God is a jealous God, and stands upon small things in matters of Worship":

> tis likely Nadab and Abihu thought, if they put fire in the Censer, it might serve, though it were not fire from the Altar; but God calls it strange fire, and therefore he burns them with strange fire, Leviticus 10:2-3.[79]

For these Baptists, baptism was vitally important. Their defense of the practice of believer's baptism by immersion was driven by their commitment to the regulative principle of worship. In their view, infant baptism simply could not be found in Scripture, and therefore had to be rejected at any cost. Believer's baptism by immersion, they believed, was the plain testimony of Scripture and was therefore to be defended at all costs.

---

[77] Calvin, "The Necessity of Reforming the Church," 133.
[78] Spilsbery, *A Treatise Concerning the Lawfull Subject of Baptism*, unnumbered page 3 of "The Epistle to the Reader."
[79] Norcott, *Baptism Discovered Plainly and Faithfully*, 19.

CHAPTER 5
The Antipaedobaptism of John Tombes
Michael T. Renihan, Ph.D.*

There is an untold chapter from the book of the Westminster Assembly in particular and Puritanism more generally. It is about a Puritan academic and pastor named John Tombes. He was a noted polemicist for the baptism of disciples alone. In this role he was engaged actively with some of the Divines seated at the Assembly. Tombes sought needed reform in the churches of England and beyond. That reform was a return to the apostolic and post-apostolic practice of disciple baptism. This essay will examine the historical background and setting, the engagement with Westminster, and the fallout that followed.[1]

Biographical Background

John Tombes was born in Bewdley, Worcestershire, England, in or about the year 1603. Not much is known about his early life other than to assume the proper foundational grammar school education was in place for a child who would eventually enter the halls of the University at Oxford at the age of fifteen. Such an education was uncommon and expensive. It was sought for promising children.

Tombes matriculated at Magdelan Hall, Oxford University, in 1618. In the typical three years he finished a Bachelor of Arts (1621).

---

*Michael T. Renihan, Ph.D., is pastor of Heritage Baptist Church, Worcester, MA, and author of *Antipaedobaptism in the Thought of John Tombes: An Untold Story from Puritan England*. Chapters five and six of this book first appered in *RBTR* and are used with permission.

[1] In large measure, this essay is from my work entitled, *Antipaedobaptism in the Thought of John Tombes*. The published work is based on a doctoral thesis at Wycliffe Hall, Oxford University, entitled, *Infant Baptism in the Thought of John Tombes*. The published work is available from B and R Press, Auburn, MA, mike_renihan@yahoo.com, originally published, 2001.

He continued as a student under William Pemble, the well-respected Puritan. Tombes completed the Master of Arts in 1624. Upon the death of his tutor that year, Tombes succeeded Pemble as Catechetical Lecturer at Magdelan Hall. Tombes was but twenty-one years of age at that succession. While teaching at Magdelan Hall, he pursued a Bachelor in Divinity degree. He finished it in 1631. This was a seven-year process to assure one's mastery of things divine. It was a time full of lectures attended and given, disputes and debates, with a life centered in the hub-bub of the university.

Between the years 1624 and 1630, Tombes lectured at St. Martin Carfax, a church whose tower still stands as a tourist attraction in downtown Oxford. In November of 1630 he was made vicar of Leominster, Herefordshire. It was reported that his preaching in "Lemster" was popular with the parishioners. The next year he married Mary Scudder, daughter of Henry Scudder, the much admired author of *A Christian's Daily Walk*. "Father" Scudder would later deliver Tombes' thoughts on baptism to a committee studying the sacraments at the Westminster Assembly.

In 1641 Tombes left Leominster for Bristol as Royalist forces forced him out. Bristol had been under the control of parliamentarian sympathizers up to that time. In Bristol, Tombes had the income or support of All Saints Parish. In that city he also had a public debate with an unnamed "ingenious baptist" whose arguments and manners converted him to antipaedobaptist views. Yet, "Due to the violence of the King's Party" in Bristol, and the recommendation of his "Physitian," Tombes left for London in 1642. He was well aware that the Westminster Assembly was about to convene. He desired to clear up the issue of baptism once for all. He planned to consult libraries and scholars, dusty books and sitting divines.

After his arrival in London, Tombes was placed at Fenchurch near the Tower of London. The parishioners, aware of his antipaedobaptist views, refused to hear him preach. Tombes sought another charge through John White, chairman of a committee handling the "plundered ministers" of that time.

After some controversy with White and Stephen Marshall, Tombes was placed as Master of the Temple Church in 1643, although a recent plaque in the building names Tombes as only a "Commonwealth Preacher." Soon he was dismissed from this post after publishing a treatise against infant baptism in response to Stephen Marshall's attack.

Tombes returned to Bewdley where as the priest at a Chapel-at-ease he did not have to baptize infants. While serving in that Parish he gathered an informal society of baptized believers from within the neighborhood for mutual edification. In 1646 he was made the rector of Ross and perpetual curate of Bewdley to add to his ability to provide for himself and his family. In ecclesiastical terms, this made Tombes a pluralist – multiple parishes providing his income.

While in Bewdley a friendship with the young Richard Baxter ensued and flourished. They spoke in each other's pulpits every other week for a weekday lecture. Kidderminster and Bewdley were just a handful of miles away from each another. There was a falling out between the two when Baxter made application in a sermon to infant baptism. Letters, discussions, and controversy ensued. On January 1, 1649/50 these two champions held a day long debate on the issue of the subjects of baptism.

The controversy with Baxter caused a great alienation of affections from the townspeople in Bewdley. Tombes moved on to another position where he could function as a man of God without violating his conscience by baptizing infants. He moved to another non-parochial post as Master of the Hospital at Ledbury. He was forsaken by the Chapel in Bewdley and then restored to the income from Leominster.

In 1653 Tombes, a known antipaedobaptist, received the respect of the Protectorate. He was appointed a trier under the Lord Protector, Oliver Cromwell. A trier was a minister who tried or tested the fitness of other ministers as they sought to be appointed or elected to pulpits. This was a position with great prestige religiously and politically. It was reserved for well-respected men of some attainment in divinity. It speaks to the character and knowledge of a man like Tombes.

The Antipaedobaptism of John Tombes

Depending on the political sympathies of the day, it was at either the Restoration of the Monarchy or the Great Ejection of the Ministers (1662) when Tombes laid down his living forever. He repudiated his ordination, since he could not in good conscience accept the Anglican Settlement. Tombes moved to Salisbury as a widower. He met and married Elizabeth Combs, a widow of some means. While living there he attended St. Edmonds Church. In 1672 his house was licensed as a "Presbyterian Meeting Place" under the second of the Conventicles Acts. In this case, "Presbyterian" was merely a synonym for non-conformist. On May 26, 1676, Tombes passed on from this world. He was buried in the churchyard of St. Edmonds. Although his body is dead, his words continue to speak and inform the thoughts of subsequent generations including our own. His legacy is a vigorous defense of believer's baptism that covers more published pages than any other writer since the dawn of the printing press. Yet, into obscurity he has fallen and remained.

Tombes' Baptismal Theology

Fifteen out of Tombes' thirty main literary works touch upon the subject of baptism. The majority of these books interact with his contemporaries according to the scholastic methodology of his era. Only two of these works present his baptismal theology in a direct and popular manner, though still in Puritan academic fashion. He uses the structure of the syllogism to give substance to his arguments along with *sola Scriptura* as his authority to "straighten" the truth.

His first work is also his first published piece on the issue. Tombes' *Exercitations* were presented to a committee of the Westminster Assembly commissioned to examine the issue of proper baptism.[2] In the *Exercitations*, Tombes presents his case

---

[2] John Tombes, *An Exercitation about Infant-Baptisme; Presented in certaine Papers, to the Chair-man of a Committee of the Assembly of Divines, Selected to consider of that Argument, in the yeers, 1643, and 1644, London, 1646. Published in Two Treatises and an Appendix to them Concerning Infant-Baptisme. The former Treatise being an Exercitation presented to the Chair-man of a Committee of the Assembly of Divines. The*

through twenty-five arguments in English for the popular dissemination of the matter, that are equivalent to nine arguments presented in the original Latin to the Westminster Divines.³ The arguments break out into four categories: (1) exegetical, where he dealt with the meaning of texts; (2) historical, where he interacted with beliefs and practices in antecedent ages; (3) theological, where he reflected upon the basis for and reasoning about truths asserted; and (4) practical, where he considered the ecclesiastical and pastoral implications of the practice. Among the arguments presented, eleven are exegetically based, five are predominantly theological, four are historical, and the remaining five are driven by practical and pastoral concerns within a theological and historical framework.

The second clear, and positive, presentation of Tombes' theology of baptism comes as his last work on the matter. In 1659, after many years of reflection, Tombes dropped his rigid scholastic methodology from his Oxford "experience" in order to present more popularly his thoughts in the form of a catechism. In forty questions and answers, Tombes gives a digest of his ever-maturing thought to facilitate an understanding of the basic issues.⁴ Or, in his words "To the Christian Reader":

---

later an Examen of the Sermon of Mr Stephen Marshall, about Infant-Baptisme, in a letter sent to him. London, 1646.

³ Tombes gives his reason for the original Latin form of the *Exercitations* in these words: "I had resolved not to publish my writings in *English*, but in *Latine*, and therefore I first framed my Exercitation in *Latine*, conceiving the Assembly would have apprehended my aime and intention, to be to deale only with Schollars in this matter: but all things falling out crosse to my expectation, I conceive it was the will of God it should be printed as it was. This much for the justifying the publishing of my treatise." See John Tombes, B.D. *An Apology or Plea for the Two Treatises, and Appendix to them concerning Infant-Baptisme; Published Decemb. 15, 1645. Against the unjust charges, complaints, and censures of Doctor Nathaniel Homes, Mr Iohn Geree, Mr Stephen Marshall, Mr John Ley, and Mr William Hussey; together with a Postscript by way of reply to Mr Blakes answer to Mr Tombes his letter, and Mr Edmund Calamy, and Mr Richard Vines Preface to it. Wherein the principall heads of the Dispute concerning Infant-Baptism are handled, and the insufficiency of the writings opposed to the two Treatises manifested*, London, 1646, 15ff.

⁴ John Tombes, *A Short Catechism about Baptism*, London, 1659. Due to the difficulty of obtaining this significant work, it was manually reproduced and

> Many are the things at this day charged on Antipoedobaptists in their Doctrine and Practise, which have been proved to be unjustly imputed to them, by many large Treatises extant in print. For a more facile understanding of the truth than by reading larger Tracts, is this Compendium, in a manner of a catechism composed and published in this time, wherein others of different judgment, have thought fit to declare their way to the world, which is done, not because the disagreement in other things is either small, or of particular persons (whose cause is to be severed from that which is commonly held) and therefore requires not a distinct Confession or Declaration from that which is by others published.[5]

Tombes, however, also prejudices the reader of his *Catechism* toward his own position by poisoning the well filled with his opponent's writings with these prefatory remarks:

> [T]he Doctrine of which is one article of the foundation of Christianity, Heb. 6.2. whereby we put on Christ, Gal 3.27. united to his members, Ephes. 4.5. conformed to Christ, Col 2.12. Rom. 6.3, 4, 5. required with faith to salvation, Mark

---

reprinted with identical pagination and spelling by the author. Copies are retained by me and a copy was deposited in the *Joseph Angus Library* at Regents Park College, Oxford, June 1994. It also appears in my *Antipaedobatism in the Thought of John Tombes*.

[5] Tombes, *Catechism*, first two unnumbered pages. It is worth noting Tombes' comments in three areas: (1) He draws attention to those whose cause is to be severed from the National Church because of views that didn't conform to the majority opinion. His desire was to reform the church to bring about credobaptism as that opinion; (2) He makes a passing mention of a Confession and Declaration which appear to be the Presbyterian *Westminster Confession of Faith* (1646) and the Congregationalist *Savoy Declaration of Faith* (1658); (3) As an advocate of a National Church he leaves an interesting inference to be drawn – that there is enough theological agreement among these diverse groups so that only a catechism on "right baptism" is needed. ". . . I have thought this necessary to be done because of the importance of restoring right baptism", second unnumbered page. Given the legitimacy of this inference, Tombes makes modern readers consider the basic implications of theological unanimity and diversity.

16.26. with repentance to remission of sins, Acts 2.38. with express profession of the Baptized's faith required, Acts 8.37. upon manifestation of conversion, Acts 10.47. Acts 11.17. as the duty of the Baptized, and not a meer priviledge, Acts 22.16. most solemly administered in the Primitive times, with strict examination and greatest engagement of persons baptized, accounted the chief evidence of Christianity, of as much or more moment than the Lord's Supper; insomuch that some conceived from Heb. 6.4. that falling away after it irreparable. But the pretended Baptism of Infants, as now used slightly and profanely done, quite different from Christ's Institution and the Apostles practise by Ministers and people in so wholy and carnal manner as that, it is upon and with gross untruths and perverting of holy Scripture, obtruded on unwary souls with a pretence of a Baptismal Vow, which is a meer fiction, and so many ill consequents both in Christian conversation and communion and church-constitution and Government, that were men sensible to their evil as they should be, they would tremble at such mockery of God, and abuse of so holy an Ordinance of God's worship and men's souls by it, and with such arrogant presumption in avowing such a manifest invention of men as God's precept. The aim of the composer of it is the manifestation of the truth, wherein doth he rejoyce, and desires thou mayest rejoyce with him.[6]

A brief taste of Tombes' baptismal theology can be gleaned by the many and varied responses to his work. Almost all of the theologians and churchmen who wrote on baptism in the last sixty years of the seventeenth century did so with Tombes as the

---

[6] Tombes, *Catechism*, unnumbered pages 2-3. Behind the rhetoric lies Tombes' initial concern–to reform the Church by the Word of God. His invective can be understood as venting frustration over the many injustices he experienced due to his beliefs or, perhaps, as a device of the time for gaining one's attention towards influencing them or pacification through education of the points in the matter, or as a mixture somewhere in between.

whetstone. They sought to redeem him or refute him. They all succeeded in a vast output on the printed page.

The Consequence of Public Discourse

After nearly twelve years of ministry in "Lemster, in Herefordshire," Tombes and his family left due to the "violence of the Kings Party." After "much wandering" and "much danger," Tombes set out for London. As he wrote, "I resolved to adventure a journey to London through Wiltshire, to conferre with Brethren of the Assembly."[7]

This Assembly was the Westminster Assembly. Tombes seemed to have been a bit naïve. He was idealistic, thinking that his purely academic query would be met with objectivity. He was sorely mistaken. Through his inquiries, discussions, publications, and debates, an irretrievable flood of interaction was set in motion.

Tombes' motivation in moving to London was stated as:

> Wherefore I resolved if ever I came to *London*, to search further into those two points of meaning of *I Cor. 7. 14*. and the History of Paedobaptisme.... [B]eing come to *London September* 22, 1643. I applied my selfe to enquire into the points forenamed.[8]

As part of this inquiry, Tombes met with a number of ministers in London about January 1643[9] to discuss his scruples as regards infant baptism. According to Tombes, some of the ministers there present believed him to have been convinced of his error because he had nothing to say in reply.[10]

---

[7] Tombes, *Apology*, 6.
[8] Tombes, *Apology*, 6.
[9] This date corresponds to January 1643 according to the modern reckoning. In the seventeenth century, they changed the year in March. So January 1643 (modern reckoning) is chronologically after July 1643 (old reckoning).
[10] Tombes, *Apology*, 8.

Tombes continued by presenting the motivation for those first and second literary works on the subject, both of which are lost. He wrote:

> Not long after the Conference, my most loving and reverend Father in law, Master *Henry Scudder,* fearing the event of the matter, after some writing that past betweene us, advised me to draw up the reasons of my doubts, and he undertook to present them to the Committee chosen (as I conceived it) to give satisfaction about that point.... ...I first drew up nine first arguments in my Excercitation, which were delivered as I relate in my Examen in *February* and *March* 1643. and after in July following, the other three.[11]

The first literary works by Tombes on baptism were the letters to Henry Scudder. The second was the original *Exercitation* expressing nine arguments penned in Latin for the Westminster Assembly sitting in London. The third is also lost to posterity. It was a one-page work also given to Henry Scudder. This one-page, in quarto, contained, as Tombes explained, "the main ground of my doubt."[12]

Controversy from Without

Tombes then met with a challenge from the pulpit. He gave the background and a firsthand account of that day's events:

> Now the Papers[13] before named, I perceived were tossed up and down from one to another, and it seemes *Master Edwards* the Controversie Lecturer at *Christ-Church* got them, and picking out some passages, but concealing others that would have cleared them under pretence of refuting them, with the

---

[11] Tombes, *Apology,* 9.
[12] Tombes, *Apology,* 9. Tombes stated that this work was less than forty lines long.
[13] Principally the original Latin *Exercitation* and the one page letter to Scudder.

writing of another that be joined with mine, meerly abused me in the Pulpit at *Christ-Church*: which I immediately charged him with after his Sermon in the Vestry, and he only excused it by telling me he named me not, though there were sundry Ministers there that knew he meant me.[14]

While in Oxford, Tombes attended Thomas Goodwin's lectures on the subject of infant baptism and went again to hear Master Edwards and his discourse at Christ Church College. He also read "many Treatises and Sermons." Tombes distilled all of this activity with the phrase, "in many of which I found rather invectives than arguments."[15]

Tombes' controversial views were becoming known. The Church to which he had been assigned in London, Fenchurch, refused to hear him preach, even though Tombes "meddled not with that matter in the Pulpit." Yet his reputation preceded him in that place. One of Tombes' "loving friends," a member of the Assembly, "understanding the Honourable Societies of the Temples wanted a Preacher, solicited the bringing of [him] thither."[16]

The Master of the Temple had been traditionally appointed directly by the Crown. During the uncertain time of Parliamentarian rule in London, this prerogative of selection was given over to the House of Commons. The issue of Tombes' appointment was given over to the Assembly of Divines sitting at Westminster. The Divines selected a committee to nominate a "Preacher" for the Temple's societies. Stephen Marshall was on the committee. Marshall did not like Tombes' theological peculiarity. Tombes was rejected.[17]

---

[14] Tombes, *Apology*, 9. See also William Kiffin, *To Mr. Thomas Edwards [A Public Challenge of a Sermon]*, n.p., 1645. This was Thomas Edwards, author of the controversial *Gangraena; or a Catalogue and Discovery of Many Errours, Heresies, Blasphemies, and pernicious Practises of the Sectaries of this Time vented and acted in England in these four last years*, London, 16 February 1646.

[15] Tombes, *Apology*, 10.

[16] Tombes, *Apology*, 10.

[17] Tombes, *Apology*, 10.

The Antipaedobaptism of John Tombes

Tombes was without an ecclesiastical charge. He had contact with John White, Chairman of the Committee for Plundered Ministers. Master White's desire was to dispute with Tombes on baptism before recommending him or supporting him further. This occasioned Tombes' fourth unpublished literary work on the matter. Tombes tells posterity of his action: "Which occasion I tooke to open my condition to him in a letter." This exchange brought forth a book by John White entitled *Infant Baptisme proved lawfull by Scripture*.[18]

While still without means to earn a living, Tombes continued the narrative of his misfortunes. "Shortly after in *August*. 1644, I met with Marshall's Sermon." This must have been a handwritten copy of Stephen Marshall's sermon, not published until 1645, entitled, in publication, *A Sermon on the Baptizing of Infants; preached in the Abbey-Church at Westminster, at the Morning Lecture*.[19] This encounter with Marshall's sermon provoked Tombes' fifth literary work on baptism. Tombes justified his action in this way:

> [A]nd finding the vehemancy of his spirit against Antipaedobaptists, and having had experience both of his, and Master Whites inflexiblenesse by my former writings, and seeing no likelihood of imploiment and maintenance for me and mine, except I would gather a separated Church, which I durst not do, as not knowing how to justifie such a practise, I resolved to make a full answer to Master Marshals Sermon, and finished it November 11. and having with much difficulty transcribed one Copy, and gotten another written for me, I sent my own to Master Marshall, who received it December 9, 1644.[20]

---

[18] Tombes, *Apology*, 10. John White, *Infant Baptisme proved Lawfull by Scripture*, London, 1644.

[19] Stephen Marshall, B.D., *A Sermon on the Baptizing of Infants, preached in the Abbey-Church at Westminster, at the Morning Lecture, appointed by the Honourable House of Commons*, London. 1645. Tombes first read the sermon sometime in 1644.

[20] Tombes, *Apology*, 10.

Marshall agreed to see Tombes. Tombes did not ask for a response to his work, but for a conversation about the pulpit at the Temple. Tombes asked Marshall, "Whether he held me fit for the Ministry or not, notwithstanding my dissent from him on that point." Marshall's reply was, in Tombes' words, "[H]e desired to know first whether I would keep my opinion to my selfe." Tombes returned this answer in writing carried by "Father Scudder":

> I request you return this answer to Master Marshall, that whereas I requested him to declare whether he thought me fit for the Ministry or not, notwithstanding my dissent about Paedobaptisme, and he demands of me a promise of silence in that point, I conceive he is bound by the rules of justice, mercy and prudence to do it without requiring that condition, and that he hath no reason to be jealous of me considering my carriage in this manner. Neverthelesse when I shall understand what promise he would have from me, and what is intended to be done by him for the discussing the point, and clearing of Truth, to which I ought not be wanting, and what advantage I may have by his agency for my imployment and maintenance, I shall give him a punctual answer, and am resolved for peace sake to yield as farre as I may without violating the solemne Covenant I have taken, and betraying truth and innocency, Decem. 26.[21]

Marshall and Tombes met on December 30, 1644 for a "friendly conference...in the morning before the [Westminster] Assembly sat." Tombes recapitulated the essence of that meeting:

> At the beginning of that Conference, Master Marshall having this last written message in his hand, & reading those words, [*and he demands of me a promise of silence in that point*] told me *that he did not demand of me a promise of silence in that point; for that was beyond his line*: this was his very expression. As soon as ever I heard those words, I conceived my selfe

---

[21] Tombes, *Apology*, 11.

freed from the snare I most feared of making a promise, which as the case might stand, I could not keep with a good conscience. Then Master *Marshall* spake to this effect, that *yet for the satisfaction of those who should enquire of him concerning me, he desired to know my intentions.* Whereupon I dealt freely, that I intended not to publish my opinion in the Pulpit, if I might be where I should not be put to baptize: for I conceived it not likely, that there would be a Reformation of that thing in this Age, there having been so long a practise of Infant-Baptisme, and such a prejudice in men against the opposers of it: yet I told him that if any should preach to that people I had charge of, that which I conceived to be an errour, I did resolve to oppose it there, otherwise mens preaching abroad should be of no provocation to me: So that it is clear, I made no promise, and that intimation of mine intentions which I made was only, that I intended not to preach my opinion in that place unlesse provoked there.[22]

Tombes added a condition:

[T]hat if Lawes were likely to be enacted to make the deniall of Infant-Baptisme penall, I held my selfe bound in conscience to appeare in publique about the matter: yea, and Master *Marshall* told me he intended me some animadversions on my *Examen*; whence it may be collected, that neither Master *Marshall* nor my selfe had agreed to lay aside the dispute it selfe.[23]

The foregoing was not without controversy. Tombes believed he had removed any restraints to ministering at the Temple, save one concession; Marshall believed Tombes to have been silenced in the matter of antipaedobaptism in order to have an ecclesiastical appointment and income. Stephen Marshall pressed home one

---

[22] Tombes, *Apology*, 11ff.
[23] Tombes, *Apology*, 12.

point, "That the Reformation of Congregations might be without altering the use of Infant-Baptisme."[24]

Tombes repeated his pledge before Obadiah Sedgwicke, his "loving friend" from their days at Oxford. "[A]fter a triall of me three Lords-daies at the *Temple*, I was at the end of January chosen by the Treasurers, and sundry others of the members of both the honourable Societies of the *Temples* to be their Preacher for a yeare."[25]

Another Front

On another front, news came from New England that a law had been passed "against those that denied baptizing of Infants," making the neglect of infant baptism penal. To mollify the civil and church authorities in New England, Tombes sent another handwritten copy of an augmented version of the *Examen* of Marshall's sermon, yet unpublished.[26] This was also in direct response to Master John Cotton's work published under the title *The Groundes and Endes of the Baptisme of the Children of the Faithfull*.[27]

Three of the Westminster Divines heard of Tombes' "act" in sending his work to New England. Thomas Goodwin, Richard Vines, and Stephen Marshall "showed scorne" towards Tombes. This public display and "sundry things happened which induced me to yeeld to the importunity of those that solicited earnestly the publishing of my writings for the publicke good." Tombes also sent to Marshall an enquiry as to whether Master Marshall would

---

[24] Tombes, *Apology*, 12.

[25] Tombes, *Apology*, 13.

[26] Tombes, *Apology*, 13. The text of the accompanying introductory letter is included in the text, 13ff.

[27] John Cotton, *The Groundes and Endes of the Baptisme of the Children of the Faithfull*, Boston, 1644. Part 3, Section 3, 42ff. Additional correspondence between Tombes and Cotton is housed at the American Antiquarian Society, Salisbury Street, Worcester, MA. These exchanges show the mid-seventeenth-century interdependence between England and her colonies. The intellectual life in England had consequences for Colonial America. See also, Richard Baxter, *Saint's Rest*, Introduction, where he appeals to certain miraculous births in New England as a sign of God's judgment on "Anabaptists."

answer the "point of difference" expressed in the handwritten epilogue to Tombes' *Examen*. The "best of the answer" Tombes received was, in Tombes' words, "since I had now a place for my Ministery without baptizing Infants, he expected I would be quiet."[28]

Tombes was aware that some in the Assembly "did have scruple in Conscience, the giving approbasion to me because of my opinion" and a growing response to antipaedobaptism in pulpit and in print. This added pressure to Tombes' personal quest to clear the truth and to publish his work. Tombes gives historical insight:

> The people of the city much inquired into this matter. A publique disputation was once allowed about it to which I was earnestly solicited, but for weighty reasons refused it. Sundry came to me to request the perusall of my papers for their satisfaction many learned, godly, and prudent persons, both of them that differed in judgement, as well as those that agreed with me, moved me to have them printed for the bringing of truth to light. I saw not wherein any danger to the State or Church might be created by the printing of them, and which was beyond all to me. I was confirmed it was a truth I held, had tried all fit meanes to have it examined, had been guided in the searching of it, and preserved for the businesse by many remarkable providences, and thereupon after prayer to God by my selfe, and with others for direction, I yeelded to the printing of them....[29]

This first published work actually included three works that introduced Tombes' antipaedobaptist theology to the reading public in a comprehensive, yet polemical, manner. The title page read, *Two Treatises and an Appendix to them concerning Infant-*

---

[28] Tombes, *Apology*, 14.
[29] Tombes, *Apology*, 15.

Baptisme.[30] The first treatise was an English translation of the Latin *Exercitation* Tombes had delivered to the Westminster Assembly. His second unpublished work was presented in a popularized format to facilitate discussion and comprehension of the issues at hand. The second of the two treatises was the *Examen of the Sermon of Mr Stephen Marshall, about Infant-Baptisme, in a letter sent to him*. They were published on December 15, 1645, nearly a year and a week after it was presented to Marshall in its handwritten form.

The publication "to cleare the truth" provoked a number of replies. Thomas Bakewell produced *A Justification of the two points now in Controversy with the Anabaptists....*[31] John Geree published a gracious reply under the short title of *Vindiciae Paedobaptismi; or a vindication of Infant Baptism....*[32] Doctor Nathaniel Homes (also Holmes) contributed *A Vindication of Baptizing Beleevers Infants....*[33] Marshall produced his own public reply, *A Defence of Infant Baptism....*[34] John Saltmarsh wrote *The Smoke in the Temple.Wherein is*

---

[30] John Tombes, *Two Treatises and an Appendix to them Concerning Infant-Baptisme, The former Treatise being an Exercitation presented to the Chair-man of a Committee of the Assembly of Divines. The later an Examen of the Sermon of Mr Stephen Marshall, about Infant-Baptisme, in a letter sent to him,* London, 1645. The Appendix was a short work to show Colossians 2:11-12 "proves not Infant-Baptisme."

[31] Thomas Bakewell, *A Justification of Two Points now in Controversy with the Anabaptists concerning baptism; with a briefe answer to Master Tombes argument, in his Exercitation about Infants baptisme. Also a briefe answer to Captaine Hobsons arguments in his Falacy of Infants baptisme,* London, 1646. Although the title page has only T. B. to denominate the author, Wing attributes the work to Bakewell. This is uncertain. The arguments addressed are closer to the concerns of Thomas Bedford, yet the printer is the same as Bakewell used on other occasions within the same decade. Neither Tombes, nor Hobson, engage this work – an anomalous reaction by Tombes. Bakewell wrote this as "a briefe Answer to Master Tombes twelve doubtful Arguments against it in his *Exercitation* about Infants' Baptisme."

[32] John Geree, M.A. Late of Tewkesbury, *Vindiciae Paedobaptismi: or a vindication of infant baptism in a full answer to Mr. Tombs his twelve arguments alleaged against it in his Exercitation and whatever is rational in his answer to Mr. Marshals sermon,* London, 1646.

[33] Nathaniel Homes, *A Vindication of Baptizing Believers Infants. In some animadversions upon Mr. Tombes his ex-exercitations about infant-baptisme,* London, 1646.

[34] Steven Marshall, B.D., *A Defence of Infant-Baptism: in Answer to two Treatise, and an Appendix to them concerning it; Lately published by Jo. Tombes. Wherein that*

a designe for peace and reconciliation of believers of the several opinions of these lines about ordinances....[35] John Ley replied to Saltmarsh mentioning Tombes in *Light for Smoak....*[36] William Hussey added his *An Answer to Mr. Tombes, His special Examination of Infants-Baptisme.*[37] Lastly, Thomas Blake answered a letter from Tombes with a preface from Edmund Calamy and Richard Vines entitled *Mr. Blakes answer to Mr. Tombes his letter....*[38]

Tombes could not disengage. The controversy was now not only public, but in print. Tombes gathered the materials and replied to each objection specifically after clearing the history of the dispute in the first section of his next published work, *An Apology, or Plea for the Two Treatises, and Appendix to them concerning Infant-Baptisme....*[39]

Controversie is fully discussed, the ancient and generally received use of it from the Apostles dayes, until the Anabaptists sprung up in Germany, manifested. The Arguments for it from the holy Scripture maintained, and objections against it answered, London, 1646.

[35] John Saltmarsh, *The Smoke in the Temple. Wherein is a designe for peace and reconciliation of believers of the several opinions of these lines about ordinances, to a fore bearance of each other in love, and meeknesse, and humility, etc. With one argument for liberty of conscience, etc.,* London, 1646.

[36] John Ley, Prebendary of Chester, *Light for Smoak, or a ...reply to Smoke in the Temple,* London, 1646.

[37] William Hussey, of Chislehurst, *An Answer to Mr. Tombes, His special Examination of Infants-Baptisme,* London, 1646.

[38] Thomas Blake, *Mr. Blakes Answer to Mr. Tombes his letter. In Vindication of the birth-priviledge or covenant holinesse of beleevers and their issue, together with the right of infants to baptisme,* London. 1646. The work included prefaces by Edmund Calamy and Richard Vines. From the content of this work, Blake was responding to the letter previously mentioned as Tombes' fourth unpublished work – the one page letter of forty lines in quarto. Blake is misattributed as the author of *A Moderate Answer to these Two Questions, 1. Whether ther be sufficient Ground in Scripture to Warrant the Conscience of a Christian to present his infants to the sacrament of Baptism: 2. Whether it be not sinfull for a Christian to receive the sacrament in a mixt Assembly,* London, 1645 by Alexander Gordon in "Blake, Thomas", *DNB,* Vol. II, 642, and Donald Wing in *Short Title Catalogue 1641-1700,* (MLA, New York, 1972), 177. The title page simply attributes the work to T. B. Holifield argues for Thomas Bedford as the proper source of this work in the appendix of *The Covenant Sealed* (Yale University Press, New Haven and London, 1974), 231. Bedford does not engage Tombes directly.

[39] The full title is: *An Apology or Plea for the Two Treatises, and Appendix to them concerning Infant-Baptisme; Published Decemb. 15, 1645. Against the unjust charges,*

Tombes answered particular questions and interacted with comments at length in an ingenious popularly written piece in narrative form. John Bachiler, who licensed the work for the press said, "Having perused this milde *Apology*, I conceive that the ingenuity, learning and piety therein contained deserve the Presse."[40]

Due to the publication of the *Apology*, Tombes was forced to leave the Temple Church. He moved to Worcestershire where he was made "Rector at Ross and perpetual Curate at Bewdley.[41] Stephen Marshall agitated for Tombes' dismissal, believing Tombes had broken his pledge not to go public with the point in controversy.[42] The inference had been drawn at some point and then remembered by Marshall.

In 1647, Robert Baillie (also Bailey and Bayley) published *Anabaptism, the True Fountain of Independency, Antinomy, Brownisme, and Familisme, and most of the other Errours, which for the time doe trouble the Church of England, Unsealed*.[43] In the same year, Tombes replied in a lengthy personal reply to Baillie, demonstrating how he had been wronged and his reputation tarnished by invectives in Baillie's work. This work was dated July 22, 1647.[44] Having no

---

complaints, and censures of Doctor Nathaniel Homes, Mr Iohn Geree, Mr Stephen Marshall, Mr John Ley, and Mr William Hussey; together with a Postscript by way of reply to Mr Blakes answer to Mr Tombes his letter, and Mr Edmund Calamy, and Mr Richard Vines Preface to it. Wherein the principall heads of the Dispute concerning Infant-Baptism are handled, and the insufficiency of the writings opposed to the two Treatises manifested, London, 1646.

[40] Tombes, *Apology*, inside cover.

[41] T. L. Underwood, "John Tombes" in Greaves and Zaller, *Biographical Dictionary*, Vol. III, 245ff.

[42] Stephen Marshall, *John Tombes, Praecursor, or a Forerunner to a large Review of the Dispute concerning Infant-Baptism; wherein many things both Doctrinall and personal are cleared: about which Mr. Richard Baxter, In a Book Mock-titled Plain Scripture Proof of Infants Church Membership and Baptism} hath Darkened the Truth*, London, 1652. First unnumbered page in the initial dedication.

[43] Robert Baillie, *Anabaptism, the True Fountain of Independency, Antinomy, Brownisme, and Familisme, and most of the other Errours, which for the time doe trouble the Church of England, Unsealed*, London, 1647.

[44] John Tombes, *An Addition to the Apology For the two Treatises concerning Infant-Baptisme, Published December 15. 1645. In which the Author is vindicated from 21. unjust Criminations in the 92. page book of Robert Baillie Minister of Glasgow, Intitled*

settlement from Baillie in the matter, Tombes sent another copy of the personal reply to Samuel Rutherford to take up the matter with Baillie, a fellow Scotsman and Covenanter.[45] Having still no resolution, Tombes sent a copy of the letter to the "Moderator and Commissioners in the Next Nationall Assembly of the Church of Scotland" on September 24, 1650.[46] Hearing nothing from Scotland to resolve the matter, Tombes went into print with *An Addition to the Apology*, five years after he penned it as a private matter to Baillie.

In the intervening five years, many set out to refute the new challenges manifest by the publication and preaching of antipaedobaptist theology. Two paedobaptist refutations directed at Tombes' previous writings were, William Hussey, *A 1st Provocation of Master Tombes to make good his generall charge against Mr. W. Husseys satisfaction to his scepticall exercitation*, in 1647[47] and John Geree, *Vindiciae Vindicarum; or a vindication of Infant Baptism....*[48]

A New Venue

A difficult epoch in Tombes' life started in 1649 while he ministered in Bewdley. A friendship was kindled with the young Richard Baxter, ministering a few miles away in Kidderminster. It was well-known at that time that Tombes was an ardent antipaedobaptist.[49] It was also known that Baxter had had previous public dealings

---

Anabaptisme. And sundry material points concerning the Covenant, Infants-interest in it, and Baptisme by it, Baptism by an unbaptized person, Dipping, Erastianism, and Church-Government, are argued, in a letter (now enlarged) sent in September 1647. to him, by..., London, 1652.

[45] Tombes, *Addition*, 38.

[46] Tombes, *Addition*, fourth unnumbered page.

[47] William Hussey, *A 1st Provocation of Master Tombes to make good his generall charge against Mr. W. Husseys satisfaction to his scepticall exercitation*, London, 1647.

[48] John Geree, *Vindiciae Vindicarum; or a vindication of Infant Baptism from the exceptions of Mr. Harrison in his Paedobaptism Oppugned and from the exceptions of Mr. Tombes*, London, 1646.

[49] Tombes came to Bewdley because, as a chapel-at-ease, he would not be required to baptize.

with other antipaedobaptists.⁵⁰ In spite of this, Tombes and Baxter had a working relationship wherein they freely preached in each other's pulpits for weekly lectures.⁵¹

As the theological issue over baptism arose, Tombes requested something from Baxter in writing in order to study and refute it. By this time, Tombes was well aware of the variety of foundations upon which paedobaptism was based. When written reasons for the practice were not forthcoming, Tombes' disciples pressed Baxter for his words. Baxter decided to bring ten reasons for infant baptism to the minds of the Bewdlians at the end of a week-night sermon preached in their chapel. Tombes sought to counteract the sermon by preaching another from 1 Corinthians 7:14 against the federated holiness of children and their claim to baptism therefrom. After multiple letters and a few private meetings, Tombes and Baxter agreed to a public debate on the matter to be held at 9:00am on

---

⁵⁰ Benjamin Coxe, *Some Mistaken Scriptures Sincerely Explained, in a letter, to one infected with Pelagian errours*, London, 1643. In the preface, Coxe gives the context for the work as being his imprisonment after a public disputation on baptism with Baxter. Whether or not the dispute led to Coxe's incarceration is a matter of historical interpretation. Whether or not Baxter is the "friend" to whom Coxe wrote this brief work is also a disputable matter.

⁵¹ Tombes, *Praecursor*, 15ff. (Sect. VII). And, *A Discussion of Mr. Richard Baxter's Ten Reasons of his Practise of about Infant-Baptism, delivered in a Sermon at Beudley; on Colos. 2. 11.* in *Antipaedobaptism, Part Three*. London. 1659. Tombes did not publish this reply for nine years as part of his final part of the comprehensive review. See also Richard Baxter, *The true History of the Conception and Nativity of this Treatise: being the Authors Apology for his attempt of this unpleasant task* in *Plain Scripture Proof of Infants Church-membership and Baptism: being arguments prepared for (and partly managed in) the publick Dispute with Mr. Tombes at Bewdley on the first day of Jan. 1649. With a full reply to what he then answered, and what is contained in his sermon since preached, in his Printed Books, his M.S. on 1 Cor. 7. 14. which I saw, against Mr. Marshall, against these Arguments. With a Reply to his Valedictory Oration at Bewdley; and a corrective against his Antidote*, London, 1656, Fourth Edition (First Edition, 1650), thirteenth unnumbered page. This can be found immediately after the twin letters to the Churches at Kidderminster and Bewdley. The fourth edition includes Baxter's work, *Plain Scripture Proof*, and another ten smaller works. Pagination is standardized from page one of the main work.

January 1, 1649. It was held in the chapel at Bewdley.[52] As one biographer recorded:

> [H]e went up to Beudley, at what time Mr. Rich. Baxter preached at Kidderminster, another market town three miles distant from that place. And 'tis verily thought that he was put upon the project of going there, purposefully to tame Baxter and his party, who then carried all the country before them. They preached against one another's doctrines, Tombes being then a preacher at Beudley, which he kept with Lemster, newly restored to him, being before forced thence by the royal party, and published books against each other. Tombes was the Coryphaes of the anabaptists, and Baxter of the presbyterians. Both had a great company of auditors, who came many miles on foot round about, to admire them. Once, I think oftner, they disputed face to face, and their followers, were like two armies: and at last it came to pass that they fell together by the ears, whereby hurt was done, and the civil magistrate had much to quiet them. All scholars there and then present, who knew the way of disputing and managing arguments, did conclude that Tombes got the better of Baxter by far.[53]

The public debate produced a prolonged dispute in print between Baxter and Tombes. Many theological writers were drawn into this disagreement. In these years the foundational theological bedrock of antipaedobaptism was established and codified for generations of Baptists who used Tombes' arguments without citation. As one paedobaptist wrote in 1698, "If you desire an

---

[52] T. L. Underwood, "Tombes, John" in Greaves and Zaller, *Biographical Dictionary of British Radicals*, 245.

[53] Anthony Wood, from *Tombes, John*, in *Athenae Oxonienses*, new edition, 1813-20, found in the *British Biographical Archive*, London, K C Saur, microfilm plates 427, 428.

answer to Mr. Tombs, the most Learnedst Champion for your Way, which most that have Written after him, have Copy'd from...."[54]

During this period Tombes found profound affirmation when the Oxonian establishment produced a paper that corroborated what Tombes had been saying for many years. In Tombes' words:

> Yea, the Oxford Divines in their late Reasons of the present Judgement of the University about the Solemne Covenant, [etc.] Approved by generall consent in a full Convocation, June 1, 1647. say, *that Without the consentient Judgement and Practise of the Universall Church,* (which we are not able to prove) *they shoulde be at a losse, when they are called upon for proofe in the Point of baptizing Infants.*[55]

Baxter used the introduction in *The Saints Everlasting Rest* (1650) to attack "Anabaptists" in general.[56] Tombes took exception to what Baxter included. He produced a work with a most evocative title, *An Antidote against the Venome of a Passage, in the 5th direction of the Epistle Dedicatory....*[57] Baxter followed with his first work on the

---

[54] *A Discourse of Infant-Baptism, By way of Dialogue, between Paedobapatsta, A Minister, for Infant Baptism. Antipaedobaptista, his Friend, against it. Aporeticus, An Ingenious Doubter,* London, 1698, 54. This work is an honest attempt to deal with the lingering issues at the end of the seventeenth century. It also shows some adaptation on the part of the author to antipaedobaptist concerns. Therein is found a repudiation of the prejudicial use of alleged connections between Continental Anabaptists and Antipaedobaptists, 57ff. An example of this "copy'd" use of Tombes' argumentation is found in Samuel Chandler and William Leigh, *A Dialogue between a Paedo-Baptist, and an Anti-Paedo-Baptist: Containing the strength of Arguments Offered on both sides at the Plymouth Disputation: with The Addition of a few more Arguments, then ready to be offered, in Vindication of Infant-Baptism,* London, 1699, 6ff.

[55] John Tombes, *An Antidote Against the venome of a Passage, in the 5th direction of the Epistle Dedicatory to the whole Book of Mr. Richard Baxter Teacher at Kederminster in Worcestershire, intitled, The Saints Everlasting Rest, containing a Satyricall invective against Anabaptists,* London, 1650, 28. In the original minutes of the convocation in the Bodleian Library, Oxford, see section 4:9.

[56] Richard Baxter, *The Saints Everlasting Rest,* London, 1650. Sixth unnumbered page.

[57] Tombes, *Antidote,* London, 1650.

The Antipaedobaptism of John Tombes

issue titled, *Plain Scripture Proof of Infants Church-Membership and Baptism*.[58]

Baxter argued for paedobaptism from a different foundation than Blake, Geree, and Marshall. His basic argument was: since infants are already church members by birth, they have the same birthright to baptism that Jews had to circumcision. Tombes worked through Baxter's arguments to produce what became the starting point for his multiple thousand page "full review" of the dispute as regards baptism. Tombes, in early 1652, published his *Praecursor, or a Forerunner To a large Review of the Dispute concerning Infant-Baptism*.[59]

Between 1650 and 1656, Baxter's *Plain Scripture Proof* went through four editions. Each edition added new fuel to the raging dispute. Some of these additions were: *An Answer to Mr. Tombes his Valedictory Oration to the People of Bewdley* (1651), *Letters that passed between Mr. Baxter and Mr. Tombes concerning the Dispute* [of 1649] (1652), *Praefestinantis Movator, Or, Mr. Tombes, his Praecursus, staid and examined, and proved not to be from Heaven, but of men* (1652), *A Briefe Confutation of divers other of Mr. T. his mistakes* (n.d.), *A Corrective For a Circumforaneous Antidote Against the Verity of a Passage in the Epistle before my Treatise of Rest* (1656), *An Addition to the twentieth Chapter of the First Part* (n.d.), *Arguments to prove that Baptism is a standing Ordinance for entering of all Church-Members (ordinarily,) and not first Discipling of a Nation*.[60]

The letters between Baxter and Tombes show the issues leading up to and flowing from the disputation. The other additional works give ever-increasing insight into Baxter's state of mind. Later that same year, 1652, Tombes would release the first part of his *Magnum opus*. In the subtitle we see his wit and his true perspective of Baxter's position. The work was called *Antipaedobaptism, or No Plain nor Obscure Scripture Proof of Infants Baptism or Church Membership. Being the first part of the full review of the dispute about Infant*

---

[58] Richard Baxter, *Plain Scripture Proof*, fourth edition, London, 1656, first edition, 1650.
[59] Tombes, *Praecursor*, London, 1650.
[60] Baxter, *Plain Scripture Truth*, fourth edition.

*Baptism....*⁶¹ Tombes set out to refute all who opposed his position in order to give a "full review" of the issue. He discussed the arguments put forth in earlier works by Stephen Marshall, John Geree, Richard Baxter, T. Cobbet, Mr. Thomas Blake, Josiah Church, and N. Stephens. Between the *Apology* in 1646 and *Antipaedobaptism, Part One* in 1652, Tombes received many replies via personal letters from his theological inquirers and opponents. Most of these are lost to posterity. We only have the answers to the letters incorporated by way of direct citation in Tombes' work. This makes a degree of reconstruction of the letters possible due to Tombes' methodology of quoting his opponent extensively while answering them. Tombes did not generalize in his replies. He set up no straw men. He sought to refute each separate strand of an argument. Those nuances were often many.

The work of Thomas Cobbet that gained the attention of Tombes was *A Just Vindication of the Covenant and Church-Estate of Children of Church-Members as also their right unto Baptisme: wherein such things as have been brought by divers to the contrary, especially by Ioh. Spilsbury, A.R., Ch. Blackwood, and H. Den are revised and answered: hereunto is annexed a refutation of a certain pamphlet styled The plain and wel-grounded treatise touching baptism.*⁶² This work had been published in 1648. Tombes replied in 1652.

In 1650, after preaching his Valedictory Oration (farewell sermon), Tombes moved from Bewdley to Ledbury to direct St. Catherine's Hospital. This was another non-parochial post. During this time, Tombes heard back from the General Assembly of the

---

⁶¹ John Tombes. *Antipaedobaptism, or No Plain nor Obscure Scripture Proof of Infants Baptism or Church Membership. Being the first part of the full review of the dispute about Infant Baptism...whereby the expositions and arguings ... for infant baptism by Mr. Stephen Marshall, Mr. John Geree, Mr. Baxter, Mr. T. Cobbet, Mr. T. Blake, Mr. J. Church; and the arguments of Mr. N. Stephens...are fully refuted,* London, 1652.

⁶² Thomas Cobbet, *A Just Vindication of the Covenant and Church-Estate of Children of Church-Members as also their right unto Baptisme: wherein such things as have been brought by divers to the contrary, especially by Ioh. Spilsbury, A.R., Ch. Blackwood, and H. Den are revides and answered: hereunto is annexed a refutation of a certain pamphlet styled The plain and wel-grounded treatise touching baptism,* London, 1648.

Scottish Kirk as regards his complaint against fellow covenanter Robert Baillie. The Assembly said:

> That Jesus Christ be Lord over his own house, and that his ministers keep Courts and exercise Jurisdiction and discipline, and all the censures of the Kirk from the lowest to the highest, in his name only, against all that depart from and do oppose the truth; or that walk loosely as doth not become the Gospell.[63]

The political situation between Scotland and England had begun to unravel. The Kirk would not hear Tombes' complaint. The implication to be drawn – Tombes opposed the truth. Tombes had only tried to act according to his conscience and in harmony with his understanding of what the Scriptures required of him to seek restoration. Seeing nothing else could be gained by keeping the matter private, and since Baillie's work was already in print, Tombes published a work written in 1645 as his reply to Robert Baillie. It was called *An Addition to the Apology For the two Treatises concerning Infant-Baptisme* (1652).

Antipaedobaptism was on the minds of churchmen in England. At the Oxford Act, the annual academic convocation at the University in that city, in July 1652, Henry Savage delivered a dissertation on Tombes' antipaedobaptist views. The work was published in 1655 in its original Latin after Tombes published his reply. Savage's work was entitled *Thesis Doctoris Savage nempe paedobaptismum esse licitum, confirmatio, contra refutationem mri Tombes.*[64] Tombes' reply to Savage was published in London as *Refutatio Positionis ejusq; Confirmationis Paedobaptistmum esse licitum affirmantis ab Henrico Savage SS.T.D. Coll. Ball.*[65] This exchange is noted for its pointed brevity. It must be said, however, that Tombes

---

[63] Tombes, *Addition*, 2.

[64] Henry Savage, *Thesis Doctoris Savage nempe paedobaptismum esse licitum, confirmatio, contra refutationem mri Tombes*, Oxford, 1655.

[65] John Tombes, *Refutatio Positionis ejusq; Confirmationis Paedobaptistmum esse licitum affirmantis ab Henrico Savage SS.T.D. Coll. Ball. in Comitioorum Vesperiis Oxon. Mense Julio, anni, 1652*, London, 1653.

had not yet finished his full review of antipaedobaptism when Savage decided to criticize his views.

Others took up the paedobaptist mantle to publish more works against Tombes. In 1653 and 1654 works came from Thomas Blake,[66] John Howe of Lynn,[67] and a work that gives insight into the form and content of the public disputations of the day, published by John Cragge, though often misattributed to Tombes in bibliographies, *A Publick Dispute betwixt John Tombes, respondent, John Cragge and H. Vaughan, opponents, touching Infant Baptism*.[68]

Tombes published a response to this specific work in short time. He called it *A Plea of Anti-paedobaptists against, the vanity and falshood of scribled papers, entitled, The Anabaptists Anatomiz'd and silenc'd in a publique dispute... betwixt John Tombes, John Cragg, and Henry Vaughan, touching infant-baptism*.[69] He also published the second part of his complete review as *Antipaedobaptism: or, the second part of the full review of the dispute concerning Infant-Baptism*.[70] In this work,

---

[66] Thomas Blake, *Three Scripture Texts, by John Tombes in the first part of his Antipaedobaptism solely handled and totally perverted, fully vindicated*, London, 1653.

[67] J[ohn] H[owe], of Lynn, *diatribh peri paido-baptismou: or, a Consideration of Infant Baptism; wherein the grounds of it are laid down, and the validity of them discussed, and many things of Mr. Tombes about it scanned, etc.*, London, 1654.

[68] John Cragge, M.A., of Lantilio-Pertholy, *A Publick Dispute betwixt John Tombes respondent, John Cragge and H. Vaughan, opponents, touching infant baptism ... Also a sermon ... wherein the necessity of dipping is refuted, and infant baptism asserted*. The frontispiece bears another title more popularly used in bibliographic information: *The Anabaptists Anatomiz'd and Silenced in a Publick Dispute*, London, 1654, reprinted 1741. Tombes' name appears first in the title. Therefrom, the wrong implication for attribution has been made. The work should be attributed to Cragge. The purpose of the work is to promote paedobaptism. Tombes was an antipaedobaptist.

[69] John Tombes, *A Plea for Anti-paedobaptists against, the vanity and falshood of scribled papers, entitled, The Anabaptists Anatomiz'd and silenc'd in a publique dispute ... betwixt John Tombes, John Cragg, and Henry Vaughan, touching infant-baptism*, London, 1654.

[70] John Tombes, *Anti-paedobaptism, or the Second Part Of the full Review of the Dispute Concerning Infant-Baptism: In which the invalidity of Arguments inferring a Duty from a positive Rite of the Old Testament concerning a positive Rite of the New, by reason of Analogy between them, is shewed; and the Argument against Infant-baptism, from Christs institution, Matth. 28. 19. the sayings and practise in the New Testament is made good against the writings of Mr. Stephen Marshall, Mr. Richard Baxter, Mr. Thomas Blake, Mr. Thomas Cobbet, Mr. John Cotton, Dr. Nathaniel Homes, Mr. Robert Bailee, Dr.*

Tombes engaged the writings old and new, those published in books and sent to him as personal letters, of Stephen Marshall,[71] Richard Baxter,[72] Thomas Blake,[73] Thomas Cobbet, John Cotton, Nathaniel Homes, Robert Baillie, Daniel Featley, John Brinsley, Cuthbert Sydenham, Henry Hammond, and Thomas Fuller. This *Second Part* provoked exponentially more responses.

In 1655 and 1656 more works came forth to deal with Tombes' arguments, attacks, and conjectures with greater specificity. His foe of ten plus years, Robert Baillie, published a work written in 1645 entitled, *The Disswasive from the Errours of the time*[74] along with *A vindication from the exceptions of Mr. Cotton and Mr. Tombes.*[75] Another mentioned in the *Second Part* published as a review of his own was Henry Hammond, *The Baptizing of Infants Reviewed, and Defended from the exceptions of Mr. Tombes, in Antipedobaptisme.*[76] Henry Savage's work on Tombes from the Oxford Convocation of 1652 was published.[77] John Cragge replied with *The Arraignment and Conviction of Anabaptism; or a Reply to Master Tombes his Plea for Anti-paedobaptists.*[78] James Nayler, the Quaker, brought forth the provocative title, *The Foot yet in a Snare* in reply to an essay Tombes had published in a work by John Tolderuy.[79] Even in Ireland, Tombes' ideas were considered a danger. Samuel Winter preached, then published *The summe of diverse sermons preached in Dublin, before the Lord Deputie Fleetwood... wherein the doctrine of Infant-Baptism is*

Daniel Featley, Mr. John Brinsley, Mr. Cuthbert Sydenham, Dr. Henry Hammond, Mr. Thomas Fuller, and others, London, 1654.

[71] Marshall, *Defence*.

[72] Baxter, subsequent editions of *Plain Scripture Proof*.

[73] Blake, *Three Scripture texts*.

[74] Robert Bailey [Baillie, or Bayley], *The Disswasive from the Errours of the time vindicated from the exceptions of Mr. Cotton and Mr. Tombes*, n.p., 1655.

[75] Baillie, *Disswasive*, n.p. 1655.

[76] Henry Hammond, D.D. *The Baptizing of Infants Reviewed, and Defended from the exceptions of Mr. Tombes, in Antipedobaptisme*, London, 1655.

[77] Savage, *Thesis*.

[78] John Cragg[e], *The Arraignment and Conviction of Anabaptism; or a Reply to Master Tombes his Plea for Anti-paedobaptists*, London, 1656.

[79] James Nayler, *The Foot yet in a Snare... discovered in answer to John Tombes*. London, 1656. John Tombes in John Tolderuy, *The Foot out of the Snare, or a Restoration of the Inhabitants of Zion into their place*, London, 1655.

asserted and the main objections of Mr. Tombes, Mr. Fisher, Mr. Blackwood and others Answered.[80]

There was a single event that prompted much of the literary output of those years. In 1654, by an executive act of the Lord Protector, Oliver Cromwell, Tombes was declared one of the "triers" for approbation of ministers. This was a high profile position in the Commonwealth period and politics. Tombes was one of thirty-eight central triers charged to examine ministers who applied for pulpits as to their fitness for ministry.[81] Perhaps the question in some minds was, "How could an antipaedobaptist be fit to try others?" Tombes' work as a trier was not without its controversy. Tombes and Philip Nye examined a royalist, Anthony Sadler, for the ministry. Sadler did not like the treatment he received from their hands so he penned *Inquisitio Anglicana: or the disguise discovered, showing the proceedings of the commissioners at White Hall, for the approbation of ministers, in the examinations of A. Sadler.*[82]

From 1657 onward there were greater common foes for the Puritan and Reformed party to fight: Catholicism, Quakerism, Antinomianism, and subtle variations on the Reformed doctrine of justification by faith alone. There were political questions in the air as well. In this transitional context, Tombes published *Antipaedobaptism; or the third part. Being a full review of the dispute concerning infant baptism.*[83] In this work alone, Tombes interacted

---

[80] Samuel Winter, *The summe of diverse sermons preached in Dublin, before the Lord Deputie Fleetwood ... wherein the doctrine of Infant-Baptism is asserted and the main objections of Mr. Tombes, Mr. Fisher, Mr. Blackwood and others Answered*, London, 1656.

[81] Protector and Council, *An Ordinance appointing commissioners for approbation of public preachers*, London, 1654.

[82] Anthony Sadler, *Inquisitio Anglicana: or the disguise discovered, showing the proceedings of the commissioners at White Hall, for the approbation of ministers, in he examinations of A. Sadler*, London, 1654. Sadler was eventually placed after the Restoration of the Monarchy.

[83] John Tombes, *Anti-Paedobaptism: or the Third Part. Being, A full Review of the Dispute concerning Infant-Baptism. In which, the Arguments for Infant-Baptism from the Covenant and Initial Seal, Infants Visible Church-membership, Antiquity of Infant-Baptism, are repelled. and the Writings of Mr. Stephen Marshal, Mr. Richard Baxter, Mr. John Geree, Mr. Thomas Blake, Mr. Thomas Cobbet, Dr, Nathaniel Homes, Mr. John Drew, Mr Josiah Church, Mr. William Lyford, Dr. Daniel Featley, Mr. John Brinsley, Mr.*

with arguments from thirty-one writers who sent letters or published works on the matter. He had exhausted the arguments for antipaedobaptism and had answered to his own satisfaction the concerns of his detractors. There was but one man who still purposed, yet again, to engage Tombes on the issue – Richard Baxter.

On May 4, 1656, Baxter preached a sermon which presented ten reasons for the practice of infant baptism. Tombes, upon perusing the notes sent to him by Baxter, wrote *Felo de Se. or Mr. Richard Baxters Self-destroying*....[84] The time between replies shows the urgency of the debate had been lost. Tombes was amazed that Baxter had not acquiesced at all. Tombes was nonplussed that Baxter still believed, "[T]hat after 1625 years use of Christian Baptism, the Ministers of the Gospel should be as yet unresolved."[85] He was compelled to reply.

In the same year, Tombes presented a more popular work to the public. Dropping his rigid scholastic methodology for the second time, he produced *A Short Catechism about Baptism*.[86] In forty questions and answers Tombes presented a popular argument for his antipaedobaptist convictions in another genre. He thus presented convictions with thirty-two years of maturation.

Religious freedoms would wane as Cromwell died and his son, Richard, after proving himself inept at running the Commonwealth, resigned. Charles II had allowed for religious toleration in the Declaration at Breda, but that too came to naught. The openness wherein the debate on baptism thrived would come to a halt. Restraints and conformity in religion became part and parcel of the restored monarchy. Tombes, as a matter of conscience, could not

---

Cuthbert Sidenham, Mr. William Carter, Mr. Samuel Rutherford, Mr. John Crag, Dr. Henry Hammond, Mr. John Cotton, Mr. Thomas Fuller, Mr John Stalham, Mr. Thomas Hall, and others, are examined; and many points about the Covenants, and Seals, and other Truths of weight, are handled, London, 1657.

[84] John Tombes, *Felo de Se. or Mr. Richard Baxters Self-destroying; Manifested In twenty Arguments against Infant-Baptism, Gathered out of his own Writing, in his Second Disputation of Right to Sacraments*, London, 1659.

[85] Baxter quoted by Tombes in *Felo de Se*, A2.

[86] John Tombes, *A Short Catechism about Baptism*, London, 1659.

conform theologically to the expectations implied in the Anglican Settlement after 1660. Therefore he laid down his living, repudiating his ordination, to live as a lay communicant in the National Church. His belief in the authority of Scripture for all areas of thought and life prompted his position as regards the restored King. Tombes wrote a controversial work entitled *A Serious Consideration of the oath of the King's Supremacy*.[87] Coming from a former Cromwellian trier, this seemed folly. It showed Tombes to be a man of conviction, not of mere convenience. This work eventually won Tombes an audience with King Charles II, through Lord Clarendon.[88]

The breakdown of prejudice against Tombes is seen in the commendations prefixed to two of Tombes' other works in 1660. His major disputant, a decade before, was asked to commend Tombes' anti-Catholic[89] and anti-Quaker[90] books to the reading public. In his prefatory comments in *True Old Light*, Baxter wrote:

> [T]he reverend author hath very judiciously handled in this Treatise, and therefore I shall say no more of it. The truth is here opened (to the showing of their errours) with great Scripture evidence; which impartially considered, may easily convince all that believe the Scriptures: And make it appear that the Light that is in these men is Darknesse; (Luke 11. 35.) Though the difference, and too-eager Disputations

---

[87] John Tombes, *A Serious Consideration of the oath of the King's Supremacy: wherein these six propositions are asserted. 1. That some swearing is lawful. 2. That some promissory oaths are lawful. 3. That a promissory oath of allegiance and due obedience to a king is lawful. 4. That the King in his realm, is the onely supreme governour over all persons. 5. That the King is the governour of the realm, as well in all spiritual or ecclesiastical things, or causes, as temporal. 6. That the jurisdictions, priviledges, preeminences, and authorities in that oath, may be assisted and defended,* London, 1660.

[88] A. J. Gordon, "Tombes, John (1603?-1676)" in *Dictionary of National Biography* (Smith, Elder and Co., London, 1909), Vol. XIX, 930, col. 2. Lord Clarendon introduced Tombes to Charles II in 1664.

[89] John Tombes, *Romanism Discussed; or an answer to the first nine articles of H[enry] T[urberville] his manual of controversies*, London, 1660.

[90] John Tombes, *True Old-Light Exalted above pretended new-light; a Treatise of Jesus Christ, as He is the light that enlightens every one that comes into the World. Against the Quaker, Arminian, etc...*, London, 1660.

between the Reverend Author and my self, about the point of Infant-Baptism, be well known, yet it is our desire that it be as much known, that we desire to hold the Unity of the Spirit in the bond of Peace; as Members of the same Head and Body, uniting our force for the common Truths against the pernicious adversaries thereof: And though we own not each other, or our selves, the discerned errours in doctrine and life, which through human frailty we may be guilty of; Nevertheless, whereto we have already attained, we desire to walk by the same Rule, and mind the same things; holding that if in any thing we be otherwise minded, God shall reveal even this unto us.[91]

To show resolution in the face of hostile theological opinion, Baxter continued:

I have already told the Episcopal Brethren, that Bishop Usher and I did fully agree in half an hour, and therefore it is not long of us, that our wound is yet unhealed. And (though I never treated with Mr. Tombes about such a matter) I am confident that he and I should agree in one daies treaty, upon terms of communion, charity, and forebearance, among those of several waies. And therefore if we continued unhealed, let the shame and horror lie on them that are obstinate in their uncharitable waies.[92]

Tombes did not publish publicly against paedobaptism again for sixteen years. At that time, 1675, he wrote *A Just Reply*.[93] This work answered objections brought to the fore by Mr. Wills[94] and Mr. Blinman. Baxter used the publication of this work to publish his largest work on the issue, *More Proofs of Infants Church-membership*

---

[91] Richard Baxter in Tombes, *True Old Light*, ninth page of preface.
[92] Baxter in Tombes, *True Old Light*, tenth page of preface.
[93] John Tombes, *A Just Reply to the Books... of Mr. Wills, and Mr. Blinman: in a letter*, London, 1675.
[94] H. Wills. *An Essay tending to issue the controversie about Infant Baptism*, London, n.d.

The Antipaedobaptism of John Tombes

*and Consequently their Right to Baptism: Or a Second Defence of Our Infant Rights and Mercies. In Three Parts.*⁹⁵ In the subtitle, Baxter wrote:

> The first is, The plain Proof of God's Statute, or Covenant for Infants Church-membership from the Creation, and the Continuation of it till the Institution of Baptism; with the Defence of the Proof against the Frivolous Exceptions of Mr. Tombes. And a Confutation of Mr. Tombes his Arguments against Infants Church-membership....⁹⁶

Tombes' Death and Legacy

John Tombes died on May 22, 1676. Within months, Baxter published the final chapter in the exchange with Tombes. He produced *Review of the State of Christian Infants.*⁹⁷ With Tombes was almost buried a now neglected chapter in the rich history of Puritan theology – the story of antipaedobaptism in the theology of the archetypical Anglican antipaedobaptist. This is truly a wonderfully rich part of a previously untold story from Puritan England.

---

⁹⁵ Richard Baxter, *More Proofs of Infants Church-membership and Consequently their Right to Baptism: Or a Second Defence of Our Infant Rights and Mercies. In Three Parts. The first is, The plain Proof of God's Statute, or Covenant for Infants Church-membership from the Creation, and the Continuation of it till the Institution of Baptism; with the Defence of the Proof against the Frivolous Exceptions of Mr. Tombes. And a Confutation of Mr. Tombes his Arguments against Infants Church-membership...*, London, 1675.

⁹⁶ Baxter, *More Proof*, Title page.

⁹⁷ Richard Baxter, *Review of the State of Christian Infants. Whether they should be entered in Covenant With God by Baptism, and be Visible Members of His Church, and have any Covenant-Right to Pardon and Salvation? Or whether Christ, the Saviour of the World, hath shut all Mankind out of his Visible Kingdom, and Covenant-Rights and Hopes, till they come to Age? And whether he did so from the beginning of the world, or after his Incarnation? Occasioned by the Importunity of Mr. E. Hutchinson, (and of Mr. Danvers, and Mr. Tombes, (who called him to this review in order to his Reaction. An Impartial Reading is humbly requested, of those Dissenters who would not be found Despisers of holy Truth, not such as judge before they hear*, London, 1676.

Chapter 6
The Abrahamic Covenant in the Thought of John Tombes
Michael T. Renihan, Ph.D.

Individual anecdotes are not normative, but illustrative of the fruit of men's labors. The fruit of a belief will be seen in how it manifests itself in practice. Ideas have consequences. Let me illustrate. A friend with whom I attended seminary called me to discuss a matter affecting the life of the church he pastored. The church is Presbyterian. My friend has always been a traditionally conservative Presbyterian pastor holding to all of the Westminster Standards – even the Directory for Publick Worship. His recent experience struck at the heart of how the infant's interest in the covenant of grace via the Abrahamic Covenant is working itself out in *some* covenantal Presbyterian or paedobaptist circles. A young woman in her late teens had become a nightmare to her Christian parents. She was disruptive at home and rebellious to the authority figures in her life. Her church prayed for her regularly over the course of almost two years. In fact, they prayed so regularly that it seemed to the pastor that the congregation had given her over as a hopeless cause. They had become desensitized through familiarity with her condition. A Christian friend of this young woman, however, also showed concern for her. She "reached out to her with a lifeline" (as the evangelical cliché says). This friend invited her to a church other than her family's where there were special summer evangelistic meetings. She agreed to attend. The rebellious one was struck by the force of the preaching and made a public profession of faith. (Let's not get lost in a visceral reaction to methodology at this point.) Late that night, she announced to her parents with tears of repentance interspersed with her words that everything was going to be okay from now on because she was now a Christian. Sounds good, doesn't it?

Her father went into a tirade. He had presumed his daughter was already regenerate by virtue of her election and her place as a "covenant child." He would not be shown to be wrong. His hyper-covenantal theology blinded him to the possibility that his daughter might have been unregenerate. In his view, she had "broken the covenant again" by making such a public profession of faith. After all, he had professed faith for her at her baptism sixteen or so years earlier. What might have been a merciful answer to the church's prayers was perceived as a greater evil than her two years of rebellion. For this act she was cast from the home. It was the proverbial last straw. The father's real grief was that his child had become "a [expletive deleted] Baptist." In those words the father conveyed his horror to his pastor, my friend. For the first time in his ministry, my friend saw the consequences of "pressing too much out of covenant theology." He asked in desperation, "What's a pastor to do?" Since he knows my dry sense of humor, I replied, "Become a Reformed Baptist." I also sent him John Tombes' work on the Abrahamic Covenant.

Tombes' Measuring Rod for Doctrine and Practice

For Tombes, the positive, codified law of God found in Scripture was the measuring rod for all doctrine and practice. He used regal language to illustrate the responsibility of those who would carry forth the sovereign Lawgiver's decrees:

> For as it is a perogative of a King to appoint the wayes of his owne service and honour, and he should be taken to be very presumptuous and arrogant that should take upon him to prescribe a fashion of attendance, suite, and service to his prince without consent, when he hath otherwise declared his will; so is it much more intolerable pride, and presumption in a mortall man, to appoint a way of service to God, which he never consented to, but hath otherwise directed his owne service. And for the same reason it is a transferring of God's

The Abrahamic Covenant in the Thought of John Tombes

perogative on a man, when he doth servilly consent by subjecting his conscience to such usurpation.¹

Tombes' view of the church and her need for divine governance accentuates the spirituality of the church over against her material existence alone. The church was more than a human society of people with mutual beliefs and concerns. It was God's domain on the earth, a realm in which God ruled, subduing the hearts of men in order to make them different – his unique people. In a summary of the practical issues as regards his regulating principle of God governing his church by the Scriptures, Tombes concluded:

> And although I know Ceremonies invented by men are pretended to serve for edification, yet I must professe that I never found in my reading, or experience, that ever any person by such rites and observances was wonne to the profession of Christ, or brought to any spirituall knowledge of Christ, any true faith or sincere obedience to him. Possibly they may beget some kinde of raptures of carnall delight, through melodious soundes or pleasant sights, some kinde of womanish pity, and teares, such as the acting of a stage play will draw from some persons: but that ever they begat sanctifying knowledge, sound repentance, holy mortification of sinne, lively faith, fruitfull living to God, I assure my selfe cannot be shewed: But it is certain on the contrary that the teaching for doctrines commandments of men hath occasioned men to oppose the principall point of the Gospel of Christ, to wit, justification by faith in him, and contrary to the covenant of grace in Christ to conceive a righteousnesse in themselves by the observation of men's commands, as in the Pharisees and Papists, and all sorts of superstitious persons it doth abundantly appear.²

---

¹ *Fermentum Pharisaeorum or, The Leaven of Pharisaical Will-Worship:declared in a sermon on Matth.xv.,* November 24, 1641, at Leominster in Herefordshire. London: 1641, 6.

² *Fermentum Pharisaeorum,* 7.

Tombes, then, was no iconoclast. He was concerned with evangelical concerns for the ultimate well-being of the souls of those who attended the church's worship. His deeply held concern was that people realize the effects of sin and find themselves eclipsed by the power of God found in the Christian gospel (Tit. 2:11-14). He also labored that God's glory would not be obscured by some novelty of man's creative mind. A rigid application of this principle drove Tombes to examine everything in his Christian belief system by the standard of Scripture alone, aided by reason, including baptism.

The recovery of right baptism was Tombes' personal, yet godly, obsession. He was concerned with the right practice of this ordinance for the good of man's soul, not to win a theological point. The debate that raged in the seventeenth century was more than the mere academic production of print on paper. Tombes really believed that the right doctrine would have major repercussions in the church-at-large. I believe that Tombes was right on target. These ripples still affect the churches of our day.

Tombes' Starting Point and the Argument from Genesis 17:7

The first argument is one that examines the case for infant baptism from the interest of believers' children in the promise given to Abraham in Genesis 17:7. It also serves as the all-important starting point for Tombes' theological reflection:

> Major premise: That which hath no testimony in Scripture for it, is doubtfull.
> Minor premise: But this Doctrine of Infant-Baptisme, hath no testimony of Scripture for it;
> Conclusion: *Ergo*, it is doubtfull.[3]

Tombes' first exegetical argument is a comprehensive, yet properly basic argument designed to examine any and all of the biblical

---

[3] Tombes, *Exercitation*, 1. See also, John Tombes, *An Apology or Plea for the Two Treatises*, London, 1646, 6.

evidence for infant baptism. The remaining arguments are applications of the first argument to specific Scriptures, theological constructions, or historical precedents. Tombes then used his conclusions to support the doctrine or practice. However, in the context of this first argument, he went on to consider what he saw as the underlying biblical texts for the practice of paedobaptism:

> The Minor is proved by examining the places that are brought for it, which are these: Genesis 17.7, etc. Acts 2.38, 39. 1 Cor. 7.14. Mark. 10.14. 16. Acts 16.15. 32. 1 Cor. 1.16. The Argument from Gen 17.7, etc. is almost the first and the last in this businesse; and therefore is the more accurately to be examined.[4]

Tombes often added color to the debate with maxims and Latin phrases. The first argument did not escape his cutting wit. Speaking of the argument for infant baptism from Genesis 17:7, etc., he added, "[B]ut it hath so many shapes, that I may here take up that Speech, *With what knot shall I hold shape-shifting Proteus?*[5] But in the issue, it falls into one or other of these forms."[6]

Tombes went on to build his foundation against the interest of believers' children in the promises of the Abrahamic Covenant. He

---

[4] John Tombes, *Two Treatises; and an Apendix to them Concerning Infant Baptisme. The Former Treatise being an Exercitation presented to the Chair-man of a Committee of the Assembly of Divines. The latter an Examen of the Sermon of Mr. Stephen Marshall, about Infant-Baptisme, in a letter sent to him.* London: 1645. The work includes an appendix to show that Col. 2:11-12 "proves not Infant-Baptisme", 1.

[5] Proteus is a striking analogy borrowed from mythology. As a shape-shifting being who possessed knowledge of the past, present and future, he would not answer questions from mortals unless bound and compelled to do so. Thomas Bulfinch, *Bulfinch's Mythology, The Age of Fable*. Nelson Doubleday, New York, 1968. Italics mine.

[6] Tombes, *Exercitation*, 1. These interjections were typical in the debates Schoolmen would enter. They were utilized to express ideas and to evoke emotions within the argumentation of the day. They were verbal symbols. Here Tombes is using a written device to display his frustration in framing an argument that it might be understood and owned by its promoters. These interjections were taken as offensive by Stephen Marshall. Because of that offense, Tombes explains the use of these sayings in *Apology*, esp. 12-30 (first ¶).

The Abrahamic Covenant in the Thought of John Tombes

did not give multiple forms of the opposing argument but one form from which he drew four sub-arguments. He thus supported his refutation of the one argument from Genesis 17:7. This was an application of his overriding principle expressed in Argument One – that there is no Scripture to warrant the baptizing of infants. He continued with another syllogism as if arguing for paedobaptism:

> Major premise: To whom the Gospel-covenant agrees, to them the sign of the Gospel-covenant agrees also.
> Minor premise: But to Infants of Believers the Gospel-covenant agrees,
> Conclusion: [A]nd consequently Baptisme.[7]

Tombes added, "The Minor is proved from Gen. 17.7. where God promiseth to *Abraham, I will be a God to thee and to thy seed after thee*."[8]

Tombes proceeded to four sub-arguments that he believed exposed the basic assumptions of the greater argument presented. By way of introduction to his main point, they were: (1) the covenant with Abraham is not identical to the Gospel (New) Covenant; (2) Abraham's seed has more than one meaning; (3) the promise of the gospel has always been the same irrespective of the age; and (4) some were circumcised who had no part in the promise made to Abraham. These four parts were intended to undermine the credibility of infant baptism by way of analogy from the Abrahamic Covenant to the New, or in Tombes' favorite phraseology, the "Euangelicall [using the Greek alliteration]" or "Gospel-Covenant."[9] These also form the foundation of all of Tombes' arguments. They were points that were non-negotiable for him. It is important to see the detail in these sub-arguments in order to understand his inferences within other constructions. Tombes kept coming back to two foundational points: (1) the lack of positive instruction in special revelation for the practice of infant

---

[7] Tombes, *Exercitation*, 1ff. Argument structural components mine.
[8] Tombes, *Exercitation*, 1ff.
[9] Tombes, *Exercitation*, first appearance on 2, then throughout.

baptism and (2) an alternative (and creative) explanation of the biblical texts, which became the foundation of his emerging covenantal and credobaptist theology.

On the first of these sub-arguments, Tombes declared:

> 1. The Covenant made with *Abraham*, is not a pure Gospel-covenant, but mixt, which I prove; The Covenant takes its denomination from the promises; but the promises are mixt, some Euangelicall, belonging to those to whom the Gospel belongeth, some are Domestique, or Civill promises, specially respecting the House of *Abraham*, and of *Israel*; *Ergo*.[10]

Explaining his distinction between evangelical and domestic or civil promises in the Abrahamic Covenant, Tombes implied there were some spiritual promises and some physical or material promises that had to be distinguished. Tombes explained what he means by "Euangelicall promises":

> That was Euangelicall which we read, *Gen 17.5. I have made thee a father of many nations;* and that which we find, *Gen 15.5. so shall thy seed be;* in which it is promised, that there shall be of all Nations innumerable that shall be *Abrahams* children by believing, Rom. 4.17,18. It was Euangelicall, which we find, *Gen 12.3. & Gen. 18.18.* and in thy seed shall all the kindreds of the earth be blessed; for in these is promised blessing to Believers, of whom *Abraham* is father, *Gal. 3.16. Acts 3.25.*[11]

Tombes then proceeded to the "Domestique" or "Civill" promises:

---

[10] Tombes, *Exercitation*, 2.

[11] Tombes, *Exercitation*, 2. Tombes assumes a high degree of biblical literacy on the part of his readers. He quotes only the essential parts of verses of Scripture as his authority when needed to make the case. In other cases, he just asserts the reference as his authority assuming one's familiarity with these texts.

> Domestique and Civill promises were many; of the multiplying the seed of *Abraham*, the birth of *Isaac'* of the coming of Christ out of *Isaac;* the bondage of the *Israelites* in *Egypt,* and deliverance thence; of possessing the Land of *Canaan, Gen. 15.13. 18. Gen. 17.7, 8. 15.16. Act. 7.4, 5, 6, 7, 8.* and many other places.[12]

The distinction is between the spiritual blessings (which are called evangelical) which accrue to believers as believers, and physical (or natural) consequences pertaining to Abraham's descendants as domestic (or civil). This distinction is also between a spiritual seed brought about by heavenly activity and a natural seed brought about by the earthly procreative act. Tombes continued to legitimize this distinction as he invoked a rigorous trinitarianism to clarify and balance the issues of continuity and discontinuity within the two aspects of the Abrahamic Covenant (and the same issues as regards other covenants):

> Yea, it is to be noted, that those promises which were Euangelicall, according to the more inward sense of the Holy Ghost, do point at the priviledges of *Abrahams* House, in the outward face [sense] of the words; whence it may be well doubted, whether this Covenant made with *Abraham,* may be called simply Euangelicall, and so pertain to Believers, as Believers. There were annexed to the Covenant on *Mount Sinai*, sacrifices pointing at the sacrifice of Christ, and yet we call not that Covenant simply Euangelicall, but in some respect.[13]

Based on the distinction that the Abrahamic Covenant is not one and the same with the New or Gospel Covenant, Tombes went on to answer the remaining three of his original four questions that paralleled the concerns already stated: "(2) Who is the seed? (3)

---

[12] Tombes, *Exercitation*, 2.
[13] Tombes, *Exercitation*, 2ff. Clarification in brackets mine.

What is the promise? (4) What of those who were circumcised who had no part in Abraham's covenant?"

Coming to his second question (Who is the seed?), Tombes says:

> Secondly, The seed of *Abraham* is many wayes so called: First, Christ is called the seed of *Abraham*, by excellency, Gal 3.16. Secondly, all the Elect, Rom. 9.7. all believers, Rom. 4.11,12. 16.17, 18. are called the seed of *Abraham*, that is spiritual seed. Thirdly, there was a natural seed of *Abraham*, to whom the inheritance did accrue; this was *Isaac*. Gen. 21.12. Fourthly, a natural seed, whether lawfull, as the sons of *Keturah*, or base, as *Ishmael*, to whom the inheritance belonged not, Gen 15.5. But no where do I find, that the Infants of Believers of the Gentiles are called *Abrahams* seed, of the three former kinds of *Abrahams* seed, the promise recited, is meant, but in a different manner thus: that God promiseth, he will be a God to Christ, imparting in him blessing to all nations of the earth, to the spiritual seed of *Abraham* in Euangelicall benefits, to the natural seed inheriting, in domestick and politicall benefits.[14]

Tombes extended the blessings of the New Covenant back upon the Abrahamic Covenant in both aspects of the covenant – spiritual and civil. He saw this as part of the promise of the New Covenant expressed in the time before Christ. He attempted to explain himself as he answered the third question (What is the promise?):

> 3. That the promise of the Gospel, or Gospel-covenant, was the same in all ages, in respect of the thing promised, and condition of the covenant, which we may call the substantiall and essentiall part of that covenant, to wit, *Christ, Faith, Sanctification, Remission of sins, Eternall life;* yet this Euangelicall covenant had divers forms in which these things were signified, and various sanctions, by which it was confirmed: To *Adam*, the promise was made under the name

---

[14] Tombes, *Exercitation*, 3.

of the seed of the woman, bruising the head of the Serpent; to *Enoch, Noah,* in other forms; otherwise to *Abraham,* under the name of his seed, in whom all nations should be blessed; otherwise to *Moses,* under the obscure shadows of the Law; otherwise to *David,* under the name of a successor in the kingdome; otherwise in the New Testament, in plain words, 2 Cor. 3.6. Heb. 8.10. It had likewise divers sanctions. The Promise of the Gospel was confirmed to *Abraham* by the sign of circumcision, and by the birth of *Isaac*; to *Moses* by the Paschall Lamb, and the sprinkling of blood on the [door], the rain of Mannah, and other signs; to *David* by an oath; in the New Testament, by Christ's blood, 1 Cor. 11.25. Therefore circumcision signified and confirmed the promise of the Gospel, according to the form and sanction of the covenant with *Abraham,* Baptisme signifies and confirms the same promise according to the form, sanction and accomplishments of the new Testament.[15]

Tombes admitted that each of these covenants has a sign to confirm the promise made. However, he maintains a distinction between the specific sign of circumcision given in the Genesis 17 covenant (given to Abraham as part of that specific covenant) and the specific sign of baptism given in the New Covenant. He went on to contrast other aspects of these covenants to demonstrate there was not a *quid pro quo* relationship between them. There was some continuity; there was also discontinuity. If they were identical in all things, they would be the same in essence, character, and name. Since there was at least one difference, the sign, it was, for Tombes' theological opponents, fallacious to impose a view of radical

---

[15] Tombes, *Exercitation,* 3. Brackets and 'door' inserted. The original has 'book.' Since this article makes no correction in the *errata,* and since this author knows of no narratve in the Pentateuch that deals with blood being sprinkled on a 'book,' the word has been changed. However, considering the context of Tombes' comments, the Passover, and having personally perused examples of his handwriting from which a printer or printer's apprentice (devil) would have copied, I believe it is no violence to the work in form or content to make this change.

The Abrahamic Covenant in the Thought of John Tombes

continuity between the covenant made with Abraham and the covenant brought about by Christ, the New Covenant. Tombes continued by looking at the elements involved:

> ...[N]ow these forms and sanctions differ many wayes, as much as concerns our present purpose in these: First, circumcision confirmed not Euangelicall promises, but also Politicall; and if we may believe *Mr. Cameron*, in his *Theses*, of the threefold Covenant of God, *Thesi. 78. Circumcision did primarily separate the seed of* Abraham *from other nations, sealed unto them the earthly promise; Secondarily, it did signifie sanctification:* But Baptisme signifies only Euangelicall benefits. Secondly, circumcision did confirm the promise concerning Christ to come out of *Isaac*; Baptisme assures Christ to be already come, to have been dead, and to have risen again. Thirdly, circumcision belonged to the Church, constituted in the House of *Abraham*, Baptisme to the Church gathered out of all nations; whence I gather, that there is not the same reason of circumcision and baptisme, in signing the Euangelicall covenant; nor may there be an argument drawn from the administration of the one to the like manner of the other.[16]

For Tombes, circumcision sealed an earthly promise and identified Abraham's seed as set apart to God for his purpose. A great part of that purpose was the incarnation of Christ from the line of Isaac. Tombes was not denying Israel's prized position as God's special ancient people; he was affirming it. However, for Tombes, it was important to understand the pre-incarnational covenants in the brighter light of the fulfillment in the New Covenant. Salvific aspects of the New Covenant were found in types and shadows within the older covenants (especially the Abrahamic), but their primary purpose was to anticipate the day when God would bring redemption. The New Covenant, however, looked back to the reality of redemption accomplished and applied. It was through

---

[16] Tombes, *Exercitation*, 3ff.

these New Covenant glasses that Tombes saw the salvific aspects of all antecedent covenants. In Tombes' theological scheme, circumcision was the sign of the former, pointing to, among other things, the spiritual realities that will be the certain possession of Abraham's spiritual seed. Baptism is the sign of the latter, looking back at what has been done by the Mediator of the New Covenant for his people.

Tombes demonstrated even more discontinuity between the Abrahamic and New Covenants while anticipating the question as regards the subjects of circumcision:

> 4. That some there were circumcised, to whom no promise in the covenant made with *Abraham* did belong; of *Ishmael*, God had said, that his covenant was not to be established with him, but with *Isaac*; and yet he was circumcised, *Gen. 17.29, 21. 25. Rom. 9.7, 8, 9. Gal. 4.29, 30.* the same may be said of *Esau*: All that were in *Abrahams* house, whether strangers, or born in his house, were circumcised, *Gen. 17.12, 13.* of whom nevertheless, it may be doubted, whether any promises of the covenant made with *Abraham*, did belong to them; there were other persons, to whom all, or most of the promises in the covenant pertained, that were not circumcised; this may be affirmed of the Females, coming from *Abraham*, the Infants dying before the eighth day, of just men, living out of *Abrahams* house, as *Melchisedech, Lot, Job*. If any say, that the females were circumcised in the circumcision of the Males, he saith it without proof; and by like, perhaps greater, reason it may be said, that the children of Believers are baptized in the persons of their own parents, and therefore are not to be baptized in their own persons. But it is manifest that the *Jewes* comprehended in the covenant made with *Abraham*, and circumcised, were nevethelesse not admitted to Baptisme by *John Baptist*, and Christs Disciples, till they professed repentance, and faith in Christ. Hence I gather, first, that the right to Euangelicall promises, was not the adequate reason of circumcising these or those, but God's

precept, as is expressed, *Gen. 17.23. Gen. 21.4.* Secondly, that those terms are not convertible, *[federated and to be signed]*.[17]

Tombes' conclusions were drawn from the positive, declarative use of circumcision and baptism in Scripture. His rigid adherence to the meaning of texts as God's words for his people and his governing principles for all matters of faith and practice compelled him to demand positive evidence for paedobaptism beyond mere theological constructions. Tombes demanded some evidence from "God's precept[s]" for the practice. He also saw more discontinuity between the Abrahamic and the New Covenant through the assertion "those terms were not convertible." By "convertible," Tombes meant synonymous. There may be some similarities; yet great differences remained.

Review and Conclusion

In review, Tombes' original, foundational argument was stated thus:

> Major premise: That which hath no testimony in Scripture for it, is doubtfull.
> Minor premise: But this Doctrine of Infant-Baptisme, hath no testimony of Scripture for it;
> Conclusion: *Ergo*, it is doubtfull.[18]

Applying this argument to baptism, he suggested a second:

> Major premise: To whom the Gospel-covenant agrees, to them the sign of the Gospel-covenant agrees also.
> Minor premise: But to Infants of Believers the Gospel-covenant agrees,
> Conclusion: [A]nd consequently Baptisme.[19]

---

[17] Tombes, *Exercitation*, 4. Italics and brackets in original.
[18] Tombes, *Exercitation*, 1.
[19] Tombes, *Exercitation*, 1ff.

After giving the four reasons above why this is not exegetically or theologically accurate, he concluded his first and most fundamental argument:

> Whereupon I answer to the Argument: First, either by denying the *Major,* if it be universally taken, otherwise it concludes nothing: or by granting it with this limitation; it is true of that sign of the covenant which agrees universally in respect of form and sanction, to them that receive the Gospel, but it is not true of that sign of the covenant, which is of a particular form or sanction, of which sort is circumcision.
>
> Secondly, I answer by denying the *Minor,* universally taken, the reason is, because those children only of believing *Gentiles,* are *Abrahams* children, who are his spiritual seed, according to the election of grace by faith, which are not known to us, but by profession, or speciall Revelation.[20]

Here, Tombes, in a summary, has given his refutation of the argument from Genesis 17:7. He denied the major premise to be universal. Circumcision was a particular part of a particular covenant made with Abraham. Circumcision fits within the structure of that narrow covenantal application to Abraham's descendants physically. It was a sanction or stipulation from God to Abraham for his house through procreation. Baptism, for Tombes, was a covenantal stipulation through the New Covenant because of, and not antecedent to, regeneration.

However, within Tombes' conclusion there is this explanatory comment, "[T]he reason is, because those children only of believing *Gentiles,* are *Abrahams* children, who are his spiritual seed, according to the election of grace by faith."[21] The true children of Abraham are those who are brought into his family through an act of God. They are the professors of faith because they have known something of the work of God and, as much as man can tell from

---

[20] Tombes, *Exercitation*, 5.
[21] Tombes, *Exercitation*, 5.

their fruit, they are possessors of faith. Based on these realities, the professors should receive the sign of the New Covenant, baptism.

Baptism ought to be administered after the new birth has been given and a credible profession of faith, backed by a life transformed and being transformed by God's discipling grace. In that regard, perhaps, infants are the ones to be baptized – not infants by natural descent, but spiritual babes, who have been born again and now rest in the bosom of Christ. This fits the pattern of the early church, the testimony of Scripture, and a system of truth that honors the covenants God made within himself, with various men, families and nations, and his own unique people.

CHAPTER 7
John Owen on the Mosaic Covenant
Thomas E. Hicks, Jr., Ph.D.*

Covenant theology has not been uniform in its understanding of the nature of the Mosaic Covenant. While today many of the adherents of popular covenant theology speak as though "true" covenant theology interprets the Mosaic Covenant to be a gracious administration of the covenant of grace, that way of speaking is historically inaccurate. Part of the reason for this one-sided expression may be covenant theology's present orientation against Dispensationalism. In reaction to the dispensational insistence on identifying the Mosaic Covenant with a covenant of works, some contemporary expressions of covenant theology have tended exclusively to assert the gracious character of the Mosaic Covenant. In today's academic literature on covenant theology, John Murray's writings strongly advocate interpreting the Mosaic Covenant exclusively as an administration of the covenant of grace, while Meredith Kline's work favors the view that formulates it as a republication of the covenant of works at the earthly typological level on the principle of inheritance by works righteousness.[1] The

---

* Thomas E. Hicks, Jr., Ph.D., is a pastor at Morningview Baptist Church, Montgomery, AL (www.morningview.org), and author of "The Doctrine of Justification in the Theologies of Richard Baxter and Benjamin Keach" (Ph.D. diss, The Southern Baptist Theological Seminary), and of chapters in *Ministry by His Grace and for His Glory* and *Whomever He Wills*, both published by Founders Press. This chapter first appeared as an article in *RBTR* and is used with permission. It has been revised and updated.

[1] Peter Golding, *Covenant Theology: The Key of Theology in Reformed Thought and Tradition* (Ross-Shire, Scotland: Mentor, 2004), 164-70. John Murray flatly rejected the idea that the Mosaic covenant was a "repetition of the so-called covenant of works," calling that view a "grave misconception" and "an erroneous construction of the Mosaic covenant." John Murray, "The Adamic Administration," *in Collected Writings, 4 vols.* (Edinburgh: Banner of Truth, 1977), 2:50. Meredith Kline on the other hand wrote, "The old (Mosaic) covenant order, though in continuity with the

present dispute in covenant theology calls for historians to study what mainstream covenant theology actually affirmed in the past. The historical picture, however, is far from uniform, since covenant theology never really settled the question. The reality is that orthodox covenant theologians affirmed various positions on the nature of the Mosaic Covenant.

Ernest Kevan, a scholar of Puritan theology, divided historic covenant theologians into two groups: those who affirmed that the Mosaic Covenant is a covenant of works and those who affirmed that it is a covenant of grace.[2] Sinclair Ferguson, however, in a description of John Owen's view of the Mosaic Covenant, took Kevan to task on his assessment and wrote, "In view of this, and some of the statements quoted, Dr. Kevan might have more accurately divided Puritan opinion on the Sinaitic Covenant into three groups."[3] If Ferguson is right, John Owen is part of a third group, which held that the Mosaic Covenant is neither strictly a covenant of works nor a covenant of grace, but a third kind of covenant which embodies principles of both the covenant of works and the covenant of grace, but is identical to neither.[4] This study will explore whether Kevan, Ferguson, neither, or each is correct in his characterization of classical covenant theology's understanding of the Mosaic Covenant. We will use Owen's doctrine of the Mosaic Covenant as the test case, since Ferguson points to him as an example of a covenant theologian who defies the twofold categorization of Kevan.

The thesis of this study is that Ferguson is correct to identify John Owen's understanding of the Mosaic Covenant as a third kind of covenant, which is neither a mere republication of the covenant of works nor simply an administration of the covenant of grace. The

---

Abrahamic covenant of promise . . . was nevertheless itself governed by a principle of works." Meredith G Kline, *Kingdom Prologue: Genesis Foundations for a Covenantal Worldview* (Oakland Park, KS: Two Age Press, 2000), 318.

[2] Ernest F. Kevan, *The Grace of Law: A Study in Puritan Theology* (Morgan, PA: Soli Deo Gloria, 1993), 113-14.

[3] Sinclair B. Ferguson, *John Owen on the Christian Life* (Edinburgh: Banner of Truth, 1987), 28.

[4] Ferguson, *John Owen*, 29.

study will discuss the relevance of the question and argue that this inquiry is important. It will then describe the views of two historic covenant theologians, one who affirmed that the Mosaic Covenant is substantively the covenant of grace, and another who affirmed that it contains the principle of the covenant of works. Next, it will present John Owen's own theology of the Mosaic Covenant and determine whether his view fits into one of the two categories or demands a third category of its own. Finally, some possible objections to the conclusion will be considered and answered.

Importance of this Study

A clear understanding of the precise nature of the Mosaic Covenant is important in the fields of biblical studies, systematic theology, and historical theology. In biblical studies the precise nature of the Mosaic Covenant is important because of Paul's discussion of the "law" and the "works of the law" in the books of Romans, 1 Corinthians, Galatians, and also in the discussions of the writer to the Hebrews on the relationship between the Old and New Covenants. These biblical authors refer to the Mosaic Covenant and the New Covenant in passages where the Old Covenant is contrasted with the New Covenant, therefore, answering the question of the nature of the Mosaic Covenant will greatly color New Testament interpretation.

In systematic theology, the nature of the Mosaic Covenant is relevant to the doctrine of justification. If the Mosaic Covenant is strictly a covenant of grace and if justification is a verdict rendered on the basis of one's conformity to the terms of the covenant of grace, then theologians may find sufficient warrant to conclude that it is reasonable to include good works in the verdict of justification. On the other hand, if the Mosaic Covenant is a covenant of works, and if Paul and others are arguing against justification by obedience to that covenant, then an argument against justification by good works clearly emerges in the scriptural corpus.

In terms of historical theology, understanding the various positions on the Mosaic Covenant could help to explain various historical positions on the relationship between the church and the state in England, and some motivations for political action and theory. It may be worth investigating whether certain aspects of the Mosaic Covenant were held by those who were more prone to seeing a unity of the church and the state, while other views of the Mosaic Covenant were held by those who advocated strong doctrines of separation between church and state. Mark Karlberg has written:

> Since the time of the Reformation there has been a Reformed consensus that there is an interconnection between OT laws, personal Christian life, and national public policy. But the relationship has not always been clearly defined, which accounts in part for the current intense debate on the role of OT laws in the formation of public policy in America's pluralistic society.[5]

Careful study of Owen's doctrine of the Mosaic Covenant could be useful in clearly delineating his political theory and explaining some of the theological motivation for his political action.

Two Historic Perspectives on the Mosaic Covenant

Some covenant theologians believed that the Mosaic Covenant is the covenant of grace, while others thought of it as being some kind of republication of the covenant of works. The view of one major proponent of each position will be presented in order to provide general descriptions of the two perspectives. They will also function as background against which Owen's own thought on the matter can be evaluated later. Francis Turretin held that the Mosaic Covenant was the covenant of grace, legally administered, while Herman Witsius believed the Mosaic Covenant was a national covenant that also reiterated the covenant of works.

---

[5] Mark W. Karlberg, *Covenant Theology in Reformed Perspective* (Eugene, OR: Wipf and Stock, 2000), 59.

Francis Turretin

Following Calvin, Turretin divided the covenant of grace into two gracious economies: the old and the new.[6] According to Turretin, there is no grace-works distinction between the covenants with Abraham and Moses. Instead, the whole Old Testament, after the fall, was a dispensation of grace in which the Mosaic Covenant was simply a gracious continuation, renewal, and expansion of the Abrahamic administration of the covenant of grace (Deut. 5:2). Turretin said that the giving of the Mosaic Covenant was "terrific, smiting with fear their consciences and by the severity of its threatenings removing them from the sight of God," but he also affirmed that "it is rightly said that the Decalogue belonged to the covenant of grace."[7] That is, the substance of the Mosaic Covenant was the covenant of grace, even though its accidental form or administration was somewhat legal. Turretin argued that God administered the Mosaic Covenant in a twofold manner, one according to the external or legal relationship, and the other according to the internal relationship of grace and promise. He wrote, "According to that twofold relation, the administration can be viewed either as to the external economy of legal teaching or as to the internal truth of the gospel promise underlying it."[8] Thus, for those Israelites who were related to the wholeness of the Mosaic Covenant because they had faithfully grasped and internalized the gracious promise of eternal life repeated in it, the Mosaic Covenant functioned as it was actually given: as a covenant of grace. But for those who did not believe and embrace the gospel extended in the Mosaic Covenant and therefore only related to the external legal

---

[6] William Ames and John Calvin are two more examples of historic Reformed theologians who affirmed the Mosaic Covenant was substantively a covenant of grace rather than a covenant of works. See William Ames, *The Marrow of Theology* (Grand Rapids: Baker, 1968), 202-05; John Calvin, *Institutes of the Christian Religion*, ed. John T. McNeil, trans. Ford Lewis Battles (Philadelphia: Westminster Press, 1960), 2.7-11 (340-449); and David L. Puckett, *John Calvin's Exegesis of the Old Testament* (Louisville, KY: Westminster John Knox, 1995), 37-44.

[7] Francis Turretin, *Institutes of Elenctic Theology*, ed. James T. Dennison, Jr., trans. George Musgrave Giger (Phillipsburg: P&R, 1994), 2:226.

[8] Turretin, *Institutes*, 2:227.

requirement, it was a killing letter and functioned to condemn them because of its revelation of the law. However, "this [legal] stipulation in the Israelite covenant was only accidental," since the substance of the Mosaic Covenant was the covenant of grace and not the covenant of works.[9]

Herman Witsius

Herman Witsius, on the other hand, affirmed that the Mosaic Covenant was a national covenant made with Israel that also reiterated the principle of the covenant of works.[10] Witsius wrote, "What was [the Mosaic covenant] then? It was a national covenant between God and Israel. . . . This agreement therefore is a consequent both of the covenant of grace and of works; but was formally neither the one nor the other."[11] The Mosaic Covenant was formally a national covenant, but it also promised the reward of eternal life. J. V. Fesko writes, "Witsius believed that God set forth a legal covenant before the nation of Israel, one by which they could earn their salvation through their obedience. Given man's sinfulness, however, the Mosaic covenant as the republished covenant of works only revealed Israel's sinfulness."[12] Witsius wrote:

> And first, we observe, that, in the ministry of Moses, there

---

[9] Turretin, *Institutes*, 2:227.

[10] Other classic Reformed theologians affirmed that the Mosaic Covenant republished the covenant of works. For example, the work of Edward Fisher (though there is some dispute about whether or not that is his real name) was influential in seventeenth- and eighteenth-century Britain during the Neonomian and Marrow controversies. He wrote a little manual of covenant theology which taught a clear law-gospel distinction and interpreted the Mosaic Covenant as a covenant of works. See Edward Fisher, *The Marrow of Modern Divinity: In Two Parts* (Edmonton, AB: Still Waters Revival, 1991) 68-83.

[11] Herman Witsius, *The Economy of the Covenants Between God and Man* (Kingsburg, CA: den Dulk Christian Foundation, 1990), 2:186.

[12] J. V. Fesko, "Calvin and Witsius on the Mosaic Covenant" in *The Law is Not of Faith: Essays on Works and Grace in the Mosaic Covenant*, ed. Bryan D. Estelle, J. V. Fesko, and David VanDrunen (Philipsburg: P&R, 2009), 37.

was a repetition of the doctrine concerning the law of the covenant of works. For both the very same precepts are inculcated, on which the covenant of works was founded, and which constituted the condition of the covenant; and that sentence is repeated, "which if a man do he shall live in them," Lev 18:5. . . . And the terror of the covenant of works is increased by repeated comminations; and that voice heard, "cursed be he that confirmeth not all the words of this law to do them," Deut 27:26.[13]

Elsewhere, Witsius said that the Mosaic Covenant "undoubtedly contained the sanction of the covenant of works."[14] That is, the Mosaic Covenant itself promised eternal condemnation to those who failed to keep all the words of the law. Thus, according to Witsius, the Mosaic Covenant had the work-for-life principle in it, though it was not formally the covenant of works.

According to Witsius, Israelites were promised both temporal and eternal spiritual blessings, not just from the covenant of grace, but also from the national Mosaic Covenant. Brenton Ferry writes, "[Witsius] explains that the reward for obedience to this national covenant is received in both this life and the next, benefitting both body and soul."[15] Witsius remarked, "He promises to them not only temporal blessings . . . but also spiritual and eternal, when he says that he will be their God and they his people . . . these words comprise life eternal and the resurrection of the body."[16]

When contrasting the Old and New Testaments, Witsius did not distinguish between two economies of a single covenant of grace like Turretin (old and new administrations of the covenant of grace); rather, he believed that the Old Covenant and the New Covenant were two different covenants. According to Witsius, when the New Covenant is contrasted with the Mosaic Covenant, "a new better covenant is opposed to that Israelitish covenant,

---

[13] Witsius, *The Economy of the Covenants*, 182.
[14] Witsius, *The Economy of the Covenants*, 359.
[15] Brenton C. Ferry, "Works in the Mosaic Covenant: A Reformed Taxonomy" in *The Law is Not of Faith*, 102.
[16] Witsius, *The Economy of the Covenants*, 182.

John Owen on the Mosaic Covenant

which is not formally the covenant of grace."[17] By denying that the Mosaic Covenant is of the same substance with the covenant of grace, Witsius distinguished his own position from theologians like Calvin and Turretin.[18]

Some representatives of historic Reformed covenant theology affirmed that the Mosaic Covenant is an administration of the covenant of grace, like Turretin, while others affirmed that it republishes the covenant of works, like Witsius. The focus of the remainder of this study will be to analyze John Owen's doctrine of the Mosaic Covenant and to determine whether Owen affirmed a third option, which denied that the Mosaic Covenant could be identified as the covenant of grace or the covenant of works.

John Owen's Doctrine of the Mosaic Covenant: A Third Perspective?

John Owen was a major figure in the development of Reformed and covenant theology.[19] Like Witsius, Owen explicitly denied that the Mosaic Covenant is identical to the covenant of works or the covenant of grace. However, unlike Witsius, the reason for Owen's denial was that he did not believe that the Mosaic Covenant extended the promise of spiritual or eternal life at all. Owen wrote, "This covenant called, 'the old covenant,' was never intended to be of itself the absolute rule and law of life and salvation to the church, but was made with a particular design, and with respect to

---

[17] Witsius, *The Economy of the Covenants*, 336.

[18] Though the preceding discussion emphasized the discontinuities between Turretin and Witsius, there is also significant continuity between them, since both recognized a distinctive works principle operating in the Mosaic Covenant. For similar continuity between Calvin and Witsius, see Fesko, "Calvin and Witsius on the Mosaic Covenant," in *The Law is Not of Faith*, 25-43.

[19] For more information on John Owen, see William Barker, *Puritan Profiles* (Ross-Shire, Scotland: Mentor, 1999), 295-300; Errol Hulse, *Who are the Puritans?* (Auburn: Evangelical Press, 2000), 97-99; Robert W. Oliver, ed., *John Owen: The Man and his Theology* (Philipsburg: P&R, 2002), 1-190; Peter Toon, *God's Statesman: The Life and Work of John Owen*, Pastor, Educator, Theologian (Exeter: Paternoster, 1971), 1-178; Carl Trueman, *The Claims of Truth* (Carlisle: Paternoster, 2001), 1-281.

particular ends."[20] Owen repeated that assertion throughout his commentary on Hebrews and in various portions of his other works as well. So, if the Mosaic Covenant did not extend the promise of life, then how did it relate to the covenant of works and the covenant of grace?

Owen said that the Mosaic Covenant did not renew, replace, or abrogate the covenant of works.[21] He believed that to assert that the Mosaic Covenant was "the" or "a" covenant of works would overthrow Paul's argument in Galatians 3, which teaches that if the Mosaic Covenant promised eternal life on the basis of the works of the law, as did the covenant of works, then the gracious promise of life by faith given to Abraham in the Abrahamic Covenant would be nullified. Paul wrote, "This is what I mean: the law, which came 430 years afterward, does not annul a covenant previously ratified by God, so as to make the promise void. For if the inheritance comes by the law, it no longer comes by promise, but God gave it to Abraham by a promise" (Gal. 3:17-18). Therefore, Owen said that it is wrong to say that the Mosaic Covenant is the covenant of works "absolutely."[22]

On the other hand, Owen denied that the Mosaic Covenant is properly considered an administration of the covenant of grace. In fact, he spent several pages in his commentary on Hebrews describing that view, which he readily admits that Calvin and most Reformed divines held, demonstrating his thorough acquaintance with that gracious perspective on the Mosaic Covenant. But then, he spent twice as many pages refuting it. In fact, his chief concern in the Hebrews commentary seems to be not so much to distance himself from the idea that the Mosaic Covenant is a republication of the covenant of works, though he does that. Instead, he was primarily interested in separating his understanding from Calvin's view, which taught that the Mosaic Covenant and the New

---

[20] Coxe and Owen, *Covenant Theology*, 188.
[21] Michael William Bobick, "Owen's Razor: The Role of Ramist Logic in *The Covenant Theology of John Owen* (1616-1683)" (Ph.D. diss., Drew University, 1996), 57-60.
[22] John Owen, *The Works of John Owen: An Exposition of the Epistle to the Hebrews*, ed. William H. Goold, vol. 19 (Edinburgh: Banner of Truth, 1965), 389.

John Owen on the Mosaic Covenant

Covenant were simply two administrations of the covenant of grace. First, Owen outlined points of agreement with Calvin: the way of justification is the same under both covenants; the writings of both Testaments contain the doctrine of justification by faith alone; and the Mosaic Covenant reveals and points to Jesus Christ.[23] Second, Owen explained why he did not adhere to Calvin's viewpoint. Owen argued that if it were a covenant of grace, then Scripture's contrasts between Mosaic law and the gospel promise in Galatians 3, Romans 3, 2 Corinthians 3, and Hebrews 8 would be nearly unintelligible. This concern to uphold the biblical distinction between the "old" and the "new" is in fact Owen's main objection to the idea that the Mosaic Covenant is identical to the covenant of grace. The New Testament makes too much of the difference between the Mosaic Covenant and the New Covenant for them to be satisfactorily explained as merely two administrations of the same covenant. It says that one is a "ministry of condemnation" and the other is a "ministry of righteousness" (2 Cor. 3:9). One is temporary, but the other is permanent (2 Cor. 3:11). One is faulty and obsolete, while the other is enacted on better promises (Heb. 8:6-7, 13). Owen believed that fidelity to the text of Scripture and particularly to the whole argument of the book of Hebrews required that the Mosaic Covenant not be identified with the covenant of grace.

Therefore, according to Owen, the Mosaic Covenant must be a "third kind of covenant," which neither promises eternal life in the covenant of works nor the covenant of grace. Owen's view of the Mosaic Covenant as a third kind of covenant grew out of his wrestling with two seemingly contradictory principles. The two apparently contradictory principles that Scripture teaches regarding the Mosaic Covenant are, first, that it cannot be the covenant of works, lest the promise be overthrown (Gal. 3:17-18). But, second, and in seeming opposition to this, the New Testament apparently demands that the Mosaic Covenant contain the work-for-life principle of the covenant of works: "Cursed be everyone who does not abide by all thing things written in the Book of the Law and do

---

[23] Coxe and Owen, *Covenant Theology*, 181.

them . . . But the law is not of faith; rather the one who does them shall live by them. Christ redeemed us from the curse of the law becoming a curse for us" (Gal. 3:10-13).

Owen resolves this apparent tension by arguing that the commands, curse and promise of the covenant of works were "revived" in the Mosaic Covenant. Regarding the "do this and live" promise of Leviticus 18:5, Owen says, "Now this is no other but the covenant of works revived," and that the Mosaic Covenant "revived the promise of that covenant that of eternal life on perfect obedience."[24] But by asserting the "revival" of the covenant of works, Owen in no way intended to say that the Mosaic Covenant is identical to the covenant of works, but only that part of the Mosaic Covenant contains a reminder of that covenant which was given to Adam in the garden before the fall. In this sense, Owen said that there is both "renovation" and "innovation" of the covenant of works.[25] He wrote, "Nor had this covenant of Sinai any promise of eternal life annexed to it, as such, but only the promise inseparable from the covenant of works, which it revived, saying, 'Do this and live.'"[26] He then concluded:

> Therefore it follows also, that it was not a new covenant of works established in the place of the old, for the absolute rule of faith and obedience to the whole church; for then would it have abrogated and taken away that covenant, and all the force of it, which it did not.[27]

This explains the relationship of the Mosaic Covenant to the covenant of works and also explains the New Testament's citation of the "do this and live" promise contained in the Mosaic Covenant. The Mosaic Covenant contained a reminder of the covenant of works, announcing the terms that belonged not to itself, but to the original covenant of works with Adam.

---

[24] Coxe and Owen, *Covenant Theology*, 189.
[25] John Owen, *The Works of John Owen*, ed. William H. Goold, vol 6 (Edinburgh: Banner of Truth, 1965), 471.
[26] Coxe and Owen, *Covenant Theology*, 189.
[27] Coxe and Owen, *Covenant Theology*, 189.

But, the Mosaic Covenant also stood in a special relationship to the covenant of grace. According to Owen, the covenant of grace was initiated and established in the protoevanglium immediately after the fall in God's promise of the Seed who would crush the head of the serpent (Genesis 3:15). The Abrahamic Covenant, revealed in Genesis 12, 15, and 17, was this same covenant of grace in which the stipulations and blessings were expanded and clarified. Israelites who were living under the Mosaic Covenant were justified and saved by the covenant of grace which had already been revealed. The Mosaic Covenant functioned as a covenantal overlay, a covenant layer that God placed on top of the already existing covenant of grace. Ferguson correctly notes, "It was *under* the covenant of grace that Old Testament saints were justified, and not *by virtue* of the old covenant (Sinai) in which the substance of the covenant of works was renewed."[28] But, even though the Mosaic Covenant did not provide the means of salvation, it still clearly pointed to the one way of salvation by means of the covenant of grace. It both revealed and repeated the promises which God had already made in earlier times, and anticipated the ultimate consummation of those promises in the first and second comings of Christ. Owen said that the Mosaic Covenant pointed to the covenant of grace:

> by representing the way and means of the accomplishment of the promise, and of that on what all the efficacy of it to the justification and salvation of sinners does depend. . . . To that end it was so far from disannulling the promise or diverting the minds of the people of God from it, that by all means it established and led to it.[29]

Thus, the sacrificial system of the Mosaic Covenant was a Christocentric depiction of the covenant of grace, and it anticipated the New Covenant which was yet to come.[30]

---

[28] Ferguson, *John Owen on the Christian Life*, 30. Emphasis is original.
[29] Coxe and Owen, *Covenant Theology*, 190.
[30] This Christocentric perspective is characteristic of Owen's entire theological

The question then becomes what the Mosaic Covenant actually is. If it is neither the covenant of works nor the covenant of grace, but merely reminds those under its administration of the terms, stipulations, and ends of those covenants, preaching their terms so to speak, but not embodying them, then the Mosaic Covenant itself must still be defined. Owen wrote, "That if it did neither abrogate the first covenant of works, and come in the room of it, nor disannul the promise made to Abraham, then to what end did it serve, or what benefit did the church receive by that means?"[31]

Like Witsius, Owen concluded that the Mosaic Covenant was a covenant uniquely designed for national Israel.[32] It was a national covenant, which God made to be subservient to the promises he made to Abraham 430 years earlier. A national covenant was necessary in order for it to be clear to subsequent generations that in the fullness of time, God kept his promise by sending Jesus the Messiah through the line and seed of Abraham, who God promised would have a multitude of children and be a blessing to the nations. Owen says that the Abrahamic promise rendered it necessary "that [Israel] should have a certain abiding place or country, which they might freely inhabit, distinct from other nations, and under a rule or scepter of their own."[33] Also, the mark of Yahweh had to remain on them and they had to be required to trust and obey him for blessings and curses, lest the Christological reason for their election and existence be obscured to future generations, and God's integrity as a promise-keeper be called into question. Also, since God chose them to be his special people, God's own holiness required him to demand their obedience and submission according to a specific and temporally appropriate pattern of worship.[34] Thus,

---

methodology and covenantal framework. See Carl. R. Trueman, *The Claims of Truth: John Owen's Trinitarian Theology* (Carlisle: Paternoster, 1998), 60-64.

[31] Coxe and Owen, *Covenant Theology*, 191.

[32] For a helpful orientation on John Owen's doctrine of the Mosaic Covenant see David Wai-Sing Wong, "The Covenant Theology of John Owen" (Ph.D. diss., Westminster Theological Seminary, 1998), 203-23.

[33] Coxe and Owen, *Covenant Theology*, 194.

[34] Coxe and Owen, *Covenant Theology*, 194-197. See also Sebastian Rehnman, *Divine Discourse: The Theological Methodology of John Owen* (Grand Rapids: Baker, 2002), 173-74.

God's goal in making the Mosaic Covenant with the people of Israel was both eschatological and Christological, but it does not explain the nature of the Mosaic Covenant.

Since the Mosaic Covenant is not about eternal life,[35] it must be an earthly covenant, which is temporary and typical of spiritual things. Owen writes, "there was ordained in it a typical representation,"[36] which was a picture of spiritual things. The Mosaic Covenant required faith, love, and actual acts of obedience, but it contained no gracious enablement for anyone under its administration actually to perform its requirements. It delivered the Israelites out of captivity in the land of Egypt (physical picture), but it did not deliver them from bondage to their sinful natures (spiritual reality); therefore, the Israelites were not capable of keeping the terms of the Mosaic Covenant by virtue of the Mosaic Covenant. Furthermore, what was promised to the Israelites for their faith, love, and obedience under the Mosaic Covenant was not eternal life (spiritual reality), but temporal, earthly blessings, including land and physical prosperity (physical picture).[37] Owen helpfully summarized his understanding of the constitution of the Mosaic Covenant:

> This covenant, thus made, with these ends and promises, did never save nor condemn any man eternally. All that lived under the administration of it did attain eternal life, or perished for ever, but not by virtue of this covenant as

---

[35] According to Richard C. Barcellos, "Owen did not view the Old Covenant as a covenant of works in itself. He viewed it as containing a renewal of the original covenant of works imposed upon Adam in the Garden of Eden . . . Moreover, Owen did not teach that Christ 'kept the Old Covenant for us and earned every blessing it promised.' On the contrary, Owen taught that obedience or disobedience to the Old Covenant in itself neither eternally saved nor eternally condemned anyone and that its promises were temporal and only for Israel while the Old Covenant lasted. According to Owen, what Christ kept for us was the original Adamic covenant of works, not the Old covenant as an end in itself." Richard C. Barcellos, "John Owen and New Covenant Theology," *RBTR*, I:2 (July 2004): 13-14.

[36] Coxe and Owen, *Covenant Theology*, 198.

[37] Coxe and Owen, *Covenant Theology*, 178.

formally such. It did, indeed, revive the commanding power and sanction of the first covenant of works; and in that respect, as the apostle speaks, was the 'ministry of condemnation,' . . . And on the other hand, it directed also to the promise, which was the instrument of life and salvation to all that did believe. But as to what it had of its own, it was confined to things temporal. Believers were saved under it but not by virtue of it. Sinners perished eternally under it, but by the curse of the original law of works.[38]

Contrary to Kevan, the views of Reformed covenant theologians on the Mosaic Covenant were not limited to "grace" or "works." Owen taught that the Mosaic Covenant is neither the covenant of works nor the covenant of grace, but a third kind of national covenant of promise, which God specially designed to keep the people of Israel together as a nation to be a visible display of God's promise-keeping by eventually bringing Jesus Christ from that nation, and to be a typical, earthly picture of both the covenant of works and the covenant of grace.[39] Therefore, Ferguson's assertion that Reformed covenant theologians should be divided into three groups, rather than two, is correct.

Objections Proposed and Answered

Three possible counter arguments could be made against the above thesis. One might argue that Owen really believed that the Mosaic Covenant was really (1) a covenant of works or (2) a covenant of grace, which would mean that Kevan, rather than Ferguson, may be right about traditional Reformed positions on the covenant. Also, one might argue that (3) both Kevan and Ferguson are correct, but in different ways. If any of these objections is substantive, the above thesis would be proven incorrect. All three counter-arguments will

---

[38] Coxe and Owen, *Covenant Theology*, 197-98.
[39] For a nearly identical Puritan perspective, see Samuel Bolton, *The True Bounds of Christian Freedom* (Edinburgh: Banner of Truth, 1994), 99.

be presented, and then all three will be answered.

First, one might argue that since on Owen's view, the Mosaic Covenant contains a revival of the terms of the covenant of works, it must itself be that covenant of works. This is in fact the view of biographer Peter Toon who argued that on Owen's view, the Mosaic Covenant is essentially the covenant of works. He said:

> Further [Owen believed the Mosaic Covenant] revived the sanction, curse and sentence of death for transgressors and the promise of eternal life as a reward for perfect obedience. So the Mosaic Covenant was related in essence to the original covenant of works.[40]

Owen's insistence on the revival of the terms of the covenant of works in the Mosaic Covenant could easily be construed as making the Mosaic Covenant the covenant of works. How can a covenant contain the stipulations, sanctions, and promises of a covenant without actually being that covenant? Owen's own denial that the Mosaic Covenant is the covenant of works is inconsistent with his own affirmation that the covenant of works is revived in the Mosaic Covenant.

Second, one might argue that Owen's doctrine of the Mosaic Covenant is essentially the covenant of grace because like the covenant of grace, it commands its members to trust the coming redeemer, and manifests the grace and mercy of God both in the gracious establishment of the covenant and in its merciful sacrificial system. The Mosaic Covenant itself does not require strict and perfect obedience for blessing like the covenant of works, but only a pattern of covenant faithfulness. Wong thinks that Owen believed the Mosaic Covenant was essentially the covenant of grace, though the legal principle of the covenant of works was intermixed as a superadded element. He writes, "According to Owen . . . from Abrahamic covenant to Mosaic covenant, they are in essence the covenant of grace."[41] If either Toon or Wong is correct, then the

---

[40] Toon, *God's Statesman*, 170. Emphasis mine.
[41] Wong, "The Covenant Theology of John Owen," 206-204. Emphasis mine.

thesis of this study fails, since Kevan would be correct about Owen, rather than Ferguson.

Third, one might argue that both Ferguson and Kevan are correct because they are talking about two different things. Kevan is saying that Reformed covenant theologians thought that the Mosaic Covenant is either gracious or legal, generally speaking, while Ferguson is saying that their views on the Mosaic Covenant are not limited to identifying it with the covenant of grace or the covenant of works. Kevan's statement uses the indefinite article "a" rather than the definite article "the" when referring to the Mosaic Covenant as "a covenant of works or a covenant of grace." Kevan wrote that some "regarded the Mosaic Covenant as a Covenant of Works, and [others] regarded it as a Covenant of Grace."[42] Given the wording of the statement, one might argue that while on Owen's view the national, Mosaic Covenant was not "the covenant of grace," properly speaking, it was nevertheless "a national covenant of grace" because God graciously initiated it and caused it to realize its ultimately gracious purpose: that Christ came from that nation to be the redeemer of the world.

In response to the first two counter arguments, two things need to be said. First, and most importantly, John Owen himself denied that the Mosaic Covenant is identical to the covenant of works or the covenant of grace. Some might object that Owen's system was inconsistent, but the fact remains that if Owen is taken on his own terms, then the Mosaic Covenant cannot be identified with either the covenant of works or the covenant of grace. Second, Owen positively offered a third alternative, which he carefully constructed. Owen's third alternative is that the Mosaic Covenant did not promise eternal life, but was a national covenant, which merely made earthly, typical, and temporal promises. It was a mere picture of heavenly things. Since both the covenant of grace and the covenant of works actually promise eternal life on some condition, Owen's understanding of the Mosaic Covenant cannot properly be called either. Therefore, the first two counter arguments fail.

The third counter argument is interesting, but Owen himself

---

[42] Kevan, *The Grace of Law*, 113-14.

never refers to the national, Mosaic Covenant as "a national covenant of grace." In fact, he seems very much to want to distance himself from specifically identifying it as exclusively gracious or legal. Instead, it was national, typical, and subservient to God's whole design, preaching the terms of the covenant of works and the covenant of grace. Furthermore, it seems unlikely that Kevan himself intended such a nuanced understanding of his words, since he argued that all Reformed covenant theologians either affirm that the Mosaic Covenant was a covenant of works or a covenant of grace. The reality is that the vast majority did affirm that the Mosaic Covenant was either the covenant of works republished or the covenant of grace administered to national Israel; therefore, the article is not likely significant.

Conclusion

A careful reading of John Owen reveals that he understood the Mosaic Covenant to be neither the covenant of works nor the covenant of grace, but a third kind of national covenant of promise. At the same time, the Mosaic Covenant revived and republished the terms of the covenant of works and revealed the stipulations and ends of the covenant of grace by prescribing faithfulness and anticipating the New Covenant in various types and shadows. The Mosaic Covenant was specially made to keep the people of Israel together as a nation, preventing their total destruction, until Christ came through them, fulfilling God's promise to Abraham. Though counter arguments can be offered, none of them are ultimately successful in overthrowing the thesis that Sinclair Ferguson, rather than Ernest Kevan, is correct in asserting that the opinion of Reformed covenant theology on the Mosaic Covenant is best divided into three groups, rather than two.

CHAPTER 8
A 'Novel' Approach to Credobaptist and Paedobaptist Polemics
Jeffrey A. Massey*

During the nineteenth century, credobaptists and paedobaptists in America employed a new weapon in their polemics with each other over the proper subjects for baptism.[1] This new weapon was the use of theological/historical novels. These novels, with such titles as *Theodosia Ernest; Or, The Heroine of Faith* and *Theophilus Walton; Or, The Majesty of Truth*, combined fictional stories with theological/historical arguments in an attempt to persuade their readers of the credobaptist or paedobaptist position. These novels had some polemical force in their day and were received with both criticism and praise.

The purpose of this study is to determine the significance and influence of these novels by examining three important factors. First, we will examine their literary significance and use by Evangelical Christians during the nineteenth century. Second, we will survey some of the novels written in this period to show how they combined fiction with theological/historical claims. And third, we will consider some of the responses that these novels received from opponents and supporters alike in the years following their publication.

---

* Jeffrey A. Massey is one of the pastors of Sovereign Grace Reformed Baptist Church, Ontario, CA. This chapter first appeared as an article in *RBTR* and is used with permission.

[1] A credobaptist is one who believes that a statement of faith or belief in Christ is necessary before a person is baptized (the Latin word *credo* means "I believe, trust"). A paedobaptist is one who believes that the proper subjects for baptism are believers and their children (from the Greek word *paidion* which means "a young child or an infant"). See Richard C. Barcellos, *Paedoism or Credoism?* (Fullerton: Reformed Baptist Publications, n.d.), 2.

The Literary Significance of these Novels

In one respect, the appearance of theological/historical novels in America during the nineteenth century was of limited significance. With the increasing proliferation of novels during this period, the introduction of this new and relatively small group of works probably drew little attention outside of Christian circles.[2] Yet, in another respect, their appearance was of considerable significance for several reasons. First, the appearance of theological/historical novels was significant because prior to their appearance, most Evangelical Christians in America were suspicious of, if not opposed to, the use of fiction.[3] Fiction was suspect because it was

---

[2] The increase in the growth and popularity of novels in the nineteenth century, especially in secular America, has been well documented. Lillie Deming Loshe wrote that from the period 1789 to 1830 alone, novels grew in America from a few amateurish works to an established form in American literature. See Lillie Deming Loshe, *The Early American Novel* (New York: Columbia University Press, 1907), v. As for the latter nineteenth century, Esther Jane Carrier wrote that by the third quarter of the century, fiction, mostly in novel form, had become the dominant literary form. Esther Jane Carrier, *Fiction in Public Libraries 1876-1900* (New York & London: The Scarecrow Press, 1965), 27. Christian fiction, on the other hand, did not begin to grow until around 1840. Any Christian fiction published before then would have hardly been noticed, except within Christian circles. For more information on the growth of Christian fiction in the 19th Century, see David S. Reynolds, *Faith in Fiction: The Emergence of Religious Literature in America* (Cambridge, MA and London: Harvard University Press, 1981), 1-6, 197-215; Jan Blodgett, *Protestant Evangelical Culture and Contemporary Society* (Westport and London: Greenwood Press, 1997), 11-32; Beatrice A. Batson, *A Reader's Guide to Religious Literature* (Chicago: Moody Press, 1968), 124-54.

[3] This Christian opposition began in the eighteenth century and continued well into the nineteenth century. Many of the opposition leaders were Christian ministers, such as Jonathan Edwards (1703-1758), Timothy Dwight (1752-1817), and Samuel Miller (1770-1840). For a critical, though helpful, treatment of this opposition, see G. Harrison Orians, "Censure of Fiction in American Novels and Magazines 1789-1810." *Publications of the Modern Language Association of America* 50 (March 1937): 195-214. Many Christian publishing societies also refused to publish fiction until the middle of the nineteenth century. For more information, see Lawrence Thompson, "The Printing and Publishing Activities of the American Tract Society from 1825-1850." *The Papers of the Bibliographical Society of America* 25 (2nd Quarter 1941): 111-13, and Lemuel Call Barnes and Mary Clark Barnes,

believed to encourage the reader's use of imagination, direct thoughts away from heaven, corrupt virtue, exalt worldly tastes, and cause readers, especially women, to be unfit for their proper duties.[4] Another reason that fiction was suspect was that it promoted romantic idealism in place of rationalism.[5] Thus, some Christians were convinced of a need to speak out against the evils of novel-reading.

One outspoken Christian opponent of fiction in America during the mid-to-late nineteenth century was Robert Lewis Dabney, a Southern Presbyterian minister and scholar.[6] In an article entitled

---

Pioneers of Light: The First Century of the American Baptist Publication Society, 1824-1924 (Philadelphia: The American Baptist Publication Society, 1925), 40.

[4] Blodgett, 22. The use of imagination was not encouraged by many Christians during this period because they were convinced that if something was imaginative, it never happened; and if it never happened, it must not be true.

[5] This suspicion was not without some warrant. Much of the fiction written in the early nineteenth century clearly set aside the rational approach which had characterized eighteenth-century literature, and promoted romanticism instead. Beatrice Batson says, "In the early nineteenth century a discernable revolt occurred against the rationalism and strict form of eighteenth century writers. Romantic idealism pervaded the philosophical world in the early part of the century, and in literature a Romantic revolt set in against the dominant tendencies of the eighteenth century. Rather than emphasizing order and lucidity, the Romanticists stressed freedom and imagination. They accorded a high place to the productions of the imagination and often rebelled against the Classical emphasis on the authority of reason. Individualism, personal experience, a love of humble folk and zeal to remake the world were concerns of the Romanticists." Baston, *A Reader's Guide to Religious Literature*, 124.

[6] Robert Lewis Dabney (1820-1898) served as a teaching elder in the Southern Presbyterian Church and as a professor at Union Seminary, VA (1853-1883) and the University of Texas (1883-1894). The *Encyclopedia of the Presbyterian Church in the United States of America*, 1884, 173, described him in this way, "Dr. Dabney is an accomplished scholar, an instructive and forcible preacher, and a writer of marked ability. He is firm in his convictions of truth and duty, and always ready to maintain them." Over one hundred years later, Douglas Kelly summarized Dabney's contributions as follows, "Robert Lewis Dabney was perhaps the greatest, and certainly the most prolific, Southern Presbyterian theologian of nineteenth-century America." Douglas Floyd Kelly, "Robert Lewis Dabney" in *Reformed Theology in America*, ed., David F. Wells (Grand Rapids: William B. Eerdmans Publishing Company, 1985), 208. The fact that an accomplished theologian like Dabney wrote against novel-reading shows that it was considered a

On Dangerous Reading, Dabney briefly summarized what he observed to be the dangers of fiction, and urged heads of families to rid their homes of all such reading material.[7] Dabney wrote:

> The results of such reading are neither vague, slight nor imaginary. They are as real and practical, as palpable and direct, as the common results of drunkenness. The writer of these remarks could point to a decided case of *lunacy*, neither remote or obscure, which was notoriously produced by prolonged novel-reading. When a tragedy was enacted in one of our cities, which shocked the whole country with sudden murder and the final desolation of a home, the grey-haired father of the wretched woman whose delinquency had produced the catastrophe, stood up in a court of justice and testified on oath that the ruin was attributable to his daughter's indulgence in novel-reading. When the learned, pious, amiable and noble head of our University fell by the hand of an assassin, his death thrilling the community with horror and almost overturning the institution of which he was the pillar and ornament, the work of so many years of enlightened and patriotic exertion, the miscreant who shed his blood without cause boasted that his atheistical callousness to danger and to the value of human life was imbibed from the poisonous pages of Bulwer. And though catastrophes so shocking do not usually result from such reading, there are few or none who have indulged in it who have not suffered some injury in weakened principles, morbid feelings, and partial unfitness for the duties of actual life. Had a wise parental restraint been placed upon the youthful reading of the writer of these columns, it would have added no little to the equanimity, happiness and usefulness of his life.

---

real and present danger; and a danger which both the theologians and the ministers of the church needed to actively combat.

[7] This article appeared in the *Watchman and Observer*, Richmond, VA, 1849.

I would, then, exhort all heads of families especially to be inexorable in cleansing their households of all such literary poison. We all know well that, however the young are in the habit of indulging this dangerous taste may be convinced of its evils, there is little hope that *they* will be firm enough to wean themselves from it. And in this fact alone there is surely a sufficient argument of its danger, that its fascinations are so great, and its consequences so insidious, that even rational and ingenuous persons, though convinced of the mischief, cannot forego the indulgence. It devolves, therefore, on the heads and guides appointed for youth by God and by nature to protect them from the intoxicating evil, by the strong arm of parental authority. Parents should feel that their station both authorized and required them to remove such evils, as much as intoxicating liquors or opium. Fictions are the intoxicating stimulants of the immortal part. As parents love the souls of their children, they should snatch away the poison more rigidly than those nuisances which deprave and ruin the body.[8]

Given Dabney's remarks, it is easy to see why the appearance of theological/historical novels was so significant. At a time in American history when many Evangelical Christians thought of fiction as a threat to society and good morals, these novels appeared, claiming to further the truths of Christianity, but employing the same literary devices that most non-Christian novels did. For this reason, some Evangelical Christians eventually spoke out against their use.[9]

A second reason that the appearance of theological/historical novels was significant is that it revealed that some Christians had reached the conclusion that fiction could be used effectively to

---

[8] Robert Lewis Dabney, "On Dangerous Reading" in *Discussions: Evangelical and Theological*, *Volume 2*, ed., C.R. Vaughn (Richmond, VA: Whittet and Shepperson, 1891: reprint ed., Harrisonburg, VA: Sprinkle Publications, 1982), 167-68.

[9] We will look at some of the criticisms waged against these novels later in this study.

A 'Novel' Approach to Credobaptist and Paedobaptist Polemics

further the truth of God, despite the misuse of fiction by ungodly men. These Christians defended their position by pointing to the example of Christ, who used parables (allegorical stories) in his teachings; therefore, justifying the right use of fiction by his own followers. Furthermore, they pointed to the powerful effects that fiction had on its readers, as well as to the increasing demand for fiction among nineteenth-century readers.

One example of this kind of defense appeared in the preface to *Theodosia Ernest, Or, Ten Day's Travel in Search of the Church*. The editors boldly defended their use of fiction in the following manner:

> And what if it be true that wicked men have made fiction the instrument of most terrible evil? What if they have used it to pander to the vilest passions of depraved humanity? What if they have employed it as a vehicle of false philosophy and false religion? What if they have prostituted it to minister to a morbid and mawkish sensibility? What if they have flooded the land with the filthy outpourings of the vilest and most loathsome stews of profligacy and impiety? What if the infidel has seized on it and wielded it as his most powerful weapon against Christianity? Shall we leave it to the exclusive possession of the enemies of God and man? True, they have degraded and polluted it, but it is still a weapon of tremendous power. We will wrest it from their grasp. We will sanctify it, by consecrating it to God and souls. We will increase its energies by earnest prayer for Heaven's blessing. And we will turn it against vice and infidelity. We will use it against error. We will make it the exponent and defender of the truth as it is in Jesus. Why should we not? Do we hesitate to make poetry the medium of truth, because the vicious and the dissolute have sometimes stolen her beautiful garments to cover up the most licentious conceptions of the veriest profligates that have ever been blessed with intellect? Do we cast aside our sacred songs because the lyre has been degraded, and made to sing what modesty would not dare to speak in simple prose? No such thing. If others deface her beauty, misconceive her purpose, and misapply her power,

we will weep over the perversion of so glorious a gift, but we will not refuse to employ the mighty energies of poetry and song in the soul-elevating work for which they were intended. Nor will we, for a similar cause, abandon to the vicious the exclusive use of the fictitious narrative. *We cannot conscientiously refuse to employ a weapon at once so effective and so necessary to the present condition of the reading world* (emphasis original).[10]

Thus, by the time these novels appeared, some Christians viewed fiction, not as the exclusive tool of the opponents of God and men, but as a powerful weapon which could be used in the promotion and the defense of basic Christian teachings. This new and growing appreciation for the power and use of fiction led to a growth in the publication of Christian fiction, especially during the second half of the nineteenth century.[11]

In summary, the appearance of theological/historical novels in the nineteenth century revealed that while some Evangelical Christians remained firm in their opposition to the use of fiction in any form, others resolved to utilize it for the advance of God's kingdom on earth. Their willingness to use fiction proved that they had come to terms with the power and popularity of novels in their day. In addition, the willingness of some Christian groups to use fiction in their polemics with other Christians confirmed that they were confident in the power of fiction to persuade.

---

[10] Amos Cooper Dayton, *Theodosia Ernest, Or, Ten Day's Travel in Search of the Church* (Philadelphia: American Baptist Publication Society, [1857]; reprint ed., Nappanee, IN: The Baptist Bookshelf, 1996), vii-viii.

[11] This growth in the publication of Christian fiction, especially after 1840, was in large part due to the establishment of publishing houses by mainline Christian denominations. Three Christian denominations actively involved in publishing Christian fiction during the latter half of the nineteenth century were the Baptists, the Methodists, and the Presbyterians. For more specifics on this, see Jan Blodgett, *Protestant Evangelical Literary Culture and Contemporary Society*, 23-25.

A Survey of Some of the Nineteenth-Century Theological/Historical Novels used in Credobaptist/Paedobaptist Polemics

Having seen the literary significance of the appearance of theological/historical novels in the nineteenth century, we will now focus on the use of fiction by both credobaptists and paedobaptists in their polemics over the subject of baptism. The most effective way to do this is to survey briefly several of the novels written during this period, with particular attention to the way that fiction was used to convey theological/historical arguments.

Theodosia Ernest, Or, The Heroine of Faith (1856)[12]

One of the earliest theological/historical novels to appear in defense of credobaptism was *Theodosia Ernest, Or, The Heroine of Faith*, written by Amos Cooper Dayton (but originally published anonymously).[13] Dayton wrote this novel to show that immersion, not sprinkling or pouring, is the divinely appointed mode for baptism in the New Testament and that only believers in Christ are the proper subjects for baptism.[14] It was also written to expose the spiritual evils of paedobaptism.

---

[12] This book was first published in 1856 by Graves, Marks and Company of Nashville, TN. Prior to this, it appeared in serial form in the *Tennessee Baptist* newspaper beginning on December 1, 1855.

[13] According to Leo T. Crismon, *Theodosia Ernest, Or, the Heroine of Faith* was not the first theological/ historical novel written by a Credobaptist. In 1854, Joseph Banvard (1810-1887) wrote *Priscilla; or trials for the truth. An historic tale of the Puritans and the Baptists*, published in Boston, MA. (I was not able to obtain a copy of this book for review). See Leo T. Crismon, "General Literature of the Baptists," *Baptist History and Heritage* (August 1965): 62. James E. Taulman, however, identifies *Theodosia Ernest, Or, the Heroine of Faith* as the first theological/historical novel written to disseminate Baptist doctrine from the South. James E. Taulman, "The Life and Writings of Amos Cooper Dayton (1813-1865)," *Baptist History and Heritage* (Jan. 1975): 43.

[14] Amos Cooper Dayton (also known as A. C. Dayton) was a former Presbyterian, a dentist by profession, but he eventually left dentistry and became a writer and editor. He was a frequent contributor to the *Tennessee Baptist*. He later served as an associate editor of the *Tennessee Baptist* (May, 1858 to October, 1859)

To present a moving and persuasive case for the credobaptist position, *Theodosia Ernest, Or, The Heroine of Faith* relates the fictional account of a Presbyterian girl who desires to know if she has been properly baptized, after witnessing a group of Baptists baptizing by immersion in a nearby river.[15] She requests the help of her fiancé, mother, uncle, and minister (all are Presbyterians), but none of them can give her the answers that she is looking for. In time Theodosia and her associates turn to a Baptist minister (who was once a Presbyterian) and he agrees to meet with them over a series of evenings to find out what the Bible teaches regarding baptism. By the end of the sixth evening, Theodosia is convinced of the credobaptist position, requests baptism, and is baptized on the next day; despite opposition from her fiancé, her minister, and others. In addition, Theodosia's resolve to obey Christ and to be baptized properly inspires others to continue their investigations into the subject of baptism; no matter what it costs. Eventually, Theodosia's fiancé, mother, uncle, and aunt seek membership in the Baptist church and are baptized as believers by immersion.

---

and the *Baptist Banner* (1863-64). Besides *Theodosia Ernest*, Dayton wrote other books, such as the polemical book *Pedobaptist and Campbellite Immersion* (1858) and the fictional book *Emma Livingston, the Infidel's daughter; or Conversations upon Atheism, Infidelity, and Universalism* (1859). As for his theological views, Dayton was a Landmark Baptist. For a good definition of Landmark Baptists, see H. Leon McBeth, "Landmark Baptists," in *Dictionary of Baptists in American*, ed. Bill J. Leonard (Downers Grove, IL: InterVarsity Press, 1994), 166-67. Dayton's influence as a writer and editor within the Landmark Baptist movement was so significant that McBeth called Dayton the third member of the "Landmark Triumvirate"; the other two men were J.R. Graves (1820-1893) and J.M. Pendleton (1811-1891). See H. Leon McBeth, *The Baptist Heritage* (Nashville: Broadman Press, 1987), 449. W.W. Barnes described Dayton as the "sword bearer" of the Landmark movement, with J.R. Graves the "warrior" and J. M. Pendleton the "prophet." William Wright Barnes, *The Southern Baptist Convention: 1845-1953* (Nashville: Broadman Press, 1954), 103. For more complete information on Dayton, see McBeth, *The Baptist Heritage*, 434-435, 448-450; Taulman, *The Life and Writings of Amos Cooper Dayton (1813-65)*, 36-43.

[15] Dayton surely intended to use symbolism in the name which he chose for his main character, Theodosia Ernest. Since Theodosia means "love of God," and she was earnest in her quest for the truth, Theodosia Ernest lived up to her name perfectly.

A 'Novel' Approach to Credobaptist and Paedobaptist Polemics

The major arguments in *Theodosia Ernest, Or, The Heroine of Faith* against the practice of paedobaptism are: (1) the mode used by paedobaptists (sprinkling or pouring) is not the biblical mode, (2) paedobaptism was not the practice of the early church, but was introduced later, and (3) those who practice paedobaptism are either ignorant of the Bible and of church history, or rebels against the commands of Christ.[16] In addition, Dayton accuses paedobaptist leaders, especially "Doctors of Divinity," of keeping most of the members of paedobaptist churches in ignorance regarding the right mode and subjects of baptism.

Theodosia Ernest, Or, Ten Day's Travel in Search of the Church (1857)[17]

Identified on its title page as the second volume of the *Christian Heroine Series*, Dayton continues the story of Theodosia Ernest (now married and the wife of a Baptist preacher) as she and her husband begin another search for truth.[18] Only in this volume, their search is not over the question of baptism, but over the question of which church, of the many churches in existence, is the true church of Jesus Christ.

In the story, Theodosia and her husband are traveling on a steamboat to Nashville when they encounter a fellow passenger who is confused over which church is the true church. Theodosia and her husband begin an investigation into this question with this passenger, but they soon seek assistance from the same Baptist minister who had assisted them earlier, and who just happens to be on the same steamboat with them. Over the next nine days, the

---

[16] The Baptist preacher who helps Theodosia and her associates goes so far as to proclaim that "the baptism of an infant is an act of high-handed rebellion against the Son of God." Amos Cooper Dayton, *Theodosia Ernest, Or, The Heroine of Faith* (Philadelphia: American Baptist Publication Society, [1866]), 319.

[17] This novel was first published in 1857 by Graves, Marks and Rutland of Nashville, TN. Later, it was combined with *Theodosia Ernest, Or, The Heroine of Faith* and published in one volume.

[18] Theodosia's husband was her fiancé in *Theodosia Ernest, Or, The Heroine of Faith*. Shortly before their marriage, he revealed that he felt called to the ministry, and she gladly consented to be a Baptist minister's wife.

Baptist minister leads this group and some occasional listeners, including a Protestant Episcopal bishop and a Methodist elder, through a study of the nine marks of a true church of Jesus Christ, eventually insisting that the Baptist church is the only church that possesses all nine of these marks.[19] The Baptist minister is not successful in winning the minds and hearts of all his listeners, but by the end of the story, the passenger, who first started the search with Theodosia and her husband, is fully persuaded that the Baptist church is the only true church of Jesus Christ, and he is baptized at the next meeting of a Baptist church near his home in Nashville.[20]

In this novel, Dayton's criticism of paedobaptists goes beyond what he asserts in the first novel of the *Christian Heroine Series*. Not only are paedobaptists unbiblical in their practice of infant baptism, but their churches are not true churches of Jesus Christ, since they do not display all the marks of a true church as defined in Scripture.[21] Thus, paedobaptist churches possess no authority to baptize or to ordain men to the ministry. The rightful authority to perform these solemn, sacred acts belongs to Baptist churches only.

---

[19] These nine marks are not listed here. However, a diagram of these marks, and how the Baptist church displays them all, is located in A. C. Dayton, *Theodosia Ernest, Or, Ten Day's Travel in Search of the Church* (Philadelphia: American Baptist Publication Society, 1886, reprint ed., Nappanee, IN: The Baptist Bookshelf, 1996), 480. It must also be pointed out that the teaching that Baptist churches are the only true churches is a major tenet of Landmarkism. For more information on this teaching, see McBeth, *The Baptist Heritage*, 450-53. Since this novel, and its predecessor *Theodosia Ernest, Or, The Heroine of Faith*, incorporated Landmark teachings into their story lines, James Tull credits these theological/historical novels with popularizing the characteristic tenets of Landmarkism. James E. Tull, *The Shapers of Baptist Thought* (Valley Forge, PA: Judson Press, 1972), 131.

[20] This passenger is identified in the story as Dr. Thinkwell. Apparently, he was given this name because he thoughtfully considered the arguments offered to him by Theodosia, her husband, and the Baptist preacher and did well by coming to the Baptist position.

[21] This includes the Roman Catholic Church, the Episcopal Church, the Methodist Episcopal Church, the Free Methodist churches, the Presbyterian Church, the Congregational churches, and the Lutheran Church.

A 'Novel' Approach to Credobaptist and Paedobaptist Polemics

Theophilus Walton; Or, The Majesty of Truth (1858)[22]

Subtitled *A Reply to Theodosia Ernest*, this novel was the first fictional contribution by nineteenth-century Methodists in their polemics against those who opposed paedobaptism. Written by "A Member of the Alabama Conference," it tries to refute the many arguments made against non-immersionist baptism and the Methodists in the *Christian Heroine Series*, published by the Baptists.[23] It also appeals for more charity and catholicity between Christian churches, as opposed to the exclusivist practices of the Baptists.[24]

Theophilus Walton; Or, The Majesty of Truth tells the story of a promising young man who risks his inheritance and the love of his fiancé in his quest to find out the truth about baptism.[25] Theophilus

---

[22] This novel was first published for the author in 1858 by Stevenson & Owen of Nashville, TN.

[23] Although the novel indicates that it was written by "A Member of the Alabama Conference," the actual author of the novel was William Pope Harrison (1830-1895). Harrison was a minister and scholar in the Methodist Episcopal Church, South. He wrote *Theophilus Walton; Or, The Majesty of Truth* when he was 28 years of age and an active member of the Alabama Conference. Harrison later served as president of the Auburn Female College, chaplain in the United States House of Representatives, Book Editor of the Methodist Episcopal Church, South, and Editor of the *Quarterly Review* (1882-1894). He was also twice elected Secretary of the General Conference, the highest governing council of his Church. In addition to his fictional work *Theophilus Walton; Or, The Majesty of Truth*, Harrison wrote two nonfiction books in defense of Methodist doctrine/practice, *A High-Churchman Disarmed: A Defense of our Methodist Fathers* (1886) and *The Scriptural Mode of Baptism* (1888). For more information on the life and character of William Pope Harrison, see Warren A. Chandler, *High Living and High Lives* (Nashville and Dallas: Publishing House of the M. E. Church, South, 1902), 159-70.

[24] The exclusivist practices most criticized are the Baptists' refusal to accept sprinkling and pouring as valid modes of baptism, and their refusal to allow their members to take the Lord's Supper in non-Baptist churches. The refusal to accept sprinkling or pouring is practiced by almost all Baptist groups. However, the refusal to allow Baptist Church members to partake of the Lord's Supper in non-Baptist churches is more characteristic of Landmarkism.

[25] The name Theophilus means "friend of God." The main character, therefore, is portrayed as a friend of God, while Baptists are portrayed as opposing the unity and cooperation that God desires among his churches.

A 'Novel' Approach to Credobaptist and Paedobaptist Polemics

(who was raised in Baptist circles, but became disillusioned with the Baptists) is attending the Methodist church and is about to request baptism by immersion.[26] However, when a Baptist minister in town begins to disrupt the unity of the churches by preaching against paedobaptism, Theophilus feels compelled to study further the question of immersion versus pouring. To find the answers that he is seeking, Theophilus participates in a series of evening meetings held by the minister of the Methodist church on the subject of baptism, as well as some informal meetings held by that same minister's daughter for the purpose of exposing errors in the Baptist novel, *Theodosia Ernest*.[27] Over the course of these meetings, Theophilus becomes convinced that immersion is not the biblical mode of baptism, and that baptism by pouring, as it is practiced by the Methodists, is the correct mode. Theophilus' change of mind regarding baptism, however, does not come without threats of retaliation. His father, a Baptist, threatens to disinherit him if he joins the Methodist church, and his fiancé's father, a local Baptist minister, tries to force his daughter to withhold her love if Theophilus becomes a Methodist. Yet, in the end, Theophilus holds firm to his beliefs regarding baptism, gains assurance from his fiancé that she will remain faithful to him, reveals he is called to ministry, and is baptized by the minister of the Methodist church.

As for its portrayal of credobaptists, this novel portrays them in a very poor light. Not only are they wrong regarding the biblical mode of baptism, they are also arrogant, disturbers of the peace among the churches, and manipulative. If they cannot convince others of their views, they condemn them and break fellowship with them. If one of their members dares to share the Lord's Supper with other Christians in non-Baptist churches, he is forced to trial

---

[26] Theophilus was disillusioned with the Baptists because they placed too much emphasis on immersion as the only mode of baptism. Theophilus was going to request baptism by immersion because it was the only baptism that he knew and he had yet to begin his study on the subject of immersion versus pouring.

[27] For the criticisms of *Theodosia Ernest*, see William Pope Harrison, *Theophilus Walton; Or, The Majesty of Truth* (Nashville: Southern Methodist Publishing House, 1859, reprint ed., Nashville and Dallas: Publishing House of the M.E. Church, South, 1904), 46, 79-91, 140-48, 185-95, and 239-46.

A 'Novel' Approach to Credobaptist and Paedobaptist Polemics

and commanded to repent upon threat of excommunication. Thus, credobaptists exhibit few, if any, of the spiritual virtues that foster true unity and cooperation among Christ's churches, regardless of denomination.[28]

Common Objections to the Baptist Denomination Considered and Replied To *(1860)*

This novel, identified on the top of its title page as "Prize Essay No. 2 of the Southern Baptist Sabbath School Union," was written by Miss Mary Jane Welsh of Selba, Mississippi.[29] Its main purpose was to answer nine objections against Baptists which were commonly voiced by paedobaptists during the period.[30] A second purpose was to exhort Baptist readers to remain firm in their convictions despite any persecution they might receive.[31]

---

[28] It is clear that the credobaptists in this novel were adherents of Landmarkism. They are referred to once in this novel as "Baptists of the Graves Stamp" (244).

[29] According to McBeth, the Southern Baptist Sabbath School Union (SBSSU) was founded in Nashville in 1857 by a group of Landmark Baptists led by J. R. Graves and A. C. Dayton. It helped to polarize Southern Baptists, fanning a major theological controversy. The SBSSU, plus the paper edited by Graves, the *Tennessee Baptist,* helped spread Landmarkism throughout the West and Southwest. The SBSSU later was decimated in the Civil War and eventually ceased operations. McBeth, *The Baptist Heritage*, 435. Apparently, the SBSSU held essay contests and *Common Objections to the Baptist Denomination Considered and Replied To* was one of the prizewinners. It was first published in book form in 1860 by the St. Louis Baptist Publishing Company. As for the author, Miss Mary Jane Welsh of Selba, MS, I could not find any information about her, except that she lived from 1846-1875.

[30] These nine objections are that (1) Baptists are of recent origin, (2) Baptists are ignorant, (3) Baptists are bigots--rejecting other churches and their baptisms, (4) Baptists are poor, (5) Baptists practice illiberality and close communion, (6) Baptists exclude non-Baptists from their pulpits, (7) Baptists allow indecency in their baptisms, (8) Baptists can be rightly charged with drunkenness, and (9) Baptists are stingy.

[31] The last paragraph of the book states, "Now, my young readers, you will in the course of your life, hear many hard things said of the Baptists, but take nothing for granted. Search the Bible to see if these things are so; examine our doctrines by that standard alone and not by systems of men. Never return railing for railing, or

To provide a story-line for its defense of the Baptist denomination, this novel tells a fictional story about the Blackwell family. This Baptist family holds a week of evening discussions in their home after their eldest son hears someone in town speaking abusively of the Baptists. During these discussions, Mr. Blackwell, the head of the family, answers most of the common objections voiced against the Baptists to the entire family's delight and satisfaction. Also present at some of these meetings are two men who work for Mr. Blackwell. These men express their own concerns and objections against the Baptists; however, by the end of the week's discussions, they are convinced of the Baptist position and join the local Baptist church through believer's baptism by immersion. Thus, the Baptist cause is not hindered by the unfair objections of its opponents, but continues to be furthered as the truth is told.

As for its portrayal of paedobaptists, it accuses them as being of a much more recent origin than the credobaptists, and of being persecutors and false accusers of Christ's true church. For these reasons, paedobaptists are guilty of much greater crimes against God and mankind than those which Baptists are unfairly accused of committing.

William the Baptist (1877)[32]

The most significant theological/historical novel published by the Presbyterians during the last half of the nineteenth century was *William the Baptist*.[33] James McDonald Chaney wrote this novel

---

persecution for persecution, but, like our Savior, forgive your enemies, and pray for them, even though they persecute you unto death. Be sure you are right; that your doctrines, and practices are supported by the Scriptures; then be FIRM (capitalization original)." Miss Mary Jane Welsh, *Common Objections to the Baptist Denomination Considered and Replied To* (St. Louis: St. Louis Baptist Publishing Company, 1860), 210.

[32] This novel was first published in 1877 by the Presbyterian Committee of Publication, Richmond, VA.

[33] This novel is the most significant because of its popularity and the number of times it has been reprinted since its first publication. This will be discussed more under the last heading.

A 'Novel' Approach to Credobaptist and Paedobaptist Polemics

primarily to communicate, in a plain and simple way, the scriptural case for paedobaptism and for baptism by sprinkling.[34] However, there are also hints that the author was responding, at least in part, to positions set forth in earlier credobaptist publications.[35]

William the Baptist relates the story of a young, promising lawyer from a Baptist upbringing who desires to unite in membership with a Presbyterian church of which his new wife has long been a member; only he insists that his baptism into the church be by immersion only.[36] However, the minister of this Presbyterian church refuses to baptize William by immersion on the ground that he does not believe that immersion in water is the scriptural mode of baptism. This refusal does not satisfy William, and so he begins

---

[34] James McDonald Chaney (1831-1909) was a minister in the Southern Presbyterian Church, officially known as the Presbyterian Church in the United States (PCUS). He pastored several churches and served as president of the Female Institute of Lexington, MO (1871-1876) and the Ladies College of Independence, MO (1885-1891). In addition to writing *William the Baptist*, Chaney wrote three other fictional works; *Agnes, daughter of William the Baptist, or The Young Theologian*; *Poliopolis and Polioland, or a Trip to the North Pole*; and *Mac and Mary, or the Young Scientist*. (I am indebted to Mr. Wayne Sparkman, the director of the PCA Historical Center in St. Louis for this biographical information on James McDonald Chaney). Regarding his plain style and appeal to the Scriptures in *William the Baptist*, Chaney wrote, "What people want is, not a learned discourse in the classic meaning of words in a language that they know nothing, but a simple exposition of the passages in the Bible with which they are familiar." James MacDonald Chaney, *William the Baptist* (Richmond, VA: Presbyterian Committee of Publication, 1877, reprint ed., Greenville, SC: Reformed Academic Press, 1994), 2.

[35] One hint that the teachings of the Landmark Baptists were on Chaney's mind is found on p. 94. Here the main character, William, reveals that he has adopted the Paedobaptist view on baptism in Romans 6:2-4, and by doing so, "the old landmarks had been removed." Doubtless, this was a not so veiled reference to Landmark Baptist teachings, which had been popularized in a book entitled *An Old Landmark Reset* (1854) by Landmark Baptist leader, J. M. Pendleton. Another hint that Chaney was responding to Landmark Baptist views is a reference to a lexical work by Professor Moses Stuart, a notable Paedobaptist scholar, which had been republished by Graves, Marks & Company of Nashville (a Landmark Baptist publishing company) and which was being used by Landmark Baptists in the nineteenth century to support their claims.

[36] Chaney first describes young William as "a most zealous Baptist, proselyting in his disposition, always ready to contend for the peculiarities of this church, even to a disagreeable degree." Chaney, *William the Baptist*, 6.

to meet with the Presbyterian minister over the course of seven evenings to discuss the case against immersion and in favor of baptism by sprinkling. During these discussions, William gradually comes to the conviction that immersion is not the scriptural mode of baptism and that he needs to be baptized by the correct mode. Thus, just two weeks after their discussions cease, William is baptized by sprinkling and gladly unites with the Presbyterian church. Shortly afterward, William also meets with the minister over the subject of paedobaptism, and he is soon convinced that "the denial of infant baptism, and the refusal to receive it as a divine command, is taking away from what God has given us to observe."[37]

As for its evaluation of credobaptists, this novel is far more restrained than earlier paedobaptist novels, such as *Theophilus Walton, Or, The Majesty of Truth*. Credobaptists are not portrayed in this novel as being arrogant, disturbers of the peace, or manipulative. However, they are accused of misinterpreting key passages of Scripture on baptism, and of relying far too often on the wrong sources in their defense of their positions.[38] Thus, credobaptists are portrayed as needing to return to the Word of God, so that they might re-examine their teachings on baptism and to determine if they are correct or not.[39]

---

[37] Chaney, *William the Baptist*, 131.

[38] These wrong sources are Greek lexicons and quotes from paedobaptist commentators who appear to be sympathetic to Baptist views on immersion. These sources, according to the author of *William the Baptist*, mean nothing, if the Bible is wholly ignored.

[39] It should be noted that a fictional response to *William the Baptist* was published in 1888 by the American Baptist Publication Society. This novel, written by "a Baptist woman," is entitled *William the Baptist's Aunt: a sequel and reply to William the Baptist.*" I was not able to obtain a copy of this novel for review, nor could I find any information as to its story line or content. However, I think that it would be safe to assume that William the Baptist's aunt is or becomes a heroine for the Baptist cause.

A 'Novel' Approach to Credobaptist and Paedobaptist Polemics

Agnes, daughter of William the Baptist, or, The Young Theologian *(1894)*

Also written by James McDonald Chaney, this novel was published by the Presbyterians in 1894, seventeen years after the publication of *William the Baptist*.[40] *Agnes, daughter of William the Baptist, or The Young Theologian* builds on the basic story-line found in the first novel, but does not lay out a detailed case for paedobaptism or try to refute the teachings of Baptists.[41] Rather, while there is an appeal for the practice of paedobaptism based on a Presbyterian understanding of covenant theology, the novel's purpose is to show that the children of believers are, by birth, rightful members of the church of Jesus Christ, and are capable of learning the truths of Scripture, so as to become, in their own right, young theologians.

As for the story-line, this novel relates the story of young Agnes, William the Baptist's daughter, as she begins to question her minister whether she is old enough to be a Christian and a member the Presbyterian church that her family attends.[42] The minister assures Agnes that she is already a member of the church and that she has been from birth, because she is the daughter of believing parents. Yet, he also makes it clear that salvation is not something that she received at birth, nor at her baptism as an infant, but is something that God works in his people through regeneration. Agnes informs the minister that she already possesses assurance that she is a true Christian, and shares her desire to know more about the Bible.

At this point, the minister agrees to meet periodically with Agnes and to teach her the basic truths of Scripture. Thus, over the course of these meetings, the minister instructs Agnes on such vital

---

[40] This novel was published in 1894 by the Presbyterian Committee of Publication, Richmond, VA.

[41] In fact, the only direct reference to the Baptists is a negative remark about a Baptist preacher who was "specially severe in his denunciation of the notion that morality can, in any degree, be a foundation for a hope of acceptance with God." James MacDonald Chaney, *Agnes, daughter of William the Baptist, or, The Young Theologian* (Richmond, VA: Presbyterian Committee of Publication, 1894), 96.

[42] Agnes is 13 years old at the time of this discussion.

topics as the authority of Scripture, the sinfulness of man, the fallen condition of mankind, the active and passive obedience of Christ, the state of believers in this life and the next, and predestination. At one point in the discussions, a young friend of Agnes also joins them, and shortly thereafter uses what she has learned to instruct her own father on the way of salvation. In the end, the minister commends his young students for being apt scholars, admonishes them not to cease their studies, and suggests that as a group they might renew their studies in the future, if the Lord so wills.[43]

Agnes, daughter of William the Baptist, or, The Young Theologian is the least polemic of all the theological/historical novels from the nineteenth century surveyed in this study. The tone is not critical or defensive. However, its fictional story-line makes an emotional case for the cause of paedobaptism.

Some Responses to these Theological/Historical Novels

Now that we have surveyed the content of some of the theological/historical novels written during the nineteenth century, it would be helpful to consider some of the responses that these novels received by both critics and supporters during the same period. Unfortunately, I was unable to find written responses to all of the novels surveyed in this study.[44] However, several of these novels did receive written responses from critics, and several were so well-received by supporters that they were promoted widely and reprinted often.

---

[43] The closing paragraph of this book implies that a continuation of the story might be forthcoming. However, to the best of my knowledge and research, James MacDonald Chaney never wrote another book, fiction or non-fiction, after this one.

[44] Although I researched the matter thoroughly, I could not find written responses, critical or supportive, to *Common Objections to the Baptist Denomination Considered and Replied To* or to *Agnes, the daughter of William the Baptist, or, The Young Theologian*. It is possible that no responses to these novels were ever written. It is also possible that responses were written, but that they have not been preserved.

Critical responses

The first novel from credobaptists to garner critical reviews was *Theodosia Ernest*.[45] This novel fired the first volley in the battle of novels between credobaptists and paedobaptists; and so, it received the most criticisms of any of the novels surveyed. The first critical review of *Theodosia Ernest* was written by Nathan Lewis Rice.[46] While editor of *The St. Louis Presbyterian* newspaper, Rice wrote a critical review of *Theodosia Ernest* simply entitled, "Notice of Theodosia." Rice says that *Theodosia* is instructive and amusing; but that it suffers from several peculiarities. First, Rice argues that *Theodosia* shows throughout the weakness of the Baptist doctrines that it is intended to advocate and promote. Instead of laying out the case for immersion from the Scriptures, the author of *Theodosia* made a heroine of a sensitive young girl of eighteen who simply wants to do what is right; thus, trying to get as much sympathy from his readers as possible.[47] Second, Rice says that *Theodosia* was not fair and honest in its portrayal of paedobaptists. Instead of responding to the actual arguments made by them to support their practices, the novel made up arguments that it can easily refute.[48]

---

[45] From this point forward in this study, all references to *Theodosia Ernest* refer to *Theodosia Ernest, Or, The Heroine of Faith* and *Theodosia Ernest, Or, Ten Day's Travel in Search of the Church* in one volume.

[46] Nathan Lewis Rice, D.D. (1807-1875) was a popular minister and editor in the Southern Presbyterian Church. He was a beloved pastor, founder of *The Western Protestant* newspaper, editor of *The St. Louis Presbyterian* newspaper, and the author of several books. The *Encyclopedia of the Presbyterian Church in the United States of America*, 1884, 761, eulogized Rice as follows, "Dr. Rice was truly a great man. He impressed all who heard him preach, the most cultured and the most cultivated, with a sense of his power. He was great in intellect, great in labors, great in goodness."

[47] Rice wrote, "The author of the novel judged rightly that the cause of immersion and anti-paedobaptism claims all this sympathy and more. If he had been a hero, instead of a youthful heroine, his hearers would have weighed his arguments, instead of being carried away with sympathy." Nathan Lewis Rice, "Notice of Theodosia" in *Theodosia Ernest, Or, The Heroine of Faith* (Philadelphia: American Baptist Publication Society, 1866), 420.

[48] Rice wrote, "It [the novel] keeps out of view the facts and arguments on which Paedobaptists rely, or caricatures them to make them appear ridiculous. It

Third, Rice states that the author of *Theodosia* used fiction to defend his views because his views are fictional in themselves and could not possibly prevail against real-life Presbyterians.[49] Thus, in Rice's view, the novel revealed that credobaptists were incapable of defending their views in real-life, and that the cause of anti-paedobaptism seemed to be "on its last legs."

It was not long, however, before credobaptists responded to Rice's review. A short time later, Dayton reviewed Rice's "Notice of Theodosia." Dayton's response was promoted by its publisher as "the most powerful argument in favor of Baptist positions" when read in connection with Dr. Rice's notice.[50] Dayton once again used fiction to argue his case; only this time, he inserted Rice into his fictional account. In the story, the author recalls a dream in which he saw the minister who had tried unsuccessfully to convince Theodosia Ernest to remain a paedobaptist reading a copy of Dr. Rice's review, and becoming upset about the way that he was portrayed.[51] Thus, he decides to go to St. Louis to talk with Dr. Rice. Once he meets him, the minister informs Dr. Rice that he has done more to destroy his confidence, and that of his congregation, than

---

puts into their mouths arguments they never use. It manufactures history to suit the occasion." Rice, *Notice of Theodosia*, 433.

[49] Rice wrote, "The author could not successfully assail *real, living* Presbyterians; and therefore, being resolved on battle and a victory, he manufactures a few to suit him, and then chooses their weapons for them, and directs them on how to use them, so they will be sure not to hurt them. Brave man! Don Quixote was scarcely his equal." Rice, *Notice of Theodosia*, 433 (emphasis original).

[50] The published name of this review is *A Dream, in Review of N.L. Rice's Notice of the Theodosia Ernest*. Although the review does not include the author's name, it seems apparent that this review was written by A. C. Dayton since it continues the story of *Theodosia Ernest* and is based on some of the same characters. When he published the review in 1857, J. R. Graves said it (combined with Rice's notice) was the "most powerful argument in favor of Baptist positions." To read the review, see A. C. Dayton, "A Dream In Review of N. L. Rice's Notice of Theodosia Ernest," in *Theodosia Ernest* (Philadelphia: American Baptist Publication Society, [1857]), 419-23.

[51] This minister is named Mr. Johnson. He is upset because Rice declared in his review that the minister was "a fool," and that so much so, that "there is not so great a fool in our whole denomination." See Dayton, *A Dream*, 428. To compare with Rice's actual remarks about the minister, see Rice, *Notice of Theodosia*, 421.

A 'Novel' Approach to Credobaptist and Paedobaptist Polemics

all of the Baptists' arguments that he has heard. On hearing this report, Rice appeals to the minister not to have a falling out with his friends, but to work together with him to try to refute the Baptist arguments. Dr. Rice also suggests that a good way to destroy the influence of the Baptists would be to ridicule them. So Dr. Rice and the minister begin working on their responses to the Baptist arguments, but after a short while, the minister concludes that Dr. Rice has no integrity or reasonable answers, and he decides to go home. Once he is home, the minister begins to study the Scriptures for himself and reaches the conclusion that he has been wrong. Not long after this, this former paedobaptist minister requests baptism from a Baptist minister and is baptized in a nearby river. As soon as they come out of the water, the author of the review awakens, and he wonders if it really was a dream.

As creative as this review of Rice's notice was, it did not put an end to paedobaptist criticisms of *Theodosia Ernest*. Shortly after the publication of Dayton's review of Rice's "Notice of Theodosia," Robert Lewis Dabney wrote a book critiquing *Theodosia Ernest*, expressing his disdain over the way that credobaptists slighted Rice's notice.[52] This book, entitled *A Review of Theodosia Ernest*, criticized the novel in several ways. First, Dabney declared that *Theodosia Ernest* was hardly worth criticizing because of its style and the feebleness of its arguments.[53] Second, he stated that *Theodosia Ernest* misrepresented Presbyterians to make them sound intolerant, stupid, easily deceived, and manipulated by their

---

[52] Robert Lewis Dabney has already been mentioned. It is not surprising that Dabney wrote a critique of *Theodosia Ernest*, given his earlier published remarks about the dangers of novel-reading. Dabney's *A Review of Theodosia Ernest* first appeared as a series of articles in the *Central Presbyterian* (June and July, 1859) and eventually went through three editions in book form. I was not able to obtain copies of the first or second editions of this book, but used the third edition (printed in 1869 by Shepperson and Graves of Richmond, VA).

[53] Dabney's actual words were, "The paltry style, the literary blunders, and the feeble argument of this work which our gallantry requires us to leave nameless, place it beneath criticism." Robert Lewis Dabney, *A Review of Theodosia Ernest* (Richmond, VA: Shepperson and Graves, 1869), 6.

A 'Novel' Approach to Credobaptist and Paedobaptist Polemics

teachers.⁵⁴ Third, he accused Dayton of trying to create anger in Immersionists against Presbyterians by using wild assertions and flimsy arguments.⁵⁵ Fourth, he criticized Dayton's use of fiction to communicate sacred truth.⁵⁶ Fifth, he asserted that *Theodosia Ernest* sought to take advantage of the "gullibility" of mankind.⁵⁷ Dabney viewed *Theodosia Ernest* in the worst possible light, and he pleaded that any fair discussion of sacred truth should not be denigrated to the level of fiction.

As far as other critical responses are concerned, we should note that, in their efforts to refute paedobaptism, credobaptists not only directed criticisms against the Presbyterians, but also against the Methodists and their writings. One example of the type of criticisms that credobaptists directed at Methodists is found in a book written in response to *Theophilus Walton; Or, The Majesty of Truth*. This book, entitled *Baptist facts against Methodist fictions*, also was written by Dayton.⁵⁸ He believed that the author of *Theophilus Walton; Or, The*

---

⁵⁴ Dabney wrote, "The tenour of both of these works (*Theodosia Ernest* and *A Dream*) is to represent Presbyterians as given to persecution, intolerant, ignorant of the reasons of their own faith, and almost stupidly foolish in their defense of them, an easy prey to proselyters, and priest-ridden by their doctors of divinity." Dabney, *A Review of Theodosia Ernest*, 8.

⁵⁵ Dabney wrote, "We denounce, therefore, with deserved indignation, this odious, false and wicked attempt to create angry blood in Immersionists against Presbyterians. Heaven knows, there is heat enough already, while the question of baptism is debated in the fiery and reckless spirit of this novel. Its unholy purpose, it seems, demanded the inflaming of bad passions, in order to blind its readers to the wildness of its assertions and the flimsiness of its arguments." Dabney, *A Review of Theodosia Ernest*, 17.

⁵⁶ Dabney wrote, "And, indeed, what is the intrinsic absurdity of sending Christian people to hunt for *truth* (and that sacred truth,) in a *work of fiction*? It is an insult to the understanding of readers; and a disgrace to the denomination which is judged to need such a mode of defense. No seeming triumph gained over an imaginary antagonist can prove anything; for, as the same author constructed both his adversary's argument and his own, of course he would make the victory fall on his side." Dabney, *A Review of Theodosia Ernest*, 19-20 (emphasis his).

⁵⁷ Dabney wrote of *Theodosia Ernest*, "The whole enterprise is a calculation on the gullibility of mankind; and it must be confessed, a calculation which was certain of realization to a large degree." Dabney, *A Review of Theodosia Ernest*, 23.

⁵⁸ The book *Baptist facts against Methodist fiction* was published in 1859, just one year after the release of *Theophilus Walton; Or, The Majesty of Truth*. It was

Majesty of Truth had unfairly and inaccurately criticized *Theodosia Ernest* and he wanted to restate the facts in defense of that work. In his attempt to do so, Dayton made some admissions and claims. First, he admitted that he may have made some mistakes in history and reasoning in *Theodosia Ernest*, but those mistakes had not been deliberate.[59] Second, he said that he did not use fiction because a non-fictional approach was more useful to his purpose: which was to provide more proofs and facts to support the claims made in *Theodosia Ernest*.[60] Third, Dayton stated that *Theophilus Walton; Or, The Majesty of Truth* contained many misstatements of simple facts, misstatements which could only be the result of lying, deceit, or bad memory.[61] Fourth, he complained that the author of *Theophilus Walton; Or, The Majesty of Truth* had accused him of dishonesty over what had turned out to be a simple typographical error.[62] Fifth, he provided additional facts and proofs to support the claims made in

---

published by the South-Western Publishing House: Graves, Marks and Co. in Nashville. Obviously, since this book was published by J. R. Graves, it teaches Landmark Baptist doctrines.

[59] Dayton wrote concerning himself, "From ignorance in some areas, and careless in others, he may have unconsciously done wrong to the truth of history or to the reasonings of an opponent." A. C. Dayton, *Baptist facts against Methodist fictions* (Nashville: South-Western Publishing House: Graves, Marks and Co., 1859), 5.

[60] Dayton wrote, "We therefore determined to enlarge our design somewhat, and to present to our readers *in another form*, with copious proofs, those facts which had been relied upon in Theodosia, and which had been disputed and perverted by this writer." Dayton, *Baptist facts against Methodist fictions*, 6 (emphasis mine).

[61] Dayton was willing to credit it to the latter. He wrote, "We take it for granted that the man intended to tell the truth, but that a treacherous memory deceived him." Dayton, *Baptist facts against Methodist fictions*, 9.

[62] The author of *Theophilus Walton; Or, The Majesty of Truth* had accused Dayton of being dishonest, since one of Dayton's references could not be found in the original source. However, Dayton replied that the problem was not dishonesty, but that he had simply failed to insert some quotation marks where they needed to be. Dayton wrote, "The charge of 'dishonesty,' against the author of *Theodosia*, based on the omission of some extra quotation marks, which, if they had been inserted, would not at all have modified the sense of the extracts. . . comes with ill grace from one who is so careless in his own statements." Dayton, *Baptist facts against Methodist fictions*, 62.

Theodosia Ernest. These facts and proofs occupy the bulk of the book.

These critical responses demonstrate how hotly debated the subject of baptism was in the nineteenth century. In addition, they show that much of the love and respect that had existed between these groups two centuries earlier had sadly deteriorated into inflamed rhetoric and harsh accusations.[63] Thus, it seems highly likely, that while some credobaptists and paedobaptists probably grew more steadfast in their beliefs from having to respond to criticisms, these critical responses did little to foster good relations between them. Instead, they most likely strengthened the animosities which already existed between these groups.

Positive responses

Many of these novels were greeted positively. Yet, determining the nature and extent of these responses is difficult. With several of them, there is no record of how they were received, even by those who were supportive of the positions advocated.[64] With others, the only information on record is the number of times the novel was reprinted.[65] In the case of one novel, there is enough information on record to reveal how positively it was received and why.[66] In the following paragraphs, we will consider only those novels which have some record as to how they were received, either in terms of published copies or reprints.

We start with the novel with the most information on record – *Theodosia Ernest*. According to the *Encyclopedia of Southern Baptists*, this novel quickly went through several editions; 14,000 selling in

---

[63] For an example of the kind of love and respect that seventeenth-century credobaptists showed their paedobaptist brethren, see the preface to the Second London Confession. This preface is located in William L. Lumpkin, *Baptist Confessions of Faith* (Valley Forge, PA: Judson Press, 1959), 244-48.

[64] These novels are the credobaptist novel, *Common Objections to the Baptist Denomination Considered and Replied To*, and the paedobaptist novel, *Agnes, daughter of William the Baptist, Or, The Young Theologian*.

[65] These novels are the paedobaptist novels, *Theophilus Walton, Or the Majesty of Truth* and *William the Baptist*.

[66] This novel is *Theodosia Ernest*.

A 'Novel' Approach to Credobaptist and Paedobaptist Polemics

the first month and 18,000 in the first year.[67] By 1858, two years after the first volume was released, the second volume had reached its 28th edition.[68] In addition, it was in great demand across the Atlantic, being printed in at least two other languages.[69] Several factors clearly contributed to this success. First, it appeared at a time in history when there was an increasing interest in fiction.[70] Second, it contained enough drama and romance to keep the novel appealing and interesting.[71] Third, the novel was written at a level that appealed to the common people, many of whom had little education.[72] Fourth, it provided simplistic answers to a complex

---

[67] J. Clark Hensley and Homer L. Grice, "Amos Dayton Cooper," *Encyclopedia of Southern Baptists*, ed. Norman Wade Cox (Nashville: Broadman Press, 1958), 352. While these sales figures may seem low by today's standards, they were impressive for a theological/historical novel in the nineteenth century. Concerning the number who read the book, James E. Tull wrote, "In the late 1850's, and for three or four decades thereafter, many thousands of Baptists all over the South read *Theodosia Ernest*." James E. Tull, *Shapers of Baptist Thought*, 131.

[68] Hensley and Grice, *Encyclopedia of Southern Baptists*, 352. We should recall that *Theodosia Ernest* was published in two volumes before it was combined into one.

[69] William Cathcart, writing in 1888, stated that this novel was "received with unusual favor and rapidly ran through several editions, whose popularity is now evinced by its being sought for on both sides of the Atlantic." William Cathcart, editor, "Rev. A.C. Dayton, M.D." In *Baptist Encyclopedia* (Philadelphia: Louis H. Everts, 1881; reprint ed., Paris, AR: The Baptist Standard Bearer, 1998), 320.

[70] This point was made more fully earlier in this article.

[71] In the case of this novel, the romance between Theodosia Ernest and her fiancé, along with the drama over whether Theodosia's change in convictions would end their planned marriage, gave readers a reason to be interested in the book, despite its seemingly endless number of quotes from Greek lexicons, Church histories, and commentators. Regarding the use of drama and romance in *Theodosia Ernest*, Dabney wrote, "He (the author) did not believe, it seems, that his principles were important and interesting enough, to make Christian people read an honest and straightforward discussion of them for its own sake: he must needs sugar the nauseous dose, to make it go down." Dabney, *A Review of Theodosia Ernest*, 19.

[72] Dabney remarked that *Theodosia Ernest* had evidently "gotten up for the million" (Dabney, *A Review of Theodosia Ernest*, 6) since it appealed so directly to the masses, instead of educated, thinking people. Yet what Dabney saw as a weakness of the book turned out to be one of its greatest strengths. It had been written for the people in the pews, and the people in the pews loved it.

A 'Novel' Approach to Credobaptist and Paedobaptist Polemics

theological debate.[73] Fifth, it reinforced a distrust of "learned clergy" and ministerial education, sentiments that were already spreading among some Baptist groups at that time.[74] Yet, despite its weaknesses, *Theodosia Ernest* gave voice to many popular Baptist sentiments and had a profound impact on Baptist thinking in the late nineteenth century.[75] Interest in this book even continued into the early twentieth century, and other novels by credobaptists (patterned after the style of *Theodosia Ernest*) began to surface addressing other important theological controversies.[76] Thus, the evidence shows that this novel was a literary success in the late nineteenth and early twentieth centuries and that it was gladly received by many of its readers; the majority of whom were probably sympathetic to the credobaptist position before reading the book.

---

[73] The debate between credobaptism and paedobaptism had been going on for centuries prior to the release of *Theodosia Ernest*, and some of the greatest minds in Church history had participated in these debates. Yet, the author of *Theodosia Ernest* suggests that the answers to the debate are so simple that a teenage girl, with her Bible in hand, can discover them before her minister, church, and denominational leaders and teachers can.

[74] Concerning *Theodosia Ernest*, McBeth writes, "the book abounds with subtle antiintellectualism, with many a sharp dig at 'learned clergy' and 'doctors of divinity.' The clear message of the book is that ministerial education is dangerous." McBeth, *The Baptist Heritage*, 449.

[75] McBeth, *The Baptist Heritage*, 450.

[76] In fact, the continuing demand for *Theodosia Ernest* in the early twentieth century was large enough to inspire the American Baptist Publication Society in Philadelphia to reprint it in 1902 and in 1903. One theological/historical novel which appeared in 1908, and which successfully employed the same fictional style as *Theodosia Ernest*, was entitled *Mabel Clement*. This novel by Baptist author, J. M. Sallee, was written against the doctrines of former Baptist, Alexander Campbell (1788-1866) and his followers. It was advertised as "an anti-dote for all the pernicious heresies of those who believe in salvation by works, salvation by water, salvation by grace and works, falling from grace and open communion." J. M. Sallee, *Mabel Clement* (1903: reprint ed., Asland, KY: Economy Printers, 1956), introduction. Concerning the influence of this novel, John R. Gilpin, Editor of *The Baptist Examiner*, wrote, "It is doubtful if any book printed on American soil has influenced more people for God and the Truth of His Word, as held by Baptists, than has this book." J.M. Sallee, *Mabel Clement*, introduction. Yet Gilpin does not give an estimate, or an actual figure, of how many copies of *Mabel Clement* were published or sold by the time of his writing.

A 'Novel' Approach to Credobaptist and Paedobaptist Polemics

Two other novels, both by paedobaptist writers, were also received positively; if the number of times that they were reprinted is a fair indication. These novels were *Theophilus Walton; Or, The Majesty of Truth* and *William the Baptist*. *Theophilus Walton* was first printed in 1858, and then reprinted seven times over the next forty-six years.[77] This number of reprints suggests that *Theophilus Walton* was clearly in demand in Methodist circles, and that they viewed it as an effective polemic for their views. *William the Baptist* was also reprinted numerous times. From 1877 to 1920 it was reprinted at least five times by Presbyterian publishers.[78] In addition, the novel was also reprinted several times during the mid-to-late twentieth century; strongly indicating that it was still valued for its polemical force a full century after it was written.[79]

Conclusion

The purpose of this study has been to determine the significance and influence of a series of theological/historical novels written by credobaptists and paedobaptists during the nineteenth century. These novels employed fiction as a vehicle for communicating arguments in support of doctrine. This method was obviously seen as an effective way to conduct polemics in an age when many

---

[77] The Southern Methodist Publishing House in Nashville reprinted the novel in 1859, 1860, 1885, 1886, 1888, and 1893. The Publishing House for the M.E. Church, South, reprinted the novel once more in 1904.

[78] I say "at least five times" here because it is possible that the book was reprinted more times than this. These are the only known reprints of *William the Baptist* during the 19th Century. Mr. Wayne Sparkman of the PCA Historical Center in St. Louis states that there could have been more reprints. The publishers and dates of these reprints were, Virginia Conference Depository, Richmond, VA (1877); Presbyterian Board of Christian Education, Philadelphia (1877, 1902); M.R. Wright Printing Co., Independence, MO (1886); Presbyterian Committee of Publication, Richmond, VA (1892).

[79] Twentieth-century reprints of *William the Baptist* were published by the Committee of Publications of the Bible Presbyterian Church, Walker, IA (1950-1959?); Department of Publication, Reformed Presbyterian Church Evangelical Synod, Wilmington, Delaware (1965-1982); Reformed Academic Press, Greenville, SC (1994).

readers wanted more than mere theological arguments; they also wanted an entertaining story.

We have seen that the appearance of these novels was quite significant. At a time when the majority of Christian sentiments were against the use of fiction in any form (and especially not as a means of communicating sacred truth), these novels appeared, revealing that the attitudes of many Christians toward fiction had changed. Many Christians now viewed fiction, righteously used, as an effective tool for defending truth and satisfying the tastes of readers.

In addition, we have seen that these novels exercised considerable influence in their day. One of them, *Theodosia Ernest*, became a powerful polemic for the credobaptist cause on both sides of the Atlantic. Several of the paedobaptist novels have been reprinted numerous times as their usefulness was rediscovered. Thus, the use of theological/historical novels by credobaptists and paedobaptists alike during the nineteenth century signaled a new way of thinking about how polemics should be done. No longer were polemics limited to debates or textbooks; now the truth was to be taken to the people in a form that they enjoyed.

A 'Novel' Approach to Credobaptist and Paedobaptist Polemics

CHAPTER 9
The Fatal Flaw of Infant Baptism: The Dichotomous Nature of the Abrahamic Covenant
Jeffrey D. Johnson, D.Min.*

Baptist covenant theology, Michael Horton, and twenty minutes are three things which, considered individually, might not make you nervous. Yet when all three are combined, it becomes a different story.[1] Recently I was given the special privilege to speak alongside Dr. Michael Horton at the 2012 *Semper Reformanda* conference (hosted by Voddie Baucham and Grace Family Baptist Church) on the differences between credobaptist and paedobaptist covenant theology. In this joint session, Horton and I were each allotted twenty minutes to explain the uniqueness of our particular covenantal position, and then another five minutes to give our respective rebuttals. Horton was to represent paedobaptist covenant theology, while I was asked to represent credobaptist covenant theology.

Twenty minutes is not a lot of time to speak upon such a weighty and controversial subject. To make things even more difficult, I realized there likely would be some in the audience who were being introduced to covenant theology for the first time. I therefore wanted to keep things simple while still getting to the

---

*Jeffrey D. Johnson, D.Min., is the author of *The Fatal Flaw of the Theology Behind Infant Baptism*, *The Church: Why Bother?*, *Behind the Bible: A Primer in Textual Criticism*, and *The Kingdom of God: A Baptist Expression of Covenant and Biblical Theology*. He is a regular contributor to the Reformed Baptist Blog and is the pastor of preaching at Grace Bible Church in Conway, Arkansas (gbcconway.com), where he resides with his wife, Letha, and their two sons, Martyn and Christian.

[1] Most of the material presented in this essay has been taken from my book, *The Kingdom of God: a Baptist Expression of Covenant and Biblical Theology* (Conway, AR: Free Grace Press, 2014) and is used with permission.

heart of the fatal flaw of the theology behind infant baptism. My goal was to be direct, clear, and pointed in my explanation of the basic error of paedobaptist covenant theology, consequently highlighting the uniqueness of Baptist covenant theology.

As I contemplated how best to accomplish my objective, I knew I needed to stay clear of many of the peripheral issues attached to the debate, such as household baptisms and the lack of a New Testament mandate. These things are important, but they are only secondary issues that often only bog down the conversation. I also wanted to stay clear of the typical Baptist approach of only talking about the newness of the New Covenant, because I do not believe that issue gets to the true heart of the debate.

The fundamental difference between Baptist and paedobaptist covenant theology, in my opinion, is each system's position on the relationship between the covenant of grace and Abraham's infant children. No doubt, when the New Covenant replaced the Old Covenant, there were some major changes. The New Covenant is not merely a new administration of the covenant of grace that is now restricted to believers only. No, Baptist covenant theology is different from paedobaptist covenant theology in its claim that unbelieving infants were never members of the covenant of grace. The covenant of grace, in both the Old and New Testament periods, has always consisted of believers, and believers alone.

The fundamental reason paedobaptists baptize their children is rooted in the presupposition that the Abrahamic Covenant, which included the physical offspring of those already in the covenant, is merely an administration of the covenant of grace. Reformed paedobaptists may disagree among themselves about the nature of the Old Covenant and the degree to which the New Covenant differs from it, but they all firmly hold to the idea that the Abrahamic Covenant established the covenant of grace with believers and their infant children.

According to Baptist covenant theology, however, believers alone belong to the covenant of grace, and this was true even under the Abrahamic Covenant. Therefore, it was at this point that I felt that I should place my energy and focus. I needed to prove within twenty minutes that the Abrahamic Covenant did not incorporate

The Fatal Flaw of Infant Baptism: The Dichotomous Nature of the Abrahamic Covenant

Abraham's unbelieving children into the covenant of grace. If this could be proven, then the practice of infant baptism would be shown to have no biblical foundation. By explaining why the Abrahamic Covenant did not place unbelieving infants into the covenant of grace, my goal was not to only pinpoint the exact spot were the paedobaptist covenantal system unravels, but to also show the unique cohesiveness of Baptist covenant theology.

The Dichotomous Nature of the Abrahamic Covenant

It is overly simplistic to view the Abrahamic Covenant as merely an administration of the covenant of grace. There is no doubt that the promises were given to Abraham unconditionally. There is also no doubt that Abraham's faith in God's promises was accounted to him for righteousness (Gen. 15:6; Rom. 4:22). Furthermore, any of Abraham's descendants who trusted in the coming promised seed also would be justified by faith alone. Because of the fidelity of God, the fulfillment of the Abrahamic promises was certain (Gal. 3:18).

However, this is only one side of the story. Although the eternal blessings foreshadowed by the covenant were unconditional for believers like Abraham, and these promised blessings were secured because of Christ's obedience, there is no textual or theological evidence indicating that Abraham's physical seed were naturally and automatically born into an unconditional covenantal relationship with God.

Rather, it was quite the opposite. Although Abraham's physical seed were born with the privilege of having access to the knowledge of the gospel, they also were born with a covenantal condition to fulfill – circumcision of the flesh. Without their obedience to this covenantal condition, the promises of the covenant, even the gospel itself, would go unfulfilled. The hope of the gospel was dependent upon the physical seed of Abraham keeping the condition. In short, the Abrahamic Covenant promised the covenant of grace by means of the physical seed of Abraham keeping a covenant of works.

Oh, how Israel and the rest of the world needed Christ! All of salvation depended upon the coming of this one promised seed. For blessing to be poured out upon the nations, Abraham's seed would have to fulfill the demands and curses of the law. Thankfully, Christ, the true promised seed of Abraham, did just that in his life and death, as proven by his resurrection.

Understanding the dichotomous nature of the Abrahamic Covenant is not something novel. Historically, the early Baptists of the seventeenth century understood that *both* the covenant of grace *and* the covenant of works were exhibited in the Abrahamic Covenant. The principle of the covenant of works was manifested in Abraham's physical seed while the covenant of grace was made known to and through Abraham's spiritual seed.

Particular Baptists such as Nehemiah Coxe, Robert Howell, John Spilsbury, Thomas Patient, Henry Lawrence, Philip Cary,[2] and Benjamin Keach taught that the Abrahamic Covenant consisted of two distinct parts: the physical and the spiritual.[3] For instance, Hercules Collins claimed, "We must know the Covenant made with Abraham had two parts…"[4] John Spilsbury remarked, "There was in Abraham at that time a spiritual seed and a fleshly seed. Between which seeds God has ever distinguished through all their Generations."[5] Henry Lawrence echoed this understanding of the dual nature of the Abrahamic Covenant, when he said, "Here you have a distinction as it were of two Abrahams, a begetting Abraham, and a believing Abraham, and also two seeds, the children of the flesh, that is by carnal generation onely, and the children of the promise."[6] Benjamin Keach stated, "God made a two-fold covenant with Abraham, and that circumcision appertained not to the covenant of grace, but to the legal covenant

---

[2] For an interesting account of the Philip Cary and John Flavel debate over the proper subjects of baptism, see Joel R. Beeke and Mark Jones, *A Puritan Theology: Doctrine for Life* (Grand Rapids: Reformation Heritage Books, 2012), 729-39.

[3] See Pascal Denault, *The Distinctiveness of Baptist Covenant Theology: A Comparison Between Seventeenth-Century Particular Baptist and Paedobaptist Federalism* (Birmingham, AL: Solid Ground Christian Books, 2013), 117-25.

[4] Denault, *Distinctiveness of Baptist Covenant Theology*, 117.

[5] John Spilsbury, *A Treatise Concerning the Lawful Subject of Baptisme*, (repr., Magazine, AR: The Old Faith Baptist Church, 1993), 31.

[6] Cited in Denault, *Distinctiveness of Baptist Covenant Theology*, 120-21.

God made with Abraham's natural seed..."[7] John Tombes, the seventeenth-century Anglican who opposed infant baptism, came to the same conclusion:

> The Covenant made with *Abraham*, is not a pure Gospel-covenant, but mixt, which I prove;
> The Covenant takes its denomination from the promises; but the promises are mixt, some Euangelicall, belonging to those to whom the Gospel belongeth, some are Domestique, or Civill promises, specially respecting the House of *Abraham*, and of *Israel*.[8]

Not only did the seventeenth-century Baptists understand the dual nature of Abraham's covenant; they also understood this dual nature to be the ground of the *continuity* and *discontinuity* of the rest of the divine covenants. It was for this reason Nehemiah Coxe stated:

> Abraham is to be considered in a double capacity: he is the father of all the true believers and the father and root of the Israelite nation. God entered into covenant with him for both of these seeds and since they are formally distinguished from one another, their covenant interest must necessarily be different and fall under distinct consideration. The blessings appropriate to either must be conveyed in a way agreeable to their peculiar and respective covenant interest. And these things may not be confounded without a manifest hazard to the most important articles in the Christian religion.[9]

---

[7] From the title of an unpublished book by Benjamin Keach, *The Ax Laid to The Root, or, One Blow at the Foundation of Infant Baptism, and Church Membership*, Part 1 (London: B. Keach, 1693).

[8] John Tombes, *Two Treatises; and an Appendix to them Concerning Infant Baptisme. The Former Treatise being an Exercitation presented to the Chair-man of a Committee of the Assembly of Divines. The latter an Examen of the Sermon of Mr. Stephen Marshall, about Infant-Baptisme, in a letter sent to him* (London: 1645).

[9] Coxe and Owen, *Covenant Theology*, 72-73.

The Fatal Flaw of Infant Baptism: The Dichotomous Nature of the Abrahamic Covenant

A Single Covenant with Two Dimensions

To help us understand why the seventeenth-century Baptists came to such a conclusion we must turn our attention to the nature of the Abrahamic Covenant.

The Abrahamic Covenant promised three basic things: (1) a land, (2) a kingship, and (3) a people (Gen. 17:6-8). Interestingly, a region of dominion, a king, and a people are the three major elements that constitute a kingdom. Thus, in essence, in the Abrahamic Covenant, God vowed to establish a kingdom through the seed of Abraham.

The Abrahamic Covenant can be spoken of as having two dimensions:

Natural Dimension
- ଊ Temporal
- ଊ Type
- ଊ Conditional

Supernatural Dimension
- ଊ Eternal
- ଊ Antitype
- ଊ Unconditional

It is important to note that the Abrahamic Covenant is not two covenants, but a single covenant. Like a coin, it is a single entity with two sides. These two sides, for the most part, coincide with the different emphases within the Old and New Testaments.

In the Old Testament, we see the unfolding and fulfillment of the physical and conditional side of the Abrahamic Covenant. The physical seed of Abraham inherited the physical land of Canaan, and they became a physical and geopolitical nation that was eventually ruled by the royal line of King David. The prosperity of this kingdom depended upon national obedience to God.

In the New Testament, we see the unfolding of a spiritual or heavenly kingdom. By faith, Abraham's spiritual seed inherit and secure a place in the heavenly kingdom. King Jesus, at his death and resurrection, began the process of taking dominion and subduing all things to himself.

Notwithstanding these differences in emphasis, we observe in both the Old and New Testaments the two dimensions of the kingdom of God, one natural and the other supernatural. We need to remember that both dimensions have their roots in the Abrahamic Covenant.

Physical Kingdom	Spiritual Kingdom
ೞ Natural	ೞ Supernatural
ೞ Canaan	ೞ Heaven
ೞ Physical Seed	ೞ Spiritual Seed
ೞ David's Royal Line	ೞ King Jesus
ೞ Israel	ೞ Christ & the Church

Dichotomous Covenants

To help explain the dichotomous nature of the Abrahamic Covenant, we only need to observe the unfolding of the covenantal history of redemption. After Adam sinned and broke God's law (the covenant of works), the curse of the law was poured out justly upon Adam and all his posterity. In Adam, all died. Universal depravity is the proof that all mankind has already been judged guilty in Adam. Out of this judgment, thankfully, came mercy and the promise of grace. The moment God issued forth judgment upon the world was the moment he also revealed the gospel to the world (Gen. 3:15). In judging the Serpent, the Lord vowed that the seed of the woman (i.e., the coming Messiah) would crush the Serpent's head. Therefore, from the very beginning, we see that grace comes out of judgment. The message is clear: if there is no judgment, there can be no grace.

The Covenantal History of Redemption

This is also true regarding salvation. Salvation is not free. We are justified by works, but the works that justify us are not our own. The high cost of our salvation was paid by Christ's own blood. The law could not be removed until it was fulfilled in both its conditions and penalties. For God to be just and the justifier of the ungodly, the legal demands of the law had to be satisfied (Rom. 3:21-26). A life of perfect, righteous obedience was needed. Therefore, salvation is free for the sinner but not for the Savior. Christ merited perfect righteousness by keeping the conditions of the law of God perfectly. He paid for his people's sins by taking on the curses of the law while upon the cross (Gal. 3:13).

Thus, we see the covenant of grace could not have been established without the full satisfaction and fulfillment of the covenant of works. After sin entered the historical narrative, it was not possible for the covenant of works and the conditions of the law to fade away. Rather, the demands of the law had to remain in force. If there had been no covenant of works to fulfill, then there could not have been a covenant of grace to reveal. Therefore, until the cross of Calvary, the covenant of works had to be a major component in the overall history of redemption.

What is a covenant? Basically, a divine covenant consists of the legal and binding terms of a relationship with God.[10] Since God is God, he sets the terms of the relationship. Because God is morally perfect, the terms of the relationship can be nothing other than perfect righteousness. Without righteousness, no one can see God. The consequence of sin is always separation from God. These terms never change. Therefore, reconciliation with God requires the establishment of perfect righteousness.

The covenant of works and the covenant of grace both contain the legal terms for a relationship with God. The covenant of works contains the terms of God's relationship with those outside of Christ, thus condemning its membership. The covenant of grace

---

[10] Walter Chantry defines a covenant as "a sovereignly given arrangement by which man may be blessed." See Walter Chantry, "The Covenants of Works and of Grace" in *Covenant Theology: A Baptist Distinctive* (Birmingham, AL: Solid Ground Christian Books, 2013), 91. Michael Horton defines a covenant as "a relationship of 'oaths and bonds' [that] involves mutual, though not necessarily equal, commitments." See Michael Horton, *God of Promise: Introducing Covenant Theology* (Grand Rapids: Baker Books, 2006), 10. O. Palmer Robertson likewise states, "This closeness of relationship between oath and covenant emphasizes that a covenant in its essence is a bond. By the covenant, persons become committed to one another." See O. Palmer Robertson, *The Christ of the Covenants* (Phillipsburg, NJ: P & R Publishing, 1980), 7.

The Fatal Flaw of Infant Baptism: The Dichotomous Nature of the Abrahamic Covenant

contains the terms of the relationship upon those in Christ, thus forgiving its membership. The law exists in both the covenant of works and the covenant of grace. However, the law is yet to be fulfilled for those in the covenant of works, and the law has already been fulfilled in Christ for those in the covenant of grace. As Walter Chantry observes:

> You live under either the Covenant of Works or the Covenant of Grace. There are none but these two... Under the Covenant of Grace, the identical demand must be met. No lesser obedience will be accepted. Under the Covenant of Works the curse pronounced for sin is death. Man sinned and death must be the result. Under the Covenant of Grace a Mediator must fulfill perfect righteousness for men who cannot provide it of themselves. The Mediator will also die under the curse of the Covenant of Works in the place of sinners. The heel of the Seed of the woman is bruised, "Christ hath redeemed us from the curse of the law, being made a curse for us..." (Gal 3:13). He did this not by abolishing law or by invalidating the Covenant of Works, but by "being made a curse for us." He met all the demands of the Covenant of Works. He fulfilled all its terms.[11]

Chantry also notes:

> The Lord required perfect and universal righteousness in both. The definition of righteousness is unchanged from the Covenant of Works to the Covenant of Grace. But in another sense everything is at opposite poles. In the Covenant of Works man must earn *by his doing*. In the Covenant of Grace, man must receive the free gift from a Mediator *by believing*.[12]

---

[11] Chantry, "The Covenants of Works and Grace," 103.
[12] Chantry, "The Covenants of Works and Grace," 97-98.

So then, there is no grace without judgment, and the overall history of redemption plays out these two covenants, one of works and one of grace, in which history finds its ultimate fulfillment in the cross of Calvary, where justice and mercy embrace.

The Davidic Covenant

Our effort to understand the dichotomous nature of the Abrahamic Covenant may be helped by observing a similar dichotomy in the Davidic Covenant. Was the Davidic Covenant a covenant of works or a covenant of grace? That is to say, was the promise to David conditional or unconditional? The answer depends upon who is asked. If we asked King David, he would respond by saying that the promise of an eternal kingship was unconditional. Yet if we asked any of David's children, they would have to answer by saying that they had been given a legal condition to obey.

These unconditional and conditional dimensions of the Davidic Covenant are clearly seen in Psalm 132:11-12:

> The LORD swore [*unconditionally*] to David a sure oath from which he will not turn back: 'One of the sons of your body I will set on your throne. If your sons [*conditionally*] keep my covenant and my testimonies that I shall teach them, their sons also forever shall sit on your throne.'[13]

David understood that although God would be faithful in fulfilling his promise to him, his royal line would be obligated to obey the Mosaic Law in order to remain upon the throne. For this reason, David sternly warned his son, Solomon, to obey God:

> When David's time to die drew near, he commanded Solomon his son, saying, "I am about to go the way of all the earth. Be strong, and show yourself a man, and keep the charge of the LORD your God, walking in his ways and

---

[13] Words in brackets are the present writer's. Scripture citations are from the ESV.

keeping his statutes, his commandments, his rules, and his testimonies, as it is written in the Law of Moses, that you may prosper in all that you do and wherever you turn, that the Lord may establish his word that he spoke concerning me, saying, 'If your sons pay close attention to their way, to walk before me in faithfulness with all their heart and with all their soul, you shall not lack a man on the throne of Israel.' (1 Kings 2:1-4)

Years later, Jeremiah reminded the sons of David that they were under the covenant of works:

> Thus says the Lord: "Go down to the house of the king of Judah and speak there this word, and say, 'Hear the word of the Lord, O king of Judah, who sits on the throne of David, you, and your servants, and your people who enter these gates. Thus says the Lord: Do justice and righteousness, and deliver from the hand of the oppressor him who has been robbed. And do no wrong or violence to the resident alien, the fatherless, and the widow, nor shed innocent blood in this place. For if you will indeed obey this word, then there shall enter the gates of this house kings who sit on the throne of David, riding in chariots and on horses, they and their servants and their people. But if you will not obey these words, I swear by myself, declares the Lord, that this house shall become a desolation. For thus says the Lord concerning the house of the king of Judah: "'You are like Gilead to me, like the summit of Lebanon, yet surely I will make you a desert, an uninhabited city. I will prepare destroyers against you, each with his weapons, and they shall cut down your choicest cedars and cast them into the fire. "'And many nations will pass by this city, and every man will say to his neighbor, "Why has the Lord dealt thus with this great city?" And they will answer, "Because they have forsaken the covenant of the Lord their God and worshiped other gods and served them."'" (Jer. 22:1-9)

Admittedly, it would have been pointless for God to give a promise to David that was dependent upon David's children keeping the law if it were not for the fact that the promise was speaking of Christ Jesus and his future obedience. Solomon succeeded David, but it was not Solomon whom God ultimately had in mind when he established the Davidic Covenant. Rather, it was Jesus Christ. For Christ was not only a descendant of David, he was the only descendant of David that perfectly kept the law, as evidenced by his resurrection from the dead.

Peter picked up this theme in his famous sermon on the day of Pentecost. After pointing out that David was convinced that one of his descendants would sit upon his throne forever, Peter went on to proclaim that this promise was fulfilled at the resurrection of Christ from the dead:

> Brothers, I may say to you with confidence about the patriarch David that he both died and was buried, and his tomb is with us to this day. Being therefore a prophet, and knowing that God had sworn with an oath to him that he would set one of his descendants on his throne, he foresaw and spoke about the resurrection of the Christ, that he was not abandoned to Hades, nor did his flesh see corruption. This Jesus God raised up, and of that we all are witnesses. Being therefore exalted at the right hand of God, and having received from the Father the promise of the Holy Spirit, he has poured out this that you yourselves are seeing and hearing. For David did not ascend into the heavens, but he himself says, "The Lord said to my Lord, 'Sit at my right hand, until I make your enemies your footstool.'" Let all the house of Israel therefore know for certain that God has made him both Lord and Christ, this Jesus whom you crucified. (Acts 2:29-36)

Christ, the son of David, is qualified to sit upon an everlasting throne because he was declared righteous in his resurrection. Without this legal righteousness, Christ would have remained in the grave, and the establishment of the kingdom, promised to Abraham and David, would not have been accomplished.

Many other parallels could be pointed out between the Abrahamic and Davidic Covenants, such as the types and antitypes, temporal and eternal elements, and the natural and supernatural dimensions of each. Nevertheless, this understanding of the unconditional and conditional sides of the Davidic Covenant is sufficient to help us better understand the dichotomous nature of the Abrahamic Covenant.

The important thing to note is that Abraham's physical seed belonged to the conditional side of the Abrahamic Covenant, and Abraham's spiritual seed belong to its unconditional side.

Conditional	**Unconditional**
☙ Canaan	☙ Heaven
☙ Kings of Judah	☙ King Jesus
☙ Physical Seed	☙ Spiritual

Understanding the dual nature of the Abrahamic Covenant is vital to understanding the *continuity* and *discontinuity* between the divine covenants. Ultimately, it helps us to answer two questions: *Who are the true people of God? What is the true nature of the kingdom of God?* In the remainder of this essay, we will attempt to prove the dichotomous nature of the Abrahamic Covenant by observing the wording, the fulfillment, the New Testament interpretation, and the two memberships of the Abrahamic Covenant.

The Wording of the Abrahamic Covenant

The first place to turn in understanding the nature and terms of the Abrahamic Covenant is to the canonical text in which the covenant was originally recorded. The promises and terms of the covenant are found in Genesis 17:6-14.[14] In this Scripture passage, we uncover the basic *unconditional* and *conditional* dimensions of the Abrahamic Covenant.

Unconditional promises

In verses 6-8, we notice the certainty and *unconditional* nature of these promises:

> *I will* make you exceedingly fruitful, and *I will* make you into nations, and kings shall come from you. And *I will* establish my covenant between me and you and your offspring after you throughout their generations for an everlasting covenant, to be God to you and to your offspring after you. And *I will* give to you and to your offspring after you the land of your sojournings, all the land of Canaan, for an everlasting possession, and *I will* be their God. (Genesis 17:6-8)[15]

The certainty of these promises is seen in the fact that it is God himself who has made them. The words "I will" are consistently repeated in these verses, and they are powerful words when coming from a God who cannot lie. Abraham trusted God, for he knew the foundation of the promises was based upon the fidelity of God. In this way, the promises were certain and unconditional to the one who received them.

Conditional promises

The language in the next few verses shifts away from certain fulfillment to the real possibility of some of Abraham's physical seed being "cut off" and separated from the people of God. In verses 9-14, we observe the *conditional* side of the covenant:

---

[14] While Gen.12:1-7; 15; and 17:1-21 are all important and relevant passages when speaking of the Abrahamic Covenant, at present the focus will center on Gen. 17:6-14.

[15] Emphasis is the present writer's.

The Fatal Flaw of Infant Baptism: The Dichotomous Nature of the Abrahamic Covenant

And God said to Abraham, "As for you, *you shall keep* my covenant, you and your offspring after you throughout their generations. This is my covenant, which *you shall keep*, between me and you and your offspring after you: Every male among *you shall be circumcised*. [...] Any uncircumcised male who is not circumcised in the flesh of his foreskin *shall be cut off* from his people; he *has broken* my covenant." (Gen. 17:9-10, 14)[16]

The language turns from "I will," to "you shall." The responsible party has shifted from God to Abraham and his physical seed. Even more telling is that this covenant is said to be *breakable*. Those who are not circumcised have "broken" the covenant. Even Moses almost died in the wilderness because he neglected his duty to circumcise his children (Exod. 4:24-26). In this, we see all the ingredients of a covenant of works: (1) a condition – circumcision; (2) covenant breakers – the uncircumcised; (3) covenant blessings and curses – being either united or "cut off" from God and his people.

The conditional nature of the Abrahamic Covenant would seem contradictory and pointless if it were not for the fact that the promised seed was restricted to only one "seed" in particular. However, since the promised seed was Christ, then both the promise and condition of the Abrahamic Covenant were certain to be fulfilled.

"Now the promises were made to Abraham and to his offspring. It does not say, 'And to offsprings,' referring to many, but referring to one, 'And to your offspring,' who is Christ" (Gal. 3:16). In other words, God *did not* promise Abraham that every physical descendant of his (i.e., Ishmael, Esau, and all his children from his second wife – Keturah) would be counted among the children of promise. Rather, the promised seed was in reference to one child in particular – Jesus Christ. Other than Jesus Christ, the rest of Abraham's physical descendants *were not given* any unconditional guarantee that they would not be "cut off" from the

---

[16] Emphasis is the present writer's.

The Fatal Flaw of Infant Baptism: The Dichotomous Nature of the Abrahamic Covenant

covenant. Paul made this clear when he said, "not all who are descended from Israel belong to Israel, and not all are children of Abraham because they are his offspring..." (Rom. 9:6b-7a).

Nevertheless, every physical descendant of Abraham, even Christ, was placed under the legal condition of obedience. However, as we shall see, Christ was the only physical seed of Abraham who kept the covenant. Thus, only Christ and those who are united to him by faith are the fulfillment of the promised seed.

The significance of circumcision

The condition of the Abrahamic Covenant was circumcision, yet this condition implied more than the outward cutting of the flesh. For example, the single command given to Adam and Eve not to eat of the forbidden fruit included full obedience to the moral law of God. The law demands that we love God with all of our heart, soul, and mind, and that we love our neighbor as ourselves (Matt. 22:37-40). By one act of disobedience, Adam broke the entire law (James 2:10). Adam's single act of rebellion displayed a fundamental lack of love for God and a lack of love for his neighbor.

In the same way, keeping the condition of circumcision implied more than one simple act of outward obedience. Rather, it symbolized full obedience of the law from the heart (Deut. 30:6). This was the assessment of the Lord Jesus: "Moses gave you circumcision (not that it is from Moses, but from the fathers), and you circumcise a man on the Sabbath. ...on the Sabbath a man receives circumcision, so that the law of Moses may not be broken..." (John 7:22-23).

Moreover, the apostle Paul understood that circumcision could not be disjoined from the law of God: "I testify again to every man who accepts circumcision that he is obligated to keep the whole law" (Gal. 5:3). "For circumcision indeed is of value if you obey the law, but if you break the law, your circumcision becomes uncircumcision" (Rom. 2:25).

This connection between circumcision and perfect obedience is not merely a New Testament understanding of circumcision, for even the Old Testament explained that the blessings of the

Abrahamic Covenant were contingent upon the righteousness of the physical seed of Abraham:

> The LORD said, "Shall I hide from Abraham what I am about to do, seeing that Abraham shall surely become a great and mighty nation, and all the nations of the earth shall be blessed in him? For I have chosen him, that he may command his children and his household after him *to keep the way of the* LORD *by doing righteousness and justice, so that the* LORD *may bring to Abraham what he has promised him.*" (Gen. 18:17-19)[17]

In other words, in order for the nations of the world to be blessed, the seed of Abraham was required not only to be circumcised, but also to be righteous.

Covenantal Presbyterians are correct, therefore, when they press the importance of the spiritual and inward significance of circumcision. Circumcision meant more than an outward act of obedience; it also signified the cutting away of the old fleshly nature and loving God from a renewed heart (Col. 2:11-12). For instance, G. K. Beale states, "Circumcision represented…the 'cutting off of the flesh' to designate that the sinful flesh around the heart was cut off, signifying the regeneration of the heart and the setting apart of a person to the Lord."[18] In essence, this means outward circumcision spoke of the need for the Jews to have a circumcised heart.

The problem, however, was that circumcision of the flesh did not promise, produce, or secure a circumcised heart. There was no saving efficacy in fleshly circumcision. In other words, fleshly circumcision demanded love for God but was unable to produce a love for God. This is why Moses told the unbelieving children of Abraham to circumcise the foreskins of their heart (Deut. 10:16).

---

[17] Emphasis is the present writer's.

[18] G. K. Beale, *A New Testament Biblical Theology: The Unfolding of the Old Testament in the New* (Grand Rapids: Baker, 2011) 812-13.

The Fatal Flaw of Infant Baptism: The Dichotomous Nature of the Abrahamic Covenant

Moses understood that outward circumcision alone was inadequate in setting apart a people for God.

Jeremiah also understood this (Jer. 4:4). He therefore warned the Jews that those who did not circumcise their hearts would be "cut off" from God: "Behold, the days are coming, declares the LORD, when I will punish all those who are circumcised merely in the flesh..." (Jer. 9:25).

The apostle Paul confirmed this Old Testament teaching by explaining the reason why outward circumcision alone was insufficient in producing the children of God:

> For no one is a Jew who is merely one outwardly, nor is circumcision outward and physical. But a Jew is one inwardly, and circumcision is a matter of the heart, by the Spirit, not by the letter. His praise is not from man but from God." (Rom. 2:28-29)

In short, being placed under the law of circumcision did not produce the ability to obey the law that was signified by circumcision.

Moreover, the impossibility of circumcising one's own heart did not nullify the responsibility for the Jews to love God with all their heart, mind, and soul. Moral inability does not render God's commands hypothetical; the condition is binding even if it is impossible. It is impossible to have a relationship with God without holiness (Heb. 12:14).

Therefore, as we have seen, circumcision explained that perfect righteousness was needed to have a relationship with God. For instance, because Abraham was circumcised after he believed, his circumcision was the "seal of the righteousness that he had by faith while he was still uncircumcised" (Rom. 4:11). In other words, *credocircumcision* signified the blessings of the law for those who have been given the imputed righteousness of Christ by faith. Yet for those who received circumcision without faith, their circumcision signified the righteousness that was still required of them. In other words, *paedocircumcision* signified the curses of the law that remained upon those without faith. As Beale acknowledges, circumcision also represented being 'cut off' from the Lord.[19] Thus, circumcision signified the blessing and curses of the law depending upon if it was administered with or without faith.

The good news is that even though circumcision placed the Israelites under unbearable demands they could not satisfy, they still had hope of salvation. The same covenant that demanded obedience also promised the gospel. By believing the unconditional promise that was given to Abraham, Abraham's physical children could legally be declared righteous. Like Abraham, they could be declared righteous apart from outward circumcision and apart from obedience to the law (Rom. 4:9-12). Abraham's physical seed could become Abraham's spiritual seed. By the Holy Spirit's gift of faith, their outward circumcision could be transformed into inner circumcision. By faith, the law that was externally engraven upon their flesh could be internally written upon their hearts.

Though Abraham's physical seed were born under the covenant of works, they were blessed with access to the gospel. By faith, apart from circumcision, the Jews could be declared righteous in Christ and receive the imputed reality of what was outwardly commanded of them by circumcision (Rom. 3).

However, it is important to note that even though salvation in the Old Testament was by grace through faith, there still remained the necessity for Abraham's physical seed (Christ Jesus) to keep the law. As it is written, salvation would come from the Jews (John 4:22). All hope for salvation in the Old Testament would be lost if this did not occur. To bring salvation and blessings to the nations, including the nation of Israel, the law had to be satisfied. The circumcision of the Abrahamic Covenant demanded that the heirs of the promises be holy and set apart before God. There was no way around this. This is why, although the Abrahamic Covenant promised the gospel, it also placed all of Abraham's physical seed under a covenant of works.

Thankfully, the seed of Abraham did come and fulfill the righteous demands of the law. "For I tell you that Christ became a

---

[19] Beale, *A New Testament Biblical Theology*, 812-13.

servant to the circumcised to show God's truthfulness, in order to confirm the promises given to the patriarchs, and in order that the Gentiles might glorify God for his mercy" (Rom. 15:8-9a). This is why Genesis 18:19 says the physical seed of Abraham had to "keep the way of the LORD by doing righteousness and justice, so that the LORD may bring to Abraham what he has promised him."

The Fulfillment of the Abrahamic Covenant

Not only does the wording of the Abrahamic Covenant reveal its dichotomous nature, but the actual working out and fulfillment of the covenant in redemptive history serve to verify its two-sided (conditional and unconditional) character.

Abraham's two seeds

The promises to Abraham concerning a coming kingdom were slowly and progressively fulfilled in the Old Testament in a conditional, typological, and temporal fashion. In the New Testament, the promised kingdom is being progressively established in an unconditional, antitypical, and eternal fashion. The physical descendants of Abraham were established into a geopolitical nation which eventually crumbled because of their disobedience. Abraham's spiritual seed, on the other hand, have been born again into a spiritual kingdom which is eternal because of the imputed righteousness of Christ to its citizenship.

However, these two kingdoms (physical and spiritual) do not represent two distinct and separate plans of God. Rather, these two kingdoms work together to fulfill God's overall covenantal plan of redemption. As we shall see, the physical kingdom foreshadowed, served, and eventually assisted in the establishment of the spiritual kingdom. Thus, the spiritual kingdom does not *replace* the physical kingdom, but rather *fulfills* it.

Abraham's two sons

The two-pronged fulfillment of the Abrahamic Covenant is immediately seen in the two sons of Abraham: Ishmael and Isaac. Ishmael was born of the flesh, while Isaac was born of the promise. These two children represent the two types of seeds (physical and spiritual) of Abraham (Gal. 4:21-31). According to the apostle Paul, Ishmael represents the physical descendants of Abraham that occupy the storyline of the Old Testament, while Isaac represents the spiritual children of Abraham that occupy the storyline of the New Testament.

- Ishmael = The Natural Seed of Abraham
- Isaac = The Supernatural Seed of Abraham

The physical seed are the *natural* children of Abraham; the spiritual seed are the *supernatural* children of Abraham. The physical seed were circumcised in the *flesh*; the spiritual seed have been circumcised in *heart*. The physical seed inherited an *earthly* land; the spiritual seed are heirs to a *heavenly* city whose builder and maker is God. The physical seed became a geopolitical nation, an *earthly kingdom*; the spiritual seed have been birthed into the *kingdom of God*.

The natural seed and the Mosaic Covenant

To understand the role of Abraham's natural offspring, we must keep in mind that the condition of the Abrahamic Covenant could not have been removed until it was fulfilled. Therefore, every physical descendant of Abraham, even Christ, was born under its legal and binding obligation, symbolized by circumcision. Circumcision was a boundary marker that separated Abraham's seed from the rest of the world and distinguished them as the family through which the Messiah would come. Those who were not circumcised were cut off from God and his people.

Yet, as we have seen, circumcision called for more than just the outward cutting of the flesh. It demanded circumcision of the heart.

A circumcised heart is the sign of the child of God, for inward *holiness*, not mere outward conformity, has always been the true identifying mark of God's people.

The problem, however, with all of Abraham's physical children, (excepting Christ) was that they were born with uncircumcised hearts. Due to their inward depravity, they were born already spiritually "cut off" from God. Being physically and outwardly circumcised children of Abraham did not change their legal standing before God (Rom. 2:6-29). Abraham's children may have been born privileged, having access to the gospel, but they were also born depraved. Because of Adam's sinful nature, which passed to them through Abraham, the children of Abraham were born into a state of condemnation and under the wrath of God (Rom. 3:9).

Thankfully, hope for salvation remained for the Israelites. As with Abraham and the rest of the believing remnant in the Old Testament, Abraham's physical seed could turn from trusting in their own righteousness by looking to and trusting in the coming Messiah. They could forsake all confidence in the flesh (which would include not trusting in their status as outwardly circumcised children of Abraham) and place their full confidence in the promised seed who would keep the condition of the covenant on their behalf. Like Abraham, an Old Testament Jew could certainly be saved, but it had to be by faith, not simply because they were Jewish.

To point Abraham's physical and fallen seed to the coming Messiah, God established the Mosaic Covenant with the house of Israel. The Mosaic Covenant was given to Israel to manifest their innate sinfulness (Rom. 3:20). The law was given, not to *save* the children of Israel, but to *condemn* them. That is, God gave them the law to help them see that they were already unrighteous and guilty before him (Rom. 3:19).

The law was also designed to be a schoolmaster to lead Israel to Christ (Gal. 3:21-25). The law was not given to nullify faith in the promise but to point Abraham's children away from faith in themselves (Gal. 3:22). Being circumcised children of Abraham was of no value to the Jews unless they could keep the whole law (Rom. 2:25). Therefore, the Law of Moses was instituted to call them to repent, and the promise to Abraham was given to call them to believe the gospel. "But the Scripture imprisoned everything under sin, so that the promise by faith in Jesus Christ might be given to those who believe" (Gal. 3:22).

In some ways, therefore, the Mosaic Covenant was unlike the Abrahamic Covenant. Yet in other ways, it was nothing more than the outworking of the covenant of works that had already been placed upon the physical seed of Abraham in Genesis 17:9-14.

The discontinuity between the Abrahamic and Mosaic Covenants

As the outworking of the conditional side of the Abrahamic Covenant, the Mosaic Covenant stood in direct contrast to the unconditional side of the Abrahamic Covenant. That is, unlike the Abrahamic Covenant, the Mosaic Covenant contained no unconditional promises (Gal. 3:16-18). For this reason, Moses made sure the Israelites understood the difference between law and promise when he distinguished the Mosaic Covenant from the Abrahamic Covenant:

> And Moses summoned all Israel and said to them, "Hear, O Israel, the statutes and the rules that I speak in your hearing today, and you shall learn them and be careful to do them. The LORD our God made a covenant with us in Horeb. Not with our fathers did the LORD make this covenant, but with us, who are all of us here alive today." (Deut. 5:1-4)

In distinguishing the Israelite children from the fathers (Abraham, Isaac, and Jacob), Moses highlighted the discontinuity between the Abrahamic and Mosaic Covenants. Abraham, Isaac, and Jacob were promised that the Messiah would be one of their personal descendants. Yet, after Israel was divided into twelve tribes, the average Israelite could not assume that he might be the father of the Messiah. What could be said of Abraham, Isaac, and Jacob – "in your seed all the nations of the earth shall be blessed" – could not be said for the children of Dan, Reuben, or the majority of the other

Israelites. The unconditional promise was established with the fathers, not with every physical child of Abraham.

The Mosaic Covenant was different from the Abrahamic Covenant in that it was established, not just with the direct genealogical line of Christ, but with every Israelite without exception. The Mosaic Covenant was a national covenant. The fathers were given a promise, while the nation of Israel was given the law.

Moreover, the promise given to Abraham was not to be confused with the law given by Moses. The law and the gospel are not the same. The Abrahamic Covenant promised the covenant of grace, but as we shall see, the Mosaic Covenant was a republication of the covenant of works. This was a major distinction between the Abrahamic and Mosaic Covenants.

The continuity between the Abrahamic and Mosaic Covenants

Yet it is the *discontinuity* between the promise of the Abrahamic Covenant and the law of the Mosaic Covenant that leads to the *continuity* between these two covenants. For instance, the promise of the Abrahamic Covenant was that the physical seed of Abraham would fulfill the law of the Mosaic Covenant and thus bring blessings to the nations. To understand the nature of the *continuity* between the Abrahamic and the Mosaic Covenants, we must remember that the oath that was established with Abraham, and personally reaffirmed with Isaac and Jacob, guaranteed that the coming Messiah would be one of their direct descendants (Gen. 26:2-5; 28:13-15). We must also keep in mind that, though the promise was given to the fathers, the condition was given to their children. In other words, the unconditional promise that God gave to Abraham, Isaac, and Jacob would not come to fruition unless their seed fulfilled the condition of the covenant.

The condition of the covenant was circumcision, but the full implications of circumcision remained murky until God gave the physical seed of Abraham the law at Mount Sinai. Importantly, the Mosaic Covenant did not replace, alter, or add to the condition placed upon the physical seed of Abraham in Genesis 17. It merely gave clarity to what was already required by circumcision. In other words, the Mosaic Covenant grew out of and codified the conditional side of the Abrahamic Covenant. There are at least five theological reasons why the law did not and could not replace, alter, or add to what was already demanded by circumcision.

First, the Mosaic Covenant was established with the physical children of Abraham – the same group of people who were placed under the conditions of the Abrahamic Covenant. If the Abrahamic Covenant had been purely a covenant of grace for the physical seed of Abraham, then it would have been unjust for God to place that same group of people under the Mosaic Covenant of works.[20] Therefore, the only way the covenant of works (republished in the Mosaic Covenant) could have been established with the physical seed of Abraham was for the physical seed of Abraham to have already been obligated to obey the moral law of God in the Abrahamic Covenant.[21]

Second, the covenantal blessings were conditional from the beginning of the Abrahamic Covenant, and they continued to be so under the Mosaic Covenant.

> Thou shalt therefore keep the commandments, and the statutes, and the judgments, which I command thee this day, to do them. Wherefore it shall come to pass, *if ye hearken to these judgments, and keep, and do them*, that the LORD thy God shall keep unto thee the covenant and the mercy which he sware unto thy fathers... (Deut. 7:11-12, KJV)[22]

---

[20] No doubt, within the Old Testament dispensation, there was a remnant of Jewish believers, the spiritual children of Abraham, who were subject to the legal regulations of the Mosaic Covenant. Though they were members of the covenant of grace by faith, they were outwardly under the Mosaic Covenant and were "enslaved to the elementary principles of the world" (Gal. 4:1-7).

[21] This is where paedobaptists who claim that the Mosaic Covenant is a republication of the covenant of works are inconsistent. According to these paedobaptists, the physical offspring of Abraham were born into the covenant of grace under the Abrahamic Covenant, but later they were placed into the covenant of works under the Mosaic Covenant.

[22] Emphasis is the present writer's.

The Promised Land, the eternal kingship, and the establishment of the people of God all were predicated on the fulfillment of the Mosaic Covenant.

> Now therefore, if you will indeed obey my voice and keep my covenant, you shall be my treasured possession among all peoples, for all the earth is mine; and you shall be to me a kingdom of priests and a holy nation. (Exod. 19:5-6)

Thus, the kingdom promised in the Abrahamic Covenant remained conditional under the Mosaic Covenant. Without the fulfillment of the Mosaic Covenant, the covenant promises to Abraham would go unfulfilled.

Third, obedience to the moral law of God was already the condition of the Abrahamic Covenant. About four hundred years prior to the establishment of the Mosaic Covenant, the Lord explained that the blessings promised to Abraham were predicated upon the obedience of the physical seed of Abraham:

> The LORD said, "Shall I hide from Abraham what I am about to do, seeing that Abraham shall surely become a great and mighty nation, and all the nations of the earth shall be blessed in him? For I have chosen him, that he may command his children and his household after him *to keep the way of the* LORD *by doing righteousness and justice, so that the* LORD *may bring to Abraham what he has promised him.*" (Gen. 18:17-19)[23]

Since the conditions listed in Exodus 19 are the same as the conditions that we read of in Genesis 18, it is evident that the Mosaic Covenant did not alter the terms of the blessings of the Abrahamic Covenant. Once the covenant was ratified with the physical seed of Abraham in Genesis 17, the terms and conditions of that covenant could not have been changed four centuries later.

---

[23] Emphasis is the present writer's.

Any alteration to the terms placed upon the physical seed of Abraham would have been unjust (Gal. 3:15).

Fourth, the New Testament teaches that the condition of the Mosaic Covenant was the same as the condition of the Abrahamic Covenant. "Moses gave you circumcision (not that it is from Moses, but from the fathers), and you circumcise a man…so that the law of Moses may not be broken…" (John 7:22-23). "For circumcision indeed is of value if you obey the law, but if you break the law, your circumcision becomes uncircumcision" (Rom. 2:25). "[I]f you accept circumcision, Christ will be of no advantage to you. I testify again to every man who accepts circumcision that he is obligated to keep the whole law" (Gal. 5:2-3). If circumcision was a sign and seal of the covenant of *grace*, then the Lord Jesus and the apostle Paul misspoke when they equated circumcision with the Mosaic *Law*.

Fifth, in Romans 3, Paul teaches that the physical seed of Abraham were privileged to have the gospel (Rom. 3:1-2), but ontologically and soteriologically they were no better off than the Gentiles who were condemned by the law (Rom. 3:9-18). Therefore, the physical seed of Abraham could not have been born into a covenant of grace, as some suppose, since Paul clearly states that the physical seed of Abraham were under the curse of the covenant of works (Rom. 3:19-20).

Again, if the blessings were *unconditional* for the physical seed in the Abrahamic Covenant, then it would have been unjust for God to make those same blessings *conditional* in the Mosaic Covenant. However, if the Abrahamic Covenant had already placed the physical children of Abraham under the obligation to obey the law of God, then the Mosaic Covenant did no injustice to the Israelites. The Mosaic Covenant simply added clarity to what was already demanded of them in the Abrahamic Covenant.

In seeking to comprehend the relationship between the Old and New Covenants, it is vital that we understand that the Abrahamic Covenant, although promising the covenant of grace, was a conditional covenant that was established with the physical seed of Abraham. The condition of the Abrahamic Covenant was clarified and codified in the Mosaic Covenant, and the gospel that was promised in the Abrahamic Covenant was contingent upon the fulfillment of the law of the Mosaic Covenant.

So far, we have seen that there are two seeds of Abraham. One was physical and under the obligation of a covenant of works; the other is spiritual, the heirs of the promises of the gospel.

The New Testament Interpretation of the Abrahamic Covenant

The dichotomous nature of the Abrahamic Covenant is not restricted to being gleaned only from the wording of the Abrahamic Covenant (Gen. 17:4-14). It is also clearly affirmed in the New Testament. In fact, the apostle Paul – the quintessential covenant theologian – had a lot to say about the relationship between the Old and New Testaments. Therefore, to further understand the nature of the Abrahamic Covenant, we now turn to the writings of Paul. As we shall discover, Paul understood and taught the dichotomous nature of the Abrahamic Covenant.

The two covenants of Abraham (Galatians 4:22-31)

In Galatians 4:22-31, Paul gives a quick and concise overview of his inspired view of the Abrahamic Covenant. Paul succinctly stated his position by explaining the allegorical differences between Abraham's two sons (i.e., Ishmael and Isaac), then went on to explain their analogous relationships with the two separate covenants that find their roots in Abraham. According to Paul, the first covenant was conditional and led to bondage, and the second covenant was unconditional and leads to freedom. The first covenant proceeding from Abraham was ultimately the Mosaic covenant of works delivered at Mount Sinai. The second covenant proceeding from Abraham is the ultimately the New Covenant of grace.

Paul began his allegory by claiming that Abraham's two wives, Sarah and Hagar, represent two different covenants:

> For it is written that Abraham had two sons, one by a slave woman and one by a free woman. But the son of the slave

was born according to the flesh, while the son of the free woman was born through promise. Now this may be interpreted allegorically: these women are two covenants. (Gal. 4:22-24a)

Paul demonstrated the typical nature of Abraham's two sons by showing how each of their mothers and the nature of their births were symbolic as well. Ishmael, the nature of his birth, and Hagar represent the covenant of works. Isaac, the nature of his birth, and Sarah represent the covenant of promise and grace.

According to Paul, the main difference between these two children was their mothers. Importantly, it was their respective mothers that determined which of the two received the promised inheritance. Being born of a free or slave woman determined if the child himself would be born into slavery or freedom.

According to Paul, Hagar, the mother of Ishmael, represents the conditional covenant made with Abraham. Ishmael's mother and the nature of Ishmael's birth depict a conditional covenant that leads to bondage. Just as Ishmael was born from Hagar, the slave woman, so it is for all those who are born into the covenant of works. Ishmael was born under the law and in slavery to the dominion of sin, as are all those who are born after the flesh (Rom. 6).

Ishmael also represents the covenant of works because of the nature of his birth, of which there was nothing supernatural. Ishmael's birth required no faith on Abraham's part, and therefore, he was *not* the child of promise. Similarly, just as Ishmael was *not* the promised 'seed,' so it is with all Abraham's physical children who are not born again by the Spirit, for there is nothing supernatural or spiritual for those born after the flesh. "That which is born of the flesh is flesh, and that which is born of the Spirit is spirit" (John 3:6). "This means that it is not the children of the flesh who are the children of God…" (Rom. 9:8).

The details of Isaac's birth were the opposite of Ishmael's. Isaac's mother represents the unconditional covenant of grace revealed to Abraham. Isaac was born (1) supernaturally, (2) by the free woman, and (3) according to the promise. In a sense, these characteristics are true for all those who have been born again by the Spirit into the covenant of grace.

In the verses above (Gal. 4:22-24), Paul focused upon the differences between the births of these two children. Although both of them were the physical children of Abraham and circumcised in the flesh, only one was the child of promise. This, being allegorical, shows the great difference between the covenant of works and the covenant of grace. Those who are born into the covenant of works are born slaves, while those born into the covenant of grace are born free.

The important thing to note, according to Paul, is that these two mothers are representative of "two covenants" (Gal. 4:24). Paul went on to explain how these different mothers (i.e., Hagar and Sarah) represent the difference between the physical seed and spiritual seed of Abraham. In so doing, Paul linked the physical seed with the covenant of works, while linking the spiritual seed with the covenant of grace.

> Now this may be interpreted allegorically: these women are two covenants. One is from Mount Sinai, bearing children for slavery; she is Hagar. Now Hagar is Mount Sinai in Arabia; she corresponds to the present Jerusalem, for she is in slavery with her children. But the Jerusalem above is free, and she is our mother. For it is written, "Rejoice, O barren one who does not bear; break forth and cry aloud, you who are not in labor! For the children of the desolate one will be more than those of the one who has a husband." Now you, brothers, like Isaac, are children of promise. (Gal. 4:24-28)

Hagar, the Arabian bondwoman, represents the physical seed of Abraham and the Mosaic Covenant of works, for "she is in slavery with her children." Hagar shows that the physical children of Abraham, those who were "born according to the flesh," were born into bondage under the dominion of sin. The historical covenant established with Abraham's physical seed was the Mosaic Covenant, and Paul linked the Mosaic Covenant with Hagar and her son, when he stated, "One is from Mount Sinai, bearing children for slavery; she is Hagar. Now Hagar is Mount Sinai in Arabia" (Gal. 4:24-25).

This is why the Lord told the Jews that, despite their Abrahamic heritage, they were actually born in slavery to sin (John 8:34-38). Thus, Paul concluded that unbelieving Jews were not any better off than the unbelieving Gentiles: "What then? Are we Jews any better off? No, not at all. For we have already charged that all, both Jews and Greeks, are under sin" (Rom. 3:9).

In contrast, Sarah represents the New Covenant. Sarah, unlike Hagar, was a free woman and the mother of the child of promise. Sarah represents "the Jerusalem above," which is also free, and the mother of Abraham's spiritual seed.

Just as the slave woman represents the Mosaic Covenant of bondage, the free woman represents the New Covenant of freedom. Just as Isaac was born free as the supernatural child of promise, so are the spiritual children of Abraham born free by their supernatural birth. This is in agreement with what Paul said earlier in Galatians: "And if you are Christ's, then you are Abraham's offspring, heirs according to promise" (Gal. 3:29).

Just as Abraham had two sons from two different wives, Abraham had two different seeds that were born from two different covenants, which are the Old and New Covenants, and the two seeds are his physical and spiritual children. This dual covenantal framework is in harmony with Paul's application and conclusion:

> But just as at that time he who was born according to the flesh persecuted him who was born according to the Spirit, so also it is now. But what does the Scripture say? "Cast out the slave woman and her son, for the son of the slave woman shall not inherit with the son of the free woman." So, brothers, we are not children of the slave but of the free woman. (Gal. 4:29-31)

The Two Memberships of the Abrahamic Covenant

The apostle Paul had a deep love for his own kinsmen. He was not ashamed of being a Jew, and he realized the Jewish people were born privileged. Yet Paul also knew being born from Jewish parents alone did not bring a child into the covenant of grace. Paul understood "that it is not the children of the flesh who are the children of God, but the children of the promise are counted as offspring" (Rom. 9:8). Paul knew even Jews had to be born again by the Spirit.

The physical seed and the covenant of works

As a race of people, Paul placed the physical children of Abraham in the same category as the Ishmaelites. According to Jonathan Edwards:

> They were rejected and cast off from being any longer God's visible people. They were broken off from the stock of Abraham, and since then have no more been reputed his seed than the Ishmaelites or Edomites, who are as much his natural seed as they.[24]

Ishmael was Abraham's physical seed, but he was not the child of promise. Because of this, after Isaac was born, Ishmael and his mother, Hagar, were driven out into the wilderness, for it is written: "Cast out the slave woman and her son, for the son of the slave woman shall not inherit with the son of the free woman" (Gal 4:30).

Although this was historically true for Ishmael, when Paul said, "The son of the slave woman shall not be heir with the son of the free woman," he was not referring to Ishmael or the Ishmaelites. Rather, he was referring to the *Israelites*, "the present Jerusalem." Just as Ishmael was not the seed God had in mind when he promised Abraham a son, the physical children of Abraham were never intended to be the children of promise (Rom. 9:8).

In point of fact, God commanded Abraham to drive Hagar and his own physical son Ishmael away into the wilderness. Abraham

---

[24] Jonathan Edwards, *A History of the Work of Redemption* (Edinburgh: Banner of Truth Trust, 2003), 297.

then deserted the Arabian bondwoman and her child, driving them out into the desert sands. In the same way, God has deserted the house of Israel: "See, your house is left to you desolate" (Matt. 23:38).

Just as the Mosaic Covenant was established in the desert, its members, because they were the children of bondage, were ultimately deserted there as well. This may sound harsh, but without the righteousness of Christ, no one will see God. Similarly, just as the full inheritance went to Isaac and not Ishmael, the kingdom promised to Abraham has been given solely to the spiritual seed of Abraham, while the unbelieving physical seed of Abraham have been completely cut off from the promised inheritance (Matt. 21:43).

Paul explained that for the same reason the Ishmaelites persecuted the Israelites, so now the Israelites are the persecutors of the church: "But just as at that time he who was born according to the flesh persecuted him who was born according to the Spirit, so also it is now" (Gal. 4:29). Just as Ishmael had no inheritance with Isaac, the nation of Israel has no spiritual inheritance with those who have been quickened together with Christ.

The spiritual seed and the covenant of grace

Abraham's physical children, because they were born by the works of the flesh, are the children of bondage. They are not the children of promise, for there was nothing supernatural about their birth. On the other hand, the spiritual seed of Abraham are the *true* fulfillment of the Abrahamic Covenant: "Now you, brothers, like Isaac, are children of promise" (Gal. 4:28). "And if you are Christ's, then you are Abraham's offspring, heirs according to promise" (Gal. 3:29). "So, brothers, we are not children of the slave but of the free woman" (Gal. 4:31). The Jerusalem from above is the mother of Abraham's spiritual seed, for believers have not come to Mount Sinai but to Mount Zion. They have come "to the city of the living God, the heavenly Jerusalem, and to innumerable angels in festal gathering, and to the assembly of the firstborn who are enrolled in heaven…" (Heb. 12:22-23).

With this in mind, we happily agree with Michael Horton when he correctly concludes:

> Personal obedience to commands is a radically different basis for an inheritance than faith in a promise. While the Scriptures uphold the moral law as the abiding way of life for God's redeemed people, it can never be a way to life. Every covenant has two parties, and we assume the responsibilities of faithful partners, but the basis of acceptance with God is the covenant-keeping of another, the Servant of the Lord: and because of his faithfulness, we now inherit all of the promises through faith alone, as children of Sarah and citizens of the heavenly Jerusalem.[25]

Conclusion

According to Paul, the physical seed of Abraham were not naturally born into the covenant of grace. Instead, Abraham's physical seed were born into the covenant of works. This means the true children of promise are only those who have been supernaturally born again by the Spirit of God. In other words, the promised children of Abraham are those who have the faith of Abraham. Apart from faith, the physical offspring of Abraham remain the children of darkness and will be condemned for their sins on the Day of Judgment. It is Abraham's spiritual offspring – the elect, believing church, consisting of regenerate saints throughout all history – who comprise the true people of God, and the fulfillment of the Abrahamic promise.

---

[25] Horton, *God of Promise*, 76.

Chapter 10
The Difference Between the Two Covenants
John Owen, D.D.*

> But now he has obtained a more excellent ministry, by how much also he is the mediator of a better covenant, which was established on better promises. (Heb. 8:6)[1]

There is no material difference in any translators, ancient or modern, in the rendering of these words; their significance in particular will be given in the exposition.

In this verse begins the second part of the chapter, concerning the difference between the two covenants, the old and the new, with the pre-eminence of the latter above the former, and of the ministry of Christ above the high priests on that account. The whole church-state of the Jews, with all the ordinances and worship of it, and the privileges annexed to it, depended wholly on the covenant that God made with them at Sinai. But the introduction of this new priesthood of which the apostle is discoursing, did necessarily abolish that covenant, and put an end to all sacred ministrations that belonged to it. And this could not well be offered to them without the supply of another covenant, which should excel the

---

* This is a slightly revised version of Owen's exposition taken from Nehemiah Coxe and John Owen, *Covenant Theology from Adam to Christ* (Palmdale, CA: RBAP, 2005) and is used with permission. The footnotes are the ones in the Coxe/Owen volume. Those bracketed with [ ] were provided by the editors of the Coxe/Owen volume.

[1] Νυνὶ δὲ διαφορωτέρας τέτυχεν λειτουργίας ὅσῳ καὶ κρείττονός ἐστιν διαθήκης μεσίτης ἥτις ἐπὶ κρείττοσιν ἐπαγγελίαις νενομοθέτηται

Exposition.- Turner remarks that νυνὶ, *now*, is not here so much a mark of time, as a formula to introduce with earnestness something which has close, and may have even logical, connection with what precedes. See also for this use of the term, ch. xi.16, 1 Cor. xv.20, xii.18, 20; in which passages it does not refer to time, but implies strong conviction grounded upon preceding arguments.- Ed. [Banner of Truth Edition.]

former in privileges and advantages. For it was granted among them that it was the design of God to carry on the church to a perfect state, as has been declared on chap. 7; to that end he would not lead it backward, nor deprive it of any thing it had enjoyed, without provision of what was better in its room. This, therefore, the apostle here undertakes to declare. And he does it after his usual manner, from such principles and testimonies as were admitted among them.

Two things to this purpose he proves by express testimonies out of the prophet Jeremiah:

1. That besides the covenant made with their fathers in Sinai, God had promised to make another covenant with the church, in his appointed time and season.

2. That this other promised covenant should be of another nature than the former, and much more excellent, as to spiritual advantages, to them who were taken into it.

From both these, fully proved, the apostle infers the necessity of the abrogation of that first covenant in which they trusted and to which they adhered, when the appointed time was come. And on this he takes occasion to declare the nature of the two covenants in various instances, and in which the differences between them did consist. This is the substance of the remainder of this chapter.

This verse is a transition from one subject to another; namely, from the excellence of the priesthood of Christ above that of the law, to the excellence of the new covenant above the old. And in this also the apostle skillfully comprises and confirms his last argument, of the pre-eminency of Christ, his priesthood and ministry, above those of the law. And this he does from the nature and excellence of that covenant of which he was the mediator in the discharge of his office.

There are two parts of the words: First, An assertion of the excellence of the ministry of Christ. And this he expresses by way of comparison; "He has obtained a more excellent ministry:" and after he declares the degree of that comparison; "By how much also." Secondly, He annexes the proof of this assertion; in that he is "the mediator of a better covenant, established on better" or "more excellent promises."

The Difference Between the Two Covenants

An Assertion of the Excellence of the Ministry of Christ

In the first of these there occur these five things: 1. The note of its introduction: "But now;" 2. What is ascribed in the assertion to the Lord Christ: and that is a "ministry;" 3. How he came by that ministry: "He has obtained it;" 4. The quality of this ministry: it is "better" or "more excellent" than the other; 5. The measure and degree of this excellence: "By how much also." All which must be spoken to, for the opening of the words.

The Introduction of the Assertion

The introduction of the assertion is by the particles νυνὶ δέ, "but now." Νῦν, "now," is a note of time, of the present time. But there are instances where these adverbial particles, thus conjoined, do not seem to denote any time or season, but are merely adversative, Rom. 7:17; 1 Cor. 5:11; 7:14. But even in those places there seems a respect to time also; and therefore I know not why it should be here excluded. As, therefore, there is an opposition intended to the old covenant, and the Levitical priesthood; so the season is intimated of the introduction of the new covenant, and the better ministry by which it was accompanied; '"now," at this time, which is the season that God has appointed for the introduction of the new covenant and ministry.' To the same purpose the apostle expresses himself, treating of the same subject, Rom. 3:26: "To declare ἐν τῷ νῦν καιρῷ, "at this instant season," now the gospel is preached, "his righteousness."

First Practical Observation

God, in his infinite wisdom, gives proper times and seasons to all his dispensations to and towards the church. So the accomplishment of these things was in "the fullness of times," Eph. 1:10; that is, when all things rendered it seasonable and suitable to the condition of the church, and for the manifestation of his own glory. He hastens all his works of grace in their own appointed time, Isa. 60:22. And our duty it is to leave the ordering of all the concerns of the church, in the accomplishment of promises, to God in his own time, Acts 1:7.

What is Ascribed to Christ in the Assertion

That which is ascribed to the Lord Christ is λειτουργία, a "ministry." The priests of old had a ministry; they ministered at the altar, as in the foregoing verse. And the Lord Christ was "a minister" also; so the apostle had said before, he was λείτουργος τῶν ἁγίων, verse 2, "a minister of the holy things." To that end he had a "liturgy," a "ministry," a service, committed to him. And two things are included in this:

(1.) That it was an office of ministry that the Lord Christ undertook. He is not called a minister with respect to one particular act of ministration; so are we said to "minister to the necessity of the saints," which yet denotes no office in them that do so. But he had a standing office committed to him, as the word imports. In that sense also he is called διάκονος, a "minister" in office, Rom. 15:8.

(2.) Subordination to God is included in this. With respect to the church his office is supreme, accompanied with sovereign power and authority; he is "Lord over his own house." But he holds his office in subordination to God, being "faithful to him that appointed him." So the angels are said to minister to God, Dan. 7:10; that is, to do all things according to his will, and at his command. So the Lord Christ had a ministry.

Second Practical Observation

And we may observe that the whole office of Christ was designed to the accomplishment of the will and dispensation of the grace of God. For these ends was his ministry committed to him. We can never sufficiently admire the love and grace of our Lord Jesus Christ, in undertaking this office for us. The greatness and glory of the duties which he performed in the discharge of it, with the benefits we receive by that means, are unspeakable, being the immediate cause of all grace and glory. Yet we are not absolutely to rest in them, but to ascend by faith to the eternal spring of them.

The Difference Between the Two Covenants

This is the grace, the love, the mercy of God, all acted in a way of sovereign power. These are everywhere in the Scripture represented as the original spring of all grace, and the ultimate object of our faith, with respect to the benefits which we receive by the mediation of Christ. His office was committed to him of God, even the Father; and his will did he do in the discharge of it.

Third Practical Observation

Yet also, the condescension of the Son of God to undertake the office of the ministry on our behalf is unspeakable, and for ever to be admired. Especially will it appear so to be, when we consider who it was who undertook it, what it cost him, what he did and underwent in the pursuance and discharge of it, as it is all expressed, Phil. 2:6-8. Not only what he continues to do in heaven at the right hand of God belongs to this ministry, but all that he suffered also on the earth. His ministry, in the undertaking of it, was not a dignity, a promotion, a revenue, Matt. 20:28. It is true, it is issued in glory, but not until he had undergone all the evils that human nature is capable of undergoing. And we ought to undergo any thing cheerfully for him who underwent this ministry for us.

Fourth Practical Observation

The Lord Christ, by undertaking this office of the ministry, has consecrated and made honorable that office to all that are rightly called to it, and do rightly discharge it. It is true, his ministry and ours are not of the same kind and nature; but they agree in this, that they are both a ministry to God in the holy things of his worship. And considering that Christ himself was God's minister, we have far greater reason to tremble in ourselves on an apprehension of our own insufficiency for such an office than to be discouraged with all the hardships and contests we meet in the world on the account of it.

The Difference Between the Two Covenants

How Christ Came into this Ministry

The general way in accordance with which our Lord Christ came to this ministry is expressed: Τέτευχε, "He obtained it." Τυγχάνω is either *"sorte contingo,"* "to have a lot or portion;" or to have any thing happen to a man, as it were by accident; or *"assequor," "obtineo,"* to "attain" or "obtain" any thing which before we had not. But the apostle intends not to express in this word the especial call of Christ, or the particular way in accordance with which he came to his ministry, but only in general that he had it, and was possessed of it, in the appointed season, which before he had not. The way in accordance with which he entered on the whole office and work of his mediation he expresses by κεκληρονόμηκε, Heb. 1:4, he had it by "inheritance;" that is, by free grant and perpetual donation, made to him as the Son. See the exposition on that place.[2]

There were two things that concurred to his obtaining this ministry: (1.) The eternal purpose and counsel of God designing him to that – an act of the divine will accompanied with infinite wisdom, love, and power. (2.) The actual call of God, to which many things did concur, especially his unction with the Spirit above measure for the holy discharge of his whole office. Thus did he obtain this ministry, and not by any legal constitution, succession, or carnal rite, as did the priests of old.

Fifth Practical Observation

And we may see that the exaltation of the human nature of Christ into the office of this glorious ministry depended solely on the sovereign wisdom, grace, and love of God. When the human nature of Christ was united to the divine, it became, in the person of the Son of God, fit and capable to make satisfaction for the sins of the church, and to procure righteousness and life eternal for all that believe. But it did not merit that union, nor could do so. For as it

---

[2] [Owen's complete Exposition of Hebrews, as well as his Miscellaneous Works, is available from Banner of Truth. The reader is often directed to his previous writings.]

was utterly impossible that any created nature, by any act of its own, should merit the hypostatical union,[3] so it was granted to the human nature of Christ antecedently to any act of its own in way of obedience to God; for it was united to the person of the Son by virtue of that union. To that end, antecedently to it, it could merit nothing. Therefore its whole exaltation and the ministry that was discharged in that respect depended solely on the sovereign wisdom and pleasure of God. And in this election and designation of the human nature of Christ to grace and glory, we may see the pattern and example of our own. For if it was not on the consideration or foresight of the obedience of the human nature of Christ that it was predestinated and chosen to the grace of the hypostatical union, with the ministry and glory which depended for that reason, but of the mere sovereign grace of God; how much less could a foresight of any thing in us be the cause why God should choose us in him before the foundation of the world to grace and glory!

The Quality of this Ministry

The quality of this ministry, thus obtained, as to a comparative excellence, is also expressed: Διαφορωτέρας, "More excellent." The word is used only in this epistle in this sense, chap. 1:4, and in this place. The original word denotes only a difference from other things; but in the comparative degree, as here, it signifies a difference with a preference, or a comparative excellence. The ministry of the Levitical priests, was good and useful in its time and season; this of our Lord Jesus Christ so differed from it as to be better than it, and more excellent; πολλῷ ἄμεινον.[4]

---

[3] ["…the union of the two natures in the person of Christ. …the assumption of a human nature by the preexistent eternal person of the Son of God in such a way as to draw the human nature into the oneness of the divine person without division or separation of natures…, but also without change or confusion of natures…; yet also in such a way that the attributes of both natures belong to the divine-human person and contribute conjointly to the work of salvation" (Muller, *Dictionary*, 316).]

[4] [Greatly the best.]

The Preeminence of this Ministry

And, there is added to this the degree of this pre-eminence, so far as it is intended in this place and the present argument, in the word ὅσῳ, "by how much." "So much more excellent, by how much." The excellence of his ministry above that of the Levitical priests, bears proportion with the excellence of the covenant of which he was the mediator above the old covenant in which they administered; of which afterwards.

So we have explained the apostle's assertion, concerning the excellence of the ministry of Christ. And by this means he closes his discourse which he had so long engaged in, about the pre-eminence of Christ in his office above the high priests of old. And indeed, this being the very hinge on what his whole controversy with the Jews did depend, he could not give it too much evidence, or too full a confirmation.

Sixth Practical Observation

And as to what concerns ourselves at present, we are taught by that means, that it is our duty and our safety to consent universally and absolutely in the ministry of Jesus Christ. That which he was so designed to, in the infinite wisdom and grace of God; that which he was so furnished for the discharge of by the communication of the Spirit to him in all fullness; that which all other priesthoods were removed to make way for, must needs be sufficient and effectual for all the ends to which it is designed. It may be said, "This is that which all men, all who are called Christians do fully consent in the ministry of Jesus Christ." But if it be so, why do we hear the bleating of another sort of cattle? What mean those other priests, and reiterated sacrifices, which make up the worship of the church of Rome? If they rest in the ministry of Christ, why do they appoint one of their own to do the same things that he has done, namely, to offer sacrifice to God?

The Difference Between the Two Covenants

The Proof of the Assertion

Secondly, the proof of this assertion lies in the latter part of these words: "By how much he is the mediator of a better covenant, established on better promises." The words are so disposed, that some think the apostle intends now to prove the excellence of the covenant from the excellence of his ministry in that respect. But the other sense is more suited to the compass of the place, and the nature of the argument with which the apostle presses the Hebrews. For on supposition that there was indeed another, and that a "better covenant," to be introduced and established, than that which the Levitical priests served in, which they could not deny, it plainly follows, that he on whose ministry the dispensation of that covenant did depend must of necessity be "more excellent" in that ministry than they who appertained to that covenant which was to be abolished. However, it may be granted that these things do mutually testify to and illustrate one another. Such as the priest is, such is the covenant; such as the covenant is in dignity, such is the priest also.

In the words there are three things observable: 1. What is in general ascribed to Christ, declaring the nature of his ministry – he was a "mediator;" 2. The determination of his mediatory office to the new covenant – "of a better covenant;" 3. The proof or demonstration of the nature of this covenant as to its excellence, it was "established on better promises."

The Office of Mediator

His office is that of a mediator, μεσίτης, one that interposed between God and man, for the doing of all those things in accordance with which a covenant might be established between them, and made effectual. Schlichtingius[5] on the place gives this description of a mediator: "Being a mediator is nothing other than being the negotiator of God and the go-between in settling (his) covenant

---

[5] [Jonas Schlichtingius, a Socinian author. His works form one volume in the "Bibliotheca Fratrum Polonorum".]

The Difference Between the Two Covenants

with men; through whom, in other words, both, God might disclose his (own) will to men, and they, in turn, might agree with God, and having been reconciled with him, they might experience peace for the future..."[6] And Grotius speaks much to the same purpose.

But this description of a mediator is wholly applicable to Moses, and suited to his office in giving of the law. See Exod. 20:19; Deut. 5:27, 28. What is said by them does indeed immediately belong to the mediatory office of Christ, but it is not confined to that; yea, it is exclusive of the principal parts of his mediation. And although there is nothing in it but what belongs to the prophetical office of Christ, which the apostle here does not principally intend, it is most improperly applied as a description of such a mediator as he does intend. And therefore, when he comes afterwards to declare in particular what belonged to such a mediator of the covenant as he designed, he expressly places it in his "death for the redemption of transgressions," Heb. 9:15; affirming that "for that cause he was a mediator." But of this there is nothing at all in the description they give us of this office. But this the apostle does in his writings elsewhere, 1 Tim. 2:5, 6, "There is one God, and one mediator between God and men, the man Christ Jesus; who gave himself a ransom for all." The principal part of his mediation consisted in the "giving himself a ransom," or a price of redemption for the whole church. On that ground this description of a mediator of the new testament is pretended only, to exclude his satisfaction, or his offering himself to God in his death and blood-shedding, with the atonement made by that means.

The Lord Christ, then, in his ministry, is called μεσίτης, the "mediator" of the covenant, in the same sense as he is called ἔγγυος, the "surety," of which see the exposition on Heb. 7:22. He is, in the new covenant, the mediator, the surety, the priest, the sacrifice, all in his own person. The ignorance and lack of a due consideration of this are the great evidence of the degeneracy of Christian religion.

---

[6] *Mediatorem foederis esse nihil aliud est, quam Dei esse interpretem, et internuntium in foedere cum hominibus pangendo; per quem scilicet et Deus voluntatem suam hominibus declaret, et illi vicissim divinae voluntatis notitiâ instructi ad Deum accedant, cumque eo reconciliati, pacem in posterum colant.*

The Difference Between the Two Covenants

Although this is the first general notion of the office of Christ, that which comprises the whole ministry committed to him, and contains in itself the especial offices of king, priest, and prophet, in accordance with which he discharges his mediation, some things must be mentioned that are declarative of its nature and use. And we may to this purpose observe,

(1.) That to the office of a mediator it is required that there be different persons concerned in the covenant, and that, by their own wills; as it must be in every compact,[7] of whatsoever sort. So says our apostle, "A mediator is not of one, but God is one," Gal. 3:20; that is, if there were none but God concerned in this matter, as it is in an absolute promise or sovereign precept, there would be no need of, no place for a mediator, such a mediator as Christ is. To that end our consent in and to the covenant is required in the very notion of a mediator.

(2.) That the persons entering into covenant be in such a state and condition as that it is no way convenient or morally possible that they should treat immediately with each other as to the ends of the covenant; for if they are so, a mediator to go between is altogether needless. So was it in the original covenant with Adam, which had no mediator. But in the giving of the law, which was to be a covenant between God and the people, they found themselves utterly insufficient for an immediate treaty with God, and therefore desired that they might have an internuncio to go between God and them, to bring his proposals, and carry back their consent, Deut. 5:23-27. And this is the voice of all men really convinced of the holiness of God, and of their own condition. Such is the state between God and sinners. The law and the curse of it did so interpose between them, that they could not enter into any immediate treaty with God, Psa. 5:3-5. This made a mediator necessary, that the new covenant might be established; of which we will speak afterwards.

(3.) That he who is this mediator be accepted, trusted, and rested in on either sides of the parties mutually entering into covenant. An absolute trust must be reposed in him, so that each

---

[7] [Covenant.]

The Difference Between the Two Covenants

party may be everlastingly obliged in what he undertakes on their behalf; and such as admit not of his terms, can have no benefit by, no interest in the covenant. So was it with the Lord Christ in this matter. On the part of God, he reposed the whole trust of all the concernments of the covenant in him, and absolutely rested in that respect. "Behold," says he of him, "my servant, whom I uphold; mine elect, in whom my soul delights," or is "well pleased," ἐν ᾧ εὐδόκησα, Isa. 42:1; Matt. 3:17. When he undertook this office, and said, "Lo, I come to do your will, O God," the soul of God rested in him, Exod. 23:21; John 5:20-22. And to him he gives an account at last of his discharge of this thing, John 17:4. And on our part, unless we resign ourselves absolutely to a universal trust in him and reliance on him, and unless we accept of all the terms of the covenant as by him proposed, and engage to stand to all that he has undertaken on our behalf, we can have neither share nor interest in this matter.

(4.) A mediator must be a middle person between both parties entering into covenant; and if they be of different natures, a perfect, complete mediator ought to partake of each of their natures in the same person. The necessity of this, and the glorious wisdom of God in this, I have elsewhere at large demonstrated, and will not therefore here again insist on it.

(5.) A mediator must be one who voluntarily and of his own accord undertakes the work of mediation. This is required of every one who will effectually mediate between any persons at variance, to bring them to an agreement on equal terms. So it was required that the will and consent of Christ should concur in his reception of this office; and that they did so, himself expressly testifies, Heb. 10:5-10. It is true, he was designed and appointed by the Father to this office; by reason of this he is called his "servant," and constantly witnesses of himself, that he came to do the will and commandment of him that sent him: but he had that to do in the discharge of this office, which could not, according to any rule of divine righteousness, be imposed on him without his own voluntary consent. And this was the ground of the eternal compact that was between the Father and the Son, with respect to his mediation, which I have elsewhere explained. And the testification[8] of his own will, grace, and love, in the reception of this office, is a principal motive to that faith and trust which the church places in him, as the mediator between God and them. On this his voluntary undertaking does the soul of God rest in him, and he reposes the whole trust in him of accomplishing his will and pleasure, or the design of his love and grace in this covenant, Isa. 53:10-12. And the faith of the church, on what salvation does depend, must have love to his person inseparably accompanying it. Love to Christ is no less necessary to salvation, than faith in him. And as faith is resolved into the sovereign wisdom and grace of God in sending him, and his own ability to save to the uttermost those that come to God by him; so love arises from the consideration of his own love and grace in his voluntary undertaking of this office, and the discharge of it.

(6.) In this voluntary undertaking to be a mediator, two things were required:

[1.] That he should remove and take out of the way whatever kept the covenanters at a distance, or was a cause of enmity between them. For it is supposed that such an enmity there was, or there had been no need of a mediator. Therefore in the covenant made with Adam, there having been no variance between God and man, nor any distance but what necessarily ensued from the distinct natures of the Creator and a creature, there was no mediator. But the design of this covenant was to make reconciliation and peace. On this therefore depended the necessity of satisfaction, redemption, and the making of atonement by sacrifice. For man having sinned and apostatized from the rule of God, making himself by that means subject to his wrath, according to the eternal rule of righteousness, and in particular to the curse of the law, there could be no new peace and agreement made with God unless due satisfaction were made for these things. For although God was willing, in infinite love, grace, and mercy, to enter into a new covenant with fallen man, yet would he not do it to the prejudice of his righteousness, the dishonor of his rule, and the contempt of his law. To that end none could undertake to be a

---

[8] [The action or an act of testifying; the testimony borne.]

The Difference Between the Two Covenants

mediator of this covenant, but he that was able to satisfy the justice of God, glorify his government, and fulfill the law. And this could be done by none but him, concerning whom it might be said that "God purchased his church with his own blood."

[2.] That he should procure and purchase, in a way suited to the glory of God, the actual communication of all the good things prepared and proposed in this covenant; that is, grace and glory, with all that belong to them, for them and on their behalf whose surety he was. And this is the foundation of the merit of Christ, and of the grant of all good things to us for his sake.

(7.) It is required of this mediator, as such, that he give assurance to and undertake for the parties mutually concerned, as to the accomplishment of the terms of the covenant, undertaking on each hand for them:

[1.] On the part of God towards men, that they will have peace and acceptance with him, in the sure accomplishment of all the promises of the covenant. This he does only declaratively, in the doctrine of the gospel, and in the institution of the ordinances of evangelical worship. For he was not a surety for God, nor did God need any, having confirmed his promise with an oath, swearing by himself, because he had no greater to swear by.

[2.] On our part, he undertakes to God for our acceptance of the terms of the covenant, and our accomplishment of them, by his enabling us to that.

Seventh Practical Observation

These things, among others, were necessary to a full and complete mediator of the new covenant, such as Christ was. And the provision of this mediator between God and man was an outworking of infinite wisdom and grace; yea, it was the greatest and most glorious external accomplishment of them that ever they did produce, or ever will do in this world. The creation of all things at first out of nothing was a glorious work of infinite wisdom and power; but when the glory of that design was eclipsed by the entrance of sin, this provision of a mediator, one in accordance with which all things were restored and retrieved to a condition of bringing more glory to God, and securing for ever the blessed estate of them whose mediator he is, is accompanied with more evidences of the divine excellencies than that was. See Eph. 1:10.

Further Description of His Mediatory Office

Two things are added in the description of this mediator: (1.) That he was a mediator of a covenant; (2.) That this covenant was better than another which respect is had to, of which he was not the mediator:

(1.) He was the mediator of a "covenant." And two things are supposed in this:

[1.] That there was a covenant made or prepared between God and man; that is, it was so far made, as that God who made it had prepared the terms of it in a sovereign act of wisdom and grace. The preparation of the covenant, consisting in the will and purpose of God graciously to bestow on all men the good things which are contained in it, all things belonging to grace and glory, as also to make way for the obedience which he required in this, is supposed to the constitution of this covenant.

[2.] That there was need of a mediator, that this covenant might be effectual to its proper ends, of the glory of God and the obedience of mankind, with their reward. This was not necessary from the nature of a covenant in general; for a covenant may be made and entered into between different parties without any mediator, merely on the equity of the terms of it. Nor was it so from the nature of a covenant between God and man, as man was at first created of God; for the first covenant between them was immediate, without the interposition of a mediator. But it became necessary from the state and condition of them with whom this covenant was made, and the especial nature of this covenant. This the apostle declares, Rom. 8:3, "For what the law could not do, in that it was weak through the flesh, God sending his own Son in the likeness of sinful flesh, and for sin, condemned sin in the flesh." The law was the moral instrument or rule of the covenant that was made immediately between God and man: but it could not continue to be so after the entrance of sin; that is, so as that God might be glorified

The Difference Between the Two Covenants

by that means, in the obedience and reward of men. To that end he "sent his Son in the likeness of sinful flesh;" that is, provided a mediator for a new covenant. The persons with whom this covenant was to be made being all of them sinners, and apostatized from God, it became not the holiness or righteousness of God to treat immediately with them any more. Nor would it have answered his holy ends so to have done. For if when they were in a condition of uprightness and integrity, they kept not the terms of that covenant which was made immediately with them, without a mediator, although they were holy, just, good, and equal; how much less could any such thing be expected from them in their depraved condition of apostasy from God and enmity against him! It therefore became not the wisdom of God to enter anew into covenant with mankind, without security that the terms of the covenant should be accepted, and the grace of it made effectual. This we could not give; yea, we gave all evidences possible to the contrary, in that "GOD saw that every imagination of the thoughts of man's heart was only evil continually," Gen. 6:5. To that end it was necessary there should be a mediator, to be the surety of this covenant. Again, the covenant itself was so prepared, in the counsel, wisdom, and grace of God, as that the principal, yea, indeed, all the benefits of it, were to depend on what was to be done by a mediator, and could not otherwise be accomplished. Such were satisfaction for sin, and the bringing in of everlasting righteousness; which are the foundation of this covenant.

(2.) To proceed with the text; this covenant, of which the Lord Christ is the mediator, is said to be a "better covenant." To that end it is supposed that there was another covenant, of which the Lord Christ was not the mediator. And in the following verses there are two covenants, a first and a latter, an old and a new, compared together. We must therefore consider what was that other covenant, of which this is said to be better; for on the definition of it depends the right understanding of the whole ensuing discourse of the apostle. And because this is a subject wrapped up in much obscurity, and attended with many difficulties, it will be necessary that we use the best of our diligence, both in the investigation of the truth and in the declaration of it, so as that it may be distinctly understood. And I will first explain the text, and then speak of the difficulties which arise from it:

[1.] There was an original covenant made with Adam, and all mankind in him. The rule of obedience and reward that was between God and him was not expressly called a covenant, but it contained the express nature of a covenant; for it was the agreement of God and man concerning obedience and disobedience, rewards and punishments. Where there is a law concerning these things, and an agreement on it by all parties concerned, there is a formal covenant. To that end it may be considered two ways:

1st. As it was a law only; so it proceeded from, and was a consequent of the nature of God and man, with their mutual relation to one another. God being considered as the creator, governor, and benefactor of man; and man as an intellectual creature, capable of moral obedience; this law was necessary, and is eternally indispensable.

2dly. As it was a covenant; and this depended on the will and pleasure of God. I will not dispute whether God might have given a law to men that should have had nothing in it of a covenant, properly so called; as is the law of creation to all other creatures, which has no rewards nor punishments annexed to it. Yet God calls this a covenant also, inasmuch as it is an accomplishment of his purpose, his unalterable will and pleasure, Jer. 33:20-21. But that this law of our obedience should be a formal, complete covenant, there were moreover some things required on the part of God, and some also on the part of man. Two things were required on the part of God to complete this covenant, or he did so complete it by two things:

(1st.) By annexing to it promises and threats of reward and punishment; the first of grace, the other of justice. (2dly.) The expression of these promises and threats in external signs; the first in the tree of life, the latter in that of the knowledge of good and evil. By these God did establish the original law of creation as a covenant, gave it the nature of a covenant. On the part of man, it was required that he accept of this law as the rule of the covenant which God made with him. And this he did in two ways:

The Difference Between the Two Covenants

[1st.] By the innate principles of light and obedience co-created with his nature. By these he absolutely and universally assented to the law, as proposed with promises and threats, as holy, just, good, what was fit for God to require, what was equal and good to himself.

[2dly.] By his acceptance of the commands concerning the tree of life, and that of the knowledge of good and evil, as the signs and pledges of this covenant. So it was established as a covenant between God and man, without the interposition of any mediator.

This is the covenant of works, absolutely the old, or first covenant that God made with men. But this is not the covenant here intended; for,

1st. The covenant called afterwards "the first," was διαθήκη, a "testament." So it is here called. It was such a covenant as was a testament also. Now there can be no testament, but there must be death for the confirmation of it, Heb. 9:16. But in the making of the covenant with Adam, there was not the death of any thing, from what cause it might be called a testament. But there was the death of beasts in sacrifice in the confirmation of the covenant at Sinai, as we will see afterwards. And it must be observed, that although I use the name of a "covenant," as we have rendered the word διαθήκη, because the true signification of that word will be more properly presented to us in another place, yet I do not understand by that means a covenant properly and strictly so called, but such a one as has the nature of a testament also, in which the good things of him that makes it are bequeathed to them for whom they are designed. Neither the word used constantly by the apostle in this argument, nor the design of his discourse, will admit of any other covenant to be understood in this place. Although, therefore, the first covenant made with Adam was in no sense a testament also, it cannot be here intended.

2dly. That first covenant made with Adam, had, as to any benefit to be expected from it, with respect to acceptance with God, life, and salvation, ceased long before, even at the entrance of sin. It was not abolished or abrogated by any act of God, as a law, but only was made weak and insufficient to its first end, as a covenant. God had provided a way for the salvation of sinners, declared in the first promise. When this is actually embraced, that first covenant ceases towards them, as to its curse, in all its concerns as a covenant, and obligation to sinless obedience as the condition of life; because both of them are answered by the mediator of the new covenant. But as to all those who receive not the grace tendered in the promise, it does remain in full force and efficacy, not as a covenant, but as a law; and that because neither the obedience it requires nor the curse which it threatens is answered. Therefore, if any man believes not, "the wrath of God abides on him." For its commands and curse depending on the necessary relation between God and man, with the righteousness of God as the supreme governor of mankind, they must be answered and fulfilled. To that end it was never abrogated formally. But as all unbelievers are still obliged by it, and to it must stand or fall, so it is perfectly fulfilled in all believers, not in their own persons, but in the person of their surety. "God sending his own Son in the likeness of sinful flesh, and for sin, condemned sin in the flesh, that the righteousness of the law might be fulfilled in us," Rom. 8:3, 4. But as a covenant, obliging to personal, perfect, sinless obedience, as the condition of life, to be performed by them, so it ceased to be, long before the introduction of the new covenant which the apostle speaks of, that was promised "in the latter days." But the other covenant here spoken of was not removed or taken away, until this new covenant was actually established.

3dly. The church of Israel was never absolutely under the power of that covenant as a covenant of life; for from the days of Abraham, the promise was given to them and their seed. And the apostle proves that no law could afterwards be given, or covenant made, that should disannul that promise, Gal. 3:17. But had they been brought under the old covenant of works, it would have disannulled the promise; for that covenant and the promise are diametrically opposite. And moreover, if they were under that covenant, they were all under the curse, and so perished eternally: which is openly false; for it is testified of them that they pleased God by faith, and so were saved. But it is evident that the covenant intended was a covenant in which the church of Israel walked with God, until such time as this better covenant was solemnly

The Difference Between the Two Covenants

introduced. This is plainly declared in the following context, especially in the close of the chapter, where, speaking of this former covenant, he says, it was "become old," and so "ready to disappear." To that end it is not the covenant of works made with Adam that is intended, when this other is said to be a "better covenant."

[2.] There were other federal transactions between God and the church before the giving of the law on Mount Sinai. Two of them there were into which all the rest were resolved:

1st. The first promise given to our first parents immediately after the Fall. This had in it the nature of a covenant, grounded on a promise of grace, and requiring obedience in all that received the promise.

2dly. The promise given and sworn to Abraham, which is expressly called the covenant of God, and had the whole nature of a covenant in it, with a solemn outward seal appointed for its confirmation and establishment. Of this we have treated at large on the sixth chapter.

Neither of these, nor any transaction between God and man that may be reduced to them as explanations, renovations, or confirmations of them, is the "first covenant" here intended. For they are not only consistent with the "new covenant" so as that there was no necessity to remove them out of the way for its introduction, but did indeed contain in them the essence and nature of it, and so were confirmed in that respect. Therefore the Lord Christ himself is said to be "a minister of the circumcision for the truth of God, to confirm the promises made to the fathers," Rom. 15:8. As he was the mediator of the new covenant, he was so far from taking off from, or abolishing those promises, that it belonged to his office to confirm them. To that end,

[3.] The other covenant or testament here supposed, to which that of which the Lord Christ was the mediator is preferred, is none other but that which God made with the people of Israel on Mount Sinai. So it is expressly affirmed, verse 9: "The covenant which I made with your fathers in the day when I took them by the hand to lead them out of the land of Egypt." This was that covenant which had all the institutions of worship annexed to it, Heb. 9:1-3; of which we must treat afterwards more at large. With respect to this it is that the Lord Christ is said to be the "mediator of a better covenant," that is, of another distinct from it, and more excellent.

It remains to the exposition of the words that we inquire what this covenant was of which our Lord Christ was the mediator, and what is here affirmed of it.

Of What Covenant Was Christ the Mediator?

This can be no other in general but that which we call "the covenant of grace." And it is so called in opposition to that of "works" which was made with us in Adam; for these two, grace and works, do divide the ways of our relation to God, being diametrically opposite, and every way inconsistent, Rom. 11:6. Of this covenant the Lord Christ was the mediator from the foundation of the world, namely, from the giving of the first promise, Revelation 13:8; for it was given on his interposition, and all the benefits of it depended on his future actual mediation.

Difficulties of the Context Answered

But here arises the first difficulty of the context and that in two things; for,

[1.] If this covenant of grace was made from the beginning, and if the Lord Christ was the mediator of it from the first, then where is the privilege of the gospel-state in opposition to the law, by virtue of this covenant, seeing that under the law also the Lord Christ was the mediator of that covenant, which was from the beginning?

[2.] If it be the covenant of grace which is intended, and that be opposed to the covenant of works made with Adam, then the other covenant must be that covenant of works so made with Adam, which we have before disproved.

The answer to this is in the word here used by the apostle concerning this new covenant: νενομοθέτηται, of which meaning we must inquire into. I say, therefore, that the apostle does not here consider the new covenant absolutely, and as it was virtually administered from the foundation of the world, in the way of a

The Difference Between the Two Covenants

promise; for as such it was consistent with that covenant made with the people in Sinai. And the apostle proves expressly, that the renovation of it made to Abraham was no way abrogated by the giving of the law, Gal. 3:17. There was no interruption of its administration made by the introduction of the law. But he treats of such an establishment of the new covenant as by which the old covenant made at Sinai was absolutely inconsistent, and which was therefore to be removed out of the way. To that end he considers it here as it was actually completed, so as to bring along with it all the ordinances of worship which are proper to it, the dispensation of the Spirit in them, and all the spiritual privileges by which they are accompanied. It is now so brought in as to become the entire rule of the church's faith, obedience, and worship, in all things.

This is the meaning of the word νενομοθέτηατι, "established," say we; but it is, "reduced into a fixed state of a law or ordinance." All the obedience required in it, all the worship appointed by it, all the privileges exhibited in it, and the grace administered with them, are all given for a statute, law, and ordinance to the church. That which before lay hid in promises, in many things obscure, the principal mysteries of it being a secret hid in God himself, was now brought to light; and that covenant which had invisibly, in the way of a promise, put forth its efficacy under types and shadows, was now solemnly sealed, ratified, and confirmed, in the death and resurrection of Christ. It had before the confirmation of a promise, which is an oath; it had now the confirmation of a covenant, which is blood. That which before had no visible, outward worship, proper and peculiar to it, is now made the only rule and instrument of worship to the whole church, nothing being to be admitted in that respect but what belongs to it, and is appointed by it. The apostle intends this by νενομοθέτηται, the "legal establishment" of the new covenant, with all the ordinances of its worship. On this the other covenant was disannulled and removed; and not only the covenant itself, but all that system of sacred worship in accordance with which it was administered. This was not done by the making of the covenant at first; yea, all this was added into the covenant as given out in a promise, and was consistent with that. When the new covenant was given out only in the way of a promise, it did not

The Difference Between the Two Covenants

introduce worship and privileges expressive of it. To that end it was consistent with a form of worship, rites and ceremonies, and those composed into a yoke of bondage which belonged not to it. And as these, being added after its giving, did not overthrow its nature as a promise, so they were inconsistent with it when it was completed as a covenant; for then all the worship of the church was to proceed from it, and to be conformed to it. Then it was established. Therefore it follows, in answer to the second difficulty, that as a promise, it was opposed to the covenant of works; as a covenant, it was opposed to that of Sinai. This legalizing or authoritative establishment of the new covenant, and the worship to that belonging, accomplished this alteration.

The Proof of the Nature of this Covenant as to its Excellence

In the last place, the apostle tells us on what this establishment was made; and that is ἐπὶ κρείττοσιν ἐπαγγελίαις, "on better promises." For the better understanding of this we must consider somewhat of the original and use of divine promises in our relation to God. And we may observe,

Every Covenant Established on Promises

That every covenant between God and man must be founded on and resolved into "promises." Therefore essentially a promise and a covenant are all one; and God calls an absolute promise, founded on an absolute decree, his covenant, Gen. 9:11. And his purpose for the continuation of the course of nature to the end of the world, he calls his covenant with day and night, Jer. 33:20. The being and essence of a divine covenant lies in the promise. Therefore they are called "the covenants of promise", Eph. 2:12; such as are founded on and consist in promises. And it is necessary that so it should be. For,
 [1.] The nature of God who makes these covenants requires that it should be so. It becomes his greatness and goodness, in all his voluntary transactions with his creatures, to propose that to them in which their advantage, their happiness and blessedness, does

The Difference Between the Two Covenants

consist. We inquire not how God may deal with his creatures as such; what he may absolutely require of them, on the account of his own being, his absolute essential excellencies, with their universal dependence on him. Who can express or limit the sovereignty of God over his creatures? All the disputes about it are fond. We have no measures of what is infinite. May he not do with his own what he pleases? Are we not in his hands, as clay in the hands of the potter? And whether he make or mar a vessel, who will say to him, What are you doing? He gives no account of his matters. But on supposition that he will condescend to enter into covenant with his creatures, and to come to agreement with them according to the terms of it, it becomes his greatness and goodness to give them promises as the foundation of it, in which he proposes to them the things in which their blessedness and reward do consist. For, 1st. In this he proposes himself to them as the eternal spring and fountain of all power and goodness. Had he treated with us merely by a law, he had in that respect only revealed his sovereign authority and holiness; the one in giving of the law, the other in the nature of it. But in promises he reveals himself as the eternal spring of goodness and power; for the matter of all promises is somewhat that is good; and the communication of it depends on sovereign power. That God should so declare himself in his covenant was absolutely necessary to direct and encourage the obedience of the covenanters; and he did so accordingly, Gen. 15:1, 17:1, 2. 2dly. By this means he reserves the glory of the whole to himself. For although the terms of agreement which he proposes between himself and us be in their own nature "holy, just, and good," which sets forth his praise and glory, yet if there were not something on his part which has no antecedent respect to any goodness, obedience, or merit in us, we should have in which to glory in ourselves; which is inconsistent with the glory of God. But the matter of those promises in which the covenant is founded is free, undeserved, and without respect to any thing in us in accordance with which it may in any sense be procured. And so in the first covenant, which was given in a form of law, attended with a penal sanction, yet the foundation of it was in a promise of a free and undeserved reward, even of the eternal enjoyment of God: which no goodness or obedience in the creature

The Difference Between the Two Covenants

could possibly merit the attainment of. So that if a man should by virtue of any covenant be justified by works, though he might have of which to glory before men, yet could he not glory before God, as the apostle declares, Rom. 4:2; and that because the reward proposed in the promise does infinitely exceed the obedience performed.

[2.] It was also necessary on our part that every divine covenant should be founded and established on promises; for there is no state in which we may be taken into covenant with God, but it is supposed we are not yet arrived at that perfection and blessedness of which our nature is capable, and which we cannot but desire. And therefore when we come to heaven, and the full enjoyment of God, there will be no use of any covenant any more, seeing we will be in eternal rest, in the enjoyment of all the blessedness of which our nature is capable, and will immutably adhere to God without any further expectation. But while we are in the way, we have still somewhat, yea principal parts of our blessedness, to desire, expect, and believe. So in the state of innocence, though it had all the perfection which a state of obedience according to a law was capable of, yet the blessedness of eternal rest, for which we were made, did not consist in that respect. Now, while it is thus with us, we cannot but desire and look out after that full and complete happiness, which our nature cannot come to rest without. This, therefore, renders it necessary that there should be a promise of it given as the foundation of the covenant; without which we should lack our principal encouragement to obedience. And much more must it be so in the state of sin and apostasy from God; for we are now not only most remote from our utmost happiness, but involved in a condition of misery, without a deliverance from which we cannot be in any way induced to give ourselves up to covenant obedience. To that end, unless we are prevented in the covenant with promises of deliverance from our present state, and the enjoyment of future blessedness, no covenant could be of use or advantage to us.

[3.] It is necessary from the nature of a covenant. For every covenant that is proposed to men, and accepted by them, requires somewhat to be performed on their part, otherwise it is no

The Difference Between the Two Covenants

covenant; but where any thing is required of them that accept of the covenant, or to whom it is proposed, it does suppose that somewhat be promised on the behalf of them by whom the covenant is proposed, as the foundation of its acceptance, and the reason of the duties required in it.

All this appears most evidently in the covenant of grace, which is here said to be "established on promises" and that on two accounts. For,

[4.] At the same time that much is required of us in the way of duty and obedience, we are told in the Scripture, and find it by experience, that of ourselves we can do nothing. To that end, unless the precept of the covenant is founded in a promise of giving grace and spiritual strength to us, in accordance with which we may be enabled to perform those duties, the covenant can be of no benefit or advantage to us. And the lack of this one consideration, that every covenant is founded in promises, and that the promises give life to the precepts of it, has perverted the minds of many to suppose ability in ourselves of yielding obedience to those precepts, without grace antecedently received to enable us to that; which overthrows the nature of the new covenant.

[5.] As was observed, we are all actually guilty of sin before this covenant was made with us. To that end unless there be a promise given of the pardon of sin, it is to no purpose to propose any new covenant terms to us. For "the wages of sin is death" and we having sinned must die, whatever we do afterwards, unless our sins be pardoned. This, therefore, must be proposed to us as the foundation of the covenant, or it will be of no effect. And in this lies the great difference between the promises of the covenant of works and those of the covenant of grace. The first were only concerning things future; eternal life and blessedness on the accomplishment of perfect obedience. Promises of present mercy and pardon it stood in need of none, it was not capable of. Nor had it any promises of giving more grace or supplies of it; but man was wholly left to what he had at first received. Therefore the covenant was broken. But in the covenant of grace all things are founded in promises of present mercy, and continual supplies of grace, as well as of future blessedness. Therefore it comes to be "ordered in all things, and sure."

And this is the first thing that was to be declared, namely, that every divine covenant is established on promises.

The New Covenant is Established on Better Promises

These promises are said to be "better promises." The other covenant had its promises peculiar to it, with respect to which this is said to be "established on better promises." It was, indeed, principally represented under a system of precepts, and those almost innumerable; but it had its promises also, into the nature of which we will immediately inquire. With respect, therefore, to them is the new covenant, of which the Lord Christ is the mediator, said to be "established on better promises." That it should be founded in promises was necessary from its general nature as a covenant, and more necessary from its especial nature as a covenant of grace. That these promises are said to be "better promises" respects those of the old covenant. But this is so said as to include all other degrees of comparison. They are not only better than they, but they are positively good in themselves, and absolutely the best that God ever gave, or will give to the church. And what they are we must consider in our progress. And various things may be observed from these words.

Eighth Practical Observation

There is infinite grace in every divine covenant, inasmuch as it is established on promises. Infinite condescension it is in God that he will enter into covenant with dust and ashes, with poor worms of the earth. And in this lies the spring of all grace, from out of which all the streams of it do flow. And the first expression of it is in laying the foundation of it in some undeserved promises. And this was that which became the goodness and greatness of his nature, the means in accordance with which we are brought to adhere to him in faith, hope, trust, and obedience, until we come to the enjoyment of him; for that is the use of promises, to keep us in

The Difference Between the Two Covenants

adherence to God, as the first original and spring of all goodness, and the ultimate satisfactory reward of our souls, 2 Cor. 7:1.

Ninth Practical Observation

The promises of the covenant of grace are better than those of any other covenant, as for many other reasons, so especially because the grace of them prevents any condition or qualification on our part. I do not say the covenant of grace is absolutely without conditions, if by conditions we intend the duties of obedience which God requires of us in and by virtue of that covenant; but this I say, the principal promises of it are not in the first place remunerative of our obedience in the covenant, but efficaciously assumptive of us into covenant, and establishing or confirming in the covenant. The covenant of works had its promises, but they were all remunerative, respecting an antecedent obedience in us; (so were all those which were peculiar to the covenant of Sinai). They were, indeed, also of grace, in that the reward did infinitely exceed the merit of our obedience; but yet they all supposed it, and the subject of them was formally reward only. In the covenant of grace it is not so; for several of the promises of it are the means of our being taken into covenant, of our entering into covenant with God. The first covenant absolutely was established on promises, in that when men were actually taken into it, they were encouraged to obedience by the promises of a future reward. But those promises, namely, of the pardon of sin and writing of the law in our hearts, on which the apostle expressly insists as the peculiar promises of this covenant, do take place and are effectual antecedently to our covenant obedience. For although faith be required in order of nature antecedently to our actual receiving of the pardon of sin, yet is that faith itself produced in us by the grace of the promise, and so its precedence to pardon respects only the order that God had appointed in the communication of the benefits of the covenant, and intends not that the pardon of sin is the reward of our faith.

The Difference Between the Two Covenants

A Discourse of Some Things in General

This entrance has the apostle made into his discourse of the two covenants, which he continues to the end of the chapter. But the whole is not without its difficulties. Many things in particular will occur to us in our progress, which may be considered in their proper places. In the meantime there are some things in general which may be here discoursed, by whose determination much light will be communicated to what does follow.

A Dispute Concerning Two Covenants

First, therefore, the apostle does evidently in this place dispute concerning two covenants, or two testaments, comparing the one with the other, and declaring the disannulling of the one by the introduction and establishment of the other. What are these two covenants in general we have declared, namely, that made with the church of Israel at Mount Sinai, and that made with us in the gospel; not as absolutely the covenant of grace, but as actually established in the death of Christ, with all the worship that belongs to it.

Here then arises a difference of no small importance, namely, whether these are indeed two distinct covenants, as to the essence and substance of them, or only different ways of the dispensation and administration of the same covenant. And the reason of the difficulty lies in this: We must grant one of these three things: 1. That either the covenant of grace was in force under the old testament; or, 2. That the church was saved without it, or any benefit by Jesus Christ, who is the mediator of it alone; or, 3. That they all perished everlastingly. And neither of the two latter can be admitted.

Some, indeed, in these latter days, have revived the old Pelagian imagination, that before the law men were saved by the conduct of natural light and reason; and under the law by the directive doctrines, precepts, and sacrifices of it, without any respect to the Lord Christ or his mediation in another covenant. But I will not here contend with them, as having elsewhere sufficiently refuted

The Difference Between the Two Covenants

these imaginations. To that end I will take it here for granted, that no man was ever saved but by virtue of the new covenant, and the mediation of Christ in that respect.

Suppose, then, that this new covenant of grace was extant and effectual under the old testament, so as the church was saved by virtue of it, and the mediation of Christ in that respect, how could it be that there should at the same time be another covenant between God and them, of a different nature from this, accompanied with other promises, and other effects?

On this consideration it is said, that the two covenants mentioned, the new and the old, were not indeed two distinct covenants, as to their essence and substance, but only different administrations of the same covenant, called two covenants from some different outward solemnities and duties of worship attending of them. To clear this it must be observed,

1. That by the old covenant, the original covenant of works, made with Adam and all mankind in him, is not intended; for this is undoubtedly a covenant different in the essence and substance of it from the new.

2. By the new covenant, not the new covenant absolutely and originally, as given in the first promise, is intended; but in its complete gospel administration, when it was actually established by the death of Christ, as administered in and by the ordinances of the new testament. This, with the covenant of Sinai, would be, as most say, but different administrations of the same covenant.

But on the other hand, there is such express mention made, not only in this, but in various other places of the Scripture also, of two distinct covenants, or testaments, and such different natures, properties, and effects, ascribed to them, as seem to constitute two distinct covenants. This, therefore, we must inquire into; and will first declare what is agreed to by those who are sober in this matter, though they differ in their judgments about this question, whether two distinct covenants, or only a twofold administration of the same covenant, be intended. And indeed there is so much agreed on, as that what remains seems rather to be a difference about the expression of the same truth, than any real contradiction about the things themselves. For,

The Difference Between the Two Covenants

Four Agreements about the Two Administrations

1. It is agreed that the way of reconciliation with God, of justification and salvation, was always one and the same; and that from the giving of the first promise none was ever justified or saved but by the new covenant, and Jesus Christ, the mediator of it. The foolish imagination before mentioned, that men were saved before the giving of the law by following the guidance of the light of nature, and after the giving of the law by obedience to the directions of it, is rejected by all that are sober, as destructive of the Old Testament and the New.

2. That the writings of the Old Testament, namely, the Law, Psalms, and Prophets, do contain and declare the doctrine of justification and salvation by Christ. The church of old believed this, and walked with God in the faith of it. This is undeniably proved, in that the doctrine mentioned is frequently confirmed in the New Testament by testimonies taken out of the Old.

3. That by the covenant of Sinai, as properly so called, separated from its figurative relation to the covenant of grace, none was ever eternally saved.

4. That the use of all the institutions in accordance with which the old covenant was administered, was to represent and direct to Jesus Christ, and his mediation.

These things being granted, the only way of life and salvation by Jesus Christ, under the old testament and the new, is secured; which is the substance of the truth in which we are now concerned. On these grounds we may proceed with our inquiry.

The Judgment of Most Reformed Divines

The judgment of most Reformed divines is, that the church under the old testament had the same promise of Christ, the same interest in him by faith, remission of sins, reconciliation with God, justification and salvation by the same way and means, that believers have under the new. And although the essence and the substance of the covenant consist in these things, they are not to be said to be under another covenant, but only a different

The Difference Between the Two Covenants

administration of it. But this was so different from that which is established in the gospel after the coming of Christ, that it has the appearance and name of another covenant. And the difference between these two administrations may be reduced to the ensuing heads.

Five Differences Between The Two Administrations

1. It consisted in the way and manner of the declaration of the mystery of the love and will of God in Christ; of the work of reconciliation and redemption, with our justification by faith. For in this the gospel, in which "life and immortality are brought to light," does in plainness, clearness, and evidence, much excel the administration and declaration of the same truths under the law. And the greatness of the privilege of the church in this is not easily expressed. For by this means "with open face we behold as in a glass the glory of the Lord," and "are changed into the same image," 2 Cor. 3:18. The man whose eyes the Lord Christ opened, Mark 8:23-25, represents these two states. When he first touched him, his eyes were opened, and he saw, but he saw nothing clearly; by reason of which, when he looked, he said, "I see men as trees, walking," verse 24: but on his second touch, he "saw every man clearly," verse 25. They had their sight under the old testament, and the object was proposed to them, but at a great distance, with such an interposition of mists, clouds, and shadows, as that they "saw men like trees, walking," nothing clearly and perfectly: but now under the gospel, the object, which is Christ, being brought near to us, and all clouds and shadows being departed, we do or may see all things clearly. When a traveler in his way on downs or hills is encompassed with a thick mist and fog, though he be in his way yet he is uncertain, and nothing is presented to him in its proper shape and distance; things near seem to be afar off, and things afar off to be near, and every thing has, though not a false, yet an uncertain appearance. Let the sun break forth and scatter the mists and fogs that are about him, and immediately every thing appears quite in another shape to him, so as indeed he is ready to think he is not where he was. His way is plain, he is certain of it and the entire

The Difference Between the Two Covenants

region about lies evident under his eye; yet is there no alteration made but in the removal of the mists and clouds that interrupted his sight. So was it with them under the law. The types and shadows that they were enclosed in, and which were the only medium they had to view spiritual things in, represented them not to them clearly and in their proper shape. But they being now removed, by the rising of the Sun of righteousness with healing in his wings, in the dispensation of the gospel, the whole mystery of God in Christ is clearly manifested to them that do believe. And the greatness of this privilege of the gospel above the law is inexpressible; of which, as I suppose, we must speak somewhat afterwards.

2. In the plentiful communication of grace to the community of the church; for now it is that we receive "grace for grace," or a plentiful effusion of it, by Jesus Christ. There was grace given in an eminent manner to many holy persons under the old testament, and all true believers had true, real, saving grace communicated to them; but the measures of grace in the true church under the new testament do exceed those of the community of the church under the old. And therefore, as God winked at some things under the old testament, as polygamy, and the like, which are expressly and severely interdicted under the new, nor are consistent with the present administrations of it; so are various duties, as those of self-denial, readiness to bear the cross, to forsake houses, lands, and habitations, more expressly enjoined to us than to them. And the obedience which God requires in any covenant, or administration of it, is proportional to the strength which the administration of that covenant does exhibit. And if those who profess the gospel do content themselves without any interest in this privilege of it, if they endeavor not for a share in that plentiful effusion of grace which does accompany its present administration, the gospel itself will be of no other use to them, but to increase and aggravate their condemnation.

3. In the manner of our access to God. In this much of all that is called religion does consist; for on this depends all our outward worship of God. And in this the advantages of the gospel-administration of the covenant above that of the law is in all things

very eminent. Our access now to God is immediate, by Jesus Christ, with liberty and boldness, as we will afterwards declare. Those under the law were immediately conversant, in their whole worship, about outward, typical things, the tabernacle, the altar, the ark, the mercy-seat, and the like obscure representations of the presence of God. Besides, the manner of the making of the covenant with them at Mount Sinai filled them with fear, and brought them into bondage, so as they had comparatively a servile frame of spirit in all their holy worship.

4. In the way of worship required under each administration. For under that which was legal, it seemed good to God to appoint a great number of outward rites, ceremonies, and observances; and these, as they were dark in their signification, as also in their use and ends, so were they, by reason of their nature, number, and the severe penalties under which they were enjoined, grievous and burdensome to be observed. But the way of worship under the gospel is spiritual, rational, and plainly subservient to the ends of the covenant itself; so as that the use, ends, benefits, and advantages of it are evident to all.

5. In the extent of the dispensation of the grace of God; for this is greatly enlarged under the gospel. For under the old testament it was on the matter confined to the posterity of Abraham according to the flesh; but under the new testament it extends itself to all nations under heaven.

Various other things are usually added by our divines to the same purpose. See Calvin. Institut. lib. 2:cap. xi.; Martyr. Loc. Com. loc. 16, sect. 2; Bucan. loc. 22, etc.

The Lutheran Arguments

The Lutherans, on the other side, insist on two arguments to prove, that not a twofold administration of the same covenant, but that two covenants substantially distinct, are intended in this discourse of the apostle.

1. Because in the Scripture they are often so called, and compared with one another, and sometimes opposed to one another; the first and the last, the new and the old.

The Difference Between the Two Covenants

2. Because the covenant of grace in Christ is eternal, immutable, always the same, subject to no alteration, no change or abrogation; neither can these things be spoken of it with respect to any administration of it, as they are spoken of the old covenant.

Five Things Concerning This Matter

To state our thoughts aright in this matter, and to give what light we can to the truth, the things ensuing may be observed:

1. When we speak of the "old covenant," we intend not the covenant of works made with Adam, and his whole posterity in him; concerning which there is no difference or difficulty, whether it is a distinct covenant from the new or no.

2. When we speak of the "new covenant," we do not intend the covenant of grace absolutely, as though that were not before in being and efficacy, before the introduction of that which is promised in this place. For it was always the same, as to the substance of it, from the beginning. It passed through the whole dispensation of times before the law, and under the law, of the same nature and efficacy, unalterable, "everlasting, ordered in all things, and sure." All who contend about these things, only except the Socinians, do grant that the covenant of grace, considered absolutely, that is the promise of grace in and by Jesus Christ, was the only way and means of salvation to the church, from the first entrance of sin. But for two reasons it is not expressly called a covenant, without respect to any other things, nor was it so under the old testament. When God renewed the promise of it to Abraham, he is said to make a covenant with him; and he did so, but it was with respect to other things, especially the proceeding of the promised Seed from his loins. But absolutely under the old testament it consisted only in a promise; and as such only is proposed in the Scripture, Acts 2:39; Heb. 6:14-16. The apostle indeed says, that the covenant was confirmed of God in Christ, before the giving of the law, Gal. 3:17. And so it was, not absolutely in itself, but in the promise and benefits of it. The νομοθεσία, or full legal establishment of it, by reason of which it became formally a

covenant to the whole church, was future only, and a promise under the old testament; for it lacked two things to that:

(1.) It lacked its solemn confirmation and establishment, by the blood of the only sacrifice which belonged to it. Before this was done in the death of Christ, it had not the formal nature of a covenant or a testament, as our apostle proves, Heb. 9:15-23. For neither, as he shows in that place, would the law given at Sinai have been a covenant, had it not been confirmed with the blood of sacrifices. To that end the promise was not before a formal and solemn covenant.

(2.) This was lacking, that it was not the spring, rule, and measure of all the worship of the church. This does belong to every covenant, properly so called, that God makes with the church, which it be the entire rule of all the worship that God requires of it; which is that which they are to estipulate in their entrance into covenant with God. But so the covenant of grace was not under the old testament; for God did require of the church many duties of worship that did not belong to that. But now, under the new testament, this covenant, with its own seals and appointments, is the only rule and measure of all acceptable worship. To that end the new covenant promised in the Scripture, and here opposed to the old, is not the promise of grace, mercy, life, and salvation by Christ, absolutely considered, but as it had the formal nature of a covenant given to it, in its establishment by the death of Christ, the procuring cause of all its benefits, and the declaring of it to be the only rule of worship and obedience to the church. So that although by "the covenant of grace," we oftentimes understand no more but the way of life, grace, mercy, and salvation by Christ; yet by "the new covenant," we intend its actual establishment in the death of Christ, with that blessed way of worship which by it is settled in the church.

3. While the church enjoyed all the spiritual benefits of the promise, in which the substance of the covenant of grace was contained, before it was confirmed and made the sole rule of worship to the church, it was not inconsistent with the holiness and wisdom of God to bring it under any other covenant, or

prescribe to it what forms of worship he pleased. It was not so, I say, on these three suppositions:

(1.) That this covenant did not disannul or make ineffectual the promise that was given before, but that that does still continue the only means of life and salvation. And that this was so, our apostle proves at large, Gal. 3:17-19.

(2.) That this other covenant, with all the worship contained in it or required by it, did not divert from, but direct and lead to, the future establishment of the promise in the solemnity of a covenant, by the ways mentioned. And that the covenant made in Sinai, with all its ordinances, did so, the apostle proves likewise in the place before mentioned, as also in this whole epistle.

(3.) That it be of present use and advantage to the church in its present condition. This the apostle acknowledges to be a great objection against the use and efficacy of the promise under the old testament, as to life and salvation; namely, "To what end then serves the giving of the law?" to which he answers, by showing the necessity and use of the law to the church in its then present condition, Gal. 3:17-19.

4. These things being observed, we may consider that the Scripture does plainly and expressly make mention of two testaments, or covenants, and distinguish between them in such a way, as what is spoken can hardly be accommodated to a twofold administration of the same covenant. The one is mentioned and described, Exod. 24:3-8, Deut. 5:2-5, namely, the covenant that God made with the people of Israel in Sinai; and which is commonly called "the covenant," where the people under the old testament are said to keep or break God's covenant; which for the most part is spoken with respect to that worship which was peculiar to that. The other is promised, Jer. 31:31-34, 32:40; which is the new or gospel covenant, as before explained, mentioned Matt. 26:28; Mk. 14:24. And these two covenants, or testaments, are compared one with the other, and opposed one to another, 2 Cor. 3:6-9; Gal. 4:24-26; Heb. 7:22; 9:15-20.

These two we call "the old and the new testament." Only it must be observed, that in this argument, by the "old testament," we do not understand the books of the Old Testament, or the writings

The Difference Between the Two Covenants

of Moses, the Psalms, and the Prophets, or the oracles of God committed then to the church, (I confess they are once so called, 2 Cor. 3:14, "The veil remains untaken away in the reading of the Old Testament," that is, the books of it; unless we should say, that the apostle intends only the reading of the things which concern the old testament in the Scripture;) for this old covenant, or testament, whatever it be, is abrogated and taken away, as the apostle expressly proves, but the word of God in the books of the Old Testament abides for ever. And those writings are called the Old Testament, or the books of the Old Testament, not as though they contained in them nothing but what belongs to the old covenant, for they contain the doctrine of the New Testament also; but they are so termed because they were committed to the church while the old covenant was in force, as the rule and law of its worship and obedience.

5. To that end we must grant two distinct covenants, rather than a twofold administration of the same covenant merely, to be intended. We must, I say, do so, provided always that the way of reconciliation and salvation was the same under both. But it will be said, and with great pretense of reason, for it is that which is the sole foundation they all build on who allow only a twofold administration of the same covenant, "That this being the principal end of a divine covenant, if the way of reconciliation and salvation be the same under both, then indeed are they for the substance of them but one." And I grant that this would inevitably follow, if it were so equally by virtue of them both. If reconciliation and salvation by Christ were to be obtained not only under the old covenant, but by virtue of it, then it must be the same for substance with the new. But this is not so; for no reconciliation with God nor salvation could be obtained by virtue of the old covenant, or the administration of it, as our apostle disputes at large, though all believers were reconciled, justified, and saved, by virtue of the promise, while they were under the covenant.

The Difference Between the Two Covenants

Three Things Related to the First Covenant that Prove that It Was Not an Administration of the Covenant of Grace

As therefore I have showed in what sense the covenant of grace is called "the new covenant," in this distinction and opposition, so I will propose various things which relate to the nature of the first covenant, which manifest it to have been a distinct covenant, and not a mere administration of the covenant of grace.

First, It Was Not for the Life and Salvation of the Church

This covenant, called "the old covenant," was never intended to be of itself the absolute rule and law of life and salvation to the church, but was made with a particular design, and with respect to particular ends. This the apostle proves undeniably in this epistle, especially in the chapter foregoing, and those two that follow. Therefore it follows that it could abrogate or disannul nothing which God at any time before had given as a general rule to the church. For that which is particular cannot abrogate any thing that was general, and before it; as that which is general does abrogate all antecedent particulars, as the new covenant does abrogate the old. And this we must consider in both the instances belonging to this. For,

(1.) God had before given the covenant of works, or perfect obedience, to all mankind, in the law of creation. But this covenant at Sinai did not abrogate or disannul that covenant, nor in any way fulfill it. And the reason is, because it was never intended to come in the place or room of it, as a covenant, containing an entire rule of all the faith and obedience of the whole church. God did not intend in it to abrogate the covenant of works, and to substitute this in the place of it; yea, in various things it re-enforced, established, and confirmed that covenant. For,

[1.] It revived, declared, and expressed all the commands of that covenant in the Decalogue; for that is nothing but a divine summary of the law written in the heart of man at his creation. And in this the dreadful manner of its delivery or promulgation, with its writing in tables of stone, is also to be considered; for in them the

The Difference Between the Two Covenants

nature of that first covenant, with its inexorableness as to perfect obedience, was represented. And because none could answer its demands, or comply with it in that respect, it was called "the ministration of death," causing fear and bondage, 2 Cor. 3:7.

[2.] It revived the sanction of the first covenant, in the curse or sentence of death which it denounced against all transgressors. Death was the penalty of the transgression of the first covenant: "In the day that you eat of it, you will die the death." And this sentence was revived and represented anew in the curse by which this covenant was ratified, "Cursed be he that confirms not all the words of this law to do them," Deut. 27:26; Gal. 3:10. For the design of God in it was to bind a sense of that curse on the consciences of men, until he came by whom it was taken away, as the apostle declares, Gal. 3:19.

[3.] It revived the promise of that covenant that of eternal life on perfect obedience. So the apostle tells us that Moses thus describes the righteousness of the law, "That the man which does those things will live by them," Rom. 10:5; as he does, Leviticus 18:5.

Now this is no other but the covenant of works revived. Nor had this covenant of Sinai any promise of eternal life annexed to it, as such, but only the promise inseparable from the covenant of works which it revived, saying, "Do this, and live."

Therefore it is, that when our apostle disputes against justification by the law, or by the works of the law, he does not intend the works peculiar to the covenant of Sinai, such as were the rites and ceremonies of the worship then instituted; but he intends also the works of the first covenant, which alone had the promise of life annexed to them.

And therefore it follows also, that it was not a new covenant of works established in the place of the old, for the absolute rule of faith and obedience to the whole church; for then would it have abrogated and taken away that covenant, and all the force of it, which it did not.

(2.) The other instance is in the promise. This also went before it; neither was it abrogated or disannulled by the introduction of this covenant. This promise was given to our first parents immediately after the entrance of sin, and was established as containing the only way and means of the salvation of sinners. Now, this promise could not be abrogated by the introduction of this covenant, and a new way of justification and salvation be by that means established. For the promise being given out in general for the whole church, as containing the way appointed by God for righteousness, life, and salvation, it could not be disannulled or changed, without a change and alteration in the counsels of him "with whom is no variableness, neither shadow of turning." Much less could this be accomplished by a particular covenant, such as that was, when it was given as a general and eternal rule.

Second, It Did Not Disannul the Promise Made to Abraham

But although there was an especial promise given to Abraham, in the faith of which he became "the father of the faithful," he being their progenitor, it should seem that this covenant did wholly disannul or supersede that promise, and take off the church of his posterity from building on that foundation, and so fix them wholly on this new covenant now made with them. So says Moses, "The LORD made not this covenant with our fathers, but with us, who are all of us here alive this day," Deut. 5:3. God made not this covenant on Mount Sinai with Abraham, Isaac, and Jacob, but with the people then present, and their posterity, as he declares, Deut. 29:14, 15. This, therefore, should seem to take them off wholly from that promise made to Abraham, and so to disannul it. But that this it did not, nor could do, the apostle strictly proves, Gal. 3:17-22; yea, it did in various ways establish that promise, both as first given and as afterwards confirmed with the oath of God to Abraham, in two ways especially:

(1.) It declared the impossibility of obtaining reconciliation and peace with God any other way but by the promise. For representing the commands of the covenant of works, requiring perfect, sinless obedience, under the penalty of the curse, it convinced men that this was no way for sinners to seek for life and salvation by. And by this means it so urged the consciences of men, that they could have no rest or peace in themselves but what the promise would afford them, to which they saw a necessity of committing themselves.

The Difference Between the Two Covenants

(2.) By representing the ways and means of the accomplishment of the promise, and of that on what all the efficacy of it to the justification and salvation of sinners does depend. This was the death, blood-shedding, oblation, or sacrifice of Christ, the promised seed. This all its offerings and ordinances of worship directed to; as his incarnation, with the inhabitation of God in his human nature, was typed by the tabernacle and temple. To that end it was so far from disannulling the promise, or diverting the minds of the people of God from it, that by all means it established it and led to it.

Third, It Had Other Benefits for the Church

But it will be said, as was before observed, "That if it did neither abrogate the first covenant of works, and come in the room of it, nor disannul the promise made to Abraham, then to what end did it serve, or what benefit did the church receive by that means?" I answer,

(1.) There has been, with respect to God's dealing with the church, οἰκονομία τῶν καιρῶν, a "certain dispensation" and disposition of times and seasons, reserved to the sovereign will and pleasure of God. Therefore from the beginning he revealed himself πολυτρόπως[9] and πολυμερῶς,[10] as seemed good to him, Heb. 1:1. And this dispensation of times had a πλήρωμα, a "fullness" assigned to it, in which all things, namely, that belong to the revelation and communication of God to the church, should come to their height, and have as it were the last hand given to them. This was in the sending of Christ, as the apostle declares, Eph. 1:10, "That in the dispensation of the fullness of times he might bring all to a head in Christ." Until this season came, God dealt variously with the church ἐν ποικίλῃ σοφίᾳ, "in manifold" or "various wisdom," according as he saw it needful and useful for it, in that season which it was to pass through, before the fullness of times came. Of this nature was his entrance into the covenant with the church at Sinai; the reasons of which we will immediately inquire into. In the

---

[9] [In various times.]
[10] [In various ways.]

meantime, if we had no other answer to this inquiry but only this, that in the order of the disposal or dispensation of the seasons of the church, before the fullness of times came, God in his manifold wisdom saw it necessary for the then present state of the church in that season, we may well consent in that respect. But,

(2.) The apostle acquaints us in general with the ends of this dispensation of God, Gal. 3:19-24: "To what end then serves the law? It was added because of transgressions, until the seed should come to whom the promise was made; and it was ordained by angels in the hand of a mediator. Now a mediator is not of one, but God is one. Is the law then against the promises of God? God forbid; for if there had been a law given which could have given life, verily righteousness should have been by the law. But the Scripture has concluded all under sin that the promise by faith of Jesus Christ might be given to them that believe. But before faith came, we were kept under the law, shut up to the faith which should afterwards be revealed. To that end the law was our schoolmaster to bring us to Christ, that we might be justified by faith." Much light might be given to the mind of the Holy Spirit in these words, and that in things not commonly discerned by expositors, if we should divert to the opening of them. I will at present only mark from them what is to our present purpose.

A Double Inquiry Concerning the Covenant of Sinai

There is a double inquiry made by the apostle with respect to the law, or the covenant of Sinai: [1.] To what end in general it served. [2.] Whether it was not contrary to the promise of God. To both these the apostle answers from the nature, office, and work of that covenant. For there were, as has been declared, two things in it: [1.] A revival and representation of the covenant of works, with its sanction and curse. [2.] A direction of the church to the accomplishment of the promise. From these two does the apostle frame his answer to the double inquiry laid down.

And to the first inquiry, "to what end it served," he answers, "It was added because of transgressions." The promise being given, there seems to have been no need of it, why then was it added to it

The Difference Between the Two Covenants

at that season? "It was added because of transgressions." The fullness of time was not yet come, in which the promise was to be fulfilled, accomplished and established as the only covenant in which the church was to walk with God; or, "the seed" was not yet come, as the apostle here speaks, to whom the promise was made. In the meantime some order must be taken about sin and transgression that all the order of things appointed of God might not be overflowed by them. And this was done two ways by the law:

[1.] By reviving the commands of the covenant of works, with the sanction of death, it put awe on the minds of men, and set bounds to their lusts, that they should not dare to run forth into that excess which they were naturally inclined to. It was therefore "added because of transgressions;" that, in the declaration of God's severity against them, some bounds might be fixed to them; for "by the law is the knowledge of sin."

[2.] To shut up unbelievers, and such as would not seek for righteousness, life, and salvation by the promise, under the power of the covenant of works, and curse attending it. "It concluded" or "shut up all under sin," says the apostle, Gal. 3:22. This was the end of the law, for this end was it added, as it gave a revival to the covenant of works.

To the second inquiry, which arises out of this supposition, namely, that the law did convince of sin, and condemn for sin, which is, "whether it be not then contrary to the grace of God," the apostle in like manner returns a double answer, taken from the second use of the law, before insisted on, with respect to the promise. And,

[1.] He says, "That although the law does thus rebuke sin, convince of sin, and condemn for sin, so setting bounds to transgressions and transgressors, yet did God never intend it as a means to give life and righteousness, nor was it able so to do." The end of the promise was to give righteousness, justification, and salvation, all by Christ, to whom and concerning whom it was made. But this was not the end for which the law was revived in the covenant of Sinai. For although in itself it requires a perfect righteousness, and gives a promise of life for that reason, ("He that does these things, he will live in them,") yet it could give neither righteousness nor life to any in the state of sin. See Rom. 8:3; 10:4. To that end the promise and the law, having diverse ends, they are not contrary to one another.

[2.] He says, "The law has a great respect to the promise; and was given of God for this very end, that it might lead and direct men to Christ." This is sufficient to answer the question proposed at the beginning of this discourse, about the end of this covenant, and the advantage which the church received by that means.

The Substance of the Whole Truth

What has been spoken may suffice to declare the nature of this covenant in general; and two things do here evidently follow, in which the substance of the whole truth contended for by the apostle does consist:

(1.) That while the covenant of grace was contained and proposed only in the promise, before it was solemnly confirmed in the blood and sacrifice of Christ, and so legalized or established as the only rule of the worship of the church, the introduction of this other covenant on Sinai did not constitute a new way or means of righteousness, life, and salvation; but believers sought for them alone by the covenant of grace as declared in the promise. This follows evidently on what we have discoursed; and it secures absolutely that great fundamental truth, which the apostle in this and all his other epistles so earnestly contends for, namely, that there neither is, nor ever was, either righteousness, justification, life, or salvation, to be attained by any law, or the works of it, (for this covenant at Mount Sinai comprehended every law that God ever gave to the church,) but by Christ alone, and faith in him.

(2.) That although this covenant being introduced in the pleasure of God, there was prescribed with it a form of outward worship suited to that dispensation of times and present state of the church; on the introduction of the new covenant in the fullness of times, to be the rule of all relationship between God and the church, both that covenant and all its worship must be disannulled. This is that which the apostle proves with all sorts of arguments, manifesting the great advantage of the church by that means.

These things, I say, do evidently follow on the preceding discourses, and are the main truths contended for by the apostle.

Six Reasons for the First Covenant

There remains one thing more only to be considered, before we enter on the comparison between the two covenants here directed to by the apostle. And it is how this first covenant came to be an especial covenant to that people: in which we will manifest the reason of its introduction at that season. And to this end various things are to be considered concerning that people and the church of God in them, with whom this covenant was made; which will further evidence the nature, use, and necessity of it:

(1.) This people were the posterity of Abraham, to whom the promise was made that in his seed all the nations of the earth should be blessed. To that end from among them was the promised Seed to be raised up in the fullness of time, or its proper season, from among them was the Son of God to take on him the seed of Abraham. To this end various things were necessary:

[1.] That they should have a certain abiding place or country, which they might freely inhabit, distinct from other nations, and under a rule or scepter of their own. So it is said of them, that "the people should dwell alone, and not be reckoned among the nations," Num. 23:9; and "the scepter was not to depart from them until Shiloh came," Gen. 49:10. For God had regard to his own glory in his faithfulness as to his word and oath given to Abraham, not only that they should be accomplished, but that their accomplishment should be evident and conspicuous. But if this posterity of Abraham, from among whom the promised Seed was to rise, had been, as it is at this day with them, scattered abroad on the face of the earth, mixed with all nations, and under their power, although God might have accomplished his promise really in raising up Christ from among some of his posterity, yet could it not be proved or evidenced that he had so done, by reason of the confusion and mixture of the people with others. To that end God provided a land and country for them which they might inhabit by themselves, and as their own, even the land of Canaan. And this was so suited to all the ends of God towards that people, as might be declared in various instances, that God is said to have "espied this land out for them," Ezek. 20:6. He chose it out, as most fit for his purpose towards that people of all lands under heaven.

[2.] That there should be always kept among them an open confession and visible representation of the end for which they were so separated from all the nations of the world. They were not to dwell in the land of Canaan merely for secular ends, and to make as it were a mute show; but as they were there maintained and preserved to evidence the faithfulness of God in bringing forth the promised Seed in the fullness of time, so there was to be a testimony kept up among them to that end of God to which they were preserved. This was the end of all their ordinances of worship, of the tabernacle, priesthood, sacrifices, and ordinances; which were all appointed by Moses, on the command of God, "for a testimony of those things which should be spoken afterwards," Heb. 3:5.

These things were necessary in the first place, with respect to the ends of God towards that people.

(2.) It becomes not the wisdom, holiness, and sovereignty of God, to call any people into an especial relation to himself, to do them good in an eminent and peculiar manner, and then to suffer them to live at their pleasure, without any regard to what he has done for them. To that end, having granted to this people those great privileges of the land of Canaan, and the ordinances of worship relating to the great end mentioned, he moreover prescribed to them laws, rules, and terms of obedience, on what they should hold and enjoy that land, with all the privileges annexed to the possession of it. And these are both expressed and frequently inculcated, in the repetition and promises of the law. But yet in the prescription of these terms, God reserved the sovereignty of dealing with them to himself. For had he left them to stand or fall absolutely by the terms prescribed to them, they might and would have utterly forfeited both the land and all the privileges they enjoyed in that respect. And had it so fallen out, then the great end

The Difference Between the Two Covenants

of God in preserving them a separate people until the Seed should come, and a representation of it among them, had been frustrated. To that end, although he punished them for their transgressions, according to the threats of the law, yet would he not bring הדס, "curse of the law," on them, and utterly cast them off, until his great end was accomplished, Mal. 4:4-6.

(3.) God would not take this people off from the promise, because his church was among them, and they could neither please God nor be accepted with him but by faith in that respect. But yet they were to be dealt with according as it was proper. For they were generally a stiff-necked people, of a hard heart and lifted up with an opinion of their own righteousness and worth above others. This Moses endeavors, by all manner of reasons and instances to the contrary, to take them off from, in the book of Deuteronomy. Yet it was not performed among the generality of them, nor is to this day; for in the midst of all their wickedness and misery, they still trust to and boast of their own righteousness, and will have it that God has an especial obligation to them on that account. For this cause God saw it necessary, and it pleased him to put a grievous and heavy yoke on them, to subdue the pride of their spirits, and to cause them to breathe after deliverance. This the apostle Peter calls "a yoke that neither they nor their fathers were able to bear," Acts 15:10; that is, with peace, ease, and rest: which therefore the Lord Christ invited them to seek for in himself alone, Matt. 11:29, 30. And this yoke that God put on them consisted in these three things:

[1.] In a multitude of precepts, hard to be understood, and difficult to be observed. The present Jews reckon up six hundred and thirteen of them; about the sense of most of which they dispute endlessly among themselves. But the truth is, since the days of the Pharisees they have increased their own yoke, and made obedience to their law in any tolerable manner altogether impracticable. It would be easy to manifest, for instance, that no man under heaven ever did, or ever can, keep the Sabbath according to the rules they give about it in their Talmud. And they generally scarce observe one of them themselves. But in the law, as given by God himself, it is certain that there are a multitude of arbitrary precepts, and those in themselves not accompanied with any spiritual advantages, as our apostle shows, Heb. 9:9, 10; only they were obliged to perform them by a mere sovereign act of power and authority.

[2.] In the severity by which the observance of all those precepts was enjoined them. And this was the threat of death; for "he that despised Moses' law died without mercy," and "every transgression and disobedience received a just recompense of reward." Therefore was their complaint of old, "Behold, we die, we perish, we all perish. Whosoever comes any thing near to the tabernacle of the LORD will die: will we be consumed with dying?" Num. 17:12, 13. And the curse solemnly denounced against every one that confirmed not all things written in the law was continually before them.

[3.] In a spirit of bondage to fear. This was administered in the giving and dispensation of the law, even as a spirit of liberty and power is administered in and by the gospel. And as this respected their present obedience, and manner of its performance, so in particular it regarded death not yet conquered by Christ. Therefore our apostle affirms, that "through fear of death they were all their lifetime subject to bondage."

This state God brought them into, partly to subdue the pride of their hearts, trusting in their own righteousness, and partly to cause them to look out earnestly after the promised deliverer.

(4.) Into this estate and condition God brought them by a solemn covenant, confirmed by mutual consent between him and them. The tenor, force, and solemn ratification of this covenant, are expressed, Exod. 24:3-8. To the terms and conditions of this covenant was the whole church obliged indispensably, on pain of extermination, until all was accomplished, Mal. 4:4-6. To this covenant belonged the Decalogue, with all precepts of moral obedience from there drawn. So also did the laws of political rule established among them, and the whole system of religious worship given to them. All these laws were brought within the verge of this covenant, and were the matter of it. And it had especial promises and threats annexed to it as such; of which none did exceed the bounds of the land of Canaan. For even many of the laws of it were such as obliged nowhere else. Such was the law of the sabbatical year, and all their sacrifices. There was sin and obedience in them or about them in the land of Canaan, none elsewhere. Therefore,

(5.) This covenant thus made, with these ends and promises, did never save nor condemn any man eternally. All that lived under the administration of it did attain eternal life, or perished for ever, but not by virtue of this covenant as formally such. It did, indeed, revive the commanding power and sanction of the first covenant of works; and in that respect, as the apostle speaks, was "the ministry of condemnation," 2 Cor. 3:9; for "by the deeds of the law can no flesh be justified." And on the other hand, it directed also to the promise, which was the instrument of life and salvation to all that did believe. But as to what it had of its own, it was confined to things temporal. Believers were saved under it, but not by virtue of it. Sinners perished eternally under it, but by the curse of the original law of works. And,

(6.) On this occasionally fell out the ruin of that people; "their table became a snare to them, and that which should have been for their welfare became a trap," according to the prediction of our Savior, Psa. 69:22. It was this covenant that raised and ruined them. It raised them to glory and honor when given of God; it ruined them when abused by themselves to ends contrary to express declarations of his mind and will. For although the generality of them were wicked and rebellious, always breaking the terms of the covenant which God made with them, so far as it was possible they should, while God determined to reign over them to the appointed season, and repining under the burden of it; yet they would have this covenant to be the only rule and means of righteousness, life, and salvation, as the apostle declares, Rom. 9:31-33; 10:3. For, as we have often said, there were two things in it, both which they abused to other ends than what God designed them:

[1.] There was the renovation of the rule of the covenant of works for righteousness and life. And this they would have to be given to them for those ends, and so sought for righteousness by the works of the law.

[2.] There was ordained in it a typical representation of the way and means in accordance with which the promise was to be made effectual, namely, in the mediation and sacrifice of Jesus Christ; which was the end of all their ordinances of worship. And the outward law of it, with the observance of its institution, they looked on as their only relief when they came short of exact and perfect righteousness.

Against both these pernicious errors the apostle disputes expressly in his epistles to the Romans and the Galatians, to save them, if it were possible, from that ruin they were casting themselves into. On this "the elect obtained," but "the rest were hardened." For by that means they made an absolute renunciation of the promise, in which alone God had enwrapped the way of life and salvation.

This is the nature and substance of that covenant which God made with that people; a particular, temporary covenant it was, and not a mere dispensation of the covenant of grace.

The Difference between the Two Covenants

That which remains for the declaration of the mind of the Holy Spirit in this whole matter, is to declare the differences that are between those two covenants, by reason of which fact the one is said to be "better" than the other, and to be "built on better promises."

The Opinion of the Church of Rome

Those of the Church of Rome do commonly place this difference in three things: 1. In the promises of them: which in the old covenant were temporal only; in the new, spiritual and heavenly. 2. In the precepts of them: which under the old, required only external obedience, designing the righteousness of the outward man; under the new, they are internal, respecting principally the inner man of the heart. 3. In their sacraments: for those under the old testament were only outwardly figurative; but those of the new are operative of grace.

But these things do not express much, if any thing at all, of what the Scripture places this difference in. And besides, as by some of them explained, they are not true, especially the two latter of them. For I cannot but somewhat admire how it came into the heart or mind of any man to think or say, that God ever gave a law or laws, precept or precepts, that should "respect the outward man only, and the regulation of external duties." A thought of it is contrary to all the essential properties of the nature of God, and fit only to ingenerate[11] apprehensions of him unsuited to all his glorious excellencies. The life and foundation of all the laws under the old testament was, "You will love the LORD your God with all your soul;" without which no outward obedience was ever accepted with him. And for the third of the supposed differences, neither were the sacraments of the law so barely "figurative," but that they did exhibit Christ to believers: for "they all drank of the spiritual rock; which rock was Christ." Nor are those of the gospel so operative of grace, but that without faith they are useless to them that do receive them.

The Scripture's Doctrine on the Difference Between the Covenants Expounded on 17 Particulars

The things in which this difference does consist, as expressed in the Scripture, are partly circumstantial, and partly substantial, and may be reduced to the heads ensuing:

1. These two covenants differ in the circumstance of time as to their promulgation, declaration, and establishment. This difference the apostle expresses from the prophet Jeremiah, in the ninth verse of this chapter, where it must be more fully spoken to. In brief, the first covenant was made at the time that God brought the children of Israel out of Egypt, and took its date from the third month after their coming up from there, Exod. 19, 24. From the time of what is reported in the latter place, in which the people give their actual consent to the terms of it, it began its formal obligation as a covenant. And we must afterwards inquire when it was abrogated and ceased to oblige the church. The new covenant was declared and made known "in the latter days," Heb. 1:1, 2; "in the

---

[11] [Not generated, self-existent; inborn, innate.]

dispensation of the fullness of times," Eph. 1:10. And it took date, as a covenant formally obliging the whole church, from the death, resurrection, ascension of Christ, and sending of the Holy Spirit. I bring them all into the epoch of this covenant, because though principally it was established by the first, yet was it not absolutely obligatory as a covenant until after the last of them.

2. They differ in the circumstance of place as to their promulgation; which the Scripture also takes notice of. The first was declared on Mount Sinai; the manner of which, and the station of the people in receiving the law, I have in my Exercitations to the first part of this Exposition at large declared, and to that place the reader is referred,[12] Exod. 19:18. The other was declared on Mount Zion, and the law of it went forth from Jerusalem, Isa. 2:3. This difference, with many remarkable instances from it, our apostle insists on, Gal. 4:24-26: "These are the two covenants; the one from Mount Sinai, which gives birth to bondage, which is Agar." That is, Agar, the bondwoman whom Abraham took before the heir of promise was born, was a type of the old covenant given on Sinai, before the introduction of the new, or the covenant of promise; for so he adds: "For this Agar is Mount Sinai in Arabia, and answers to Jerusalem which now is, and is in bondage with her children." This Mount Sinai, where the old covenant was given, and which was represented by Agar, is in Arabia, cast quite out of the verge and confines of the church. And it "answers," or "is placed in the same series, rank, and order with Jerusalem," namely, in the opposition of the two covenants. For as the new covenant, the covenant of promise, giving freedom and liberty, was given at Jerusalem, in the death and resurrection of Christ, with the preaching of the gospel which ensued for that reason; so the old covenant, that brought the people into bondage, was given at Mount Sinai in Arabia.

3. They differ in the manner of their promulgation and establishment. There were two things remarkable that accompanied the solemn declaration of the first covenant:

(1.) The dread and terror of the outward appearance on Mount Sinai, which filled all the people, yea, Moses himself, with fear and

---

[12] See vol. i, of this Exposition, p. 446. – Ed. [Banner Edition.]

trembling, Heb. 12:18-21; Exod. 19:16; 20:18, 19. Together by this means was a spirit of fear and bondage administered to all the people, so as that they chose to keep at a distance, and not draw nigh to God, Deut. 5:23-27.

(2.) That it was given by the ministry and "disposition of angels," Acts 7:53; Gal. 3:19. Therefore the people were in a sense "put in subjection to angels," and they had an authoritative ministry in that covenant. The church that then was, was put into some kind of subjection to angels, as the apostle plainly intimates, Heb. 2:5. Therefore the worshipping or adoration of angels began among that people, Col. 2:18; which some, with an addition to their folly and superstition, would introduce into the Christian church, in which they have no such authoritative ministry as they had under the old covenant.

Things are quite otherwise in the promulgation of the new covenant. The Son of God in his own person did declare it. This he "spoke from heaven," as the apostle observes; in opposition to the giving of the law "on the earth," Heb. 12:25. Yet did he speak on the earth also; the mystery of which himself declares, John 3:13. And he did all things that belonged to the establishment of this covenant in a spirit of meekness and condescension, with the highest evidence of love, grace, and compassion, encouraging and inviting the weary, the burdened, the heavy and laden to come to him. And by his Spirit he makes his disciples to carry on the same work until the covenant was fully declared, Heb. 2:3. See John 1:17, 18.

And the whole ministry of angels, in the giving of this covenant, was merely in a way of service and obedience to Christ; and they owned themselves the "fellow-servants" only of them that have "the testimony of Jesus," Rev. 19:10. So that this "world to come," as it was called of old, was not put in subjection to them.

4. They differ in their mediators. The mediator of the first covenant was Moses. "It was ordained by angels in the hand of a mediator," Gal. 3:19. And this was no other but Moses, who was a servant in the house of God, Heb. 3:5. And he was a mediator, as designed of God, so chosen of the people, in that dread and consternation which befell them on the terrible promulgation of the law. For they saw that they could no way bear the immediate

presence of God, nor treat with him in their own persons. To that end they desired that there might be a go-between, a mediator between God and them, and that Moses might be the person, Deut. 5:24-27. But the mediator of the new covenant is the Son of God himself. For "there is one God, and one mediator between God and men, the man Christ Jesus; who gave himself a ransom for all," 1 Tim. 2:5. He who is the Son, and the Lord over his own house, graciously undertook in his own person to be the mediator of this covenant; and in this it is unspeakably preferred before the old covenant.

5. They differ in their subject-matter, both as to precepts and promises, the advantage being still on the part of the new covenant. For,

(1.) The old covenant, in the preceptive part of it, renewed the commands of the covenant of works, and that on their original terms. Sin it forbade, that is, all and every sin, in matter and manner, on the pain of death; and gave the promise of life to perfect, sinless obedience only: from what cause the Decalogue itself, which is a transcript of the law of works, is called "the covenant," Exod. 34:28. And besides this, as we observed before, it had other precepts innumerable, accommodated to the present condition of the people, and imposed on them with rigor. But in the new covenant, the very first thing that is proposed is the accomplishment and establishment of the covenant of works, both as to its commands and sanction, in the obedience and suffering of the mediator. On this the commands of it, as to the obedience of the covenanters, are not grievous; the yoke of Christ being easy, and his burden light.

(2.) The old testament, absolutely considered, had, [1.] No promise of grace, to communicate spiritual strength, or to assist us in obedience; [2.] Nor of eternal life, no otherwise but as it was contained in the promise of the covenant of works, "The man that does these things will live in them;" and, [3.] Had promises of temporal things in the land of Canaan inseparable from it. In the new covenant all things are otherwise, as will be declared in the exposition of the ensuing verses.

The Difference Between the Two Covenants

6. They differ, and that principally, in the manner of their dedication and sanction. This is that which gives any thing the formal nature of a covenant or testament. There may be a promise, there may be an agreement in general, which has not the formal nature of a covenant, or testament, and such was the covenant of grace before the death of Christ, but it is the solemnity and manner of the confirmation, dedication, and sanction of any promise or agreement, that give it the formal nature of a covenant or testament. And this is by a sacrifice, in which there is both blood shedding and death ensuing for that reason. Now this, in the confirmation of the old covenant, was only the sacrifice of beasts, whose blood was sprinkled on all the people, Exod. 24:5-8. But the new testament was solemnly confirmed by the sacrifice and blood of Christ himself, Zech. 9:11; Heb. 10:29; 13:20. And the Lord Christ dying as the mediator and surety of the covenant, he purchased all good things for the church; and as a testator bequeathed them to it. Therefore he says of the sacramental cup, that it is "the new testament in his blood," or the pledge of his bequeathing to the church all the promises and mercies of the covenant; which is the new testament, or the disposition of his goods to his children. But because the apostle expressly handles this difference between these two covenants, chap. 9:18-23, we must to that place refer the full consideration of it.

7. They differ in the priests that were to officiate before God in the behalf of the people. In the old covenant, Aaron and his posterity alone were to discharge that office; in the new, the Son of God himself is the only priest of the church. This difference, with the advantage of the gospel-state for that reason, we have handled at large in the exposition of the previous chapter.

8. They differ in the sacrifices on what the peace and reconciliation with God which is tendered in them depends. And this also must be spoken to in the following chapter, if God permits.

9. They differ in the way and manner of their solemn writing or enrolment. All covenants were of old solemnly written in tables of brass or stone, where they might be faithfully preserved for the use of the parties concerned. So the old covenant, as to the principal, fundamental part of it, was "engraved in tables of stone," which

were kept in the ark, Exod. 31:18; Deut. 9:10; 2 Cor. 3:7. And God did so order it in his providence, that the first draft of them should be broken, to intimate that the covenant contained in them was not everlasting or unalterable. But the new covenant is written in the "fleshy tables of the hearts" of them that do believe 2 Cor. 3:3; Jer. 31:33.

10. They differ in their ends. The principal end of the first covenant was to discover sin, to condemn it, and to set bounds to it. So says the apostle, "It was added because of transgressions." And this it did several ways:

(1.) By conviction: for "by the law is the knowledge of sin"; it convinced sinners, and caused every mouth to be stopped before God.

(2.) By condemning the sinner, in an application of the sanction of the law to his conscience.

(3.) By the judgments and punishments by which on all occasions it was accompanied. In all it manifested and represented the justice and severity of God.

The end of the new covenant is, to declare the love, grace, and mercy of God; and therefore to give repentance, remission of sin, and life eternal.

11. They differed in their effects. For the first covenant being the "ministration of death" and "condemnation," it brought the minds and spirits of them that were under it into servitude and bondage; but spiritual liberty is the immediate effect of the new testament. And there is no one thing in which the Spirit of God does more frequently give us an account of the difference between these two covenants, than in this of the liberty of the one and the bondage of the other. See Rom. 8:15; 2 Cor. 3:17; Gal. 4:1-7, 24, 26, 30, 31; Heb. 2:14, 15. This, therefore, we must explain a little. To that end the bondage which was the effect of the old covenant arose from several causes concurring to the effecting of it:

(1.) The renovation of the terms and sanction of the covenant of works contributed much to that. For the people saw not how the commands of that covenant could be observed, nor how its curse could be avoided. They saw it not, I say, by any thing in the covenant of Sinai; which therefore "gave birth to bondage." The entire prospect they had of deliverance was from the promise.

(2.) It arose from the manner of the delivery of the law, and God's entering for that reason into covenant with them. This was ordered on purpose to fill them with dread and fear. And it could not but do so, whenever they called it to remembrance.

(3.) From the severity of the penalties annexed to the transgression of the law. And God had taken on himself, that where punishment was not exacted according to the law, he himself would "cut them off." This kept them always anxious and solicitous, not knowing when they were safe or secure.

(4.) From the nature of the whole ministry of the law, which was the "ministration of death" and "condemnation," 2 Cor. 3:7, 9; which declared the punishment of every sin to be death, and denounced death to every sinner, administering by itself no relief to the minds and consciences of men. So was it the "letter that killed" them that were under its power.

(5.) From the darkness of their own minds, in the means, ways, and causes of deliverance from all these things. It is true, they had a promise before of life and salvation, which was not abolished by this covenant, even the promise made to Abraham; but this belonged not to this covenant, and the way of its accomplishment, by the incarnation and mediation of the Son of God, was much hidden from them, yea, from the prophets themselves who yet foretold them. This left them under much bondage. For the principal cause and means of the liberty of believers under the gospel arises from the clear light they have into the mystery of the love and grace of God in Christ. This knowledge and faith of his incarnation, humiliation, sufferings, and sacrifice, in accordance with which he made atonement for sin, and brought in everlasting righteousness, is that which gives them liberty and boldness in their obedience, 2 Cor. 3:17, 18. While they of old were in the dark as to these things, they necessarily have been kept under much bondage.

(6.) It was increased by the yoke of a multitude of laws, rites, and ceremonies, imposed on them; which made the whole of their worship a burden to them, and unendurable, Acts 15:10.

The Difference Between the Two Covenants

In and by all these ways and means there was a spirit of bondage and fear administered to them. And this God did, thus he dealt with them, to the end that they might not rest in that state, but continually look out after deliverance.

On the other hand, the new covenant gives liberty and boldness, the liberty and boldness of children, to all believers. It is the Spirit of the Son in it that makes us free, or gives us universally all that liberty which is any way needful for us or useful to us. For "where the Spirit of the Lord is, there is liberty;" namely, to serve God, "not in the oldness of the letter, but in the newness of the spirit." And it is declared that this was the great end of bringing in the new covenant, in the accomplishment of the promise made to Abraham, namely, "that we being delivered out of the hand of our enemies, might serve God without fear ...... all the days of our life," Luke 1:72-75. And we may briefly consider in which this deliverance and liberty by the new covenant does consist, which it does in the following things:

(1.) In our freedom from the commanding power of the law, as to sinless, perfect obedience, in order to righteousness and justification before God. Its commands we are still subject to, but not in order to life and salvation; for to these ends it is fulfilled in and by the mediator of the new covenant, who is "the end of the law for righteousness to every one that believes," Rom. 10:4.

(2.) In our freedom from the condemning power of the law, and the sanction of it in the curse. This being undergone and answered by him who was "made a curse for us," we are freed from it, Rom. 7:6; Gal. 3:13, 14. And in that respect also we are "delivered from the fear of death," Heb. 2:15, as it was penal and an entrance into judgment or condemnation, John 5:24.

(3.) In our freedom from conscience of sin, Heb. 10:2, that is, conscience disquieting, perplexing, and condemning our persons; the hearts of all that believe being "sprinkled from an evil conscience" by the blood of Christ.

(4.) In our freedom from the whole system of Mosaic worship, in all the rites, and ceremonies, and ordinances of it; which what a burden it was the apostles do declare, Acts 15, and our apostle at large in his epistle to the Galatians.

The Difference Between the Two Covenants

(5.) From all the laws of men in things pertaining to the worship of God. 1 Cor. 7:23.

And by all these, and the like instances of spiritual liberty, does the gospel free believers from that "spirit of bondage to fear," which was administered under the old covenant.

It remains only that we point out the heads of those ways in accordance with which this liberty is communicated to us under the new covenant. And it is done,

(1.) Principally by the grant and communication of the Spirit of the Son as a Spirit of adoption, giving the freedom, boldness, and liberty of children, John 1:12; Rom. 8:15-17; Gal. 4:6, 7. From this place the apostle lays it down as a certain rule, that "where the Spirit of the Lord is, there is liberty," 2 Cor. 3:17. Let men pretend what they will, let them boast of the freedom of their outward condition in this world, and of the inward liberty or freedom of their wills, there is indeed no true liberty where the Spirit of God is not. The ways in accordance with which he gives freedom, power, a sound mind, spiritual boldness, courage, contempt of the cross, holy confidence before God, a readiness for obedience, and growth of heart in duties, with all other things in which true liberty does consist, or which any way belong to it, I must not here divert to declare. The world judges that there is no bondage but where the Spirit of God is; for that gives that meticulous fear of sin, that awe of God in all our thoughts, actions, and ways, that careful and circumspect walking, that temperance in things lawful, that abstinence from all appearance of evil, in which they judge the greatest bondage on the earth to consist. But those who have received him do know that the whole world does lie in evil, and that all those to whom spiritual liberty is a bondage are the servants and slaves of Satan.

(2.) It is obtained by the evidence of our justification before God, and the causes of it. Men were greatly in the dark to this under the first covenant, although all stable peace with God does depend for that reason; for it is in the gospel that "the righteousness of God is revealed from faith to faith," Rom. 1:17. Indeed "the righteousness of God without the law is witnessed by the law and the prophets," Rom. 3:21; that is, testimony is given to it in legal institutions and the promises recorded in the prophets. But these things were obscure to them, who were to seek for what was intended under the veils and shadows of priests and sacrifices, atonements and expiations. But our justification before God, in all the causes of it, being now fully revealed and made manifest, it has a great influence into spiritual liberty and boldness.

(3.) By the spiritual light that is given to believers into the mystery of God in Christ. This the apostle affirms to have been "hid in God from the beginning of the world," Eph. 3:9. It was contrived and prepared in the counsel and wisdom of God from all eternity. Some intimation was given of it in the first promise, and it was afterwards shadowed out by various legal institutions; but the depth, the glory, the beauty and fullness of it, were "hid in God," in his mind and will, until it was fully revealed in the gospel. The saints under the old testament believed that they should be delivered by the promised Seed, that they should be saved for the Lord's sake, that the Angel of the covenant would save them, yea, that the Lord himself would come to his temple; and they diligently inquired into what was signified before concerning "the sufferings of Christ, and the glory that should follow." But all this while their thoughts and conceptions were exceedingly in the dark as to those glorious things which are made so plain in the new covenant, concerning the incarnation, mediation, sufferings, and sacrifice of the Son of God, concerning the way of God's being in Christ reconciling the world to himself. Now as darkness gives fear, so light gives liberty.

(4.) We obtain this liberty by the opening of the way into the holiest, and the entrance we have by that means with boldness to the throne of grace. On this also the apostle insists peculiarly in various places of his following discourses, as chap. 9:8; 10:19-22: where it must be spoken to, if God permits, at large; for a great part of the liberty of the new testament does consist in this.

(5.) By all the ordinances of gospel-worship. How the ordinances of worship under the old testament did lead the people into bondage has been declared; but those of the new testament, through their plainness in signification, their immediate connection to the Lord Christ, with their use and efficacy to guide believers in

The Difference Between the Two Covenants

their communion with God, do all conduce to our evangelical liberty. And of such importance is our liberty in this instance of it, that when the apostles saw it necessary, for the avoiding of offense and scandal, to continue the observance of one or two legal institutions, in abstinence from some things in themselves indifferent, they did it only for a season, and declared that it was only in case of scandal that they would allow this temporary abridgment of the liberty given us by the gospel.

12. They differ greatly with respect to the dispensation and grant of the Holy Spirit. It is certain that God did grant the gift of the Holy Spirit under the old testament, and his operations during that season, as I have at large elsewhere declared;[13] but it is no less certain, that there was always a promise of his more distinguished effusion on the confirmation and establishment of the new covenant. See in particular that great promise to this purpose, Joel 2:28, 29, as applied and expounded by the apostle Peter, Acts 2:16-18. Yea, so sparing was the communication of the Holy Spirit under the old testament, compared with his effusion under the new, as that the evangelist affirms that "the Holy Spirit was not yet, because that Jesus was not yet glorified," John 7:39; that is, he was not yet given in that manner as he was to be given on the confirmation of the new covenant. And those of the church of the Hebrews who had received the doctrine of John, yet affirmed that "they had not so much as heard whether there were any Holy Spirit" or no, Acts 19:2; that is, any such gift and communication of him as was then proposed as the chief privilege of the gospel. Neither does this concern only the plentiful effusion of him with respect to those miraculous gifts and operations by which the doctrine and establishment of the new covenant was testified to and confirmed: however, that also gave a distinguished difference between the two covenants; for the first covenant was confirmed by dreadful appearances and operations, accomplished by the ministry of angels, but the new by the immediate operation of the Holy Spirit himself. But this difference principally consists in this, that under the new testament the Holy Spirit has graciously

---

[13] See vol. iii. p. 125, of his miscellaneous works. – Ed. [Banner Edition.]

condescended to bear the office of the comforter of the church. That this unspeakable privilege is peculiar to the new testament, is evident from all the promises of his being sent as a comforter made by our Savior, John 14-16; especially by that in which he assures his disciples that "unless he went away" (in which going away he confirmed the new covenant) "the Comforter would not come; but if he so went away, he would send him from the Father," chap. 16:7. And the difference between the two covenants which resulted from this is inexpressible.

13. They differ in the declaration made in them of the kingdom of God. It is the observation of Augustine, that the very name of "the kingdom of heaven" is peculiar to the new testament. It is true, God reigned in and over the church under the old testament; but his rule was such, and had such a relation to secular things, especially with respect to the land of Canaan, and the flourishing condition of the people in that respect, as that it had an appearance of a kingdom of this world. And that it was so, and was so to be, consisting in empire, power, victory, wealth, and peace, was so deeply fixed on the minds of the generality of the people, that the disciples of Christ themselves could not free themselves of that apprehension, until the new testament was fully established. But now in the gospel, the nature of the kingdom of God, where it is, and in which it consists, is plainly and evidently declared, to the unspeakable consolation of believers. For although it is now known and experienced to be internal, spiritual, and heavenly, they have no less assured interest in it and advantage by it, in all the troubles which they may undergo in this world, than they could have in the fullest possession of all earthly enjoyments.

14. They differ in their substance and end. The old covenant was typical, shadowy, and removable, Heb. 10:1. The new covenant is substantial and permanent, as containing the body, which is Christ. Now, consider the old covenant comparatively with the new, and this part of its nature, that it was typical and shadowy, is a great debasement of it. But consider it absolutely, and the things in which it was so were its greatest glory and excellence; for in these things alone was it a token and pledge of the love and grace of God. For those things in the old covenant which had most of

The Difference Between the Two Covenants

bondage in their use and practice, had most of light and grace in their signification. This was the design of God in all the ordinances of worship belonging to that covenant, namely, to typify, shadow, and represent the heavenly, substantial things of the new covenant, or the Lord Christ and the work of his mediation. The tabernacle, ark, altar, priests, and sacrifices did this; and it was their glory that so they did. However, compared with the substance in the new covenant, they have no glory.

15. They differ in the extent of their administration, according to the will of God. The first was confined to the posterity of Abraham according to the flesh, and to them especially in the land of Canaan, Deut. 5:3, with some few proselytes that were joined to them, excluding all others from the participation of the benefits of it. And therefore it was, that although the personal ministry of our Savior himself, in preaching of the gospel, was to precede the introduction of the new covenant, it was confined to the people of Israel, Matt. 15:24. And he was the "minister of the circumcision," Rom. 15:8. Such narrow bounds and limits had the administration of this covenant affixed to it by the will and pleasure of God, Ps. 147:19, 20. But the administration of the new covenant is extended to all nations under heaven; none being excluded, on the account of tongue, language, family, nation, or place of habitation. All have an equal interest in the rising Sun. The partition wall is broken down, and the gates of the New Jerusalem are set open to all comers on the gospel invitation. This is frequently taken notice of in the Scripture. See Matt. 28:19; Mark 16:15; John 11:51, 52; 12:32; Acts 11:18; 17:30; Gal. 5:6; Eph. 2:11-16; 3:8-10; Col. 3:10, 11; 1 John 2:2; Rev. 5:9. This is the grand charter of the poor wandering Gentiles. Having willfully fallen off from God, he was pleased, in his holiness and severity, to leave all our ancestors for many generations to serve and worship the devil. And the mystery of our recovery was "hid in God from the beginning of the world," Eph. 3:8-10. And although it was so foretold, so prophesied of, so promised under the old testament, yet, such was the pride, blindness, and obstinacy, of the greatest part of the church of the Jews, that its accomplishment was one great part of that stumbling-block whereat they fell; yea, the greatness and glory of this mystery

was such, that the disciples of Christ themselves comprehended it not, until it was testified to them by the pouring out of the Holy Spirit, the great promise of the new covenant, on some of those poor Gentiles, Acts 11:18.

16. They differ in their efficacy; for the old covenant "made nothing perfect," it could accomplish none of the things it did represent, nor introduce that perfect or complete state which God had designed for the church. But this we have at large insisted on in our exposition of the previous chapter. Lastly,

17. They differ in their duration: for the one was to be removed, and the other to abide for ever; which must be declared on the ensuing verses.

It may be other things of like nature may be added to these that we have mentioned, in which the difference between the two covenants does consist; but these instances are sufficient to our purpose. For some, when they hear that the covenant of grace was always one and the same, of the same nature and efficacy under both testaments, that the way of salvation by Christ was always one and the same, are ready to think that there was no such great difference between their state and ours as is pretended. But we see that on this supposition, that covenant which God brought the people into at Sinai, and under the yoke of which they were to abide until the new covenant was established, had all the disadvantages attending it which we have insisted on. And those who understand not how excellent and glorious those privileges are which are added to the covenant of grace, as to the administration of it, by the introduction and establishment of the new covenant, are utterly unacquainted with the nature of spiritual and heavenly things.

A Response to the Socinians

There remains yet one thing more, which the Socinians give us occasion to speak to from these words of the apostle, that the new covenant is "established on better promises." For from this place they do conclude that there were no promises of life under the old testament; which, in the latitude of it, is a senseless and brutish opinion. And,

1. The apostle in this place intends only those promises on what the new testament was legally ratified, and reduced into the form of a covenant; which were, as he declares, the promises of especial pardoning mercy, and of the efficacy of grace in the renovation of our natures. But it is granted that the other covenant was legally established on promises which respected the land of Canaan. To that end it is granted, that as to the promises in accordance with which the covenants were actually established, those of the new covenant were better than the other.

2. The old covenant had express promise of eternal life: "He that does these things will live in them." It was, indeed, with respect to perfect obedience that it gave that promise; however that promise it had, which is all that at present we inquire after.

3. The institutions of worship which belonged to that covenant, the whole ministry of the tabernacle, as representing heavenly things, had the nature of a promise in them; for they all directed the church to seek for life and salvation in and by Jesus Christ alone.

4. The question is not, What promises are given in the law itself, or the old covenant formally considered as such? But, What promises had they who lived under that covenant, and which were not disannulled by it? For we have proved sufficiently, that the addition of this covenant did not abolish or supersede the efficacy of any promise that God had before given to the church. And to say that the first promise, and that given to Abraham, confirmed with the oath of God, were not promises of eternal life, is to overthrow the whole Bible, both Old Testament and New.

Tenth Practical Observation

And we may observe from the previous discourses that although one state of the church has had great advantages and privileges above another, yet no state has had of which to complain, while they observed the terms prescribed to them. We have seen in how many things, and those most of them of the highest importance, the state of the church under the new covenant excels that under the old; yet that was in itself a state of unspeakable grace and privilege. For,

    1. It was a state of near relation to God, by virtue of a covenant. And when all mankind had absolutely broken covenant with God by sin, to call any of them into a new covenant relation with himself, was an act of sovereign grace and mercy. In this were they distinguished from the rest of mankind, whom God permitted to walk in their own ways, and winked at their ignorance, while they all perished in the pursuit of their foolish imaginations. A great part of the Book of Deuteronomy is designed to impress a sense of this on the minds of the people. And it is summarily expressed by the psalmist, Psa. 147:19, 20; and by the prophet, "We are *yours*: you never bore rule over them; they were not called by your name," Isa. 43:19.

    2. This covenant of God was in itself holy, just, and equal. For although there was in it an imposition of various things burdensome, they were such as God in his infinite wisdom saw necessary for that people, and such as they could not have been without. Therefore on all occasions God refers it even to themselves to judge whether his ways towards them were not equal, and their own unequal. And it was not only just, but attended with promises of unspeakable advantages above all other people whatever.

    3. God dealing with them in the way of a covenant, to which the mutual consent of all parties covenanting is required, it was proposed to them for their acceptance, and they did accordingly willingly receive it, Exod. 24, Deut. 5; so as that they had not of which to complain.

    4. In that state of discipline in which God was pleased to order them, they enjoyed the way of life and salvation in the promise; for, as we have showed at large, the promise was not disannulled by the introduction of this covenant. To that end, although God reserved a better and more complete state for the church under the new testament, having "ordained better things for us, that they without us should not be made perfect;" yet was that other state in itself good and holy, and sufficient to bring all believers to the enjoyment of God.

The Difference Between the Two Covenants

Eleventh Practical Observation

The state of the gospel, or of the church under the new testament, being accompanied with the highest spiritual privileges and advantages that it is capable of in this world, two things follow from there:

1. The great obligation that is on all believers to holiness and fruitfulness in obedience, to the glory of God. We have in this the utmost condescension of divine grace, and the greatest effects of it that God will communicate on this side of glory. That which all these things tend to, that which God requires and expects on them, is the thankful and fruitful obedience of them that are made partakers of them. And they who are not sensible of this obligation are strangers to the things themselves, and are not able to discern spiritual things, because they are to be spiritually discerned.

2. The heinousness of their sin by whom this covenant is neglected or despised is therefore abundantly manifest. The apostle particularly asserts and insists on this, Heb. 2:2, 3; 10:28, 29.

CHAPTER 11
The Newness of the New Covenant: Better Covenant, Better Mediator, Better Sacrifice, Better Ministry, Better Hope, Better Promises (Part 1)
James R. White, Th.D.*[1]

The epistle to the Hebrews embodies one of the strongest apologetic defenses of the supremacy of Christ's work in all of the New Testament. The purpose of the book, its intended audience, its historical setting, and its deep use of the Old Testament, provide a rich treasure of inspired teaching on the work of Christ, especially in his office as high priest.

For those who take seriously the consistency of God's self-glorification in his progressive revelation of the covenant of grace throughout history, the discussion of the διαθήκη καινή, "new covenant," drawn from Jeremiah 31:31-34, must be given its due prominence in answering the question, "Exactly what is the nature of the covenant in the blood of Christ (Luke 22:20; Heb. 13:20), and how does it differ from other divine covenants with men?" A full-orbed investigation into the nature of the New Covenant has led many to conclude that the "newness" of this covenant leads inevitably to conclusions that impact many other areas of theological inquiry. If this New Covenant is, in fact, based upon better promises, and has a better Mediator with a better ministry, who offers a better sacrifice, resulting in a better hope, so that all

---

[*] James R. White, Th.D., is an Elder at Phoenix Reformed Baptist Church, Phoenix, AZ, Adjunct Professor of Columbia Evangelical Seminary, Director of Alpha and Omega Ministries, and author of *The Forgotten Trinity*, *The Potter's Freedom*, and *The God Who Justifies*, among others.

[1] This chapter first appeared in *RBTR* and is used with permission with slight modifications.

those who are within the boundaries marked out by its very identification as a covenant made *in* the blood of Christ know him and experience the forgiveness of their sins, then it follows that such issues as covenant *membership,* its relationship to the external church, and our understanding of apostasy, must *start* with these truths. If we approach the topic backwards, beginning with traditions regarding covenant membership, signs, or a particular view of apostasy, we run a great danger of turning the direct and plain exegesis of the text of Hebrews upon its head.

Recent Developments

P&R Publishing released a compendium of articles edited by Gregg Strawbridge titled *The Case for Covenantal Infant Baptism*[2] in 2003. In this work the issue of the nature of the New Covenant comes up often and is in fact the subject of an entire chapter, written by Pastor Jeffrey D. Niell of Emmanuel Covenant Church (CRE), Phoenix, Arizona, titled "The Newness of the New Covenant." Pastor Niell and I co-authored a publication for Bethany House Publishers, *The Same Sex Controversy*, which was released in 2002. We are both graduates of the same college (both having an emphasis in the study of Greek under the same professor, one year apart from one another) and seminary, and both came into a knowledge of, and acceptance of, the doctrines of grace at the same time. He visited the Phoenix Reformed Baptist Church with me before I became a member, and I was involved in his ordination. To say that we "go back" a long way is to make an understatement. And yet our journeys in Reformed theology have taken us to very different conclusions regarding the nature of the New Covenant, and hence to disagreement on the membership of the covenant, the nature of apostasy, and the giving of the covenant sign. It is my hope to model proper Christian disagreement between brothers, based upon a common belief in the ultimate authority of God's Word, its perspicuity, and the over-riding need to engage in consistent

---

[2] Gregg Strawbridge, ed., *The Case for Covenantal Infant Baptism* (Phillipsburg, NJ: P&R Publishing, 2003).

exegesis of the inspired text so as to lay the only foundation upon which disagreements can be resolved.

In this and the next chapter, we will examine the concept of the New Covenant in the context of Hebrews, focusing upon its classic expression in chapter 8, but likewise noting other passages (especially Heb. 10:10-22) that directly impact our understanding of this vital truth. We will look at the broad contextual background, specifics regarding significant textual variants, and the relevance of the theme of the "better" in this section of Hebrews. Then the key passages will be exegeted. Exegesis will be followed by interpretational conclusions. Then we will respond to the presentation made by Pastor Niell, and contrast some comments offered by Richard Pratt in his chapter in the same volume.

Hebrews: There is Nothing to Go Back To – Christ is All in All

The context of the book of Hebrews is, obviously, central to a proper understanding of such phrases as διαθήκη καινή, "new covenant," or κρείττονος διαθήκης, "better covenant." This is an *apologia,* a defense offered in the form of an exhortation to those Hebrew Christians who would be subject to the pressures created by their cultural context. That is, the work is written to those who would hear the siren call of the old ways and, upon seeing the difficulties inherent in following Christ, be tempted to give in and "go back" to the old ways. The constant emphasis upon exhortation to continuance and perseverance speaks directly to this issue, and explains the format of the book's progressive explanation of Christ's superiority to each of the chief aspects of the "old way" of a Judaism that stood firmly opposed to the messiahship of Jesus Christ. By demonstrating the superiority of Christ to all aspects of the "old way," and that by arguing from the Holy Scriptures themselves, the writer to the Hebrews provides a solid foundation upon which to stand against the temptation to "go back." When one is truly convinced in one's soul that Jesus Christ is superior to every aspect of the old Judaism, the heart of the temptation is removed, and the call to go back is rendered powerless.

The Newness of the New Covenant (Part 1)

Any work of apologetic weight, however, must provide some kind of compelling argumentation. And when one examines a major element of such an apologetic argument, a simple question suggests itself, one that should always be asked of any interpretation offered. "What is the role of this particular concept or passage in the over-all apologetic of the author? And does my interpretation strengthen, or weaken, the attempted argumentation?" This is important in examining the New Covenant concept in Hebrews, for surely it is part of the writer's demonstration of the supremacy of the work of Christ over the "old." If we allow deeply held traditions to influence our exegesis, so that the apologetic element of the author's presentation of the New Covenant is compromised, we can see by this that we have erred and must "practice what we preach" and alter our views in accordance with our motto, *semper reformanda*.

The narrative context is that of the fulfillment of the types and shadows and, in particular, those embodied in the priesthood and the sacrifices of the tabernacle, in the Messiah, Jesus Christ. The author has opened and addressed numerous aspects of Christ's superiority as high priest, interweaving various themes around the major presentation of Christ as the one and only perfect high priest. Practical exhortations and warnings are attached to each aspect of Christ's priesthood as it is presented. After presenting Christ's priesthood after the order of Melchizedek in chapter 5, for example, the warnings of Hebrews 6:1-8 follow, concluded by the encouragement and exhortation of 6:9-12, where we read in closing:

> And we desire that each one of you show the same diligence so as to realize the full assurance of hope until the end, so that you will not be sluggish, but imitators of those who through faith and patience inherit the promises. (Heb. 6:11-12)

The text then moves back into another demonstration of an important aspect of Christ's superiority, in this instance moving toward the extended discussion of the supremacy of the *work* of the one high priest, which forms the substance of chapters 7 through

10. The discussion of the New Covenant is inextricably linked with this demonstration of the supremacy of Christ's priesthood *and salvific work* (Heb. 7:22-25; 9:15, 23-25; 10:10-18). It is important to follow the connections inherent in the text itself. Considering the covenant apart from such issues as Christ's priesthood, mediation, sacrifice, and resultant salvific work, is to mishandle the author's words and to isolate one contextual element to the detriment of the others. Our author thinks holistically, not in the Western "pigeon hole" style wherein doctrines and beliefs exist separately from one another and do not come together to form a coherent fabric of truth. As such, his view of the New Covenant as "better" must be seen in light of the perfection of Christ's work of mediation and every other aspect of the argument as he presents it.

Exegetically Significant Textual Variants

In focusing upon the description of the New Covenant in chapters 8 through 10 of Hebrews, we encounter two highly significant textual variants that directly impact the translation, and hence interpretation, of the text. The first is found in Hebrews 8:8a, and the second involves a variant between the Massoretic Hebrew (MT) text and the Greek Septuagint (LXX). None of the other variants in the relevant passages are overly difficult to decide.[3]

The first variant touches on whether the text is indicating that God was finding fault "with them," i.e., with those who had lived under the Old Covenant in the days of Jeremiah, as most translations have it, or, whether it would be better to render the text as, "For, finding fault [with the Old Covenant], He says to them...." The difference in the reading is between αὐτοὺς and αὐτοῖς, between the accusative plural and the dative plural. While some see little

---

[3] Most of the variants in the actual citation of the LXX flow from later scribes possessing a different "stream" of Septuagint readings and seeking harmonization on that basis. There are some interesting, but not overly relevant, variants in how the text is cited in Hebrews 8 and 10, but these do not impact the exegesis.

difference between the readings,[4] it is important to consider the possibilities inherent in the two readings. The external data can be argued either direction,[5] and internal argumentation can go both ways as well, making it a particularly difficult variant. The NA27/UBS4 texts adopt αὐτούς, while Philip Hughes argues for αὐτοῖς.[6]

I would like to suggest that one aspect of this variant needs to be allowed consideration in the exegetical process. In Hebrews 8:7 the writer uses the Greek term ἄμεμπτος, "blameless," which, of course, is merely the negation of μέμψις, which in its verbal form is μέμφομαι, the very term which appears at the beginning of verse 8 and which may, if we read the variant as αὐτοῖς, govern the translation, as the verb μέμφομαι can take its object in the dative or the accusative (hence the translations "finding fault with them" or "finding fault, he said to them"). The connection between saying the first *covenant* (the term διαθήκη does not appear and is understood) was not *without fault* (ἄμεμπτος) is maintained strongly by reading the dative αὐτοῖς and rendering it, "For finding fault [with the first covenant] he says to them." The only other way to make a meaningful connection with "finding fault" (μέμφομαι) in Hebrews 8:8a is to connect it with "for they did not continue in my

---

[4] Bruce Metzger, *A Textual Commentary on the Greek New Testament* (Stuttgart: United Bible Societies, 1994), 597, says the variant "makes very little difference in sense, though the latter may be construed with either μεμφόμενος or λέγει."

[5] αὐτούς is the original reading of a, A, the original reading of D, some early uncials, most early versions in other languages, and a few early Fathers. αὐτοῖς is the corrected reading of a and D, and is the reading of the early papyrus p[46], along with B, 1749, 1881, and is the reading of the vast bulk of later minuscule manuscripts. Metzger indicated that "the direction in which scribal corrections moved" determined the acceptance of αὐτούς by the UBS translation committee (Metzger, *Textual Commentary*, 597), but one is left wondering what factors influenced such a general "directional" tendency. The conjunction of p[46], B, the early correction of a, and the consideration that other ancient language translations would not necessarily reflect an understanding of the fact that μέμφομαι can take its object in the dative or the accusative, seems to this writer to give a slight edge to αὐτοῖς.

[6] Philip Edgecombe Hughes, *A Commentary on the Epistle to the Hebrews* (Grand Rapids: Eerdmans, 1977), 298-99.

covenant, and I did not care for them" at the end of verse 9. But the connection here is much more tenuous, both for the reason that the terminology differs substantially as well as the fact that the phrase "I did not care for them" is a variant between the MT and the LXX (the second major variant we will examine). While this is not enough to make a firm decision, it is relevant to the statement of the writer that the first covenant was to be "faulted," while the New Covenant is placed in a position of direct contrast thereto. As we will note in the exegesis, the Old Covenant was "faulted" in that "they did not continue in My covenant" hence, for the New Covenant to be superior, it would have to be inviolable, as the exegesis itself suggests. This point is strengthened if we take the dative plural αὐτοῖς and read it with λέγει, "he says to them."

The second major variant involves the always challenging area of differences between the Hebrew MT and the Greek LXX. It is important to note this variant, as this author has encountered Jewish apologists who refer to it as a means of attacking the veracity and accuracy of the New Testament text. Given the general ignorance of even trained ministers on the subject of textual criticism and the textual history of the Old Testament, springing such a surprise (using the differing translations found in Jeremiah and in Hebrews) can result in a very awkward, difficult situation. Though the variant seems quite major (in the sense made of the passage), in reality it is probably based upon a single letter in the Hebrew. As rendered by the NASB, the MT reads, "'My covenant which they broke, although I was a husband to them,' declares the LORD." However, the LXX, cited in Hebrews 8:9, reads, "'for they did not continue in My covenant, and I did not care for them,' says the LORD." The difference between "I was a husband to them" and "I did not care for them" could be construed as presenting a complete opposite. Now, it is true that the writer to the Hebrews does not repeat the phrase, nor base any particular statement upon it. However, it does seem that the LXX rendering could be seen as more consistent with the point being made, especially with the strong contrast between the Old and New Covenants and those who participate therein.

The Newness of the New Covenant (Part 1)

But the variant can be fairly easily explained, as suggested by the textual apparatus of *Biblia Hebraica Stuttgartensia*. The verb "to be a husband to" in the MT is בָּעַלְתִּי. One may recognize the root *ba-al*, here, to be master, lord, husband. But there is another verb in Hebrew, *ga-al*, or as it would possibly have appeared here, גָּעַלְתִּי, which means "to despise, abhor." The visual similarity of B with G is clear to anyone. This might explain the origination of the LXX reading. But the question arises, did the writer to the Hebrews know of the variant, and if so, would this not mean the choice of the LXX was purposeful? But if the LXX is simply the "default" translation being used, one could not put any weight upon the variation. These issues go beyond our scope here, but they do touch upon a number of important passages in the New Testament.

Better: No, Really

When a writer repeats a particular term we must always take into consideration the possibility that he is indeed seeking to communicate a particular concept through that term. The writer to the Hebrews uses the term "better" in key passages throughout his work. This is hardly surprising, in light of the fact that the writer is engaged in a comparison of the old and the new, the old law and its fulfillment in Christ. Looking at the comparative form, "better," here are those things which are "better" in Hebrews:

> having become as much better than the angels, as He inherited a more excellent name than they (Heb. 1:4)

> We are convinced of better things concerning you, and things that accompany salvation (Heb. 6:9)

> and on the other hand there is a bringing in of a better hope, through which we draw near to God (Heb. 7:19)

> so much more also Jesus has become the guarantee of a better covenant (Heb. 7:22)

The Newness of the New Covenant (Part 1)

But now He has obtained a more excellent ministry, by as much as He is also the mediator of a better covenant, which has been enacted on better promises (Heb. 8:6)

Therefore it was necessary for the copies of the things in the heavens to be cleansed with these, but the heavenly things themselves with better sacrifices than these (Heb. 9:23)

But as it is, they desire a better *country*, that is, a heavenly one (Heb. 11:16)

Women received *back* their dead by resurrection; and others were tortured, not accepting their release, so that they might obtain a better resurrection; (Heb. 11:35)

And all these, having gained approval through their faith, did not receive what was promised, because God had provided something better for us, so that apart from us they would not be made perfect (Heb 11:39-40)

and to Jesus, the mediator of a new covenant, and to the sprinkled blood, which speaks better than *the blood* of Abel" (Heb 12:24)

The term "better" can be understood in various ways. One can argue that one item in a class is "better" than another item *in the same class*. That is, one can argue that one kind of motorcycle is superior to, better than, another kind of motorcycle. Both, however, are motorcycles by nature. Or, one could say that something is better *qualitatively*. One might say that a high quality diamond is *better* than a cubic zirconium, and such a statement would be making a comparison differentiating between the items *on the ground of nature*. The *nature* of the diamond is better than that of the cubic zirconium.

When we look at the use of this term in Hebrews, the kind of "betterness" can be clearly discerned. When the writer says that Jesus is "better than" the angels (Heb. 1:4), is he not saying that

The Newness of the New Covenant (Part 1)

Jesus is better than the angels *qualitatively*, on the level of being? Surely he is not saying that Jesus and the angels are in the same category, and Jesus is simply a better kind of angel than any others. In Hebrews 6:9 the writer refers to "better things concerning you, things which accompany salvation." There the distinction is between things which do not of necessity accompany salvation and things which do. Are actions which accompany salvation merely "better works" than those which are non-salvific, or is there a qualitative difference? In Hebrews 7:19, is the "better hope" ushered in by Christ just a larger, grander hope than that provided by law, but a hope of the same kind? Could anyone truly draw near to God by means of the law? No, for "the Law made nothing perfect." The hope inaugurated by Christ is *qualitatively different*. In Hebrews 11:16, when "they desire a better *country*, that is, a heavenly one," is the heavenly country of the same *kind* as an earthly country? Is it just *better* as in bigger, or brighter? Or is the heavenly country *better* on the level of *nature* and *quality*?

The reason for these considerations comes into play when we consider what it means to speak of *better* promises, *better* sacrifices, and a *better* covenant. When Christ is said to be "the guarantee of a better covenant" in Hebrews 7:22, is the covenant that is here described as "better" merely "better" in the sense of being "bigger" or "larger" or "more grand," or is it "better" on a substantial, *qualitative* basis? Does this really mean that there are just more of the elect in the "better covenant," and this is why it is "better"? Or is there a more fundamental distinction? Likewise, in Hebrews 8:6 the term appears twice. First, Jesus is said to be "the mediator of a better covenant which has been enacted on better promises." This is all placed in the context of describing a "more excellent ministry." Is this ministry simply of the same *kind* as the ministry of the old priests, only, in some fashion, "more excellent"? Or is the point of the passage that the Messiah's ministry, the covenant in his blood, and the promises upon which the covenant stands – all these things are *substantially* different, *better*, than that which came before?

This is plainly brought out in Hebrews 9:23 when the writer speaks of the "better sacrifices" by which the heavenly things are cleansed. Here Christ's sacrifice (as the following context makes plain) is said to be "better" than the animal sacrifices, those of goats and bulls. Surely, at this point there can be no argument that the betterness of the sacrifice of Christ is *qualitatively superior* to that of the animal sacrifices of the Old Covenant. His death is not just *more effective* or in some fashion *greater* than the sacrifice of a lamb or a bull. That sacrifice differs on a fundamental, foundational level. It is better *by nature and definition*.

This is important to our examination of the New Covenant, for it is said to be a *better* covenant, with a *better* mediator, with *better* promises, based upon a *better* sacrifice, resulting in a *better* hope. So when we look at the description of the New Covenant in Hebrews 8:8ff, we must see how each of these elements of the New Covenant are "better" than those of the Old Covenant.

Exegesis of Hebrews 8:6-13

The immediately preceding argument, leading to the key presentation of the New Covenant in Hebrews 8:6-13, flows from the identification of Christ with the superior priesthood of Melchizedek (Psa. 110:4, cited in Heb. 7:17, 21), leading to the description of Christ as the ἔγγυος ("guarantee" or "guarantor")[7] of the New Covenant, and also bringing the first use of κρείττονος διαθήκης, "better covenant," in 7:22, "so much the more also Jesus has become the guarantee of a better covenant." Hebrews 7:23-8:5 comprises a demonstration of the basis for the apologetic assertion that the New Covenant is, in fact, "a better covenant" (part and parcel of the purpose of the letter), one that flows from the priestly nature of Christ's work. Hebrews 7:23-25 proves this by the contrast of the mortal priests with the one priest, Jesus Christ; and 7:26-28 does so in light of the sinfulness of the many priests and hence their

---

[7] ἔγγυος is a *hapax legomenon* in the New Testament, appearing only in the Apocryphal books of Sirach and 2 Maccabees prior to this. It has semantic connections to ἀρραβών (*down payment*) in Ephesians 1:14, for in common secular usage it refers to providing security or a guarantee, normally in a financial or business transaction. The *guarantee* then of the *better* covenant is introduced here within the context of Christ's superior priesthood, his indestructible life, and divine ability to save to the uttermost (Heb. 7:24-35).

repeated sacrifices versus the singular sacrifice of the innocent, undefiled Christ. Hebrews 8:1-6, then, provides first a summary statement of the preceding arguments (i.e., our one high priest has entered into the heavenlies) and then provides the thesis statement for the description of the superiority of the New Covenant from Jeremiah 31 with the assertion that Christ has obtained "a more excellent ministry" than that of the old priests, that he is the mediator (in contrast, in context, to Moses, v. 5; Gal. 3:19; John 1:17) of "a better covenant" enacted on "better promises." Some brief exegetical comments should be offered on these texts.

First, Christ's role as singular and never dying high priest, and the resulting assurance of the perfection of his work, is seen by the writer as part of the demonstration of why the covenant of which he is the guarantee is "better" (Heb. 7:23-25). While our English translations normally say something like, "The *former* priests existed in greater numbers" at Hebrews 7:23, the literal reading is simply, "the priests," contrasting[8] the plural with the singular "he" (οἱ vs. ὁ) in verse 24. The work of the many priests is, of necessity, imperfect, for they are "prevented by death" from "continuing" or "abiding." But, in contrast, he "abides forever," he is no longer subject to death. Hence, he, unlike the old priests under the Old Covenant, holds his priesthood (which has been shown to be superior in the preceding arguments) ἀπαράβατον, "permanently," or, in some sources, "without successor." Both translations fit the context, for he never lays aside this priesthood, hence, it is "permanent" in contrast to the former priests. But likewise he has no successor in his office. The entire concept is meant to be in contrast to the old priests and their inherently temporary nature. As a result of the permanence of his priestly position,[9] Christ has an ability the old priests did not possess. He is able to save. The profundity of the words may deflect proper attention. The permanence of his life and position as high priest grants to him the ability to save. He is active in saving, and he is capable of so doing.

---

[8] Using the common μέν/δέ. form translated "on the one hand/on the other hand."

[9] ὅθεν, "for which reason."

As noted above, the soteriological content of the superiority of Christ's work as high priest and of the New Covenant cannot be dismissed or overlooked. The extent of his salvific work is noted by the phrase εἰς τὸ παντελὲς, which can be translated "forever" in the sense of permanence, or "to the uttermost" in the sense of completely, similar, in fact, to ἀπαράβατον above. Owen noted the propriety of seeing both senses in the text:

> Take the word in the first sense, and the meaning is, that he will not effect or work out this or that part of our salvation, do one thing or another that belongs unto it, and leave what remains unto ourselves or others; but "he is our Rock, and his work is perfect." Whatever belongs unto our entire, complete salvation, he is able to effect it. The general notion of the most that are called Christians lies directly against this truth….That this salvation is durable, perpetual, eternal… and there is nothing hinders but that we may take the words in such a comprehensive sense as to include the meaning of both these interpretations. He is able to save completely as to all parts, fully as to all causes, and for ever in duration.[10]

Just as the Father's will for the Son revealed in John 6:38-39 demands perfection in his role as Savior, so too here the very same soteriological perfection and completion is central to the work of the eternal high priest. This is brought out with strong force in the rest of the verse, for the author indicates both the object of the salvific work and the basis thereof, and both are intensely priestly statements. The singular priest saves "those who draw near to God through Him." This clearly harkens back to the people who drew near in worship to God in the temple, and their representative, the high priest on the day of atonement. There is specificity to the salvific work of the priest. He does not make a general plan of salvation available, he saves a specific people (cf. Matt. 1:21). And secondly, "He always lives to make intercession for them" points to

---

[10] John Owen, *An Exposition of the Epistle to the Hebrews,* in *The Works of John Owen,* ed., William Goold, ed. (Ages Digital Library, 2000), 20:646-47.

the same perfection of the high priest. His indestructible life means he never lays aside his priestly role, hence, since the high priest interceded (ἐντυγχάνειν, Rom. 8:34) for those for whom he offered sacrifice, Christ ever lives to make intercession for those who draw near to God through him, resulting in the perfection of their salvation. The work of intercession guarantees the salvation of a specific people in this passage. This is vital to remember as we look at the key text in Hebrews 8.

Similar themes appear in Hebrews 7:26-28, including the perfect character of the high priest (v. 26), which establishes another element of his supremacy over the old priests, for Christ does not have to offer sacrifice for his own sins, and then the sins of the people. But here also appears a concept that will be expanded upon greatly at a later point, for the author says, "because this He did once for all when He offered up Himself." Self-offering is yet another aspect of what sets the priesthood of Christ apart, for obvious reasons, from the priesthood of old. The high priest presents the offering in his own body, a concept expanded upon in chapter nine. But he did so "once for all." The sacrifice is a singularity in time, for the author uses the temporal adverb, ἐφάπαξ, to strongly emphasize this concept. The old priests sacrificed often for themselves, while Christ offered one sacrifice (i.e., himself) for the people.

Chapter 8 begins with a summary of the preceding argument, focusing upon the ascended Savior who has "taken His seat" (v. 1) in heaven itself. The writer then notes that in light of the parallels he is drawing, the heavenly priest would need to have "something to offer" (v. 3) just as the old priests did. While he would not have been a priest while on earth (v. 4), he has "obtained a more excellent ministry" (v. 6). How is it a better ministry? And how is this related to his sacrifice, which is clearly in the preceding context (see above) as well as in that which follows? To that we now turn in exegesis.

The Newness of the New Covenant (Part 1)

Hebrews 8:6

> But now He has obtained a more excellent ministry, by as much as He is also the mediator of a better covenant, which has been enacted on better promises. (Heb. 8:6)

The writer is contrasting the priestly ministry in the tabernacle with the heavenly ministry of Christ, using the technical term λειτουργίας, "ministry." This is the term used in the LXX for the priestly "service" in the tabernacle. It is not only "more excellent," but the term διαφορωτέρας also contains within its lexical meaning the idea of "difference" and "distinction," so that we have grounds to say it is not just superior but of the same kind, but superior and greater in kind as well (which fits with the discussion of "better" presented above). How much more excellent is this ministry of the single high priest? The ESV captures the essence of the comparison (using the correlative pronoun ὅσῳ) by rendering the phrase, "Christ has obtained a ministry that is as much more excellent than the old as the covenant he mediates is better, since it is enacted on better promises." That is, his ministry is as much more excellent as the covenant he mediates is better. This is truly the phrase that transitions the text into the citation of Jeremiah 31, for it draws a direct parallel between the superior nature of Christ's priestly ministry and connects it firmly to the "betterness" of the New Covenant.

Some comment must be made on the use of the term μεσίτης, "mediator."[11] The term appears with reference to Christ specifically in 1 Timothy 2:5-6, "For there is one God, *and* one mediator also between God and men, *the* man Christ Jesus, who gave Himself as a ransom for all, the testimony *given* at the proper time," and three times in Hebrews (8:6; 9:15; 12:24). The use in Hebrews 9:15 establishes that the "better covenant" with "better promises" is indeed the New Covenant, by saying:

---

[11] See the extended discussion of Owen in *Hebrews*, 21:66ff.

The Newness of the New Covenant (Part 1)

For this reason He is the mediator of a new covenant, so that, since a death has taken place for the redemption of the transgressions that were *committed* under the first covenant, those who have been called may receive the promise of the eternal inheritance. (Heb. 9:15)

Note as well the consistency of the author in connecting mediation, the New Covenant, Christ's work as high priest, his death, and redemption of transgressions (cf. Heb. 8:12), with the result that "those who have been called" may receive the promise. Here it is difficult to argue against the conclusion that the author is consistently connecting the work of Christ in atonement (mediation, intercession), which "perfects" those for whom the atonement is made (10:10, 14), with the electing grace of God ("those who are called"). We will note this further in our conclusions.

That it is the intention of the author to connect the superior nature of Christ's priestly ministry with the "betterness" of the New Covenant is further borne out by the fact that he then insists that this "better covenant" of which Christ is mediator *"has been enacted on better promises"* (emphasis mine). It is important to see that for the writer, the New Covenant has been, as a past-tense action, officially enacted. The term used is νενομοθέτηται, the perfect passive of νομοθετέομαι, "to enact on the basis of legal sanction, ordain, found by law" (BDAG). The New Covenant is not something that will someday be established but has already, as a completed action, been founded, established, enacted, and that upon "better promises" than "the first" (v. 6). There is nothing in the text that would lead us to believe that the full establishment of this covenant is yet future, for such would destroy the present apologetic concern of the author; likewise, he will complete his citation of Jeremiah 31 by asserting the obsolete nature of the first covenant, which leaves one to have to theorize, without textual basis, about some kind of intermediate covenantal state if one does not accept the full establishment of the New Covenant as seen in the term νενομοθέτηται, "has been enacted."

For the moment, we emphasize that the author lays, as the groundwork of his citation of Jeremiah 31:31-34, a solid foundation in the assertion that Christ is the mediator of a better covenant, based upon better sacrifices, with a more excellent ministry, based upon better promises, which include, he will later assert, the very promise of the eternal inheritance for those in the New Covenant (Heb. 9:15), which has been established: it is a present reality. This is the immediate context of the citation, and must be allowed to have its determinative status.

Hebrews 8:7

> For if that first *covenant* had been faultless, there would have been no occasion sought for a second. (Heb. 8:7)

Hebrews 8:7 contains the expansion of the implied apologetic claim of verse 6: if Christ has obtained a better ministry, is mediator of a better covenant, enacted on better promises, then that which is "better" means that which is "less" is, by definition, inferior. Hence the writer simply draws out the only logical conclusion, for if "that first" (the term "covenant" is not included in the text, but is implied by the use of the article with "first") "had been faultless, there would have been no occasion sought for a second." Here the writer moves us to the context of Jeremiah 31:31-34, and indicates that the passage he is about to cite amounts to a seeking for a second, faultless covenant. But there would be no need for this if, in fact, the first covenant was ἄμεμπτος, "without fault" or "blame." What is the nature of this blame in a covenant that was established by God himself? The answer can be discerned by recalling the preceding context; Christ's ministry is more excellent, though it is being compared to a ministry established by God *as a picture* of the greater fulfillment to come. Even so the New Covenant is better than the Old, though the Old had likewise been established by God and served a particular purpose. But the contrast with the New Covenant about to be described from Jeremiah explains the "fault" of the Old: that which the New Covenant provides in perfection the Old only provided in part or in picture. Those aspects of the New Covenant about to be enumerated must be seen in the light of this context: where something is found in both covenants, it will be seen to be partial and incomplete in the Old, finished, total, and perfect in the New.

Hebrews 8:8

> For finding fault with them, He says, "BEHOLD, DAYS ARE COMING, SAYS THE LORD, WHEN I WILL EFFECT A NEW COVENANT WITH THE HOUSE OF ISRAEL AND WITH THE HOUSE OF JUDAH; (Heb. 8:8)

The first question posed by the text of verse 8 is related to the textual variant noted above. I will proceed on the grounds that the best logical connection, in light of the fairly evenly balanced external and internal considerations, is to read, "For finding fault, He says to them," following the thought of the preceding verse. The idea then is that the scriptural citation about to be provided, almost word-for-word from the LXX in Jeremiah 31, encompasses a finding of "fault" in the first covenant, announcing in the coming covenant which is "not like" the first (v. 9) the perfection not found in the Old. The meaning is not greatly altered if we read the other variant, "for finding fault with them, He says," though we would be in error to think that the fault then spoken of, which is in contrast to the New Covenant, was specific only to the context of those in Jeremiah's day. The contrast between Old and New is firm no matter how the variant is read in light of the first words of verse 9, but the continuity of the text is better served reading as suggested.

The citations of the LXX are almost verbatim aside from the interesting replacement of the normal LXX reading of διαθήσομαι with συντελέσω. The first term is actually a cognate of "covenant," while the verb the author of Hebrews chooses is related more strongly to the categories of finishing, establishing, or completing. The difference may be purposeful, textual, or stylistic.

Thus begins the citation of Jeremiah. Verse 8 announces, on the authority of Yahweh himself, that he will establish "a new covenant." It is his work, his initiative, and it is born of divine and sovereign freedom. He will make this covenant "with the house of Israel and with the house of Judah," a united kingdom, obviously transcending the political divisions of the days of Jeremiah, pointing to the future singular people of God.

Hebrews 8:9

> NOT LIKE THE COVENANT WHICH I MADE WITH THEIR FATHERS ON THE DAY WHEN I TOOK THEM BY THE HAND TO LEAD THEM OUT OF THE LAND OF EGYPT; FOR THEY DID NOT CONTINUE IN MY COVENANT, AND I DID NOT CARE FOR THEM, SAYS THE LORD. (Heb. 8:9)

The New Covenant announced by Yahweh is οὐ κατὰ, "not like," the covenant made with their fathers at Sinai. The force of the phraseology cannot be diminished. The phrase continues the context of contrast from verses 6 and 7, and in fact explains how the New differs from the Old in what follows. While God had initiated the Old Covenant as well ("I took them by the hand") and did so in power (the Exodus), "they did not continue in My covenant, and I did not care for them." The Old Covenant was, by nature, breakable. Why? Because it did not, in and of itself, effect the change in the heart and mind of each member thereof that would cause them to "continue" therein. We have noted the variation between the MT and the LXX at this point. Following the reading in Hebrews, there is, as a result of the defection and faithlessness of the people a resultant response from God, as there always is in response to sin. A violated covenant brings the curses promised in Deuteronomy 28 and 29. The history of Israel illustrates the constant cycle of judgment, repentance, blessing, and violation. While there were those who knew the Lord and followed his statutes, they were the remnant, not the norm. For every David there were a dozen Ahabs, though all were part of the Old Covenant. So how does the New Covenant differ? How is the New Covenant "not like" the Old? What is the result of a more excellent priestly ministry, better sacrifices, a better mediator, better promises, all comprising a better covenant? The next three verses lay out the answer.

The Newness of the New Covenant (Part 1)

Hebrews 8:10

> "FOR THIS IS THE COVENANT THAT I WILL MAKE WITH THE HOUSE OF ISRAEL AFTER THOSE DAYS, SAYS THE LORD: I WILL PUT MY LAWS INTO THEIR MINDS, AND I WILL WRITE THEM ON THEIR HEARTS. AND I WILL BE THEIR GOD, AND THEY SHALL BE MY PEOPLE. (Heb. 8:10)

The language used in verse 10 is well-known covenantal language, used by Yahweh in establishing the very covenant to which he is now drawing a contrast (Exod. 6:7; 29:45, 46; Deut. 26:18), just as the priestly, sacrificial language up to this point in the book has been taken over, expanded, and gloriously fulfilled in Christ. In the great fulfillment of God's purposes with Israel ("after those days") God promises to "put My laws into their minds, and I will write them on their hearts." Here we encounter a vital exegetical key to a proper understanding of the function of this text for the author: in verse 9 (and possibly v. 8 in the variant) we see "them," those under the Old Covenant, those who did not continue in his covenant, those for whom God did not care ("I did not care for them"). Verse 10 introduces a new "them" that is in view consistently in verses 10-12. The "them" here are those in the New Covenant, the "house of Israel" with whom God makes this new and better covenant (v. 10a). A consistent reading of the text then reveals the following actions on God's part in this verse: 1) God puts his laws in *their* minds; 2) God writes his laws on *their* hearts; 3) God will be *their* God; and 4) *they* will be God's people. The contrast then is seen in the all-extensive nature of the New Covenant, for the text demands the continuation of the contrast begun in verse 6, expanded in verse 7, and boldly proclaimed in verse 9. What the Old Covenant had only pictured and hinted at, but failed to produce in *them*, God fulfills in the better covenant with the better sacrifices and better promises and better mediator. All those with whom he makes this covenant experience what the remnant experienced under the Old: true internal conversion resulting in a love for God's law and a true relationship with him. Quite simply, there is no "remnant" in the

New Covenant, and all those with whom God makes this covenant experience its fulfillment. This is why it is better, and hence proves the author's apologetic presentation of the supremacy of Christ over the old ways.

Hebrews 8:11

> "AND THEY SHALL NOT TEACH EVERYONE HIS FELLOW CITIZEN, AND EVERYONE HIS BROTHER, SAYING, 'KNOW THE LORD,' FOR ALL WILL KNOW ME, FROM THE LEAST TO THE GREATEST OF THEM. (Heb. 8:11)

The faithful ones in the Old Covenant by nature sought to speak about their God and call those around them to repentance and faith in him. The entire ministry of the prophets of old could be summed up in the constant revelation of the knowledge of God to a hard-hearted and stubborn people. The phrase "know the LORD" or "did not know the LORD" appears a number of times in the Scriptures (Exod. 5:2; Judg. 2:10; 1 Sam. 2:12; 3:7; Isa. 19:21; Hos. 2:20; 5:4; 6:3). Interestingly, though Eli's sons were members of the Old Covenant, and in fact, were priests, they did not "know the LORD" (1 Sam. 2:12). Obviously, Eli's sons knew the name of Yahweh; they knew of his existence. But they did not *know* him. The only meaningful way of seeing this is that they knew him externally, but not internally. In Isaiah 19:21 a prophecy is found in which even the Egyptians come to know the Lord and engage in worship. The Egyptians surely knew about Yahweh (He had despoiled their gods in the Exodus.) but they did not know him personally and internally, so this prophecy of a future healing in which the Egyptians will know the Lord would indicate a personal knowledge, an internal knowledge, leading to true worship. Likewise, the phrase appears in Hosea 2:20, 5:4, and 6:3 in the same kind of context, where knowing the Lord is internal, salvific, while not knowing him is likened to a "spirit of harlotry" that precludes them from returning "to their God." So while members of the Old Covenant could bear the name of Yahweh, and even serve as priests

The Newness of the New Covenant (Part 1)

in his worship, and still not know him, the New Covenant will not be like this.

Rather than the natural desire to announce the truth of Yahweh that would exist in the hearts of the remnant in the Old Covenant, in the New Covenant this internal, salvific knowledge of the Lord is universal. "For all will know Me, from the least to the greatest of them." The great contrast with the Old Covenant, that contained some who did know the Lord, but so many more who did not, is that the covenant that has a better mediator, better sacrifices, better promises, and a better hope, is made with the people of God who know him, each and every one, "from the least to the greatest of them." Surely this is the continued contrast that is carried on from the preceding context, and this is seen because of the continuation of the same audience: "and *they* shall be my people" posits the same audience as "from the least to the greatest of *them*." The audience does not all of a sudden change in mid-citation, indeed, it continues, consistently, into the next verse, "For I will be merciful to *their* iniquities." The knowledge obviously, then, is as salvific and full as the mercy shown to the iniquities of the very same people. And, as we saw by following the soteriological thought from chapter 7 into this discussion, the relationship of "better covenant" with "better mediator" and "intercession" clearly comes into play here as well. The contrast drawn here between the old "faulted" covenant and the new faultless one is simple: the New Covenant brings salvific knowledge and relationship to *all* who are in it, "from the least to the greatest of them." This would be a vital apologetic assertion, again harmonizing with the text perfectly. A New Covenant that did not bring the fullness of the knowledge of God to the covenant members would hardly be superior to the Old, and we must always remember that this book was written for a particular purpose with a particular audience in view. The Old Covenant should not attract one who understands the supremacy and perfection of the New. All of these contextual issues establish the simple reading of the text as the best: salvific knowledge is universal in the New ("better") Covenant that God has established in the work of Christ.

The Newness of the New Covenant (Part 1)

Hebrews 8:12

"FOR I WILL BE MERCIFUL TO THEIR INIQUITIES, AND I WILL REMEMBER THEIR SINS NO MORE." (Heb. 8:12)

The citation of Jeremiah concludes with the fullest expression of salvific accomplishment. It is important to see that the connection between "they shall know Me" and "I will be merciful to their iniquities" is expressed very strongly through the use of ὅτι, "*for* I will be merciful...." The reason all in the New Covenant know the Lord savingly is because God will be merciful to their iniquities and will remember their sins no more. How else can the ὅτι be understood? This soteriological fulfillment of the promised covenant explains how the law can be written upon the hearts and minds of those in its fellowship, and how he will be their God and they his people in a fashion superior to and greater than the first covenant. The writer plainly sees in these words a prophetic proclamation of what Christ, the one high priest, would accomplish through his better sacrifice so as to initiate a better covenant based upon better promises leading to a better hope. The singular offering of Christ (Heb. 7:27) and the acceptance of that offering pictured in his entrance into the holy place and his being seated at the right hand of the throne of the Majesty in the heavens (Heb. 8:1) has made it possible for God to be merciful to the iniquities of those for whom the high priest now intercedes (Heb. 7:24-35). This will be expanded upon and illustrated in chapters 9 and 10 as well.

Hebrews 8:13

> When He said, "A new *covenant*," He has made the first obsolete. But whatever is becoming obsolete and growing old is ready to disappear. (Heb. 8:13)

The writer, having concluded the citation, begins his application. The reference to "the new" (καινὴν) means "the first" (πρώτην) has been made obsolete (πεπαλαίωκεν, perfect active, "to declare old, obsolete"). The word "covenant" does not appear in the text. The very enunciation in Jeremiah of God's intention to enact the New Covenant indicates that the Old will be rendered "obsolete." There is some discussion as to whether we should take the viewpoint of Jeremiah, or of the writer to the Hebrews, here and in verse 8, though there is little difference in the resulting meanings either direction. Some see in the present participle παλαιούμενον, "becoming obsolete," a historical reference that places Hebrews prior to the destruction of the Temple in A.D. 70. In any case, apologetically, the writer is establishing the fact that one cannot return to the old ways for they are growing old, obsolete, and are passing away. The New Covenant has come, and the New has replaced the Old. It is superior in every way, and thus the writer to the Hebrews encourages believers to remain steadfast in their confession of Christ.

The New Covenant and the Singular Sacrifice that Perfects

The announcement of the New Covenant in Jeremiah re-appears in the argument of the writer in the presentation encapsulated in Hebrews 10:15-18. Between its appearance in the latter half of chapter 8 and its reappearance in chapter 10, the writer has developed his argument on a broad plane. He has delved into the arrangement of the sacred furnishings in the tabernacle, the significance of the holy place, all as part of the Spirit's demonstration of the preparatory and incomplete nature of the shadows and types that were the substance of the Old Covenant "until a time of reformation" (Heb. 9:10). He focuses upon the fulfillment of these types and shadows in the perfect ministry of Christ who has entered into the holy place in heaven. His mediation of the New Covenant continues to hold central place (Heb. 9:15). The cleansing of the earthly sanctuary, which is but a shadow, with the sacrifices of goats and bulls, is contrasted with the "better sacrifice" of Christ.

The emphasis then moves to the singularity of that sacrifice in time over against the repetitive sacrifices of the Old Covenant (Heb. 9:25-10:4). Verses 5 through 9 form a biblical argument drawn from Psalm 40:6-8 (as found in the LXX). The argument is fairly simple, for the writer sees in this passage the same contrast that he has just drawn in the first four verses. Specifically, he contrasts the sacrifices and burnt offerings, which he points out were offered in accordance with the law, with the coming of the one who does God's "will." He concludes that he (Christ) takes away the first (the offerings and sacrifices) "in order to" (ἵνα, purpose clause) establish the second, which would be the "will" of God accomplished in the death of Christ.

We have already established the deeply soteriological nature of the New Covenant. This is displayed in the very section of Hebrews that argues so strongly for the perfection of the atoning work of Christ. Hence we will invest some space in establishing that connection in the immediate context of Hebrews chapter 10.

The author concludes his argument in verse 10 by stating that it is by "this will" (ἐν ᾧ θελήματι, the will of God for Christ, interpreted by the writer as having "taken away" the first which was made up of the old offerings and sacrifices) that "we have been sanctified through the offering of the body of Jesus Christ once for all." The writer is speaking within the context of sacrifice and tabernacle, offering and cleansing, and we should not, as a result, immediately import a systematized meaning into the text. That is, many will think of the idea of "progressive sanctification," whereby we are conformed to the image of Christ and our fleshly lusts mortified. But this is surely not the intention of the writer, nor is that the meaning of the term as it is used in Hebrews. To sanctify something, within the context of the tabernacle and sacrifice, is to set it aside as holy unto God. We note two other important aspects of interpreting this term: as it is used here it is the immediate result of the sacrificial offering of the physical body of Jesus Christ, and this is a once-for-all, singular event (expressed by ἐφάπαξ). These considerations are important for this is something that has been accomplished by the death of Christ.

The specific construction the author uses is called a periphrastic. The phrase is ἡγιασμένοι ἐσμὲν, "we have been sanctified." One of the key elements in grasping the tremendous message of Hebrews chapter 10 is to hear it not in the modern parlance but in the ancient context, as the author intended. The phrase the author uses to

The Newness of the New Covenant (Part 1)

describe the result of Christ's work carries a particular meaning. Periphrastics combine the ever-expressive Greek participle with a finite verbal form (normally of εἰμί). The result is an enhanced or emphasized "tense meaning." In this case, when you combine a perfect participle with a present tense form of εἰμί, the result is a perfect tense periphrastic construction.

While some grammarians today do not see the periphrastic as containing an added emphasis, many do. In this case, the periphrastic would emphasize the completedness of the action (which makes perfect sense in light of the argument the author is presenting). The writer is then emphasizing the fact that the "will" fulfilled or accomplished by Christ in his offering of his own body upon Calvary has sanctified us as a completed action in the past. This is not a conditional statement. It is not a provisional statement. It is not a theoretical statement. It is a statement of fact, placed firmly in the past with perfective emphasis. "We have been sanctified." We have been made holy, we have been set apart unto God. This must be kept in mind when we read verse 14 and its description of those who are sanctified.

Hebrews 10:11-18

Verses 11 through 13 form a parenthesis, repeating in another fashion the argument already enunciated regarding the Old Covenant and its repetitious sacrifices. The same sacrifices are offered over and over and over again, all in accordance with God's law. The writer will contrast the standing priest (ἕστηκεν) whose work is never done with the seated Savior whose work is finished and accomplished. He likewise makes sure the on-going, repetitive nature of the old sacrifices is seen (καθ᾽ ἡμέραν λειτουργῶν) by including "daily" and using the present tense of the participle "ministering." He piles term upon term to make sure we see the entirety of the long line of priests, offering sacrifices that can never take away sins. How can the congregants go back to a system such as this, when they have come to understand the singularity of the finished sacrifice of Christ? These repetitive sacrifices lack the power or ability to take away sins (οὐδέποτε δύνανται).

In verse 12 we have the very purposeful "but He" in contrast to "every priest." Christ "offered," past tense (προσενέγκας), one sacrifice for sins forever, this over against the regular offering of the priests of the Old Covenant. And the contrast is made complete in stating that Christ sat down at the right hand of God, fulfilling, in verse 13, the great Messianic Psalm 110. He does not go in and out, as the old priests, but he waits, rests, his work as high priest now defined as the passive presentation of his finished work in his own body: indeed, he is the Lamb "standing, as if slain" before the throne (Rev. 5:6). His work of intercession is not a further work that adds to his sacrifice: his people are united to him in his death, and his death avails for them. As the risen Victor he is seated at the right hand of the Father, his ever-present resurrected body still bearing the marks of the sacrifice, "pleading effectual prayers," in the words of the hymn-writer, the constant testimony to the finished work accomplished on Calvary.

Verse 14 is closely related to verse 10. Both verses speak of the offering of Christ. Both emphasize the singularity of the event, verse 10 by using "once for all" and verse 14 using "one [offering]." Verse 10 tells us the offering of the body of Jesus Christ "sanctifies" as a perfective action; verse 14 says it "perfects" or "completes," this time using the perfect tense verb, τετελείωκεν. The intriguing difference between the verbs is the use of "sanctified." In verse 10 it is the result of the "will" of God fulfilled through the offering of the body of Christ. "We have been sanctified." But in verse 14 it becomes the identifier of the objects of the action of making perfect, "those who are sanctified." So the question becomes, how can the offering of Christ be the means of creating the group who are sanctified and also be the means of perfecting that same group? The participle "those who are sanctified" should be understood in light of the emphasis that has already been made regarding the perfective result of the work of Christ: "we have been sanctified," and hence, we *are* sanctified. It is a simple statement of fact: this singular offering perfects those who are sanctified. It is not the author's intention for the participle to add a further statement about the nature of sanctification, as that has already been stated in

The Newness of the New Covenant (Part 1)

verse 10. So the NASB's translation correctly identifies the function of the participle with the rendering, "those who are sanctified."

Having announced the tremendous perfection of the work of Christ (plainly a soteriological context), the writer calls upon the Scriptures as another witness in Hebrews 10:15-18. He does so, however, by identifying the words of Jeremiah 31 as the very testimony of the Holy Spirit (an impressive witness to the view of the writers of Scripture themselves regarding the nature of the Word). The New Covenant passage from Jeremiah is again cited, with minor variations from the form found in Hebrews 8,[12] but the material embodied in Hebrews 8:11 is not repeated. The introductory statement, "for after saying," has led the NASB to insert the phrase "He then says" in italics prior to verse 17 and the final element of the Jeremiah citation regarding the forgiveness of sins. This insertion would be based upon the need to complete the thought in English implied by the introduction, "after saying." It seems logical to see the break in the citation of Jeremiah as the place to insert "He then says."

The point in the use of the text regarding the New Covenant is focused upon the soteriological element. Just as we saw in examining the text of Hebrews 8, so here the placing of the law upon the heart and writing it upon the mind is connected directly to the forgiveness of sins. The same audience is in view throughout the text. In Hebrews 10:16-18 the point of the writer is to see in the fulfillment of Jeremiah's prophecy in the priestly ministry and offering of Christ the very ending of all of the types and shadows that reflected that coming singular sacrifice that "perfected for all time those who are sanctified." The writer says, "where there is forgiveness of these things" (τούτων), referring to the substance of verse 17, "there is no longer any offering for sin." Such

---

[12] The differences raise a number of issues regarding the citation of translations, the role of the LXX in the New Testament, etc. In this instance, given the reorganization of the material of Jeremiah 31:34 (38:34 LXX) and the fact that the more literal rendering found in the LXX is found just a little earlier at Hebrews 8:12, it would seem that the form of Hebrews 10:17 is best explained as a paraphrase focusing attention upon sins and lawless deeds in a more compact statement, leading to the conclusion in verse 18.

argumentation makes no sense unless this covenant has been established and is thereby rendering the Old obsolete, so that there is no longer any offering for sin outside of the completed, finished work of Christ. The old ways cannot attract the true believer, for there is no longer any sacrifice for sin in the old system. It has been done away, fulfilled, in the one-time-offering of Jesus Christ. This then lays the foundation for the author's encouragement to enter into the holy place by the blood of Jesus (v. 19), for the work is finished, the better covenant is in place, and its promises valid and applicable. Truly we see here the fulfillment of the words of our faithful high priest on the night of his betrayal, when he established the covenant meal for his people, "This is the new covenant *in My blood*" (Luke 22:20).

Exegetical Summary

To summarize what we have seen on the basis of the text:

1) The context of Hebrews as a whole is apologetic and exhortational. It is seeking to encourage fidelity to the faith through the demonstration of the supremacy of Christ in every aspect of his ministry and person. Any interpretation that leads away from such an argument has missed the thrust of the epistle.
2) The use of the term "better" by the author is part of his apologetic approach. The complex of phrases seen in "mediator of a better covenant," "better sacrifices," "better promises," "better hope," and "more excellent ministry" are tied intimately to the work of Christ *and* to the establishment, nature, application, and fulfillment of the New Covenant. The New Covenant has distinct, unquestionably *soteriological* ramifications.
3) The audiences addressed in the citation from Jeremiah remain consistent throughout. Those who were under the Old Covenant are not confused with those under the New. Beginning in verse 10 the same audience is in view throughout the rest of the citation. This means that those who have the law

written upon their hearts and minds (v. 10) are those who know the Lord savingly (v. 11) and who have their sins forgiven (v. 12). There is no textual basis (linguistically or contextually) for positing separate, distinct audiences for differing descriptions of God's activities as recorded in Hebrews 8:10-12.
4) As a result of the third point, we discover that *all* who are in the New Covenant, "from the least to the greatest of them," experience the fullness of all of the blessings of the covenant. There is no "remnant" as with the Old Covenant, but, due to its soteriological nature, those in the New Covenant receive remission of sins and know the Lord savingly. This is part and parcel of the New Covenant's superiority to the Old.
5) This consistent theme is continued on and comes to expression again in chapter 10 when the New Covenant passage from Jeremiah is again cited and attached directly to the finished, sanctifying, perfecting work of Christ in his once for all offering of himself. The ending of offerings for sin is proven by reference to the fact that Christ has offered himself once for all, and that this, through the testimony of the Holy Spirit regarding the New Covenant, brings about remission of sins.

Relevance for Reformed Baptists

The relevance of the preceding exegetical inquiry for Reformed Baptists is rather obvious. One of the key issues separating credobaptists from paedobaptists is the nature of the New Covenant, and its relationship to the covenant of grace. In my work as an apologist, I have engaged in more than three dozen moderated, public debates against Roman Catholic apologists, and a number of those have been focused upon the issue of the Mass. As an elder in a Reformed Baptist church, I have approached the issue as one seeking to be consistent in my defense of the faith, but realizing that I must create my apologetic based upon a fully biblical and consistent theology. I believe in particular redemption, and hence am automatically drawn to Hebrews 10 in defining the perfection of the work of Christ in behalf of his people. But it was in pondering this very truth in light of the Roman Catholic claim that the Mass is a *re-presentation* of the *one* sacrifice of Calvary (and hence not a re-sacrificing of Christ) that I was struck by the inconsistency of holding to both the concept of particular redemption *and* to the idea that the New Covenant, the covenant in Christ's blood, the better covenant with a better mediator, a mediator whose intercession saves to the uttermost, could be entered into by those who will fail to receive eternal salvation. And so it was natural for me to see the truths of Christ's mediatorial perfection and his sacrificial offering in behalf of *the members of the New Covenant* as standing in opposition to those who would, on the one hand, affirm particular redemption but, then, make the covenant in Christ's blood one that, like the Old Covenant, contained both regenerate and unregenerate individuals.

In the next chapter, we will examine some of the arguments presented in defense of making the New Covenant a mixed covenant, containing both regenerate and unregenerate people. As noted in the introduction, we will do this with reference to *The Case for Covenantal Infant Baptism*, focusing primarily on the presentation of Pastor Jeff Niell, but also contrasting the perspective offered by Richard Pratt. Specifically, Pastor Niell insists that the newness of the New Covenant is to be construed in a tremendously more limited fashion than our exegesis has indicated. We will present a number of citations directly from the work and interact with them based upon the exegesis just provided.

The Newness of the New Covenant (Part 1)

CHAPTER 12
The Newness of the New Covenant: Better Covenant, Better Mediator, Better Sacrifice, Better Ministry, Better Hope, Better Promises (Part 2)
James R. White, Th.D.*

In the first part of this study we examined the text of Hebrews, focusing on the "new covenant," taking special note of the term "better," and following closely the argument of the writer in chapters 8 and 10, where the key prophetic passage Jeremiah 31:31-34 is cited, applied, and interpreted within the context of the author's presentation. In this part of our study we will recap our exegetical conclusions and then interact with the presentations of various paedobaptist writers, all reflecting on the issue of the New Covenant, focusing on the presentation given by Pastor Jeff Niell in *The Case for Covenantal Infant Baptism*.[1] Pastor Niell co-authored *The Same Sex Controversy* with me, and hence this topic provides an opportunity for modeling exegetically based dialogue and even disagreement regarding important issues, while honoring our common bond in Christ.

Recapitulation of Exegesis

Throughout his epistle, the writer of Hebrews presents a defense of the supremacy of Christ, seeking to demonstrate that in every aspect he is superior to the Old Covenant, so that there is nothing in the "old ways" to attract the believer in him. We also saw that the

---

* This chapter first appeared in *RBTR* and is used with permission with slight modifications.

[1] Gregg Strawbridge, ed., *The Case for Covenantal Infant Baptism* (Phillipsburg, NJ: P&R Publishing, 2003).

complex of terms related to "better" (mediator of a "better covenant," "better sacrifices," "better promises," "better hope" and "more excellent ministry") are found in distinctively soteriological contexts. The writer introduced the citation of Jeremiah within a context of contrast (Heb. 8:6-7), continued it within the citation itself ("not like the covenant which I made with their fathers," v. 9), and made the contrast explicit in his conclusion at 8:13. The text presents an apologetic argument that unlike the Old Covenant, where "they did not continue in My covenant" (v. 9), the New Covenant presents a perfect, full work of God which includes the internal renovation of the heart, salvific knowledge of God, and the forgiveness of sins. There is nothing in the text that suggests that there are different audiences envisioned in verses 10-12; those who have God's law written on their hearts are also those who know the Lord savingly, and whose sins are remembered no more. Unlike the Old Covenant, in the New all know the Lord, "from the least to the greatest of them." That we have accurately discerned the writer's intention in seeing the New Covenant soteriologically is borne out by reference to the second citation of Jeremiah 31 in Hebrews 10:16-17, for not only does the author cite the passage in support of one of the central soteriological arguments of the entire book (Heb. 10:10-14), but his interpretation of the final words regarding forgiveness of sins is clearly expressed in the same context.

Reformed Baptists have asserted that this passage is directly relevant to the commonly presented arguments of covenantal paedobaptists. Arguing from the common ground of a covenant of grace, Reformed credobaptists have asserted that if this passage teaches that the New Covenant differs from the Old in the matter of the extensiveness of the work of grace in the lives of the members (i.e., the New Covenant is not a mixed covenant of regenerate and unregenerate, elect and non-elect), then the most needed element of the paedobaptist argument regarding the continuity of the covenants and the covenant sign is disrupted at its most vital point. The "continuity" of the covenant of grace is seen in the expansion of God's work of grace, so that the New Covenant in the blood of the Son encompasses all of God's elect, with the Old Covenant's ceremonies pointing forward to the perfection that would come in

Christ. The New Covenant is soteriologically extensive in scope: all who are in it receive eternal life. The giving of the covenant sign, then,[2] must reflect the nature of the New Covenant as the covenant in the blood of Christ, a covenant which fulfills, and hence a covenant that differs on the level of membership. If the New Covenant is extensive in that all those who are in it know the Lord and have forgiveness of sins in the blood of Christ, this fact must be allowed to speak directly to the question, "To whom do we give the sign of the New Covenant?" While the common theme in paedobaptist writings emphasizes *continuity* (while other writings go to the opposite extreme seeking to create complete *discontinuity*), the biblical emphasis is on *fulfillment* and *completion.* The "not like" of Hebrews 8:9 points to a perfect covenantal work in the blood of the Son of God shed in behalf of his people.

Classically, credobaptists have seen the elect filling the New Covenant (due to its nature), and hence have recognized that the visible church is a mixed body, not to be seen as fully co-extensive with it. Apostasy, then, is viewed as apostasy from a profession of faith, not from membership in the New Covenant. The visible church contains true covenant members and false: but since the New Covenant is inherently soteriological in nature, and is made in the blood of Christ himself, its members cannot apostatize anymore than Christ can lose his sheep (John 10:27-30) or fail to do the Father's will (John 6:38-39). Apostasy, then, is not from the New Covenant, but from false profession of faith in Christ, which may include membership in the visible church. As we interact with the paedobaptist position, we will note that its understanding of the classic apostasy passages is, we believe, allowed to overturn the presentation of the inspired writer regarding the perfection and extent of the New Covenant.

---

[2] We do not here engage the argument over whether water baptism, in and of itself, is the best candidate for the "covenant sign" in light of the importance of the presence of the Spirit as the *down payment* in the life of all of the elect, and in light of the intimate connection between the Spirit's presence and the intention of God in the atoning work of Christ. The discussion here proceeds on the basis of the assumed paedobaptist argumentation, and contrasts it with the viewpoint of Hebrews on the nature of the New Covenant.

The Newness of the New Covenant (Part 2)

Niell's "The Newness of the New Covenant"

Jeffrey Niell's contribution to *The Case for Covenantal Infant Baptism* is entitled "The Newness of the New Covenant." The thesis of the chapter can be summarized briefly. Its fundamental assertion is that of the things listed in Hebrews 8:10-12, only the content of verse 11 is truly "new." Since men experienced the writing of God's law on their hearts under the Old Covenant, and since God's mercy was expressed under the Old Covenant as well, these are not "new." The essence of the newness of the covenant is in the doing away with the mediating Jewish priesthood that was involved in teaching the people. As Niell writes, "One can see that Hebrews 8:11 is referring to the removal of the old covenant priesthood and the people and duties associated with it."[3] His thesis is that the Old and New Covenants are substantially the same in reference to the fact that both present a mixture of regenerate and unregenerate members, leading to the assertion that "God has implemented no change whatsoever in covenant membership in the new covenant."[4]

Pastor Niell rightly points out:

> Many misunderstandings arise because of the failure to properly understand the experience of the regenerate in the older covenant....The entire quotation is concerned with its newness, not just Hebrews 8:11.[5]

This is perfectly in line with our own exegesis. The entire quotation is indeed concerned with newness, as our exegesis showed. But this truth must be kept in mind when seeing the *contrast* inherent in the context before and after the citation of Jeremiah 31. The only way to remove this element is to bring in outside considerations, and this is what Pastor Niell does. Responding, seemingly, to Paul Jewett's oft-

---

[3] Niell, "The Newness of the New Covenant" in *The Case for Covenantal Infant Baptism*, 148.
[4] Niell, "The Newness of the New Covenant," 130.
[5] Niell, "The Newness of the New Covenant," 131.

repeated (and documented) assertion regarding the reading of the New Testament as if it were the Old, and vice-versa, Niell writes:

> All too often, covenant theologians have been accused of treating the New Testament as if it were the Old. This misrepresentation of covenant theology is not helpful. But the question remains, How is the new covenant different? Does the newness pertain to its *essential* nature, making it qualitatively different from the previous covenant, or does the newness pertain to *membership* – or both? Those who would utilize the Hebrews passage to argue against paedobaptism would say that the new covenant is new in both respects.[6]

This assumes that "covenant theology" must, as a necessary element, include the assertion that the essential nature and membership of all postlapsarian biblical covenants are identical (and therefore that credobaptists cannot, despite the claims of Reformed Baptists, truly hold to "covenant theology"). Yet even if one rightly believes the covenant of grace was first revealed to Adam, does it necessarily follow that it was formally established with him? Was the constituted membership of the people of God the same from Adam to Abraham? From Abraham to Moses? From Moses to Christ? From Christ to the present? What covenant sign was given to covenant members from Adam to Abraham? Unless one limits the essential nature of the covenant of grace to merely that which consists of God acting graciously, supposed differences in administration (let alone the qualitative difference inherent in the covenant in the blood of the Son of God) would be contrary to the needed foundation that underlies the paedobaptist's insistence that the covenant sign should be given to all offspring of covenant members. When credobaptists look at the insistence that we change our hermeneutical process solely in this one area of investigation, and when we insist that outside traditions are operational in paedobaptist interpretations so that they are reading *out* of the text

---

[6] Niell, "The Newness of the New Covenant," 132.

The Newness of the New Covenant (Part 2)

the very distinctions emphasized *by* the text, we are not being "unhelpful." We must identify violations of proper hermeneutical process, and when deeply held traditions are very likely to impact our reading, we should be quick to recognize and consider them.

A common element of paedobaptist discussions of the New Covenant is the prioritizing of a particular view of apostasy above the direct teaching of Hebrews 8 and 10 regarding the nature of the New Covenant. That is, we are told that since apostasy from the New Covenant is taught elsewhere (the exegesis of said passages is, of course, questionable on many grounds), this consideration must become the *a priori* interpretational grid through which Hebrews 8 must be seen. This is seen in these words:

> Hebrews 8:11 cannot mean that every single member of the new covenant knows the Lord savingly, for that would be contrary to the rest of the New Testament. We must avoid equating covenant membership with election while we recognize that Scripture exhorts new covenant disciples to continue on in the faith. We will see that the distinction between the new covenant and the previous one does not relate to its essential nature or membership.[7]

When the final conclusion of the argument provides the foundation for its own annunciation, we have encountered a hermeneutical circle. We believe that the direct teaching of the text should determine the nature of the New Covenant first and foremost. Then, we can look at other passages *assumed* to be about it and determine, from a solid foundation, if in fact we are addressing apostasy *from the New Covenant* or apostasy *from an empty profession of faith*. But when we have clear, compelling, didactic revelation concerning the nature and extent of the New Covenant, we surely are working backwards to mitigate such teaching on the basis of an assumed doctrine of apostasy from highly questionable passages in foreign contexts. It is unlikely that in any other area of exegetical study (Trinity, deity of Christ, justification, etc.) would Niell allow

---

[7] Niell, "The Newness of the New Covenant," 133.

this kind of *a priori* interpretational methodology to go unchallenged.

At this point in his study, Pastor Niell addresses the views of various writers[8] and concludes, "These writers surprisingly assert that the internal operations of divine grace were not present for the old covenant saint."[9] Whether this is an accurate summary of the positions of each individual is itself an interesting question, but not one to be pursued here. The point is that for Niell, the "counterpoint" to which he is responding is an either/or situation: either the elements of the New Covenant described in Hebrews 8:10 were *completely* absent under the Old Covenant (as he understands the citations he presents to assert) or they were present *and hence cannot be definitional of what is "new" in the New Covenant.* But it is just here that the position of Reformed Baptists in general, and that seen in our exegesis, must be allowed to speak to the issue. We must agree that considered individually, each of the elements of the New Covenant listed in Hebrews 8:10-12 can be found in particular individuals under the Old Covenant. Surely, David knew of the work of God's law in his heart, knew God intimately and personally and salvifically, and experienced the forgiveness of sins. Our exegesis of the text has not led us to conclude that no one prior to the establishment of the New Covenant ever experienced these demonstrations of divine favor. But that is hardly the issue, for it is just as clear that for every David there were a dozen Ahabs; for every Josiah a legion of Manassehs. Unfaithfulness, the flaunting of God's law, the rejection of the role of truly being God's people, the rejection of his knowledge, and the experience of his wrath, were the *normative* experiences seen in the Old Covenant, which is why the writer to the Hebrews says that they did not keep his covenant and that he did not care for them. So, if *some* under the Old Covenant experienced these divine works of grace, but *most* did not, what then is to be concluded? That the newness of the New Covenant is seen partially in the *extensiveness* of the expression of God's grace to *all* in it. It is an *exhaustive* demonstration of grace, for

---

[8] John MacArthur, Leon Morris, and Philip E. Hughes.
[9] Niell, "The Newness of the New Covenant," 134.

The Newness of the New Covenant (Part 2)

all in the New Covenant experience *all* that is inherent in the covenant in the blood of the Son of God. It is not merely a remnant that experiences these things, but all, so that the saying, "They did not keep my covenant" cannot be said of them, for unlike the Old Covenant where there were many who did not have the law in their hearts and minds, did not know the Lord, and did not know the forgiveness of their sins, *this is not the case in the New Covenant*. Therefore, Pastor Niell's comments are not relevant to the Reformed Baptist position. We are not saying there were *none* who experienced God's grace under the Old Covenant, but rather that the Old Covenant, *in and of itself,* did not administer the eternal benefits of salvation by the blood of Christ. The newness of the New Covenant is therefore found in the reality that the better mediator, better hope, and better sacrifices mean that *all*, from the least to the greatest of them, know the Lord savingly. This is its glory, for it reflects the power of the blood in which it is sealed. Hence, when we read, "God's law, the transcript of his holiness and his expectations for his people, was already on the hearts of his people, and so is not new in the new covenant,"[10] we respond by saying it is not the mere existence of the gracious act of God writing his law on the heart that is new, but it is the *extensiveness* of that work that is new. While *some* under the Old Covenant experienced this, *all* in the New Covenant do so. This fulfills each and every element of the apologetic argument of the writer to the Hebrews that we identified in our exegesis of the passage. The importance of this point is seen repeatedly in examining the position presented by Niell:

> To state the matter as simply as possible, the writing of the law of God on the hearts of his people is *not new* in the new covenant, nor are the internal operations of God's Holy Spirit upon the hearts and minds of his people new in the new covenant. These were precious realities for the old covenant saint as well.[11]

---

[10] Niell, "The Newness of the New Covenant," 132.
[11] Niell, "The Newness of the New Covenant," 136.

We agree that the Old Covenant *saint* experienced the writing of God's law upon his or her heart. Obviously, Psalm 119 gives elegant testimony to this reality. But the point is not the presence of the elect as a sub-group in the Old Covenant anymore than it would be that the elect are a mere sub-group in the New Covenant. Ahab was an Old Covenant member but God's law was not written upon his heart so that he delighted in it. The newness of the New Covenant, as we have seen exegetically, is that *all* of these divine actions are true for *all* of those in it. *All* who receive forgiveness of sins (Heb. 8:12) likewise have God's law written upon their hearts, for there is no textual disruption of the audience in view from verse 10 to verse 12. For Niell's thesis to be established, the text would have to demand a break in audience through 8:10-12, but it does not.

Having asserted that the writing of God's law on the hearts of the members of the New Covenant is not "new," Pastor Niell moves to the central part of his presentation: the concept that Hebrews 8:11 does not mean that all members of the New Covenant know God savingly. Instead, he argues, the passage is about the removal of the Old Covenant priesthood. This concept is built upon insisting that something that was going on under the Old Covenant would cease. He writes:

> Nonetheless, the phraseology is stated negatively: 'They shall *not*.' Something is going to cease; it will disappear in the new covenant era, and it will pertain to teaching and the knowledge of the Lord. It has to do with a form of teaching that occurred among the covenant people of the Lord.[12]

What is the essence of the "newness" introduced by Hebrews 8:11? We are told that verse 11 "is referring to the removal of the old covenant priesthood and the people and duties associated with it."[13] Or, again in Pastor Niell's words:

---

[12] Niell, "The Newness of the New Covenant," 138-39.
[13] Niell, "The Newness of the New Covenant," 148.

To state it negatively: the newness of the new covenant is seen in *the cessation of the ceremonial aspects of the law.* To state it positively: Jesus Christ has fulfilled the law. He has become our perfect High Priest and has accomplished our redemption (atonement) through the perfect sacrifice of himself.[14]

What does this mean? The thesis is that the "newness" of the New Covenant is found in the cessation of the priestly office, described in verse 11 in terms of teaching.

These priests, in dealing with the ceremonial aspects of the law, revealed the gospel in pictures and illustrated the way of salvation. Their unique teaching was to cease at the time of the new covenant….Therefore, when God removed the priesthood (the persons and the work), the new covenant is precisely described with these words, "I will be their God, and they shall be My people. And…all will know Me, from the least to the greatest of them" (Heb 8:10-11)….Hebrews 8:11 explains that part of the newness of the new covenant is found in the removal of the Levitical priesthood – an office that was especially engaged in teaching and representing the knowledge of the Lord to the people.[15]

While the case can surely be made that, in a sense, the ministry of priests included elements of "teaching" through the institutions in which they ministered, our exegesis has shown the text from Jeremiah to be a consistent whole, with all of the descriptions of its newness having the same audience and the same soteriological implications. There simply is no contextual reason to look for this distant application, one that would require some level of explication on the part of the author (in which we would expect the application to be made with significantly greater clarity and force), when the context itself points us in the opposite direction. When a

---

[14] Niell, "The Newness of the New Covenant," 143.
[15] Niell, "The Newness of the New Covenant," 149, 151, 153.

consistent interpretation of the passage is at hand that requires no disruption of the flow of thought, we need a truly compelling reason to look for anything other than the plainest meaning of the words as they would have been read by the original audience. In this instance, while all agree that priesthood terminology in the context of shadow and fulfillment is central to the argument of the author, the specific idea of priests as teachers is far removed from the immediate discussion of the New Covenant as better and superior because of its accomplishment of that which the Old could not. Further, as we saw before, there is no reason to think the knowledge spoken of here is anything other than that seen in 1 Samuel 2:12, which states that Eli's sons "did not know the LORD." Ironically, here you have *priests* who, by their actions, would be engaged in the very types and shadows that are involved in teaching the knowledge of the Lord to the people of Israel, and yet they did not *know the Lord*. Was this because they did not perform their duties correctly? No, it is because they were "worthless men," men who did not have the law written on their hearts and minds, did not know Yahweh, and hence did not experience his mercy and forgiveness. There simply is no contextual reason to think that any other kind of knowledge was in view in Jeremiah 31, or that the writer to the Hebrews applied such a construct to this one verse without informing his audience of his meaning or intention.

It is important to understand that this interpretation has wider ramifications than simply throwing into question the actual nature of what is "new" in the New Covenant. Pastor Niell includes a footnote regarding what it means to "know the LORD" in Hebrews 8:11:

> It has been asserted that Heb. 8:11 refers to saving knowledge, but it must be recognized that *know* can refer to nonsaving knowledge (Jer. 16:21; Gen. 4:1). As argued throughout this chapter, the context deals with the removal of the ceremonial aspects of the law and refers to the knowledge that is possessed and published by the priests. This is true whether or not they were elect before the foundation of the world. With the author of Hebrews, we

The Newness of the New Covenant (Part 2)

must be careful to avoid equating covenant membership with election. This is shown by the warnings of apostasy that are given to new covenant members throughout this epistle – referring to apostasy from the covenant, not apostasy from election....[16]

What is the exegetical basis for seeing the knowledge of Hebrews 8:11 as non-salvific? The alleged foundation is two-fold: the already addressed idea that nothing in verses 10 or 12 is "new" to the New Covenant (i.e., they were present in some, but not in all, of the members of the Old Covenant), along with the continued pre-eminence of a particular understanding of apostasy texts. In other words, we do not find the argument to be exegetically derived, but instead to be an argument based on an overriding theological grid that predetermines the outcome of the study. The text has not driven us to divide up the audience envisioned in the New Covenant in this fashion; it has instead shown its consistency and harmony through its emphasis upon the "better" way in Christ. The soteriological thrust of the entire passage is not interrupted here, and is instead carried on through verse 12. But it is just here that Pastor Niell introduces a most interesting idea. When initially presenting the thesis that the newness of the New Covenant is limited in Hebrews 8, he says, "God's full pardon for sinners was just as present and real for saints in the Old Testament as it is for saints in the New."[17] So it seems here that in saying this is not new in the New Covenant the words are understood to refer to pardon for sinners. But, once you claim that the knowledge of God in Hebrews 8:11 is not salvific, how can you then revert back to a context of salvation? When addressing this, Pastor Niell says:

> The ceremonial aspects of the covenant of grace are also in view in Hebrews 8:12. Since God's grace, mercy, and forgiveness are not new in the new covenant, this passage must refer to something else and must accord with the

---

[16] Niell, "The Newness of the New Covenant," 153.
[17] Niell, "The Newness of the New Covenant," 140.

> context. Hebrews 8:12 refers to the abrogation of the ceremonies of sacrifice, the priestly duties, of the old covenant....God has always been merciful to his people, to their iniquities. Psalm 103 declares that he will separate our sins from us, as far as the east is from the west. He has always offered full pardon, but now, in the new covenant, the continual reminder is removed.[18]

Hebrews 10:3-4 is cited as evidence of this function of the old priesthood "reminders" of the sin of the people. Surely the writer to the Hebrews does contrast the once for all, completed, finished sacrifice of Christ with the repetitive sacrifices of the Old Covenant which did, indeed, function as an annual reminder of sin. One of the great truths of the New Covenant is that while those repetitive sacrifices were an ἀνάμνησις of sin, a regular reminder, built into the economy of the priesthood worship by God himself, there is no such ἀνάμνησις in the New Covenant, for all those in that covenant have received forgiveness of sins. The "remembrance" of the New Covenant is the Lord's Supper, in which we proclaim the Lord's death till he comes as an ἀνάμνησις of him (1 Cor. 11:25-26). Evidently, the function of a reminder of sins is no longer needed in the New Covenant; but, if it, like the Old, is a mixed covenant, this introduces an odd discontinuity, unless we recognize the utter superiority of the covenant in the blood of Christ. This is the very point of the writer to the Hebrews. As we noted in our exegesis, the reason all in the New Covenant know the Lord is laid out in verse 12, "*for* I will be merciful to their iniquities." This is not merely the removal of sacrifices. It is the removal of the very sins of the people so that they are brought into relationship with God through their Savior, Jesus Christ.

We must further note that the contrast in Hebrews 10 is between the repetitive sacrifices of the Old Covenant, which could never take away sins, and the singular sacrifice of the New, which not only *can* but in reality *does* do so for those who are in the covenant (Heb. 10:10-18)! This is the reason why the writer again

---

[18] Niell, "The Newness of the New Covenant," 154.

The Newness of the New Covenant (Part 2)

introduces the Jeremiah passage and connects these very words to the "one offering" which "perfected for all time those who are sanctified" (Heb. 8:14).

Do the Apostasy Passages Provide an Overriding Theological Matrix?

Though we can hardly enter into a full discussion of all the passages cited in support of a particular theory of apostasy, and though it seems clear that not all of the writers represented in *The Case for Covenantal Infant Baptism* would agree with Pastor Niell on this topic, a brief response to the key passage that is related to our central text (Heb. 10:29) may make our response fuller and more useful.

> For if we go on sinning willfully after receiving the knowledge of the truth, there no longer remains a sacrifice for sins, but a terrifying expectation of judgment and the fury of a fire which will consume the adversaries. Anyone who has set aside the Law of Moses dies without mercy on the testimony of two or three witnesses. How much severer punishment do you think he will deserve who has trampled under foot the Son of God, and has regarded as unclean the blood of the covenant by which he was sanctified, and has insulted the Spirit of grace? (Heb. 10:29)

Following John Owen's understanding of the context, we will assume the essential correctness of the position that sees the context of Hebrews 10:29 as an act of apostasy on the part of a baptized, confessing member of the congregation of Jewish Christians to which the author is writing.[19] Recognizing this immediate context protects the passage from its most common misapplications and brings us to the key issue in our inquiry: in the case of those who knowingly reject their profession of faith and return to Judaism,

---

[19] John Owen, *An Exposition of the Epistle to the Hebrews* (reprint ed., Edinburgh: Banner of Truth Trust, 1991), 6:530, 531.

were these individuals, in the thinking of the writer to the Hebrews, members of the New Covenant, perfected by the death of Christ, sanctified by his blood, who then became imperfect and were lost? Who is the object of the phrase ἐν ᾧ ἡγιάσθη ("by which he was sanctified"): the apostate or the Son of God? Those who press this passage as a clear indication that the New Covenant can be entered into and yet violated assume that the phrase, which can grammatically be attached to either antecedent, *must* be applied to the apostate.

The exegesis that we have offered, together with the compelling argumentation (that reaches its climax in Heb. 10:10-18) regarding the perfection that flows from the singular, completed sacrifice of the New Covenant, provides a very strong ground on which to argue that the writer would hardly turn around and vitiate the central core of his apologetic argument within a matter of only a few sentences by robbing the New Covenant of its intrinsically perfect soteriological content. We would actually be in very good company to assert that the depth of the sin of apostasy here noted is magnified by recognition that the one who is sanctified by the blood treated as common or unclean (κοινὸν) by the apostate through returning to the sacrifice of goats and bulls is actually Christ, the very Son of God who has set himself apart as high priest as well as offering. Owen expressed it forcefully:

> The last aggravation of this sin with respect unto the blood of Christ, is the nature, use, and efficacy of it; it is that "wherewith he was sanctified." It is not *real* or *internal sanctification* that is here intended, but it is a *separation* and *dedication unto God*; in which sense the word is often used. And all the disputes concerning the total and final apostasy from the faith of them who have been really and internally sanctified, from this place, are altogether vain; though that may be said of a man, in aggravation of his sin, which he professeth concerning himself. But the difficulty of this text is, concerning whom these words are spoken: for they may be referred unto the person that is guilty of the sin insisted on; he counts the blood of the covenant, wherewith he

himself was sanctified, an unholy thing. For as at the giving of the law, or the establishing of the covenant at Sinai, the people being sprinkled with the blood of the beasts that were offered in sacrifice, were sanctified, or dedicated unto God in a peculiar manner; so those who by baptism, and confession of faith in the church of Christ, were separated from all others, were peculiarly dedicated to God thereby. And therefore in this case apostates are said to "deny the Lord that bought them," or vindicated them from their slavery unto the law by his word and truth for a season, 2 Peter 2:1. But the design of the apostle in the context leads plainly to another application of these words. It is Christ himself that is spoken of, who was sanctified and dedicated unto God to be an eternal high priest, by the blood of the covenant which he offered unto God, as I have showed before. The priests of old were dedicated and sanctified unto their office by another, and the sacrifices which he offered for them; they could not sanctify themselves: so were Aaron and his sons sanctified by Moses, antecedently unto their offering any sacrifice themselves. But no outward act of men or angels could unto this purpose pass on the Son of God. He was to be the priest himself, the sacrificer himself, — to dedicate, consecrate, and sanctify himself, by his own sacrifice, in concurrence with the actings of God the Father in his suffering. See John 17:19; Hebrews 2:10, 5:7, 9, 9:11, 12. That precious blood of Christ, wherein or whereby he was sanctified, and dedicated unto God as the eternal high priest of the church, this they esteemed "an unholy thing;" that is, such as would have no such effect as to consecrate him unto God and his office.[20]

Owen's exegesis is only strengthened by the considerations raised in our own study of the text. It should be noted that some might be unaware that Owen took this viewpoint, in light of the fact that in the more popular work, *The Death of Death in the Death of*

---

[20] Owen, *An Exposition of the Epistle to the Hebrews*, 6:545-46.

Christ,[21] he did not even mention this exegetical possibility, but took the phrase to refer to the apostate. Why this inconsistency? The answer is easy to ascertain: Owen wrote *The Death of Death* as a young man; it was his second work, and his first widely received polemic effort. But his massive commentary on Hebrews came many years later, and is the work of a mature exegete. It is clear that he had not even considered the possibility in his younger days.

In light of this exegesis and its consistency with the apologetic argument of the epistle, it is interesting to note that though a number of the authors featured in *The Case for Covenantal Infant Baptism* cite Hebrews 10:29 as evidence of apostasy from the New Covenant with accompanying New Covenant curses, only two even note this other interpretation, and then only in footnotes, and none make any note of Owen's words. Gregg Strawbridge writes:

> A minority of interpreters take the implied "he" in "the blood of the covenant by which *he was sanctified* (*hegiasthe* [third person singular]" as referring to Christ. However, the grammar certainly does not necessitate that interpretation. Such a view seems to be an *ad hoc* response to the theological difficulties of a baptistic Calvinism, which are alleviated in the general Reformed view of the covenant with its internal and legal dimensions.[22]

Surely Owen would not be guilty of coming up with an *ad hoc* response due to his holding a baptistic Calvinism, so perhaps it is better to see this view as flowing from a contextual exegesis that is driven by maintaining the apologetic thrust and argument of the epistle to the Hebrews while likewise refusing to allow an external tradition or practice to become an overriding consideration in our interpretation. Likewise, Randy Booth provides a footnote to his use of Hebrews 10:29:

---

[21] John Owen, *The Death of Death in the Death of Christ* (reprint. Ed., Edinburgh: Banner of Truth Trust, 1985), 252-56.
[22] Strawbridge, ed., *Case for Covenantal Infant Baptism*, 281.

> Some contend that the words "by which he was sanctified" refer to Jesus (see John 17:19). Such an interpretation cannot be sufficiently supported. Moreover, even if they did refer to Jesus, it must be admitted that the word "sanctify" is used in a different way than it is earlier in Heb. 10:14. Surely the sanctification experience of Jesus is far different from that which we experience.[23]

One cannot respond to the assertion that "such an interpretation cannot be sufficiently supported" since the author does not expand upon the statement. In light of the above provision of what seems to be more than sufficient support for the position, we cannot accept the assertion. And while the "self-sanctifying" of Christ by his sacrifice must, by nature, be "far different from that which we experience," it is hard to see how this is relevant to the point at issue, i.e., who is "sanctified" by the blood of the covenant and how this relates to the great guilt of the apostate. It is our firm conviction that this understanding of the text not only comports better with the context, but it has not at all been allowed to have a sufficient voice in the use of the text by paedobaptist authors seeking to establish the case for apostasy from the New Covenant. Further, in reference to Pastor Niell's thesis, and the centrality of an overarching concept of apostasy to his entire reading (Heb. 10:29 figuring prominently in the listing of passages supporting his view as he sees it), these considerations seriously undermine the position, especially in light of the positive exegetical thrust of the passage established in the first part of this study.

The New Covenant as Future Fulfillment?

Other authors in *The Case for Covenantal Infant Baptism* present the thesis that the New Covenant experiences a gradual growth or fulfillment over time, so that the final establishment awaits the consummation of the ages in the coming of Christ. In fact, Richard

---

[23] Strawbridge, ed., *Case for Covenantal Infant Baptism*, 198. Prior to this, Booth had stated, "The old and new covenants are essentially one."

L. Pratt, Jr. supports the exegetical conclusions we presented regarding the inherent *soteriological* nature of the New Covenant in his presentation. Directly contrary to Pastor Niell, Dr. Pratt writes:

> A second feature of Jeremiah's prophecy that is often used to oppose infant baptism is that *the new covenant is fully internalized*. Jeremiah 31:33 speaks plainly in this regard: "I will put my law in their minds and write it on their hearts." This feature of the new covenant demonstrates that God himself will bring about deep internal transformation of his covenant people. The words "mind" and "heart" often denote the inner person, the deeper recesses of personality, or, in contemporary parlance, "the soul." Jeremiah did not see entrance into the new covenant community as entrance into an external environment, but as undergoing a spiritual, inward change.[24]

In reference to "knowing" the Lord as cited in Hebrews 8:11, Pratt says, "In a word, to know God as Jeremiah spoke of it would be to receive eternal salvation. In the covenant of which Jeremiah spoke, salvation would come to each participant."[25] We note this simply to demonstrate that the exegesis we have offered of the *nature* of the new covenant is surely not to be relegated to something that is derived from the uncritical application of "baptistic" presuppositions to the text, since obviously Dr. Pratt brings no such presuppositions. In light of these statements, then, how does Pratt maintain a paedobaptist commitment in light of the nature of the New Covenant? He does so by differentiating between the inauguration of the New Covenant and the final establishment thereof, putting that final consummation off until the return of Christ. He writes:

---

[24] Richard L. Pratt Jr., "Infant Baptism in the New Covenant" in Strawbridge, ed., *Case for Covenantal Infant Baptism*, 169.
[25] Pratt, "Infant Baptism in the New Covenant," 161.

> The new covenant was inaugurated in Christ's first coming; it progresses in part during the continuation of Christ's kingdom; but it will reach complete fulfillment only when Christ returns in the consummation of all things. We must approach Jeremiah 31:31-34 just as we approach all prophecies regarding the restoration after exile: with the understanding that the restoration of the kingdom and the renewal of the covenant will not be complete until Jesus returns....When we apply the basic pattern of New Testament fulfillment to Jeremiah's prophecy of the new covenant, it becomes clear that his expectations provide no basis at all for opposing infant baptism.[26]

This means that the perfect fulfillment of God's purpose, seen in the New Covenant, is, from the vantage point of both Jeremiah *and* the author of Hebrews, a future reality. While acknowledging the indefectibility of New Covenant membership, Pratt does not believe this is yet a reality for Christ's people in the church. "In the consummation of Christ's kingdom, this prediction will be completely fulfilled. Once Christ returns, it will not be possible to break the new covenant and thereby to enter into another exile."[27] Evidently, until then, the New Covenant, while inaugurated, is not fully established.

> We can have confidence that after Christ returns in glory, everyone in the new creation will have the law of God written on his or her heart. We will all love and delight in his ways, just as Christ already does....In this sense, we expect Jeremiah's prophecy to find complete fulfillment when Christ returns.
>
> At the present time, however, this expectation is only partially fulfilled. To be sure, the hearts and minds of believers have been renewed by God's grace....At the same time, however, we are commanded to be guided by the

---

[26] Pratt, "Infant Baptism in the New Covenant," 169.
[27] Pratt, "Infant Baptism in the New Covenant," 169.

Scriptures and to watch for corruption in our thinking....The New Testament speaks this way because, while the internalization of the law of God has begun within believers, it has not yet been completed.[28]

Based upon this "partial fulfillment" motif, Pratt can affirm the perfection of the New Covenant but only as it is finally and completely established in the future.

> The promise that the new covenant will grant salvation to all who participate will be fulfilled by the removal of the unbelievers at the time of judgment. Only true believers will be left, and thus all who remain in the new covenant will be saved.
>
> But prior to the judgment that Christ will render at his return, the new covenant community is not restricted to believers only. If it were, there would be no separation of people at Christ's return....Until the consummation, the new covenant will continue to be a mixture of true believers and sanctified unbelievers.[29]

Before interacting briefly with this concept, it is important to understand *why* Pratt says the New Covenant is only "partially" fulfilled. He refers to the fulfillment pattern of Jeremiah 31. "In a word, the fulfillment of the new covenant depended on the fulfillment of the other predictions of chapter 31."[30] Specifically, Pratt identifies three sections to Jeremiah's prophecy:

- Future planting of God's people in the land (vv. 27-30)
- Future new covenant with God's people (vv. 31-37)
- Future rebuilding and permanence of the holy city (vv. 38-40)

---

[28] Pratt, "Infant Baptism in the New Covenant," 171.
[29] Pratt, "Infant Baptism in the New Covenant," 173.
[30] Pratt, "Infant Baptism in the New Covenant," 165.

Pratt sees the fulfillment of the first and third portions of the prophecy as yet future, and hence the middle portion cannot yet have come to full completion. He writes:

> Because the New Testament does not explicitly apply this threefold fulfillment pattern to Jeremiah's prophecy of the new covenant, the fulfillment of that particular prophecy is often misunderstood. Often interpreters approach this text as if the new covenant was realized in its fullness when Christ first came to earth, but this is a serious error.[31]

The two elements of this presentation, then, that need to be examined in light of the exegesis already offered are *first*, is there warrant to insist that a particular theory of fulfillment of prophetic material surrounding the Jeremiah passage must be obtained before the New Covenant it promises can be fully realized? And, *second*, what are the ramifications of creating a dichotomy between "partial fulfillment" and "final fulfillment" with reference to the use of the passage by the writer to the Hebrews?

With reference to fulfillment themes in the New Testament, we note that there are numerous passages that its writers saw as fulfilled completely in the ministry of Christ that are plainly part of a larger narrative that has not yet been fulfilled in a particular fashion. One can think of Psalm 22 and the fact that its entire thrust leads us from the suffering Messiah (vv. 1-18) through to the resurrected and conquering King (vv. 27-31). Can one section be fulfilled without the other? Surely.

Moving to Jeremiah, a close contextual passage is found in Jeremiah 32:40. "I will make an everlasting covenant with them that I will not turn away from them, to do them good; and I will put the fear of Me in their hearts so that they will not turn away from Me." Here Jeremiah re-states the New Covenant theme from the preceding chapter (indeed, Pratt likewise saw the element of indefectibility in the Jeremiah 31 prophecy that is here laid out with greater clarity). Yet, the immediate context is very closely tied to

---

[31] Pratt, "Infant Baptism in the New Covenant," 168.

Jerusalem (v. 36), restoration (v. 37), and the very internal promises of the New Covenant (vv. 38-39). Though the context continues in close proximity with the historic Jerusalem motif (v. 42), clearly these promises are fulfilled in the church. So if particular elements of the prophecy can be fulfilled in the coming of the Spirit and his ministry in the church, upon what basis are we to insist upon a particular "level" of fulfillment of surrounding prophetic material before allowing a "full" fulfillment for the New Covenant?

Further, one could argue that it is artificial to insist upon such a strong connection between the elements Pratt lists. There is a clear break after Jeremiah 31:26, followed by two "days are coming" oracles. It is hard to insist that the first oracle is to be connected to the second, especially in light of the "sour grapes" saying (v. 29). After verse 34 we have another break, with the form of the text changing once again to a poetic revelation motif. The real question that must be asked is, does the writer to the Hebrews see the same three-part fulfillment motif that Pratt insists must be followed? We can only answer that we see no evidence that he does.

But far more compelling is the consideration of the result of making the New Covenant something that is yet future in its fulfillment. We noted in our exegesis that central to the thrust of the writer is the establishment of the supremacy of Christ over the old ways, and in our key texts, he does this through the assertion of a better ministry, a better and New Covenant, with better sacrifices, and a better hope. We are never given the slightest indication that this better covenant is only *partly* better now, and will get *much* better in the future. When the writer says in 8:6 that this covenant "has been enacted" (νενομοθέτηται), there is nothing in the verb used, or in the tense form, to indicate a progressive action that has been "inaugurated" but is still in process and will not come into full force until far in the future. Instead, he chooses the very form of the term that is the most difficult to fit with such a concept. The covenant "has been enacted" (perfect tense) as a completed action. This establishment of a second covenant (in contrast with the "first," Heb. 8:7) is related to the passing away of the first (Heb. 8:13). But if the first passes away, and the second is not fully established, are we left with some form of "partial covenantalism"

The Newness of the New Covenant (Part 2)

that is to fill the description of the "better" covenant to which the people should cling rather than returning to the old ways? Is this really how we are to read the writer to the Hebrews? We have insisted that any interpretation that diminishes the apologetic weight of the epistle is to be questioned. Surely the introduction of partiality (and hence imperfection) into the original readers' experience of the New Covenant falls into this category. How could it not, when the writer concludes his citation with the assertion that the old ways are "about to disappear" (Heb. 8:13) and yet must then, in the next breath, say that all the promises of the New Covenant are yet future in their final fulfillment, and that the partial covenant that he is offering to them continues to have the very same faults in it that the passage in Jeremiah had addressed (specifically, the fact that they did not keep the covenant, hence, there were apostates and unfaithfulness and individuals for whom the Lord "did not care")? We suggest that any concept of partiality stands in direct opposition to the apologetic thrust of the writer himself. If we take the inspired interpretation of the New Testament as our norm, we must reject the partial fulfillment theory based upon the usage of the text itself.

But there is another immediate problem with this theory. As we noted, Jeremiah 31 is not cited only in Hebrews chapter 8. It appears also in chapter 10. There we saw that it was once again intimately tied to the salvific purpose of God in the sacrifice of Jesus Christ. The writer cites it once again as the Holy Spirit's testimony to the truthfulness of the point he just established, i.e., the once for all offering of Jesus Christ that perfects those who are sanctified. The writer's conclusion is, "Now where there is forgiveness of these things, there is no longer *any* offering for sin" (Heb. 10:18). Consider well what the "only inaugurated, but only partially fulfilled" theory of the New Covenant means in a passage such as this. Is not the very forgiveness of sins dependent upon the *completed* sacrifice of Jesus Christ? Is it not a part of the writer's argument that the old offerings have been done away with because the *one* offering of Christ (the blood of the New Covenant!) has brought about forgiveness? Surely it is. So where is this concept of partiality in the text that directly addresses the nature and result of the New Covenant? It is nowhere to be found. Indeed, we are left to wonder exactly how this "partiality" would be applied in light of the fact that Pratt has clearly seen that the New Covenant is exhaustive and perfect in its soteriological element. Evidently Pratt believes the full establishment of the New Covenant implies sinless perfection on the part of its members. But this means that while the audience of the Jeremiah prophecy, as applied by the writer to the Hebrews, remains the same from verses 10 through 12 (as Pratt seems to agree), the actual fulfillment of the divine blessings differs along the line: there is a partial writing of the law upon the heart, a partial knowledge, but full forgiveness. We are again forced to point out the inconsistency created by not allowing the New Covenant to be fully established by the shed blood of Jesus Christ or to in any way seek to make room within its perfection for the unregenerate. The impact upon the apologetic thesis of the book of Hebrews of such a theory of "partiality," along with the simple fact that we do not have the first word of description of the covenant in this form as something that will only truly *become* better in the final completion of all things, argues convincingly against this theory.

Conclusion

Semper reformanda is a phrase that, despite its repetition, is often set aside in the service of tradition. The concept underlying the phrase is the unfathomable riches of the Word of God, the very words of God inscripturated and given as a gift to Christ's body, the church. And while *semper reformanda* does not mean that we never set down boundary markers of truth, it does mean that the highest authority for the church is always the Scripture, and the church is constantly to be examining her faith in the light of God's Word, knowing our penchant for apathy, our love of the comfortable, the ease with which we confuse human traditions with divine revelation and call them "good." Engaging the text of Scripture afresh, seeking to hear only what the Holy Spirit has given us in it, eschewing the myriad forms of pious unbelief that mar the work of exegesis in modern times (and question its truly divine nature and clarity), is truly the highest form of obedience to the divine truth contained in the phrases *sola Scriptura* and *semper reformanda*.

We have sought to engage, fairly and honestly, the text of the tremendous epistle to the Hebrews and to do justice to the themes and concerns of the writer. The text is clear, compelling, and once again captivates the heart with the glory of its self-consistency. The New Covenant is seen as a divine work, comprehensive in its perfection, reflecting the radiance of the one who defines its every contour, the Lord Jesus Christ, its mediator and its sacrificial offering.

We have likewise sought to be fair to those we have reviewed as we view them as our fellow heirs of grace, our brothers in Christ, even when our exegesis has led us to question, and reject, the substance of their position. We have written in the firm conviction that Christ's Word is truth, and Christian unity can only be forged when his people seek his truth there, and nowhere else. It is our hope that this interchange will aid those who seek to examine the issues of baptism, the covenant, and the proper place of these beliefs in the ministry of the church.

The Newness of the New Covenant (Part 2)

Chapter 13
Acts 2:39 in its Context (Part 1): An Exegetical Summary of Acts 2:39 and Paedobaptism
Jamin Hübner, Th.D.*

Acts 2:39 is one of the most controversial texts in the paedobaptist vs. credobaptist debate. Reformed scholars treat the text as though it supports the necessary grounds for paedobaptism, while Reformed Baptists do not see it as such. In fact, the text may even lend support to the Baptist position.

In general, the paedobaptism assertion is that "the promise" and the phrase "for you and for your children" in Acts 2:39 is primarily referring to the covenant of grace revealed to Abraham and the "you and your seed" in Genesis 17.[1] There may be other secondary meanings in the text, but, as Joel Beeke put it:

---

* Jamin Hübner, Th.D., is the founding chair of the Christian Studies Program at John Witherspoon College. He is a graduate of Dordt College (B.A. Theology), Reformed Theological Seminary (M.A. Religion) and the University of South Africa (Th.D. Systematic Theology). In addition to being a prolific author, Jamin has taught at several educational and church institutions, participated in several moderated debates, and plays drums primarily for jazz and big band settings. He and his wife, Jessica (B.S. Biology, M.S. Counseling), enjoy the outdoors, gardening, tea, photography (blackhillsphoto.org), and exploring the wonders of God's creation.

[1] Joseph Nally even found Acts 2:39 as supporting a connection between baptism and circumcision. He says, "The clear link is seen in Acts 2:39, where Peter gives the reason for this action: "the promise is to you and to your children, and all who are far off" (cf. "and thy seed after thee in their generations"; Gen. 17). The Apostle Peter consciously uses the same formula (because it is an everlasting covenant) as the LORD himself used when he instituted the sign of circumcision in Genesis 17. The Jews listening understood this precisely. Thus, as they understood circumcision was for Abraham and his seed, they understood that baptism was for those that believe and their seed. Thus, it seems clear that Peter and his audience understood there to be a link between circumcision and Baptism." Joseph R Nally.

Peter uses the term *the promise* as rhetorical shorthand for the covenant of grace, which embodies the promise of salvation he calls upon his hearers to embrace (see Acts 2:21). This promise is the same as those made to Abraham, to David, to Israel, and even to the Gentiles.[2]

Calvin himself went as far as to say that

> This place [Acts 2:39], therefore, doth abundantly refute the manifest error of the Anabaptists, which will not have infants, which are the children of the faithful, to be baptized, as if they were not members of the Church.[3]

As such, Acts 2:39 functions for the paedobaptist as a bridge between the Testaments that re-asserts a basic principle of the Abrahamic Covenant: parents stand as the covenant representative of their family, and the children of believing parents are to be included among God's covenant people.

This essay will demonstrate that a consistent exegesis of Acts 2:39 does not uphold these claims. The meaning of "the promise" and the phrase "for you and for your children" refers *not* primarily to the Abrahamic Covenant or the covenant of grace, but to the specific promise of the Holy Spirit and the "sons and daughters" cited earlier from Joel (Acts 2:17-21). This fact alone has numerous implications that question the legitimacy of paedobaptist interpretations of the verse. Acts 2:39 is undoubtedly *related* to the

---

"A Brief Critique of Fred Malone's "The Baptism of Disciples Alone"." *Reformed Perspectives Magazine*. 7:49 (2005).

[2] Joel R. Beeke and Ray B. Lanning. "Unto You, and to Your Children" in Gregg Strawbridge, ed., *The Case for Covenantal Infant Baptism* (Phillipsburg: P&R, 2003), 49. J. V. Fesko recently asserted essentially the same: "To what promise does Peter refer? The promise is undoubtedly weighted on the whole of redemptive history: the *protoevangelium* (Gen. 3:15); God's promise to Abraham (Gen. 12:1-3; 15; 17:1-14); and his promise to David (1 Sam. 7:14)." J. V. Fesko. *Word, Water, and Spirit: A Reformed Perspective on Baptism* (Grand Rapids: Reformation Heritage Books, 2010), 357.

[3] John Calvin, *Commentary on Acts*. Christian Classics Ethereal Library. http://www.ccel.org/ccel/calvin/calcom36.html (Accessed February 29, 2012).

covenant of grace revealed to Abraham – just as countless other blessings are part and parcel of this broad gospel "preached beforehand to Abraham" (Gal. 3:8). But when priority is given to the original context and primary meaning of the verse, it becomes clear that Acts 2:39 cannot and should not be *equated* with the covenant of grace, nor can the specific features of the Abrahamic Covenant (e.g., infants receive the sign of the covenant) be forced into the verse and its surrounding context – precisely because Acts 2:39 is describing a *New Covenant* reality ("And in the last days it shall be, God declares, that I will pour out my Spirit on all flesh," Acts 2:17). Whatever "covenantal language" that does exist between Acts 2:39 and any part or aspect of the Old Testament must be understood as Peter applies it. The phrase "everyone whom the Lord God shall call" in verse 39 and the whole of verse 41 further establishes that Acts 2:39 provides more support for the credobaptist position (i.e., "believer's baptism") than the paedobaptist position.

Background to the Text

Acts 2:37-41 comes immediately after the second speech in Acts, the speech of Peter at Pentecost (Acts 2:14-36). The Holy Spirit finally comes as it had been specifically promised in both the Old and New Testament Scriptures (Joel 2, Acts 1:4, John 15, etc.) and was particularly manifested by speaking in tongues (Acts 2:1-4). Verse 5 continues from there:

> Now there were dwelling in Jerusalem Jews, devout men from every nation under heaven. And at this sound the multitude came together, and they were bewildered, because each one was hearing them speak in his own language. And they were amazed and astonished, saying, "Are not all these who are speaking Galileans?" (Acts 2:5-7)

Peter then gives a speech in response to these Jews in Jerusalem. It contains three major citations from the Old Testament, each making a specific point.

Acts 2:39 in its Context (Part 1): An Exegetical Summary of Acts 2:39 and Paedobaptism

The first citation in verses 17-21 from Joel 2:28-32 (Joel 3:1-5, LXX) vindicates the immediate fact of Pentecost. The pouring out of the Spirit is promised in the Old Testament prophets. The second citation from Psalm 16:8-11 vindicates the crucified and resurrected Lord. The very suffering and death of Jesus "by the hands of lawless men" was the direct result of "the definite plan and foreknowledge of God" (Acts 2:23). Furthermore, the resurrection demonstrates that Jesus was even greater than "the patriarch David" before Him (Acts 2:29). Verse 33 then summarizes the conclusions from these two Old Testament texts: "Being therefore exalted at the right hand of God [referring to the argument in vv. 22-31, Psa. 16], and having received from the Father the promise of the Holy Spirit [referring to vv. 15-21, Joel 2], he has poured out this that you yourselves are seeing and hearing." Finally, Peter finalizes his speech with Psalm 110 (Acts 2:34-35) and concludes in verse 36: "Let all the house of Israel therefore know for certain that God had made him both Lord and Christ, this Jesus whom you crucified."

A few preliminary remarks are in order. First, Peter's audience in this entire context is primarily Jewish. Not only does Peter's speech contain more of the Old Testament than Peter's own words, but the first assertion following all of the three Old Testament quotations are Peter's explicit confirmation of his listening audience.[4]

Second, it seems clear that "the promise of the Holy Spirit" in verse 33 refers to the giving of the Holy Spirit that the Jews and Jerusalem are witnessing. The same term, "promise" (ἐπαγγελία), is also used in Acts 2:39 in the same sense.[5] Nevertheless, the promise of the Spirit does not come isolated from the fact of general salvation; verse 21 says "everyone who calls upon the name of the Lord shall be saved."

---

[4] Quote of Joel 2 in Acts 2:17-21 followed by "Men of Israel, hear these words" (2:22). Quote of Psalm 16 in Acts 2:25-28 followed by "Brothers, I may say to you" (2:29). Quote of Psalm 110 in Acts 2:34-35 followed by "Let all the House of Israel therefore know" (Acts 2:36).

[5] The next occurrence of the word does not come until Acts 7:17 (where Stephen explicitly refers to the Abrahamic promise).

Acts 2:39 in its Context (Part 1): An Exegetical Summary of Acts 2:39 and Paedobaptism

Up to this point (Acts 2:33), Peter has essentially cleared up the primary objections of the Jews that were given in Acts 2:5-13. Pentecost is not as foreign as the Jews had originally thought. But Peter does not stop there. He goes on to make a third and more assertive argument, namely, the argument from Psalm 110 that "God has made him both Lord and Christ, this Jesus whom you crucified." Not only was the odd behavior of the church at Pentecost justified, but the accusation of the Jews was thoroughly *unjustified* – for they had actually killed the Son of God! This was more information than the Jews asked for. They were confronted with the major facts of the Christian gospel (i.e., death, resurrection, deity, and Lordship of Christ).

The event of Pentecost provided a unique opportunity for witnessing. This is clearest in verses 37-38, where Peter commands his audience to repent and be baptized.

Acts 2:37-38

> Now when they heard this, they were pierced to the heart, and said to Peter and the rest of the apostles, "Brethren, what shall we do?" Peter said to them, "Repent, and each of you be baptized in the name of Jesus Christ for the forgiveness of your sins; and you will receive the gift of the Holy Spirit." (Acts 2:37-38, NASB)

Peter is undoubtedly calling the Jews to embrace the gospel and convert to Christianity. But, it is important to note that the *specific promise of the Spirit* is still on his mind. The command to repent (imperative) is used three times in Acts (in 2:28; 3:19; 8:22), but only here is it immediately followed by the gift of the Spirit. The reason is obvious: Pentecost is the context.

Before moving into verses 37-38 in more detail, it should be mentioned that there has been much debate over the meaning of "for" (εἰς) in the phrase "for the forgiveness of your sins." It has been used by some to justify a "salvation by baptism" position with εἰς interpreted in a causal sense. This position continues to be refuted,⁶ and it is also not an issue that usually divides Reformed (paedobaptist or credobaptist) interpretations of Acts 2:37-41, so a full discussion will not be taken up here. It is sufficient enough for our purposes to simply state that the precondition for receiving forgiveness of sins and receiving the Holy Spirit is repentance. A person "will receive the gift of the Holy Spirit" when repentance takes place. Unrepentant individuals do not receive the gift (or "promise," v. 39) of the Spirit.

Both "repent" (μετανοήσατε) and "be baptized" (βαπτισθήτω) are imperatives. However, the former is 2nd person plural (matching the 2nd person plural, "of you") while the latter is 3rd person singular (matching the singular, "each of you").⁷ So the verse is more precisely rendered, "You all repent and each one of you all (who repent) be baptized."⁸ It is clear that the ones to be baptized are to be the same ones who repent.⁹ As I. Howard Marshall summarized: "Repentance and faith are two sides of the same coin. So it is that here repentance is linked with being baptized."¹⁰

But Peter could have expressed this general point by simply saying "you all repent and be baptized." Why the inclusion of "each of you" (ἕκαστος ὑμῶν). The specificity of Peter's words at this point – that is, his extension from the general "you all" to the more exhaustive "every/each one of you" – is no surprise given the context. The preceding arguments regarding the giving of the Holy Spirit clearly assert the same concept of expansion. God will pour out his Spirit "on all flesh…sons and daughters…young men…old men…even on my male servants and female servants" (vv. 17-18). The following verse expresses the same idea: "The promise is for

---

⁶ The most concise treatments of this issue can be found in the *NET Bible* footnotes on this text, and in the *PCNT* and *BECNT* commentaries on Acts.

⁷ David Williams seems to have missed the plurality of μετανοήσατε ("you all repent") when he said in his exegetical discussion that both terms are singular: "The call to repentance and baptism – the individual's response to God's grace – is in the singular." David J. Williams. *Acts, NIBC* (Peabody, MA: Hendrickson, 1990), 54.

⁸ The ESV renders it, "repent and be baptized every one of you."

⁹ If that was not true, "repent" would not have the same number, plural, as "of you" (ὑμῶν).

¹⁰ I. Howard Marshall. *Acts, TNTC* (Downers Grove, IL: InterVarsity, 2008), 81.

Acts 2:39 in its Context (Part 1): An Exegetical Summary of Acts 2:39 and Paedobaptism

you [2nd p. pl.] and for your children and for all who are far off, everyone..." (v. 39). Therefore, both the larger context of Peter's speech and the immediate context of verses 38-39 contain the same idea of expansion and inclusiveness; the filling of the Spirit (and of course, the total salvation it is associated with[11]) is not merely for the Jews or even for their children, but ultimately for all who have faith in Jesus, who is "both Lord and Christ" (v. 36).

But to whom does "each of you" (ἕκαστος ὑμῶν) specifically refer? There is no question that Peter is talking primarily to Jewish men[12] and that this class also makes up the majority of the crowd.[13] But the very inclusion of Peter's words "each one of you" seems to imply that the ones Peter is addressing are not *solely and exhaustively* Jewish men.[14] Obviously, Peter wants to avoid confusion lest anyone in his audience think that only *some* should be baptized instead of "each one of" them. Whether he is referring to Jewish children, Jewish women, foreign servants, or Gentiles of any kind is not entirely clear. But one thing is for certain, whatever group(s) that *were* listening to Peter are included by these words.

Therefore, if any children of any age were present (and since "children" are then mentioned in verse 39, this seems like an acute possibility), those children are unquestionably told to be baptized via "each one of you" (v. 38), given – as it was shown above – that they "repent."

---

[11] See Acts 2:21.

[12] See vv. 14, 22, 29.

[13] See. v. 5. It should be noted that the association with maleness to Peter's audience is particularly strong throughout the whole chapter: "Jerusalem Jews, devout men" (v. 5); "Men of Judea" (v. 14); "Men of Israel" (v. 22); "Brothers" (v. 29). The pattern shifts at v. 36 where there is expansion: "Let *all the house of Israel* therefore know..." (emphasis mine).

[14] Of course, it is possible that there are sub-groups within the Jewish men Peter is speaking to. But the context simply does not give any indication that this is the case. Verses 17-21 and v. 39, however, explicitly identify various groups. This fact will be discussed below.

Acts 2:39

For the promise is for you and for your children and for all who are far off, everyone whom the Lord our God calls to himself. (Acts 2:39, ESV)

The adverbial conjunction γάρ ("for"[15]) connects verse 38 to verse 39. Thus, "the promise" in Acts 2:39 is the specific promise of the pouring forth of the Spirit prophesied by Joel (Acts 2:17-21), which is the same promise of verse 33. As Nehemiah Coxe summarized in 1681, "The promise which he refers to is the one cited earlier of the salvation of all who in the day of the gospel call on the name of the Lord, and the pouring out of his Spirit on all flesh (see verses 17-21)."[16] A variety of today's scholars concur with this interpretation.[17]

If this is true – that Peter is directly reasserting and concluding (not merely "echoing" or "alluding to") the "promise" of the Spirit in Joel that he had just quoted – then it logically follows that "for your children" in verse 39 is as equally a reference to "sons and daughters" in that same context (v. 17).[18] The same is true for the phrase, "everyone whom the Lord our God calls to himself" in verse 39, which clearly refers back to "everyone who calls upon the

---

[15] James Swanson, *Dictionary of Biblical Languages With Semantic Domains: Greek (New Testament)*, electronic ed. (Oak Harbor: Logos Research Systems, Inc., 1997).

[16] Coxe and Owen, *Covenant Theology*, 115.

[17] For example: "The 'promise' is, of course, the promise of the gift of the Spirit (cf. 2:33) made by Joel" in G. K. Beale and D. A. Carson, eds., *Commentary on the New Testament Use of the Old Testament* (Grand Rapids: Baker, 2007), 543; "'The promise' is most obviously the promise of the Spirit about which Jesus spoke during his earthly ministry (cf. Luke 24:49; Acts 1:4)" in James Peterson, *The Acts of the Apostles, PNTC* (Grand Rapids: Eerdmans, 2009), 156; "The promise's scope is what Peter notes next. The promise certainly alludes back to the Spirit (vv. 33, 38) and possibly forgiveness as well (v. 38)" in Darrell Bock, *Acts*, BECNT (Grand Rapids: Baker Academic, 2007), 145.

Whether or not such a promise is enveloped in a larger scheme of the unfolding promises given to Abraham will be taken up in the section below dealing with biblical theology.

[18] See G. R. Beasley-Murray, *Baptism in the New Testament* (Grand Rapids: Eerdmans, 1973), 342.

name of the Lord shall be saved" in verse 21[19] and/or the rest of Joel 2:32 that was not immediately cited ("among the survivors shall be those whom the Lord calls").[20]

In short, the entire thrust and substance of Acts 2:39 is virtually identical to that of Acts 2:17-21. Peter has in mind the specific fulfillment of the promise of the Spirit as told by the prophet Joel and the ultimate salvation of God's called people who call out to him (that is, those who are repentant). Thus, Acts 2:39 is primarily an assertion about a New Covenant (not Old Covenant) reality: "in the last days it shall be, God declares, that I will pour out my Spirit on all flesh" (Acts 2:17).[21]

It should be obvious that the "your sons and your daughters" and "your old men" and "young men" in Joel 2 *are* the "you and your children" in Acts 2:39. Joel 2 predicts a time in the future, and that time has come in Acts 2. Peter wants to make that point clear, which is why he mentions children again in verse 39. It is not as if the promise of the Spirit prophesied in Joel only refers to a certain age or generation of Jewish believers, as if the Spirit would come for a while, and then leave (e.g., the Spirit that came and left Saul and Sampson). Not at all! The Spirit continues to be poured out from that point of Pentecost forward, from generation to generation. And it is not as if the promise of the Spirit is only for leaders since it expands to children and even "male and female servants." As Wellum remarked:

---

[19] "With these words Peter rounds off the quote from Joel 2:32 with which his discourse had begun." Marshall, *Acts*, 82.

[20] "The idea of the Lord calling echoes, to a degree, what was not cited from Joel 2:32b (3.5b LXX), and so the Joel passage is still present in the backdrop." See Bock, *Acts*, 145.

[21] Additionally, combined with the general gospel call of repentance and the consequent forgiveness of sins in vv. 37-38, v. 39 partly functions as representing the more specific fruit of conversion. Just as the same kind of repentance in the book of Acts "leads to life" (Acts 11:18), blots out sins (Acts 3:19), and results in "performing deeds" (Acts 26:20), so too, does repentance lead to receiving "the promise" and "gift of the Spirit."

Acts 2:39 in its Context (Part 1): An Exegetical Summary of Acts 2:39 and Paedobaptism

Under the old covenant, the "tribal" structure of the covenant community meant that the Spirit was uniquely poured out on leaders. But what the prophets anticipate is a crucial change: the coming of the new covenant era would witness a *universal* distribution of the Spirit (see Joel 2:28-32; Acts 2). God would pour out his Spirit on *all* flesh, namely, *all* those within the covenant community. Thus, *all* those "under the new covenant" enjoyed the promised gift of the eschatological Holy Spirit (see Eph. 1:13-14)...In this age, the Spirit is sent to *all* believers and thus becomes the precious seal, down-payment, and guarantee of the promised inheritance to the last day. To be "in Christ" is to have the Spirit for, as Paul reminds us, "if anyone does not have the Spirit of Christ, he does not belong to Christ" (Rom. 8:9).[22]

But *more* than that is that the promise of the Spirit is "for all who are far off." This obviously introduces a more popularly disputed phrase. What does it mean? How does this fit with verses 17-21 like the rest of 2:39?

Scholars are divided. Peterson,[23] Williamson,[24] Keener[25] and others assert that the phrase is referring to the scattered Jewish Diaspora. I. Howard Marshall asserts that it should not be limited to the Jewish race.[26] Calvin,[27] Bavinck,[28] Thielman,[29] Kaiser,[30]

---

[22] Stephen J. Wellum, "Baptism and the Relationship between the Covenants" in *Believer's Baptism*, Shawn Wright and Thomas Schreiner, eds. (Nashville: B&H, 2006), 133.

[23] Peterson, *Acts*, 156.

[24] Williamson, *Acts*, 56.

[25] Craig S. Keener. *The IVP Bible Background Commentary: New Testament* (Downers Grove, IL: InterVarsity, 1993), 330.

[26] I. Howard Marshall, "Acts," in Beale and Carson, eds., *Commentary on the New Testament Use of the Old Testament*, 543.

[27] John Calvin, *Commentary on Acts*, vol. 1. Calvin even goes as far as to say that "For those which refer it unto those Jews which were exiled afar off, (and driven) into far countries, they are greatly deceived."

[28] Herman Bavinck, *Reformed Dogmatics: Holy Spirit, Church, and New Creation* (Grand Rapids: Baker, 2008), 529.

[29] Frank Thielman, *Theology of the New Testament: A Canonical and Synthetic Approach* (Grand Rapids: Zondervan, 2005), 147, 705.

Polhill,[31] Tannehill,[32] the *ESV Study Bible*, etc. assert that the phrase refers to Gentiles. Joel Beeke says it means "afar off from the covenant community and its divine covenant promises."[33] F. F. Bruce, similar to Darrell Bock's position,[34] believes that it refers to those in "distant lands (and, as appears later in Luke's narrative, not only to Jews but to Gentiles also)."[35] Marshall agrees, when he says, "[It is] a phrase which certainly includes Jews scattered throughout the world and (in Luke's eyes, whether or not Peter had yet reached this insight) the Gentiles also."[36] Finally, Ben Witherington has the somewhat unusual interpretation that "it is more likely that in context Peter is referring to future generations, not far-off Gentile peoples or Diaspora Jews who were in fact present and represented in number on that day in Jerusalem."[37]

The word "far off" or "far away" (μακράν) is used two other times in Acts. The first is in Acts 17:27, which is in the middle of Paul's speech on Mars hill: "Yet he is actually not far from each one of us." The second is in Acts 22:21, where Paul is quoting Jesus: "And he said to me, 'Go, for I will send you far away to the Gentiles.'" Outside Acts, the term is found only seven times, used in similar ways that refer to both a geographical farness (e.g., Luke 7:6, John 21:8), and a spiritual farness (e.g., Mark 12:34, "not far

---

[30] Walter C. Kaiser Jr., "My Heart is Stirred by a Noble Theme" in *Introduction to Biblical Hermeneutics: The Search for Meaning* (Grand Rapids: Zondervan, 2007), 149.

[31] John Polhill, *Acts*, NAC 26 (Nashville: Broadman, 1992), 117.

[32] R. C. Tannehill, *The Narrative Unity of Luke-Acts A Literary Interpretation* (Minneapolis: Fortress, 1990) 2-27, 134.

[33] Beeke and Lanning, "Unto You, and to Your Children," 49-69.

[34] "The language "far off"...echoes Isa. 57:19 and, in Peter's mind, possibly alludes to responding Diaspora Jews and God-fearers, since, until the vision in Acts 10, he does not think of Gentiles who are unconnected to Israel's God...In the development of Luke, however, the expression looks to anyone who responds, which would eventually include Gentiles." See Bock, *Acts*, 145.

[35] F. F. Bruce, *The Book of Acts*, NICNT . Revised ed. (Grand Rapids: Eerdmans, 1988), 71.

[36] Marshall, *Acts*, 82.

[37] Ben Witherington, *Troubled Waters: The Real New Testament Theology of Baptism* (Waco: Baylor University Press, 2007), 56-57.

Acts 2:39 in its Context (Part 1): An Exegetical Summary of Acts 2:39 and Paedobaptism

from the kingdom of God"). It is used specifically in referring to the Gentiles four times (Eph. 2:13, 17; Acts 22:21; Luke 15:20).

Word studies alone are not enough to understand the meaning of the phrase.[38] Context is the better guide. And given the tight relationship between Acts 2:39 and the text of Joel 2 cited in Acts 2:17-21 examined above and how 2:39 is generally a summation or conclusion, it seems fair to assume that Peter is not introducing any new content to his argument. That is, one would expect that this phrase ("and for those who are far off") would refer back to something after "sons and daughters" (v. 17, corresponding to "children" in v. 39) and before "everyone" (v. 21, corresponding to "everyone" in v. 39) since "for all who are far off" rests between each of those assertions in verse 39 respectively. Indeed, "if Peter cites the whole text [in this case, Joel 2:28-32], then we should reckon with the whole; and since Peter finds use for the first and last parts of the text, then we should expect he finds use for the middle."[39]

Of course, this does not *need* to be true. For example, "for all who are far off" could simply be a restatement of "everyone who calls upon the name of the Lord" in verse 21. But that seems somewhat out of place and redundant since Peter immediately says "everyone whom the Lord God calls" in the next phrase of Acts 2:39. "For those who are far off" seems to be asserting something more specific than "everyone." Another possibility is that Peter *could* have introduced an entire new idea or category that has no connection with his previous argument from Joel or from anywhere else in his speech. But, given how the gift of the Spirit in verse 38 is the same gift of the Spirit in Acts 2:15-21, which is the same "promise" in 2:39, and the groups in 2:39 ("you," "your children,"

---

[38] Although, it is legitimate to say – given the statistical information provided above – that the term (μακράν) is used twice as often in referring to Gentiles than in referring to spatial/geographical locations in the New Testament.

[39] C. Godwin Sathianathan, "Redemptive Expansion Through the Testaments: Joel 2:28-32 as Sinaitic Program" (Grand Rapids: Grand Rapids Theological Seminary, 2009), 17.

Acts 2:39 in its Context (Part 1): An Exegetical Summary of Acts 2:39 and Paedobaptism

"everyone")[40] are specifically mentioned – and in the *same order* – in 2:15-21, this seems a highly improbable conclusion.

Therefore, the phrase "for those who are far off" would logically refer to some category or group given in the citation of Joel 2 since everything else in Acts 2:39 comes from that text as well. As it turns out, the only group between verse 17 and 21 is verse 18 (Joel 2:29): "even on my male and female servants."[41] One must then ask, what do slaves and servants have in common with "all who are far off"? There could be many things. But if this parallel between Acts 2:18 and 2:39 is legitimate it would probably suggest that Peter has in mind those who are not in the same social class as the Jews (adult and children) to which both Peter and Joel were speaking. This does not answer whether or not what category (e.g., Diaspora Jews, Gentiles, etc.) fits best with "for all who are far off." Nevertheless, it demonstrates that interpreting the phrase ("for all who...") within the text of Joel (v. 17-21) – like one would interpret the rest of 2:39 – is helpful (if not essential) in understanding what Peter is trying to communicate when he says "for all who are far off."

The last part of verse 39 has been cited several times already. But its significance should not be overlooked. Indeed, it is not merely the concluding remark to Acts 2:39, but the key to understanding its meaning: "everyone whom the Lord our God calls to himself." The sovereign choice of God is the final and ultimate determiner of the person who receives the promise of the Spirit. No category matters, whether age, social status, geographical location, etc. Only God's elect people will receive the promise *which is* the Spirit.[42] So, one might paraphrase the text this way: "For the

---

[40] The "you" in Acts 2:39 are obviously the same "sons and daughters" in Joel 2. They are the Jewish descendants of the original hearers of Joel's prophecy.

[41] It should be noted that Peter (as told by Luke) does not follow the LXX reading (Joel 3:2).

[42] Notice the genitive of apposition in Acts 2:33 (ἐπαγγελίαν τοῦ πνεύματος) and Acts 2:38 (δωρεὰν τοῦ ἁγίου πνεύματος). It is not the usual "ownership" idea as if to say "the Spirit's promise" or "the Spirit's gift." Rather, as the *NET Bible* textual footnotes remark, "the promise consists of the Holy Spirit" in Acts 2:33, and the gift consists of the Spirit in 2:38. This is important to remember since, as the next part of this discussion will show, an argument in Beeke and Lanning's essay on

promise is, ultimately, for everyone whom the Lord our God calls to himself."

It should also be noted that while Acts 2:39 says, "For the promise is for...everyone whom the Lord God calls to Himself," its referent, Acts 2:21 (Joel 2:32a[43]), says "everyone *who calls upon the name of the Lord* shall be saved" (emphases mine). There are two possible options at this point. First, two different aspects of the same divine event are being described. The calling of Acts 2:39 is the efficacious, elective, sovereign calling of God while Acts 2:21 contains the calling of man out to God (repentance and faith).[44] One is what God does; the other is what man does. The second option is that Peter may be referring to the rest of Joel 2:32 that was not cited: "among the survivors shall be those whom the Lord calls." If that is the case, then the phrase in Acts 2:39 is obviously referring to the same idea (and not a different aspect) of Joel 2:32 – God is doing the calling. Whatever one may conclude, Acts 2:39 is still directly referring to Joel 2, and the "everyone" is still all of God's chosen people.

Let us then summarize verse 39 in relation to verses 17-21. The text says, "For the promise is for you and for your children and for all who are far off, everyone whom the Lord our God calls to himself." The "promise" refers to the specific promise of the Spirit (v. 38, v. 33) prophesied in Joel (vv. 17-21), which is nothing less than the Spirit himself.[45] "For you and for your children" harkens back to the "sons and daughters" in verse 17. "And for all who are far off" (possibly) refers to "even on your male and female servants" in verse 18. "Everyone" refers to either the "everyone" in

---

Acts 2:39 in *The Case for Covenantal Infant Baptism* completely ignores this fact, and renders it invalid.

[43] Paedobaptists usually acknowledge this connection. For example, Fesko says, "Peter concludes by saying, 'as many as the Lord our God will call,' which comes from Joel 2:32 and stresses God's gracious initiative in the proclamation of salvation and its universal scope." See Fesko, *Word, Water, and Spirit*, 358.

[44] See Alan Conner, *Covenant Children Today: Physical or Spiritual?* (Owensboro, KY: RBAP, 2007), 76.

[45] See note above regarding "of the Spirit" being a genitive of apposition.

verse 21 (Joel 2:32), or the rest of Joel 2:32 that was not cited ("those whom the Lord calls").

	Peter's Argument from Joel 2 (Acts 2:14-21)	Peter's Summary and Application 1A (Acts 2:38)	Peter's Summary and Application 1B (Acts 2:39)
Jews and Their Children	"your sons and your daughters" (v. 17; Joel 2:28)	"You all repent and each one of you be baptized and you will receive the gift of the Holy Spirit."	"For the promise is for you and for your children…"
Those Not in Same Class as Immediate Jewish Audience (Gentiles? Diaspora?)	"Even on my male servants and female servants" (v. 18; Joel 2:29)	"…and *each one of you* be baptized and you will receive the gift of the Holy Spirit."	"and for all who are far off…"
Everyone ("All Flesh)	"Everyone who calls up on the name of the Lord shall be saved" (v. 21; Joel 2:32a) ["among the survivors shall be those whom the Lord calls."] (Joel 2:32b)		"…everyone whom the Lord our God calls to himself."

Acts 2:39 in its Context (Part 1): An Exegetical Summary of Acts 2:39 and Paedobaptism

Acts 2:40-41: The Promise Fulfilled

The question now is, *what happens*? How is this Old Testament promise of Joel fulfilled in the "last days"[46] of the New Testament times? Peter has given his argument (vv. 12-36). The Jews have listened (v. 37). Peter has told the Jews what to do in response ("repent and be baptized," v. 38) – all on the grounds of "for the promise is for you and for your children and for all who are far off, everyone whom the Lord God calls to himself" (v. 39). How is the response of the audience going to *correspond* to the prophecy of Joel and to Peter's assertions in Acts 2:39?

We should be able to answer this question by Acts 2:14-39 alone. If "the promise is for" the Jews, their "children and for all who are far off," and in fact for "*everyone*," it would seem as if *absolutely everyone* would receive the gift of the Spirit. But it is then that we remember that verse 39 begins with the adverbial conjunction "for" (γάρ), and thus connects with verse 38. Verse 38, as it was demonstrated, asserts that the Holy Spirit is received when a person repents. There is no reason to suggest that the Holy Spirit will be received by/poured out upon a person if that person is unrepentant. If *that* is true, then the pouring out of the Spirit prophesied in Joel and essentially restated in Acts 2 is limited to those who repent and receive the gospel – or, as the next phrase says, to "everyone whom the Lord God will call." Its probable referent verse (v. 21, "everyone who calls on the name of the Lord") obviously re-affirms that the people being referred to are repentant.

Therefore, if what has been said above is true, the only people that should be baptized in Acts 2, *according* to Acts 2, are the repentant people of God – that is, people who hear the gospel and accept it. There is no other option. And that, of course, is precisely what occurs:

> And with many other words he bore witness and continued to exhort them, saying, "Save yourselves from this crooked generation." *So those who received his word were baptized*, and

---

[46] These words (ἐν ταῖς ἐσχάταις ἡμέραις) are Peter's insertion into Joel.

there were added that day about three thousand souls. (Acts 2:40-41, emphasis mine)

Conclusions Pertaining to the Recipients of Baptism

Verse 41 is highly significant for the question as to who should be baptized. Peter has brought up several categories and groups of people in Acts 2:17-21 and 2:39, including "children." But the final precondition that was met before any in Peter's audience were baptized is the receiving of the word, not social status, Old Covenant status, or the faith of any parent. "Those who received his word and their children were baptized" is not in the text, nor would it fit any concept asserted in Acts 2.[47] Baptism in Acts 2, in Acts in general, and in *all* the New Testament is consistently associated with repentance and faith.[48] Furthermore, as Conner argues, when Peter specifically says "for you and your children" he "does not have specifically Christian parents in mind, but all Jews in general…This rules out any notion of making this promise apply just to Christian parents."[49] He goes on:

> …the promise was made in general to all Israel, but it will only be fulfilled in those whom the Lord chooses to call to

---

[47] Fesko asserts the opposite in his discussion of Acts 2:39: "The inclusion of infants had been a practice of the covenant community for nearly 2,000 years…For there to have been a change in this covenantal practice without so much as a syllable of explanation would not have gone over well with first century Jews." See Fesko, *Word, Water, and Spirit*, 358. Fesko is correct that it would not have gone over well–if the Jews were assuming that baptism was no different in purpose and participants than Old Covenant circumcision. But is there really adequate indication that they thought of one replacing the other? Furthermore, Fesko is assuming the non-newness of the New Covenant. Does not Jeremiah 31 and Hebrews 8, *at the very least*, assert a change in the "covenant community"? If not, what are we to make of the argument *for* the newness of the New Covenant by the author of Hebrews? If so, would it not be expected to see a change in the *sign* of a covenant if the substance of the convent itself changed?

[48] See chapters 1-3 in *Believer's Baptism*, Wright and Schreiner, eds.

[49] Conner, *Covenant Children Today*, 75.

himself. These alone will repent, be forgiven, and receive the gift of the Holy Spirit.[50]

Indeed, the point of Acts 2:39 is not to re-establish any Old Testament principle, as if to assert that the recipients of the sign of the promise are somehow determined by *someone else's* repentance. Rather, in the fulfillment of Joel 2 ("all flesh"), it is to demonstrate that the promise is ultimately for the church – those who call upon the name of the Lord and those who are called by the Lord. In the church, in the New Covenant, the "last days" of Joel 2 and "those days" of Jeremiah 31, the covenant members are "all flesh" – or, more specifically, "everyone whom the Lord our God calls to himself." God's *repentant and chosen people* are baptized and receive the promise of the Spirit; "all who call upon the name of the Lord shall be saved" (2:21). Gone are the days of a mixed covenant where the sign was given to unrepentant individuals (e.g., infants) who may or may not actually be called by God to take part in God's plan of salvation. The New Covenant has come, and due to its genuine newness, the sign and criteria for receiving the sign of the covenant change.[51] The reason why baptism (and not circumcision[52]) is a sign of new life (Col. 2:12), forgiveness and cleansing from sin (Acts 22:16, 1 Pet. 3:21), and being identified with Christ (Rom. 6:3-4; Col. 2:10-14) is precisely because those who are to be baptized have been regenerated (Heb. 8:11), forgiven (Heb. 8:12), and united to Christ. That is, those who are in the New Covenant (believers) are to

---

[50] Conner, *Covenant Children Today*, 76.

[51] See John Owen's exposition of Hebrews 8 in Coxe and Owen, *Covenant Theology*, as well as both segments in James White's series, "The Newness of the New Covenant" in the *Reformed Baptist Theological Review* (July 2004 and January 2005). White's series is particularly helpful as it deals with the best of contemporary paedobaptist material, such as Richard Pratt, Jeff Neil, and Gregg Strawbridge's exegetical works on Jeremiah 31 and Hebrews 8. These two articles comprise chapters 11 and 12 of the present work.

[52] J. V. Fesko disagrees and argues that circumcision signifies the same realities and has the same purpose as New Covenant baptism. See Fesko, *Word, Water, and Spirit*, 342-44, and compare with the opposite view of Wellum, "Relationship Between the Covenants," 157-58.

Acts 2:39 in its Context (Part 1): An Exegetical Summary of Acts 2:39 and Paedobaptism

receive the sign of the New Covenant (baptism).[53] Such was never the case in the Old Covenant – whether with Abraham's descendants/servants (Gen. 17:23) or in the Mosaic economy – since the sign was given *regardless* of spiritual status.

Thus, Samuel Waldron summarizes:

> In the Old Covenant, covenant status was conferred irrespective of spiritual qualifications. Thus the covenant blessing could and would be lost (Acts 3:25, cf. v. 23; Deut. 5:2-3, 27-29; Jer. 31:31-32). In the New Covenant, the conferring and consequent possession of covenant status assures the bestowal of the required response (Jer. 31:33-34; 32:40; 2 Cor. 3:1-9). Paul is not saying in 2 Corinthians 3:1-9 that the Old Covenant is a covenant of works. He is saying that it did not effectively confer life and righteousness on its beneficiaries. Many who possessed the Old Covenant status did not attain the required response and fell short of the promised blessing. The New Covenant confers the required response on all those brought into it. "They all shall know me" is its tenor. Old Covenant status did not assure life. New Covenant status does (2 Cor. 3:3). Unless we are willing to say that life and righteousness are the assured and inalienable possession of all the children of believers, we cannot say that the New Covenant is made with believers *and their physical seed*.[54]

In reading that last sentence by Waldron, one recalls Galatians 4.

> But the son of the slave was born according to the flesh, while the son of the free woman was born through promise. Now this may be interpreted allegorically: these women are two covenants. One is from Mount Sinai, bearing children

---

[53] This is not to mention receiving the Lord's Table, the second ordinance of New Covenant members.

[54] Samuel E. Waldron, *A Modern Exposition of the 1689 Baptist Confession of Faith* (New York: Evangelical Press, 2005), 120.

> for slavery; she is Hagar. Now Hagar is Mount Sinai in Arabia; she corresponds to the present Jerusalem, for she is in slavery with her children. But the Jerusalem above is free, and she is our mother. For it is written, "Rejoice, O barren one who does not bear; break forth and cry aloud, you who are not in labor! For the children of the desolate one will be more than those of the one who has a husband." Now you, brothers, like Isaac, are children of promise. But just as at that time he who was born according to the flesh persecuted him who was born according to the Spirit, so also it is now. But what does the Scripture say? "Cast out the slave woman and her son, for the son of the slave woman shall not inherit with the son of the free woman." So, brothers, we are not children of the slave but of the free woman. (Gal. 4:23-31)

First Peter 1:23 should also be recalled, "You have been born again, not of perishable seed but of imperishable, through the living and abiding word of God (1 Pet. 1:23)."

Believer's today – members of the New Covenant – are "children of promise" who are not "born according to the flesh" (Gal. 4:23, 29) or of "perishable seed" (1 Pet. 1:23) but of "imperishable seed" (v. 23), "born through promise" (Gal. 4:23), and "born according to the Spirit" (v. 29). It is a total contradiction to say that those born according to the flesh (i.e., physical children of believers) are always the same children "born through promise" (v. 23) and "born according to the Spirit" (v. 29) and therefore should be baptized, just as it is wrong to say that those born of "perishable seed" are children born of "imperishable seed." Yet, that is essentially what the paedobaptist is obligated to teach: children of the flesh *are* children of the promise in the New Covenant; believers' children are essentially "like Isaac" (Gal. 4:28). But Scripture teaches the opposite: "*if you* [not just your parents] *are Christ's*, then you are Abraham's offspring, heirs according to promise" (Gal. 3:29, emphasis mine).

Jewett makes a keen observation regarding Acts 2:39 in this discussion of covenant theology:

Whether we think of Peter's listeners or of their children or of those far removed from the immediate scene of this first Christian *kerygma,* the point is that the promise is to all whom God shall call. This fact puts the whole matter on a rather different theological axis from that which is traditionally assumed in the interest of infant baptism. It becomes no more a question of one's natural birth, as Paedobaptists have often implied; there is nothing in this Scripture passage of "visible church membership" and "external covenant privilege." Rather, the passage is concerned with the call of God, that inner work of the Spirit...The Paedobaptist ear is so attuned to the Old Testament echo in this text that it is deaf to its New Testament crescendo. It fails to perceive that the promise is no longer circumscribed *by birth* but by the call of God.[55]

If there were *any* children in Peter's audience, they were not baptized unless they "received his word" – that is, embraced the gospel preached by Peter. And this obviously does not apply to children only, but to everyone in each of the categories that Peter has addressed.[56] The same ones who were baptized in verse 41 are the same "everyone whom the Lord our God calls to himself" in verse 39.[57] Therefore, unless we are to believe Peter was commanding infants to repent in verse 38, it is clear that he does not have infants in mind when he says "children" in verse 39. The

---

[55] Paul Jewett, *Infant Baptism and the Covenant of Grace: An Appraisal of the Argument that as Infants were Once Circumcised, So They Should Now Be Baptized* (Grand Rapids: Eerdmans, 1978), 120-22.

[56] "The indication is that they are such as can repent and be baptized for the remission of sins and the reception of the Holy Ghost, according to v. 38." Beasley-Murray, *Baptism in the New Testament,* 342.

[57] "The promise in Acts 2:39 need not mean that children are to be baptized; the promise may mean no more than that the gospel is a blessing not only for the present generation but to their descendants as well – not only to people in Jerusalem but also to those of distant lands – and is analogous to "your sons and daughters" in 2:17. The "children" are limited by the following phrase, "every one whom the Lord our God calls to him."See George Eldon Ladd, *A Theology of the New Testament* (Grand Rapids: Eerdmans, 1993), 387.

Acts 2:39 in its Context (Part 1): An Exegetical Summary of Acts 2:39 and Paedobaptism

"children," as it has been demonstrated, fall under the "every one of you" in verse 38, the same "each of you" (ἕκαστος ὑμῶν) that refers to "repent" and "be baptized." Moreover, as it was also demonstrated, the "children" (v. 39) most likely refer to "sons and daughters" in verse 17:

> The prophecy in verse 17 thinks of children who are old enough to prophesy, and that verse 38 speaks of receiving forgiveness and the Spirit; in neither case are infants obviously involved. The point of the phrase is rather to express the unlimited mercy of God which embraces the hearers and subsequent generations of their descendents and in addition *all that are far off*.[58]

Additionally, Peter does not use the specific word for "infants" (βρέφος) used eight times in the New Testament, the vast majority of which are usually translated as "infants" and "babies" as he does elsewhere (e.g., 1 Pet. 2:2). Nor does Peter use the word νήπιος which usually means "infant" and sometimes "child." Peter says "children" (τέκνοι), which is used 99 times in the New Testament and is virtually never translated as "infants." In fact, the term is used by Peter elsewhere (cf. 1 Pet. 1:14) to mean "class of persons."[59] This fits precisely with the usage and context of Acts 2:39.

Therefore, it seems wholly unjustified for any interpreter to use Acts 2:39 to make any specific application for *infants*. But this is exactly what occurs in defenses of infant baptism. For example, John Murray said, "The seals of the covenant pertain to those to whom the covenant itself pertains. But that the covenant pertains to infants is clear from Genesis 17:7 and Acts 2:39."[60] On the contrary, it is clear that Peter is *not* speaking of infants in this text. Even if he

---

[58] Marshall, *Acts*, 81-82.

[59] See James Swanson, *Dictionary of Biblical Languages With Semantic Domains : Greek (New Testament)*, electronic ed. (Oak Harbor: Logos Research Systems, Inc., 1997).

[60] John Murray, "Covenant Theology" in *Collected Writings of John Murray* (Edinburgh/Carlisle, PA: Banner of Truth, 1982), 4:239-40.

was, the requirement for both the entrance into the New Covenant and the sign of being in the New Covenant is the same: *personal* repentance (and faith[61]), not *parental* repentance and faith.

Even the Canons of Dort misuse Acts 2:39 in this way:

> ...the children of believers are holy, not by nature, but in virtue of the covenant of grace, in which they together with the parents are comprehended, godly parents ought not to doubt the election and salvation of their children whom it pleases God to call out of this life in their infancy (Gen. 17:7; Acts 2:39; I Cor. 7:14).[62]

Acts 2:39 in no way supports such an assertion. There is no reason to suspect that Peter was speaking of those "in their infancy," let alone somehow giving "godly parents" assurance that all of their children are God's elect people. Acts 2:37-41 asserts something much different: the fulfillment of the actual promise (and thus, the giving of the sign) comes through repentance.

This fits with Waldron's statement about the New Covenant in general. "The New Covenant confers the required response on all those brought into it." That "response," of course, is the gift of faith and repentance – everyone in the covenant "shall know [God], from the least of them to the greatest" (Heb. 8:11). And that, again, is why verse 41 says "those who received his word were baptized" and not "those who received his word and their children were baptized."

But it is also why Peter comes to this same conclusion in his next speech in Acts 3. He asserts that *repentance* is the fulfillment of the Messiah promised in the Abrahamic Covenant.

---

[61] This particular aspect of conversion has not been fully addressed in this essay because it is beyond its scope. For an argument that the New Testament teaches that baptism comes after repentance and faith, see chapters 1-3 in Schreiner and Wright's *Believer's Baptism*.

[62] Article 17 of "The First Head of Doctrine," cited in Louis Berkhof, *Systematic Theology* (Grand Rapids: Eerdmans, 1996), 638.

Approaching Biblical Theology: Acts 2:39 and Acts 3:25

> You are the sons of the prophets and of the covenant that God made with your fathers, saying to Abraham, 'And in your seed shall all the families of the earth be blessed.' God, having raised up his servant, sent him to you first, to bless you by turning every one of you from your wickedness. (Acts 3:25-26, author's translation)

God sent Christ to save. How? "To bless you by turning every one of you from your wickedness." God sent Christ so that his people *will repent* and thereby "be blessed" (v. 25).[63] The Jews may have had a number of things going through their minds when hearing about Christ and the fulfillment of the Abrahamic promises; a political leader, physical land promises, physical expansion of a people, etc. They may have even believed that being Jewish was enough to secure their salvation. But Peter quotes from Genesis 12:22 (It is conflated. See the quote of Peterson below.), not to make any of those assertions. He argues that the Abrahamic Covenant and its ultimate fulfillment in Christ points to something more personal – turning away from wickedness. That is why God "raised up his servant" and "sent him to" the Jews first.

> [Peter] also claims that they are heirs of '*The covenant God made with your fathers*', meaning that they are in line to experience the ultimate blessing of the covenant made with Abraham, Isaac, and Jacob (cf. v. 13 note). This last point is so foundational to Peter's understanding of Scripture and its revelation of God's purposes that he develops and expands it as the climax of his appeal. In so doing, he conflates the promise of Genesis 12:3 LXX ('and all peoples on earth will

---

[63] The dual-aspect of Peter's theology in both of his speeches should be noted. Just as in Peter's speech in Acts 2, there is the divine perspective and the human perspective to the act of faith and repentance. In Acts 2, there is first the calling of man to God (Acts 2:21) and then the sovereign calling of man by God (Acts 2:39). Likewise, in Acts 3, there is first the human turning away from sin (Acts 3:19) and then God himself turning his people away from their wickedness (v. 26).

Acts 2:39 in its Context (Part 1): An Exegetical Summary of Acts 2:39 and Paedobaptism

be blessed through you') with the promise of Genesis 22:18 LXX ('and through your offspring all nations on earth will be blessed'). It is clear, however, 'that they do not have a right to the covenant itself irrespective of their reaction to Jesus.' [Barrett 1994, 212][64]

This stress on repentance is nothing new, even in the context of Acts 3. Peter already asserted the centrality of repentance in the context of Old Testament promises in 3:17-19:

> And now, brothers, I know that you acted in ignorance, as did also your rulers. But what God foretold by the mouth of all the prophets, that his Christ would suffer, he thus fulfilled. Repent therefore, and turn again, that your sins may be blotted out, that times of refreshing may come from the presence of the Lord, and that he may send the Christ appointed for you, Jesus, (Acts 3:17-20)

As it was observed earlier, the continual insistence to repent and turn from sin and embrace Christ against the backdrop of the promises given in the Old Testament, whether from Joel and the Psalms (Acts 2) or Genesis (Acts 3), points to the present reality of the New Covenant where those promises are fulfilled: when "no longer shall each one teach his neighbor and each his brother, saying, 'Know the LORD,' for they shall all know me, from the least of them to the greatest" and when "I will pour out my Spirit on all flesh…everyone who calls on the name of the Lord shall be saved" (Acts 2:17, 21). Unlike the Old Covenant, the New Covenant confers the requirements of the covenant to those who are in the covenant – which includes repentance. Since Christ and the pouring out of his Spirit, there is no longer a mixed "covenant community," there is the church – repentant believers in Christ.

Indeed, as Peterson and Barrett pointed out above, no one has a right to the New Covenant and its promise of the Spirit if the fulfillment of that covenant (the Seed) is rejected. Entering into the

---

[64] Peterson, *The Acts of the Apostles*, 184.

Acts 2:39 in its Context (Part 1): An Exegetical Summary of Acts 2:39 and Paedobaptism

covenant requires more than being the carnal seed of Abraham (and obviously more than believing parents). One must personally turn away from sin in order to be united to Christ, who is the fulfillment of the covenant given to Abraham. That is why the next verse (Acts 3:26) confirms the primacy of repentance even in the context of being "sons of the prophets and of the covenant that God made with your fathers." It says, "God, having raised up his servant, sent him to you first, to bless you by turning every one of you from your wickedness" (Acts 3:26).

It is evident, then, Acts 2:39 and 3:25 have much more in common than the fact that they both mention "children"/"offspring."[65] At the very least, they teach (1) salvific expansion to the Gentiles[66] and (2) the need for repentance and turning towards Christ, both of which are part and parcel of the

---

[65] Briefly stated, the similarities (in no particular order) of context between Peter's speech in Acts 2 and his speech in Acts 3 include (1) the same speaker – Peter, (2) a Jewish audience, (3) an intention to see Jews become Christians. The similarities of the speeches include (1) a summary of the events of Christ – trial, crucifixion, resurrection and affirmation of Christ's deity and (2) a call to repentance. The differences in context include (1) immediate context of the speech – post-Pentecost vs. post-healing of a lame man at the Beautiful Gate and therefore, (2) the expectation and concerns of the audience. The differences in the speeches include (1) Acts 3 contains no reference to the Holy Spirit, or "promise" and (2) all of the citations from Acts 3 come from the Pentateuch, while none of the citations from Acts 2 come from the Pentateuch.

In short, the speech of Acts 2 comes after Pentecost and is a response to the Jewish concern regarding that event. Acts 3 comes after the healing of a lame man and is a response to the Jewish concern regarding that event. Thus, Acts 2 begins pneumatological and ends Christological and soteriological (pointing towards repentance in 2:38), while Acts 3 begins Christological and ends Christological and soteriological (also, pointing towards repentance in 3:26).

[66] "God...sent [Christ] to you *first*," (Acts 3:26, emphasis mine). Obviously, this implies a sending of Christ to non-Jews second (hence, Paul says things such as, "I am not ashamed of the gospel, for it is the power of God for salvation to everyone who believes, to the Jew *first* and also to the Greek" (Rom. 1:16, emphasis mine). Marshall says, "In view of the next verse ('to you first'), it is likely that the word 'families' is meant to refer to both Jews and Gentiles, although the reference to the Gentiles is at this stage a quiet hint" (Marshall, *Acts*, 96). In other words, the idea of expansion (from Jews to Gentiles) is (possibly) asserted in Acts 3 just as it is in Acts 2 (if "for all who are far off" is referring to Gentiles).

Acts 2:39 in its Context (Part 1): An Exegetical Summary of Acts 2:39 and Paedobaptism

conferred blessings of the New Covenant (the fulfillment of Old Testament promises).

The Promise of the Spirit, the Abrahamic Covenant, and Galatians 3:14

Having addressed the contextual similarities and differences, what then, is the *theological* relationship between the promise of the Spirit and the Abrahamic Covenant? Does not Galatians 3:14 assert that the promise of the Spirit *is* the Abrahamic Covenant?

> Christ redeemed us from the curse of the law by becoming a curse for us--for it is written, "Cursed is everyone who is hanged on a tree"-- so that in Christ Jesus the blessing of Abraham might come to the Gentiles, so that we might receive the promised Spirit through faith. (Gal. 3:13-14, ESV)

The first thing to note is the instrumental means by which the Spirit is received: faith (διά τῆς πίστεως). Whose faith? It refers to the "us" and "we" in the context – Christians (that is, those who exercise saving faith). There simply is no idea in the context that the faith *of a parent* somehow ensures the fulfillment of the promise of the Spirit for an unrepentant individual (i.e., infant).

In any case, the text maintains both a clear distinction between the "blessing of Abraham" and "the promised Spirit" as well as a tight connection between them. Many argue (e.g., Fung,[67] Bruce,[68] Schreiner[69]) that 2:13-14 is structured by the main clause (v. 13) supported by the coordinate purpose (ἵνα) clauses (vv. 14a, 14b). This conclusion is mostly drawn from the assumption that Paul may be alluding to Isaiah 44:3 ("For I will pour water on the thirsty land, and streams on the dry ground; I will pour my Spirit upon

---

[67] Ronald Fung, *Epistle to the Galatians*, NICNT (Grand Rapids: Eerdmans, 1988).

[68] F. F. Bruce, *Epistle to the Galatians*, NIGTC (Grand Rapids: Eerdmans, 1982), 167.

[69] Thomas Schreiner, *Galatians*, ZECNT (Grand Rapids: Zondervan, 2010), 219.

your offspring, and my blessing on your descendants"), where the "Spirit" *is* the "blessing." Thus, it is further suggested that Paul is asserting the exact same concept in his letter to the Galatians; the "Spirit" is the "blessing of Abraham." Verse 14a is talking about the same reality as 14b so that there is no substantive difference between the two.

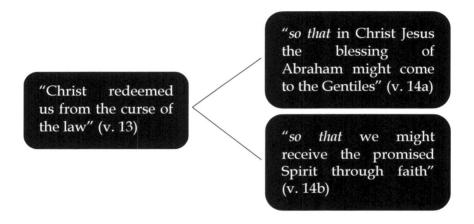

This interpretation is possible, but not entirely consistent. First of all, *possible allusions* to the Old Testament are not in and of themselves sufficient to (a) interpret a New Testament text, nor (b) enough to downplay the importance of the immediate context (see "third of all" below). Regarding (a), not only do New Testament authors use Old Testament allusions and concepts to suite their purposes as authors of inspired Scripture, but it is even possible for Paul to quote the Old Testament and apply it in a somewhat different sense than was originally intended by the original author of the Old Testament quotation (e.g., Rom. 9 and applying the concept of national election of Edom and Israel from Mal. 1:2-3 to individuals such as Pharaoh, etc.[70]).

---

[70] See Beale and Carson's work in *Commentary on the New Testament Use of the Old Testament* for dozens of examples of this phenomenon.

Second of all, two coordinate purpose clauses supporting a main clause as it does here does not automatically erase the theological distinction between the two. If a person said, "The firefighter saved us from the building *so that* we might live and *so that* we might see our family again," the first purpose clause and the second one are related but do not contain the same concepts; being alive is not the same concept as seeing a family. In the same way, the possibility that Galatians 3:14a is a first purpose clause and 14b is a second, and both are coordinate clauses, does not mean they are communicating one and the same concept.[71] Further exegesis and context must determine what is being said for each.

Third of all (see (b) above), the immediate context may actually stand against the two clauses being coordinate.[72] It is obvious that Galatians 3:13-14 should be interpreted in the context of what has been said immediately before it. And two things are clear from these earlier portions: (1) Christ "supplies the Spirit to you" (v. 5) and (2) the "blessing of Abraham" is "that God would justify the Gentiles by faith" (v. 8). Some scholars conclude from this that "in Paul's thinking the blessing of justification is almost synonymous (it is certainly contemporaneous) with the reception of the Spirit."[73] But it is more probable that Paul is describing two different concepts and connecting *those* clauses together. That is, the second purpose clause is attached to the first, perhaps "expressing the moral dependence on the one on the other,"[74] or simply identifying the connection between the promised Spirit and "the blessing of Abraham" without collapsing the distinction between the two. After all, none of the Abrahamic promises in Genesis mention (at least, explicitly) the promise of the Spirit. Paul's audience knows

---

[71] Fung asserts something similar, although not exactly the same. He says that the first clause "makes a statement from the perspective of salvation history" while the "second clause expresses the same truth in terms of individual spiritual experience." See Fung, *Galatians*, 151.

[72] See Hans Deiter Betz, *Galatians: A Commentary on Paul's Letter to the Churches of Galatia* (Augsburg: Fortress Publishers, 1979), 152.

[73] Fung, *Galatians*, 152.

[74] J. B. Lightfoot, *Saint Paul's Epistle to the Galatians* (London: MacMillan, 1865), 133-34.

Acts 2:39 in its Context (Part 1): An Exegetical Summary of Acts 2:39 and Paedobaptism

that. It probably would have confused the Galatians if Paul was asserting in such a short space that the promise of the Spirit simply *is* the Abrahamic Covenant and that we are not to understand them as being two distinct concepts.

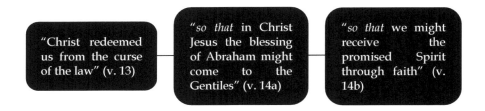

Therefore, whether the clauses are coordinate or not, the "promised Spirit" cannot be simply equated with "the blessing of Abraham," at least in Galatians 3. They are two related but different realities, not merely different words to describe the same reality.[75] The promised Spirit is one of the many blessings that comes from and with Christ (v. 5) and his work (vv. 6-14), both of which (Christ and his work) are the fulfillment of the Abrahamic Covenant.[76] Thus, the Abrahamic Covenant *contains in the sense described by Paul* – because of the nature of Christ's work and the inseparability of the Spirit during/after the work of justification – the promise of the Spirit. When the Gentiles have faith and are justified, they receive the Spirit.

In *that* sense, can we say that the promise of the Spirit is part and parcel of the blessings in the Abrahamic Covenant? To go beyond this by rashly equating the two and making no distinctions between them risks committing the horrible practice of eisegesis –

---

[75] See the thorough study of Chee-Chiew Lee, "The Blessing of Abraham and the Promise of the Spirit: The Influence of the Prophets on Paul in Galatians 3:1-14," Ph.D. diss. (Wheaton, IL: Wheaton College Graduate School, 2010).

[76] Sanders says something similar: "Verse 14 summarizes the preceding argument in chiastic fashion, the first *hina* clause…reiterating the positive point of 3:8 (the blessing of Abraham for the Gentiles), the second, the positive assertion of 3:1-5 (the Spirit is received through faith)." E. P. Sanders, *Paul, the Law, and the Jewish People* (Augsburg: Fortress Publishers, 1983), 22.

reading into a text something that is not there, instead of reading out of it the text's original meaning.

Conclusions to Acts 2:39 and Introduction to Case Studies

Yet, this is precisely what happens with paedobaptist interpretations of Acts 2:39: the promise of the Spirit is equated whole-sale, usually with no distinction, with the Abrahamic Covenant of Genesis 17 and/or the covenant of grace. And since it is assumed that circumcision is the sign and seal of the covenant of grace, the specific participants of circumcision (i.e., infants) are directly associated with whatever is being asserted in Acts 2:39. There is, then, little need to distinguish the promise of the Spirit in Acts 2 from the Abrahamic Covenant or covenant of grace – let alone see what Peter was originally referring to (i.e., Joel 2) to interpret Acts 2:39. As a result, the Abrahamic Covenant and its features such as the recipients of circumcision are imported entirely into Acts 2:39 without any consideration as to what promise is being talked about in Acts 2:39, what the fulfillment of that promise looks like in the New Covenant, and what argument is being made in Acts 2 and how that argument is not altogether the same as Acts 3, and so on and so forth. In short, "The Paedobaptist ear is so attuned to the Old Testament echo in this text that it is deaf to its New Testament crescendo."[77] The attitude is "promise of the Spirit, Abrahamic Covenant, covenant of grace, it is all the same thing," and "children, seed, same idea" when it comes to interpreting Acts 2:39.

It would be no different if a person said, "justification, regeneration, same thing." The two are obviously related and in some ways dependent on each other due to the marvelous and radical nature of salvation. But it would be wrong to suggest that because of that relationship between the two, the distinct features of justification and regeneration can be exchanged whenever the concepts are mentioned, echoed, or alluded to in the Bible. Worse,

---

[77] Jewett, *Infant Baptism and the Covenant of Grace*, 122.

Acts 2:39 in its Context (Part 1): An Exegetical Summary of Acts 2:39 and Paedobaptism

is forcing the same words (or *different* words, in this case[78]) to mean the same thing because of such "allusions" and "echoes" with no regard to the actual context.

Indeed, the fact that "promise" and "children" occur in Acts 2:39 and "covenant" and "children" occur in Genesis 12-22 does not automatically mean that the point of Acts 2:39 is to re-establish a principle of the Old Testament.[79] An interpreter's interest in hearing Old Testament overtones should not overthrow exegesis of the actual text. To put it differently, while no exegetical theology can be isolated from biblical theology, biblical theology should not simply trump exegetical theology since biblical theology itself depends upon the prior work of exegetical theology.

For example, if the paedobaptist hermeneutic of Acts 2:39 (that will be explored in the next part of this work) were applied consistently, then Peter could not possibly have been describing the New Covenant reality of the church, when saying in 1 Peter 2:9, "you are a chosen race, a royal priesthood, a holy nation, a people for his own possession, that you may proclaim the excellencies of him who called you out of darkness into his marvelous light." But Peter certainly *was* talking about the church.[80] The same is true for "Israel" in Galatians 6:16 and "the circumcision" in Philippians 3:3, where Paul uses the most explicit Old Testament language to assert something inherent to the New Covenant, *not* to re-affirm an Old Covenant reality.[81]

Therefore, even if Peter was using "Old Testament language" or "covenantal language" in Acts 2:39 by saying "you and your children," context still determines what he meant. And as it has

---

[78] Neither "children" (τέκνοις) nor "promise" (ἐπαγγελία) is used anywhere in Gen. 3-22 (LXX), with the exception of "son" in Gen. 17:16 and 22:7-8.

[79] In fact, if one wanted to import additional "children of the promise" theology into Acts 2:39, Peter's remarks in 1 Pet. 1:23 and Paul's teaching in Gal. 4 (discussed above) would be more than appropriate.

[80] See Ladd, *A Theology of the New Testament*, 641; Beale and Carson, *Commentary on the New Testament Use of the Old Testament*, 1016; Walton, Matthew, Chavalas, *The Bible Background Commentary: Old Testament*, 281; Carson and Moo, *An Introduction to the New Testament*, 647; Grudem, *Systematic* Theology, 863; etc.

[81] See Heb. 8:6-13 and Rom. 9:24-26 for more Old Testament language being applied to the church.

Acts 2:39 in its Context (Part 1): An Exegetical Summary of Acts 2:39 and Paedobaptism

been observed, context does not suggest Peter meant the same (or even a similar) thing as Genesis 17. At the least, he was repeating what was being said in Joel 2 (Acts 2:17-21) and, perhaps for the sake of his Jewish audience, describing the New Covenant realities of the church (Acts 2:21, 2:39b, etc.) in more "Old Covenant language." Whatever he meant must first be interpreted by the immediate context (e.g., Acts 2:38 and 41) and surrounding context (the rest of Acts 2) before demanding that the verse fit a presupposed biblical-theological category.

The next part of this study will document such cases of when biblical-theological concepts overturn (instead of enlighten) a consistent exegesis of Acts 2:39 in paedobaptist interpretations.

Acts 2:39 in its Context (Part 1): An Exegetical Summary of Acts 2:39 and Paedobaptism

CHAPTER 14
Acts 2:39 in its Context (Part 2): Case Studies in Paedobaptist Interpretations of Acts 2:39
Jamin Hübner, Th.D.

In the first part of this study, we examined the text of Acts 2:39 and drew a number of conclusions that were relevant to the paedobaptist/credobaptist debate. Some of the main points of that discussion include the following:

1. The primary meaning of "the promise" in Acts 2:39 is the promise of the Spirit (Acts 2:38, 33, 17-21), which *is* the Spirit.[1] There may (or may not) be specific allusions to the Abrahamic Covenant and its mentioning of children. If there are allusions, the context is generally clear that they are not what Peter immediately has in mind.[2] His primary focus is on the New Covenant reality prophesied in Joel 2 that is specifically fulfilled in Acts 2:17-21: the Spirit's outpouring on all of God's repentant people.[3]
2. The "children" of Acts 2:39:
    a. Are perhaps a familiar category to the Jews (especially after Peter just cited Joel 2, with "sons and daughters"), but cannot be properly understood apart from the rest of the verse: "everyone whom the Lord our God calls to himself." Peter's whole argument revolves around Joel 2

---

[1] The Spirit in both ἐπαγγελίαν τοῦ πνεύματος in v. 33 and δωρεὰν τοῦ ἁγίου πνεύματος in v. 38 are genitives of apposition.

[2] Peter's direct citations of Gen. 15 and 17 in Acts 3 is an example of when Peter *does* have the Abrahamic promise "immediately in mind."

[3] We also observed how Peter has in other places used the most explicit Old Covenant language to describe New Covenant realities such as the church in 1 Pet. 2:9, or Paul, "we are the circumcision" in Phil. 3:3, etc.

and the fulfillment of those promises in the church; he is asserting something unique about the New Covenant church as a fulfillment of the promise ("Spirit will be poured out on all flesh," "everyone who calls upon the name of the Lord shall be saved," "the promise is for…everyone whom the Lord our God calls to Himself," etc.), not re-establishing or re-asserting an Old Testament feature (e.g., "covenant community" that includes children, etc.).
   b. Hence, the final result in verse 41 is that "those who received his word were baptized," not "those who received his word and their children were baptized" or some other such variant.
   c. Infants are not being discussed since (a) the children being referred to are probably the "sons and daughters" prophesying (v. 11) or are at least contained in that group, (b) "children" (τέκνοι) and not "infants" (βρέφος) nor "infants/children" (νήπιος) is used, (c) the imperatives ("repent and be baptized") in verse 38 cannot be separated from verse 39. Thus, even if the "children" refers to infants, the whole context requires that their entrance into the fulfillment of the promise depends on whether or not *they* (not their parents) repent. And if they repent, they should be baptized.
   d. Thus, there is little (if any) basis to directly apply Acts 2:39 to infants for any reason.
3. Repentance is central to Peter's thought even as he strongly grounds his arguments from the Old Testament (Acts 2:38, 3:17-20, 25-26). This is because Peter (in the aforementioned texts) is primarily talking about the fulfillment of the Old Testament promises in the New Covenant. In the New Covenant (in contrast with the Old, where spiritual qualifications were not required to enter) the required response (i.e., faith, repentance) is conferred on "all" those who are brought into it (see Jer. 31; Heb. 8).

Acts 2:39 in its Context (Part 2): Case Studies in Paedobaptist Interpretations of Acts 2:39

a. Baptism (unlike circumcision[4]) is a sign of (actual, not potential) new life (Col. 2:12), forgiveness and cleansing from sin (Acts 22:16; 1 Pet. 3:21), and being identified with Christ (Rom. 6:3-4; Col. 2:10-14). This is because those who are to be baptized have been regenerated (Heb. 8:11), forgiven (Heb. 8:12), and united to Christ. In other words, those who are to receive the *sign* of the New Covenant (baptism) are *members* of the New Covenant (believers).
   b. In Scripture, those who are "born of the flesh" (physical descendants of Abraham, "perishable seed," 1 Pet. 1:23) received the sign of circumcision, but those born "according to the Spirit" and born "through promise" (according to "imperishable seed," 1 Pet. 1:23 and Gal. 4:23-31) now receive the New Covenant sign of baptism; the "children of the promise" in Galatians 4 are "like Isaac" and like the children of promise in Acts 2:38-39. They are all in the same group.
4. The promise of the Spirit (whether in Acts 2:39 or Gal. 3:14) cannot and should not be equated with the Abrahamic Covenant of Genesis 17 or simply the covenant of grace because (a) though related, they are two distinct concepts and (b) it is undeniable that Peter's focus is the specific promise of the Spirit. As such, there is no need or grounds for inserting the specific patterns and features of the Abrahamic Covenant (or covenant of grace, if it is considered essentially the same) into Acts 2:37-41.

Having laid this vital, exegetical foundation, we are now in a better position to examine alternative interpretations of Acts 2:39. The short story is, the vast majority of the above exegetical conclusions are either ignored or rejected by Reformed paedobaptists, past and present. All of the paedobaptist

---

[4] See Stephen J. Wellum, "Baptism and the Relationship between the Covenants" in *Believer's Baptism*, Shawn Wright and Thomas Schreiner, eds. (Nashville: B&H, 2006), 158.

Acts 2:39 in its Context (Part 2): Case Studies in Paedobaptist Interpretations of Acts 2:39

interpretations mentioned below assert that Acts 2:39 does little more than re-affirm a principle of the Old Testament, such as that the physical seed is being talked about because of "you and your children." None of them see Acts 2:39 as having anything to do with the uniqueness/newness of the New Covenant, nor do they view Pentecost and the fulfillment of Joel 2 as relevant to interpreting the text. Combined with what appears to be loyalty to Calvin, there is, then, a repetitious pattern of errors in interpreting Acts 2:39 throughout much of history.

Acts 2:39 Out of Its Context:
Calvin, Owen, Turretin, WCF, à Brakel, Bavinck, Buswell

John Calvin says[5] in 4.26.15 of the Battles' translation of *The Institutes*:

> Do you see how, after Christ's resurrection also, he thinks that the promise of the covenant is to be fulfilled, not only allegorically but literally, for Abraham's physical offspring? To the same point applies Peter's announcement to the Jews (Acts 2:39) that the benefit of the gospel belongs to them and their offspring by right of the covenant; and in the following chapter he calls them "sons of the covenant" (Acts 3:25), that is, heirs.[6]

Notice that no distinction is made between the promise of the Spirit in Acts 2 and the covenant with Abraham in Acts 3. As far as Calvin is concerned, they are one and the same. This is an obvious error. They are two different speeches, in two different contexts, and context demands that the "covenant" in 3:25 cannot simply be assumed to be the same as the "promise" in 2:39.

A quote from the rest of Acts 2:39 may have caused Calvin to reconsider his assertion: "The promise is for…everyone who the

---

[5] This is the only citation of Acts 2:39 in Calvin's defense of paedobaptism in *The Institutes*.

[6] John Calvin, *The Institutes of the Christian Religion*, trans. Ford Lewis Battles (Louisville: Westminster John Knox, 1960), 4.26.15.

Acts 2:39 in its Context (Part 2): Case Studies in Paedobaptist Interpretations of Acts 2:39

Lord our God calls to Himself." Peter's goal is not to restate an Old Testament principle and let the carnal seed of Abraham rest assured, but to show the fulfillment of these promises in the New Covenant and to urge the physical children of Abraham to repent like anyone else precisely because physical descent is not enough to be saved. Hence, we read that those "who received his word were baptized" (v. 41).

When looking at his commentaries, Calvin does not acknowledge that the promise in Acts 2:39 has anything to do with the specific promise of the Spirit, Acts 2:17-21, or Joel 2. Instead, he gives the "promise" several labels that begin to relate to the immediate context, but eventually end up with something else. He first refers to the promise as "the grace of Christ," then the broader "promise of God," then "the covenant with the Jews, (Exodus 4:22)," and finally, at the end of his explanation of "for the promise pertaineth unto you," he identifies this promise as "the words of the promise: I will by thy God, and the God of thy seed after thee, (Genesis 17:7)."

Why the great variety of terms? And why does Calvin *begin* with an exclusion of the immediate context (that the promise is the Holy Spirit) and end with something foreign to the immediate context (the covenant in Gen. 17)? It almost seems as if Calvin has some kind of goal in mind that causes his thought to quickly evolve in this direction.

The very next sentence of Calvin's commentary may reveal this possible agenda:

> This place, therefore, doth abundantly refute the manifest error of the Anabaptists, which will not have infants, which are the children of the faithful, to be baptized, as if they were not members of the Church. They espy a starting hole in the allegorical sense, and they expound it thus, that by children are meant those which are spiritually begotten. But this gross impudency doth nothing help them. It is plain and evident that Peter spoke thus because God did adopt one nation peculiarly. And circumcision did declare that the

right of adoption was common even unto infants. Therefore, even as God made his covenant with Isaac, being as yet unborn, because he was the seed of Abraham, so Peter teacheth, that all the children of the Jews are contained in the same covenant, because this promise is always in force, I will be the God of your seed.[7]

The first thing to point out is that Calvin's initial words about the Anabaptists certainly do not apply to most of today's Baptists. Reformed Baptists, for example, do believe that children of the faithful are to be baptized, *but not because they are children of the faithful*. Any child old enough to repent from sin and confess Christ as Lord should be baptized and recognized as being part of God's church. That seems fairly consistent with the narrative and implications of Acts 2:37-41.

We already noted that Calvin equates the promise of the Spirit in Acts 2:39 (Joel 2) with the covenant of Abraham in Genesis 17 without making any distinctions between them. And we observed why this is problematic in the first part of this work. The only thing left to observe is the fact that the phrase "everyone who the Lord our God calls to Himself" is entirely absent from his commentary. This is particularly troublesome since he normally does not exclude entire phrases like this. Nevertheless, Calvin does address the word "call' from the last part of 2:39, but does so under his explanation of the phrase "for all who are far off":

> *And to those which are afar off.* The Gentiles are named in the last place, which were before strangers. For those which refer it unto those Jews which were exiled afar off, (and driven) into far countries, they are greatly deceived…And therefore he useth this word *call*, as if he should say: Like as God hath gathered you together into one peculiar people heretofore by his voice, so the same voice shall sound everywhere, that those which are afar off may come and join

---

[7] John Calvin, *Commentary on Acts*. Christian Classics Ethereal Library. http://www.ccel.org/ccel/calvin/calcom36.html (Accessed February 29, 2012).

Acts 2:39 in its Context (Part 2): Case Studies in Paedobaptist Interpretations of Acts 2:39

themselves unto you, when as they shall be called by a new proclamation.[8]

It seems that the reason Calvin does not quote the rest of Acts 2:39 is because he collapses "for all who are far off" and "everyone whom the Lord our God calls to himself" into the same idea (similar to how he collapses the "promise" of "the Spirit" in Acts 2:38-39 into the "I will be the God of your seed" of Genesis 17). Calvin does not mention "everyone" from 2:39, but only relates the "call" to "for those who are far off." This is what pushes readers away from the fact that Peter is talking of God's elect ("everyone the Lord God calls to Himself") – whether they are Jews or Gentiles, children or adults.

We must move on to the Puritan scholar John Owen (1616-1683), who said:

> This covenant was, that he would be "a God unto Abraham and to his seed"... The right unto the covenant, and interest in its promises, wherever it be, gives right unto the administration of its initial seal, that is, to baptism, as Peter expressly declares, Acts 2:38, 39. Wherefore, — The right of the infant seed of believers unto baptism, as the initial seal of the covenant, stands on the foundation of the faithfulness of Christ as the messenger of the covenant, and minister of God for the confirmation of the truth of his promises. In brief, a participation of the seal of the covenant is a spiritual blessing... that is, the covenant of God with Abraham, Genesis 17:7.[9]

Owen makes the same mistakes as Calvin: (1) equating the covenant in Genesis 17 with the promise in Acts 2:39 without any distinction, (2) ignoring the immediate context of the promised Spirit of the New Covenant, (3) not quoting Acts 2:39 in its entirety,

---

[8] Calvin, *Commentary on Acts*.
[9] John Owen, "Of Infant Baptism" in *The Works of John Owen*, Vol. 16 (London: Johnston and Hunter, 1938), 261.

and (4) failing to recognize the significance of verse 41, etc. It is not clear how much impact Calvin had on Owen. But given the shear similarity of content, it would not be surprising if the impact was rather substantial – and this pattern will continue through church history.

Francis Turretin (1623-1687) says in the 15th Topic of his classic work *The Institutes of Elenctic Theology*:

> XIV. The reasons [for seminal faith in infants] are: (1) the promise of the covenant pertains no less to infants than to adults, since God promises that he will be 'the God of Abraham and of his seed' (Gen. 17:7) and the promise is said to have been made 'with the fathers and their children' (Acts 2:39). Therefore also the blessings of the covenant (such as "remission of sins" and "sanctification") ought to pertain to them (according to Jer. 31 and 32) and are communicated to them by God according to their state.[10]

Turretin, like Owen, makes most of the same mistakes as Calvin. He (1) equates the "promise" of the Spirit in Acts 2 with the Abrahamic Covenant in Genesis 17 without making any real distinction, (2) quotes Acts 2:39 in a way that fits his paedobaptist purposes, paraphrasing the text to read "with the fathers and their children" instead of "for you and for your children"),[11] and (3) assumes "children" are infants. And, of course, all of this is to assert that infants can have saving faith, albeit it "seminal" saving faith. But, clearly, *none* of these conclusions can be drawn from a

---

[10] Francis Turretin, *Institutes of Elenctic Theology*, Vol. 2 (Phillipsburg: P&R, 1994), 586.

[11] The Latin reads: "XIV. Rationes cur ita statuamus sunt: 1. Quia promissio Foederis non minus ad Infantes, quam ad Adultos pertinet; siquidem Deus pollicetur se fore *Deum Abrahami, et seminis ejus*, Ge. xvii.7, et, Act. ii. 39, promissio dicitur facta *Patribus et Liberis*." Dennison's edition of Turretin's *Institutes* (in English) unfortunately places "Patribus et Liberis" ("fathers and their children") in quotation marks so that it looks like Turretin misquotes Acts 2:39, when in fact it is not a quotation but a paraphrase. Either way, this part of Turretin's work shows how confidently he feels Acts 2:39 supports paedobaptism.

consistent exegesis of Acts 2:39. The covenant of Genesis 17 is not the "promise," the "children" are not "infants," and so forth.

The *Westminster Confession of Faith* (1646) references Acts 2:39 three times:

> Elect infants, dying in infancy, are regenerated and saved by Christ through the Spirit [Acts 2:39], who worketh when, and where, and how He pleaseth. So also are all other elect persons, who are uncapable of being outwardly called by the ministry of the Word. (WCF, 10.3)

> The visible Church, which is also catholic or universal under the Gospel (not confined to one nation, as before under the law), consists of all those throughout the world that profess the true religion; and of their children [Acts 2:39]: and is the kingdom of the Lord Jesus Christ, the house and family of God, out of which there is no ordinary possibility of salvation. (WCF, 25.2)

> Not only those that do actually profess faith in the obedience unto Christ, but also the infants of one, or both, believing parents, are to be baptized [Acts 2:39]. (WCF, 28.4)

While many of the above assertions are theologically sound, it should be clear that Acts 2:39 does not genuinely support any of them (regeneration of elect infants, visible/invisible church, baptism of believer's children). The same is true for Acts 2:39 in the Synod of Dordt.[12]

---

[12] "…the children of believers are holy, not by nature, but in virtue of the covenant of grace, in which they together with the parents are comprehended, godly parents ought not to doubt the election and salvation of their children whom it pleases God to call out of this life in their infancy (Gen. 17:7; Acts 2:39; I Cor. 7:14)." Article 17 of "The First Head of Doctrine," cited in Louis Berkhof, *Systematic Theology* (Grand Rapids: Eerdmans, 1996), 638. Is Peter really suggesting that parents should not doubt the "election and salvation of their children"? Or is he saying in effect, "the work of the Spirit you are now witnessing can be yours – anyone's, just repent of your sins and be baptized."

Acts 2:39 in its Context (Part 2): Case Studies in Paedobaptist Interpretations of Acts 2:39

Wilhelmus à Brakel (1635-1711) also cites Acts 2:39 in *The Christian's Reasonable Service*:

> An external covenant does not exist, for there is but one covenant between God and believers: the covenant of grace. The children of members of the covenant are therefore in the covenant. [13] In this respect the Lord calls them His children. "Moreover thou hast taken thy sons and thy daughters, whom thou hast borne unto Me ... that thou hast slain My children" (Ezek 16:20-21). If they are in the covenant, they must also indeed receive the seal of the covenant. This is evident in Acts 2:38-39, where we read, "... be baptized every one of you ... for the promise is unto you, and to your children.[14]

Again, same set of assertions, same set of problems. Acts 2:39 is not quoted in its entirety, the immediate context and the vital connection with 2:17-21 is not acknowledged, etc.

---

[13] As an aside, notice that à Brakel specifically distinguishes the covenant that children are in (one that has two parties: "God and believers") from an external covenant – one that "does not exist." This is generally the same as Bavinck's position (see below). But this is the opposite of what many or most of today's paedobaptists believe. They believe that children of believers *are* in the external covenant (in the "visible church") and thus should be baptized. The reasons for holding this position are obvious: if à Brakel's above assertion is true, then the covenant of grace is no longer comprised of the two parties, "God and believers." Presumably, in à Brakel's view, a non-elect person can be part of the covenant of grace (or New Covenant), and thus Christ would be the mediator on behalf of someone who rejects God. Though this view (that infants of believers are *actually*, not externally, in the covenant of grace) is not normative in today's paedobaptist circles, it can be found in popular works by those who lean towards the Federal Vision. See the last segment of James R. White's debate with Gregg Strawbridge (editor of *The Case for Covenantal Infant Baptism*), which can be found at aomin.org. For more information on this subject, especially on historic Reformed theology and who are true members of the covenant of grace, see Part I of Greg Nichols, *Covenant Theology: A Reformed and Baptistic Perspective on God's Covenants* (Vestavia Hills, AL: Solid Ground Christian Books, 2011).

[14] Wilhelmus à Brakel, *The Christian's Reasonable Service*, Vol. 2, ed. Joel Beeke (Grand Rapids: Reformation Heritage Books, 1992), 509.

Acts 2:39 in its Context (Part 2): Case Studies in Paedobaptist Interpretations of Acts 2:39

The great Dutch dogmatician Herman Bavinck says in chapter 10 ("The Spirit's Means of Grace") of volume three of his *Reformed Dogmatics*:

> From the early introduction of infant baptism, the general acknowledgement it was accorded from the start and Origen's witness – from these follows the possibility and even the probability that it already was an apostolic practice. Peter, moreover, says that the promise of the old covenant that God would be the God of believers and of their children passed into the dispensation of the New Testament (Acts 2:39). This, admittingly, first of all applies to the Jews, and Gentiles are not mentioned until Peter says: "And all who are far away." But this does not alter the fact that the Jews who convert to Christ not only receive the promise of the covenants for themselves but also for their children. And the Gentiles who become believers share the same privileges and, according to the whole New Testament, are in no respect inferior to believers from the Jews.[15]

Like Calvin and Turretin, Acts 2:39 is not quoted in its entirety. Bavinck stops at "for those who are far off" and does not mention "everyone who the Lord our God calls to Himself." Verse 41 and the practical fulfillment of this promise is also absent. And like Calvin, Owen, and Turretin, nothing is said about Acts 2:39 having anything to do with the promise of the Spirit as prophesied by Joel. Consequently, the vast majority of what comes prior to verse 39 in Acts 2 is neglected as having no interpretive relevance. Bavinck also abolishes any distinctions between the promise of Acts 2:39 and the Abrahamic Covenant by saying, "Peter…says that the promise of the old covenant that God would be the God of believers and of their children." Finally, nothing is said about how Acts 2:39 is in any way connected with the introduction of New Covenant realities

---

[15] Herman Bavinck, *Reformed* Dogmatics, Vol. 4, *Holy Spirit, Church, New Creation*, trans. John Vriend (Grand Rapids: Baker, 2008), 529.

and the fulfillment of the Abrahamic Covenant in it.[16] It is truly amazing how all of the essential features of the context of Acts 2:39 can be so easily set aside in arguments for infant baptism.

J. Oliver Buswell seems to recognize some of the tension that surrounds this verse. In an attempt to salvage paedobaptist defenses based on Acts 2:39, he provides his own argument, which demonstrates even clearer that the verse simply cannot deliver for paedobaptist arguments.

> The words – "…be baptized…the promise is to you and to your children…" – would necessarily call to the mind of every instructed Jew the covenant of circumcision and the promises attached thereto. In the historical setting it would have been entirely superfluous to mention the fact that the children were included in the baptism. They are included explicitly in the scriptural "promise" to which Peter made an allusion. Note that my argument is not in the form, "Since Peter mentioned both baptism and children on the day of Pentecost, therefore the children were to be baptized!" The argument is, "Since Christians explicitly considered baptism as "Christian circumcision" and this is declared by the Apostle Paul in Colossians 2:11, 12, and since Peter's invitation on the day of Pentecost was based upon the promise given in connection with the covenant of circumcision, therefore the mention of children as recipients of the promise, would carry with it the implication that children were to be baptized." Everything in the New Testament is for it, and there is not one whisper to the contrary.[17]

---

[16] In *Our Reasonable Faith*, Bavinck also cites Acts 2:39 in support of the following statement: "Therefore baptism is ministered not only to such adults as have been won for Christ through the work of missions, but to the children of believers also, for they together with their parents are included in the covenant of grace." Herman Bavinck, *Our Reasonable Faith* (Grand Rapids: Eerdmans, 1956), 542.

[17] J. Oliver Buswell, *A Systematic Theology of the Christian Religion* (Grand Rapids: Zondervan, 1961), 2:263.

Clearly, this argument is fallacious.[18] According to Buswell, the argument for paedobaptism from Acts 2:39 rests on the assumption that New Testament replaces Old Testament circumcision (according to Col. 2:11-12). However, this assumption has been refuted time and again, more recently by Richard Barcellos and Martin Salter;[19] there is no baptism-circumcision parallel in Colossians 2:11-14, but rather, "*spiritual circumcision* [is] tied to union with Christ and *baptism*."[20] The second assumption, that "Peter's invitation on the day of Pentecost was based upon the promise given in connection with the covenant of circumcision," has already been shown to be lacking adequate grounds. The "connection" between the "covenant of circumcision" (Acts 7:8) in Genesis 17 and the promise of the Spirit in Joel 2 is highly theological and limited – if extant at all. In the end, one is once again left wanting. (And, notice again that the last phrase of Acts 2:39 is mysteriously absent from the entire discussion.)[21]

---

[18] The only exception is when he says "[Children] are explicitly in the scriptural 'promise' to which Peter made an allusion." This is true, although not in the sense Buswell means it. It is true that children are explicitly in the scriptural promise to which Peter made an allusion–that is, the "sons and daughters" in the promise of the Spirit in Acts 2:17-21. But, as it has been demonstrated, the entirety of the Abrahamic Covenant cannot be wholesale equivocated with the promise of the Spirit in Acts 2:39. It muffles the climactic crescendo of Acts 2:39 and distorts the context of repentance and faith in vv. 38 and 41. Yet, that is what Buswell does.

[19] See Richard C. Barcellos, "An Exegetical Appraisal of Colossians 2:11-12" in *Reformed Baptist Theological Review* II:1 (2005): 3-23, reprinted as chapter 15 of this work; Martin Salter. "Does Baptism Replace Circumcision? An Examination of the Relationship between Circumcision and Baptism in Colossians 2:11-12" in *Themelios* 35.1 (2010): 15:-29.

[20] Wellum, "The Relationship Between the Covenants," 158.

[21] With Robert Reymond, that finally changes. He mentions the connection of Acts 2:39 with Joel 2, and actually quotes Acts 2:39 in its entirety. This is refreshing to see! But unfortunately, Reymond evidently does not believe these things have any interpretive relevance, as he cites Murray and then ends the matter on short order. Neither ultimately exegete Acts 2:39 nor explain what the last half of Acts 2:39 might mean. See Robert L. Reymond, *A New Systematic Theology of the Christian Faith* (Nashville: Thomas Nelson, 1998), 941-42.

Acts 2:39 in its Context (Part 2): Case Studies in Paedobaptist Interpretations of Acts 2:39

Acts 2:39 Out of Its Context: Beeke and Lanning

Joel Beeke and Ray Lanning provide an extensive essay on Acts 2:39 entitled "Unto You and Your Children" on pages 49-69 of *The Covenantal Case For Infant Baptism*. While I want to give much credit to such fine authors, it is clear that this particular essay lacks any real exegesis and is bent to support the authors' assumptions.

The first direct assertion about Acts 2:39 is the following:

> Several elements stand out in the words of Acts 2:39. First, it is clear that Peter uses the term the promise as rhetorical shorthand for the covenant of grace, which embodies the promise of salvation he calls upon his hearers to embrace (see Acts 2:21). This promise is the same as those made to Abraham, to David, to Israel, and even to the Gentiles. It includes the promise of the Holy Spirit and forgiveness of sins referred to in the previous verse (Acts 2:38).[22]

Notice that no argument is given that the promise is "rhetorical shorthand for the covenant of grace." This is simply assumed. The same goes for the sentence "the promise is the same as those made to Abraham, to David, and to Israel, and even to the Gentiles." The authors literally reduce (or expand, depending on how one looks at it) the entire thrust of "the promise" in Acts 2 to the substance of Genesis 17 on the basis of assertion alone – precisely as Calvin did over four centuries ago. This has been demonstrated to be a serious error.

Beeke and Lanning then say that the Abrahamic Covenant (which they fail to distinguish in any way from the covenant of grace)[23] "*includes* the promise of the Holy Spirit and forgiveness of

---

[22] Beeke and Lanning, "Unto You, and to Your Children," 55.

[23] The Abrahamic Covenant should not be equated with the covenant of grace any more than the promise of Acts 2:39 should be equated to the covenant of grace or the Abrahamic Covenant. See Samuel Waldron. *A Modern Exposition of the 1689 Baptist Confession of Faith* (Webster, NY: Evangelical Press, 2005), 107: "None of these covenants may simply be equated with what the Confession describes as 'the covenant of grace.' Presbyterians have often spoken as if the covenant with

sins referred to in the previous verse (2:38)" (emphasis mine).[24] This assertion introduces two errors, the first logical and the second exegetical. First, if "the promise" *is* just "rhetorical shorthand for the covenant of grace" and is "the same as those made to Abraham, to David, to Israel," then how can they in any way *distinguish* between two promises, one being "included" in another? Second, asserting that the "promise" in Acts 2:39 is *not* the promise of the Spirit in 2:38 but the covenant of grace which merely "includes" the promise of the Spirit is syntactically erroneous. The "Spirit" in ἐπαγγελίαν τοῦ πνεύματος τοῦ ἁγίου ("the Holy Spirit of promise") in verse 33 is a genitive of apposition ("the promise, *which is* the Holy Spirit"[25]) just like δωρεὰν τοῦ ἁγίου πνεύματος ("the gift of the Holy Spirit") in verse 38 is also a genitive of apposition ("the gift, *which is* the Spirit"). Furthermore, the "promise" in verse 39 *is* "the gift of the Spirit" in verse 38.[26] There is no third element, nor can verse 38 be disconnected from verse 39.

Therefore, for Beeke and Lanning's interpretation to stand, they need to demonstrate that (1) the "promise of the Spirit" in verse 38 is (contra Wallace, Robertson, Moulton, Young, etc.) not a genitive of apposition and (2) that "the promise" in verse 39 is (contra Beale, Carson, Peterson, Bock, Coxe, etc.) not "the gift of the Spirit" in verse 38. Both options are essentially impossible.

Abraham were the covenant of grace, but this identification ignores its typical elements and its beginning in the lifetime of Abraham, not immediately after the Fall (note chapter 29)."

[24] One clearly sees the problem in methodology. It is first assumed that Peter means "promise" precisely as a biblical-theological category. That is, Peter *must* be talking about the Abrahamic Covenant from the outset. Then, after that assumption has been stated, the immediate context is then consulted to contribute to its own interpretation. Thus, the meaning of Acts 2 is truncated, bottlenecked into the presupposed lens of the Abrahamic Covenant so that even if Peter *were* to assert something new or different, it could never be heard. Jewett's words on this very text, written over two decades before Beeke and Lanning's work, are worth quoting again. "The Paedobaptist ear is so attuned to the Old Testament echo in this text that it is deaf to its New Testament crescendo." Jewett, *Infant Baptism and the Covenant of Grace*, 122.

[25] Daniel Wallace, *Greek Grammar Beyond the Basics* (Grand Rapids: Zondervan, 1996), 99.

[26] See exegetical summary of Acts 2:38-39 in the beginning of this essay.

Acts 2:39 in its Context (Part 2): Case Studies in Paedobaptist Interpretations of Acts 2:39

Nevertheless, Beeke and Lanning go on:

> Peter reminds his listeners that they are "the children of the covenant which God made with our fathers" and that is why God has sent His Son Jesus to them first of all (Acts 3:25-26). Stephen recalls the promise, "which God had sworn to Abraham" (7:17). In the synagogue at Antioch, Paul informs hearers that God has raised "unto Israel a Saviour, Jesus," and declares, "Men and brethren, children of the stock of Abraham, and whosoever among you feareth God, to you is the word of this salvation sent" (13:23, 36). In Acts 2, Peter proclaims that Jesus of Nazareth is "Lord and Christ" (v. 36). That fulfills the promise made to David concerning "the fruit of his loins" (Ps. 132:11) and David's own prophecies of Messiah's resurrection (Ps. 16:8-11) and ascension into heaven (Ps. 110:1). The presentation is intensely covenantal, since the covenant with David and his seed is rooted in the covenant with Abraham and his seed. Peter's words in Acts 2:39 are therefore a covenantal formulary. "Unto you, and to your children" simply restates "between me and thee and thy seed after thee" (Gen. 17:7). These words assert the identity of the covenant of grace under all dispensations, and the continuity of the covenant pattern in which promises made to believers are extended to their children. As God has always done, so He will continue to do in these last days. "I am the LORD, I change not" (Mal. 3:6).[27]

It is clear that the context of Acts 2:39 is pushed into the background. The meaning of the text is determined not by exegesis, but by broad patterns of biblical theology, echoes and allusions, etc. "Intensely covenantal" language seems to trump all – especially the immediate context.

> We have to remind ourselves that the multitude who heard Peter's sermon on Pentecost was Jewish. It included Jews

---

[27] Beeke and Lanning, "Unto You, and to Your Children," 56.

from Palestine, proselytes, and dispersed Jews from other parts of the Roman Empire and beyond. The Old Testament was all they had of the Holy Scriptures. As they listened to Peter preaching from those Scriptures (twelve of the twenty-two verses of Peter's sermon in Acts 2 contain quotations from the Old Testament), they could only have understood his words one way — as a reference to the promise in God's covenant, and the fact that that promise extended not only to believers but to their children as well. To interpret Acts 2:39 in light of the New Testament Scriptures, which did not yet exist, as do many Baptists, is to engage in exegetical error and can only lead to a serious misrepresentation of the mind of the Spirit.[28]

Of course, by "the promise of God's covenant," Beeke and Lanning mean the Abrahamic Covenant in Genesis 17. But why is nothing said about the fact that Acts 2:39 comes to readers in the context of prophetic fulfillment? Why is not acknowledged that *none* of the quotes in any of Acts 2 come from Genesis (or any book of the Pentateuch for that matter)? And why is nothing said about the fact that Peter's audience would probably understand Acts 2:39 in terms of Joel 2 (the most relevant Old Testament text in Peter's speech) instead of Genesis 17 – especially after they witnessed eye-opening events, so strange that they confused the Spirit with drunkenness? All of the essentials are missing.

The remark about "many Baptists" is baffling. Only one is cited (William Wilkinson), and even that citation does not support the authors' point. Here is the full section of Wilkinson that Beeke and Lanning reference:

> Here the promise – that is, the promise of the Holy Ghost - is said to be for the Israelites of Peter's day, together with their "children," and for as many besides these as may be "called." The Greek word for "children" is one which has not the smallest reference to age, infant or adult, of the

---

[28] Beeke and Lanning, "Unto You, and to Your Children," 56-57.

persons so designated. It simply means "posterity," "descendants." This is all that the word means; but if the word meant infants, as it does not, the only infants, as yet more it does not, still the sense of the passage would be that the Holy Spirit was promised, on a certain condition, to infants. There would be in it no possible allusion to the practice of infant baptism unless the allusion were to be found in the command, "Be baptized;" which command, in that case, being addressed in the second person to the subjects, would necessarily have to be obeyed by the subjects themselves or not to be obeyed at all. And then, as those same subjects also commanded beforehand in the same breath to "Repent," it is to be supposed that obedience to the second command would be preceded by obedience to the first, whereby infant baptism referred to would be baptism of infant believers, and thus not in the least the same practice with infant baptism known to the ecclesiastical usage of today.[29]

How do any of these words invoke Beeke and Lanning's particular objection? And how is the above quote of Wilkinson in anyway an interpretation of "Acts 2:39 in light of New Testament Scriptures, which did not yet exist"? What "New Testament Scriptures" are Beeke and Lanning referring to? Wilkinson certainly does not provide any other scriptural citations except for "be baptized" and "repent" from Acts 2:38. So, as far as the essay is concerned, the two-fold charge of "exegetical error" and "many Baptists" is without basis.

For several paragraphs, the authors continue to play the same drum-beat that the promise in Acts 2:39 is no different than the covenant of grace. Then they conclude:

---

[29] William Cleaver Wilkinson, *The Baptist Principle in its Application to Baptism and the Lord's Supper* (Philadelphia: American Baptist Publication Society, 1881), 158-59.

Thus, in Acts 2:39, after Peter assures Jewish believers that the covenant promise and covenant pattern are still in effect, and that the covenant promise continues to be in force for their children, he boldly proclaims that the promise shall also be to all that are afar off — i.e., afar off from the covenant community and its divine covenant promises. Peter is affirming that God is no longer restraining his saving purposes to one nation in the New Testament era. The gospel is to all to whom it comes without exception or distinction from this time on. God's saving purposes are to all nations, "even as many as the Lord our God shall call" (Acts 2:39b), Peter says. Wherever the gospel is preached, sinners are welcome to enter into the covenant of God that He has purposed according to His immutable promise. We have no reason to conclude that when they do so the covenant now is only with the individuals of the first generation of converts.[30]

Beeke and Lanning's particular covenant theology continues to force the text to mean something that it is not saying. As it was demonstrated in the first installment of this work, scholars agree that "those who are far off" means either (1) Gentiles, (2) the Jewish Diaspora, or (3) peoples of all kinds who are in geographically remote locations. But in an attempt to shore up additional support for their argument, Beeke and Lanning insist on their own unique interpretation: that Peter is primarily talking about the "covenant community." This, of course, is a notoriously ambiguous couplet that saturates defenses of infant baptism (though does not saturate the New Testament).[31]

---

[30] Beeke and Lanning, "Unto You, and to Your Children," 59.

[31] The phrase "covenant community" is found over 30 times in *The Covenantal Case for Infant Baptism*. This is not to say "covenant community" is always a useless phrase. But that also does not mean it is helpful or necessary in discussions of infant baptism. Grudem's assessment is particularly insightful: "The New Testament does not talk about 'a covenant community' made up of believers *and* their unbelieving children and relatives and servants who happen to live among them. (In fact, in the discussion of baptism, the phrase "covenant community" as

> Baptists often dismiss this covenantal argument by harking back to verse 38, arguing that since Peter says "repent and be baptized," baptism must always follow repentance. Since infants are not yet able to repent, they ought not be baptized. To such reasoning, we would posit three responses. First, the word "and" between "repent" and "be baptized" is a coordinate and not a causal conjunction. That is to say, though both things are true, there is not necessarily a causal connection between them. "Repent" and "be baptized" are two coordinate commands. Acts 2:38 does not require that we are to be baptized because we have repented, nor does it say that it is wrong to baptize someone who has not repented.[32]

The fact that καὶ ("and") is a coordinate and not a causal conjunction makes no difference. No one is suggesting that repentance is the *cause* of baptism. As it was demonstrated in the first part of this work that "repent" and "of you" are 2nd person plurals while "be baptized" and "each of you" are singulars; ὑμῶν matches μετανοήσατε in person and number. Hence, it is rendered "You all repent and each one of you (who repent) be baptized." Thus, the conclusion that "it [does not] say that it is wrong to baptize someone who has not repented" is fallacious. The text is clear that *the command to be baptized is for the ones repenting*. There is no exegetical basis for breaking up the text into separate groups so that baptism is being commanded to one group and repentance for another. They go together.

---

used by paedobaptists often tends to function as a broad and vague term that blurs the differences between the Old Testament and the New Testament on this matter. In the New Testament church, the only question that matters is whether one has saving faith and has been spiritually incorporated into the body of Christ, the true church. The only "covenant community" is *the church*, the fellowship of the redeemed." Wayne Grudem, *Systematic Theology* (Grand Rapids: Zondervan, 2000), 977.

[32] Beeke and Lanning, "Unto You, and to Your Children," 60.

Acts 2:39 in its Context (Part 2): Case Studies in Paedobaptist Interpretations of Acts 2:39

> Second, the causal conjunction, "for," at the beginning of Acts 2:39 indicates that verse 38 is part of a larger thought which is concluded in verse 39. Attempting to understand repentance and baptism in verse 38, therefore, without examining verse 39 is refusing to listen to the whole text. "For" in verse 39 indicates that that verse is giving the reason why we are to repent and be baptized, namely, "for the promise is to you and to your children, and to all that are afar off." In other words, those who have received the promise of God of the remission of sins and the gift of the Holy Spirit are qualified to be baptized, and, Peter clearly says, that includes them and their children.[33]

There are many problems here. First, as we observed earlier, Calvin, Turretin, Bavinck, and others have left off the last half of Acts 2:39. Beeke and Lanning follow suit and only quote the first half of the verse in this vital portion of their essay. To finish the verse and say "everyone whom the Lord our God calls to Himself" would introduce an unwelcome concept to paedobaptist exposition of Acts 2:39 – the concept of God's elect, the spiritual seed.

Second, this paragraph is very difficult to understand since "that" in "that includes them and their children" has no clear referent. Are the authors referring to "that promise" or "that remission of sins" or "that gift of the Holy Spirit," or several of these, or all of these as a concept, or the "those" who receive all of these things, or that baptism in "to be baptized"? The most probable referent is to the whole idea of "those who have received the promise of God of the remission of sins and the gift of the Holy Spirit." So, Beeke and Lanning are saying "them and their children" are "those who have received the promise of God of the remission of sins and the gift of the Holy Spirit," and therefore, "them and their children" are "qualified to be baptized." But, this seems to reverse the order. Repentance and forgiveness of sins qualifies a person for baptism, not the other way around. And if the sins of the Jews and their children are not automatically forgiven by virtue of

---

[33] Beeke and Lanning, "Unto You, and to Your Children," 60.

Acts 2:39 in its Context (Part 2): Case Studies in Paedobaptist Interpretations of Acts 2:39

being "those who have received the promise of God," what is the condition that is needed for forgiveness of sins? The first half of 2:38 answers this question – the half that the authors fail to mention at this point. They are attempting to isolate "forgiveness of sins" and "gift of the Holy Spirit" from "repent and be baptized." This is simply impossible to do since (as the authors point out, ironically) the text explicitly connects the two halves with the conjunction "for" (εἰς). This repentance and/or baptism is "for the forgiveness [εἰς ἄφεσιν] of your sins." If we are to follow the first of the two probable options Wallace proposes regarding εἰς in this text,[34] then it "should be repunctuated" to read "Repent *for/with reference* to your sins, and let each one of you be baptized." The conclusion, then, is that there is no forgiveness of sins apart from repentance. This does not square with the authors' interpretation.

The other option according to Wallace ("the idea of baptism might incorporate both the spiritual reality and the physical symbol"), asserts that "water baptism is not a cause of salvation, but a *picture*; and as such it serves both as a public acknowledgement (by those present) and a public confession (by the convert) that one has been Spirit-baptized."[35] This also does not fit with the authors' interpretation since, as it was shown above, even if εἰς was referring to "be baptized" only, that does not disconnect "be baptized each one of you" from "the ones repenting."

A final option is that of F. F. Bruce who says that εἰς ἄφεσιν τῶν ἁμαρτιῶν ὑμῶν, "for the forgiveness of your sins," is "to be taken with *metanoesate* (repent) as well as with *baptistheto* (be baptized); cf. 3:19; 5:31; Luke 24:47."[36] In other words, "for the forgiveness of your sins" has reference to both "be baptized" and "you all repent." This also does not square with Beeke and Lanning's assertion that children are somehow exempt from having to repent in order to be baptized.

---

[34] These would be options 3 and 4 on pages 370-71 of *Greek Grammar Beyond the Basics*. The first two (baptism refers only to physical or only to spiritual reality only) are less probable according to his analysis.

[35] Wallace, *Greek Grammar*, 370-71.

[36] Bruce, *Acts of the Apostles*, 98.

So no matter how one puts it, Peter is not asserting in Acts 2 that one should be baptized apart from repentance. He is asserting quite the opposite! This is a fact of the text (and all of Scripture) that stands in contradiction to infant baptism and simply will not go away: repentance from sin is a precondition to baptism.

> Third, an argument against infant baptism from Acts 2:38 is an argument against infant salvation. If infants cannot be baptized because they are incapable of repentance and faith, then they cannot be saved for the same reason. The use of such verses as Mark 16:16 and Acts 2:38 to argue that repentance and faith are required for baptism also argues that repentance and faith are required for salvation, thereby consigning all infants incapable of repentance and faith to perdition.[37]

If one is to accurately represent the Baptist objection, the authors should say "infants *should not* be baptized because they *do not and cannot* repent and exercise saving faith." If a two-week old baby repented and believed, surely she should be baptized.

Nevertheless, paedobaptists (e.g., WCF) and confessional Reformed Baptists (2LCF) both agree that the ability to repent (at least the kind of repentance Peter is talking about in Acts 2:38-39) is not always necessary for "salvation."[38] So the whole argument seems to be a rather moot point.

Beeke and Lanning continue:

> God refuses baptism to impenitent sinners (Matt. 3:7-8) because, not granting them the grace, He will not grant them the sign. If therefore God denies the sign to infants of believers, it must be because He denies them the grace. All

---

[37] Beeke and Lanning, "Unto You, and to Your Children," 60.
[38] "Elect infants, dying in infancy, are regenerated and saved by Christ through the Spirit, who worketh when, and where, and how He pleaseth. So also are all other elect persons, who are uncapable of being outwardly called by the ministry of the Word" (WCF, 2LCF, 10.3).

Acts 2:39 in its Context (Part 2): Case Studies in Paedobaptist Interpretations of Acts 2:39

children of believers who die in their infancy, then, must be hopelessly lost — not that all must be lost who are not baptized, but all must be lost whom God does not *want* baptized. Yet most Baptists will admit that the New Testament, like the Old, indicates that small children—even infants (Luke 18:15-17) — are proper subjects of Christ's kingdom (see Matt. 18:6, 19:13-15, 21:16; Luke 10:21).[39]

This is a somewhat confusing paragraph since the argument is not one that challenges any major Baptist teaching. Yes, all children who die in their infancy are hopelessly lost outside the grace of God (We agree on the doctrine of original sin.). Yes, no one is baptized or saved who God does not want to save or have baptized (We agree on the doctrine of divine election.). However, the assertion and following references about infants being "proper subjects of Christ's kingdom" are troublesome. This is a very common attempt at gathering evidence for paedobaptism. A brief refutation is in order.

First, regarding Luke 18:15-17, Matthew 18:6, and 19:13-15, the children are not even said to be "in the kingdom," let alone "in the covenant." In his commentary on Matthew, D. A. Carson concisely undercuts the paedobaptist interpretation of these texts:

> Jesus does not want the little children prevented from coming to him (v. 14), not because the kingdom of heaven belongs to them [a paedobaptist assertion], but because the kingdom of heaven belongs to those like them (so also Mark and Luke, stressing childlike faith): Jesus receives them because they are an excellent object lesson in the kind of humility and faith he finds acceptable.[40]

Second, if it is suggested that these children had faith, that undermines the very point paedobaptists are trying to demonstrate

---

[39] Beeke and Lanning, "Unto You, and to Your Children," 60.
[40] D. A. Carson, *Matthew*, EBC, ed. F. E. Gaebelein (Grand Rapids: Zondervan, 1995), 8:420.

– namely, that those *incapable* of having saving faith should be considered in the covenant and thus be baptized.[41] Third, none of the parents of the children in these texts are identified as believers. They are not even mentioned. In short, then, it does not appear these three texts can amount to what the paedobaptist asserts they amount to.

The next text referenced is Matthew 21:16.[42] According to Beeke and Lanning, this is a text that supports the assertion that infants "are proper subjects of Christ's kingdom." But, they are obviously asserting more than that. What they are really asserting is that children and infants are part of the church and so should be baptized and Matthew 21 demonstrates that infants are part of the church because they praise Jesus. But it is clear that the text is far from asserting this. All that really happens is children cry "Hosanna to the Son of David!" and this event is noted to be a fulfillment of prophecy (Psa. 8:2). Beyond that, the main thrust of the text is uncontroversial (to us, not to the original hearers): "If God can speak through babies, from the lesser to the greater, how much more through children. And if children, by the same logic, how much more ought the religious leaders to join in."[43] Of course, even if these children are "in the covenant" in some way, that does

---

[41] "These passages [Matt. 18:1-10] have nothing to do with whether infants are in the covenant because this *paidon* [little child] responded to Jesus' call, *proskaleo*, and believed in Him. This humble submission of a child to Christ as Lord was what He was trying to teach His disciples about entrance in the greatness in the kingdom." See Fred A. Malone, *The Baptism of Disciples Alone: A Covenantal Argument for Credobaptism Versus Paedobaptism* (Cape Coral, FL: Founder's Press, 2007), 141.

[42] "But when the chief priests and the scribes saw the wonderful things that he did, and the children crying out in the temple, "Hosanna to the Son of David!" they were indignant, and they said to him, "Do you hear what these are saying?" And Jesus said to them, "Yes; have you never read, '"Out of the mouth of infants and nursing babies you have prepared praise'?" And leaving them, he went out of the city to Bethany and lodged there" (Matt. 21:15-17).

[43] Craig Keener, *The Intervarsity Bible Background Commentary: New Testament* (Downers Grove, IL: InterVarsity, 1993), 503; "Yahweh is worthy of all praise and worship (thus the psalm), and now all the more because he has sent his Messiah (thus Matthew)." See Beale and Carson, *Commentary on the New Testament Use of the Old Testament*, 70.

Acts 2:39 in its Context (Part 2): Case Studies in Paedobaptist Interpretations of Acts 2:39

not mean the children of believers are supposed to be baptized. The parents of these children are not mentioned. As far as the text and narrative is concerned, the children are praising Jesus regardless of the spiritual condition of their parents. So if these children are somehow supposed to be considered part of the church, then they are included in the church on the basis of something other than the faith of their parents. Further, if the argument is that infants have visible saving faith since they praise Jesus and are therefore part of the church, that does not remove the requirement for a visible saving faith of such infants today. Again, no matter how one looks at the text, it does not and cannot support the conclusions of the paedobaptist.

The final reference listed is Luke 10:21 (cf. Matt. 11:25-30).[44] It is puzzling why Beeke and Lanning would reference this verse in support of anything related to children, covenant theology, or baptism – for "children" in this verse is referring to Jesus' disciples! As the *ESV Study Bible* remarks, "to little children, that is, to the disciples, who have childlike faith themselves (v. 23)."[45] *Nothing about biological age is even being asserted*. The use of "children" in this text has to do with spiritual maturity and knowledge (see Calvin,[46] Morris,[47] etc.) It is a desperate attempt to cite this text to support paedobaptism.

---

[44] "In that same hour he rejoiced in the Holy Spirit and said, "I thank you, Father, Lord of heaven and earth, that you have hidden these things from the wise and understanding and revealed them to little children; yes, Father, for such was your gracious will."

[45] Wayne Grudem and J. I. Packer, eds. *The ESV Study Bible* (Wheaton, IL: Crossway, 2008), Luke 10:21.

[46] "I consider that Christ here includes all who are eminent for abilities and learning, without charging them with any fault; as, on the other hand, he does not represent it to be an excellence in any one that he is a *little* child. True, humble persons have Christ for their master, and the first lesson of faith is, Let no man presume on his wisdom." See Calvin, *Commentary on Matthew, Mark, Luke*, Vol. 2, http://www.ccel.org/ccel/calvin/calcom32.html.

[47] "The Father has *hid* from the world's great and wise ones and revealed to the lowliest, those who can be called *babies*. This does not mean that all the *wise* are lost and all the *babies* are saved; it means that the knowledge of God does not depend on human wisdom and education." See Leon Morris, *The Gospel According to Matthew*, PNTC (Grand Rapids: Eerdmans, 1992), 292.

Acts 2:39 in its Context (Part 2): Case Studies in Paedobaptist Interpretations of Acts 2:39

Having examined every single reference provided on this matter, it is evident Beeke and Lanning are on their own when they say "most Baptists will admit that the New Testament, like the Old, indicates that small children – even infants (Luke 18:15-17) – are proper subjects of Christ's kingdom (see Matt. 18:6, 19:13-15, 21:16; Luke 10:21)."[48] None of these biblical references support their paedobaptist position.

After a brief historical sketch of the Reformers' view on baptism, Beeke and Lanning then conclude the section by re-stating the classic paedobaptist interpretation of Acts 2:39:

> The promise which says, "I will be your God and you will be my people," given to Abraham to embrace not just Abraham but his family, still stands; and it is still, in the words of Peter, "for you and for your children." Children would therefore naturally be regarded as subjects of baptism just as they were of circumcision in the Old Testament.[49]

At this point in our discussion, it is abundantly clear what is wrong with this conclusion, and it need not to be revisited again.

The next section ("Fourth Context: Prophecy, or the Vision of the Prophet") contains the quote of Joel 2:28-29. But, unfortunately, it is not exegeted either in its context or in the context of Acts 2:17-21.[50] To our dismay, it is virtually dismissed. Joel 2 is set side by side with other prophecies of similar content and tone, and then the following conclusion is offered:

> These prophecies are anchored in the promises of the covenant, and confirm those promises "to a thousand generations" (Ps. 105:8). They also reinforce the covenantal pattern or form which the promise takes. At every point,

---

[48] Beeke and Lanning, "Unto You, and to Your Children," 61.
[49] Beeke and Lanning, "Unto You, and to Your Children," 63.
[50] For a helpful analysis on this issue, see chapter 11, "Children in Prophecy" in Conner, *Covenant Children Today*.

Acts 2:39 in its Context (Part 2): Case Studies in Paedobaptist Interpretations of Acts 2:39

"the promise is unto you, and to your children" (Acts 2:39a).[51]

The entire weight of Joel 2 has obviously been missed. Joel presents the outpouring of the Spirit on "all flesh" and the fact that "everyone who calls upon the name of the Lord shall be saved" *as something different than the previous era*. But the only thing that seems to matter to the authors is that Joel 2 mentions "your sons and daughters" and this supports the conclusion that "At every point, 'the promise is unto you, and to your children.'" The "last days" of Joel 2, in the lens of Beeke, Lanning, and for all of the paedobaptist scholars observed in this essay, is really no different than the *those days* of the Old Covenant! Since Acts 2:39 *sounds like* Genesis 17 and other Old Testament texts, it *cannot* assert anything substantially new – even if that is the entire purpose of the text itself.[52] It is an ironic observation, indeed.

> Our response to Acts 2:39 is to set the Christ of the covenant before our children, as He is revealed in the Scriptures, trusting that He will grant them faith and repentance by His Spirit. Nor does anything said above obviate the need for personal regeneration as the experiencing of the truth and power of the covenant promise. Covenant promise is no substitute for personal regeneration.[53]

Yet, for the paedobaptist, there is a sense in which the covenant promise *is* a substitute for personal repentance and baptism. If a parent is repentant, that is sufficient enough to baptize the child of

---

[51] Beeke and Lanning, "Unto You, and to Your Children," 64.

[52] This obviously brings to mind the same phenomenon in the paedobaptist reading of Hebrews 8. Even though the whole purpose of the chapter is to stress the newness of the New Covenant and the discontinuity between the Old and the New Covenant, that argument is turned upside down for the sake of defending infant baptism and a dogma of continuity wins the day. See James White's series, "The Newness of the New Covenant" in the *Reformed Baptist Theological Review* (July 2004 and January 2005), reprinted as chapters 11 and 12 of this work.

[53] Beeke and Lanning, "Unto You, and to Your Children," 67.

Acts 2:39 in its Context (Part 2): Case Studies in Paedobaptist Interpretations of Acts 2:39

that parent – at least before the child is old enough to repent himself (then baptism is withheld and the requirement for repentance is added).[54]

> Parents who presume that their children are regenerate by virtue of the covenant may see no need to tell their children that they must be born again. William Young calls this view "hyper-covenantism," because the relation of children to the covenant is exaggerated to the point that the covenant relation replaces the need for personal conversion.[55]

But, where was the need for personal conversion in Genesis 17? If the covenant of grace in Genesis 17 is where we turn to figure out who should be baptized, then we cannot help but remember that circumcision was given regardless of conversion. So, why require it now? If the response is "because the New Testament teaches the need for personal conversion," then one ought to be consistent and say "the New Testament teaches the need for personal repentance before water baptism." For that is precisely the teaching of the New Testament and the pattern of the Apostolic church.

Acts 2:39 Out of Its Context: J. V. Fesko

In a rather splendid and informative book, J. V. Fesko adds more recent comments to the discussion on Acts 2:39 in *Word, Water, and Spirit*:

---

[54] That is, indeed, an area of inconsistency for paedobaptism. For example, if the unbelieving father in an unbelieving family totaling four people (mother, father, one month-old son, 14 year-old daughter) was to become a Christian, the paedobaptist minister would only baptize the one month-old son, regardless if "the promise" or "covenant" was equally given to both the son *and* the daughter. The paedobaptist principle in that case is that baptism should be administered when a person *cannot and does not repent* (e.g., infant son) and should not be administered when a person *can repent* (e.g., teenage daughter). Yet, the Bible teaches the polar opposite: baptism should be administered when a person *does repent* and should not be administered to a person who *cannot and does not repent*.

[55] Beeke and Lanning, "Unto You, and to Your Children," 67.

Acts 2:39 in its Context (Part 2): Case Studies in Paedobaptist Interpretations of Acts 2:39

Abraham was supposed to administer the sign of God's covenant promise to his male offspring (Gen. 17:10). Peter echoes this command in his sermon at Pentecost...[quote of text]...To what promise does Peter refer? The promise is undoubtedly weighted on the whole of redemptive history: the *protoevangelium* (Gen. 3:15); God's promise to Abraham (Gen. 12:1-3; 15; 17:1-14); and his promise to David (I Sam. 7:14). However, Peter also mentions the gift of the Holy Spirit, which invokes the fulfillment of Joel's prophecy (2:28-29) and is certainly connected to the promise of the new covenant, which included the promise to children (Jer. 31:31; 32:39; Isa. 32:15; 44:3; Ezek. 11:19; 36:26-27; 37:14). Peter echoes Joel's prophecy that God would pour out His Spirit on Israel's sons and daughters, both young and old (Joel 2:28), but also His promise that He would be the God of Abraham and of his generations to come (cf. Gen. 9:9; 13:15; 17:7; Gal. 3:16, 29; Pss. 18:50; 89:34-37; 132:11-12).[56]

As we look at Fesko's comments through the lens of church history, it is clear that there is nothing substantially new here, and old errors are repeated. Context is set aside. Genesis 17 is given primary importance. The promise of the Spirit, which has been the subject of Peter's entire speech in Acts 2, is downplayed; it merely "echoes" Joel's prophecy.

He goes on to say:

> The inclusion of infants had been a practice of the covenant community for nearly 2,000 years...For there to have been a change in this covenantal practice without so much as a syllable of explanation would not have gone over well with first century Jews.[57]

Fesko is correct that it would not have gone over well – *if the Jews were assuming that baptism was no different in purpose and participants*

---

[56] Fesko, *Word, Water, and Spirit*, 357.
[57] Fesko, *Word, Water, and Spirit*, 358.

than Old Covenant circumcision. But is there really adequate indication that they thought of one replacing the other? Did they even have a firm grasp on whether to circumcise in the New Covenant or not?

Everything we know about the early church suggests the contrary. The church was substantially confused and split over the subject of circumcision, which is why it led to the first church council (Acts 15). There is no shred of evidence that suggests that *anyone* in the Apostolic period understood baptism as replacing circumcision.[58] Furthermore, Fesko is assuming the non-newness of the New Covenant. This argument has already been adequately critiqued in previous publications of *RBTR*.[59]

Conclusion

We must be honest with Scripture, and honest with ourselves. If we gave an average Christian a Bible and five minutes to answer the question "what is the 'promise' in Acts 2:33?," chances are, there would be no hesitation in answering with, "it is the promise of the Spirit, which is prophesied in Joel 2, and quoted earlier in Acts." I believe that is the right answer, and that is the exegetical answer. Yet, for the paedobaptist, there is *always* hesitation with this kind of question. And there is hesitation when the same question is asked about "the promise" in verse 39. Why?

It is not because "the promise" is any less clear in its meaning in verses 33 and 39. It is because Acts 2:39 was supposed to be the "place" that "doth abundantly refute the manifest error of the Anabaptists, which will not have infants, which are the children of the faithful, to be baptized, as if they were not members of the Church" (Calvin). But since it clearly *is not* that place, and since paedobaptists after Calvin seem determined to continue using the

---

[58] See chapter 2 of Jeffrey D. Johnson. *The Fatal Flaw of the Theology Behind Infant Baptism* (Conway: Free Grace Press, 2010).

[59] See James White's series, "The Newness of the New Covenant" in the *Reformed Baptist Theological Review* (July 2004 and January 2005), reprinted as chapters 11 and 12 of this work.

Acts 2:39 in its Context (Part 2): Case Studies in Paedobaptist Interpretations of Acts 2:39

text (much like Col. 2:11-12[60]) to support the practice, the basic rules of context and exegesis must be suspended until the essential features of paedobaptist covenant theology can be conveniently imported into the verse. That is what history shows, and it is, quite simply, a black-eye to historic Reformed theology. Alas, the historical interpretation of Acts 2:39 has been anything but sound in the Reformed faith. Therefore, let us turn the tide by letting the Word of God speak on its own terms, and be willing to test our traditions. Only then are we truly practicing *sola Scriptura*. Amen and *semper reformanda*.

---

[60] Colossians 2:11-12 has been used since Zwingli (at least according to Fesko's historical analysis, see *Word, Water, and Spirit*, 63, and all of Part I) to support paedobaptism via a circumcision-baptism parallel. And, yet, it has become increasingly clear that this text simply does not say what Reformed paedobaptists have wanted it to say (see essays by Barcellos and Salter mentioned above). And just in passing, Fesko tries to salvage paedobaptist uses of the text, but really only manages to say that "it seems to be overly fine exegesis to eliminate the signs from the things signified. One should not have to choose between a reference to a rite or a work of the Spirit," Fesko, *Word, Water, and Spirit*, 241.

Acts 2:39 in its Context (Part 2): Case Studies in Paedobaptist Interpretations of Acts 2:39

CHAPTER 15
An Exegetical Appraisal of Colossians 2:11-12
Richard C. Barcellos, Ph.D.*

and in Him you were also circumcised with a circumcision made without hands, in the removal of the body of the flesh by the circumcision of Christ; having been buried with Him in baptism, in which you were also raised up with Him through faith in the working of God, who raised Him from the dead. (Col. 2:11-12)[1]

Colossians 2:11-12 is one text used by paedobaptists to justify their practice of baptizing infants. It is used to display the relationship between Old Testament circumcision and New Testament baptism. The conclusion drawn is that what circumcision was, baptism is. As John Murray puts it, "baptism is the circumcision of the New Testament."[2] Simply put, in paedobaptist thought, baptism replaces circumcision as the sign and seal of the covenant of grace. Since infants were circumcised under the Old Testament administration of the covenant of grace, infants should be baptized under the New Testament administration of the covenant of grace. A replacement (or maybe better said, a fulfillment) theology between circumcision and baptism is argued by this understanding of the text.

It must be admitted that a *prima facie* glance at the biblical text above seems to give credibility to such an interpretation. Our purpose in this chapter is to examine Colossians 2:11-12 in the Greek text to determine its meaning in context and to compare our

---

* A version of this chapter first appeared in *RBTR* and is used with permission and with slight modification.

[1] English Bible references are taken from *The New American Standard Bible Updated Edition*.

[2] Quoted by Joseph A. Pipa, "The Mode of Baptism" in Gregg Strawbridge, ed., *The Case For Covenantal Infant Baptism* (Phillipsburg, NJ: P&R Publishing, 2003), 123.

findings with the claim that it is a valid proof text for infant baptism. The approach will be as follows: *first*, to set the text in its context; *second*, to examine its syntactical structure and provide exegesis of its contents; *third*, to compare our conclusions with arguments used in *The Case For Covenantal Infant Baptism*; and *fourth*, to draw some pertinent conclusions.

Colossians 2:11-12 in Context

Colossians 2:11-12 comes in a larger context where Paul is exposing error and giving its remedy (Col. 2:4-3:4).[3] In the immediate context, Paul warns the Colossians: "See to it that no one takes you captive through philosophy and empty deception, according to the tradition of men, according to the elementary principles of the world, rather than according to Christ" (Col. 2:8). Verses 9-15 give the reasons why they are not to be led astray in ways not according to Christ.

Verses 9 and 10 give two (possibly three) reasons why Christ is the remedy against error. "For in Him all the fullness of Deity dwells in bodily form and in Him you have been made complete, and He is the head of all rule and authority" (Col. 2:9-10). The first reason is Christ's deity (Col. 2:9). The second reason is the completeness that Christians have in Christ (Col. 2:10). A third reason may appear in the final clause of verse 10: "and He is the head over all rule and authority."[4] This is added due to the complex heresy Paul is combating. Paul assures the Colossians that Christ is head of all rule and authority. T. K. Abbott adds:

> He is the head of all those angelic powers to whose mediation the false teachers would teach you to seek. As they are subordinate to Christ, ye have nothing to expect

---

[3] See Murray J. Harris, *Exegetical Guide to the New Testament: Colossians & Philemon* (Grand Rapids: William B. Eerdmans Publishing Company, 1991), 85-143 for his discussion on this section and reasons for his outline of this portion of the epistle.

[4] This is a relative clause and can be more literally translated "who is" (NKJV).

from them which is not given you in full completeness in Christ.[5]

Christ is the incarnate Son of God and provides everything the Colossians need for their souls.

Verses 11-15 present the means by which completeness in Christ has come.[6] The *first* means occurs in verses 11-12 (see the syntactical and exegetical discussion below). Christians are complete in Christ by means of being "circumcised with a circumcision made without hands." Christ performs this circumcision or it is Christ's circumcision in that it belongs to him as Christian or New Covenant circumcision (see below). The *second* means by which completeness in Christ has come to the Colossians is found in verses 13-15. It is due to what God did to them while they were "dead in [their] transgressions and the uncircumcision of [their] flesh." He made them "alive together with Him," that is, with Christ. This making "alive together with Him" was effected by God the Father. The verb συνεζωοποίησεν ("made you alive together") implies a subject other than the "Him" of σὺν αὐτῷ ("with Him"[i.e., Christ]). Christ, therefore, is not the subject of the verb. This would be a cumbersome tautology indeed. Taking ὁ θεὸς ("God" the Father) as the implied subject does away with the tautology and is supported by the parallel passage in Ephesians 2:4-5.[7]

The Colossians were told that Christ alone was not enough. Paul argues against such anti-Christian teaching by highlighting Christ's deity and the completeness Christians have in him.

---

[5] T. K. Abbott, *A Critical and Exegetical Commentary on the Epistles to the Ephesians and to the Colossians* in *The International Critical Commentary*, eds. S. R. Driver, A. Plummer, and C. A. Briggs (reprint ed., Edinburgh: T & T Clark, 1974), 250.

[6] "Here in 2:11-15 Paul described in more detail the fullness believers have in Christ through salvation." See Sharon Gray, ed., *Translator's Notes on Colossians* (Dallas: Summer Institute of Linguistics, 2001), 61.

[7] Cf. Harris, *Colossians and Philemon*, 106 and J. B. Lightfoot, *Saint Paul's Epistles to the Colossians and Philemon* (New York: Macmillan and Co., Limited, 1897), 183.

An Exegetical Appraisal of Colossians 2:11-12

Syntactical Structure and Exegesis of Colossians 2:11-12

Having set the verses in context, we are now prepared to uncover the relationship and meaning of their parts. As we move through the text, the completeness Christians have in Christ will become clearer.

The meaning and function of ἐν ᾧ καὶ, translated "and in Him" (NASB)

The first question is the meaning and function of the first three words in the Greek text, ἐν ᾧ καὶ, translated "and in Him" (NASB), "In Him …also" (NKJV), and literally "in [or "by"] whom also" (KJV). The "whom" (ᾧ) refers back to Christ in verse 10. Some commentators take this to mean union with Christ.[8] For instance, John Eadie says:

> …the formula ἐν ᾧ has its usual significance – union with Him – union created by the Spirit, and effected by faith; and, secondly, the blessing described in the verse had been already enjoyed, for they were and had been believers in Him in whom they are complete. Through their living union with Christ, they had enjoyed the privilege, and were enjoying the results of a spiritual circumcision.[9]

On the face of it, Eadie's comments seem appropriate. Upon further examination, however, problems arise. Notice that he is arguing that the union under discussion is vital, experiential union with Christ "created by the Spirit, and effected by faith." Commenting further, Eadie adds, "It is plain that the spiritual circumcision is not different from regeneration."[10] Assuming a causal order in Colossians 2:11 (which will become clearer below), Eadie's position would imply that the Spirit creates and faith effects union with

---

[8] Cf. Harris, *Colossians and Philemon*, 101 and John Eadie, *Colossians* (reprint ed., Grand Rapids: Klock & Klock, 1980), 149.
[9] Eadie, *Colossians*, 149.
[10] Eadie, *Colossians*, 151.

Christ, thus, ἐν ᾧ καὶ ("in whom also"), which is then followed by spiritual circumcision or regeneration. Eadie understands union with Christ here in terms of a vital union (i.e., communion) "created by the Spirit, and effected by faith." If this is so, then causally, faith precedes circumcision of the heart or regeneration. Communion with Christ through faith precedes regeneration by the Spirit. As we will see below, in this passage faith comes as a result of spiritual circumcision or regeneration (Col. 2:13; cf., John 3:3-8) and is the means through which believers are personally united to Christ (i.e., vital union and communion).

Can Paul be alluding to union with Christ by ἐν ᾧ καὶ? The answer is yes, but not without crucial qualification. To understand union with Christ in the realm of the application of redemption effected by faith is unnecessary for several reasons. *First*, the idea of faith is not found in the text until the end of verse 12. *Second*, faith itself is a result of the "circumcision made without hands" (see the discussion below). *Third*, the concept of union with Christ is not limited to the application of redemption effected by faith elsewhere in Paul.[11] John Murray says, "It is quite apparent that the Scripture applies the expression 'in Christ' to much more than the application of redemption."[12] Ephesians 1:4, for instance, says that Christians were chosen "in Him before the foundation of the world." This indicates a pre-temporal union with Christ apart from faith and void of communion with Christ. Vital union (i.e., communion with Christ), the type of union experienced in space and time, unites us to Christ in such a way that we experience personally the spiritual benefits of redemption (i.e., justification, adoption, sanctification, and glorification). *Fourth*, assuming a causal sequence in the text and assuming ἐν ᾧ καὶ refers to vital union, we would have an *ordo salutis* as follows: union with Christ by faith then spiritual circumcision (i.e., regeneration). Again, as we shall see, faith that unites one vitally to Christ is a product of the "circumcision made without hands" and proceeds from it, not the other way around.

---

[11] See the discussion by John Murray in *Redemption Accomplished and Applied* (reprint ed., Grand Rapids: Wm B. Eerdmans Publishing Company, 1987), 161-73.

[12] Murray, *Redemption*, 161.

An Exegetical Appraisal of Colossians 2:11-12

It may be better to paraphrase ἐν ᾧ καὶ as "through your relation to Him,"[13] understanding union with Christ here in a nonvital manner. This would allow for a union apart from faith that corresponds with the broader meaning of union with Christ in many other places in Paul.[14] Richard B. Gaffin argues for a "broader, more basic notion of union"[15] in his *Resurrection and Redemption*. He lists three types of union: predestinarian, redemptive-historical, and existential.[16]

There are at least two other ways to understand ἐν ᾧ καὶ. It could be understood like the ἐν αὐτῷ ("in Him") of Colossians 1:17. The ἐν ("in") would function like a dative of sphere. It would be paraphrased as "in the sphere of Christ's activity you were circumcised." Or it could be translated "by whom also." The ἐν ("by") would function like a dative of means or agency. Paul uses ἐν ᾧ 26 times in the Greek text. The NASB translates it "by which" in Romans 7:6; 8:15 ["by whom" NKJV]; 14:21; and Ephesians 4:30. He uses ἐν ᾧ καὶ seven times in the Greek text. Though the NASB does not translate it "by whom also," the NKJV does in 1 Peter 3:19a and Clarence B. Hale suggests this translation for Ephesians 2:22 (i.e., "…by whom you also are being built together…").[17] As a dative of means or agency, it would be translated "by whom also you were circumcised."

The union with Christ in Colossians 2:11 may be understood best either as a union based on election "in Him" (Eph. 1:4) and true of all the elect prior to the personal application of redemption in

---

[13] Harris, *Colossians and Philemon*, 101.

[14] Cf. Murray's discussion noted above.

[15] Richard B. Gaffin, *Resurrection and Redemption: A Study in Paul's Soteriology* (reprint ed., Phillipsburg, NJ: P&R Publishing, 1987), 53. Gaffin relies heavily on John Murray at this point. Cf., John Murray, "Definitive Sanctification" in *Collected Writing of John Murray*, vol. 2, *Selected Lectures in Systematic Theology* (Edinburgh: The Banner of Truth Trust, 1984), 277-84.

[16] Gaffin, *Resurrection*, 57.

[17] Clarence B. Hale, *The Meaning of "In Christ" in the Greek New Testament* (Dallas: Summer Institute of Linguistics, 1991), 32. Hale translates Col. 2:11 "in whom also."

space and time[18] or in one of the last two ways suggested above. Either of these views fits the context of Colossians 2:11ff. and is syntactically and theologically consistent with Paul's usage elsewhere. And either view will allow for the causal relationship between circumcision and union with Christ effected through faith, which is clear in this passage (see the discussion below).

The ἐν ᾧ καὶ refers back to Christ and our being complete in him (v. 10). Verses 11 and 12 go on to describe just how Christians are complete in him. The verb περιετμήθητε ("you were circumcised") indicates a past action in which the Colossians were passive. They were acted upon by an outsider. They did not circumcise themselves. Someone else was the subject, the circumciser, and they were the objects, the recipients of circumcision. The rest of verses 11 and 12 are subordinate to this verb and explanatory of it.

We will now examine the subordinate and explanatory aspects of verses 11 and 12.

The character or nature of "a circumcision made without hands"

The *first* thing Paul tells us about this circumcision is its character or nature. It was περιτομῇ ἀχειροποιήτῳ ("a circumcision made without hands"). It was performed without human hands, unlike the circumcision of the Old Testament and the type being promoted by Judaizers in the first century. John Eadie says, "The circumcision made without hands is plainly opposed to that which is made with hands."[19] It is a spiritual circumcision, a circumcision of the heart, and amply testified by Scripture (cf., Deut. 10:16; 30:6; Jer. 4:4; Ezek. 44:7; Rom. 2:28-29; Phil. 3:3).[20] Harris says, "It is spiritual surgery

---

[18] John Callow acknowledges that union can be understood "outside the categories of time (Eph. 1:4)" though he does not opt for this view. See John Callow, *A Semantic Structure Analysis of Colossians*, ed. Michael F. Kopesec (Dallas: Summer Institute of Linguistics, 1983), 140.

[19] Eadie, *Colossians*, 150.

[20] Eadie, *Colossians*, 149; Harris, *Colossians & Philemon*, 101; and Lightfoot, *Colossians and Philemon*, 181.

An Exegetical Appraisal of Colossians 2:11-12

performed on Christ's followers at the time of their regeneration."[21] The Colossians are complete in Christ due to being circumcised without hands.

The effects of "a circumcision made without hands"

The *second* thing Paul tells us about this "circumcision made without hands" is its effect. This spiritual circumcision was ἐν τῇ ἀπεκδύσει τοῦ σώματος τῆς σαρκός ("in the removal of the body of the flesh").[22] "[T]he body of the flesh" (τοῦ σώματος τῆς σαρκός) is also spiritual. Since the circumcision under discussion is spiritual, then its effect must be spiritual.[23] The preposition ἐν ("in") is best understood epexegetically (NASB). It could be stated as "consisting in the removal of the body of the flesh." It exegetes or explains the "circumcision made without hands." The effect of the spiritual circumcision was a spiritual "removal of the body of the flesh." But what does Paul mean by "the body of the flesh"? The noun ἀπεκδύσει ("removal") has a double prepositional prefix (ἀπο and ἐκ) which intensifies it so that it might be translated "completely off from."[24] The "removal of the body of the flesh" was a radical and spiritual act effected by the "circumcision made without hands." The "body of the flesh" is what is stripped off or radically affected. As noted above, "the flesh" (τῆς σαρκός) is best taken as spiritual. In this case, σαρκός ("flesh") is used in a moral sense. It refers to the sinful natures of the Colossians (cf., Col. 2:18; Rom. 8:5-7; 13:14; and Eph. 2:3 for similar uses). Eadie says, "Flesh is corrupted humanity."[25] The fleshly body (i.e., the entirety of their sinful

---

[21] Harris, *Colossians & Philemon*, 116.

[22] It is of interest to note that the KJV and NKJV include the noun phrase "of the sins" (Gk. τῶν ἁμαρτιῶν) after τοῦ σώματος ("of the body"), reflecting the Greek text underlying those versions.

[23] By "spiritual" I mean, primarily, non-material. I think a good case can be made that "spiritual" for Paul means wrought by the Spirit of God but that discussion is beyond the present one.

[24] Harris, *Colossians & Philemon*, 101.

[25] Eadie, *Colossians*, 150. Cf. John Calvin, *Calvin's Commentaries*, vol. XXI, *Commentaries on the Epistles of Paul the Apostle to the Philippians, Colossians, and Thessalonians* (reprint ed., Grand Rapids: Baker Book House, 1984), 184.

nature) was radically altered by this spiritual circumcision. Abbott adds, "The connection requires it to be understood passively, not 'ye have put off,' but 'was put off from you.'"[26] The sinful souls of the Colossians were radically changed. The body of the flesh was put off from them. This is a description of the radical effects of heart circumcision upon the soul within the complex of the grace of regeneration (cf. Titus 3:5).[27] Discussing regeneration, Murray says:

> There is a change that God effects in man, radical and reconstructive in its nature, called new birth, new creation, regeneration, renewal – a change that cannot be accounted for by anything that is in lower terms than the interposition of the almighty power of God. . . . The governing disposition, the character, the mind and will are renewed and so the person is now able to respond to the call of the gospel and enter into privileges and blessings of the divine vocation.[28]

Regeneration involves both cleansing from sin (Titus 3:5) and new life (John 3:3-8). Paul is saying that the Colossians have experienced regeneration. They were complete in Christ because of the radical alteration of soul effected by the "circumcision made without hands."

The author or owner of "a circumcision made without hands"

The *third* thing Paul tells us about this "circumcision made without hands" is its author or owner. This is indicated by the words ἐν τῇ περιτομῇ τοῦ Χριστοῦ ("by the circumcision of Christ"). This phrase has three possible meanings. The primary issue revolves around the function of the genitive τοῦ Χριστοῦ ("of Christ").

One option takes it as an objective genitive and translates as "the circumcision performed on Christ" or "experienced by Christ."

---

[26] Abbott, *Ephesians and Colossians*, 250.
[27] Cf. Calvin, *Colossians*, 184 and Eadie, *Colossians*, 151.
[28] Murray, *Selected Lectures*, 171.

This would refer either to Christ's physical circumcision or "to his death when he stripped off his physical body."[29] However, Paul has been talking about what has happened *in* and *to* (i.e., *ordo salutis*) the Colossians, not *for* (i.e., *historia salutis*) them.[30] Paul discusses what Christ did *for* the Colossians in verse 13b and 14. Verses 11 and 12 discuss what happens *in* the Colossians and *to* them. Callow says:

> Ingenious though this view is, it seems rather far-fetched to take circumcision as figuratively referring to Christ's death. There is no suggestion of this in such passages as Rom. 2:28f. or Phil. 3:3. And in the nearer context of Col. 2:15, it is not said that Christ put off his body of flesh, but the powers and authorities. Further, in the ethical application of the teaching here which is given in chapter 3, Paul says (3:9) that the Colossians have "put off" the old man with his (evil) deeds, a statement which is very similar to the one used here.[31]

Another option takes the genitive as subjective and translates as "a circumcision effected by Christ." The NIV reads "done by Christ." This makes Christ the circumciser of the Colossians' hearts. The last option sees the genitive as possessive. It is "Christ's circumcision" or "Christian circumcision." It is a circumcision that belongs to Christ.

Either of the last two options fits the context better than the first. The genitive of possession view, of course, does not preclude Christ from performing the circumcision, especially if we translate ἐν ᾧ καὶ (Col. 2:11a) as "by whom also."

---

[29] Harris, *Colossians & Philemon*, 102. This is the view of Peter T. O'Brien in David A. Hubbard and Glenn W. Barker, eds., *Word Biblical Commentary, Volume 44, Colossians, Philemon* (Waco, TX: Word Books, Publisher, 1982), 117-18 and David W. Pao in Clinton E. Arnold, General Editor, *Zondervan Exegetical Commentary on the New Testament, Volume 12, Colossians & Philemon* (Grand Rapids: Zondervan, 2012), 166.

[30] Though it is certainly true that what Christ does to us is based on what Christ did for us.

[31] Callow, *Semantic Structure*, 141.

In Titus 3:5-6, God is said to have "saved us…by the washing of regeneration and renewing by the Holy Spirit whom He poured out upon us richly through Jesus Christ our Lord." Regeneration is by the Holy Spirit and through Jesus Christ and all is connected to the divine trinitarian act in saving us. The Holy Spirit is the effective agent of regeneration; however, he is, nonetheless, the Spirit of Christ and God (i.e., the Father). In the economy of redemption, he convicts of sin and glorifies Christ by bringing the fruits of his redemption to the souls of elect sinners. And he does this as Christ's emissary. The application of redemption is God's act through Christ by the Spirit. Therefore, the genitive of possession option can be viewed in a way that encompasses the subjective genitive contention. It is Christ's circumcision, as opposed to Moses', the fathers', or anyone else's. It is Christian or New Covenant circumcision, because it is under the authority and administration of Christ. He commissions the Holy Spirit to perform it, yet can be viewed as the author. As God uses means to save us, so Christ uses means to circumcise us.

An important observation to make at this point is that Christian circumcision, the circumcision of the heart, is the counterpart to physical circumcision. Harris says:

> . . . v. 11 presents spiritual circumcision, not baptism, as the Christian counterpart to physical circumcision. A contrast is implied between circumcision as an external, physical act performed by human hands on a portion of the flesh eight days after birth and circumcision as an inward, spiritual act carried out by divine agency on the whole fleshly nature at the time of regeneration.[32]

Just as everyone who was physically circumcised under the Abrahamic Covenant became covenant members, so all who are spiritually circumcised become members of the New Covenant. Physical circumcision is replaced by spiritual circumcision under the New Covenant.

---

[32] Harris, *Colossians & Philemon*, 103.

The subsequent, spiritual concomitant or attendant of "a circumcision made without hands"

The *fourth* thing Paul tells us about this "circumcision made without hands" is its subsequent, spiritual concomitant or attendant. We are introduced to verse 12 by an aorist, passive participial clause, συνταφέντες αὐτῷ ἐν τῷ βαπτισμῷ ("having been buried with Him in baptism"). The participle, συνταφέντες ("having been buried"), finds as its antecedent verb περιετμήθητε ("you were circumcised") of verse 11.[33] It indicates a further and subordinate explanation of the "circumcision made without hands." Wallace calls this a dependent, adverbial, temporal participle.[34] He defines this type of participle as follows:

> In relation to its controlling verb, the temporal participle answers the question, *When*? Three kinds of time are in view: antecedent, contemporaneous, and subsequent. The *antecedent* participle should be translated *after doing, after he did*, etc. The *contemporaneous* participle should normally be translated *while doing*. And the subsequent participle should be translated *before doing, before he does*, etc. This usage is common.[35]

The *antecedent* option would translate Colossians 2:12a as "you were circumcised *after* being buried with Him in baptism." This would make the "circumcision made without hands, in the removal of the body of the flesh by the circumcision of Christ" causally dependent upon baptism and, therefore, a result of it. This would argue for post-baptismal (whether water or spiritual baptism) regeneration in the case of the Colossian believers. This seems far-fetched in light of our discussion thus far.

---

[33] Harris, *Colossians & Philemon*, 103.
[34] Daniel B. Wallace, *Greek Grammar Beyond the Basics: An Exegetical Syntax of the New Testament* (Grand Rapids: Zondervan Publishing House, 1996), 622-27.
[35] Wallace, *Greek Grammar*, 623.

The *contemporaneous* option would translate Colossians 2:12a as "you were circumcised *while* being buried with Him in baptism." This would argue either for baptismal regeneration or that burial with Christ in baptism is synonymous with and epexegetical of the circumcision made without hands. This should be discarded for the reasons mentioned in connection with the antecedent option above. As we shall see, aorist participles subordinate to aorist main verbs are not always contemporaneous. Equating circumcision and baptism is not warranted from this text as we have noted and will become more evident as our discussion proceeds.

The *subsequent* option would translate Colossians 2:12a as "you were circumcised *before* being buried with Him in baptism." This view is best for the following reasons. *First*, according to Dana and Mantey, aorist participles subordinate to aorist verbs can express subsequent action.[36] *Second*, the burial referred to in this verse is subsequent to the death of the old man in verse 11, effected by circumcision. Eadie says, "It is plain that the spiritual circumcision is not different from regeneration, or the putting off of the old man and putting on the new."[37] Though Paul does not use the same terminology as Eadie in this text, "the removal of the body of the flesh" effected by the "circumcision made without hands" does transform the old man into a new man, and thus implies the death of the old man (Col. 2:20; Rom. 6:6-7; Titus 3:5). *Third*, this view maintains the death, burial, resurrection motif of other Pauline texts (e.g., Col. 2:12, 20; 3:1, 3; Rom. 6:3-8). *Fourth*, this view comports with the rest of the verse, which sees faith as the means through which resurrection with Christ is effected (see the discussion below). *Fifth*, this view does not get one into the difficulties mentioned above in the other views. This argues for a causal (or logical) relationship between circumcision and burial with Christ in baptism. The burial with him in baptism was brought about causally subsequent to the circumcision. The subsequent, spiritual concomitant or attendant to spiritual circumcision, therefore, is

---

[36] H. E. Dana and Julius R. Mantey, *A Manual Grammar of the Greek New Testament* (New York: Macmillan Publishing Co., Inc., 1955), 230.

[37] Eadie, *Colossians*, 151.

burial with Christ in baptism. Burial with Christ in baptism came to the Colossians causally and logically subsequent to being "circumcised with a circumcision made without hands."

The application of redemption is a complex of interrelated and interdependent divine redemptive acts. Our text has shown this to be the case thus far with the relationship between heart circumcision and burial with Christ. This leads us, however, to another question. What does Paul mean by burial with him in baptism? Lightfoot takes the position that Paul is referring to physical, water baptism.

> Baptism is the grave of the old man, and the birth of the new. As he sinks beneath the baptismal waters, the believer buries there all his corrupt affections and past sins; as he emerges thence, he rises regenerate, quickened to new hopes and a new life.[38]

Commenting on συνταφέντες αὐτῷ ἐν τῷ βαπτισμῷ ("having been buried with Him in baptism"), A. S. Peake says:

> This refers to the personal experience of the Christian. The rite of baptism, in which the person baptized was first buried beneath the water and then raised from it, typified to Paul the burial and resurrection of the believer with Christ.[39]

Peake makes a crucial distinction that is necessitated by the flow of our discussion thus far. He does not equate burial with him in baptism with water baptism, as does Lightfoot. He says, "The rite of baptism [i.e., water baptism], in which the person baptized was first buried beneath the water and then raised from it, *typified* to Paul the burial and resurrection of the believer with Christ [emphasis added]." Lightfoot links regeneration with emerging from

---

[38] Lightfoot, *Colossians and Philemon*, 182.
[39] A. S. Peake, *The Epistle to the Colossians* in *The Expositor's Greek Testament*, vol. 3, ed. W. Robertson Nicoll (reprint ed., Grand Rapids: Wm. B. Eerdmans Publishing Company, 1988), 525.

baptismal waters. Peake says that water baptism *typifies* burial and resurrection with Christ. We have seen that the "circumcision made without hands" is the presupposition of and causal prerequisite to burial with Christ in baptism. On this ground, we must reject Lightfoot's view. The baptism in view here, though typified by water baptism, is not to be equated with it.[40]

Another important and related question also arises at this point. Since the circumcision the Colossians underwent was "without hands," was the burial in baptism they underwent and their being "raised up with Him" also without hands? In other words, is the baptism Paul refers to here water baptism or that which water baptism signifies – burial and resurrection with Christ or union with Christ in his burial and resurrection? From our discussion thus far, it seems obvious that it must be the latter. Paul is not teaching that burial with Christ in *water* baptism was immediately preceded by their "circumcision made without hands." How could he know that? How could he know that they were *water* baptized immediately upon their regeneration? He could not. However, he could know that all who are circumcised of heart are buried with Christ in spiritual baptism and raised with him spiritually, typified by their water baptism, effected through faith (see the discussion below). We must agree with Mark E. Ross, when he says:

> It is important to say at this point that in both verse 11 and verse 12 Paul is not speaking of any physical rite or ceremony. The baptism in view in verse 12 is just as spiritual as the circumcision in verse 11. The physical rite of baptism signifies and seals that believers are raised up with Christ by faith in the working of God, who raised him from the dead, but water baptism in and of itself does not accomplish this.[41]

---

[40] I am not claiming that Peake holds the view I'm advocating. I am using the distinction he makes and may be applying it in a different way than he would have.

[41] Mark E. Ross, "Baptism and Circumcision as Signs and Seals" in Strawbridge, ed., *Infant Baptism*, 103.

An Exegetical Appraisal of Colossians 2:11-12

Paul could know that the Colossians were buried with Christ causally subsequent to their "circumcision made without hands" because he knew that all regenerate persons express faith and are vitally united to Christ in his burial and resurrection. Murray gives eloquent comment to this:

> ...there is an invariable concomitance or co-ordination of regeneration and other fruits of grace. ...As we shall see later, this is a very significant emphasis and warns us against any view of regeneration which abstracts it from the other elements of the application of redemption.[42]

> We must not think of regeneration as something which can be abstracted from the saving exercises which are its effects. ...The regenerate person cannot live in sin and be unconverted.[43]

> There are numerous other considerations derived from the Scripture which confirm this great truth that regeneration is such a radical, pervasive, and efficacious transformation that it *immediately* registers itself in the conscious activity of the person concerned in the exercise of faith and repentance and new obedience [emphasis added].[44]

Paul knew that regeneration was logically and causally prior to faith and is its immediate precondition. He knew that those circumcised of heart expressed faith in the Son of God. This is why he tells the Colossians that, upon being spiritually circumcised, they expressed faith that united them vitally to Christ. This view is further substantiated when we understand the function of the next clause in the text.

---

[42] Murray, *Redemption*, 101.
[43] Murray, *Redemption*, 104.
[44] Murray, *Redemption*, 104-05. Murray's comments come after discussing John 3 and 1 John concerning regeneration and its effects.

The next issue is what to make of the ἐν ᾧ καὶ clause, translated "in which you...also ..." (NASB) of verse 12. Is it to be viewed as a second, parallel clause with the one in verse 11? If so, the Colossians' completeness in Christ is argued first from their "circumcision made without hands" and second from their being "raised up with Him." This view seems strained for several reasons. *First*, a general rule of Greek syntax is that clauses and phrases modify the nearest antecedent they can, unless there is good reason in the text to go further afield. There is no compelling reason to go further than the immediate antecedent ἐν τῷ βαπτισμῷ ("in baptism"). While some argue that the ἐν ᾧ καὶ clause of verse 12 is grammatically parallel with the ἐν ᾧ καὶ clause of v. 11[45] (that's the only apparently substantial argument for this view), grammatical (formal) parallels are not necessarily syntactical (functional) parallels. A *second* reason why this view is strained is because the ἐν ᾧ καὶ clause of verse 12 continues with language normally connected to what precedes it. Paul continues, ἐν ᾧ καὶ συνηγέρθητε ("in which you were also raised up with Him"). Paul is completing his thought begun in the beginning of the verse. The fact that Paul often speaks of burial, baptism, and resurrection with Christ together leans us in the direction that this clause is subordinate to ἐν τῷ βαπτισμῷ ("in baptism"). Just as the Colossians were buried with Christ in baptism, so they were raised with him in baptism.[46]

The rest of verse 12, then, is subordinate to τῷ βαπτισμῷ ("baptism"). Paul says that in spiritual baptism συνηγέρθητε διὰ τῆς πίστεως ("you were also raised up with Him through faith"). The prepositional phrase διὰ τῆς πίστεως ("through faith") indicates the means through which the Colossians were raised with Christ. Meyer says:

> Paul is describing the *subjective medium*, without which the joint awakening, though objectively and historically accomplished in the resurrection of Christ, would not be

---

[45] Abbott, *Ephesians and Colossians*, 251. This is H. A. W. Meyer's view, according to Abbot.

[46] Abbott, *Ephesians and Colossians*, 251.

An Exegetical Appraisal of Colossians 2:11-12

appropriated individually... The unbeliever has not the blessing of having risen with Christ, because he stands apart from the fellowship of life with Christ, just as also he has not the reconciliation, although the reconciliation of all has been accomplished objectively through Christ's death.[47]

Clearly, the faith here is that expressed by the Colossians. This is the first mention of human response in the text and this response comes as a result of being circumcised "without hands." Those who already possess the circumcision "made without hands" experience this complex of spiritual events, being buried and raised with Christ in baptism through faith. This is another reason why Paul cannot be speaking exclusively of water baptism in the text. Many who are water baptized do not have faith. But the ones described here exercised faith as a means or instrument through which they were united to Christ in his burial and resurrection. Commenting on Ephesians 2:5ff and Colossians 2:12, Gaffin says, "being raised with Christ is an experience with which faith is associated in an instrumental fashion."[48] Being raised with Christ, as with being buried with him, is causally dependent upon being "circumcised with a circumcision made without hands." As the Colossians' circumcision was without hands, so was their burial and rising with Christ.

The final words of verse 12 are subordinate to διὰ τῆς πίστεως ("through faith"). There are two ways to understand the words τῆς ἐνεργείας τοῦ θεοῦ ("in the working of God"). The question concerns the function of the genitive τοῦ θεοῦ ("of God"). Either it is subjective or objective. If subjective, then Paul is saying that their faith is the effect of God's working in them. God gave them faith. God worked faith in them. If objective, then their faith was in the power exercised by God in the resurrection of Christ. The working of God's power in the resurrection of Christ, according to this view,

---

[47] Heinrich August Wilhelm Meyer, *Critical and Exegetical Hand-Book to the Epistles to the Philippians and Colossians, and to Philemon* (reprint ed., Peabody, MA: Hendrickson Publishers, Inc., 1983), 301.

[48] Gaffin, *Resurrection*, 129.

is the object of their faith. The final participial clause of verse 12, τοῦ ἐγείραντος αὐτὸν ἐκ νεκρῶν ("who raised Him from the dead"), is subordinate to τοῦ θεοῦ ("of God"). God is the one who raised Christ from the dead by his power. Though it is certainly true that faith is the effect of God's working in the soul, it is best to understand τῆς ἐνεργείας τοῦ θεοῦ ("in the working of God") here as objective, as the thing believed or the content of their faith. One reason for taking this view is that "the genitive after πίστις ["faith"], when not that of the person, is always that of the object."[49] Also, elsewhere Paul makes the resurrection of Christ effected by God the object of saving faith (cf., Rom. 10:9).

Christians are complete in Christ because they have received a circumcision made without hands – regeneration. Regeneration produces faith that vitally unites souls to Christ in the efficacy of his burial and resurrection. This vital union with Christ in burial and resurrection is a spiritual baptism. Vital union brings believing sinners into the orbit of redemptive privilege and power. Every sinner circumcised in heart expresses saving faith in God's power in raising Christ from the dead. Burial and resurrection with Christ in baptism cannot be abstracted from its causal prerequisite – regeneration. If one has been buried and raised with Christ in baptism, it is only because one has been circumcised "without hands." The result of regeneration, faith, is the instrumental cause of union with Christ. And the union with Christ of Colossians 2:12 ushers the believer experientially into the complex of redemptive privileges purchased by the Lord Jesus Christ for the elect. In other words, this is the experience of all believers, though not of all those water baptized. All of this may be typified by water baptism, though it is not effected by it. Christians are complete in Christ because of regeneration and its effects in the soul.

---

[49] Abbott, *Ephesians and Colossians*, 252. Cf., Eadie, *Colossians*, 156; Harris, *Colossians & Philemon*, 105; Lightfoot, *Colossians and Philemon*, 183; Peake, *Colossians*, 526.

An Exegetical Appraisal of Colossians 2:11-12

Colossians 2:11-12 in *The Case For Covenantal Infant Baptism*

The Scripture index to *The Case For Covenantal Infant Baptism* contains 17 entries for Colossians 2:11-12. Space does not permit us to discuss every entry. However, we will examine a few of the uses in light of the exposition above.

Mark Ross

Mark Ross, in his chapter "Baptism and Circumcision as Signs and Seals," says:

> It is imperative that we look more closely at this verse in the Greek text. Colossians 2:12 is a continuation of verse 11, which itself is a continuation of the sentence begun in verse 9. Verse 12 is a series of participial phrases, all of which are related to the main verb in verse 11, "you were circumcised." Thus, in verse 12 Paul is explaining more fully just how it is that the Colossians have been circumcised in this circumcision made without hands. They were circumcised, "having been buried with [Christ] in baptism." Thus, verse 12 explains how the Colossians were "circumcised."[50]

Colossians 2:12 in fact contains only two participles. The first, συνταφέντες ("having been buried with"), is the first word of the verse and is immediately subordinate to the main verb περιετμήθητε ("you were circumcised"). The second is τοῦ ἐγείραντος ("who raised [Him from the dead]") and is immediately subordinate to τοῦ θεοῦ ("of God"). Though it is remotely related to the main verb, it is not in an immediate, adverbial relationship to it. Ross' statement makes it appear so but it is not. He oversimplifies the syntax. Further, he claims that the participle συνταφέντες ("having been buried with") begins Paul's explanation of "how the Colossians were 'circumcised.'" However, we have seen that Paul already explained

---

[50] Ross, "Baptism and Circumcision as Signs and Seals," 102.

how the Colossians were circumcised before he gets to verse 12. They were "circumcised with a circumcision made without hands, in the removal of the body of the flesh by the circumcision of Christ" (v. 11). Verse 12 reveals to us the subsequent, spiritual concomitant of their circumcision, not "how the Colossians were 'circumcised.'" It tells us *when* the Colossians were buried and raised with Christ in baptism – i.e., after they were circumcised.

On the next page, Ross says, "The baptism of Colossians 2:12 can only be the reality of the Spirit's working to regenerate the heart and free the soul from the dominion of sin."[51] But, as we have seen, verse 12 speaks of a spiritual, vital union with Christ effected through faith. This presupposes regeneration (v. 11). If both verses are describing regeneration, then Paul could be paraphrased as saying, "You were regenerated when you were regenerated." This would certainly be a cumbersome tautology and does not respect the syntax of the text. The Bible uses other words and phrases to describe regeneration that Paul could have used here (e.g., born from above). However, it is clear from the exposition above that Paul is not speaking about regeneration in verse 12. He is speaking about the fruit of regeneration – union with Christ in burial and resurrection, effected through faith.

Cornelis Venema

Cornelis Venema, in his chapter "Covenant Theology and Baptism," says:

> ...it is not surprising to find the apostle Paul treating baptism as the new covenant counterpart to circumcision (Col. 2:11-13). ...Baptism now represents the spiritual circumcision "made without hands, in the removal of the body of the flesh" (Col. 2:11).[52]

---

[51] Ross, "Baptism and Circumcision as Signs and Seals," 103.
[52] Cornelis P. Venema, "Covenant Theology and Baptism" in Strawbridge, ed., *Infant Baptism*, 222.

An Exegetical Appraisal of Colossians 2:11-12

Venema offers no exegesis, only assertions. Our exegesis above has made it clear that Colossians 2:11-12 does not warrant such statements. The New Covenant counterpart to physical circumcision is spiritual circumcision. Venema's claim, in essence, is that water baptism represents or signifies regeneration according to this text. The baptism of Colossians 2:12, however, is spiritual baptism that represents vital union with Christ. Regeneration is presupposed and effects burial and resurrection with Christ in baptism through faith. Venema is assuming that baptism has replaced circumcision by this statement. Our exegesis has shown this to be an unwarranted implication of the text.

Joel R. Beeke and Ray Lanning

In a context discussing the household baptisms of the New Testament, Joel Beeke and Ray Lanning say:

> Similarly, children of believing parents are addressed as members of churches at Ephesus (Eph. 6:1-4) and Colossae (Col. 3:20). These children were also baptized, as Paul affirms in Colossians 2:11-12, where he calls baptism "the circumcision of Christ."[53]

This appears to claim that Paul is speaking of water baptism in Colossians 2:11-12. If this is what the authors are claiming, it contradicts what we have seen Ross claim later in the book, where he says:

> It is important to say at this point that in both verse 11 and verse 12 Paul is not speaking of any physical rite or ceremony. The baptism in view in verse 12 is just as spiritual as the circumcision in verse 11.[54]

---

[53] Beeke and Lanning, "Unto You, and to Your Children," 52.

[54] Ross, "Baptism and Circumcision as Signs and Seals," 103. These kinds of seemingly contradictory statements in books by multiple authors are somewhat typical of such works. I acknowledged this in the Preface.

Also, we have already seen that all who are spiritually circumcised are spiritually buried and raised with Christ, effected through faith. Beeke and Lanning's statement would then imply that all the children Paul was addressing were also regenerate. But, of course, they do not advocate that. The main problem with their statement (not to mention their use of the word "affirms") comes in its final sentence. "These children were also baptized, as Paul affirms in Colossians 2:11-12, where he calls baptism 'the circumcision of Christ.'" They equate circumcision with baptism. But, as we have seen clearly, Paul does not do this.

Pertinent Conclusions

Baptism does not replace circumcision as the sign and seal of the covenant of grace. We have seen clearly that spiritual circumcision, not baptism, replaces (better, fulfills) physical circumcision. Baptism in Colossians 2:12 (i.e., vital union with Christ) is a result of spiritual circumcision (i.e., regeneration). Burial and resurrection with Christ is not equivalent to but causally subsequent to spiritual circumcision. Physical circumcision has been replaced or fulfilled by spiritual circumcision under the New Covenant. The correspondence between the two, however, is not one-to-one. Paul tells us this by saying that New Covenant circumcision is "a circumcision made without hands." Though physical circumcision and spiritual circumcision are related they are not equivalent. One is physical and does not affect the heart; the other is spiritual and does not affect the body (at least not initially). Both are indications of covenant membership, though not necessarily of the same covenant. But only the circumcision of the heart guarantees one's eternal destiny, for all the regenerate express faith and "are protected by the power of God through faith" (1 Pet. 1:5).

We must take issue with those who argue from this text that baptism replaces circumcision. The Lutheran scholar Eduard Lohse asserts:

> Baptism is called circumcision here… The circumcision of Christ which every member of the community has

experienced is nothing other than being baptized into the death and resurrection of Christ.[55]

We have seen, however, that the only "replacement" motif in this text is between physical circumcision and spiritual circumcision. Spiritual circumcision is not equivalent to baptism. Baptism (i.e., union with Christ) is the sphere in which burial and resurrection with Christ occurs, which is effected through faith, and a result of spiritual circumcision.

The Reformed commentator William Hendriksen says:

> Evidently Paul in this entire paragraph magnifies Christian baptism as much as he, by clear implication, disapproves of the continuation of the rite of circumcision if viewed as having anything to do with salvation. The definite implication, therefore, is that *baptism has taken the place of circumcision*. Hence, what is said with reference to circumcision in Rom. 4:11, as being a sign and a seal, holds also for baptism. In the Colossian context baptism is specifically a sign and seal of having been buried with Christ and of having been raised with him [emphasis Hendriksen's].[56]

We take issue with Hendriksen's view on several fronts. *First*, Paul is not magnifying Christian baptism in this text. He is magnifying Christian circumcision. This is evident by the fact that "you were also circumcised" is the regulating verb to which the rest of verses 11 and 12 are subordinate. *Second*, there is not a "definite implication …that *baptism has taken the place of circumcision*." Our exegesis has shown this to us clearly. *Third*, it is not true that "what is said with reference to circumcision in Rom. 4:11, as being a sign and a seal, holds also for baptism." This is so because Paul is not

---

[55] Eduard Lohse, *Colossians and Philemon* (Philadelphia: Fortress Press, 1971), 101-02.

[56] William Hendriksen, *New Testament Commentary: Galatians, Ephesians, Philippians, Colossians and Philemon* (reprint ed., Grand Rapids: Baker Books, 1995), 116.

arguing for a replacement theology between physical circumcision and water baptism and because the seal of the New Covenant is the Holy Spirit (Eph. 1:13; 4:30). *Fourth*, Paul says nothing in Colossians 2:11-12 about baptism being "a sign and seal of having been buried with Christ and of having been raised with him." He does say, though in other words, that the subsequent, spiritual concomitant of spiritual circumcision is spiritual burial and resurrection with Christ in baptism effected through faith. There is no hint of baptism being a sign and seal as argued by Hendriksen. It is of interest to note one of Hendriksen's footnotes to these statements. Notice the concession he makes.

> I am speaking here about a clear *implication*. The surface contrast is that between *literal* circumcision and *circumcision without hands*, namely, the circumcision of the heart, as explained. But the implication also is clear. Hence, the following statement is correct: "Since, then, baptism has come in the place of circumcision (Col. 2:11-13), the children should be baptized as heirs of the kingdom of God and of his covenant" (*Form for the Baptism of Infants* in *Psalter Hymnal of the Christian Reformed Church*, Grand Rapids, Mich., 1959, p. 86). When God made his covenant with Abraham the children were included (Gen. 17:1-14). This covenant, in its spiritual aspects, was continued in the present dispensation (Acts 2:38, 29; Rom. 4:9-12; Gal. 3:7, 8, 29). Therefore the children are still included and should still receive the sign, which in the present dispensation, as Paul makes clear in Col. 2:11, 12, is baptism [emphases Hendriksen's].[57]

Hendriksen's concession that "The surface contrast is that between *literal* circumcision and *circumcision without hands*" surely sheds doubt over his initial claim of "speaking here about a clear *implication*." Again, we have seen that Paul is not arguing that water

---

[57] Hendriksen, *Galatians, Ephesians, Philippians, Colossians and Philemon*, 116, n. 86.

An Exegetical Appraisal of Colossians 2:11-12

baptism replaces physical circumcision as a sign and seal of the covenant. It does not follow, then, that "the children should be baptized as heirs of the kingdom of God and of his covenant." Paul does not say or imply that the sign and seal of the covenant is baptism. If there is a sign of the covenant in this text it is regeneration. All who are spiritually circumcised are buried and raised with Christ in baptism, effected through faith. Colossians 2:11-12 is about the application of redemption to elect souls and does not imply infant baptism. If it implies anything about water baptism, it implies that it ought to be administered to those who have been circumcised of heart and vitally united to Christ through faith as a sign of these spiritual blessings.

All who are circumcised of heart are buried and raised with Christ through faith logically subsequent to their heart circumcision. Regeneration cannot be abstracted from its immediate fruits. All regenerate souls are united to Christ through faith. This is what Colossians 2:11-12 clearly teaches. Our exegesis argues for an *ordo salutis* as follows: regeneration, then union with Christ through faith. And this experience is that of all the regenerate and has nothing to do with the act of water baptism in itself.

This text neither teaches baptismal regeneration nor implies infant baptism. In context, it is displaying the completeness *believers* have in Christ. It does not apply to unbelievers or to all who are baptized by any mode and/or by properly recognized ecclesiastical administrators. It has to do with the spiritual realities that come to souls who are Christ's sheep. It has to do with the application of redemption to elect sinners. It has to do with regeneration, faith, and experiential union with Christ. These are the aspects of completeness in Christ Paul highlights here. We should gain much encouragement from these things. They were revealed to fortify believers against error. They were written to strengthen saints, those already in Christ. They were not revealed as proof for the subjects of baptism. They were not revealed to teach us that water baptism replaces physical circumcision as the sign and seal of the covenant of grace. God gave us Colossians 2:11-12 to display this fact: when you have Christ, you have all you need.

An Exegetical Appraisal of Colossians 2:11-12

CHAPTER 16
Reformed Baptist Covenant Theology and Biblical Theology
Micah and Samuel Renihan*

This material, in a slightly different form, was originally presented by the authors during their senior year at Westminster Seminary California. It was delivered to students during a lunch hour on campus in response to inquiries about how Reformed Baptists view covenant theology. Given the time constraints of a one-hour presentation, the focus of the material was on areas of positive argument for the credobaptist position where it differs from paedobaptism. Key points of covenant theology are absent from this presentation, not because they do not form a part of Reformed Baptist covenant theology, but because there is no disagreement between our position and that of the paedobaptists. For example, there is no discussion of the covenant of works, fully affirmed by the Second London and Westminster confessions, and there is no discussion of the definition of a covenant since we agree with the basic definition formulated by Meredith G. Kline: a commitment with divine sanctions between a lord and a servant.[1] Other arguments and significant points were omitted for the sake of time, such as the relation between kingdom and covenant or exegetical discussions of specific key passages around which this dialogue normally revolves. What follows are foundational assertions arguing for a Reformed Baptist view of covenant theology and biblical theology, applied specifically to credobaptism.

---

* Micah Renihan (M.Div., Westminster Seminary California) is a pastor at Grace Reformed Baptist Church, Brunswick, ME. Samuel Renihan (M.Div., Westminster Seminary California) is a pastor at Trinity Reformed Baptist Church, La Mirada, CA, and a doctoral candidate at the Free University of Amsterdam. Scripture references are taken from the ESV.

[1] Meredith G. Kline, *Kingdom Prologue Genesis Foundations for a Covenantal Worldview* (Overland Park, KS: Two Ages Press, 2000), 1-7.

Foundations of Reformed Baptist Covenant Theology

The covenant of redemption informs and unites all of redemptive history.

The *pactum salutis*[2] establishes the redemption of the elect through Christ's incarnation, life, death, resurrection, and ascension as that which is the driving purpose of history. God's decree is that from fallen humanity, the Son, empowered by the Spirit, should redeem the people given to him by the Father as a reward.

The New Covenant is the final and full accomplishment of the covenant of redemption in history.

Where do we see the accomplishment of the redemption of the elect in history through the incarnation and death of Christ? It is in the New Covenant, made in the blood of Christ.[3] What is it that Christ claims that he has come to do? He claims that he has come to redeem those whom the Father has given to him.[4] His purpose is to accomplish the *pactum salutis* in time and history. The New Covenant goes no further than the *pactum salutis*, not only because Christ specifically said that his mission was purely to redeem the elect, but also because the New Covenant is made in Christ's blood, redeeming blood whose salvific merit is determined by the *pactum salutis* and whose benefits have never been and never will be applied to any but the elect. This means that the parties of the New Covenant are none other than God and Christ, and the elect in him.

Although the *pactum salutis* has been finally and fully accomplished in history through Christ's work, what remains is entrance into the consummated blessings and rewards of Christ's kingdom. That will not occur until every last elect person for whom

---

[2] "**pactum salutis:** *covenant of redemption;* in Reformed federalism, the pretemporal, intratrinitarian agreement of the Father and the Son concerning the covenant of grace and its ramifications in and through the work of the Son incarnate." Cf. Muller, *Dictionary*, 217.

[3] Cf. Heb. 7:20-22.

[4] Cf. John 6:38-40; 10:14-16, 26-28; 17:6-11, 17-21.

Christ died has been gathered in by Christ himself through the preaching of the gospel to all nations.

The covenant of grace is the in-breaking of the covenant of redemption into history through the progressive revelation and retroactive application of the New Covenant.

Herman Bavinck says:

> The covenant of grace was not first established in time, but has its foundation in eternity, is grounded in the pact of salvation, and is in the first place a covenant among the three persons of the divine being itself.[5]

Geerhardus Vos says:

> The covenant of redemption is the pattern for the covenant of grace. However, it is more than that. It is also the effective cause for carrying out the latter. As far as its offer and application are concerned, the covenant of grace lies enclosed in the counsel of peace, so that with respect to the latter it appears completely as a gift, as a covenantal benefit.[6]

There is one uniting and driving force in redemptive history, and that is the covenant of redemption. Although it is not accomplished in history until Christ comes, we see the gathering in of the elect who believe in Christ from the fall onward. Where we see that in-gathering of the elect who believe in the gospel as it is revealed progressively in types and shadows, there we see the retroactive New Covenant, and that is the covenant of grace. What has been required of all men at all times in all places is to believe the gospel however it has been revealed in a particular moment of

---

[5] Herman Bavinck, *Reformed Dogmatics Vol. III* (Grand Rapids: Baker, 2006), 405.

[6] Geerhardus Vos, *Redemptive History and Biblical Interpretation* (Phillipsburg, NJ: P&R Publishing, 2001), 252.

redemptive history.[7] Because the covenant of grace is nothing other than the retroactive New Covenant, founded on the covenant of redemption, its parties have already been defined: Christ, and the elect in him. Vos says:

> In other words, the bond that links the Old and New Covenants together is not a purely evolutionary one, inasmuch as the one has grown out of the other; it is, if we may so call it, a transcendental bond: the New Covenant in its preexistent, heavenly state reaches back and stretches its wings over the Old, and the Old Testament people of God were one with us in religious dignity and privilege; they were, to speak in a Pauline figure, sons of the Jerusalem above, which is the mother of all.[8]

Bavinck says:

> This pact of salvation, however, further forms the link between the eternal work of God toward salvation and what he does to that end in time. The covenant of grace revealed in time does not hang in the air but rests on an eternal, unchanging foundation. It is firmly grounded in the counsel and covenant of the triune God and is the application and execution of it that infallibly follows…It is a false perception that God first made his covenant with Adam and Noah, with Abraham and Israel, and only finally with Christ; the covenant of grace was ready-made from all eternity in the pact of salvation of the three persons and was realized by Christ from the moment the fall occurred…For though God communicates his revelation successively and historically makes it progressively richer and fuller, and humankind therefore advances in the knowledge, possession, and enjoyment of that revelation, God is and remains the same….Although Christ completed his work on earth only in

---

[7] Cf. Heb. 4:2; Gal. 3:8-9; 1 Pet. 1:10-11; Eph. 3:4-6, 8-12.
[8] Vos, *Redemptive History*, 199.

the midst of history and although the Holy Spirit was not poured out till the day of Pentecost, God nevertheless was able, already in the days of the Old Testament, to fully distribute the benefits to be acquired and applied by the Son and the Spirit. Old Testament believers were saved in no other way than we. There is one faith, one Mediator, one way of salvation, and one covenant of grace.[9]

The Old Covenant is coextensive with and collectively representative of theocratic Israel, defined by the Abrahamic, conditioned by the Mosaic, and focused by the Davidic Covenants. The Old Covenant, and thus each of these three covenants, differs from the New Covenant not merely in administration, but also in substance.

The Abrahamic Covenant, called the covenant of circumcision by Stephen in Acts 7:8, promised Abraham three things primarily. It promised him a land, a people, and a kingship. In other words, Abraham's physical descendants would inherit the land and grow into an innumerable people ruled by their own kings. This was called the covenant of circumcision because circumcision was the sign of these blessings and separated Abraham's offspring from the rest of the world as the heirs of these promises.[10]

Abraham was the federal head of this covenant because the promises were made to him and to his physical seed. All those who were of Abraham, or in Abraham we might say, were heirs of the national promises. This defined the membership of the covenant.

One of the most interesting features of this covenant was that while God promised to bring about the fulfillment of his promises irrespective of merit on Abraham's part, he likewise required Abraham and all those under his federal headship to keep the covenant through circumcision. Those who were disloyal or disobedient would be cut off (Gen. 17:14). So, while God

---

[9] Bavinck, *Reformed Dogmatics Vol. III*, 215-16.
[10] This is not to say that circumcision had no further significance, but that the national promises were its primary referent.

guaranteed that the promises would be fulfilled collectively to Abraham and his offspring, the tenure of individuals or families in those blessings depended on their faithfulness to the dictates of the covenant. Considered from this perspective, can the covenant of circumcision rightly be called an administration of the covenant of grace? If the covenant of grace is the accomplishing of the covenant of redemption in history, the retroactive application of the New Covenant, then the distinction between national Israelite promises via Abraham and new creation promises via Christ should be clear. We can state confidently that although all the Abrahamic promises typologically reveal the New Covenant, in their substance and essence they are distinct from it. Abraham knew that Canaan was not heaven.

The Mosaic Covenant was added and attached to the Abrahamic Covenant in such a way that it further conditioned the enjoyment of the Abrahamic blessings. God immutably promised Abraham that the covenant blessings would be realized. The extent to which those blessings would be enjoyed, however, depended upon the obedience of the people of Israel. To put it simply, in the Abrahamic Covenant, God promised Abraham a land, nation, and kingship, and in the Mosaic Covenant God said "If you're going to be My people, this is how you must live." These conditions were strong enough that although God would inevitably realize the promises, they could be lost through disobedience. That the Mosaic Covenant conditions the Abrahamic Covenant is evident not only by virtue of the fact that its obedience is directly tied to the enjoyment of the Abrahamic promises, but also by virtue of the fact that it was made specifically with the Abrahamic people.

That the Mosaic Covenant is not one in essence and substance with the covenant of grace is further recognized by the fact that, as Hebrews tells us, the sacrifices had no power to remove sin. "The law has but a shadow of the good things to come instead of the true form of these realities" (Heb. 10:1). Hebrews 8:5 calls the Mosaic system a "copy and shadow of the heavenly things." Paul, speaking in Colossians of Mosaic rites such as new moons, festivals, and Sabbaths, says that "These are a shadow of the things to come, but the substance belongs to Christ" (Col. 2:17). Continuing the same argument that was applied to the Abrahamic Covenant, the conditioning of national promises by law is not the accomplishing of the redemption of the elect in history by the blood of Christ. Hence, the Mosaic Covenant is separate from the covenant of grace in its essence. However, every single element of the Mosaic economy typologically revealed and set before the eyes of the Jews the covenant of grace wherein true righteousness, true forgiveness of sins, and true holiness could be found. Since tenure in the land was what was in view in the Mosaic law, offenses against that covenant could be addressed within that covenant and sacrificial system. But concerning true spiritual realities, concerning offenses committed against a Holy God, the sacrifices could do nothing but point ahead to that one true sacrifice, Jesus Christ.

Even until today, many have wrestled with how it could be that the covenant of grace was being administered by a strict works principle. This difficulty is simply and rightly avoided when one recognizes that the Mosaic Covenant is not an administration of *the* covenant of grace, but rather typologically reveals it in its law and worship. The Mosaic Covenant is then free to be affirmed as a graciously administered works principle, controlling the extent to which the Abrahamic blessings are enjoyed. "The one who does them shall live by them" (Gal. 3:12).

The Mosaic Covenant lacked a federal head until the kingship was established. The Abrahamic people as a whole were judged on different levels, sometimes the individual, sometimes the family, sometimes the tribe, sometimes the nation. Everyone did what was right in his own eyes, and there was no king in Israel.

The Davidic Covenant brings all of the Abrahamic promises to consummation and focuses the Mosaic Covenant into one person. It was under the line of David, specifically Solomon, that at last the nation of Israel reached the fulfillment of being the Abrahamic people ruling all of the Abrahamic land, under Abrahamic, specifically Judean, kings. The biblical authors are careful to record when these promises are fulfilled (Josh. 21:43-45 and 1 Kings 4:20). Under David and his line, the national people of Abraham enjoyed the blessings and benefits of the Promised Land to the extent to which the Davidic king obeyed the Mosaic law. This is the concern of the records of the kings. They did what was right in the eyes of the Lord, or they did what was evil. Israel was blessed or cursed accordingly.

Because the Mosaic Covenant controls both the Abrahamic and the Davidic Covenants, it is the primary referent of the New Testament when speaking about the Old Covenant. However, the Mosaic Covenant cannot be divided or disconnected from the Abrahamic and Davidic Covenants, and thus all three combine to form the Old Covenant, in every aspect typological of the covenant of grace, yet in every aspect different in substance from the covenant of grace.

The Old Covenant is related to the New Covenant historically and typologically.

Is the Old Covenant entirely unrelated to the covenant of grace? Have we utterly divested the Old Covenant of its theological richness and significance? No, we are merely making careful distinctions. There is historical and typological unity between the Old and the New.

There is historical unity in that Abraham was also promised that the nations would be blessed through him. Israel was designated the mother of the Messiah, the guardian of the gospel in its shadowy forms. The birth of Christ was a fulfillment of the Abrahamic Covenant.[11] Israel's disobedience to the law of Moses could not prevent this immutable promise of God from coming to pass.

There is typological unity in that every single part of the Old Covenant, that is, every single part of the Abrahamic, Mosaic, and Davidic Covenants, typologically revealed the New Covenant, whether through what was lacking or what was being commended. This allows us to affirm heartily every single aspect of a redemptive-historical hermeneutic and approach to preaching. Christ is everywhere, the gospel is everywhere, the covenant of grace is everywhere, because it is God's driving and uniting

---

[11] Luke 1:55, 73.

purpose to gather the elect in history. But Abraham's people in Canaan are not the gospel, nor are they the covenant of grace. They reveal it, they progress history toward it, and those who looked past the types to the reality participated in it, but the type is not the antitype.

Therefore, the Abrahamic, Mosaic, and Davidic Covenants were national, temporary, and typological covenants that placed Israel in an external relationship with God and in which the New Covenant was revealed through types and shadows. On the one hand they are, in their substance and essence, distinct from the covenant of grace, and on the other hand they are related to it through rich typology and historical progression.

Kline says:

> When Paul, in Romans 9-11, defends God's covenantal faithfulness in the face of Israel's fall, he bases his case on the identification of the promised seed as the individual election, a remnant-fullness of Jews and Gentiles, spiritual children of Abraham, all like him justified by faith. The apostle finds within the Lord's revelation of the promises to Abraham explicit warrant for distinguishing this spiritual seed of Abraham from the physical offspring. What is remarkable is how he bypasses the more literal first level significance of Abraham's seed and takes for granted the second, spiritual level of meaning as *the* meaning of the promise.[12]

What are these two levels? They are the physical offspring and the spiritual offspring of Abraham, the first being a "provisional and prototypal" people, and the other being a "messianic and eternal" people.[13] Where do they come from? The two circles of the internal and external distinction are the result of two different covenants. As was shown by Vos previously, the paradigm for the

---

[12] Kline, *Kingdom Prologue*, 335, emphasis his. Kline makes the same point with regard to Gal. 3:16.

[13] Kline, *Kingdom Prologue*, 334.

covenant of grace is not the Abrahamic Covenant, but the covenant of redemption. We are not arguing that the unregenerate have never been or can never be in a covenantal relationship with God. Rather, we are arguing that the covenant of grace has always been an internal covenantal relationship with God through Christ, while the national covenants were an external covenantal relationship with God through Abraham.

In Galatians 4, Paul distinguishes between two covenants, Jerusalem above and Jerusalem below, contrasting them as being born according to the flesh and according to the Spirit. One is clearly a physical covenant; the other is clearly spiritual. Paul is contrasting the difference between Old Covenant Israel and New Covenant Israel. The difference is the Spirit and the flesh, the external and the internal, the law and the gospel, *and they are two different covenants*.

Furthermore, Paul's distinction is not purely between the Abrahamic and Mosaic Covenants, because as Kline has pointed out, when Paul speaks of the Abrahamic promises he is deliberately ignoring the national Abrahamic promises and looking at the Messianic promises. We are asserting that those Messianic promises point to the Messianic Covenant, that is the New Covenant, the covenant of grace, and that as such they point to a covenant distinct from the covenant of circumcision with Abraham and his natural offspring. This means that not only has that typical, external covenantal relationship been abrogated and passed away, but also that the Messianic and eternal relationship was always active, embedded within that external covenant. The internal and external circles, visible in the Old Testament, are not the result of two levels of covenantal membership, but are the result of two different covenants, the covenant of circumcision and the covenant of grace.

With the triangular shape of typology in mind,[14] using the type (Abrahamic, Old Covenant Israel) to shape the antitype (covenant of grace, New Covenant Israel), not only reverses the progress of redemptive history, but also fails to understand the New Covenant

---

[14] See Vos, *The Teaching of the Epistle to the Hebrews* (Grand Rapids: Eerdmans, 1965), 55-65.

antype as it is founded in the archtype (i.e., the covenant of redemption).

Covenant of Redemption (Archtype)

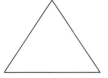

Old Covenant (Type)   New Covenant (Antitype)

To be in a covenant, you must be united to the federal head of that covenant. Federal headship is immediate in every covenant.

Nehemiah Coxe says:

> This is also worthy to be noted by us: that when God has made covenants, in which either mankind in general or some elect number of men in particular have been involved, it has pleased him first to transact with some public person, head, or representative for all others that should be involved in them.[15]

He adds:

> The right of the remotest generation was as much derived from Abraham and the covenant made with him, as was that of his immediate seed, and did not at all depend on the faithfulness of their immediate parents. Thus, the immediate seed of those Israelites that fell in the wilderness under the displeasure of God were made to inherit the land of Canaan by virtue of this covenant with Abraham. They never could

---

[15] Coxe and Owen, *Covenant Theology*, 39.

have enjoyed it by virtue of their immediate parent's steadfastness in the covenant.[16]

Because covenant membership and covenant blessings depend on the federal head, immediately, every member of every covenant, according to the terms of a given covenant, is entitled to every blessing or curse incurred by the federal head. Every human being stands on equal ground in the covenant of works because they are Adam's offspring, no matter how far removed. Each human being is directly and immediately federally united to Adam. We are in Adam, not because of our parents, but because of our direct federal relation to Adam. The same principle applies with Christ as federal head of the covenant of grace.

Jesus Christ has been and always will be the federal head of the covenant of grace/New Covenant. To be federally united to him you must be 1) promised to him outside of time in the covenant of redemption and 2) brought into union with him in time by the Holy Spirit.

The Son was the one elected by the Father to win the redemption of the elect. All of this is accomplished in the New Covenant, which is the historical climax of the covenant of grace. To be in the covenant of grace/New Covenant, you must be united to Christ, its federal head.[17]

Since the covenant of grace is the retroactive application of the New Covenant, if we posit that Christ is the mediator of the covenant of grace, we can only understand the terms of his role as mediator, and our relation to him as such, through the way that he is presented in the New Covenant. That Christ is the mediator of the covenant of grace, the New Covenant, no Reformed theologian denies. Thus, in line with New Testament doctrine, the only way to be under Christ's federal headship is to be united to him by the Holy Spirit. This union finds its roots outside of time as we are

---

[16] Coxe and Owen, *Covenant Theology*, 97.
[17] Cf. WLC 57-59.

chosen in Christ in the covenant of redemption and is applied to the elect in time by the Spirit, begun in effectual calling and consummated in the faith of the believer. Apart from saving faith there can be no union with Christ, because the Spirit does not indwell any except the elect, those who have been justified by faith.[18] Christ is the one and only federal head of the covenant of grace, the New Covenant. Federal headship is never mediate, thus none can enter the covenant other than those who are directly or immediately under his federal headship by the Holy Spirit.[19]

Vos says:

> However narrowly or widely the boundary of the covenant of grace be drawn, in any case it involves a relationship with Christ, whether external or internal, by which it is tied to the covenant of redemption.[20]

He adds:

> One is first united to Christ, the Mediator of the covenant, by a mystical union, which finds its conscious recognition in faith. By this union with Christ all that is in Christ is simultaneously given. Faith embraces all this too; it not only grasps the instantaneous justification, but lays hold of Christ as Prophet, Priest, and King, as his rich and full Messiah.[21]

Bavinck says:

> On the Christian position there can be no doubt that all the benefits of grace have been completely and solely acquired by Christ; hence, they are included in his person and lie prepared for his church in him...And since these benefits are all covenant benefits, were acquired in the way of the

---

[18] Cf. Acts 2:38, Eph. 1:13.
[19] Cf. WLC 65-69.
[20] Vos, *Redemptive* History, 252.
[21] Vos, *Redemptive History*, 256.

covenant, and are distributed in the same covenantal way, *there is no participation in those benefits except by communion with the person of Christ*, who acquired and applies them as the mediator of the covenant.[22]

Fairbairn says:

> Here, precisely as in the rending of the veil for the ceremonials of Judaism, the exclusive bond for the people was broken at the center: Christ's very mother and brothers were to have no precedence over others, nor any distinctive position in His kingdom; spiritual relations alone should prevail there, and the one bond of connection with it for all alike, was to be the believing reception of the gospel and obedience to it...So far, therefore, as regards Israel's typical character, their removed and isolated position is plainly at an end: all tribes and nations are on a footing as to the kingdom of God – members and fellow-citizens if they are believers in Christ, aliens if they are not.[23]

Fairbairn adds, "And wherever there is found a soul linked in vital union with Christ, there also are found the essential characteristics of Abraham's seed, and title to Abraham's inheritance."[24]

Consider the following portions of Scripture.

> Anyone who does not have the Spirit of Christ does not belong to him. (Rom. 8:9)

> For the Scripture says, "Everyone who believes in him will not be put to shame." [12] For there is no distinction between Jew and Greek; for the same Lord is Lord of all, bestowing

---

[22] Bavinck, *Reformed Dogmatics Vol. III*, 591, emphasis added.
[23] Patrick Fairbairn, *The Interpretation of Prophecy* (London: The Banner of Truth, 1964), 261-62.
[24] Fairbairn, *Interpretation of Prophecy*, 270.

his riches on all who call on him. [13] For "everyone who calls on the name of the Lord will be saved." (Rom. 10:11-13)

All these are empowered by one and the same Spirit, who apportions to each one individually as he wills. [12] For just as the body is one and has many members, and all the members of the body, though many, are one body, so it is with Christ. [13] For in one Spirit we were all baptized into one body--Jews or Greeks, slaves or free--and all were made to drink of one Spirit. (1 Cor. 12:11-13)

for in Christ Jesus you are all sons of God, through faith. [27] For as many of you as were baptized into Christ have put on Christ. [28] There is neither Jew nor Greek, there is neither slave nor free, there is no male and female, for you are all one in Christ Jesus. (Gal. 3:26-28)

And he put all things under his feet and gave him as head over all things to the church, [23] which is his body, the fullness of him who fills all in all. (Eph. 1:22-23)

There is one body and one Spirit--just as you were called to the one hope that belongs to your call-- [5] one Lord, one faith, one baptism, [6] one God and Father of all, who is over all and through all and in all. (Eph. 4:4-6)

The covenant of grace is so called because its blessings are freely given to its members. Those blessings are free because they have been won solely by Christ's obedience in fulfillment of his commission in the covenant of redemption. Thus understood, the covenant of grace arises in history in contradistinction to the covenant of works. That covenant having been broken, all mankind is born immediately federally united to Adam, under the curse of the law. When man is liberated from this condemnation, his liberation comes through the propitiatory satisfaction of Christ on his behalf and the gracious imputation of Christ's righteousness to his account, appropriated by faith. In other words, as Genesis 3

Reformed Baptist Covenant Theology and Biblical Theology

shows, the covenant of grace is the solution to the curses of the covenant of works.

The fact that we see this redemption promised and typified from the fall onward has led Reformed theologians to see God's grace extending into history prior to the incarnation and death of Christ. Where God's grace extended into the past, it came by way of covenant, wherein Christ's blood of the New Covenant was retroactively applied to those who believed in the promise, and that retroactivity of the New Covenant was and remains distinct from the Old Covenant. Thus, Christ's people have always been those who were promised to him by the Father, and it is those people for whom he spilled his blood.

Scripture teaches that Christ brings his own to himself through the work of the Spirit, and that he dwells in his own by the Spirit. Therefore, without the Spirit, none belong to Christ. If you belong to Christ, you are in the covenant of grace. If you do not belong to Christ, you are in the covenant of works. You cannot be in both.[25] If it is possible to be born into the covenant of grace through the mediated federal headship of a parent, then, unless regeneration is presumed, one is both in Adam and in Christ at the same time. However, this is impossible. One man sinned and brought death to all mankind; another obeyed and brought life to his people. You are either in Adam or in Christ.

To bring this to a conclusion, a right understanding of the membership of the covenant of grace is founded on the covenant of redemption and the New Covenant. Those who are in the covenant of grace are those who were promised to the Son by the Father in the covenant of redemption, won by the Son's life, death, and resurrection, and sealed by the Holy Spirit, uniting them to their federal head, Jesus Christ. Laying claim to Christ and his benefits is a serious matter, and as Scripture shows, only those who have saving faith can truly make that claim. There is no external federal relation to Jesus Christ. In terms of membership or qualification, there are no distinctions in the body of Christ, that is, the church. All are sons of God through faith, under one head, indwelt by one

---

[25] Cf. Rom. 7:4-6.

Spirit. "Anyone who does not have the Spirit of Christ does not belong to him" (Rom. 8:9). In spite of the false professions, unbelief, and lies of apostates, God knows his own, Christ knows his sheep, and the Spirit of adoption knows the children of God.[26] The covenant people of God are "a chosen race, a royal priesthood, a holy nation, a people for his own possession" (1 Pet. 2:9). The glorious New Covenant does not look to the Old for its pattern and people but stands on the eternal foundation of the covenant of redemption and comes to the elect as a covenant of grace, purchased, mediated, and eternally kept by "our great God and savior Jesus Christ who gave himself for us to redeem us from all lawlessness and to purify for himself a people" (Titus 2:14).

The Biblical-Theological Basis for Credobaptism

Redemptive history moves forward progressively, giving rise to new revelation.

Geerhardus Vos famously argued that we must view revelation as a progressive unfolding coinciding with the progressive unfolding of redemptive history itself. In other words, this progressive unfolding of redemptive history gives rise to new revelation. One of the primary applications of that point is that we must look at the various parts of Scripture in the specific context of their period of redemptive history. Thus the New Testament believer must be careful about how the Old Testament is read and even how the Gospels are read since they refer to a redemptive historical era prior to the one in which we now live.

The different epochs of redemptive history are governed by their own covenantal canons.

Meredith Kline continued this idea by relating it more specifically to covenant documents. He argued that the Old Testament itself made up the covenant document of the Old Covenant. Likewise,

---

[26] Cf. 2 Tim. 2:19, John 10:27, Matt. 7:15-23, Rom. 8:16.

the New Testament is the covenant document of the New Covenant. Kline says:

> The Old and New Testaments, which respectively define and establish these two structures, will be clearly seen as two separate and distinct architectural models for the house of God in two quite separate and distinct stages of its history. The distinctiveness of the two community organizations brings out the individual integrity of the two Testaments which serve as community rules for the two orders. The Old and New Testaments are two discrete covenant polities, and since biblical canon is covenantal polity-canon, they are two discrete canons in series.[27]

Kline draws out some of the implications of this idea.

> The old covenant is not the new covenant. The form of government appointed in the old covenant is not the community polity for the church of the new covenant, its ritual legislation is not a directory for the church's cultic practice.[28]

Kline is not saying that the Old Testament is of no use for New Testament Christians. Instead, he is saying that as a defining covenant document that includes all of the pertinent sanctions and stipulations for the covenant, the New Covenant people of God must look to the New Testament and not the Old Testament.[29]

---

[27] Meredith G. Kline, *The Structure of Biblical Authority* (Eugene, OR: Wipf & Stock, 1997), 98-99.

[28] Kline, *Structure*, 99.

[29] Michael Horton says essentially the same thing. "The new covenant is constituted by its own canon...the New Testament...It has its own stipulations (both doctrines and commands) and sanctions (life and death)." Cf. Horton's *The Christian Faith* (Grand Rapids: Zondervan, 2011), 153. He goes on to say, "There can be no covenant without a canon or canon without a covenant. In fact, the covenant *is* the canon and vice versa," (155, emphasis his).

As we will mention in a moment, this has obvious implications for baptism. Baptism is the sign of the New Covenant. It is not a sign of the Old Covenant. To understand the correct administration of the sign of the New Covenant, we must look to its own covenant document – the New Testament.

Positive law elements of different covenant-canons are restricted to their particular covenant-canons.

Richard Muller defines natural law in this way:

> the universal moral law either impressed by God upon the mind of all people or immediately discerned by the reason in its encounter with the order of nature.[30]

Moral law endures throughout all of the covenants, but positive laws do not. A positive law may be generally defined as "something that is dependent on direct revelation for its obligation."[31] In other words, without some form of special revelation, we would not know of these positive laws and we would not be required to obey them. For example, the civil and ceremonial laws of the Old Testament are positive laws. There was no requirement placed on other nations to follow the same civil laws as Israel. These are not laws that are morally binding on all people in all places at all times. They are binding only for a particular people and for a particular time. This is because they are positive laws.[32]

---

[30] Muller, *Dictionary*, 174.

[31] From IRBS PT 600 lecture by Dr. James M. Renihan.

[32] This can be seen in the Sabbath command. The 4th commandment has both a moral and positive aspect to it. This was affirmed by the Synod of Dordt in their resolutions regarding the Sabbath:

1. "In the fourth Commandment of the divine law, part was ceremonial, part is moral."

2. "The rest of the seventh day after creation was ceremonial and its rigid observation peculiarly prescribed to the Jewish people."

3. "Moral in fact, because the fixed and enduring day of the worship of God is appointed, for as much rest as is necessary for the worship of God and holy

When it comes to positive laws we should not assume they are in effect unless rescinded. Positive laws, instead, end with the termination of the covenant in which they were given. Positive laws are given in a particular redemptive-historical setting and in a particular covenant document. Positive laws only apply to the covenantal context in which they are given. This is why we no longer are obligated to follow the ceremonial laws of the Old Testament.[33]

In order to understand a particular covenantal-canon's stipulations and sanctions we can only look to that particular covenant.

It follows that if different covenants have their own covenant-canons and those covenant-canons contain positive laws, then we should only look to those particular covenant-canon documents to understand their corresponding sanctions and stipulations. As Kline says, "The treaty canon that governs the church of the new covenant as a formal community is the New Testament alone."[34]

This point has the potential to be misunderstood. It does not say that the Old Testament has no bearing on the New Testament. We certainly do not want to suggest that. The Old and New Testaments do have a very intimate connection, but it is one of promise and fulfillment. Nevertheless, while there is unity between the Old and New Testaments, the fact remains that they are separate and distinct periods of redemptive history with separate and distinct

---

meditation of him." (translation by R. Scott Clark, http://clark.wscal.edu/dortsabbath.php).

These theologians at the Synod of Dordt affirmed that the observance of a Sabbath rest, a one day in seven ceasing from all work and worshipping God was required by moral law. However, they also affirmed that the particular day upon which God is to be worshipped is a matter of positive (or ceremonial) law. In the Old Testament it was the seventh day of the week, but in the New Testament it is the first day of the week.

[33] Col. 2:16-17, "Therefore let no one pass judgment on you in questions of food and drink, or with regard to a festival or a new moon or a Sabbath. These are a shadow of the things to come, but the substance belongs to Christ."

[34] Kline, *Structure*, 100.

covenant-canons. For this reason, when we want to understand the particular requirements of a particular covenant, we must look at that covenant's particular covenant document.

Patrick Fairbairn says:

> It is implied that the revelations by prophecy, respecting the gospel age and its realities, were necessarily defective as to clearness and precision, and are not capable of bearing so exact an interpretation, or yielding so explicit a meaning, in respect to the affairs of Christ's kingdom, as is conveyed by the writings of the New Testament. But such, precisely, is the result that was to be expected, from the place and calling of the Old Testament prophets...There cannot be a surer canon of interpretation, than that *everything which affects the constitution and destiny of the New Testament Church has its clearest determination in New Testament Scripture*.[35]

To summarize so far, our understanding of redemptive history as articulated by men such as Vos, Owen, and Ridderbos, tells us that the redemptive-historical context in which Scripture is written *must* be taken into account when understanding that passage of Scripture. Kline and others have combined this with the idea of covenant and canon, showing that the Old Testament and New Testament are separate covenantal documents governing separate covenants. When understanding essential elements of a particular covenant, we must look to that covenant's own document to properly understand those essential covenantal elements.

Circumcision is a positive law from the Old Covenant canon and thus applies only to that covenant except insofar as it acts as a type.

Circumcision must be a positive law since it is neither commanded in the New Testament nor was it commanded prior to Abraham.[36]

---

[35] Fairbairn, *Interpretation of Prophecy*, 157-58, emphasis his.
[36] Cf. Gal. 5:6; Acts 7:8; 1 Cor. 7:19; Rom. 2:25-27.

Baptism is a New Covenant ordinance established by Christ through positive law. Our understanding for the carrying out of this requirement, therefore, is restricted to the covenantal-canon under which it was given.

Baptism is a positive law since it is not commanded in the Old Testament. As 2LCF 28.1 says, "Baptism and the Lord's Supper are ordinances of positive and sovereign institution, appointed by the Lord Jesus, the only Lawgiver, to be continued in His church to the end of the world."

We should remind ourselves here that baptism is a key component of the covenant. As one of the two sacraments of the New Covenant, it is not a minor point. It is precisely the type of thing for which you would want to look to the New Covenant document. The New Covenant document, the New Testament, ought to dictate how its own sacraments are administered.[37]

Furthermore, the regulative principle of worship necessitates that we look only to the explicitly prescribed way of administering baptism. The 2LCF (22.1), in almost identical language to the WCF (21.1) articulates this principle, saying:

> The acceptable way of worshipping the true God is instituted by himself, and so limited by his own revealed will, that he may not be worshipped according to…any other way not prescribed in the Holy Scriptures.

Since the sacraments of baptism and the Lord's Supper are elements of worship, they too must fall under this criteria of the regulative principle. The administration of baptism must be limited by God's own revealed will according to the way prescribed in Scripture.[38]

---

[37] This is the same principle as is exercised with the Lord's Supper. While we acknowledge a typological connection between Passover and the Lord's Supper, our understanding of the observance of the Supper comes from the New Testament, not from the Old Testament observance of Passover.

[38] Cf. Fred A. Malone, *The Baptism of Disciples Alone* (Cape Coral, FL: Founders Press, 2003), xv.

Since the baptism of infants is not prescribed in Scripture, it ought not to be done.

Compare this to what B. B. Warfield said:

> It is true that there is no expressed command to baptize infants in the New Testament, no express record of the baptism of infants, and no passages so stringently implying it that we must infer from them that infants were baptized. If such warrant as this were necessary to justify the usage we should have to leave it incompletely justified. But the lack of this express warrant is something so far short of forbidding the rite; and if the continuity of the church through all ages can be made good, the warrant for infant baptism is not to be sought in the New Testament but in the Old Testament when the church was instituted, and nothing short of an actual forbidding of it in the New Testament would warrant our omitting it now.[39]

While we certainly disagree with Warfield's conclusions that infant baptism may still be justified, we appreciate his admission that the New Testament itself does not adequately justify the practice of infant baptism. Warfield admits that it is necessary to rely on the teaching of the Old Testament to arrive at the practice of infant baptism. However, as we have shown, the nature of redemptive history, as well as the covenantal character of the New and Old Testament canons, shows that we need to look to the New Testament canon to understand this practice.

Proper weight must be given to the newness of the New Covenant.

Speaking of the Old and New Covenants, Kline says:

> They are of course, indissolubly bound to one another in organic spiritual-historic relationship. They both unfold the same principle of redemptive grace, moving forward to a

---

[39] B. B. Warfield, *Studies in Theology* (Grand Rapids: Baker, 2003), 399-400.

common eternal goal in the city of God. The blessings of old and new orders derive from the very same works of satisfaction accomplished by the Christ of God, and where spiritual life is found in either order it is attributable to the creative action of the one and selfsame Spirit of Christ. According to the divine design the old is *provisional* and *preparatory* for the new, and by divine predisclosure the new is prophetically anticipated in the old. External event and institution in the old order were divinely fashioned to afford a systematic representation of the realities of the coming new order, so producing a type-antitype correlativity between the two covenants in which their unity is instructively articulated.[40]

When dealing with types we must acknowledge a basic and fundamental unity, yet not such as to ignore the typological and thus different character of the type. The Old Testament covenants do indeed reveal the New Covenant, but in a progressive, typological way. The New Covenant is further revealed by various steps throughout the Old Testament era, first in the *protevangelium*, and then throughout all of the Old Testament covenants. Just as the gospel was revealed step by step, so also is the New Covenant because it is in essence the gospel.

This is basically what the 2LCF says in 7.3.

> This covenant is revealed in the gospel; first of all to Adam in the promise of salvation by the seed of the woman, and afterwards by farther steps, until the full discovery thereof was completed in the New Testament.

This is also not far from what Vos says:

> The successive stages of God's redemptive and revealing work in the pre-Christian era are measured by successive covenants, each introducing new forces and principles and

---

[40] Kline, *Structure*, 98, emphasis added.

each imparting to the ensuing period a distinctive character of its own. Thus the covenant-idea is an eminently historical idea, most intimately associated with the gradual unfolding of God's self-disclosure to His people.[41]

So, there is a basic unity which begins at the fall, well before Abraham ever appeared on the scene, as the various covenants in the Old Testament progressively and typologically reveal the New Covenant which is made when Christ's blood is shed on the cross. But because the Old Testament covenants are types of the New Covenant, we must recognize the discontinuity that also exists between them. This explains the language of Jeremiah 31 or Joel 2:28-29.

> And it shall come to pass afterward, that I will pour out my Spirit on all flesh; your sons and your daughters shall prophesy, your old men shall dream dreams, and your young men shall see visions. 29 Even on the male and female servants in those days I will pour out my Spirit. (Joel 2:28-29)[42]

Proper weight must be given to the *newness* of the *New* Covenant by seeing it as something that has not yet come about from the perspective of the Old Testament. This is not merely a scale in which the New Covenant is "more of the same." It is not merely quantitatively different from the Old Covenant. It is something qualitatively different. There will be things that are true in the New Covenant that are not true when any Old Testament author writes.

---

[41] Vos, *Redemptive History*, 192.

[42] Jeremiah 31:33-34 **33**"But this is the covenant that I will make with the house of Israel after those days, declares the LORD: I will put my law within them, and I will write it on their hearts. And I will be their God, and they shall be my people. And no longer shall each one teach his neighbor and each his brother, saying, 'Know the LORD,' for they shall all know me, from the least of them to the greatest, declares the LORD. For I will forgive their iniquity, and I will remember their sin no more."

Similarly, there are things that will no longer be true in the New Covenant that are true in the Old Covenant.

When the Old Testament speaks of the New Covenant, it speaks of it as something future and as something truly different from what is currently in place. The language of both Joel and Jeremiah clearly indicate that things will be different in this future New Covenant from how they were in their day.

Again, Vos says this very well:

> The revelation of the New Covenant is not only better comparatively speaking; it is final and eternal because delivered in a Son, than whom God could send no higher revealer.[43]

The most essential difference between the New Covenant and all the covenants of the Old Testament is that it is made and sealed in the blood of Christ and it is revealed in Christ (Heb. 9:15-16). For this reason, the New Covenant is different in substance from all the Old Testament covenants.

As Vos goes on to say, the New Covenant is necessarily connected to the new age, the consummation. With the inauguration of the New Covenant, the new age breaks forth into this current age. Vos says, "The New Covenant, then, coincides with the age to come; it brings the good things to come; it is incorporated into the eschatological scheme of thought."[44] If the New Covenant truly coincides with the new age, we should not look back at the Old Covenant to understand this New Covenant. Instead we should look forward to the consummation. True, we live in the "not yet." But it is just as true that we live in the "already." For these reasons, we must conclude that theologies that rely too heavily on the Old Covenant for their description and articulation of the New Covenant demonstrate an under-realized eschatology. They do not give enough weight to the "already."

---

[43] Vos, *Redemptive History*, 194.
[44] Vos, *Redemptive History*, 195.

Thus the discipline of biblical theology, the study of redemptive history, and the nature of revelation teach us that we ought to treat the New Covenant as different in substance from the Old Testament covenants.

Furthermore, the New Testament treatment of the Old Testament Scripture as mystery, shadows, and types indicates that the New Testament must be the lens through which we view the Old Testament and not vice versa.

Any Reformed theologian speaking of hermeneutics will agree that the New Testament is the lens through which we must interpret the Old Testament. Usually the famous saying attributed to Augustine is quoted, "The New is in the Old concealed; the Old is in the New revealed." So trying to understand the antitype by looking at the type causes difficulties. It is difficult to know which aspects of the type are carried over into the antitype and which aspects are to be cast aside.

The New Testament affirms the difficulty of understanding the Old Testament types. Paul has a well-developed theology of mystery.[45]

> the mystery hidden for ages and generations but now revealed to his saints. 27 To them God chose to make known how great among the Gentiles are the riches of the glory of this mystery, which is Christ in you, the hope of glory. (Col. 1:26-27)

> making known to us the mystery of his will, according to his purpose, which he set forth in Christ 10as a plan for the fullness of time, to unite all things in him, things in heaven and things on earth. (Eph. 1:9-10)

---

[45] Cf. Herman Ridderbos *Paul: An Outline of His Theology* (Grand Rapids: Eerdmans, 1977), 44-49.

because of his own purpose and grace, which he gave us in Christ Jesus before the ages began, ¹⁰and which now has been manifested through the appearing of our Savior Christ Jesus, who abolished death and brought life and immortality to light through the gospel. (2 Tim. 1:9-10)[46]

Ridderbos points out that this mystery now revealed has both "a noetic and a historical connotation."[47] So, there is both a greater understanding and new revelation (especially in the form of new redemptive-historical events). If we follow Warfield in looking at the Old Testament as our basis for how we administer baptism, we violate this fundamental principle of hermeneutics.

Promise and Fulfillment

For our last point, we want to notice a couple of the elements of promise and fulfillment, of type and antitype, that we find in the Old and New Testaments.

Ridderbos says:

> God's people are those for whom Christ sheds his blood of the covenant. They share in the remission of sins brought about by him and in the unbreakable communion with God in the new covenant that he has made possible…The rejection of Israel as God's people does not annihilate the idea of covenant, but imparts to it a *new*, or at least a *more definite content*. The particular character of grace and of communion with God is fully maintained. But the circle in which it is granted and where God's people are found, is no longer that of the empirical Israel, but it is that of those who

---

[46] Cf. Titus 1:2-3 "in hope of eternal life, which God, who never lies, promised before the ages began 3and at the proper time manifested in his word through the preaching with which I have been entrusted by the command of God our Savior."

[47] Ridderbos, *Paul*, 46.

are given remission of sins in Christ's death, and whose hearts have been renewed by the Holy Spirit.[48]

The point Ridderbos wants to make here is that a fundamental change has taken place from the Old Covenant to the New Covenant. The people of God in the Old Testament were made up of an empirical people. Ridderbos explicitly speaks of a "new formation of God's people."[49] He recognizes that there is something very different about the people of God in the New Covenant from the people of God in the Old Covenant. The people of God in the New Covenant are characterized by faith, by remission of sins, and by regeneration. Ridderbos continues:

> The special relation between God and Israel as his people is one of the foundations of the gospel…At the same time we have noticed a transition in this basic idea, in the sense that, by the side of and in the place of empirical Israel, those who believe the gospel are considered as the flock of the Lord, the seed of Abraham, and the children of the kingdom.[50]

Fairbairn says it this way:

> The seed of Israel, as an elect people, placed under covenant with God, represented the company of an elect church, redeemed from the curse of sin, that they might live forever in the favour and blessing of Heaven: and when the redemption came, the representation passed into reality.[51]

Ridderbos continues his argument by saying:

> This result is of the greatest importance for the question under discussion. For this rejection of Israel and this new

---

[48] Herman Ridderbos, *The Coming of the Kingdom* (Philadelphia: P&R, 1976), 202, emphasis added.
[49] Ridderbos, *Kingdom*, 351.
[50] Ridderbos, *Kingdom*, 351-52.
[51] Fairbairn, *Interpretation of Prophecy*, 267.

formation of God's people is not simply something of the eschatological future, but has already begun to be realized with the coming of Jesus.[52]

He goes on to say:

> The *ekklesia* in all this is the people who in this great drama have been placed on the side of God in Christ by virtue of the divine election and covenant. They have been given the divine promise, have been brought to manifestation and gathered together by the preaching of the gospel, and will inherit the redemption of the kingdom now and in the great future...So there is no question of *basileia* and *ekklesia* as being identical.[53]

Let's pull together some of these strands. In the Old Testament, the Old Covenant was a type and shadow of the fullness to come. That fullness was shrouded in mystery and types waiting for its revelation in Christ. With the coming of Christ we now have that fullness. The external, typological elements of the Old Covenant are cast off. The mystery and shadows are gone. With the New Covenant comes the in-breaking of the eschatological age in its "already-not yet" form. The Old Covenant people were naturally generated and marked by circumcision of the flesh. The New Covenant people are Spiritually generated, thus circumcised in heart, the antitype of circumcision. Thus, baptism should only be administered to those who are Spiritually born into the covenant. The only way prescribed in Scripture to evaluate if someone is in the covenant is by a profession of faith. Upon profession of faith baptism is administered. This is precisely the pattern we see in the New Testament – baptism follows a profession of faith.[54]

---

[52] Ridderbos, *Kingdom*, 352.
[53] Ridderbos, *Kingdom*, 354-55.
[54] Louis Berkhof says that the New Testament "points to faith as a prerequisite for baptism," *Systematic Theology* (East Peoria, IL: Versa Press Inc., 2005), 637. Cf. Acts 2:41; 10:44-48; 18:8.

This fits exactly with our understanding of covenant theology. All of those who are in the covenant have Christ as their federal head. The only way to be "in Christ" is to have the Holy Spirit (Rom. 8:9), and those who have the Spirit are those who have faith. All of this is rooted and grounded in the great covenant of redemption, the *pactum salutis*, where the Father covenanted with the Son to give him an elect people. Thus baptism as a sign of the covenant is administered only to those who make a profession of faith. It is an effectual means of grace for those who receive it in faith. Apart from faith it does nothing.

Conclusion

In closing we want to consider a quotation from Charles Hodge.

> The difficulty on this subject is that baptism from its very nature involves a profession of faith; it is the way in which by the ordinance of Christ, He is to be confessed before men; but infants are incapable of making such confession; therefore they are not the proper subjects of baptism. Or, to state the matter in another form: the sacraments belong to the members of the Church; but the Church is the company of believers; infants cannot exercise faith, therefore they are not members of the Church, and consequently ought not to be baptized. In order to justify the baptism of infants, we must attain and authenticate such an idea of Church as that it shall include the children of believing parents.[55]

Hodge recognizes that the doctrine of baptism itself excludes the idea of baptizing infants, and so he resorts to defining the church in such a way that it may allow for this practice. However, as we have shown, the movement of redemptive history, the full revelation in Christ, the in-breaking of the eschatological age, the regulative principle, the nature of covenant, the nature of positive law, and the

---

[55] Charles Hodge, *Systematic Theology*, Vol. 3 (Peabody, MA: Hendrickson, 2003), 546-47.

basic principles of biblical hermeneutics all show that this move by Hodge simply cannot be made. Instead we must recognize the newness of the New Covenant in its fulfillment of the types and shadows of the Old Testament as well as in its connection to the consummation.

Scripture Index

Genesis

1:28, *17*
2:16–17, *38*
2:17, *30*
3, *489*
3:15, *24, 26, 30, 31, 32, 39, 40, 43, 67, 186, 230, 384, 446*
3:21, *102*
3:22 ff, *30*
3–22, *414*
4:1, *367*
4:4, *102*
6:5, *272*
8:20, *102*
9:9, *446*
12, *95*
12, *15, 95, 186*
12:1–3, *384, 446*
12:3, *406*
12:22, *406*
12–22, *414*
13:15, *446*
15, *166, 384, 417, 446*
15:6, *226*
17, *78, 95, 96, 163, 164, 166, 168, 170, 171, 247, 249, 383, 413, 415, 419, 421, 422, 423, 424, 425, 429, 430, 433, 444, 445, 446*
17:1–14, *384, 446, 473*
17:4–14, *250*
17:6–8, *229, 237*
17:6–14, *236*
17:7, *77, 162, 163, 164, 172, 404, 405, 421, 423, 424, 425, 432, 446*
17:9–10, *14, 238*
17:9–14, *246*
17:10, *446*
17:14, *105, 480*
17:16, *414*
17:23, *401*
18, *165, 249*
18:17–19, *240, 249*
18:19, *242*
21, *167, 171*
22:13, *102*
22:18, *407*
26:2–5, *247*
28:13–15, *247*
46:1, *102*

Exodus

3, *78*
4:22, *421*
19, *249*

Leviticus

10:2–3, *115, 125*
18:5, *72, 100, 185*

Deuteronomy

5, *324*
5:1–4, *246*
5:2, *179*

5:2–3, *27–29, 401*
5:2–5, *294*
7:11–12, *248*
10:16, *455*
26:18, *344*
28, *101, 344*
30:6, *239, 455*

Joshua

21:43–45, *481*

Judges

2:10, *345*

1 Samuel

2:12, *345, 367*
3:7, *345*
7:14, *384*

1 Kings

2:1–4, *234*
4:20, *481*

Psalms

16, *386*
16:8–11, *385, 432*
22, *378*
40:6–8, *349*
103, *369*
105:8, *443*
110, *351, 386*
110:1, *432*
119, *365*

132:11, *432*
132:11–12, *233*
147:19, *320*

Isaiah

19:21, *345*
32:15, *446*
44:3, *409, 446*
57:19, *393*

Jeremiah

4:4, *455*
16:21, *367*
22:1–9, *234*
31, *336, 341, 342, 352, 358, 360, 367, 377, 378, 380, 399, 400, 418, 424, 499*
31, f, *339*
31:26, f, *379*
31:31, *446*
31:31–32, *401*
31:31–34, *326, 341, 357, 375*
31:31–34, 32:40, *294*
31:33, *375*
31:33–34, *105, 401*
31:33–34 33, *499*
31:34, *106, 352*
32:39, *446*
32:40, *378, 401*

Ezekiel

11:19, *446*
36:26–27, *446*
37;0, *446*
44:7, *455*

14, *446*

Hosea

2:20, *345*
2:20, 5:4, *346*
5:4, *345*
6:3, *345*
6:7, *39*

Joel

2, *385, 386, 391, 394, 395, 396, 397, 400, 413, 415, 417, 418, 420, 421, 422, 429, 433, 443, 444, 447*
2:28, *397, 446*
2:28–29, *443, 499*
2:28–32, *385, 392, 394*
2:29, *395, 397*
2:32, *390, 391, 396, 397*
3:1–5, *385*
3:2, *395*

Zechariah

9:11, *312*

Malachi

1:2–3, *410*
3:6, *432*

Matthew

1:21, *338*
3:4, *123*
3:7–8, *439*
7:15–23, *490*
11:25–30, *442*
18:1–10, *441*
18:6, *440*
18:6, 19:13–15, 21:16, *440, 443*
21, *441*
21:15–17, *441*
21:16, *441*
21:43, *255*
22:37–40, *239*
23:38, *255*
26:28, *294*
28:18, *121*
28:18–20, *121*
28:19, *116, 120, 121*
28:19–20, *122*

Mark

8:23–25, *288*
12:34, *393*
16, *133*
16:15–16, *121*
16:16, *122, 439*

Luke

1:55, *73, 482*
7:6, *393*
10:21, *440, 442, 443*
11, *156*
15:20, *394*
18:15–17, *440, 443*
22:20, *326, 353*
24:47, *438*
24:49, *390*

John

1:16–17, *104*
1:17, *336*
3, *464*
3:3–8, *453, 457*
3:6, *252*
3:23, *123*
4:22, *242*
6:38–39, *338, 359*
6:38–40, *476*
7:22–23, *239, 249*
8:34–38, *253*
10:14–16, 26–28, *476*
10:27, *490*
10:27–30, *359*
15, *385*
17:6–11, 17–21, *476*
17:19, *372, 373*
21:8, *393*

Acts

1:4, *385, 390*
2, *133, 163, 391, 392, 398, 399, 406, 407, 408, 413, 415, 420, 424, 427, 430, 431, 432, 433, 439, 446*
2 f, *413*
2:1–4, *385*
2:5–7, *385*
2:5–13, *386*
2:14–21, *397*
2:14–36, *385*
2:14–39, *398*
2:15–21, *394*
2:17, *385, 391*
2:17, 21, *407*
2:17–21, *384, 390, 391, 394, 399, 415, 417, 421, 429, 443*
2:17–21 f, *386*
2:18, *395*
2:21, *383, 389, 396, 406, 430*
2:21, 2:39, *415*
2:23, *386*
2:25–28 f, *386*
2:29–36, *235*
2:33, *386, 395, 447*
2:34–35, *386*
2:34–35 f, *386*
2:36, *386*
2:37–38, *387*
2:37–41, *385, 387, 405, 419, 422*
2:38, *395, 397, 415, 430, 434, 436, 439, 486*
2:38, 3:17–20, 25–26, *418*
2:38, 29, *473*
2:38, 33, 17–21, *417*
2:38, 39, *423*
2:38–39, 11, *419, 423, 426, 431, 439*
2:39 –, *437*
2:39, *10, 292, 382, 383, 384, 385, 386, 389, 390, 391, 394, 395, 396, 397, 398, 399, 400, 402, 403, 404, 405, 406, 408, 413, 414, 415, 417, 418, 419, 420, 421, 422, 423, 424, 425, 426, 427, 428, 429, 430, 431, 432, 433, 434, 435, 437, 443, 444, 445, 447, 448*
2:39 f, *384*
2:40–41, *397, 398*
2:41, *504*

3, *165, 405, 406, 407, 408, 413,
417, 420*
3:17–20, *407*
3:19, *391, 406*
3:25, *401, 405, 420*
3:25–26, *406, 432*
3:26, *408*
7:8, *429, 479, 495*
7:17, *386*
8, *133*
10, *133, 393*
10:44–48, *504*
11, *133*
11:18, *391*
14:15–18, *68*
15, *447*
16, *163*
17:22 ff, *68*
17:27, *393*
18:8, *504*
22, *133*
22:16, *400, 419*
22:21, *393, 394*
26:20, *391*

Romans

1:16, *408*
2:6–29, *245*
2:25, *239, 245, 249*
2:25–27, *495*
2:28 f, *458*
2:28–29, *92, 455*
3, *184, 250*
3:1–2, *250*
3:9, *245, 253*
3:9–18, *250*

3:19, *245*
3:19–20, *250*
3:20, *245*
3:21–26, *231*
4, *165, 167*
4:9–12, *473*
4:11, *472*
4:22, *226*
5:18–20, *101*
5:19–20, *102*
6, *133, 252*
6:2–4, *209*
6:3–4, *400, 419*
6:3–8, *461*
6:6–7, *461*
6:14, *73*
6:23, *72, 101*
7:4–6, *490*
7:6, *454*
8:3, *72, 102*
8:3–4, *101*
8:5–7, *456*
8:9, *392, 488, 490, 504*
8:15, *454*
8:16, *490*
8:34, *338*
9, *167, 170, 410*
9:6, *238*
9:6–8, *92*
9:8, *95, 252, 254, 255*
9:24–26 f, *414*
9–11, *483*
10:9, *467*
10:11–13, *488*
13:14, *456*
15:8–9, *242*

1 Corinthians

1, *163*
7, *146, 163*
7:14, *146*
7:19, *495*
11, *168*
11:25–26, *369*
12:11–13, *489*

2 Corinthians

3, *168, 184*
3:1–9, *401*
3:3, *401*
3:6–9, *294*
3:7, *313*
3:9, *184*
3:11, *184*
3:14, *294*
3:17, *315*
3:18, *288*

Galatians

3, *73, 93, 165, 183, 184, 412*
3:1–14, *412*
3:7, *8, 29, 473*
3:8, *384*
3:8–9, *478*
3:10–13, *185*
3:12, *481*
3:13, *101, 102, 231*
3:13–14, *409, 411*
3:14, *409, 411, 419*
3:15, *249*
3:16, *238, 483*
3:16, *29, 446*
3:16–18, *246*
3:17–18, *91, 92, 183, 184*
3:18, *226*
3:19, *336*
3:19–24, *98*
3:21, *72, 101, 102, 103*
3:21–25, *245*
3:22, *245*
3:22–24, *103*
3:23, *98*
3:26–28, *489*
3:29, *96, 254, 256, 402*
4, *95, 170, 401, 414, 419, 484*
4:1–7, *248*
4:4, *102*
4:4–5, *101*
4:21–31, *244*
4:22–24, *251, 252*
4:22–31, *92, 93, 96, 97, 251*
4:23, *402*
4:23, *29, 402*
4:23–31, *402, 419*
4:24, *96, 252*
4:24–25, *253*
4:24–28, *253*
4:28, *256, 402*
4:29, *255*
4:29–31, *254*
4:31, *256*
5:2–3, *250*
5:3, *239*
5:6, *495*
6:16, *414*

Ephesians

1:4, *53, 454, 455*

1:4, f, *453*
1:9–10, *501*
1:13, *473, 486*
1:13–14, *392*
1:14, f, *336*
1:22–23, *489*
2:3 f, *456*
2:4–5, *451*
2:5 ff, *466*
2:12, *86*
2:13, *17, 394*
2:22, *454*
3:4–6, 8–12, *478*
3:8–10, *321*
4:4–6, *489*
4:30, *454, 473*
6:1–4, *470*

Philippians

3:3, *414*

Colossians

1:17, *454*
1:26–27, *501*
2:4–3:4, *450*
2:8, *450*
2:9, *450*
2:9–10, *450*
2:10, *450*
2:10–14, *400, 419*
2:11, *452, 454, 458, 469*
2:11 ff, *455*
2:11, *12, 428, 473*
2:11–12, *10, 11, 142, 163, 429, 448, 449, 450, 451, 467, 468, 469, 470, 471, 473, 474*
2:11–13, *469, 473*
2:11–14, *429*
2:12, *400, 419, 460, 461, 466, 467, 468, 469, 470, 471*
2:12, *20, 461*
2:13, *453*
2:15, *458*
2:16–17, *494*
2:17, *480*
2:18, *456*
2:20, *461*
3:1, 3, *461*
3:20, *470*

1 Timothy

2:5, *267*
2:5–6, *340*

2 Timothy

1:9, *54*
1:9–10, *501*
2:15, *17*
2:19, *490*

Titus

1:2, *54*
1:2–3, *501*
2:14, *491*
3:5, *457, 461*
3:5–6, *459*

Hebrews

1:4, *333, 334*
2:2, *3, 324*
2:10, 5:7, *9, 9:11, 12, 372*
4:2, *478*
5:17–18, *89*
6, *133*
6:1–8 f, *329*
6:9, *333, 334*
6:11–12, *329*
6:14–16, *292*
7:11, *99, 101*
7:17, 21, *335*
7:19, *333, 334*
7:20–22, *476*
7:22, *294, 333, 334*
7:22–25, *329*
7:23, *336*
7:23–8:5, *336*
7:23–25, *336*
7:24–35, *336, 347*
7:26–28, *338*
7:27, *347*
7–9, *89*
8, *352*
8, *34, 168, 184, 330, 338, 352, 362, 368, 399, 400, 418, 444*
8:1, *347*
8:1–6, *336*
8:5, *480*
8:6, *10, 87, 257, 333, 335, 339*
8:6–7, *358*
8:6–7, 13, *184*
8:6–13, *72, 335, 414*
8:6–13, f, *335*
8:7, *330, 341, 379*

8:8, *329, 331, 342*
8:8 ff, *335*
8:9, *332, 343, 359*
8:10, *344, 363*
8:10–12, *354, 360, 363*
8:11, *345, 352, 360, 362, 365, 366, 367, 368, 375, 400, 405, 419*
8:12, *340, 347, 352, 365, 368, 400, 419*
8:13, *348, 379, 380*
8:14, *369*
8–9, *74*
9:10, *348*
9:15, *340, 341, 349*
9:15, 23–25, *329*
9:15–16, *500*
9:15–20, *294*
9:15–23, *86, 292*
9:16, *274*
9:23, *333, 335*
9:25–10:4, *349*
10, *355, 369*
10:1, *480*
10:1–14, *102*
10:3–4, *369*
10:10–14, *358*
10:10–18, *329, 369, 371*
10:10–22, *327*
10:11–18, *350*
10:14, *374*
10:15–18, *348, 352*
10:16–17, f, *358*
10:16–18, *353*
10:17, *352*
10:18, *380*
10:28, 29, *324*

10:29, *370, 373*
10:29 f, *374*
11:8–10, *92*
11:16, *333, 334*
11:35, *333*
12:14, *241*
12:22–23, *256*
13:20, *326*

James

2:10, *239*

1 Peter

1:5, *471*
1:10–11, *478*
1:14, *404*
1:23, *402, 414, 419*
2:2, *404*
2:9, *414, 417, 490*
3:19, *454*
3:21, *400, 419*

2 Peter

2:1, *372*

1 John

3:8, *31*

Revelation

2:7, *30*
5:6, *351*

Name and Subject Index

à Brakel, Wilhelmus, *420, 426*
Abraham, *23, 28, 35, 39, 40, 77, 78, 80, 87, 88, 89, 91, 92, 93, 94, 95, 96, 97, 98, 99, 162, 164, 165, 166, 167, 168, 169, 170, 172, 179, 183, 187, 192, 224, 225, 226, 227, 228, 235, 236, 237, 238, 239, 240, 241, 242, 243, 244, 245, 246, 247, 248, 249, 250, 251, 252, 253, 254, 255, 256, 275, 276, 278, 290, 291, 297, 298, 302, 309, 314, 315, 320, 322, 361, 383, 384, 385, 390, 401, 402, 406, 408, 409, 410, 411, 412, 419, 420, 421, 422, 423, 424, 430, 431, 432, 443, 446, 473, 478, 479, 480, 481, 482, 483, 484, 485, 488, 495, 499, 503*
Abrahamic Covenant, *9, 10, 11, 71, 91, 92, 93, 95, 96, 97, 159, 160, 163, 164, 165, 166, 167, 183, 186, 223, 224, 225, 226, 228, 229, 232, 235, 236, 237, 238, 239, 241, 242, 243, 245, 246, 247, 248, 249, 250, 253, 255, 384, 405, 406, 409, 412, 413, 417, 419, 424, 427, 429, 430, 431, 433, 459, 479, 480, 481, 482, 484*
Adam, *19, 20, 23, 28, 29, 30, 32, 33, 34, 35, 36, 37, 38, 39, 63, 65, 67, 68, 71, 73, 74, 79, 82, 85, 86, 88, 89, 98, 99, 100, 101, 102, 103, 167, 185, 188, 229, 238, 244, 257, 267, 269, 273, 274, 276, 277, 286, 291, 361, 478, 486, 489, 490, 498*
administered, *67, 75, 82, 87, 124, 133, 173, 178, 179, 192, 241, 264, 277, 278, 286, 287, 305, 310, 315, 316, 445, 474, 481, 496, 504, 505*
administration, *23, 34, 75, 76, 77, 81, 82, 84, 85, 86, 90, 92, 97, 107, 118, 169, 175, 176, 179, 182, 183, 187, 188, 224, 225, 278, 285, 286, 288, 289, 290, 291, 293, 294, 295, 306, 320, 321, 335, 357, 358, 361, 423, 449, 459, 479, 480, 481, 493, 496*
Ainsworth, Henry, *34, 47, 49, 50*
Ames, William, *20, 22, 23, 24, 34, 41, 47, 54, 57, 76, 77, 179*
antitype, *485, 498*
arch-type, *485*

baptism, *48, 52, 56, 57, 67, 69, 80, 110, 111, 112, 113, 114, 115, 116, 117, 118, 120, 121, 122, 123, 124, 125, 127, 128, 129, 130, 131, 132, 133, 135, 137, 142, 146, 149, 150, 152, 155, 160, 162, 165, 168, 171, 173, 193, 200, 201, 202, 204, 205, 207, 208, 209, 210, 214, 215, 217, 226, 359, 372, 382, 383, 385, 387, 388, 399, 400,*

405, 419, 423, 425, 428, 429,
434, 435, 436, 437, 438, 439,
442, 443, 444, 445, 446, 447,
448, 449, 459, 460, 461, 462,
463, 465, 466, 467, 468, 469,
470, 471, 472, 473, 474, 489,
493, 496, 497, 502, 504, 505
Bavinck, Herman, 392, 420,
426, 427, 428, 437, 477, 478,
479, 487, 488
Baxter, Richard, 129, 140, 144,
145, 146, 147, 148, 149, 150,
152, 153, 154, 155, 156, 157,
158, 175
Beale, G. K., 239, 240, 241, 390,
392, 410, 414, 431, 441
Beeke, Joel, 35, 36, 110, 226,
383, 384, 393, 395, 426, 430,
431, 432, 433, 434, 435, 436,
437, 438, 439, 440, 441, 442,
443, 444, 445, 470, 471
Berkhof, Louis, 405, 425, 504
Blackwood, Christopher, 55,
150, 154
Bolton, Samuel, 19, 189
Buswell, J. Oliver, 420, 428,
429

Calvin, John, 20, 21, 24, 77,
109, 115, 120, 125, 179, 180,
182, 183, 290, 384, 392, 420,
421, 422, 423, 424, 427, 430,
437, 442, 447, 456, 457
Canaan, 166, 228, 236, 303,
305, 311, 319, 320, 322, 480,
483, 485
Carson, D. A., 390, 392, 410,
414, 431, 440, 441

Chantry, Walter, 230, 231
children, 13, 66, 78, 80, 93, 94,
95, 127, 146, 162, 163, 165,
170, 172, 187, 193, 197, 210,
224, 225, 226, 232, 234, 237,
239, 240, 241, 243, 244, 245,
246, 247, 248, 249, 251, 252,
253, 254, 255, 256, 308, 309,
312, 315, 316, 383, 384, 389,
390, 391, 394, 395, 396, 397,
398, 399, 401, 402, 403, 404,
405, 408, 413, 414, 417, 418,
419, 420, 421, 422, 423, 424,
425, 426, 427, 428, 429, 432,
433, 435, 437, 438, 440, 441,
442, 443, 444, 445, 446, 447,
470, 471, 473, 474, 483, 491,
503, 505
church, 14, 24, 31, 32, 34, 40,
42, 43, 47, 48, 50, 52, 57, 69,
87, 109, 110, 112, 113, 114,
120, 128, 132, 133, 140, 149,
159, 160, 161, 162, 173, 177,
182, 185, 187, 196, 201, 202,
203, 205, 207, 208, 210, 219,
255, 256, 257, 258, 259, 260,
262, 264, 266, 269, 270, 275,
276, 278, 283, 285, 286, 287,
288, 289, 291, 292, 293, 294,
295, 296, 297, 298, 299, 300,
301, 302, 304, 305, 308, 309,
310, 312, 318, 319, 320, 321,
322, 323, 324, 326, 354, 359,
372, 376, 379, 381, 382, 383,
387, 400, 403, 407, 414, 415,
417, 418, 422, 424, 425, 426,
436, 441, 445, 446, 447, 487,

Name and Subject Index | 519

489, 490, 492, 494, 496, 497, 503, 505
circumcised, *95, 164, 167, 170, 237, 239, 240, 242, 243, 244, 252, 449, 451, 454, 455, 456, 459, 460, 461, 463, 464, 466, 467, 468, 471, 472, 474, 504*
circumcision, *67, 82, 92, 96, 98, 149, 168, 169, 170, 171, 172, 225, 226, 237, 238, 239, 240, 241, 243, 246, 249, 276, 320, 383, 399, 400, 413, 414, 417, 419, 421, 428, 429, 443, 445, 447, 448, 449, 451, 452, 453, 455, 456, 457, 458, 459, 460, 461, 462, 463, 464, 465,466, 467, 468, 469, 470, 471, 472, 473, 474, 479, 484, 504*
Clark, R. Scott, *194, 218, 451, 494*
Cocceius, Johannes, *20, 22, 23, 24, 25, 26, 27, 29, 34, 64, 77*
Collins, Hercules, *92, 109, 113, 114, 115, 117, 118, 119, 120, 121, 122, 123, 124, 125, 226*
condition, *26, 30, 37, 56, 64, 66, 70, 104, 105, 137, 138, 139, 159, 167, 181, 191, 199, 211, 225, 232, 237, 238, 240, 243, 244, 246, 248, 249, 259, 267, 270, 271, 275, 281, 284, 293, 305, 311, 316, 319, 434, 438, 442*
conditional, *55, 99, 100, 102, 105, 106, 228, 232, 235, 236, 237, 242, 245, 247, 248, 249, 250, 251, 350*

covenant, *6, 7, 8, 11, 12, 13, 15, 16, 20, 22, 23, 24, 25, 26, 27, 28, 29, 30, 32, 33, 34, 35, 36, 37, 39, 41, 42, 43, 45, 50, 52, 53, 54, 55, 56, 57, 60, 62, 63, 64, 65, 66, 67, 68, 69, 70, 71, 72, 73, 74, 75, 76, 77, 78, 79, 80, 81, 82, 84, 85, 86, 87, 88, 89, 90, 91, 92, 93, 94, 95, 96, 97, 98, 99, 100, 101, 102, 103, 104, 105, 106, 107, 143, 159, 160, 161, 164, 165, 167, 168, 169, 170, 171, 172, 175, 176, 177, 178, 179, 180, 181, 182, 183, 184, 185, 186, 187, 188, 189, 190, 191, 192, 210, 223, 224, 225, 226, 227, 228, 229, 230, 232, 233, 235, 236, 237, 238, 241, 242, 244, 245, 246, 247, 248, 249, 250, 251, 252, 254, 255, 256, 257, 258, 259, 264, 265, 266, 267, 268, 269, 270, 271, 272, 273, 274, 275, 276, 277, 278, 279, 280, 281, 282, 283, 284, 285, 286, 287, 289, 290, 291, 292, 293, 294, 295, 296, 297, 298, 299, 300, 301, 302, 305, 306, 307, 308, 309, 310, 311, 312, 313, 314, 315, 316, 317, 318, 319, 320, 321, 322, 323, 324, 325, 326, 327, 329, 330, 331, 332, 333, 334, 335, 336, 339, 340, 341, 342, 343, 344, 346, 347, 353, 354, 355, 357, 358, 359, 360, 361, 362, 363, 364, 365, 366, 368, 369, 370, 372, 373, 374, 375, 376, 377, 378, 379, 381,*

382, 383, 384, 392, 393, 399, 400, 401, 402, 403, 404, 405, 406, 407, 413, 414, 418, 419, 420, 421, 422, 423, 424, 425, 426, 427, 428, 429, 430, 432, 433, 434, 435, 440, 441, 442, 443, 444, 445, 446, 448, 449, 459, 469, 471, 473, 474, 475, 476, 477, 478, 479, 480, 481, 482, 483, 484, 485, 486, 487, 489, 490, 491, 492, 493, 494, 495, 496, 498, 499, 502, 503, 504, 505

covenant of circumcision, 35, 91, 95, 96, 98, 428, 429, 479, 484

covenant of grace, *6, 23, 25, 26, 30, 35, 39, 41, 53, 55, 62, 66, 67, 73, 75, 76, 77, 78, 79, 80, 81, 82, 84, 85, 86, 87, 88, 89, 90, 91, 92, 93, 95, 96, 97, 98, 99, 101, 104, 106, 107, 159, 161, 175, 176, 177, 178, 179, 180, 181, 182, 183, 184, 186, 187, 189, 190, 191, 192, 224, 225, 226, 230, 232, 246, 247, 249, 251, 252, 254, 255, 256, 277, 282, 283, 284, 285, 286, 287, 291, 292, 295, 301, 307, 312, 321, 325, 354, 358, 361, 368, 383, 384, 405, 413, 419, 425, 426, 428, 430, 432, 434, 445, 449, 471, 474, 476, 477, 478, 480, 481, 482, 483, 484, 486, 487, 489, 490*

covenant of redemption, *33, 39, 41, 62, 99, 101, 476, 477,* *480, 484, 485, 486, 487, 489, 490, 505*

covenant of works, *22, 23, 25, 26, 28, 29, 30, 35, 37, 39, 42, 43, 63, 69, 71, 72, 73, 74, 96, 99, 100, 101, 102, 103, 106, 175, 176, 177, 178, 179, 180, 181, 182, 183, 184, 185, 186, 187, 188, 189, 190, 191, 192, 225, 226, 229, 230, 232, 233, 237, 241, 245, 246, 247, 249, 250, 251, 252, 254, 256, 274, 275, 277, 279, 282, 284, 286, 291, 295, 296, 297, 298, 299, 300, 306, 311, 313, 401, 475, 486, 489, 490*

covenantal, *5, 6, 7, 13, 17, 19, 25, 27, 33, 53, 56, 57, 61, 62, 63, 65, 66, 67, 69, 72, 78, 159, 160, 165, 172, 186, 187, 223, 225, 229, 242, 247, 253, 340, 344, 358, 385, 399, 414, 432, 436, 443, 446, 477, 483, 484, 488, 491, 492, 494, 495, 496, 497*

Coxe, Nehemiah, *11, 18, 19, 28, 29, 30, 31, 32, 33, 34, 35, 37, 43, 63, 64, 65, 66, 72, 78, 81, 82, 84, 85, 86, 88, 89, 94, 95, 97, 105, 107, 146, 183, 184, 185, 186, 187, 188, 189, 226, 227, 257, 390, 400, 431, 485, 486*

credobaptism, *81, 132, 200, 219, 475*

credobaptist, *165, 193, 201, 208, 217, 219, 221, 223, 383, 385, 388, 417, 475*

Dabney, Robert Lewis, *77, 195, 197, 214, 215, 218*
David, *40, 45, 168, 179, 180, 187, 194, 195, 228, 232, 233, 234, 343, 363, 384, 386, 388, 430, 431, 432, 441, 446, 458, 481*
Davidic Covenant, *232, 234, 235, 479, 481, 482, 483*
Dispensationalism, *6, 14, 16, 17, 18, 175*

earthly, *48, 92, 93, 102, 166, 169, 175, 188, 189, 191, 243, 319, 334, 348, 390*
Eden, *25, 35, 38, 188*
Edwards, Jonathan, *40, 41, 42, 43, 48, 57, 135, 136, 194, 254*
eschatological, *25, 27, 34, 35, 38, 188, 392, 500, 504, 505*
eschatology, *25, 35, 38, 500*
essence, *23, 76, 77, 82, 91, 97, 138, 168, 190, 228, 230, 239, 276, 279, 285, 286, 287, 339, 360, 365, 470, 480, 483, 498*
eternal life, *26, 30, 37, 38, 55, 66, 69, 72, 179, 180, 182, 183, 184, 185, 188, 190, 191, 282, 296, 306, 311, 322, 359, 502*

Fairbairn, Patrick, *488, 495, 503*
federal, *6, 19, 20, 22, 24, 27, 28, 29, 33, 34, 35, 43, 44, 64, 67, 107, 276, 479, 481, 485, 486, 490, 505*
federal theology, *6, 20, 22, 24, 44, 107*

federalism, *20, 22, 24, 39, 44, 71, 76, 77, 84, 85, 86, 89, 90, 91, 94, 95, 101, 107, 476*
Ferguson, Sinclair, *176, 186, 189, 191, 192*
Fesko J. V., *180, 182, 384, 396, 399, 400, 445, 446, 447, 448*
First London Confession (1LCF), *46, 47, 49, 50, 51, 52, 53, 54, 55, 57, 58, 67, 68, 70, 87*
Fisher, Edward, 19, 154, 180
fulfill, *225, 226, 230, 231, 241, 242, 246, 270, 295*
fulfilled, *26, 67, 102, 105, 106, 107, 229, 231, 234, 237, 242, 243, 246, 275, 300, 315, 344, 350, 351, 353, 366, 376, 377, 378, 379, 380, 398, 399, 407, 417, 420, 471, 480, 481*
fulfillment, *68, 107, 169, 225, 228, 230, 232, 235, 236, 238, 242, 243, 248, 250, 255, 256, 328, 332, 341, 344, 347, 348, 352, 353, 359, 367, 374, 376, 377, 378, 379, 381, 391, 400, 405, 406, 407, 409, 412, 413, 418, 420, 421, 427, 433, 441, 446, 449, 479, 481, 482, 489, 494, 502, 506*

Gaffin, Richard B., *20, 454, 466*
garden, *29, 30, 185*
garden of Eden, *29*
gospel, *30, 36, 39, 41, 42, 43, 66, 67, 68, 75, 79, 82, 85, 86,*

120, 121, 162, 164, 179, 180,
184, 225, 229, 241, 244, 245,
246, 249, 250, 259, 270, 277,
285, 286, 288, 289, 290, 293,
305, 308, 309, 312, 314, 316,
317, 318, 319, 320, 324, 366,
385, 387, 390, 391, 398, 403,
408, 420, 435, 457, 477, 482,
484, 488, 495, 498, 502, 503,
504
Grudem, Wayne, 414, 435, 442

Hendriksen, William, 472, 473
historia salutis, 22, 26, 36, 39,
41, 53, 89, 458
Hodge, Charles, 77, 505
Holy Spirit, 27, 32, 69, 116,
234, 241, 299, 307, 309, 318,
321, 352, 354, 364, 380, 381,
384, 385, 386, 387, 388, 392,
395, 397, 398, 400, 408, 421,
427, 430, 434, 437, 442, 446,
459, 473, 479, 486, 490, 503,
505
Horton, Michael, 111, 223,
230, 256, 492
immersion, 110, 112, 114, 115,
116, 117, 118, 124, 125, 200,
201, 205, 207, 208, 209, 212
infant baptism, 110, 111, 114,
120, 121, 125, 129, 134, 136,
140, 142, 146, 150, 152, 154,
155, 162, 163, 164, 203, 209,
224, 225, 227, 375, 376, 403,
404, 427, 428, 434, 435, 439,
444, 450, 474, 497
Isaac, 94, 95, 96, 166, 167, 168,
169, 170, 243, 245, 246, 250,
251, 252, 253, 254, 255, 297,
402, 406, 419, 422
Ishmael, 96, 167, 170, 237, 243,
250, 251, 254, 255
Israel, 34, 39, 74, 89, 96, 100,
101, 102, 103, 105, 165, 169,
180, 187, 188, 189, 192, 225,
227, 233, 234, 238, 241, 244,
245, 246, 255, 275, 276, 285,
293, 308, 320, 342, 343, 344,
367, 384, 386, 389, 393, 399,
410, 414, 430, 431, 432, 446,
478, 479, 480, 481,482, 483,
484, 488, 493, 499, 502, 503
Israelites, 166, 179, 181, 186,
188, 241, 244, 245, 246, 249,
254, 255, 433, 485

justice, 24, 72, 138, 196, 232,
233, 239, 242, 248, 270, 273,
313, 382
justification, 26, 60, 68, 70, 79,
154, 161, 177, 184, 186, 287,
288, 296, 297, 298, 300, 301,
315, 316, 363, 411, 412, 413,
453, 487

Karlberg, Mark W., 19, 178
Keach, Benjamin, 18, 28, 69,
70, 74, 86, 89, 100, 101, 106,
110, 112, 175, 226, 227
Kevan, Ernest, 176, 189, 191,
192
kingdom, 24, 31, 42, 57, 92,
199, 228, 229, 235, 242, 243,
248, 255, 319, 342, 376, 394,
425, 440, 441, 443, 473, 474,
475, 476, 488, 495, 503, 504

Kline, Meredith G., *175, 475, 483, 484, 491, 492, 494, 495, 497, 498*

law of God, *30, 101, 160, 230, 238, 249, 364, 376, 377*
law of Moses, *30, 67, 102, 238, 249, 482*
law of nature, *38, 67*
Lawrence, Henry, *56, 80, 95, 194, 226*

Marshall, Stephen, *129, 131, 136, 137, 138, 139, 140, 142, 144, 146, 149, 150, 152, 153, 163, 227, 388, 391, 392, 393, 404, 408*
mediator, *41, 53, 55, 62, 68, 87, 98, 106, 257, 258, 264, 265, 266, 267, 268, 269, 270, 271, 272, 274, 275, 276, 277, 283, 285, 287, 299, 310, 311, 312, 315, 333, 334, 335, 336, 339, 340, 341, 343, 344, 346, 353, 355, 358, 364, 382, 426, 486, 488*
Melchizedek, *56, 328, 335*
Messiah, *67, 80, 82, 187, 229, 243, 244, 245, 246, 328, 334, 378, 405, 432, 441, 482, 487*
moral law, *29, 42, 43, 238, 247, 248, 256, 493, 494*
Mosaic Covenant, *9, 71, 77, 91, 92, 98, 99, 100, 175, 176, 177, 178, 179, 180, 181, 182, 183, 184, 185, 186, 187, 188, 189, 190, 191, 192, 243, 244, 245, 246, 247, 248, 249, 252, 253, 255, 480, 481, 482, 484*
Mosaic law, *184, 481*
Moses, *23, 30, 34, 39, 40, 42, 68, 76, 77, 98, 104, 119, 168, 179, 180, 208, 233, 237, 238, 239, 244, 245, 246, 249, 266, 294, 296, 297, 303, 304, 305, 309, 310, 336, 361, 370, 372, 459*
Mount Sinai, *29, 94, 166, 246, 250, 252, 255, 276, 285, 290, 297, 301, 309, 401*
Muller, Richard A., *33, 36, 37, 38, 263, 476, 493*

national covenant, *39, 102, 178, 180, 181, 187, 189, 191, 192, 246, 484*
natural law, *493*
New Covenant, *5, 6, 10, 11, 23, 28, 34, 43, 56, 69, 71, 72, 74, 75, 76, 77, 78, 81, 82, 85, 86, 87, 88, 89, 90, 91, 93, 96, 104, 105, 106, 107, 167, 168, 169, 170, 171, 172, 173, 177, 181, 184, 186, 188, 192, 224, 249, 250, 253, 283, 325, 326, 327, 328, 329, 331, 335, 337, 339, 340, 341, 342, 343, 344, 346, 347, 348, 349, 352, 353, 354, 355, 357, 358, 359, 360, 361, 362, 363, 364, 365, 366, 367, 368, 369, 371, 373, 374, 375, 376, 377, 378, 379, 380, 382, 385, 391, 399, 400, 401, 402, 405, 407, 409, 413, 414, 415, 417, 418, 419, 420, 421,*

423, 426, 427, 444, 447, 451,
459, 470, 471, 473, 476, 477,
478, 479, 480, 482, 483, 484,
485, 486, 490, 492, 493, 496,
497, 498, 499, 500, 501, 503,
504, 506
New Testament, 25, 26, 30, 39,
67, 68, 73, 74, 79, 80, 82, 85,
86, 87, 107, 110, 115, 118,
123, 125, 152, 168, 177, 181,
184, 185, 200, 224, 228, 235,
238, 239, 241, 242, 243, 249,
250, 287, 294, 325, 330, 331,
332, 335, 352, 361, 362, 376,
377, 378, 380, 385, 390, 392,
393, 394, 398, 399, 403, 404,
405, 410, 413, 414, 427, 428,
429, 431, 433, 434, 435, 440,
441, 443, 445, 449, 450, 454,
458, 460, 461, 470, 472, 482,
486, 491, 492, 493, 494, 495,
496, 497, 498, 501, 502, 504
Norcott, John, 113, 114, 115,
117, 118, 120, 121, 122, 123,
124, 125

Old Covenant, 23, 56, 69, 73,
74, 77, 78, 81, 89, 92, 96, 98,
99, 100, 101, 102, 103, 105,
177, 181, 188, 224, 329, 331,
335, 336, 343, 344, 345, 346,
348, 350, 351, 353, 354, 355,
358, 360, 363, 365, 368, 369,
391, 399, 401, 407, 414, 415,
417, 444, 447, 479, 482, 484,
485, 490, 491, 493, 495, 499,
500, 503, 504

Old Testament, 22, 32, 40, 41,
42, 43, 67, 78, 79, 82, 87, 93,
107, 118, 152, 179, 186, 228,
238, 239, 240, 241, 242, 243,
244, 247, 287, 293, 322, 325,
331, 368, 385, 386, 390, 392,
398, 400, 403, 407, 409, 410,
413, 414, 418, 420, 421, 429,
431, 433, 436, 441, 443, 444,
449, 455, 478, 479, 484, 491,
492, 493, 494, 495, 496, 497,
498, 499, 500, 501, 502, 503,
504, 506
ordinance, 87, 118, 162, 278,
401, 496, 505
ordo salutis, 22, 26, 36, 41, 453,
458, 474
Owen, John, 8, 9, 10, 11, 19,
20, 28, 29, 30, 31, 32, 33, 34,
35, 43, 58, 63, 64, 65, 72, 78,
80, 81, 82, 84, 85, 86, 87, 88,
89, 95, 97, 104, 105, 106, 107,
175, 176, 178, 182, 183, 184,
185, 186, 187, 188, 189, 190,
191, 192, 204, 227, 257, 262,
337, 339, 370, 371, 372, 373,
390, 400, 420, 423, 424, 427,
485, 486, 495

pactum salutis, 27, 53, 476, 505
paedobaptism, 76, 77, 146,
149, 152, 157, 163, 164, 171,
200, 202, 204, 205, 208, 209,
210, 211, 212, 213, 215, 219,
361, 383, 420, 424, 429, 440,
442, 445, 448, 475
paedobaptist, 6, 8, 11, 18, 44,
46, 50, 60, 66, 71, 73, 75, 76,

77, 78, 82, 84, 85, 89, 90, 93,
104, 107, 110, 111, 114, 124,
145, 147, 152, 159, 193, 202,
203, 209, 213, 214, 217, 220,
221, 223, 224, 225, 357, 358,
359, 361, 362, 374, 375, 383,
384, 388, 400, 402, 413, 414,
415, 417, 419, 424, 426, 428,
437, 440, 441, 442, 443, 444,
445, 447, 448, 449
Particular Baptist, 6, 8, 9, 11,
13, 21, 28, 35, 43, 44, 45, 46,
47, 50, 57, 60, 65, 68, 69, 70,
71, 73, 74, 75, 79, 81, 82, 84,
85, 86, 87, 89, 91, 92, 93, 94,
95, 96, 98, 99, 100, 101, 103,
104, 107, 110, 112, 113, 125,
226
Patient, Thomas, 70, 98, 105,
106, 226
Pelagian, 146, 285
Pentecost, 234, 385, 386, 387,
391, 408, 420, 428, 429, 432,
446, 479
Perkins, William, 20, 21, 22
Petto, Samuel, 93, 100, 102,
103
Pipa, Joseph A., 449
positive law, 67, 493, 494, 495,
496, 505
Presbyterian, 5, 16, 68, 130,
132, 159, 195, 200, 201, 203,
207, 208, 210, 212, 214, 220
Promised Land, 248
protoevanglium, 186
Purnell, Robert, 53, 54

redemption, 28, 31, 40, 41, 42,
43, 54, 102, 169, 229, 230,
232, 242, 266, 269, 288, 340,
354, 366, 453, 454, 459, 462,
464, 474, 476, 478, 481, 486,
490, 503, 504
regeneration, 172, 210, 239,
413, 425, 444, 452, 453, 456,
457, 459, 460, 461, 462, 463,
464, 467, 469, 470, 471, 474,
490, 503
republication, 69, 175, 176,
178, 183, 246, 247
republished, 75, 180, 192, 208,
247
Richardson, Samuel, 54, 55
Ridderbos, Herman, 495, 501,
502, 503, 504

sacrament, 143
sanctification, 68, 169, 349,
351, 371, 374, 424, 453
sanction, 30, 37, 168, 172, 181,
189, 190, 280, 296, 299, 300,
306, 311, 312, 313, 315, 340
Savoy Declaration (Savoy),
58, 59, 60, 62, 66, 67, 68, 72,
73, 82, 132
Second London Baptist
Confession of Faith of
1677/89 (2LCF), 11, 12, 13,
14, 28, 30, 32, 33, 51, 57, 58,
61, 62, 65, 66, 67, 69, 70, 72,
73, 74, 79, 80, 84, 85, 86, 87,
96, 439, 496, 498
seed, 23, 30, 31, 32, 77, 79, 82,
85, 93, 95, 96, 97, 100, 103,

*164, 165, 166, 167, 168, 169,
172, 187, 225, 226, 228, 229,
235, 236, 237, 238, 239, 241,
242, 243, 244, 245, 246, 247,
248, 249, 251, 252, 253, 254,
255, 256, 275, 298, 299, 300,
302, 383, 401, 402, 406, 408,
413, 419, 420, 421, 422, 423,
424, 432, 437, 479, 483, 485,
488, 498, 503*
sign, *30, 69, 78, 140, 164, 168,
170, 171, 172, 173, 244, 249,
326, 358, 359, 361, 383, 385,
399, 400, 405, 413, 419, 439,
446, 449, 471, 472, 473, 474,
479, 493, 505*
Sinai, *42, 43, 67, 86, 94, 102,
103, 185, 186, 252, 253, 257,
258, 274, 278, 279, 284, 286,
287, 292, 293, 295, 296, 298,
299, 300, 301, 309, 314, 321,
343, 372, 402*
Socinian, *79, 265*
Spilsbury, John, *50, 81, 87, 95,
96, 113, 114, 115, 116, 117,
120, 121, 125, 150, 226*
stipulation, *172, 180*
subservient, *39, 187, 192, 290*
substance, *34, 38, 47, 58, 62,
67, 74, 75, 76, 77, 78, 79, 80,
81, 82, 88, 90, 91, 92, 97, 98,
104, 105, 106, 107, 130, 179,
182, 186, 258, 285, 286, 287,
291, 292, 294, 301, 307, 319,
328, 348, 352, 382, 391, 399,
430, 479, 480, 482, 483, 494,
500, 501*

temporal, *39, 97, 156, 181, 188,
189, 191, 235, 242, 306, 307,
311, 338, 453, 460*
Tombes, John, *9, 127, 128, 129,
130, 131, 132, 133, 134, 135,
136, 137, 138, 139, 140, 141,
142, 143, 144, 145, 146, 147,
148, 149, 150, 151, 152, 153,
154, 155, 156, 157, 158, 159,
160, 161, 162, 163, 164, 165,
166, 167, 168, 169, 170, 171,
172, 227*
Trueman, Carl R., *182, 187*
Turretin, Francis, *19, 77, 78,
104, 178, 179, 180, 181, 182,
420, 424, 427, 437*
type, *34, 38, 95, 111, 123, 215,
309, 453, 455, 460, 483, 484,
485, 495, 496, 498, 501, 502,
504*
typological, *102, 175, 242, 482,
483, 496, 498, 504*
typology, *27, 34, 41, 483, 484*

unconditional, *99, 104, 105,
106, 225, 232, 235, 236, 237,
241, 242, 245, 246, 249, 250,
251*
union, *24, 262, 263, 429, 452,
453, 454, 455, 463, 467, 469,
470, 471, 472, 474, 486, 487,
488*

van Asselt, Willem J., *20, 24,
25, 26, 27*
Venema, Cornelis, *469, 470*

Vos, Geerhardus, *19, 20, 477, 478, 483, 484, 487, 491, 495, 498, 499, 500*

Waldron, Samuel, *73, 401, 405, 430*
Warfield, B. B., *13, 62, 497, 502*

Westminster Confession of Faith (WCF), *13, 58, 62, 66, 67, 68, 75, 420, 425, 439, 496*
Witsius, Herman, *19, 35, 36, 37, 38, 39, 73, 75, 76, 77, 178, 180, 181, 182, 187*

Made in United States
Troutdale, OR
12/12/2023